Integrated Coverage of Environmental Influences on the Aging Process

(continued on back endsheets)

Aging and Older Adulthood

Joan T. Erber
Florida International University

THOMSON
™
WADSWORTH

AUSTRALIA • CANADA • MEXICO • SINGAPORE • SPAIN • UNITED KINGDOM • UNITED STATES

To Lauren, Isaac, Megan, and Rebecca,
the future generation

Acquisitions Editor: Michele Sordi
Assistant Editor: Jennifer Wilkinson
Editorial Assistant: Chelsea Junget
Developmental Editor: Kristin Makarewycz
Technology Project Manager: Erik Fortier
Marketing Manager: Dory Schaeffer
Marketing Assistant: Laurel Anderson
Advertising Project Manager: Tami Strang
Project Manager, Editorial Production: Paul Wells
Art Director: Vernon Boes
Print/Media Buyer: Lisa Claudeanos
Permissions Editor: Sarah Harkrader

Production Service: Vicki Moran,
    Publishing Support Services
Photo Researcher: Stephen Forsling
Copy Editor: Pat Tompkins
Cover Designer: Denise Davidson
Cover Images: woman planting in garden © Corbis; couple
    walking in woods © Masterfile/www.masterfile.com;
    man playing piano with woman © Masterfile/www.
    masterfile.com; surfer © Masterfile/www.masterfile.com;
    Asian couple © Masterfile/www.masterfile.com
Compositor: International Typesetting and Composition
Printer: Transcontinental Printing, Louiseville

Printed in Canada
1 2 3 4 5 6 7   08 07 06 05 04

Library of Congress Control Number: 2004106306

ISBN 0-534-35636-2

Thomson Wadsworth
10 Davis Drive
Belmont, CA 94002-3098
USA

Asia
Thomson Learning
5 Shenton Way #01-01
UIC Building
Singapore 068808

Australia/New Zealand
Thomson Learning
102 Dodds Street
Southbank, Victoria 3006
Australia

Canada
Nelson
1120 Birchmount Road
Toronto, Ontario M1K 5G4
Canada

Europe/Middle East/Africa
Thomson Learning
High Holborn House
50/51 Bedford Row
London WC1R 4LR
United Kingdom

Brief Contents

Contents

Preface

Thanks in large part to advances in medical science and technology, we are living in a society that is rapidly aging, and many of us will live well into the older adult years. With the baby boom generation poised to enter older adulthood, the ranks of the older-adult age group will swell all the more. It is no wonder that developmental researchers and practitioners are turning their attention to this important period of the adult life span.

My interest in writing a book on aging and older adulthood began some time ago when, as an undergraduate psychology major at Washington University in St. Louis, I enrolled in a course on the psychology of aging taught by the late Dr. Robert Kleemeier. This was listed as a senior level undergraduate course, but it was populated mainly by graduate students, and our textbook was the original edited *Handbook of Aging and the Individual*. Challenging as this outstanding volume was for an unseasoned undergraduate, Dr. Kleemeier's obvious enthusiasm for the subject matter was inspiring.

Shortly after I earned my undergraduate degree from Washington University, I was saddened to hear that Dr. Kleemeier had passed away suddenly and unexpectedly. Several years later, as I was completing my Ph.D. degree in psychology at Saint Louis University, I obtained a temporary position at Washington University working on a research project on aging headed by Dr. Eva Kahana of the Department of Sociology. It now seems fortuitous that during the short time I spent on this project, I was introduced to Dr. Jack Botwinick, who had recently joined the psychology faculty of Washington University to head the department's longstanding Aging and Development Program. A year later,

Dr. Martha Storandt, who was working with Dr. Botwinick, asked if I would be interested in a postdoctoral fellowship in the Aging and Development Program. This was the beginning of my career in the field of aging. During my years at Washington University, including two as a postdoctoral fellow and additional time as a research associate, I conducted studies on aging and also taught upper-division undergraduate courses in the psychology of aging and social gerontology. When I joined the psychology faculty of Florida International University, I continued teaching an undergraduate course in the psychology of aging as well as a graduate proseminar on aging.

As I was teaching these courses, I began to think about a book on aging that would spark the interest of advanced undergraduates or graduate students being introduced to the topic. The thought of writing a book on aging and older adulthood remained in the back of my mind, but gradually my ideas began to take shape. The book I envisioned would focus on up-to-date theories and research on issues central to aging and older adulthood. Research findings are the basis for what we know and are the guiding force for what still needs investigating.

My book explains how research studies attempt to answer questions of both theoretical and practical importance. Because I believe it is essential to give readers a flavor for how research is conducted, I describe studies in some detail but in a way that can be clearly understood by readers who vary in their prior exposure to research. To achieve this purpose, I explain the hypotheses and findings of the studies I selected for inclusion in a manner that is not oversimplified but at the same time should be comprehensible to readers who may have limited experience in conducting research themselves. I point out that the hypotheses of a particular research study were, or in some cases were not, supported. In some instances, I describe studies that report conflicting findings, and I offer suggestions to explain why the results may have differed. Such is the nature of science and my goal is to raise students' awareness of this. At the same time, I made every effort to tie together the studies I describe so that they tell a coherent story. Also, I include examples of how knowledge gained through research studies can be applied to the everyday lives of older adults.

THEORETICAL MODELS

Another goal I set in writing this book was to present a theoretical framework that would lend cohesion to the material covered. The theoretical models I chose are able to subsume research findings that indicate people experience changes as they age. However, both models allow that aging can be a positive process with great potential for being successful. The two theoretical models I selected and describe in some detail in the initial chapter are the Selective Optimization with Compensation Model and the Ecological Model.

At the end of each chapter, I revisit these models for a brief discussion of how they relate to the topic covered. I do this to demonstrate to readers how theoretical models can be an effective mechanism for gaining a deeper understanding of what is known as well as what still needs to be discovered about aging and older adulthood.

INTEGRATED THEMES

A third goal in writing this book was to integrate all of the information into the text itself. Everything I selected for inclusion plays an important role in the story of what we know about aging and older adulthood. I steered away from placing material in boxes because in my experience, students are often unclear about the importance of boxed material in relation to the rest of the text. Instead, the book has an integrated thematic organization. These themes, which appear on the endpapers with specific examples of where information occurs throughout the book, are as follows: diversity, environmental influences on the aging process, and applications to everyday life.

LAYOUT OF THE BOOK

This book includes 12 chapters, which is ideal for a one-semester undergraduate course or graduate proseminar in aging and older adulthood. Although it is not essential, I suggest that for maximum clarity, the chapters be covered in order.

Chapter 1 introduces the topic of aging and older adulthood, and it gives a brief history of how the study of aging got started and how age is defined. In addition, it includes basic information on the characteristics of the older adult population and the influences that are assumed to play a role in the aging process. At the end of this chapter, I introduce the two theoretical models that will be revisited in a final section of each subsequent chapter.

Chapter 2 lays the groundwork for approaches taken to study aging and older adulthood as well as the advantages and disadvantages of the research designs that can be used. It also touches upon topics related to measurement, sampling, and ethics. In sum, this chapter contains basic information that is important for understanding and evaluating the research findings in substantive areas that are covered in the chapters that follow.

Chapter 3 includes topics of interest both to biologists and psychologists. How long can we expect to live, to what extent is biological aging under our control, and what can we do to ensure a high quality of life in older adulthood?

Chapter 4 focuses on recent theories and research on sensory, perceptual, and attentional processes. This chapter takes a closer look at vision and hearing with regard to changes that often occur with increasing age. Such information is basic to the understanding of age-related changes in memory, problem solving, and social processes, which subsequent chapters cover.

Chapter 5 is devoted to memory, a widely studied subject of great interest not only to researchers but also to individuals who are aging. An entire book could be written about memory and aging, but this chapter covers theoretical models about how memory works, what has been found to be characteristic of older adults' memory, and what people believe to be true about memory and aging.

Chapter 6 on intellectual functioning includes scientific views of intelligence, how level of intelligence is determined, and which intellectual abilities decline or are maintained with increasing age. In addition to psychometric approaches, the concept of intelligence is applied to older adults' competence in various aspects of their everyday lives.

Chapter 7, which explores cognition and problem solving in the everyday world, has an applied focus. For example, how do older adults use their cognitive capabilities in dealing with real-world situations such as solving social, moral, and interpersonal dilemmas or giving advice to others? How do older adults make decisions about their own health care or perhaps about more mundane consumer purchases?

Chapter 8 covers theories about personality and coping. It also discusses how laypeople (nonscientists) view the personality traits of older adults. In addition, it discusses self-concept and personal control, including strategies people use that can affect their quality of life in older adulthood.

Chapter 9 examines social interaction and social ties in older adulthood. It describes prominent theories and discusses specific relationships (marital, intergenerational, grandparenthood, siblings, and friendship). Included in this chapter is the topic of elder abuse, a social problem that in recent years is gaining the attention it deserves.

Chapter 10 highlights aspects of life planning of great significance for older adults: employment and retirement as well as living arrangements. What is typical for the work life and exit from the workforce for today's older adults and what changes are expected in the future? Also, what options do older adults have for living environments, and what are the advantages and disadvantages of each?

Chapter 11 discusses the availability of mental health services for older adults, the kinds of psychopathology that occur most frequently in the older adult population, and the types of therapy that are effective in treating problems that older adults experience.

Chapter 12 covers topics related to facing the end and looking toward the future. Death, dying, and loss are viewed as critical episodes within the experience of living, which may be quite different for older adults in the future.

ACKNOWLEDGMENTS

I wish to acknowledge the many people who played a role in my career in the field of aging and the integration of my knowledge and experience in the form of this book. My initial undergraduate course with Dr. Kleemeier at Washington University whetted my interest in the field and my brief experience working on Dr. Eva Kahana's project in social gerontology reinforced it. Subsequently, I was privileged to conduct research and teach in the Aging and Development Program at Washington University in St. Louis with Drs. Jack Botwinick and Martha Storandt. My years at Washington University were highly influential in my thinking and my motivation for writing this book. More recently, the suggestions I received from my Ph.D. advisor, Dr. Donald H. Kausler, have been invaluable.

Dr. Kausler applied his expertise in memory and cognition to the study of cognitive aging at about the time I began my postdoctoral fellowship at Washington University. Writing a textbook is a major undertaking, and his encouragement played an important role in my bringing the project to fruition. Finally, I acknowledge my students, who provided me with their views of the aging process and for whom I hope this book will open the door to continued interest and pursuit of careers in the field.

On a more personal level, I am grateful to my parents, Harriet Tatelbaum and the late Milton Tatelbaum, who took a keen interest in my work and encouraged me as I was writing this book. Over the years, they willingly shared their insights on their own aging experiences. Also, I thank Drs. Jack Botwinick and Martha Storandt, who allowed me the necessary flexibility during my time at Washington University that enabled me to pursue my career while raising my children.

I would like to thank Vicki Knight, Publisher for Psychology at Wadsworth, who first encouraged me to write this book, and Jim Brace-Thompson and Edith Beard-Brady who helped guide me through the beginning stages of the process. Kristin Makarewycz, Developmental Editor, provided suggestions that resulted in a book that is both readable and engaging. I owe much gratitude to Michele Sordi, Senior Psychology Editor, whose expertise and enthusiasm were invaluable in bringing the project down the home stretch. I thank Paul Wells, Vernon Boes, Stephen Forsling, and Vicki Moran for their professional production expertise.

About the Author

Joan T. Erber received her Ph.D. in Psychology from Saint Louis University, after which she completed a Post-Doctoral Fellowship in Aging and Development at Washington University in St. Louis. She is Professor of Psychology at Florida International University, where she was a recipient of a State University System Professorial Excellence Program (PEP) Award. Dr. Erber has extensive experience teaching undergraduate and graduate courses in adult development and aging and conducting research on the processes of aging. Her numerous publications focus on aging and memory and how age stereotypes influence our perceptions and evaluations of older adults. Her research findings, some of which were funded by grants from the National Institute on Aging, are published in scientific journals such as *Psychology and Aging, Journal of Gerontology: Psychological Sciences*, and *Experimental Aging Research*. Dr. Erber has served on the editorial boards of journals that publish research on aging. Additionally, she is a Fellow of the Gerontological Society of America (GSA) and the American Psychological Association (APA), and she is a past president of APA Division 20 (Adult Development and Aging).

Introduction to Aging and Older Adulthood

1

Corrine just turned 65 so she supposes the time has finally come when people will categorize her as an older adult. With her salt-and-pepper hair, she is not surprised when the young clerks at the local discount store automatically give her a 10 percent senior citizen discount even though she never asks for it. Actually, Corrine does not feel any different now than she did 20 years ago. In fact, when she goes for routine medical check-ups, her doctor says her blood pressure is close to that of the average 35-year-old. Corrine works full time and on the weekends she makes it a point to walk at least four miles a day. She can go faster and farther than many of her walking mates who are 10 or 15 years younger than she is. For other recreational activities, Corrine enjoys trying new restaurants rather than going back to the same old ones and she takes a vacation to a different place each year. Corrine lost her husband several years ago, but now she is dating a man she likes very much. Sometimes her grown daughters tease her about having the social life of a teenager.

THE STUDY OF AGING AND OLDER ADULTHOOD

From time immemorial, people have speculated about aging, and there have been numerous themes, or myths, about how to slow down the aging process and prolong life (Birren, 1996; Birren & Schroots, 2001). One myth revolved around speculation about the miraculous healing powers of waters or other substances in certain parts of the world. The Spanish explorer Ponce de Leon (1460–1521) is said to have discovered Florida while searching for a fountain of youth that supposedly would rejuvenate anyone who drank or bathed in its waters. People believed that drinking or bathing in such waters or partaking in other magical substances would not only restore youth but perhaps also guarantee immortality. Birren (1996) points out that the modern equivalent of the search for rejuvenation is evident in the pilgrimages people make to health spas and their willingness to follow dietary regimens touted as having special potency for ensuring long and healthy lives. The universal appeal of being able to combat aging and extend life has allowed many entrepreneurs to amass great wealth by selling antiaging products of questionable value to naive consumers (Olshansky, Hayflick, & Carnes, 2002).

History of the Scientific Study of Aging

Although interest in the aging process goes back for centuries, the scientific study of aging and older adulthood is more recent. Birren (1996), Birren and Schroots (2001), and Schroots (1996) offer detailed versions of the history of the scientific study of aging, and some of the highlights are recounted in the paragraphs that follow.

In 1835, Belgian mathematician and astronomer Adolphe Quetelet published a book describing the physical and behavioral characteristics of people at various ages. Quetelet was interested in what would best represent the average man at different stages of the life span. In 1884, Francis Galton, an Englishman trained in medicine and mathematics, sponsored a health exhibition in London during which he measured numerous physical and mental functions in more than 9,000 people who ranged from 5 to 80 years of age. Subsequently, Galton's data were analyzed by several scientists. In 1922, G.S. Hall published a book entitled *Senescence: The Second Half of Life*, which summarized what was known about aging in fields such as physiology, medicine, anatomy, and philosophy. The content of this book touched upon psychology as well.

In the latter part of the 19th century and early part of the 20th century, developmental psychologists focused mainly on children. Perhaps the concentration on children was driven by practical necessities such as training teachers and providing childrearing advice to parents (Birren & Schroots, 2001). However, in 1933, Charlotte Buhler published a book on biological and psychological processes throughout the entire course of human development. Written in German, Buhler's book is considered by many to be the foundation of life-span developmental psychology (Schroots, 1996).

In 1927, one of the first scientific laboratories to systematically study the psychology of aging was established (Birren, 1996; Birren & Schroots, 2001; Schroots, 1996). This laboratory, in the psychology department of Stanford University, was headed by Walter R. Miles, who initiated the Stanford Later Maturity Study. According to Birren's (1996) account, the main reason for establishing the Stanford laboratory was that men in California were having difficulty finding work because they were considered too old (Chapter 10 discusses the older worker). For more than five years, Miles conducted research on age and psychomotor functioning.

In 1939, E. V. Cowdry, a cytologist at Washington University in St. Louis, edited a classic volume entitled *Problems of Aging*. This book went beyond the biomedical aspects of aging to include social, psychological, and psychiatric information. In 1940, the Macy Foundation of New York, which had encouraged Cowdry to write his volume, sponsored the Club for Research on Aging where scientists could meet to discuss their ideas and findings. In 1941, the U.S. Public Health Service organized a conference on mental health and aging. That same year, the Surgeon General of the U.S. Public Health Service recruited Dr. Nathan W. Shock to head the newly established Section on Aging within the National Institutes of Health, which is an agency of the federal government.

In sum, by the late 1930s and early 1940s, the scientific study of aging was beginning to take shape in the United States. Concentrated efforts to conduct aging research were temporarily halted when the United States entered World War II. However, when the war ended, interest in aging research was revived and several professional societies for the study of aging were established. In 1945, the Gerontological Society (subsequently renamed the Gerontological Society of America) was founded. The Gerontological Society and the newly established American Geriatric Society began publishing scientific journals on aging. The International Association of Gerontology, founded at about the same time, began to organize national and international conferences on the scientific study of aging.

In 1945, a small group of psychologists petitioned the American Psychological Association (APA) to approve a new division that would be devoted to the study of human development in the later years. In a letter accompanying this petition, Dr. Sidney L. Pressey of Ohio State University argued convincingly that a new division on adulthood and later maturity would "be a natural complement to the present division on childhood and adolescence" and would "recognize that human development and change continue throughout the adult years and old age" (Pressey, 1945, as quoted by B. Birren & Stine-Morrow, unpublished manuscript). The first actual reference to this new APA division (Division 20) appeared in the minutes of an initial organizational meeting held during the 1946 APA convention and attended by 13 members. Dr. Pressey was the first President of Division 20, which was initially named "The Division on Maturity and Old Age." At various times over the years, Division 20 has been referred to as "The Division on Maturity and Old Age," "The Division of Psychology of Adulthood and Old Age," and "The Division of Psychology of Adulthood and Later Maturity." In 1973, Division 20 was officially designated in the bylaws as the "Division of Adulthood and Aging." Today, the APA Division of Adulthood and Aging has well over 2,000 members and plays an influential role in the American Psychological Association.

The National Institutes of Health (NIH) conducts in-house (intramural) research. It is also the federal agency that funds extramural research carried out at various colleges and universities. The NIH consists of a number of institutes. In 1974, the National Institute on Aging (NIA) was established with Dr. Robert Butler as its first director. As with the other institutes, the NIA oversees its own intramural research program and it also funds a great deal of the extramural research on aging and older adulthood conducted by scientists throughout the country.

As the quantity of aging research has grown over the past 25 years, so has its quality. Today's researchers are increasingly aware of the complexities of studying aging. The methods used to study aging and older adulthood are covered in Chapter 2.

Geriatrics and Gerontology

Geriatrics and gerontology refer to fields of study related to aging and older adulthood. **Geriatrics** is the branch of medicine specializing in the medical care and treatment of the diseases and health problems of older adults. **Gerontology** is the study of the biological, behavioral, and social phenomena that occur from the point of maturity to old age.

Geriatrics and gerontology each have their own definitions, but sometimes it is difficult to clearly distinguish between research studies that fall into one category or the other. The term *geriatrics* is loosely applied to the study of the disease-related aspects of aging, while *gerontology* refers to the study of healthy older adults. Studies of older adults who are hospitalized or live in nursing homes usually fall into the category of geriatric research, while studies of healthy community-living older adults fall into the category of gerontology research. However, as described in Chapter 3, most older adults, even those who live independently in the community, are not completely disease free. Also, not all research conducted in institutional settings is geriatric. For example, studies on social processes among nursing home residents could fall into the category of gerontology rather than geriatrics.

Why Was the Study of Aging Neglected?

Why did the theories and scientific study of the psychology of aging and older adulthood lag so far behind the theories and scientific study of child psychology? One likely reason was the common belief that development takes place primarily during childhood and adolescence. People assumed that by the time adulthood is reached, personality is formed and no further developmental change occurs.

Until relatively recently, a *two-stages-of-life* viewpoint was prevalent in developmental psychology (Schroots, 1996). According to this perspective, both physical and psychological functions were thought to develop up to the point of maturity, after which there would be a transition from development to aging characterized by a decline in functioning from the peak reached in young adulthood. From the two-stages-of-life perspective, there was little reason to study aging and older adulthood because development peaks in young adulthood, only to be followed by a gradual and predictable downhill progression.

More recently, the assumption of uniform decline in functioning beyond young adulthood has been called into question. The view that universal decrement characterizes all functions as age increases beyond young adulthood is considered overly simplistic by contemporary psychologists. Recognition that development is a complex process, even at the older end of the continuum, has spurred greater interest in the study of aging and older adulthood. The lifespan developmental perspective, which Chapter 2 describes in greater detail, postulates that development is an ongoing process in which the organism and the environment influence one another throughout life.

Another reason for the belated interest in the scientific study of aging and older adulthood is that in earlier times, both the number and proportion of older adults was relatively small. Historically, old age was not unknown; even in early societies, some individuals lived into advanced old age. However, the number of such individuals was small and made up only a tiny segment of the population. The phenomenal increase in the number of older adults during the 20th century in developed countries such as the United States is due to improvements in sanitation and nutrition, as well as to astounding medical advances. Chapter 3 discusses factors contributing to the expanding older adult population.

Reasons for Studying Aging and Older Adulthood

Interest in the study of aging and older adulthood stems from concerns of a scientific, personal, and practical nature. Until recently, much of our knowledge about adult development has been based on tests, observations, and interviews with young adults. From a scientific point of view, it is important to determine whether the findings of studies on these young adult samples can be applied, or generalized, to older adults. If the findings obtained with young adults do not generalize to older adults, then their scientific value may be limited. From a developmental standpoint, however, different findings for young versus older adults can have significant theoretical implications for the scientific understanding of basic developmental processes. For example, if young adults have better memory for recent events and older adults recall events that happened long ago better, it is possible that the two age groups differ in how they think.

In addition to scientific reasons for studying aging and older adulthood, personal and practical reasons are also important. From a personal standpoint, knowledge about aging and older adulthood can give us insight into the changes that we are experiencing or can expect to experience. Such insight can be helpful when we plan specific events such as our own retirement or when we make decisions about how and where we want to live in our older adult years.

Interest in aging and older adulthood may also stem from our concern about others. Information on aging and older adulthood is useful when we cope with dilemmas involving older friends and family members. Perhaps you have noticed that an older friend or relative seems to have difficulty hearing or understanding conversations. On the basis of information about age-related changes in hearing (see Chapter 4), what might be done to improve communication? Perhaps an older relative or friend is becoming forgetful. Is this a cause for concern? Chapter 5 covers age-related changes in memory, and Chapter 11 covers the cognitive symptoms of dementia that may be relevant to this concern. Perhaps an older friend or relative seems less outgoing than he or she was at an earlier time. Is this a cause for concern? Chapters 8, 9, and 10 include information on personality, social processes, and lifestyle that are relevant to such concerns.

Because older adults are such a rapidly growing segment of the population, they are bound to gain economic importance. Thus, information on aging and older adulthood has value from a practical standpoint. Health service workers can anticipate increased contact with older adults. Physicians, nurses, psychologists, social workers, physical therapists, occupational therapists, speech therapists, paramedics, and medical support staff are likely to find that much of their time is spent serving older adults. Educators will have more older adult students in their college and university classes, and providing optimal conditions for older adult learning will be a greater concern in planning university communities. Those who work in business settings will benefit from knowledge about the aging process. Employees will probably remain in the paid labor force until later in life (see Chapter 10 for further discussion of work and retirement), and managers will do well to understand the needs and abilities of older workers. Those who work in housing management, real estate, and banking will have older adult clients. Furthermore, older adults will become even more important than they are now as consumers of manufactured products, so more items will be designed for the older adult market. Those employed in architectural planning will profit from knowledge about aging when they design living environments for older adults.

Up to this point, we have made references to *aging* and *older adulthood* without being specific about the meaning of these terms. First, we will look at several ways of defining age. Then we will turn to the question of when older adulthood actually begins and what we can expect when it does.

DEFINING AGE AND OLDER ADULTHOOD

Aging begins at birth and continues throughout life. However, in this book the emphasis is on the aging that takes place from the point of maturity (once adulthood is attained) and continues into the later years. Our main focus will be on older adulthood. However, in many instances, we obtain information about older adults by comparing them with individuals from young or middle-age adult groups. Another way to study older adults is to follow the same individuals over time, observing how their patterns of behavior change as the years go by. Chapter 2 further describes the advantages and disadvantages of these two approaches. Meanwhile, let's turn our attention to how age is defined.

Definitions of Age

Most of us think about age in terms of the number of birthdays we have celebrated. **Chronological age** is measured in units of time (months or years) that have elapsed since birth. Corrine, who was described at the beginning of the chapter, is 65 years old. Although merely an index of time, chronological age is the most common measure of age and we will return to it later. However, age can be defined not only chronologically, but also biologically, functionally, psychologically, and socially. Chronological age does not always accurately predict where a particular individual falls along each of these dimensions.

Biological Age   **Biological age** has to do with where people stand relative to the number of years that they will live (that is, their longevity). One individual might live to the chronological age of 70, in which case he or she might be considered biologically old at the age of 65. Another might live to the age of 90, so he or she would probably not be considered biologically old at the age of 65 because another 25 years of life remain. Because we cannot usually predict the exact length of a particular individual's life with great accuracy, this way of conceptualizing biological age is speculative.

Another way to define biological age is in terms of the body's organ systems and physical appearance. With regard to these measures, how does one individual compare with others in the same chronological age group (that is, age peers)? Even within the same individual, different aspects of biological functioning and physical appearance must be evaluated separately because they can vary. For example, Corrine is biologically younger than her age peers in terms of blood pressure and most likely in cardiovascular functioning. However, her salt-and-pepper hair is a sign of physical aging that places her squarely with others in her chronological age group. Chapter 3 looks further at biological aging.

Functional Age   **Functional age** has to do with a person's competence in carrying out specific tasks. As with biological age, functional age involves comparison with chronological age peers. An individual might be considered functionally young when his or her competence in some aspect of functioning compares favorably with that of chronological age peers. For example, Corrine works full time, whereas many people of her chronological age (65) have retired from the labor force. Also, she is able to go faster and farther than her walking mates who are 10 or 15 years younger than she is. Functionally, Corrine would be considered young in the categories of work and physical mobility. In another example, an 85-year-old man who drives at night on a major highway would be considered functionally younger than his chronological age peers who have given up driving at night and perhaps even during the day. As described in Chapter 4, visual changes that occur with increasing age make driving at night difficult. Keep in mind that functional capabilities, and thus functional age, can vary within the same individual (Siegler, 1995). For example, the 85-year-old man who drives at night may have severe arthritis that prevents him from walking around the block. Also, functional age is often evaluated in relation to a specific context. For many sports, an athlete might be considered functionally old at the age of 35. However, a 60-year-old Chief Operating Officer of a large corporation or a 60-year-old President of the United States would not be considered functionally old.

Psychological Age   **Psychological age** generally refers to how well a person adapts to changing conditions. To what extent can an individual use cognitive, personal, or social skills to adjust to new circumstances or attempt new activities or experiences? Individuals who can adapt to changing conditions are considered psychologically younger than those who have difficulty doing so and prefer to do the same things over and over again. In short, we associate the ability to remain flexible with being psychologically young. Thus, Corrine's desire to try new restaurants and take vacations to different places would make her psychologically younger than someone who returns to the same restaurant and vacation spot over and over again. Chapters 4, 5, 6, and 7 cover topics related to adaption in the realm of perceptual, intellectual, and cognitive skills. Topics related to adaptation in the realm of personality, social skills, work, and mental health are covered in Chapters 8, 9, 10, and 11.

Social Age   In any given society, there are unwritten rules about what is expected at specific stages of life. **Social age** has to do with the views held by most members of a society about what individuals in a particular chronological age group should do and how they should behave. For example, people may be expected to complete their education by the age of 22, marry by the age of 25, have children by the age of 28, and be established in a career by the age of 40. The individual who does not marry until the age of 40 and lives with his or her parents up to that time would be considered socially younger than the individual who leaves his or her parents' home and marries at the age of 25. An individual who does not become a parent until the age of 42 would be considered socially younger than one who becomes a parent at age 28. Someone working in an entry-level job at the age of 40 would be considered socially younger than someone who is promoted to a middle-management level at the age of 40. Corrine's daughters think she is socially young because after losing her husband, she is dating again.

Krueger, Heckhausen, and Hundertmark (1995) interviewed men and women ranging from 25 to 80 years of age to determine what they thought of a middle-aged individual in the domains of both family and career. Study participants had an especially positive view of a 45-year-old woman whom they were told had been married for 20 years, had two children ages 19 and 17, and worked as a department manager in a bank. This woman conformed to their social expectations for middle adulthood. In contrast, they had a negative view of a 45-year-old woman whom they were told had been married for only 5 years, had one young child, and worked at a low-level job in a bank with the hope of getting promoted. This woman had not accomplished what was expected for someone in middle adulthood. Study participants would probably consider her socially young for her chronological age and stage in life.

Each society has its own expectations about roles to play and goals to attain in young, middle, and older adulthood. Krueger et al.'s study was conducted in Berlin, Germany, and it remains to be seen whether the same results would be found if a similar study were to be conducted in the United States. Neugarten (1977) contended that people use a social clock to evaluate whether their own progress or the progress of others is "on-time" or "off-time." In her later thinking, however, Neugarten placed less emphasis on being on time according to a social clock. She argued that in the United States, age was becoming increasingly irrelevant as a predictor of needs, lifestyle, and accomplishments (Binstock, 2002).

What Is Older Adulthood?

Clearly, older adulthood falls at the upper end of the age continuum. Although there are numerous ways to define age, we usually fall back on chronological markers when we judge whether someone has entered older adulthood or even middle age. When does middle age end and older adulthood begin?

Subjective Age   The chronological age that people select to mark the onset of middle and older adulthood seems to be colored by their own age or stage of adulthood. Individuals in their 20s often think that middle age starts in the 30s. Many think that older adulthood starts in the 50s but certainly no later than the 60s. In contrast, most individuals in their 60s consider themselves to be middle aged, and they think older adulthood is a long way off. In other words, compared with adults in their 20s, adults in their 60s tend to think that the onset of middle age and older adulthood occur later chronologically.

Montepare and Lachman (1989) compared people's subjective age identities (that is, how old they feel) with their actual chronological ages. Approximately 200 individuals ranging in chronological age from their teens to their 80s made judgments about the chronological age that they thought most closely corresponded to the way they felt. The teenagers felt that they were older than their chronological age, so they tended to have older age identities. For young adults, subjective age corresponded closely with actual chronological age. Both middle-aged and older adults felt that they were younger than their chronological ages, so they had younger age identities. This gap between subjective age and actual age was wider for middle-aged and older-adult women than it was for middle-aged and older-adult men. In a larger survey, Goldsmith and Heiens (1992) reported similar findings. From young adulthood to older adulthood, the agreement between chronological age and subjective age declines. In other words, as adults become older chronologically, the gap between their chronological age and their subjective age becomes wider. They feel younger than they are.

The Magic Age of 65   There is no set rule about when an individual is considered to be an older adult. Nonetheless, 65 has come to signify the official age of entry into older adulthood. The association of 65 with the start of older adulthood can be traced to the Social Security System that the U.S. government established in 1935. Among other functions, Social Security (discussed in more detail in Chapter 10) was intended to provide economic security in the form of a monthly pension to older adults when they retired from the paid workforce. Social Security in the United States was modeled after the German retirement system, which had designated 65 as the age when citizens were eligible for pension benefits upon retirement. Similarly, workers in the United States became eligible for Social Security pension benefits once they reached 65. The chronological age of 65 has become an arbitrary marker of older adulthood. Corrine assumes everyone will consider her an older adult now that she has celebrated her 65th birthday even though she still works full time.

As one step to ensure that the Social Security System remains financially solvent, the age at which workers become eligible to draw full pension benefits is being raised gradually from 65 to 66 and then 67. Only time will tell whether the chronological age associated with entry into older adulthood will be pushed up as the age of eligibility for Social Security benefits increases.

Categories of Older Adulthood   A great deal of information in this book is about older adults as a group. Many references are made to averages, or what most older adults are like. General statements about older adults as a group are one way of organizing what we know. At the same time, keep in mind that averages do not describe every individual in the group.

It would be a mistake to assume that once a person reaches age 65, he or she becomes a member of a homogeneous group. People in any age group are diverse. They have what psychologists call individual differences, or *interindividual variability*. Among people age 65 and older (65+), there is a tremendous amount of interindividual variability on almost every possible measure. Some 65-year-olds are fully retired from the paid labor force, while others work full time. Some 75-year-olds suffer from incapacitating health problems, while others lead active lives and are able to travel or participate in walking groups or marathon races. Some 80-year-olds have difficulty with hearing or with memory, while others can hear a pin drop and never forget a name. Study after study has shown that individual differences may be even greater in the older age group than they are in young adult or middle-aged groups.

One way to acknowledge the variability in individuals who are 65 and over (65+) is to segment older adulthood into categories based on chronological

There are great individual differences among older adults in many aspects of functioning. Some are physically active and others have physical limitations.

age: **young-old** (ages 65–74), **old-old** (ages 75–84), and **oldest-old** (ages 85+). Compared with individuals in the old-old and oldest-old categories, those in the young-old category have greater physical vigor and they are less likely to suffer from significant sensory or cognitive decline. In fact, many young-old adults differ very little from adults in late middle age. In general, old-old adults experience more of what are considered to be age-related changes in sensory, perceptual, and cognitive functioning. Compared with individuals in the young-old and old-old groups, individuals in the oldest-old group have the highest rate of health problems and the greatest need for services.

Many researchers use this three-tier categorization of older adulthood, and throughout this book there will be references to the young-old, old-old, and oldest-old age groups. Even so, keep in mind that even within these three categories, there are individual differences. Some people in the oldest-old group are healthier and more active than people in the young-old group.

In addition, while the three-tier categorization of chronological age is useful for some purposes, the fact is that chronological age is an organismic variable. As Chapter 2 describes further, an organismic variable cannot be manipulated or controlled. We may find that adults who fall into a certain chronological age range tend to behave in particular ways, solve problems using a certain type of strategy, or express certain opinions. Even so, we cannot conclude that chronological age causes them to behave, solve problems, or think as they do. Age is mixed up, or confounded, with other characteristics, or variables, such as educational exposure and life experiences.

Either separately or in combination with age, these variables could be the basis for the behavior, problem-solving strategies, or opinions held by individual members of a particular age group.

Terms for the 65+ Age Group   A number of terms refer to individuals who are age 65 and older. The term *older adults* has already been used in this chapter. The terms *old* and *elderly* may be used more often to refer to individuals in the old-old and oldest-old groups. Although there is no firm rule, *elderly* often refers to older adults who are in frail health or reside in institutional settings such as nursing homes. The terms *retired* and *retired Americans* are often used but they are not always appropriate because some individuals in the 65+ age group work part- or even full-time. Other terms include the *aged, golden-agers, older Americans,* and *senior citizens*. Some gerontology researchers jokingly refer to older adults as *chronologically challenged, chronologically gifted,* and *chronologically advantaged.*

Older adults are sensitive to the terms used by others to describe their age group. Many of them feel that some terms are less favorable than others. For example, a label such as *the aged* might be considered less favorable than *senior citizens,* which would be regarded as less favorable than *older adults* (Kite & Wagner, 2002). In general, older adults prefer that unfavorable terms be avoided because they fear they will become victims of ageism.

Ageism refers to discriminatory attitudes directed toward older adults. It implies negative beliefs, or stereotypes, about older adults as a group or what all older adults are like. Ageism can manifest itself in low expectations about an individual older adult's cognitive capabilities or in negative beliefs about an older adult's personal or social capabilities. However, a more recent and subtle form of ageism may be seen in compassionate stereotypes, which foster a view of older adults as helpless and in need of advocacy (Revenson, 1989). According to Palmore (2001), ageism is the third greatest "ism" in American society, following racism and sexism. Palmore contends that ageism is widespread in American society. He also points out that, unlike racism and sexism, all of us could become targets of ageism if we live long enough.

Palmore (1975) compared the status of older adults in Japan and America, both of which are modern industrialized societies. In Japanese society, there was greater respect for age, older adults were treated with greater deference in the work place, and there was a tradition of respect and duty toward parents and grandparents (Quadagno, 2002). Whether older adults still hold positions of elevated status in Japanese society and whether the tradition of respect and duty toward older parents and grandparents remains as strong in recent years is not clear.

Information related to attitudes toward older adults appears throughout this book (see Chapters 5, 6, 7, 8, and 10). Although ageism usually connotes discriminatory attitudes, note that views of older adults are not uniformly negative. For instance, Hummert (1990) found that young adult college students hold multiple stereotypes about older adults, some negative (for example, "set in ways" and "old-fashioned") but others positive (for example, "generous" and "loving"). Also, most people recognize that there is diversity among older adults and that not all older adults have the same characteristics (Hummert, Garstka, Shaner, & Strahm, 1994). Erber and Szuchman (2002) asked study participants to read a scenario describing an individual (target) whom they were told was either 28 years old or 67 years old. Afterward they rated the target on a series of traits. Ratings were no different for the 28- and 67-year-old target on undesirable traits such as stubborn, complaining, and bitter. Moreover, the 67-year-old target was credited with a higher degree of desirable traits such as responsible, understanding, and cheerful. The fact that the older target was not considered any worse as far as undesirable traits and was considered better on desirable ones contradicts the idea that people have a more negative view of older adults than they do of other adult age groups. Some stereotypes about older adults are positive.

Even so, because of the negative effect it can have when it does exist, ageism calls for further investigation. Are discriminatory attitudes held mainly by young adults, or do middle-aged and even older adults themselves have ageist attitudes? Within the United States, is there more ageism in some ethnic groups than in others? Perhaps ageism will decline in the United States as the older population continues to grow.

DEMOGRAPHIC PROFILE OF OLDER AMERICANS

The increase in the older population in developed countries such as the United States has been a major force in the expansion of interest in the study of aging and older adulthood. **Demography** is the scientific study of populations that focuses on broad groups within a specific population or sometimes across different populations. Demographers study past and present population trends and characteristics, including size, growth, and migration patterns. They also study population characteristics such as age, gender, marital status, living arrangements, health, educational level, economic status, and geographical distribution.

Demographic information is crucial for the study of aging and older adulthood because it can assist us in recognizing the needs of older adults as a group. As the age distribution of a population shifts, changes in the types of living environments that are available may be necessary. As described in Chapter 10, there may be an increased need for housing that offers services such as meals on the premises and van transportation. Also, information about demographic characteristics of the older adult population is useful when investigators want to recruit a sample of research participants who are representative of the older adult population. Further discussion of sampling strategies appears in Chapter 2.

Not only is demographic information essential for understanding past and present population characteristics, but it also can be used to project future trends in the size and growth of a particular segment of the population. The projections that demographers make may not be exact, but they can offer some guidelines about what the likely size and characteristics of the population will be in the future.

Demographic descriptions are usually expressed in terms of statistical measures such as the mean (average), median (point that separates one half of the population from the other), or percentage of a particular group or subgroup in the population that possess a particular characteristic. These measures provide an overall picture of a population.

The population of primary concern for those who study aging and older adulthood is the group age 65 and over (65+). In this book, the main focus is on the 65+ age group in the United States. The demography of the aged is a phrase used to describe the characteristics of the older (65+) population as well as the factors that can lead to changes in this segment of the population (Myers & Eggers, 1996).

Number and Proportion of Older Adults

In recent decades, the high birthrate in the **baby boom years** (1946 to 1964) and advances in medical care have been expected to lead to an increase in the number of Americans in the 65+ age category. This projection is fast becoming a reality. The first wave of baby boomers is poised to enter the 65+ age category in 2010, and the baby boom generation will continue to swell the ranks of the 65+ age group through the year 2030. The United States is undergoing a silent revolution: the aging of its population.

Figure 1.1 shows how many (in millions) older adults ages 65+ lived in the United States at several different points in time. Note that in 1900, the number was relatively small (3.1 million). By 2000, the number had increased more than tenfold to 35 million. According to projections, by 2010, there will be close to 40 million, by 2020 over 50 million, and by 2030 more than 70 million older adults (age 65+) in the United States.

One illustration of how the older adult population is growing is that in 1999, almost two million Americans celebrated their 65th birthday (5,422 per day). In that same year, about 1.8 million persons 65 and older died. These figures yield a net increase of approximately 200,000 (558 per day) people ages 65+ (A Profile of Older Americans: 2000).

Not only is the number of older adults growing, but so is their proportion of the U.S. population. In 1900, older adults (65+) made up 4.1 percent of the U.S. population; in 1999, they were 12.7 percent; in 2000, they were 12.8 percent. From 2000 through 2030, the proportion of older adults (65+) is expected to surge to 20.1 percent of the United States.

The projection that older adults will make up approximately 20 percent of the U.S. population by the year 2030 is based on several trends. First, the entire baby boom generation (born between 1946 and 1964) will have entered older adulthood by the year 2030, and this will swell the sheer number of people in that age group. Second, with the decline in birthrate after 1964, fewer additions were made to the younger segment of the population. A low birthrate contributes to the general aging of the population because fewer babies offset the large number of people entering the older-adult age category. If the birthrate were to increase significantly in the future, the number of older adults in the U.S. population would be more balanced by the youngest members. This would reduce the proportion of the population in the older-adult category.

Figure 1.1 | Number of Persons 65+ (in Millions) in the United States, 1900 to 2030

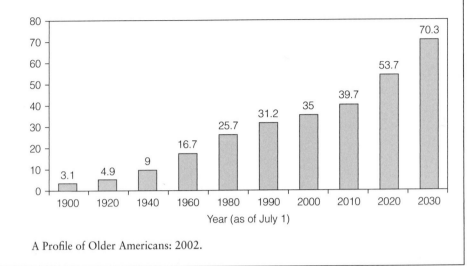

Year (as of July 1)

A Profile of Older Americans: 2002.

Demographic Transition   Demographers have described several distinct stages of transition in the aging of populations (Myers, 1990; Myers & Eggers, 1996). In an initial stage, societies have populations characterized by a high birthrate as well as a high death rate. This profile would be typical of agriculturally-based preindustrialized societies. The high birthrate is due mainly to low use or availability of birth control methods. The high death rate stems largely from poor sanitary conditions, poor nutrition, and lack of medical technology. Societies in this stage of transition consist of a large proportion of younger members and a small proportion of older ones.

As societies become more industrialized and more technologically advanced, they enter a second stage of transition. In this stage, the death rate declines due to better control of infectious and parasitic diseases. However, the birthrate remains high. The size of the population grows but younger members still predominate.

For societies in the third stage of demographic transition, the birthrate declines, contributing to a slower rate of growth in the total population. The death rate could drop as well, but the increase in the proportion of older persons is due mainly to the decline in birthrate.

Societies in the fourth and final stage of demographic transition are characterized by extremely low birthrates and death rates, at least into advanced old age. In these societies, population growth is minimal, and the proportion of the people in the various age categories is similar. Few babies will be born, but those who are have a good chance of living into old age.

Population Pyramid   A **population pyramid** is a bar graph that illustrates how a population is distributed in terms of both age and gender.

Figure 1.2 Population Pyramids for the United States in 1900, 1970, 1995, and 2030 (Projected)

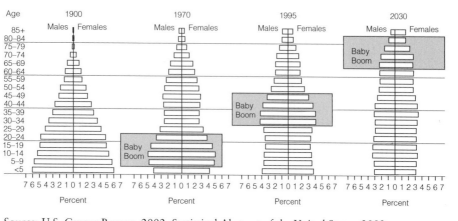

Source: U.S. Census Bureau, 2002. Statistical Abstract of the United States, 2002. Washington, DC: US Government Printing Office.

The population pyramids in Figure 1.2 show the proportion, or percentage, of the total U.S. population falling into five-year age categories in 1900, 1970, 1995, and 2030. The youngest age group (0–5) is at the base of the pyramid, with increasingly older five-year ages in the segments above. The group at the top of each pyramid includes those in the 85+ age category. Population pyramids represent proportions of a population not only by age but also by gender. The left side of each population pyramid represents the proportion of males in each age cohort, and the right side represents the proportion of females.

The shape of the graph in the year 1900 suggests why the term population pyramid came into use. Note that in 1900, each five-year category is slightly smaller in proportion compared to the one immediately beneath it, and in each age category, the proportion of males and females is almost identical. The resulting shape is a pyramid.

By 1970, the graph bears much less resemblance to a pyramid, and its shape reflects several important features of the U.S. population. First, the smaller base of the pyramid is due to the decline in birthrate. Also, a low birthrate between the years of 1925 and 1940 (possibly in response to the social and economic conditions of the Great Depression and the beginning of World War II) gives the graph a constricted middle, indicating that the proportion of the population between the ages of 30 and 45 is relatively small. Third, compared to 1900, a larger proportion of the population now falls into groups age 65 and over. In 1995, the shape of the graph is even less like a pyramid than it was in 1970. The birthrate remains steady, and the older (65+) age groups are gaining in proportion.

The shape of the population pyramid for the year 2030 is based on projections using information we have now. As mentioned earlier, projections about populations are based on a number of assumptions, one of which is birthrate. The youngest five-year segments of the graph are all similar in proportion, which indicates a projected age structure with a constant birthrate that is slightly lower than it was in 1995. At the same time, there is a dramatic increase in the population ages 65+ because by 2030 the baby boomers have all entered their older adult years. The most notable increase in proportion is for the oldest-old (85+) age category. Overall, the graph projected for the U.S. population in 2030 resembles a beanpole rather than a pyramid.

Global Considerations   At present, the proportion of older adults is larger in the more developed regions and smaller in the less developed regions of the world. According to a report published by the United Nations Population Division in 2002, the percent of the population aged 60 years and older varies from nation to nation, with a high of 24 percent in Italy and a low of 3 percent in Niger (United Nations Publication ST/ESA/SER.A/208). Other countries in which the proportion of the age 60+ population is approximately 24 percent are Japan and Germany. Countries in which the proportion of the age 60+ population is in the same low range (3–4 percent) as Niger include Yemen, Qatar, Uganda, and Somalia. In countries such as the Netherlands, Russia, the United States, Canada, and Australia, more than 15 percent of the population is age 60 and older. In China, Chile, and Brazil, the population age 60 and older is approximately 10 percent.

The Aging of the Older Adult Population   In developed countries, the age 65+ population is showing signs of aging (Myers, 1995). In the United States, the young-old (65–74) population of 18.8 million was eight times larger in 1995 than it was in 1900. However, the old-old (75–84) population of 11.1 million was 14 times larger in 1995 than it was in 1900. The oldest-old (85+) population of 3.6 million was 29 times larger in 1995 than it was in 1900 (A Profile of Older Americans, 1996). At present, the fastest-growing segment of the older-adult population in the United States is the oldest-old (85+) group.

By the year 2030, the 65+ age group will constitute approximately 20 percent of the U.S. population, and there will be more than 70 million adults age 65 and older. There is little question that in the United States, older adults will be an even more important force than they are now. Now that we have covered present and future trends in the older population, let's take a closer look at some of the characteristics of the people in this growing segment of the population.

A Snapshot of the Older Population

Populations can be described in terms of characteristics such as gender, marital status, living arrangements, health, level of education, economic status, and geographical distribution. What can be said about the older-adult (65+) population in the United States with regard to these dimensions?

Gender, Marital Status, and Living Arrangements   The population pyramids in Figure 1.2 show the proportion of males in each age group on the left and the proportion of females on the right. The symmetrical shape of the population pyramid in 1900 indicates a balanced proportion of males and females in all of the age categories. By 1970 and slightly more so in 1995, there was some

Figure 1.3 | Marital Status of Older (65+) Men and Women, 2001

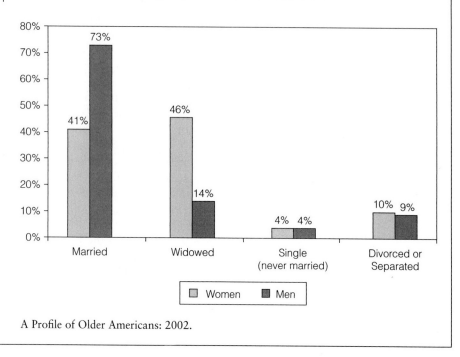

A Profile of Older Americans: 2002.

imbalance in the proportion of males and females in groups age 65 and older, with a greater proportion of females than males. By 2030, the groups above age 65 are projected to be even more heavily weighted toward females.

Not surprisingly, the proportion of men and women in the older-adult age group is reflected in their numbers. In the United States in 1995, there were 19.8 million women but only 13.7 million men ages 65 and older. With a ratio of 145 women for every 100 men, older women clearly outnumber older men (A Profile of Older Americans, 1996). Moreover, the gender gap widens from the young-old to the old-old to the oldest-old age groups. In the 65–69 group, there were 120 women for every 100 men, but in the 85+ age group there were 257 women for every 100 men (A Profile of Older Americans, 1996).

The gap between the number (and proportion) of older men and women has important implications for social factors such as marital status. In 2001, only 4 percent of older men and 4 percent of older women were single (never married). However, 73 percent of older men (age 65+) but only 41 percent of older women (age 65+) were married. Why are older men more likely to be married than older women?

Men usually marry women younger than themselves. Also, as described in Chapter 3, women tend to live longer than men do. As a result, married women lose their spouses more often than do married men. Another reason more older men are married is that men who lose their spouses are more likely to remarry than are women who lose their spouses. In 2001, almost half (46 percent) of

© Larry Williams/Corbis

Men usually marry women younger than themselves. As a result, married women lose their spouses more often than married men do.

older (65+) women were widows (lost their spouses and have not remarried), whereas only 14 percent of older men were widowers. In 2001, there were over four times as many older widows (8.49 million) as there were older widowers (2 million) (A Profile of Older Americans: 2002).

In 2001, 10 percent of older women and 9 percent of older men were divorced or separated (A Profile of Older Americans: 2002). This percentage has increased considerably since 1994, when only 6 percent of older women and 5 percent of older men were divorced or separated (A Profile of Older Americans: 1996).

The larger ratio of women in the older age group has implications for living arrangements. In 2000, 73 percent of older men but only 41 percent of older women were living with a spouse. Also, 40 percent of older women but only 17 percent of older men were living alone (A Profile of Older Americans: 2002). Some older adults live with family members other than a spouse, but this arrangement is more likely for older women than it is for older men (Pynoos & Golant, 1996).

The proportion of older (65+) adults who reside in nursing homes and other institutional settings has remained relatively stable over a number of years (Pynoos & Golant, 1996), ranging from approximately 4 percent to 6 percent. For example, approximately 4.8 percent of older (65+) adults lived in nursing homes in 1980, and approximately 5 percent were living in nursing homes in 1990 (A Profile of Older Americans, 1996). In 2000, 4.5 percent of the 65+ population were living in nursing homes (A Profile of Older Americans: 2002).

While the proportion of adults ages 65+ who live in nursing homes is not large, Kastenbaum and Candy (1973) coined the phrase **4 percent fallacy.** By this they meant that even though only 4 percent of older adults (65+) may be living

Figure 1.4 | Living Arrangements of Older (65+) Adults

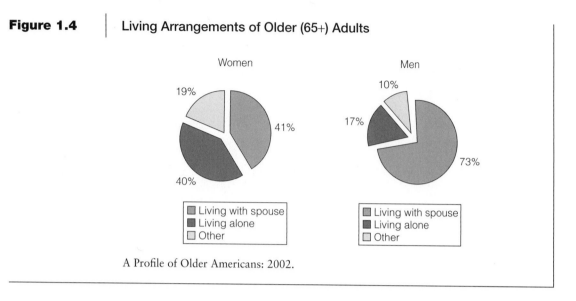

A Profile of Older Americans: 2002.

in institutional settings at a particular point in time, an individual's lifetime probability of spending at least some amount of time in a nursing home or other institution is much higher. One estimate is that up to 40 percent of older adults will spend some time in a nursing home during their lives (Mitty, 1995). Why is this true and which older adults are most likely to be found in institutional settings such as nursing homes?

When the entire age range of older adulthood (65+) is divided into the young-old, old-old, and oldest-old categories described earlier, the percent who reside in institutional settings such as nursing homes varies a great deal. In 2000, only 1.1 percent of persons ages 65–74 lived in nursing homes, but 4.7 percent of persons ages 75–84 years lived in nursing homes and 18.2 percent of persons 85+ lived in nursing homes (A Profile of Older Americans: 2002). Because the number of people living into the old-old and oldest-old (85+) age ranges is increasing, it is not surprising that the nursing home industry has been growing.

In addition to categories of older adulthood (young-old, old-old, and oldest-old), what other factors are associated with residence in nursing homes? In the United States, a substantial number of older adults live in nursing homes on a temporary basis following stays in acute care hospitals (see Chapter 10 for more discussion). Eventually some of them go back to their homes, but approximately half of those admitted to nursing homes become permanent residents (Mitty, 1995). In this regard, marital status makes a difference: Less than one-third of the married older adults admitted to nursing homes end up living there permanently compared to more than half of the unmarried residents (Mitty, 1995). Because fewer older women are married, it is not surprising that more women than men become permanent residents rather than being discharged (Mitty, 1995). Approximately 70 percent of nursing home residents are women.

Figure 1.5 | Racial and Ethnic Composition of the Older (65+) Adult Population in the United States

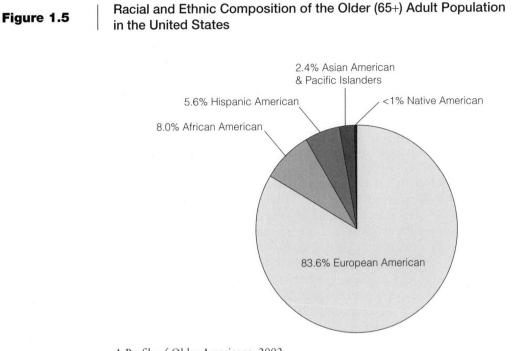

A Profile of Older Americans: 2002.

Also, the majority (91 percent) are European American, which could reflect a smaller number of family members who live nearby compared to larger and possibly closer networks in families of African American, Asian American, and Hispanic American origin. Further research is needed to help us understand how family members in various ethnic groups may serve to keep older relatives out of institutional settings (Bengston, Rosenthal, & Burton, 1996). Nonetheless, nursing homes will undoubtedly play a needed role as more people live into the oldest-old (85+) age category.

Racial and Ethnic Composition   In 2000, 83.6 percent of the older adults ages 65+ in the United States were European American, and a total of 16.4 percent were members of minority groups as follows: 8.0 percent African Americans; 5.6 percent Hispanic Americans of all races; 2.4 percent Asian Americans and Pacific Islanders; less than 1 percent Native Americans or Native Alaskans (A Profile of Older Americans: 2002). Approximately 0.8 percent of persons 65+ identified themselves as being of two or more races. Projections indicate that by 2030, the minority population will grow to represent 25.4 percent of the 65+ population (A Profile of Older Americans: 2002).

Another way to describe the older adult (65+) population from various racial and ethnic backgrounds is to look at their percentage of the population in their individual ethnic groups. In 2000, 15.0 percent of the European American population in the United States was age 65 and older, while only

6.6 percent of minority race and Hispanic populations were ages 65 and older. For the individual groups, the following percentages were ages 65 and older: 8.2 percent of African Americans; 7.8 percent of Asian American and Pacific Islanders; 6.0 percent of American Indians and Native Alaskans; and 4.9 percent of Hispanic Americans (A Profile of Older Americans: 2002).

Compared with European American older adults, African American and Hispanic American older adults are more likely to live with relatives other than a spouse (Pynoos & Golant, 1996). Also, as noted earlier, members of these groups are less likely than European Americans to live in institutional environments such as nursing homes.

Health, Education, and Economic Status   Health, education, and economic status affect where older adults live and how well they function in daily life. Many older adults are in good health, but health becomes a greater concern as people progress from their young-old to old-old to oldest-old years.

In 2000, 27.0 percent of older adults (65+) assessed their health as only fair or poor compared to only 9.0 percent for persons of all ages. However, older African Americans (41.6 percent) and older Hispanic Americans (35.1 percent) were more likely to rate their health as only fair or poor as compared to older European Americans (26 percent) (A Profile of Older Americans: 2002).

Many older adults have at least one chronic health condition. (More detailed discussion of physical changes and health appears in Chapter 3.) Limitations on activities because of chronic health conditions increase with age. In 2000, 26.1 percent of the young-old (65–74 years of age) reported a limitation caused by a chronic condition. However, almost half (45.1 percent) of those 75 years and older reported limitations due to chronic conditions (A Profile of Older Americans: 2002). Note in Figure 1.6 that the percent who have any disability, who have severe disability, and who need assistance in caring for themselves increases from the 60s to the 80s.

As a group, the old-old are more in need of help compared with the young-old. Also, older women are more likely than older men are to have chronic health problems that have caused physical limitations (Barer, 1994; Crispell & Frey, 1993). While women live longer than men on average (see Chapter 3), they are more frequently afflicted with chronic health problems such as arthritis and osteoporosis (thinning of the bones), which restrict their mobility. Also, older women are more likely than older men to live alone, so they are apt to experience greater difficulty if they do suffer from limitations in functioning.

On a more positive note, older adults of today have achieved higher levels of education compared to older adults in the past. Between 1970 and 2001, the percentage of adults ages 65+ who completed high school increased from 28 percent to 70 percent, and in 2001, approximately 17 percent had a bachelor's degree or more. However, the percent of older adults who completed high school varied depending upon race and ethnic background as follows: 74 percent of European Americans; 63 percent of Asian and Pacific Islanders; 51 percent of African Americans; and 35 percent of Hispanic Americans (A Profile of Older Americans: 2002). In the future, older adults will have even more formal education than they do today.

Figure 1.6   Percent with Disabilities by Age: 65–69, 70–74, 75–79, 80+

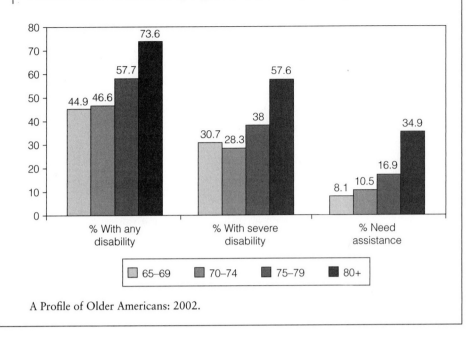

A Profile of Older Americans: 2002.

Education can affect economic status, which in turn can affect health. People once assumed that older adults in the United States were poor. In fact, one purpose of the Social Security System established by the federal government in 1935 was to provide a base level of economic security for retired older Americans. (Social Security is discussed further in Chapter 10.) Over the years, cost-of-living increases in the payments to Social Security recipients have helped to improve older adults' economic status. In 1966, the poverty rate among older adults was slightly more than double the poverty rate of the nonelderly segment of the population. By 1992 the poverty rate had fallen in the elderly population and risen in the nonelderly population, with both groups having a poverty rate of approximately 13 percent (Chen, 1996). By 1999, the poverty rate among the older population had dropped to 9.7 percent (3.2 million), although another 6.1 percent (2.0 million) were living close to the poverty level.

In sum, although the majority of older adults do not live in poverty and some older adults are affluent, a sizeable proportion fall at or below the poverty level. In 1999, there was a higher rate of poverty among older women (11.8 percent) than among older men (6.9 percent). Also, older adults living alone or with nonrelatives were more likely to be poor (20.2 percent) than older adults living with families (5.2 percent). The highest rate of poverty (58.8 percent) was among Hispanic American women who lived alone (A Profile of Older Americans: 2000). In households headed by persons 65 and older, median incomes were higher among European Americans, lower among

African Americans, and lowest among Hispanic Americans (A Profile of Older Americans: 2002).

The future economic status of older adults holds much uncertainty. Older adults will be more educated, so their incomes will probably be higher during their working years. However, the young and middle-age adult generations are saving less money so they may well have to work to older ages than today's older adult generation did. As described in Chapter 10, working to older ages is not unreasonable because older people are healthier now than they were in the past, and many jobs are less physically demanding today than in earlier years.

Geographical Distribution   In 2000, about half (52 percent) of the older adults in the United States lived in nine states (A Profile of Older Americans: 2002). The states with the largest number of older (65+) adults are as follows: California (3.6 million), Florida (2.8 million), New York (2.4 million), Texas (2.1 million), and Pennsylvania (1.9 million). Ohio, Illinois, Michigan, and New Jersey each had more than 1 million.

Another way to view the geographical distribution of older Americans is to calculate their proportion by dividing the number of older adults by the number of people in the total population of that state. Based on the 2000 U.S. Census (A Profile of Older Americans: 2002), the following nine states had at least 14 percent older adults: Florida (17.6 percent), Pennsylvania (15.6 percent), West Virginia (15.3 percent), Iowa (14.9 percent), North Dakota (14.7 percent), Rhode Island (14.5 percent), Maine (14.4 percent), South Dakota (14.3 percent), and Arkansas (14.0 percent).

In the United States, older adults who suffer from arthritis and other disabling conditions seem to be clustered in milder climates and in regions where jobs such as coal mining are dangerous and the poverty level is high (Crispell & Frey, 1993). Most of the counties with the largest share of older adults with mobility and self-care limitations are located in the southern states. An exception to this is Apache County, Arizona, the highest ranking county in this regard. More than 38 percent of the older (65+) residents in Apache County have restrictions in mobility and difficulties with self-care. Apache County is rural and poor and two-thirds of the population reside on the Navajo Reservation (Crispell & Frey, 1993).

There is a popular belief that most older adults pack up and move to warmer climates once they retire. In general, however, older adults are actually less likely than other age groups to relocate to new areas. In 1999, only 4.2 percent of elderly households had moved within the previous 12 months compared to 16.5 percent of persons under the age of 65 (A Profile of Older Americans: 2002). Even so, some older adults do relocate, and approximately 10 percent of them move across state or county lines (Longino, 1995), many to locales with warmer climates such as Arizona, Florida, and North Carolina. For the past several decades, there has been rapid growth in the number of "retired immigrants" in areas that have been developed in the Southeastern and Southwestern regions of the United States (Crispell & Frey, 1993).These retired immigrants are generally "sixty-something" and are independent, enjoy relatively good health, and tend to have higher incomes than the population native to the area. These young-old adults are able both physically and financially to enjoy the recreational and social amenities in their new communities. The economic effect of these immigrant retirees has been to stimulate the demand for goods and services. Many of them are in the market for new homes and they make other major purchases, which creates a positive economic ripple effect in surrounding areas.

As described more fully in Chapter 10, some immigrant retirees return to their states of origin when they enter the old-old category (75–84) and begin to experience economic and physical dependency (Longino, 1995). They move back to be closer to the family members they left behind when they moved to distant retirement communities in their young-old years.

In contrast to the retiree immigrants, many older adults remain in the same geographical locations where they have always lived. Some remain in the same residences where they have lived for decades. A recent phenomenon is the aging of the suburbs to which people were attracted in the 1970s during their working and childrearing years. A number of these suburbs have become havens for young-old retirees who choose not to move (Crispell & Frey, 1993).

In sum, the population of older adults in the United States is growing, and this growth is most concentrated in the oldest-old (85+) age group. Older adults are healthier, more educated, and economically better off now than in the past, but those in the oldest-old (85+) age group are likely to need some extra services. Many older adults continue to live in the same location even after they retire. A small percent of older adults do relocate, often to warmer climates, but some return to their home states when they become widowed or need help from family members. As the characteristics of the older population change, demographers will undoubtedly need to re-evaluate their description of this age group.

DEVELOPMENTAL INFLUENCES AND ISSUES

Many factors influence us over our lifetimes, and developmental investigators have divided these into three categories: normative age-graded influences, normative history-graded influences, and the influence of nonnormative life events. All three affect each of us as we grow up and move through adulthood. In addition, two issues have been prominent in the study of development. One is the relative influence of nature versus nurture. The other is the question of whether developmental change is quantitative versus qualitative.

Influences on Development

As we develop, all of us are influenced by events that happen to almost all people at a certain age or stage of life. We are also influenced by events or the environmental climate that surrounds us during the time in which we develop. Finally, our development may be influenced by events that are unexpected and do not happen to everyone.

Normative Age-Graded Influences   Normative age-graded influences are biological or environmental events and occurrences that are associated with chronological age. Examples of normative age-graded influences that are closely related to biology are puberty and menopause in women. Under the usual circumstances, puberty and menopause occur within certain age ranges during the course of development.

Normative age-graded influences can also be specific to the society in which people live. Many such influences have to do with socialization practices within a particular culture. Examples are the ages when most people go to school, marry, and retire from their jobs. In American society, schooling is normative for people between the ages of 5 and 18, and it is becoming normative for people ages 18–22 (college) as well. First-time marriage is normative in the 20s or 30s, and retirement is normative in the 60s.

Social age, described earlier in this chapter, is tied to the expectations a society has for its members, as is the idea of being "on time" in development. In contemporary American culture, there is greater flexibility in the age at which certain events are expected to occur. Schooling from ages 5 to 18 remains a normative age-graded influence. However, it is becoming more common for adults of all ages to seek opportunities for higher education, so the chronological age of college students is broader than it was in previous decades. Also, while it may still be normative for people to marry in their 20s or early 30s, more people are postponing marriage as well as childbearing to their 30s and 40s. Retirement in the 60s (especially at the age of 65) has been a normative age-graded event. In recent years, however, more people are retiring at younger or older ages.

Normative History-Graded Influences   Normative history-graded influences also play a role in development. These influences can result from an event, or they can represent a more gradual evolution of societal structure. Examples of normative history-graded influences include epidemics, wars, and the state of the economy such as depression or prosperity.

Also included in the normative history-graded category are sociocultural influences such as childrearing philosophy and practices, educational philosophy and practices, gender-role expectations, and attitudes toward sexuality and sexual behavior. Changes in these influences can be triggered by historical events such as war, disease, or the introduction of new technology. In the1940s when men were fighting in World War II, it became more acceptable for women to join the paid labor force. In the mid- to late 1980s, the AIDS epidemic led to increased conservatism in attitudes toward sexual behavior. In the 1990s, the computer revolution changed the way people communicate and obtain information. Instead of visiting the local library or shopping mall, people simply log on to a personal computer. Cell phones have made it possible to be in touch and still be mobile.

A history-graded influence of great importance for older adults is the increased availability of health care, largely attributed to the federal health insurance program for older adults (Medicare) initiated by the U.S. government in 1965. Since that time, older Americans have had greater access to medical care than they did before.

Nonnormative Life Events   Development can also be influenced by **nonnormative life events,** which do not affect all, or even most, members of a particular cohort. The influence of nonnormative life events is not necessarily associated either with chronological age or historical time, but nonetheless such events can play an important role in the development of an individual (Baltes & Smith, 1995). Examples of nonnormative life events include being diagnosed with a rare illness, being involved in an accident, winning a lottery, becoming divorced from one's spouse, and being either downsized or promoted at work.

Normative age-graded, normative history-graded, and nonnormative influences have been described separately but they do not exist in a vacuum. In reality, they can affect one another. Thus, history-graded influences may interact with a person's age and stage of development. For example, the history-graded influence of the Vietnam War had quite a different effect on young Americans of draftable age than it did on middle-aged and older Americans who were not sent off to fight. The normative history-graded influence of the stock market crash of 1929 and the economic depression that followed had a direct impact on those responsible for supporting their families. It had a lasting effect on many young adolescents who were forced to drop out of school and get jobs to help support their families. For many, future work careers were shaped by this historical economic event. The computer revolution and resulting dependence of our present-day society on computer use has impacted people of various ages differently. Computers are an integral part of our modern educational system, so children and young adults of today are highly computer-literate and at ease with using computers to obtain information. In contrast, today's older adults did not use computers in school and most did not use computers at their jobs. The majority of today's older adults kept their financial records in a notebook. They were accustomed to receiving passbooks for savings accounts at their banks, they consulted a card catalog to find books at the library, and they made purchases in small neighborhood stores that offered personal service. As described in Chapter 10, most older adults can adapt to computers, but unlike younger adults, they remember a time when everything was done without them.

Nonnormative life events are not, by definition, associated with age. Even so, their influence on development may depend upon the age when they occur. Winning the lottery at age 20 could have quite a different influence on development compared with winning the lottery at age 60. Divorce, which would probably be considered a nonnormative life event despite its increasing occurrence, is likely to have a very different effect if it occurs at the age of 25 than if it occurs at the age of 65.

Even though American society is more flexible today than it was in the past, it is still probable that an event that would be considered a normative age-graded influence at one stage of life would be considered nonnormative if it were to occur at a time when it is unexpected or uncommon. Thus, retirement from the paid labor force is a normative age-graded influence at age 65, but it would be considered a nonnormative life event if it occurs at age 35. Becoming a first-time father is a normative age-graded influence at the age of 30, but it might be considered a nonnormative life event if it occurs at age 70.

In sum, all three influences play a role in development both separately and together. Because of their complexity, a complete understanding of how they affect us would actually require the cooperative efforts of psychologists, sociologists, biologists, and social historians (Baltes & Smith, 1995).

Issues in the Study of Aging

For decades, two issues have been important themes in developmental psychology and each holds special meaning for the study of aging and older adulthood. One is the relative influence of **nature and nurture** in the aging process. Another is whether any differences that exist between people of various ages (or changes that occur within the same people as they grow older) can be characterized as **quantitative or qualitative differences.**

Nature and Nurture   In the study of development, there is often concern with the relative influence of nature (that is, hereditary, genetic, and biological factors) and nurture (that is, environmental factors and experience). Early controversies revolved around the question of whether human development is attributable to nature or whether it is attributed to nurture. More contemporary views emphasize the interaction between nature and nurture and the difficulty inherent in attributing a developmental outcome to either one or the other. In the case of older adults, nature and nurture have interacted over an extended period of time, which makes it especially difficult to disentangle the relative importance of these two sources of influence on aging. The topics of longevity, biological aging, and health (covered in Chapter 3) are closely linked with the issue of nature versus nurture. For example, the concept of primary aging is tied more to nature, while that of secondary aging is more related to nurture.

As mentioned earlier, a principle that applies to almost every aspect of aging is the extensive individual variability. Why do some people remain healthy, active, and cognitively intact well into their later years, while others succumb to physical disabilities or psychological impairment relatively early in the aging process? To what extent do physical and mental disabilities have a genetic basis (nature), and to what extent are they shaped by environmental influences, lifestyle, and experiences (nurture)?

The science of behavior genetics studies how genetic and environmental factors interact to result in behavioral differences among individuals (Bergman & Plomin, 1996). Developmental behavior geneticists often compare genetically related individuals such as twins or siblings at various times to determine which aspects of their development are similar and which are different. Are there similarities between identical twins or even siblings, especially those who have spent a large part of their lives in different environments, with regard to cognitive behavior, personality, incidence of psychopathology, physical health, and longevity? To what extent is behavior in older adulthood based solely on biological constitution regardless of environment or lifestyle habits? These fascinating questions have no easy answers.

Quantitative and Qualitative Indexes   The use of quantitative versus qualitative indexes is also an important issue in the study of aging and older adulthood. When evaluating how people in two or more age groups perform or behave, or how the same people perform or behave if they are followed over time, researchers may use measures that are either quantitative or qualitative. For example, to compare how young and older adults go about solving a problem, one researcher might use a quantitative index such as the amount of time it takes each age group to solve the problem. In contrast, another researcher might use a qualitative index, such as noting the strategy young and older adults use to solve the problem. Sometimes there is a relationship between quantitative and qualitative indexes. For example, one strategy for solving a problem might take more time than another. However, researchers who focus on quantitative measures may not include qualitative measures; similarly, researchers with a qualitative focus may not use quantitative measures.

In sum, the role of both biological and environmental influences on development, and particularly the interaction between the two, continues to be of concern to developmental investigators. Also, whether performance or behavior at various stages of development differs in quantity or in quality is of great interest to investigators of aging and older adulthood. The question of quantitative versus qualitative indexes has been a particularly prominent theme in the study of intelligence and problem solving (see Chapters 6 and 7).

THEORETICAL MODELS

Theoretical models are valuable for organizing masses of data on aging and older adulthood. Such models allow us to make sense of what might otherwise be an overwhelming mass of information. Theoretical models also guide the further study of aging and older adulthood by giving us a platform for framing questions that are important to investigate.

Two theoretical models will be revisited throughout this book: the **Selective Optimization with Compensation (SOC) Model of Aging** and the **Ecological Model of Aging.** Each offers a framework for understanding what we know about aging and older adulthood, and each can help us identify things we still need to learn. Each model has its own concepts and terminology. The SOC Model focuses on the strategies aging individuals can use, whereas the Ecological Model places more emphasis on the characteristics of the environment. Together, the two models complement one another in conceptualizing the process of aging as one of adaptation.

Before proceeding to a fuller explanation of each model, let's first consider two general perspectives on the aging process. First, the idea of *normative aging* focuses on behavioral functioning that would be considered normal, or average, as individuals approach or reach older adulthood. Recently, however, there is growing interest in a second perspective, which is referred to as *successful aging.* The idea of successful aging is that as individuals grow older, a distinction can be made between an average outcome and an outcome that would be considered ideal. In other words, aging can be differentiated into what is "usual" and what is "possible" (Baltes & Baltes, 1990; Schulz & Heckhausen, 1996). The SOC and Ecological models both encompass the second, more optimistic view, although they differ in the details of how to achieve successful aging.

The Selective Optimization with Compensation Model of Aging

The Selective Optimization with Compensation (SOC) Model (Baltes & Baltes, 1990) is founded on the basic assumption that individuals engage in adaptation throughout their lives. They are capable of learning and changing and of calling upon extra, or reserve, capacity that they might not need to use under ordinary circumstances.

Another assumption of the SOC Model is that throughout development, individuals experience gains and they also experience losses. However, as older adulthood is approached, the losses may outnumber the gains. In addition, with increasing age there may be a reduction in general reserve capacity as well as reserve capacity in specific areas, or domains, of functioning. When losses predominate in a particular domain, it may become increasingly difficult to function at a high level.

Despite the greater proportion of losses and a reduction in reserve capacity with increasing age, all is not lost. According to the SOC model, certain strategies can be called into play to maximize the chances for successful aging. One strategy for adapting to loss is to concentrate efforts on the domains in which it is most likely that a high level of functioning can be maintained. These domains are not necessarily the same for every individual.

Selection is a strategy of concentrating efforts on domains in which effective functioning is most likely to remain high. However, it might also be necessary to revise one's expectations of functioning in some domains. Optimization is a strategy of focusing on behaviors that maximize the quantity and quality of life. Compensation refers to substituting new strategies when losses occur. For example, if memory falters, a person might compensate by keeping a list of things to remember. If vision or hearing is less sharp, a person might compensate by using glasses or hearing aids.

The SOC Model stems from the lifespan developmental perspective that Chapter 2 describes in greater detail, and it is well-suited for conceptualizing how people deal with age-related changes in the sensory, perceptual, cognitive, personal, and social domains. If individuals are able to select, optimize, and compensate as they experience age-related losses in any of these domains, they have a good chance of achieving successful aging.

The Ecological Model of Aging

The Ecological Model of Aging (Lawton & Nahemow, 1973) is based on the premise that the interaction between a person and his or her environment results in some level of adaptation, which is measured in terms of a person's emotional (affective) well-being and behavior.

Figure 1.7 | The Ongoing Dynamics of Selective Optimization with Compensation

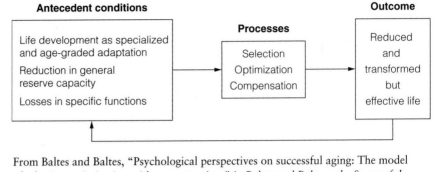

From Baltes and Baltes, "Psychological perspectives on successful aging: The model of selective optimization with compensation," in Baltes and Baltes, eds. *Successful Aging: Perspectives from the Behavioral Sciences* (pp. 1–34.), 1990. Reprinted by permission of Cambridge University Press.

As Figure 1.8 shows, a person can be characterized in terms of competence. Competence can be measured by a person's physical, sensory, cognitive, and social capabilities. An environment can be defined in terms of level of challenge, or press, which can be measured in terms of its physical demands, as well as in the level of sensory, intellectual, or social stimulation that is available. To enjoy a positive outcome (adaptation), a person's level of competence must be appropriately matched with the press of the environment in which he or she must function.

In Figure 1.8, the dotted line bisecting the shaded adaptation zone represents the ideal level of adaptation, while the shaded gray area on either side of the dotted line represents an acceptable range of positive adaptation. The white areas to the left and right of the gray zone represent zones of negative adaptation (negative affect, maladaptive behavior), which can result when environmental press is either too low or excessive.

Note in Figure 1.8 that the gray zone of positive adaptation is a function both of the person's level of competence and the degree of press in the environment. A person who is low in competence will adapt well in a narrow band of environments that are low in press, but many environments would be too challenging. At the same time, note that even for the individual who is low in competence, a small band of extremely low press environments would not offer sufficient challenge, or stimulation.

As a person's level of competence increases, a higher level of environmental press is needed for positive adaptation. The shaded gray area broadens as a person's competence increases, illustrating that someone high in competence should adapt positively to a wider range of environmental press compared to someone low in competence. At the same time, the person high in competence would adapt poorly in a broad range of environments that offer too little press.

Figure 1.8  Diagrammatic Representation of the Behavioral and Affective Outcomes of Person-Environment Transactions in the Ecological Model

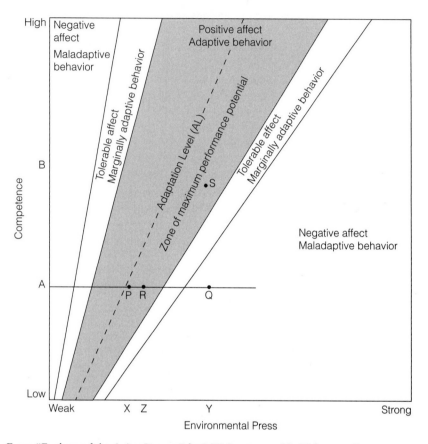

From "Ecology of the Aging Process" by M.P. Lawton and L. Nahemow. In C. Eisdorfer and M.P. Lawton (eds.) *The Psychology of Adult Development and Aging*, pp. 619–674. Copyright © 1973 American Psychological Association. Reprinted by permission.

In the original Ecological Model (Lawton & Nahemow, 1973), the older adult was viewed as a recipient of the press exerted by the environment. More recently, Lawton (1989, 1999) has emphasized the transactional nature of the person-environment interaction. Thus, rather than viewing the older adult as a passive responder to the environment, the older adult is considered capable of initiating interactions with the environment. An individual who is high in competence will be able to identify and shape the resources that are potentially available in the environment. Furthermore, an individual who is low in physical competence may have sufficient cognitive and/or social competence to take advantage of environmental resources compared to the individual who is not competent cognitively or socially. A competent individual's ability to shape the environment can result in positive adaptation, assuming that the press of the environment is not too great.

As with the SOC Model, the Ecological Model is a framework within which to consider successful aging in many domains—physical, sensory, perceptual, cognitive, personal, and social. At the end of each chapter, we will return to the SOC and Ecological models for a brief discussion of how they relate to the content covered.

KEY POINTS

- People have always been interested in how to slow down the aging process and extend life, but the scientific study of aging and older adulthood is more recent. There are more older adults today and a greater recognition that development occurs throughout the adult life span into the older adult years.
- People study aging for scientific, personal, and practical reasons. Geriatrics is the branch of medicine specializing in the medical care and treatment of the diseases and health problems of older adults. Gerontology is the study of the biological, behavioral, and social aspects of aging from maturity to old age.
- Age can be defined chronologically (number of time units since birth), but it can also be defined biologically, functionally, psychologically, and socially.
- As adults get older, there is a gap between their chronological age and their subjective feelings about age. Middle-aged and older adults, especially women, often say they feel younger than their chronological age.
- In the United States, 65 is the most common chronological marker of entry into older adulthood, but in the future this number may increase because the age of eligibility for government pensions is set to increase to 66 and then 67.
- Older adulthood is often segmented into three categories based on chronological age: young-old (ages 65–74), old-old (ages 75–84), and oldest old (ages 85+). In the United States, the fastest-growing group is the oldest-old (85+) age category.
- Ageism refers to discriminatory attitudes directed toward older adults. Further investigation is needed to determine when and how ageism affects this age group.
- In the United States, baby boomers will swell the ranks of the 65+ age group through the year 2030. At present, the largest proportion of 65+ group is European American. Also, there are more women than men, and older women are more likely than older men to be single and to live alone. There is a greater proportion of women than men in institutional settings such as nursing homes, and the majority of these women are European American.
- Older adults in the United States are healthier, more educated, and economically better off today than they were in the past.
- In the United States, the majority of older adults continue to live in the same geographic location even after they retire, but a small percentage of older

adults relocate across state lines, often to warmer climates. Some return to their home states later if they experience loss of a spouse or health difficulties.

- Over the life span, development is affected by normative age-graded influences, normative history-graded influences, and nonnormative influences. All three influences play a role in our lives as we reach maturity and move through adulthood.

- Two issues have been prominent themes in the study of development: the relative influence of nature versus nurture, and the question of whether developmental change is quantitative or qualitative.

- The Selective Optimization with Compensation (SOC) and Ecological models are two theoretical frameworks that will be used in this book to view what is known about aging and older adulthood. Both suggest ways in which people can adapt to the aging process and how they can achieve successful aging. We will return to these models at the end of each chapter.

KEY TERMS

ageism   14

baby boom years   16

biological age   9

chronological age   9

demography   15

Ecological Model of Aging   31

4 percent fallacy   21

functional age   9

geriatrics   6

gerontology   6

nature and nurture   30

nonnormative life events   29

normative age-graded influences   28

normative history-graded influences   28

oldest-old   13

old-old   13

population pyramid   17

psychological age   10

quantitative or qualitative differences   30

Selective Optimization with Compensation (SOC) Model of Aging   31

social age   10

young-old   13

To learn more about the issues discussed in this chapter, point your browser to http://www.infotrac-college.com and use the passcode from the InfoTrac College Edition card that came with your book. InfoTrac College Edition gives you access to complete articles from many different journals.

Theory and Method in Studying Aging and Older Adulthood

2

Metatheoretical Approaches to the Study of Aging
The Mechanistic Metamodel
The Organismic Metamodel
The Contextual Metamodel
The Lifespan Developmental Perspective

Developmental Research
The Age Variable
Factors in Aging Research
Research Design

Measurement
Reliability
Validity
Sampling

Approaches to Conducting Aging Research
The Experimental Approach
The Quasi-Experimental Approach
Quasi-Experimental or Experimental?
Single-Factor and Multifactor Designs
The Descriptive Approach

Ethics in Research on Human Aging

Revisiting the Selective Optimization with Compensation and Ecological Models

Key Points

Key Terms

Sylvia often wonders what ever became of her high school friends. To satisfy her curiosity, she decided to return to her hometown to attend the 50th reunion of her school's graduating class. The reunion featured a formal dinner topped off by a musical skit put on by several former classmates. Sylvia was relieved that everyone had a name tag because after 50 years, she was not sure she would recognize anyone. However, aside from some gray hair and wrinkles that might be expected after so much time had passed, she began to realize that her classmates had not changed that much since high school. Those who put on the musical skit at the reunion dinner were the same ones who had been in school plays and participated in extracurricular activities back in high school. Shy and quiet classmates were still shy and quiet, and Sylvia noticed they were less represented at the reunion compared to the more outgoing ones. Sylvia cannot help but wonder whether high school seniors today have the same wishes and fears as she and her friends had when they were 18, and whether 50 years into the future their view of life will be anything like hers is now.

METATHEORETICAL APPROACHES TO THE STUDY OF AGING

Investigators who study aging usually have a particular viewpoint about the nature of the universe in general and about developmental phenomena in particular. Such a viewpoint is referred to as a metatheoretical orientation, or a metamodel. A metamodel guides the belief researchers hold about which aspects of development are considered worthy of study (Elias, Elias, & Elias, 1977). Metamodels also influence the theories researchers propose, the hypotheses they generate, how they design their research, the nature of the sample they include in their research studies, and the method they use to analyze the research data they collect. The fact that individual researchers subscribe to different metamodels may explain, at least in part, why their findings may conflict. In some sense, scientific research is never completely objective because it is always driven by a viewpoint.

The Mechanistic Metamodel

Researchers with a **mechanistic metamodel** use a machine metaphor to study development. This is not to say that they believe that people are like machines. Rather, the machine metaphor guides their theories and hypotheses about developmental processes. Researchers with a mechanistic metamodel tend to view external environmental forces as input and the organism's behavior as output. Thus, their research tends to focus on the organism's reaction to external forces rather than on the role the organism may play in constructing the environment. With regard to the study of aging and older adulthood, if environmental forces are considered to be the main reason people age in less than ideal ways, then attempts might be made to prevent or minimize any negative aspects of aging through control of the environment (Kausler, 1982).

Researchers with a mechanistic metamodel view a whole phenomenon as equal to the sum of its parts. Therefore, their approach to the study of development is to break down a complex phenomenon into parts and then to study each one separately. Behavior is viewed as the product of many lawful associations between simple events, possibly the result of numerous stimulus-response sequences.

Researchers with a mechanistic orientation study quantitative differences, or change, between young and older adults. They might ask the following questions: "Compared with young adults, do older adults display a greater or a lesser degree of a particular behavior?" or "Do older adults demonstrate a higher or lower level of performance on a particular ability test compared to young adults?"

The Organismic Metamodel

Researchers with an **organismic metamodel** use a biological metaphor to study development. They believe that development originates from within the organism. The developing organism is viewed as acting upon, rather than reacting to, the environment. The environment is not ignored, but it is not the main focus.

According to the organismic metamodel, development is directed toward some goal, or endpoint. Development occurs in a series of stages in which new and different structures emerge. Organismic researchers focus on patterns of abilities or other characteristics as well as on the nature of the structures underlying such patterns.

In the organismic metamodel, the whole is greater than the sum of its parts. Therefore, researchers with an organismic metamodel would have little interest in studying individual behaviors in isolation. Rather, they would emphasize the importance of complex and constantly changing developmental phenomena that occur within a larger framework.

The organismic metamodel emphasizes qualitative changes in development. The main focus is on the variation in the structures, or pattern, of qualities or characteristics, at different points of the adult life span. Older organisms are not viewed as having either a lesser or a greater quantity of a characteristic or ability. Rather, characteristics and abilities are assumed to be qualitatively different at different stages of life.

The Contextual Metamodel

Researchers with a **contextual metamodel** view the organism and the environment as being in continual interaction. Thus, development is thought to consist of a series of bidirectional transactions between the organism and the environment. This is a dialectical process, which means that a constantly changing organism develops within a constantly changing environmental context. In the contextual metamodel, there is no particular direction of movement toward any single endpoint, or goal. Rather, there are multiple patterns of development, both quantitative and qualitative. These cannot be broken down into simple parts to be studied in isolation.

Developmental researchers with a contextual metamodel often look beyond the age variable. Thus, if they are studying how young versus older adults perform on a memory test, there is special concern with variables such as years of education, prior experience, present lifestyle, socioeconomic status, and cultural (ethnic) background. Also, they would consider it particularly important for

Table 2.1 | Key Theoretical Propositions of the Lifespan Development Perspective

Development occurs over the entire life span
Development occurs throughout life. No one age or stage is dominant with regard to development. At all points, from birth to death, development can be both continuous (cumulative) and discontinuous (innovative).

Development is embedded in a historical context
Development varies depending on when it occurs and the sociocultural conditions at that time.

Development is multidimensional, multidirectional, and multicausal
Development can bring change along many dimensions (physical, cognitive, social, and so on). Such change can occur in multiple directions (increases, decreases). Changes can vary as far as timing (onset, duration). Finally, multiple factors cause development.

The field of development is multidisciplinary
The study of psychological development it is greatly enhanced with information from disciplines such as biology, anthropology, and sociology.

Development includes both gains and losses
At all points of the life span, developmental processes can show both growth (gain) and decline (loss). There may be gains in some aspects of development and losses in others.

Development is plastic
Plasticity refers to intraindividual (within-person) variability and the modifiability of development. This means that individuals can change and learn during the course of development.

Adapted from Baltes, 1987.

tests of intellectual ability to consist of items with real-world relevance rather than items with limited everyday meaning.

The Lifespan Developmental Perspective

The **lifespan developmental perspective** (Baltes, 1987) draws on all three of the metamodels just described, but it bears the greatest similarity to the contextual metamodel. According to the lifespan developmental perspective, development is a multifaceted, ongoing process. A changing organism acts upon, and changes, the environment. At the same time, a dynamically changing environment acts upon, and changes, the organism. Thus, behavior is a product of the organism as well as the environment.

Because the lifespan model assumes that each individual develops in his or her own way, researchers would consider it especially important to follow the same people over time to assess intraindividual change (that is, change within the individual). The lifespan perspective can be applied to any aspect of development—cognitive, social, or biological. However, most often it has been

Figure 2.1 | Proportion of Gains and Losses

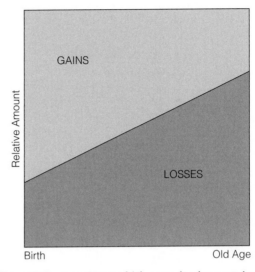

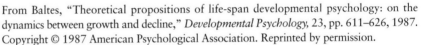

From Baltes, "Theoretical propositions of life-span developmental psychology: on the dynamics between growth and decline," *Developmental Psychology,* 23, pp. 611–626, 1987. Copyright © 1987 American Psychological Association. Reprinted by permission.

applied to the study of intellectual abilities. Chapter 6, which covers intellectual functioning, revisits the lifespan perspective.

One proposition of the lifespan perspective is that developmental processes can show both gains and losses over the life span. However, Baltes (1987) proposed that the proportion of gains to losses changes as people grow older.

Figure 2.1 shows that the proportion of gains is greater than the proportion of losses in early life through young adulthood. Toward middle age, the proportion of gains and losses is equivalent, but in older adulthood the proportion of losses outstrips the proportion of gains. Despite the greater proportion of losses in older adulthood, however, Baltes proposed that gains may be used to offset any losses that occur. This is one of the main propositions in the Selective Optimization with Compensation (SOC) Model introduced in Chapter 1.

DEVELOPMENTAL RESEARCH

Psychological research deals with variables. The term variable can refer to personal characteristics (for example, age, gender, ethnicity, socioeconomic status, level of education, group membership), environmental characteristics, observed behaviors, test performance scores, responses to questionnaires, type of test instructions that are given prior to administering a test, and so on. Variables can be categorical (that is, broken down into more than one level, each having specific boundaries) or they can be continuous (that is, having no specified boundaries). Now we will take a closer look at the age variable, which is fundamental to developmental research.

The Age Variable

In developmental research, the age variable is frequently treated as a categorical variable. Thus, when conducting a study, a researcher may include participants from two or more adult age categories, or age groups. When age is a categorical variable, there is no definite rule as to the boundaries, or span, for the separate age categories. The lower boundary for the young adult category could be set at age 18, while the upper boundary might be set at 22, 25, 30, 35, or even 40. Thus, the age span for a young adult group might be as narrow as four years (18–22), or as broad as 22 years (18–40).

In many studies, the lower boundary for the older adult age group is 65. However, the upper boundary varies widely across studies. In some studies, the age span that defines the older group is relatively narrow, such as 65–75. In other studies, the age span is extremely broad, such as 65 and older (65+). Studies that use a broad category such as 65+ most likely include individuals from the young-old (65–74), old-old (75–84), and oldest-old (85+) subcategories. As Chapter 1 states, individuals in the young-old, old-old, and oldest-old subcategories tend to differ on a number of dimensions, including health as well as sensory, perceptual, and cognitive capabilities. Depending upon which variables are of interest in a particular research study, the possible heterogeneity of a broad 65+ group may not be ideal. Also, comparing the results of two studies that differ greatly in the upper boundary of the older age category can be questionable.

Research studies in which age is a categorical variable often include young and older age categories. This so-called "extreme age groups design" (Hertzog, 1990) is used to ascertain whether older adults have less, or perhaps more, of certain kinds of abilities or characteristics compared to young adults. If the older group were to obtain lower scores than a young group on an ability test, it would not be possible with the extreme age groups design to determine whether there is a simple gradual decrease with age or whether the relationship between age and performance is more complex.

Including a middle-aged group makes it possible to estimate whether the decrease in average scores from young to older adulthood is gradual or abrupt (Elias, Elias, & Elias, 1977). However, if a middle-aged group is included, it is all the more necessary to set careful boundaries for the age categories. While there are no firm rules about age category boundaries, two guiding principles might be that (a) all categories have an equivalent chronological span (for example, 10 years) and (b) age categories are separated by a relatively equivalent number of years. A study in which the young adult category is 18–28, the middle-aged category is 42–52, and the older adult category is 65–75 comes close to meeting these guidelines.

Another strategy used in aging research is to treat the age variable as continuous, including individuals who range from young (from the age of 18 or 21) to older adulthood with no upper limit. If the age variable is continuous, there is no need to set arbitrary cutoffs or to classify participants into young, middle-aged, or older adult age categories. Also, individuals whose chronological ages might have fallen in between arbitrarily designated age category boundaries, and who might have been excluded from a categorical study, are now eligible to participate. However, when age is a continuous variable, there should be a relatively even distribution of research participants across the adult life span. This distribution requirement can be demanding, particularly if a study will have a small number of participants.

Regardless of whether the age variable is categorical or continuous, keep in mind that age is an **organismic variable.** As with variables such as gender, ethnicity, and socioeconomic status, age is inherent within the individual. As discussed further under the topic of quasi-experimental approaches to research, organismic variables cannot be controlled or manipulated.

Factors in Aging Research

Three basic factors must be considered when conducting developmental research on aging:

- Age: the chronological age, or maturational level, of the research participants
- Cohort: the cohort membership, or generation, of the research participants
- Time of measurement: when the research measures are made or the data are collected

Chronological Age   The first factor, **chronological age**, or maturational level, is defined by the number of time units that have elapsed since birth. The chronological age factor is often simply called age.

Cohort   The second factor, **cohort**, refers to a generation of individuals who were born at the same time, either having a particular year of birth or being born during a circumscribed time such as 5 years. Members of a cohort often have certain common experiences during the course of their development. For example, the lives of people in a particular cohort are influenced by the state of medical knowledge available when they were infants, young children, adolescents, and even adults. Today's older adults, for instance, were vulnerable to whooping cough and polio in their childhood years, whereas children today are vaccinated against these illnesses.

The early education of cohort members was influenced by the teaching philosophies and the technologies available during their years of schooling. Today's older adults did not use computers in school, nor were they likely to have had computers in the workplace in their young or middle adult years. For today's older adults, exposure to television during their childhood years was limited or possibly nonexistent. Today's older adults had fewer opportunities for higher education compared with the many opportunities available to the young adults of today.

The professional opportunities available to members of a particular cohort depend on the prevailing state of the general economy and the level of technological advancement when they enter the labor force and progress through their careers. Also, changing societal views mean that today's young women and members of ethnic minority groups have greater opportunities for training in the skills needed for productive careers than did women and members of minority groups in the past.

In sum, cohort members are likely to have a common set of experiences as they travel through life. Furthermore, the influence of such experiences occurs at a common stage of development for members of the same cohort. One example is war. War affects every member of a society in some way. However, the effect of war can vary considerably for different age groups, particularly when the war is waged on foreign soil. Thus, war may have a more direct impact on young adults who serve in the military than it does on middle-aged and older adults who are not serving in the military during the war. But when individuals live within a battle zone, all age groups are likely to feel the effects of war.

Before leaving the discussion of cohort, we must acknowledge that even though there are similarities among cohort members, there is also diversity. Just because individuals were born in approximately the same year does not guarantee that they all had exactly the same exposure to specific opportunities and experiences during the course of their development. Even within the same country, individuals in any given cohort may have had different educational and job opportunities and different access to health care and dietary nutrition. Some individuals grew up in cities and others in rural environments. Some were more economically advantaged than others. Cohort members vary in religious beliefs as well as in ethnic backgrounds (European American, African American, Hispanic American, Asian American, Native American), which can be associated with diverse views on childrearing and expectations about the role and importance of family.

Time of Measurement   The third factor in aging research, **time of measurement**, is related to the conditions that prevail when the research is conducted. When individuals participate in a research study, they are in a particular state of general health. They have a certain work status (for example, being employed full time) and family status (for example, being married). If a researcher were to retest these same individuals on a subsequent occasion, some of them may have experienced changes in health. Some may have experienced changes in work status such as being promoted, downsized, or retired. Some may have experienced changes in family status such as becoming separated, divorced, widowed, or perhaps remarrying, becoming parents, grandparents, or great grandparents. All of these factors could have some bearing on their questionnaire responses or their performance on the test batteries used in the study.

Not only do individual members of a research sample undergo changes over time, but there also may be changes in the tests and the methods that are available for studying the phenomena of interest. For example, a test used by a

Figure 2.2 | Cross-Sectional, Longitudinal, and Time-Lag Research Designs

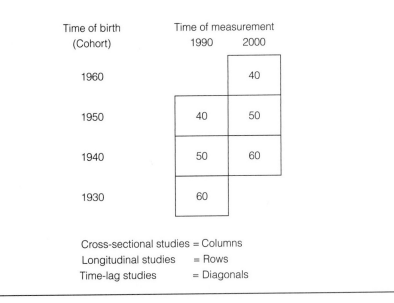

Time of birth (Cohort)	Time of measurement 1990	2000
1960		40
1950	40	50
1940	50	60
1930	60	

Cross-sectional studies = Columns
Longitudinal studies   = Rows
Time-lag studies   = Diagonals

researcher 5 years earlier may have been revised and updated. The method for presenting a visual display may be more refined than it was 5 years earlier. In addition, the personnel working on a research project could change over time. Finally, general societal attitudes and philosophies can change. For example, attitudes toward sexual behavior may have changed from the 1960s to the 1990s, partly in response to the AIDS epidemic. Time of measurement would certainly be an important factor in studies on attitudes toward sexual behavior.

Research Design

Participants in developmental research studies fall into two or more age groups. When adults from two or more age groups are studied, their responses can be compared in terms of either quantity or quality. When more than one age group is studied, researchers generally use cross-sectional or longitudinal research designs.

In some instances, however, the concern may be exclusively with individuals who fall into one age group. For example, an investigator may be interested in studying how older adults adjust to retirement from paid employment. What are the personality characteristics of older adults who report being happy and satisfied in retirement compared with those who report being unhappy and dissatisfied? Are the happy retirees of today similar in their personality characteristics to the happy retirees of 20 years ago? In this instance, only one age group is studied, and a time-lag design can be used.

Depending upon the research design, some factors are confounded with one another. The term *confounded* means that the effects of two or more factors may

Table 2.2 | "X" Indicates Factors Confounded in Cross-Sectional, Longitudinal, and Time-Lag Research Designs

	Factor		
Type of Research Design	Age	Cohort	Time of Measurement
Cross-sectional	X	X	
Longitudinal	X		X
Time Lag		X	X

be difficult or impossible to separate, or isolate, from one another. This will become clear as we take a closer look at the cross-sectional, longitudinal, and time-lag designs.

The Cross-Sectional Design   When individuals from two or more age groups are studied, the **cross-sectional research design** is the one most commonly used. In a cross-sectional study, a group of young adults (for example, 20–30 years of age) and a group of older adults (for example, 65–75 years of age) might be asked to complete a series of tests or questionnaires. If the young and older groups show differences in their level of performance or in the answers they give on the questionnaires, then we refer to *age differences,* or more appropriately to *age-related differences.*

Figure 2.2 shows examples of the cross-sectional design in the columns. For the sake of simplicity, the cohorts are defined by a specific age rather than by an age range. In one example of a cross-sectional study, data are collected in the year 1990. In a second example of a cross-sectional study, data are collected in 2000. In both examples, the youngest cohort is age 40, the middle cohort is age 50, and the oldest cohort is age 60. Note that in a cross-sectional study, data are collected at only one time, either 1990 or 2000. Because time of measurement is not a confounding factor in cross-sectional studies, there is no need for concern about changes that may take place in study participants' health, about the possibility of intervening events, or about changes in test instruments, technology, or research personnel. Moreover, attrition, or participant dropout, is minimal in cross-sectional studies because participants are tested only once.

However, the factors of age and cohort are confounded in cross-sectional research. This means that if age-related differences are found, it will not be possible to determine whether those differences can be attributed to age or to cohort membership. People who are age 40 in the year 1990 were children in the 1950s and reached young adulthood in the late 1960s. People who are age 50 in 1990 were children during the 1940s and reached young adulthood in the late 1950s. People who are age 60 in 1990 were children in the 1930s and reached young adulthood in the late 1940s. Undoubtedly, these three cohort groups were exposed to different influences and experiences throughout the course of their development. In a cross-sectional study, it would be difficult to tell whether any differences found in the responses of 40-, 50-, and 60-year-olds are due to chronological age or to cohort. Strictly speaking, the confounding of age and cohort can occur in cross-sectional research on children. However, fewer years separate children of different ages, so cohort may be less important in cross-sectional research with children than it is in cross-sectional research with adults who can vary in age by decades.

Cross-sectional studies are efficient because they are completed within a circumscribed period of time. Such efficiency is the reason that many researchers use this design. The results of cross-sectional studies allow researchers to make descriptive statements about the particular age/cohort groups that were included in the study. For example, in a cross-sectional study conducted in 1990, the 60-year-old group may perform more poorly than the 40-year-old group on a memory test. If so, then it is reasonable to conclude that there are age-related differences in memory performance. However, the findings of a cross-sectional study conducted in the year 1990 may not generalize to future cohorts of 40-year-olds and 60-year-olds. If a cross-sectional study were conducted on the memory performance of 40- and 60-year-olds in the year 2000, it is possible that the differences in the scores of these two age groups would be of lesser magnitude, possibly even nonexistent, given the increasing educational opportunities available to people of all ages in our society.

The cross-sectional design is appropriate when the purpose of a research study is to delineate the current status of young versus older adults with regard to scores on memory, problem solving, or personality tests, or to determine how young and older adults differ in their responses on self-report questionnaires or behavioral measures. If age-related differences are indeed found between two or more age groups in a cross-sectional study, then those age groups could be targeted for more time-consuming and costly longitudinal studies, which will now be described.

The Longitudinal Design In a **longitudinal research design,** the same individuals are followed over time. These individuals are tested on two or possibly more occasions. The rows in Figure 2.2 show examples of studies having a longitudinal design. A researcher sets out in the year 1990 to interview, or test, a group of 40-year-olds, who were born in 1950. In 2000, these same individuals are located and retested, at which time they will be age 50. While it is not shown in Figure 2.2, these individuals could be tested for a third time in 2010 when they reach age 60. If these research participants respond differently in 2000 than they did in 1990, we would refer to *age changes,* or more appropriately to *age-related changes.*

In studies using a longitudinal research design, age and cohort are not confounded because all participants are members of the same cohort. However, the factors of age and time of measurement are confounded. If age-related changes occur between two times of testing, it will not be possible to determine whether those changes can be attributed to participants' chronological age or to time of measurement. In longitudinal studies of adults, the points of testing are often far apart, which increases the likelihood of time-of-measurement effects. Also, since the longitudinal design calls for repeated testing of the same individuals, there may be practice effects. However, the further apart the points of testing, the less likely it will be that practice effects will influence the findings.

A different source of confounding in longitudinal studies comes from the likelihood of participant dropout, or attrition. The very nature of longitudinal studies requires that the same individuals be tested at least twice, and possibly even more times. Even with conscientious efforts on the part of longitudinal researchers to maintain the interest and motivation of study participants, it is rare that every individual from the original sample that was tested initially at Time 1 will be available for retesting at subsequent times. Attrition during the course of the study would not present any particular problem if it was random.

Unfortunately, attrition is often selective. This point was illustrated clearly in an excellent study by Siegler and Botwinick (1979), who inspected data from a longitudinal research study being conducted at Duke University in which tests of intellectual ability were administered every 6 years. Over time, some participants dropped out while others returned for retesting. Time 1 scores were available for everyone who initially participated in the study, so Siegler and Botwinick were able to compare the Time 1 scores of participants who subsequently dropped out of the study with the Time 1 scores of participants who remained in the study. The Time 1 scores of individuals who dropped out were lower than the Time 1 scores of those who returned for subsequent testing. Thus, the sample was shrinking over time, and becoming more and more positively selective because the higher performers were returning but the lower performers were not. With **selective attrition,** the composition of a longitudinal study sample fluctuates over time. The sample tested at Time 1 may have been representative of the population of interest. At subsequent times, however, the sample may become more positively selective and thus less representative of the population.

By its very nature, longitudinal research is time consuming and costly. Study participants must be located for retesting and their interest must be maintained between testing dates to ensure that they continue to take part in the study. However, a longitudinal design can provide interesting and important information about whether individuals change over time (that is, whether there is *intraindividual change*, or *intraindividual variability*). For this reason, the longitudinal method is an excellent approach for studying multidirectionality (Hoyer & Rybash, 1996), one of the propositions in the lifespan perspective described earlier in this chapter. The term *multidirectionality* refers to the possibility that some aspects of development involve growth (gain), some involve stability (no change), and some involve decline (loss). As Chapter 6 describes in more detail, some abilities (such as level of vocabulary) increase with age, while others (such as solving abstract problems) show decline. If a longitudinal study examines a range of abilities or characteristics, then it can delineate which ones increase, which ones remain stable, and which ones show age-related decline. Furthermore, if the longitudinal design calls for more than two times of testing, it will be possible to estimate the rate at which change may occur.

Some researchers who want to investigate the effects of a particular type of training or treatment use an intervention approach, and many intervention studies employ a short-term longitudinal design. For example, in an intervention study on the effect of training on certain abilities, a battery of tests would be administered to a sample of individuals at Time 1 (baseline). Then training sessions intended to increase performance on ability tests might be conducted for some period. Afterward (Time 2), the same individuals who were tested at Time 1 would be retested with a similar battery of tests to determine whether there is any improvement in their performance abilities. A similar battery of tests might be administered a third time as well to determine whether any immediate gains associated with the training are maintained over a longer period. In intervention studies, repeated testings could occur over a relatively brief interval (weeks) or over a longer time (months or more). Some researchers (for example, Schaie & Willis, 1986) have used this approach to demonstrate that older adults are capable of improving certain skills and abilities with training. Such improvement would illustrate the lifespan proposition of *plasticity,* a term that refers to the possibility that capabilities are not fixed, but rather that they can be modified (Hoyer & Rybash, 1996). Plasticity is a key proposition in the lifespan developmental perspective (Baltes, 1987).

Intervention studies are not limited to the effects of training on cognitive abilities. They have also been conducted on the effects of therapy. For example, Chapter 11 describes how a short-term longitudinal design can be used to evaluate whether therapy using pets has a positive effect on the behavior and life satisfaction of older adults who live in institutional environments.

Ideally, intervention studies include a control group that is tested at the same points in time as the trained group. However, those in the control group do not receive any skill training sessions or any therapeutic intervention. Then the test scores, behaviors, or feelings of life satisfaction of participants who received training or therapeutic intervention can be compared with control participants who did not. This comparison makes it possible to determine whether any changes in performance, behavior, or life satisfaction seen at Time 2 are due to training or therapeutic intervention or whether they are simply due to practice on the same kinds of tests or behavioral measures or to the benefits of attention received during the testing sessions. Of course, when training or treatment intervention is relatively brief (weeks or possibly months), research participants are approximately the same age both before and after the intervention. From a developmental perspective, it would be of interest to include both young- and older-adult training/treatment and control groups. This would make it possible to determine whether the pattern of improvement for the two age groups is similar or whether one age group benefits more than another from the training/treatment procedure.

The Time-Lag Design   The **time-lag research design** is not strictly developmental because all of the study participants are members of the same age group. In this design, individuals of a particular chronological age are tested at two or more different times, usually years or decades apart. Individuals of the same chronological age who are tested at different times are members of different cohorts because they were born at different times. The three diagonals in Figure 2.2 are examples of the time-lag design. Each diagonal represents a time-lag study in which all participants are either age 40, 50, or 60. In each time-lag study, the factors of cohort and time of measurement are confounded. Thus, the 40-year-olds tested in 1990 were born in 1950, whereas the 40-year-olds tested in 2000 were born in 1960. The 50-year-olds tested in 1990 were born in 1940, whereas the 50-year-olds tested in 2000 were born in 1950. The 60-year-olds tested in 1990 were born in 1930, whereas the 60-year-olds tested in 2000 were born in 1940.

As an illustration, let's suppose that an investigator conducts a study on the attitudes of 60-year-old women toward divorce. In the year 1990, the investigator administers a divorce attitude questionnaire to a group of 60-year-old women. The investigator finds that, overall, the attitude of this group is relatively negative. In 2000, the investigator administers the divorce attitude questionnaire to another sample of 60-year-old women. This time, the attitude toward divorce is less negative.

The 60-year-old women tested in 2000 were born in 1940, while the 60-year-old women tested in 1990 were born in 1930. Members of these two cohort groups may have had different experiences during the course of their development. The 60-year-old women tested in 2000 may have a less negative view of divorce due to their lifelong experiences. They may have been more exposed to divorce at various points during their lives. Perhaps their parents divorced or they themselves are divorced and have known more people their age who are divorced. In addition, women in the two cohort groups were tested at different times, 1990 and 2000. Assuming that divorce received greater media attention in 2000 than it did in 1990, it might be more accepted in 2000 than it was 1990. If the 60-year-old women tested in 2000 are less negative in their attitudes toward divorce than the 60-year-old women tested in 1990, this difference may be a time-of-measurement effect related to societal views at the time of testing. In sum, the factors of cohort and time of measurement are confounded in time-lag studies. This makes it difficult to determine whether any differences in the attitudes of the two samples of 60-year-old women can be attributed to their cohort membership or to the fact that data were collected at two different times. Clearly, investigators must exercise judgment about the possible influence of time-of-measurement factors. In the example just described, it is possible that societal views that prevail at the time of testing could influence women's attitude toward divorce.

In sum, age is not a confounding factor in time-lag studies because all participants are from the same age group. Nonetheless, individuals are characterized not only by their chronological age but also by the cohort to which they belong. Research findings obtained with older adults from one cohort may or may not generalize to findings that would be obtained from older adults some years in the future, or findings that might have been obtained from older adults in the past.

Is it possible to disentangle the factors of age, cohort, and time of measurement in studies with a cross-sectional, longitudinal, and time-lag design? One way to do so would be to conduct a logical analysis, and another would be to use complex sequential research designs.

Logical Analysis   A study by Woodruff and Birren (1972) encompassed aspects of all three designs: longitudinal, cross-sectional, and time-lag (see Figure 2.3).

Grandmothers today and grandmothers ca. 1950 may differ not only in attitudes and opinions, but also in physical appearance.

These researchers had access to data collected in 1944 on 20-year-old college students' personal adjustment as measured by a questionnaire called the California Test of Personality (CTP). These students were born in 1924. In 1969, 25 years after the initial testing, these individuals (now age 45) were contacted and asked to complete the CTP a second time. This facet of the study was longitudinal, since the same individuals were followed over time and

Figure 2.3 | Diagram of Woodruff and Birren's (1972) Study

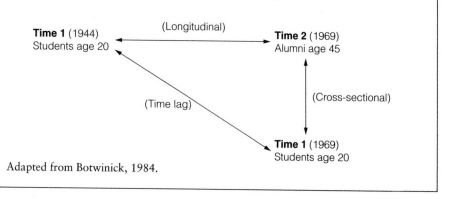

Adapted from Botwinick, 1984.

tested twice. Interestingly, there was no significant difference in the personal adjustment scores of these individuals at ages 20 and 45.

In 1969, Woodruff and Birren administered the CTP to a new sample of 20-year-old college students. Personal adjustment scores of this cohort of young adults, who were born in 1949, were compared with personal adjustment scores of the 45-year-olds, who were retested in 1969. This facet of the study is cross-sectional because two age groups from different cohorts were tested at the same time. On the cross-sectional aspect of the study, the scores of the 20-year-olds were lower than the scores of the 45-year-olds.

A time-lag comparison is built into Woodruff and Birren's study on personal adjustment in that the CTP scores were available for two different cohorts of 20-year-olds. The 20-years-olds born in 1924 (and tested in 1944) reported themselves as more adjusted than did the 20-year-olds born in 1949 (and tested in 1969).

Botwinick (1984) suggested that a logical analysis could be used to estimate which factor (age, cohort, time of measurement) was significant in Woodruff and Birren's study. In this logical analysis, the reasoning is as follows: There was no age-related change in the longitudinal comparison. Therefore, age and time of measurement can be ruled out as significant factors. However, the cross-sectional and time-lag comparisons were both significant. Because cohort is the one factor common to both cross-sectional and time-lag comparisons, it is logical to conclude that cohort is responsible for the significant cross-sectional finding. Logical analysis is a thoughtful approach for attempting to disentangle factors that are confounded in aging research. Unfortunately, few studies have longitudinal, cross-sectional, and time-lag components, so the logical analysis approach is not always feasible.

Sequential Designs   Schaie (1965) proposed that using **sequential research designs** could disentangle the effects of the three factors: age, cohort, and time of measurement. As illustrated in Figure 2.4, each of three sequential designs involves some combination of the cross-sectional, longitudinal, or time-lag comparisons.

Figure 2.4   Three Sequential Designs

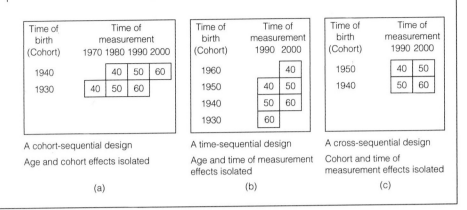

A cohort-sequential design

Age and cohort effects isolated

(a)

A time-sequential design

Age and time of measurement effects isolated

(b)

A cross-sequential design

Cohort and time of measurement effects isolated

(c)

The cohort-sequential design calls for simultaneous cross-sectional and longitudinal studies (Figure 2.4a). Note that two longitudinal studies are conducted on two different cohorts. This design separates, or isolates, age and cohort effects. However, the time-of-measurement effect cannot be isolated from the cohort effect, so this design is most useful if the researcher can assume that time of measurement effects are trivial (Elias, Elias, & Elias, 1977).

The time-sequential design (Figure 2.4b) calls for two or more cross-sectional comparisons at two or more times of measurement. This design isolates the effects of age and time of measurement, but the cohort effect cannot be isolated. Thus, this design is useful if the main concern is with separating the effects of age and time of measurement and the researcher can assume that cohort effects are trivial (Elias, Elias, & Elias, 1977).

The cross-sequential design (Figure 2.4c) consists of two or more cross-sectional and longitudinal comparisons. The effects of cohort and time of measurement are isolated but the effect of age is not. The cross-sectional part of this design involves a confound between age and cohort, while the longitudinal part involves a confound between age and time of measurement. However, this design is useful if the main concern is with separating the effects of cohort and time of measurement (Elias, Elias, & Elias, 1977).

Sequential designs require a great deal of time and effort. Furthermore, it is not clear that sequential strategies guarantee an unequivocal interpretation of the factors in aging research (Adam, 1978). However, Schaie was successful in bringing the importance of confounded factors to the attention of research investigators.

MEASUREMENT

In research studies on aging and older adulthood, data are gathered to measure the variables of interest. The type of data collected may include the responses that study participants make on instruments such as self-report questionnaires, the scores that participants earn on tests of ability, the responses participants make on tests of personality, or the ratings that others make of study participants' behavior in naturalistic or more structured laboratory settings. Regardless of the specific variables that are of interest in a particular study or the manner in which they are measured, it is essential that the measurement instruments used are both reliable and valid.

Reliability

Reliability has to do with the dependability, or consistency, of the instruments used to measure variables, or phenomena, of interest. The test-retest reliability of an instrument is related to whether the responses that research participants make on a test instrument (such as a questionnaire or a test of intellectual ability) are identical, or at least very similar, on separate occasions. When the responses of research participants are potentially ambiguous (for example, if responses are made to open-ended questions that must be evaluated later, or if observers rate research participants' behavior), then it is important to demonstrate that there is inter-rater reliability. This means that two or more independent raters, or observers, must make similar evaluations of participants' open-ended responses or similar ratings of participants' behavior.

In many cross-sectional aging studies, the same test instrument is used for the young- and older-adult research participants. In many longitudinal studies, the same test instrument is administered to research participants on various occasions over an extended time. Of special concern to developmental researchers who study aging and older adulthood is that the reliability of a particular instrument may have been established with young adults. The same instrument may now be applied to older adults with little information on whether it is reliable for that age group.

Keep in mind that the reliability of a measurement instrument must be established for all age groups regardless of whether a research study is cross-sectional or longitudinal. For cross-sectional research, the possibility of age-related differences can be entertained only if the measures have been shown to be reliable for all age groups included in the study. For longitudinal research, the possibility of age-related change within individuals over time can be entertained only if the measures are reliable for all ages/stages of adulthood.

The concept of reliability applies not only to specific test instruments but also to the findings of research studies. If an investigator conducts a study and obtains certain results, then he or she should obtain consistent results if the study is conducted a second time, assuming that the procedure used for the second study is the same as it was for the first.

Validity

Once the reliability of a measurement instrument is established, attention must turn to its **validity.** There are several different types of validity, but all have to do with whether we are measuring what we think we are measuring. Only if we are measuring what we think we are measuring do we stand a good chance of drawing appropriate conclusions from our data. The concept of validity applies both to specific measurement instruments and to the findings of research studies.

The **internal validity** of a research study refers to the accurate identification and interpretation of the factor(s), or effect(s), responsible for an observation. The **external validity** of a research study refers to whether findings obtained from the sample of study participants can be generalized to the population of interest.

One way to illustrate what internal validity means in research studies on adult development and aging is to describe situations that threaten validity. As an example, we can consider a cross-sectional study in which participants from young- and older-adult age groups take a memory test. The results indicate that, on average, the scores of the young group are higher than the scores of the older group. Can we conclude that age is the reason for this difference in memory scores? The young and older participants in a cross-sectional study differ in chronological age, but they also differ in cohort membership. The educational background and experience of a particular cohort could certainly influence scores on a memory test. If we conclude that the older group's lower memory scores are attributed solely to chronological age without acknowledging that cohort could also be important, then there is a threat to the internal validity of the study. As mentioned earlier in this chapter, age is an organismic variable. This means that age is inherent in a person and cannot be controlled. For this reason, we refer to age-related differences in a cross-sectional study rather than stating that age is the factor causing the difference in memory scores. The discussion of experimental versus quasi-experimental approaches later on in this chapter should clarify this concept further.

The internal and external validity of a research study are not totally independent. Any threat to internal validity could, in turn, represent a threat to external validity. If the memory study just described were repeated 10 years hence, young and older research participants would be members of different cohorts. If the basis for the difference between the young and older groups in the original study was actually cohort membership rather than age, then the results of that study would not be repeated, or replicated, in the more recent one. This means that the findings of the initial memory study would not be generalizable to samples of young and older adults who will be tested in the future.

Ecological Validity   **Ecological validity** is a type of external validity that has been of great interest to contemporary researchers. Ecological validity refers to whether the results obtained with a particular test instrument accurately reflect real-world functioning or real-world behavior. Scores on an intelligence test might be highly reliable for young and older adults. But do these scores inform us about the level of competence young and older adults are likely to demonstrate when they deal with real-world situations?

Of particular concern to developmental psychologists who study aging is whether a specific test has equivalent ecological validity for young adults and older adults. For example, some intelligence test items tap skills that are taught in school and needed for successful functioning in academic settings. Perhaps it is not surprising that scores on such tests are related to academic performance.

The everyday lives of many young adults involve full-time or part-time engagement in academic pursuits, so their scores on such tests may be valid measures of competence in the everyday life of a student. However, the majority of older adults are not students. The scores older adults earn on these tests may have less value, or be less ecologically valid, as far as measuring their everyday competence. Chapter 6 discusses this issue further.

Heterotypic Continuity   Heterotypic continuity has to do with whether a measure used to assess some underlying quality, or characteristic, has the same degree of internal validity for different age groups in a cross-sectional study, or for the same people as they are followed over time in a longitudinal study.

Even if individuals do possess some underlying characteristic, the behavioral manifestations may differ depending upon their age group. Heterotypic continuity is especially relevant in a clinical context. When mental disorders are assessed, the weighting of various factors could shift as a function of age or the changing contexts that accompany age (Mroczek, Hurt, & Berman, 1999). Thus, an underlying mental disorder could be stable and enduring over the adult life span, but the behavioral symptoms of that disorder could fluctuate over time. An assessment instrument that taps a narrow set of behaviors assumed to be symptomatic of a particular diagnosis could be more valid for one age group than for another.

Depression is a mental disorder discussed in greater detail in Chapter 11. Suppose that a researcher wishes to study depression in young and older adults. To measure depression in the two age groups, the researcher administers a depression questionnaire that is known to have a high level of test-retest reliability for both age groups. However, is this questionnaire an appropriate way to measure depression for both age groups? Many depression questionnaires include items about physical functioning such as loss of appetite, loss of interest in sex, or sleep disturbances. These symptoms may be indicative of depression in young adults, but in older adults they may simply be hallmarks of aging. We could be in error if we interpret a high score on this questionnaire as a valid indicator of depression in older adults.

Heterotypic continuity is relevant in areas other than clinical assessment. To illustrate, a researcher may want to measure social attachment over the adult life span (Mroczek, Hurt, & Berman, 1999). In young adulthood, attachment may be displayed by an individual's intimate relationships with a spouse and/or by involvement in close work associations. In older adulthood, however, attachment may be displayed in close relationships with adult children and grandchildren. Thus, the nature of attachments people have could differ in young and older adulthood, and they also could change as individuals progress through their adult years.

The Meaning of Rating Scales   In many aging studies, young and older participants express their beliefs or opinions using rating scales, but is it possible that these scales mean different things to different age groups? Consider the following instruction given to young and older adults who are asked to rate their own health:

Circle a number showing how you rate yourself in health. If 10 indicates excellent health and 1 indicates poor health, what do you think your present health is?

```
1     2     3     4     5     6     7     8     9     10
L__|__|__|__|__|__|__|__|__|__J
Poor                     Average              Excellent
```

Let's assume that this self-rating scale is reliable for both age groups. That is, both young and older adults rate themselves as having the same level of health on two or more occasions, assuming that there are no significant changes in medical status in the time that elapses between the two ratings. If the health self-ratings of the young and older adults are equally high, can we conclude that the young and older adults consider themselves to have the same level of health?

Before drawing such a conclusion, the possibility must be entertained that when rating their health, young and older adults each use their respective age peers as a comparison group. The average ratings of the young and older age groups may both be high (for example, "8"), but older adults may be rating themselves relative to age peers who have a greater number of health problems than do the age peers of the young adults. The average health ratings for the two age groups may be objectively similar, but ratings may represent something quite different for the young and older adults.

One way of dealing with this situation is to make the rating instructions as explicit as possible. The young and older adults could be instructed specifically as to the comparison group against which they should rate their own health (such as, "Compare yourself to others your age."). The investigator will then have to acknowledge that young and older adults are using different standards when making their self-ratings, and also that high ratings may not be truly comparable for the two age groups. Rather than concluding that the young and older adults have the same level of self-rated health, the conclusion would be that members of each age group rated themselves as having a high level of health relative to age peers.

Another way to approach young and older adults' evaluations of their own health is for the investigator to include additional measures. Not only will young and older adults complete the rating scale just described, but they also will be asked to complete a questionnaire that asks how many days in the past year that they have been ill, how many medications they are taking, and so on. By using multiple measures, the investigator will obtain more information than would be available from research participants' ratings on a single scale.

Sampling

How many individuals should be included in a research study? With a case study method, research usually consists of in-depth investigation of one person, or perhaps a small number of individuals. Open-ended interviews often result in a rich array of descriptive information. In some instances, the information obtained from in-depth case studies can be used to test hypotheses about development in larger samples of individuals.

Most studies on aging and older adulthood include a sample of individuals recruited from the population about whom a particular research question is asked (Schaie, 1995). However, obtaining a random sample can be challenging, particularly if the participants must travel to a research laboratory or complete a lengthy series of tests or questionnaires (Collins, 1996).

The way a sample is selected can affect both the internal and external validity of a research study. If selection factors vary for the different age groups included in a developmental study, then the samples may not be equally representative of the population of their respective age groups. To illustrate, we can consider a study in which an investigator administers a memory test to a sample of young adults and a sample of older adults. The young sample is recruited from the population of undergraduate students enrolled in psychology courses. The older sample is recruited from a nearby nursing home. The investigator finds out that the memory scores of the older group are lower than the memory scores of the young group. If the investigator attributes the older group's lower memory scores solely to age, this would represent a threat to the internal validity of the study. The reason for this threat is that not only do the young and older study participants differ in cohort membership, but they also almost certainly differ in health and lifestyle. Individuals in the young adult sample are probably healthy, and as students, they are actively engaged in a memory-demanding lifestyle. In contrast, the individuals in the older adult sample are likely to be in poor physical health or they would not be living in a nursing home. In addition, a sizeable proportion of nursing home residents suffer from cognitive impairment (dementia is discussed further in Chapter 11), which will definitely have a negative influence on the older sample's memory scores. Furthermore, nursing home environments make few cognitive demands compared with those inherent in college and university settings.

The likely threat to internal validity in this study will probably compromise its external validity. To illustrate, another research investigator administers the same memory test to a sample of young adult college students and a sample of older adults who live independently in the community and actively participate in continuing education programs. This investigator may well find that memory scores are no different for young and older adults. The failure of the second investigator to replicate the findings of the first investigator means that the results of the first study were not generalizable. Therefore, they lack external validity. Inconsistent findings across aging studies can often be traced to inconsistency in sampling procedures for the age groups that are included (Hertzog, 1990). Investigators may fail to recognize, or to acknowledge, that a sample in a particular study may have unique characteristics.

Threats to the internal validity of aging studies are not always as glaring as in the memory study comparing young college students with older nursing home residents. Let's suppose that another investigator conducts a study on memory. In this study, the young-adult sample consists of university undergraduates who have volunteered to participate to earn extra credit in their psychology courses. The older-adult sample has been recruited from the community with newspaper ads targeted to older people who feel that they have problems with their memory. In this study, the young-adult sample has not been self-selected for poor memory whereas the older sample has. If the purpose of the study is to compare the memory of young and older adults, and if the investigator is not explicit about the strategy used to recruit the samples of young and older adults, then the study may lack internal validity. Another investigator may conduct a similar study, this time comparing the memory of young college students and older adults who pride themselves on their good memory. The findings of this study may not replicate those of the study for which the older sample was recruited on the basis of memory problems. Therefore, the first study lacks external validity as well as internal validity.

To increase the likelihood that any differences between young and older adults in cross-sectional studies are indeed associated with chronological age, some investigators attempt to equate samples from the two age groups on various dimensions. For example, an investigator may try to control for the influence of health factors by screening study participants for specific illnesses or health problems. However, this strategy could skew the sampling in different ways for the young and older adults. The incidence of certain illnesses and health problems increases with age. Screening older study participants for these illnesses and health problems could result in greater positive bias in the older-adult sample than it would in the young-adult sample (Salthouse, 1982).

In some instances, it may be appropriate to recruit an older sample that is just as high, or perhaps even higher, on some measure compared with the young sample. To illustrate, let's suppose that an investigator conducting a study on cognitive processes purposely selects a sample of older adults whose verbal ability is just as high and perhaps even higher than the verbal ability of the young sample. If the older sample, despite being more positively selected for high verbal ability, still earns lower scores on tests of cognitive ability compared with the young sample, then the investigator can have some confidence that this age-related decrement is not simply a function of the older sample's level of verbal ability (Tun, Wingfield, Rosen, & Blanchard, 1998). In fact, the investigator may conclude that the age-related decrement obtained in this study actually underestimates the decrement that is likely to be found if the older sample were less select in terms of verbal ability (Kausler, 1982).

Some investigators have access to young college students and older college alumni. Such young and older samples are assumed to be similar in educational backgrounds. Thus, there can be some confidence that any age-related differences found are not attributable to age differences in educational background. In an early study on age-related differences in memory, I employed just such a strategy in an attempt to equate young and older research participants on as many variables as possible (Erber, 1974). Young and older nuns were recruited from the same five religious teaching orders. The women in these two age groups had comparable educational and professional backgrounds. The young nuns were full-time teachers, whereas the older nuns were either semi- or fully retired from teaching. Also, the young and older nuns had similar lifestyles. The purpose of recruiting young and older samples who were similar on a number of dimensions was to maximize the internal validity of the study. However, maximizing the internal validity of the study meant that the findings might not generalize to a broader segment of the young- and older-adult population. That is, the findings might have limited external validity. There are no simple solutions to sampling in aging research. Rather, there are trade-offs between internal and external validity. Attempts to equate young and older participants on variables other than age may increase a study's internal validity. But this may limit the external validity, or whether the findings can be generalized to broader segments of the young- and older-adult population.

Another possible threat to the internal and external validity of aging studies is posed by possible differences in the ethnic background of young- and older-adult study participants. Consider the following example:

> Professor Smith wants to conduct a survey of young and older adults' opinions about whether families are obligated to care for their elderly members. The young sample of survey participants consists of students at Professor Smith's university, most of whom are of European American background. The older sample is recruited from a local senior center that serves a population that is English-speaking but largely of Hispanic American background. The investigator finds that the older adults in the study are more likely than the young adults to think that families are obligated to care for their elderly members.

This study could lack internal validity if Professor Smith does not acknowledge the different ethnic backgrounds of the two age groups and concludes that the differences in opinion are associated with age. At a different university, Professor Allen conducts a similar survey in which both young and older adult samples are of Hispanic American background. In this study, the young and older samples do not differ in their opinions about family obligation for the care of elderly members. Thus, Professor Smith's study lacks not only internal validity, but also external validity.

APPROACHES TO CONDUCTING AGING RESEARCH

Investigators who study aging and older adulthood must have a clear idea about the questions their research studies are intended to answer. Their hypotheses serve as a guide to which variables are of interest and the approach that will be taken to analyze the research data they collect. Their studies may use an experimental, quasi-experimental, or descriptive approach.

The Experimental Approach

In studies that use an **experimental approach,** research variables are considered to be independent or dependent. The researcher manipulates the independent variable. The manipulated independent variable is usually categorical, with at least two, but sometimes more, levels, or categories.

The hallmark of the experimental method is random assignment of research participants to the various levels, or categories, of the independent variable.

The dependent variable is used to measure the outcome of the manipulated independent variable. In a true experiment, one in which participants are randomly assigned to the various levels of the independent variable, it is possible to make cause-and-effect statements regarding the influence of the independent variable on the outcome as measured by the dependent variable.

As an example of the experimental approach, let's suppose there is reason to believe that older adults who are explicitly instructed to use visual imagery when studying a list of 25 words will remember more of those words at a later time compared with older adults who are given no explicit instructions to use visual imagery when studying the same words. In an experiment designed to test this hypothesis, type of memory instructions is the independent variable, and it has two categorical levels, or treatment conditions. As older-adult research participants arrive at the laboratory, they are randomly assigned to one of the two treatment conditions: visual-imagery instructions or no-visual-imagery instructions. Those participants randomly assigned to the visual-imagery treatment condition are instructed to form visual imagery (and perhaps give an example of how to do so) when trying to remember the words they will be shown. Those assigned to the no-visual-imagery treatment condition are just told to study the list, with no instruction to use visual imagery. After receiving the treatment (instructions to use visual imagery or no such instructions), participants are shown a list of 25 words. After viewing the list for two minutes, they are asked to recall as many of the words as they can.

In this experiment, the dependent measure is the score on the memory test, or how many words the participant can recall. If those assigned to the visual-imagery treatment condition recall more words than those assigned to the no-visual-imagery treatment condition, then we can infer that visual-imagery instructions caused a higher level of memory performance.

In this research study, the experimenter manipulated the categories of the independent variable, type of instructions, and randomly assigned the older-adult research participants to one of the two instruction treatment conditions (visual-imagery instructions or no-visual-imagery instructions). After the treatment was administered, the visual-imagery instructions group recalled more words, on average, compared with the no-visual-imagery instructions group. Because research participants were randomly assigned to the two levels of the instruction variable, it is proper to assume that the only difference between the two groups was in the type of instruction received. Therefore, we can conclude that visual-imagery instructions caused the higher recall scores. Note that a statement about cause and effect is appropriate only if research participants truly are randomly assigned to the treatment levels. Random assignment ensures that all extraneous variables are evenly distributed across the levels of the independent variable. With a sufficiently large sample, it is likely that the memory ability of the participants who are randomly assigned to the two different treatments will be equivalent at the outset of the study. With smaller participant samples, the research investigator may choose to take a baseline memory measure of participants in each of the two treatment groups before administering any instruction to demonstrate that the memory performance of the two groups is equivalent at the outset.

The Quasi-Experimental Approach

In true experiments, the investigator manipulates the independent variable and randomly assigns research participants to the various levels of the independent variable. A dependent variable measures the outcome of this manipulation. Sometimes studies appear to have the same form as a true experiment, but if research participants are not randomly assigned to levels of the categorical factor, then the study is not a true experiment. Rather, it uses a **quasi-experimental approach.** For example, suppose that a group of young adults and a group of older adults are each instructed to study a list of words and remember as many as they can. On a subsequent memory test, the scores of the older group are lower than the scores of the young group.

The design of this study appears similar to that of the study just described in that age group is a categorical variable with two levels (young and older) and members of each age group have a score on a memory test. However, research participants cannot be randomly assigned to the two age categories (young or older) as was the case with the two categories of memory instruction in the true experiment. Therefore, in this study, cause-and-effect statements cannot be made. Any difference between the memory performance of the young and older groups could be caused by biological, psychological, or social factors associated with having lived more years or being born into a particular cohort. If the performance of the older group is lower than the performance of the young group, it cannot be concluded that age caused a decrement in memory performance. However, it would be appropriate to state that age is *associated with* a decrement in memory performance.

In sum, age as well as gender, ethnicity, socioeconomic status, educational level, and religious belief are organismic variables (that is, part of the person). When variables are organismic, studies are quasi-experimental. They may take the form of experiments, but they are not truly experimental because participants have not been randomly assigned to levels of the organismic variable.

Sometimes researchers want to study individuals who fall into naturally occurring groups. Research participants are not randomly assigned to these groups, so these studies are also considered to be quasi-experimental. To illustrate, suppose an investigator is interested in studying the level of life satisfaction reported by older adults who live in various housing environments. The investigator learns that the construction of two different apartment buildings is nearing completion, and the managers of both buildings are accepting applications from tenants. One building will be age integrated, meaning that residents can be any age, and no special services will be provided for the tenants. The other building will be age segregated (specifically for adults over the age of 62) and services such as transportation and planned activities will be offered to the tenants.

The investigator thinks that studying older adults who move into these two buildings will be an excellent opportunity to find out whether older adults are happier and more satisfied when they live in an age-integrated setting with no special services as opposed to an age-segregated setting in which special services are provided. The investigator waits until three months after older adults have moved into each of the two different buildings to allow time for them to get unpacked and settled. Then the investigator asks the older residents in each building to complete a life satisfaction questionnaire (on which scores can range from 0 for low life satisfaction to 30 for high life satisfaction).

Older adults in the age-integrated and age-segregated buildings are similar in age, socioeconomic status, and ethnic composition. However, there was no random assignment of the older adults to the age-integrated and age-segregated apartment buildings. Therefore, it is possible that the two groups of residents differ along one or more dimensions that have not been measured and may not be clearly apparent. Any such differences could actually be the basis for the type of building they selected as well as the degree of happiness and life satisfaction they report. If the investigator finds that older adults in the age-segregated building have higher life satisfaction than do older adults in the age-integrated building, then we can conclude that there is an association between type of apartment building and older adults' degree of happiness and satisfaction. However, it would not be appropriate to conclude that age-segregated apartments cause happiness and life satisfaction.

Quasi-Experimental or Experimental?

Consider the following hypothesis, which has sparked a great deal of interest among researchers: Older adults who have a high level of physical activity will have better memories compared to older adults who have a low level of physical activity. To test this hypothesis, a study can be designed in which activity level is either an organismic variable or an independent variable. If activity level is an organismic variable, the study is quasi-experimental. Alternatively, if activity level is an independent variable, the study is experimental. In both studies, the older participants will earn a score on a memory test.

Before initiating either type of study, it will be necessary to measure the physical activity level of potential participants. One way to do this would be to use a self-report questionnaire. Potential research participants could be given a list of activities and asked to place a check mark next to each one that applies to them. The more items they check, the higher their assumed level of activity. A second way to measure activity level would be to have potential research participants keep a diary of their daily activities. The more activities they record in the diary, the higher their assumed level of activity. A third, albeit less convenient, way to measure activity would be to have several independent observers record the behavior of potential study participants, noting the activities in which they engage over some period of time. An activity score could be tallied based on the number of activity observations recorded, perhaps with a value assigned to the various activities that were observed. For example, strolling in the mall would be worth fewer points than participating in an exercise class. To ensure reliability, we would want to make certain that at least two independent judges agree on the activity value that is assigned to the various observations.

A Quasi-Experimental Study on Activity Level   To conduct a quasi-experimental study on activity level, we can use the self-report measure of activity to select participants whose scores on a self-reported activity questionnaire fall at the two

Some researchers have found that keeping active is
associated with better memory in older adulthood.

extremes: those who checked very few activity items on the self-report scale (low
activity) and those who checked many activity items on the self-report scale
(high activity). For our present purpose, let's assume that the self-report activity measure is both reliable and valid. Also, the memory test we will administer to our study participants is a reliable and valid measure of memory
functioning, with possible scores ranging from 0 to 25.

In this study, activity level is a categorical variable with two levels, low activity and high activity. Because participants were not randomly assigned to the low
and high categories of the activity variable, the study is quasi-experimental. A
statistical analysis can be conducted to test the hypothesis that high-activity participants have higher memory scores compared to low-activity participants. If
this is found, then we can conclude that high activity level is *associated with* high
memory scores. However, we cannot conclude that high activity causes high
scores on the memory test.

A True Experimental Study on Activity Level   Now suppose we want to conduct
an experimental study to determine whether an intervention involving physical
activity affects the memory functioning of older adults who are sedentary. Using
the same self-report activity measure employed in the quasi-experimental study,
we can pinpoint a sample of older adults whose level of physical activity is low.

Then we randomly assign our low-activity older adults to one of two treatment conditions: a four-week program of daily physical activity or a four-week program that purposely excludes physical activity. At the conclusion of the four-week program, we administer a memory test. In this study, a two-level categorical treatment variable manipulates the level of activity to which research participants are exposed: physical activity versus no physical activity. Memory score is the dependent variable. Let's assume that the older adults who were randomly assigned to the physical-activity program have significantly higher memory scores than the older adults randomly assigned to the no-physical-activity program. With this design, we have grounds for concluding that the physical-activity program caused higher memory scores. Of course, we would have to make sure that study participants did not change their lifestyle outside the treatment program during the course of the study, particularly if such change involved an increased level of physical activity.

Single-Factor and Multifactor Designs

In research studies that employ both experimental and quasi-experimental designs, categorical variables are referred to as *factors*. A particular study may include one or more factors. In a quasi-experimental study, the factors are not manipulated by the researcher, but in experimental studies they are.

A study with a **single-factor research design** consists of one categorical variable. This type of design is frequently used in aging research to determine whether the manipulation of the categorical variable has any effect on some aspect of older adults' functioning or performance, as measured by the dependent variable. In the simplest case, there is only one dependent variable.

With a **multifactor research design,** there is more than one categorical variable. In many multifactor aging studies, one of the categorical variables is age. To illustrate, we can elaborate upon the single-factor study described earlier in which memory instruction was a two-level categorical independent variable (visual-imagery instructions or no-visual-imagery instructions). Older participants who received visual-imagery instructions earned higher memory scores compared with older participants who were not given visual-imagery instructions. In this single-factor study, type of instructions was an independent variable and visual-imagery instructions had a positive effect on the dependent variable, older adults' memory scores.

Researchers with developmental interests often want to ascertain whether age has anything to do with the effectiveness of a treatment. Would visual-imagery instructions have the same positive effect on young adults' memory scores, or would the positive effect of imagery instructions be limited to the older adults?

To determine whether age has anything to do with the effect of memory instructions, we could add a second categorical variable to the design: age group. Participants from each of two adult age groups, young and older, could be randomly assigned to either a visual-imagery instruction condition or to a no-visual-imagery instruction condition. After viewing a list of 25 words, participants are asked to remember as many as they can. This study has a heterogeneous multifactor design (Kausler, 1982) because the two categorical variables

Figure 2.5 | Nonsignificant and Significant Age by Memory Instructions Interactions

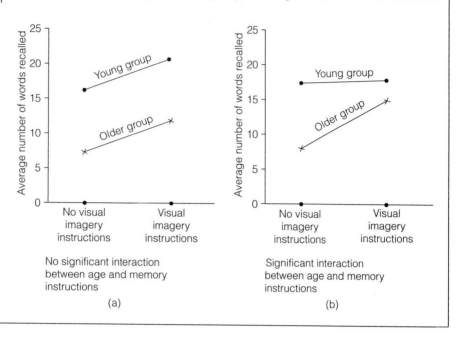

No significant interaction between age and memory instructions

(a)

Significant interaction between age and memory instructions

(b)

are from different classes: The instructions variable is manipulated and therefore it is independent; the age variable is not manipulated and therefore it is organismic.

With this heterogeneous multifactor design, several outcomes are possible. One is that, overall, the young group obtains higher memory scores compared with the older group. This would indicate that there is a significant main effect for age. In addition, let's assume that both age groups benefit from visual-imagery instructions. This would mean that there is also a significant main effect for type of memory instructions. If imagery instructions have a comparable positive effect on the young and older groups, the Age by Memory Instructions interaction effect would not be significant (see Figure 2.5a). This means that age is irrelevant as far as the effectiveness of visual-imagery instructions—the positive effect of imagery instructions applies to both age groups. If so, we can conclude that the positive effect of visual-imagery instructions generalizes across age groups. This pattern of results has some value on a practical level, but it would not be interesting from a developmental standpoint.

Another possible outcome is that visual-imagery instructions have a positive effect on one age group but not the other (see Figure 2.5b). Overall, the memory scores of the young group may be higher than those of the older group. However, type of memory instructions may have no significant effect on the young group, whose memory scores are the same regardless of which instructions they receive. In contrast, older adults who are randomly assigned to the visual-imagery condition may have higher memory scores than older adults who received no visual-imagery instructions. This pattern would indicate what psychologists refer to as "a significant Age by Memory Instructions interaction." This simply means that the older adults' memory performance is sensitive to instructions whereas young adults' memory performance is not. This interaction would be of considerable interest to researchers. They might decide to conduct additional studies to test hypotheses about why visual-imagery instructions have a positive effect only on the older age group.

The Descriptive Approach

When the variables in aging research are neither independent nor dependent, the research is considered descriptive. With the **descriptive approach,** the researcher does not attempt to manipulate any variables. Rather, data are collected on the variables of interest and the relationship between them is studied. In some instances, descriptive research is conducted only on older adults. In other instances, age may be one of many variables included. If age is a categorical variable (for example, young, middle-aged, and older groups), there may be interest in determining whether the relationship between the other variables follows the same pattern or a different pattern for the separate age groups. If age is a continuous variable, then there may be an interest in determining whether the other variables increase, decrease, or remain the same with increasing age.

Correlation is a statistical technique used to compute the extent of the relationship between variables. If two variables are related, or correlated, then knowledge about the value of one variable allows us to predict the value of the other variable with greater-than-chance accuracy. Complex correlation techniques can measure the relationship among many variables.

Correlation coefficients can range from −1.0 to +1.0. Both −1.0 and +1.0 indicate a perfect relationship between two variables. Perfect relationships between variables are rare in psychology. However, the closer a correlation is to −1.0 or +1.0, the stronger the relationship. With a strong **positive correlation** (for example, +.84), a high value on one variable is associated with a high value on the other variable. With a strong **negative correlation** (for example, −.84), a high value on one variable is associated with a low value on the other variable. The accuracy with which the value of one variable can be predicted based on knowledge about the value of the other variable is the same whether the correlation between the two variables is positive or negative.

A correlation of 0 indicates that there is no relationship between the two variables. This means that information about one variable tells us nothing about the other variable. The closer the correlation coefficient is to 0, the less accurate the prediction we can make about one variable when we have information about the other variable. Figure 2.6 illustrates a strong positive correlation between two variables, a strong negative correlation between two variables, and no correlation between two variables.

A high correlation (either positive or negative) makes it possible to predict the value of one variable with information about the other, but it does not allow any statement about cause and effect. That is, two variables may be highly

Figure 2.6 | Strong Positive, Strong Negative, and Zero Correlation Between Two Variables

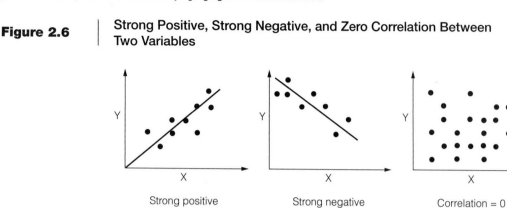

correlated, but it is not possible to determine whether one causes the other. To illustrate this point, suppose that we know there is a strong positive correlation between older adults' activity level and their satisfaction with life. Specifically, older adults with high scores on an activity questionnaire also have high scores on a life satisfaction questionnaire. Because these two variables are correlated, knowing the value of the activity score helps us to predict the life satisfaction score. However, we cannot conclude that high activity causes high life satisfaction, nor can we say that high life satisfaction causes a high level of activity. It is entirely possible that a third variable, such as health, plays a role in determining both activity level and life satisfaction.

ETHICS IN RESEARCH ON HUMAN AGING

In 1932, the U.S. Public Health Service (USPHS) initiated the Tuskegee Syphilis Study. The Tuskegee Institute, an African American university in Alabama, agreed to lend its medical facilities to the USPHS for the purpose of this study, which was to follow the natural course of the disease. Approximately 399 African American sharecroppers were recruited to participate in the study. Most of them were illiterate and underprivileged, and all were in the early stages of syphilis. Instead of being informed of their diagnosis, they were told they would be treated for "bad blood," and they were given free meals, free medical examinations, and burial insurance. They were deliberately denied medication for the disease, even when it was discovered in the 1940s that penicillin could cure it. The health of these men was purposely allowed to deteriorate to the point where they suffered from heart disease, blindness, and insanity. Over the next 40 years, many of these men died, many had infected their wives, and some of their children were born with syphilis. In 1972, journalists "blew the whistle," exposing the Tuskegee Study as the "longest nontherapeutic experiment on human beings in medical history" (see Jones, 1993).

In 1997, President Clinton issued a formal apology. However, this study left a harmful legacy—African Americans' distrust of the government and the medical profession.

Conducting research with living organisms entails considerations about ethics, and fortunately more safeguards are in place now than there were when the Tuskegee experiment was being conducted. Colleges, universities, and research institutes require that any research on living organisms be submitted to an Institutional Review Board (IRB). The IRB conducts a careful review of the purpose of the research project and the procedures the researcher plans to follow. The IRB only approves research that meets ethics criteria. What follows is a discussion of ethics as applied to research on humans.

In most cases, human research participants must sign a consent form prior to taking part in a study. The consent form must briefly describe the general nature and requirements of the study. For example, participants are informed that they will be asked to complete questionnaires, take timed tests, and so on. The consent form must also disclose approximately how long the research session will last, whether participants are expected to return for more than one session, and what compensation or benefit can be anticipated from participation in the research study.

In addition, the consent form assures participants that their responses will remain confidential, and it describes exactly how such confidentiality will be guaranteed. For example, names will not be placed on test protocols; test protocols will be coded with a number and stored separately from the consent form the participant has signed; consent forms will be kept in a locked cabinet that is accessible only to the research investigator. The consent form also gives participants an estimate of how many other individuals will be participating in the study because the number of participants could affect confidentiality. A small number of participants may mean less anonymity. Finally, the consent form indicates that participants are free to discontinue at any time.

When presenting proposals to the IRB, researchers must explain both the nature of and the reason for any "deception" that may be involved in a study. If there is deception, researchers must describe when and how research participants will be debriefed, or told about the actual purpose of the study. Also, there must be some assurance that deception will have no long-term negative effects on the research participants. If any short-term negative effects are anticipated, these must be justified. The researcher must make a convincing argument that the overall benefits of the findings are expected to outweigh any temporary discomforts participants could experience because of the deception.

Informed consent is necessary for all human research. However, special issues may arise with older-adult populations. For example, an investigator might want to study older adults who have been diagnosed with dementia. As Chapter 11 describes further, dementia is associated with compromised cognitive abilities, so individuals suffering from dementia may not be fully capable of giving informed consent. Under these circumstances, the investigator must obtain informed consent from participants' next of kin and/or from individuals who are in charge of participants' day-to-day needs and have their well-being in mind.

REVISITING THE SELECTIVE OPTIMIZATION WITH COMPENSATION AND ECOLOGICAL MODELS

How do the topics of theory and method relate to the two theoretical frameworks, or models, that were introduced in the first chapter of this book? The Selective Optimization with Compensation (SOC) Model (Baltes & Baltes, 1990) and the Ecological Model (Lawton, 1989; Lawton & Nahemow, 1973) have the closest fit with the contextual metamodel in that both conceptualize development as a series of bidirectional transactions and adjustments between the organism and the environment. However, these models can also be used to conceptualize development from mechanistic or organismic points of view, and they fit well with the propositions of the lifespan developmental perspective.

The SOC and Ecological models would both acknowledge the importance of age, cohort, and time of measurement when the aging process is studied. In developmental studies, multifactor cross-sectional comparisons of two (or more) adult age groups could be used to investigate which strategies young and older adults would select to optimize their level of functioning in any number of domains. One age group might have more losses than the other, but effective use of compensation strategies could close any gap that may exist between the functioning of the two groups. With regard to the Ecological Model, a cross-sectional design could be used to evaluate how well young and older adults adapt to living environments that present different levels of challenge, or press.

When practicable, longitudinal studies could follow the same individuals over time to ascertain whether there are any changes in the strategies people use over the adult life span to maintain their level of functioning. Using the longitudinal method, investigators can determine whether losses in some domains of functioning are compensated for by gains in other domains at various points in adult life. The longitudinal method would also be useful in determining which level of environmental press is most likely to ensure the highest possible level of adaptation at various stages of adulthood.

The time-lag method could be used to determine whether older adults from different cohorts select the same strategies to compensate for age-related losses to optimize their functioning. By testing several cohorts of older adults at different points in time, we can evaluate what kinds of losses are experienced and what types of compensatory strategies older adults use today as opposed to strategies that older adults used in the past. With regard to the Ecological Model, the time-lag method could be used to investigate whether today's cohort of older adults is similar to or different from older cohorts in previous years or decades in adapting to environments that present varying degrees of challenge, or press.

KEY POINTS

- Developmental psychologists differ in their viewpoints about the nature of the universe in general and about developmental phenomena in particular. These viewpoints, referred to as metatheoretical orientations, or metamodels, guide their beliefs about which aspects of development are most important and which theories best explain developmental phenomena.

These metamodels are mechanistic, organismic, and contextual. The lifespan developmental perspective is most closely related to the contextual metamodel.

- Developmental psychologists who conduct research on aging and older adulthood must be concerned with three factors: chronological age, cohort (generation), and time of measurement.
- Psychologists who study aging and older adulthood use cross-sectional, longitudinal, time-lag, and sequential research designs. Cross-sectional designs study age-related differences that occur at a specific point in time. They are the most efficient, but the factors of age and cohort are confounded (cannot be disentangled).
- Longitudinal designs follow individuals over time. They take a long time to complete, but they can detect age-related change within individual members of a cohort (intraindividual change). However, the factors of age and time of measurement are confounded, and there may be selective attrition, or dropout, during the course of the study.
- Time-lag designs are not truly developmental because all research participants are the same chronological age but are tested at different times. The factors of cohort and time of measurement are confounded in this design.
- The more complex sequential designs have been proposed as a means of disentangling the factors of age, cohort, and time of measurement.
- When research is conducted, the measures used must be reliable, or consistent. The measures must also be valid, or measure what we think they measure. Internal validity refers to the accurate identification and interpretation of the factor that is responsible for an observation. Heterotypic continuity has to do with whether a measure used to assess some underlying quality, or characteristic, has the same degree of internal validity for different age groups in a cross-sectional study or for the same people as they are followed over time in a longitudinal study. External validity refers to whether findings from a sample of research participants can be generalized to the population of interest. Ecological validity is a type of external validity that refers to whether the measurements using a particular test instrument accurately reflect real-world functioning or behavior.
- Research on aging and older adulthood can use an experimental, quasi-experimental, or descriptive approach. In the experimental approach, the investigator manipulates the levels of a categorical independent variable and randomly assigns research participants to each one. In the quasi-experimental approach, the categorical variable is not manipulated by the investigator and research participants cannot be randomly assigned to levels of the categorical variable. Only the experimental approach allows conclusions to be drawn about cause and effect.
- With the descriptive approach, an investigator studies two or more variables and determines how they are related to one another. Such relationships are measured by correlations. The closer these correlations are to -1.00 or $+1.00$ (the further they are from 0 in either direction), the stronger the relationship between variables.

- Guidelines for ethics in human research are meant to protect study participants from harm, including invasion of privacy and coercion to remain in a study if they wish to discontinue. Participants must be informed as to the nature and purpose of the study and they must be debriefed if any deception is involved.

KEY TERMS

chronological age   45

cohort   45

contextual metamodel   41

cross-sectional research design   48

descriptive approach   69

ecological validity   57

experimental approach   62

external validity   57

heterotypic continuity   58

internal validity   57

lifespan developmental perspective   42

longitudinal research design   49

mechanistic metamodel   40

multifactor research designs   67

negative correlation   69

organismic metamodel   41

organismic variable   45

positive correlation   69

quasi-experimental approach   64

reliability   56

selective attrition   50

sequential research designs   54

single-factor research designs   67

time-lag research design   51

time of measurement   46

validity   56

To learn more about the issues discussed in this chapter, point your browser to http://www.infotrac-college.com and use the passcode from the InfoTrac College Edition card that came with your book. InfoTrac College Edition gives you access to complete articles from many different journals.

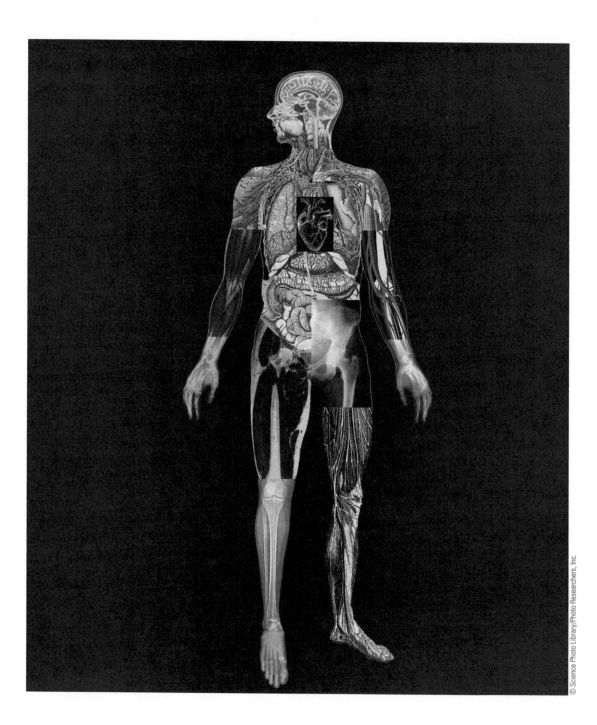

Biological Aging and Health | 3

Marcus is 70 years old and he knows his level of energy has changed from what it was when he was 40, 50, or even 60. He still gardens and works on his carpentry projects, but it is becoming more difficult to do both on the same day. Marcus often feels stiff when he wakes up in the morning, but he considers himself to be in good physical shape for his age and he knows that his family background is in his favor for living a long life. His mother lived to the age of 90 and although she took several kinds of medication, she was able to live independently with very little help until the last six months of her life. Even so, Marcus is not counting on his genetic makeup to carry him through. He makes an effort to eat plenty of fruits and vegetables and he limits his intake of alcohol to no more than one drink per day. Also, he takes walks, rides his exercise bike as often as possible, and participates in a tai chi class at the community center. Marcus gets together with his cronies to play poker every other week, and he and his wife attend church and visit with family members and friends on a regular basis. Marcus is convinced that maintaining a balance of good dietary habits, exercise, and social activities is the key to a long and healthy life.

THE MEANING OF LONGEVITY

Why does aging occur and what determines how long people will live? This chapter focuses on the biological aspects of aging. Unlike psychological aging, which includes the possibility of both increments (gains) and decrements (losses), biological aging generally involves "decremental physical changes (both structural and functional) that develop with the passage of time and eventually end with death" (Busse, 1995, p. 754). Even so, these changes do not necessarily mean that people cannot lead lives that are productive and enjoyable.

Biological aging is not confined to the final phase of the life span. Rather, it is gradual and cumulative. Schulz and Salthouse (1999) summarize some important realities about human biological aging. Biological functioning usually reaches a peak in early adulthood, after which it begins a gradual decline. However, the rate of decline is not the same for everyone, and there are considerable individual differences in biological functioning among those age 65 and over. Some adults experience noticeable declines in their mid-sixties or earlier, while others do not. The physical capabilities of some older adults are equal to those of the average middle-aged adult. Frequently we hear reports in the popular media about individuals in their 80s or even 90s who climb mountains, run in marathon races, or continue to work full time. Some older adults fit this description but they may not be in the majority. Nonetheless, despite age-related decline in biological processes, most older adults are neither helpless nor dependent.

According to some theories, biological aging occurs within the organism regardless of outside forces. Other theories contend that biological aging does not occur in a vacuum; rather, it is influenced by our environment and daily habits. Furthermore, the way we cope with life's challenges can speed up or slow down the progression of biological aging. Biological processes and behavior are most likely interrelated—just as biological processes can affect behavior, so behavior can affect biological processes (Van Dras & Blumenthal, 2000).

For the most part, scientists think biological changes are a consequence of the aging process rather than a result of disease (Hayflick, 1995). Indeed, some individuals in their 70s, 80s, and beyond show no symptoms of disease (Svanborg, 1996), and a small proportion of older adults show no discernible evidence of disease at the time of their death. Nevertheless, there is little question that the likelihood of disease increases with age. Isolating the cause of pure biological aging is a fundamental research goal. However, because aging and disease often go together, it is difficult to study pure aging.

Morbidity and mortality are terms used by those who study biological processes in large populations. **Morbidity** refers to illness and disease. **Mortality** refers to death. These two terms are related because illness and disease can result in death, and death is often preceded by illness and disease. However, morbidity does not necessarily result in mortality because people with chronic illnesses can live for a long time with the proper treatment. **Longevity** has to do with the length and duration of life. Two aspects of longevity are life expectancy and life span. As we will see shortly, life expectancy and life span are related but they are not identical.

Life Expectancy

Life expectancy is the average number of years that individuals in a particular birth cohort can be expected to live. Life expectancy figures are based on current information on mortality. As the members of a birth cohort (those born in a certain year) move through life, they face various risk factors that can result in death. Life expectancy can be calculated at any age on the basis of risk factors that members of a particular cohort are likely to face in the years ahead. Individual members of a cohort may or may not survive certain problem points. For example, those who reach their 18th birthday have survived risk factors common in infancy and childhood, while those who reach their 65th birthday have survived risk factors common in infancy, childhood, and both early and middle adulthood. Life expectancy figures give us information on what is anticipated for large numbers of people, but they do not tell us how long an individual member of a birth cohort will live (Vaupel, 1995).

Life Expectancy at Birth   Although life expectancy can be estimated at any point during life, most often it refers to the average number of years that members of a particular birth cohort (those born in a specific year) are expected to live from the time they are born, given the knowledge and conditions that prevail at that time. Not surprisingly, life expectancy at birth varies from country to country. It is affected by factors such as level of nutrition, sanitary conditions, and medical care, including antibiotics and immunizations that are available to the population of a particular country. These factors can either negatively or positively affect mortality and thus life expectancy. Again, note that the figure for life expectancy at birth represents an average for an entire cohort (people born in a certain year) and cannot be used to make an accurate forecast of how many years an individual member of the cohort will actually live.

| **Table 3.1** | Life Expectancy at Birth in the United States in 1900, 1970, 1980, 1990, and 2000 |

Year of Birth	Both Sexes	Males	Females
1970	70.8	67.1	74.7
1980	73.7	70.0	77.4
1990	75.4	71.8	78.8
2000	76.9	74.1	79.5

Source: National Vital Statistics Report (2002).

Infants born in the United States in 1900 had an average life expectancy of 47.3 years of age, while infants born in the United States in 1970 had an average life expectancy of 70.8 years. The dramatic increase in life expectancy between 1900 to 1970 is attributable chiefly to medical advances that reduced infant mortality, mortality from childhood diseases, and maternal mortality. Since 1970, life expectancy in the United States has continued to rise, but not as dramatically as it did from 1900 to 1970. Life expectancy for infants born in the United States in 1980 was 73.7. In 1990, life expectancy was 75.4, and in 2000 life expectancy was 76.9 years (see Table 3.1). The gradual increases in recent decades are due to further improvements in sanitary conditions and public health, which have resulted in further reductions in mortality from infectious diseases that affect people of all ages in the United States. In addition, medical advances in treating noninfectious cardiovascular diseases and cancer have helped to boost life expectancy.

With regard to gender, female infants born in the United States in 1900 had a life expectancy of 48.3 years, while male infants born that same year had a life expectancy of 46.3 years, a gap of only two years. Since that time, life expectancy at birth has increased for both females and males, although the gap has widened in favor of females. Female infants born in 1970 had a life expectancy of 74.7 years, while male infants born the same year had a life expectancy of 67.1 years, a gap of 7.6 years. Females born in 1980 had a life expectancy of 77.4 years, while life expectancy for males was 70.0 years, a gap of 7.4 years. Female infants born in 1990 had a life expectancy of 78.8 years, while life expectancy for male infants was 71.8, a gap of 7 years. Finally, females born in 2000 had a life expectancy of 79.5, while for males born the same year life expectancy was 74.1, a somewhat narrower gap of 5.4 years (see Table 3.1).

For future birth cohorts in the United States, life expectancy will probably continue to rise gradually with further medical advances in treating diseases, especially those that frequently occur in the older adult years. With regard to sex differences, it is difficult to predict whether the gap in life expectancy between men and women will continue to narrow. More and more women are participating in the paid workforce. Women's employment fosters independence, both socially and economically, so work could exert a positive influence on their life

Table 3.2 | Life Expectancy at Birth by Race and Sex in the United States

	European American			African American		
Year	Both Sexes	Males	Females	Both Sexes	Males	Females
1970	71.7	68.0	75.6	64.1	60.0	68.3
1980	74.4	70.7	78.1	68.1	63.8	72.5
1990	76.1	72.7	79.4	69.1	64.5	73.6
2000	77.4	74.8	80.0	71.7	68.2	74.9

Source: National Vital Statistics Report (2002).

expectancy and thus maintain or increase the gap. However, full-time employment also exposes women to increased stress, particularly if they also carry the largest share of the household responsibilities, as was the case in the 1980s for the majority of married women who worked outside the home (Berardo, Shehan, & Leslie, 1987). At this point, it would be premature to predict whether women's participation in the work force and the lifestyle habits that go with such participation will have a net positive or a net negative impact on their life expectancy.

Not only are life expectancy figures available for the total population of males and females in the United States, but as of 1970, separate statistics also were available for European American and African American groups. In 1970, the life expectancy for European American infants was 71.7, but for African American infants it was 64.1, a gap of 7.6 years. In 1980, the life expectancy for European American infants was 74.4 and for African American infants it was 68.1, a gap of 6.3 years. In 1990, the life expectancy for European American infants was 76.1 and for African American infants it was 69.1, a gap of 7 years. In 2000, the life expectancy for European American infants was 77.4 and for African American infants it was 71.7, a gap of 5.7 years. Table 3.2 shows life expectancies for European Americans and African Americans and also for males and females in each group. As in the European American group, there is also a gender gap among African American men and women, with women having a greater life expectancy at birth compared to men.

Life expectancy at birth varies throughout the world. In developed countries such as Japan, Sweden, and the United Kingdom, it is as high or slightly higher than life expectancy in the United States. In contrast, life expectancy is much lower in less developed countries in Africa (for example, Uganda).

Life Expectancy at Ages 65 and Older   Of special interest to those who study the older adult population is the life expectancy of people who reach the later years. For example, what is the life expectancy of people who celebrate their 65th birthday? These individuals represent a select group who survived obstacles that ended the lives of some of their fellow cohort members in infancy, childhood, or

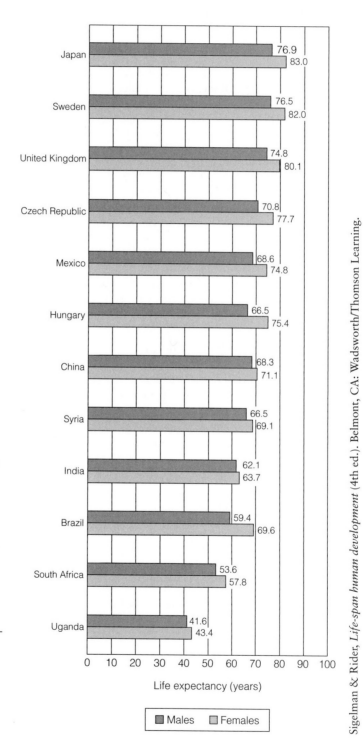

Figure 3.1   Male and Female Life Expectancies at Birth in Selected Countries

Sigelman & Rider, *Life-span human development* (4th ed.). Belmont, CA: Wadsworth/Thomson Learning.

Table 3.3	Life Expectancy at Ages 65, 75, 85, and 95 by Race and Sex in the United States

| | European American | | | African American | | |
Age	Both Sexes	Males	Females	Both Sexes	Males	Females
65	17.9	16.3	19.2	16.2	14.5	17.4
75	11.3	10.1	12.1	10.5	9.4	11.2
85	6.2	5.5	6.6	6.3	5.7	6.5
95	3.3	2.9	3.3	3.7	3.6	3.6

Source: National Vital Statistics Report (2002).

adulthood. In the United States, individuals who celebrated their 65th birthday in 2000 are expected to live an additional 17.9 more years (19.2 for females and 16.3 for males). How do these figures compare with those from earlier decades? In 1900, a woman who reached age 65 was expected to live another 12.0 years, while a man was expected to live another 11.3 years. Note that life expectancy at 65 increased from 1900 to 2000 for men and women, but the gender gap widened in favor of women.

Once people celebrate their 75th birthday, how much longer can they expect to live? In the United States in 2000, the answer is 11.3 years, 10.1 for men and 12.1 for women. Once people celebrate their 85th birthday, their life expectancy is 6.3 years, 5.6 for men and 6.7 for women. Life expectancy for those who celebrate their 95th birthday is 3.5 years, 3.1 for men and 3.5 for women. Note that as people get older and older, the gender gap in life expectancy narrows.

Table 3.3 shows life expectancy figures for European Americans and African Americans who live to ages 65, 75, 85, and 95. Note that the gap that existed between these two groups for life expectancy at birth is much narrower for life expectancy at 65 and 75. At ages 85 and 95 the gap is very small and it favors African Americans over European Americans at these late ages.

Life Span

Life span refers to the maximum longevity, or the extreme upper limit of time that members of a species can live. For humans, what is that upper limit? In the 1970s, a flurry of media attention was directed toward several isolated communities in mountainous regions of Russia, Turkey, and Ecuador. Many who resided in these communities seemed to be centenarians (living to the age of 100), some claiming to be as old as 120, 130, 150, and even 160 years of age (Beller & Palmore, 1974; Kyucharyants, 1974; Medvedev, 1974). Scientists flocked to these remote areas to unlock the secret of such long lives only to discover that the phenomenally old ages of the inhabitants had been exaggerated, so these villagers were not as old as they claimed to be. Confusion as to their exact chronological ages was due partly to the fact that accurate birth records were not kept in these villages but also to the common practice of duplicating names across several generations. When available records were examined, it was discovered that one man claiming to be 100 was actually 84 years old. Another man claiming to be 130 was actually 78 but he had used his father's name and documents to avoid serving in the Russian Army in World War I. To date, the oldest person whose birth record has been documented with a high degree of certainty is a woman named Jeanne Calment of Arles, France, who was born in 1875 and died in August, 1997 at the age of 122 (Weiss, 1997).

Despite the exaggerated chronological ages of the villagers in Russia, Turkey, and Ecuador, a number of them were living beyond average human life expectancy and many were in good health. Studying individuals who live exceptionally long and healthy lives, even if their ages are within the bounds of maximum human longevity, is an important way to explore what factors might prevent or delay the onset of diseases that commonly occur in the later years (Solomon, 1999). The older villagers in these remote communities shared certain characteristics. All of them lived in mountainous regions and led physically demanding lives. They lived on low-calorie, low-fat diets and consumed only moderate amounts of alcohol, all habits recommended today as part of a healthy lifestyle. Many were active in their communities, holding leadership positions that commanded great respect. No doubt their high level of social status fostered positive images of self-worth, which could have contributed indirectly to their good health.

Even so, general statements about lifestyles of long-lived individuals are difficult to make. For example, Wilmoth, Skytthe, Friou, and Jeune (1996) made an extensive case study of a 114-year-old man named CM (initials), who resided in San Rafael, California. As of 1996, CM was thought to be the oldest living male whose birth record could be documented, but his lifestyle prior to old age does not seem extraordinary by any means. He immigrated to the United States from Denmark at age 16. After a brief marriage in his 20s, he divorced and never remarried. He worked as a milkman, operated a small restaurant, and worked in factories, retiring in 1950. At age 96 he moved to the independent living section of a retirement community, and at 110 he entered a skilled nursing facility. When interviewed at age 114, CM had been living in the nursing facility for more than three years. He was completely blind, had difficulty hearing, and could not walk without assistance. Despite these difficulties, however, CM had no apparent signs of disease. Furthermore, his memory and reasoning abilities were largely intact, and he displayed a sense of humor during his interviews.

In the United States, the Georgia Centenarian Study has been following individuals ages 60 to 100 years of age to determine the relationships between family longevity, social and environmental support, personality characteristics, adaptational skills, satisfaction with life, loneliness, nutrition and dietary patterns, and health (Fees, Martin, & Poon, 1999; Poon, Sweaney, Clayton, & Merriam, 1992). Continued follow-up of these individuals could yield important clues about the key to a long life. Harvard Medical School researcher Thomas Perls and his colleagues have studied 150 centenarians. Based on their findings, they developed a quiz that people can use to determine their chances of living to 100 (see Table 3.4).

Table 3.4 | Will You Live to be 100?

After completing a study of 150 centenarians, Harvard Medical School researchers Thomas Perls, M.D., and Margery Hutter Silver, Ed.D., developed a quiz to help you calculate your estimated life expectancy.

LONGEVITY QUIZ

	Score
1. Do you smoke or chew tobacco, or are you around a lot of secondhand smoke? Yes (–20) No (0)	
2. Do you cook your fish, poultry, or meat until it is charred? Yes (–2) No (0)	
3. Do you avoid butter, cream, pastries, and other saturated fats as well as fried foods (e.g., French Fries)? Yes (+3) No (–7)	
4. Do you minimize meat in your diet, preferably making a point to eat plenty of fruits, vegetables, and bran instead? Yes (+5) No (–4)	
5. Do you consume more than two drinks of beer, wine, and/or liquor a day? (A standard drink is one 12-ounce bottle of beer, one wine cooler, one five-ounce glass of wine, or one and a half ounces of 80-proof distilled spirits.) Yes (–10) No (0)	
6. Do you drink beer, wine, and/or liquor in moderate amounts (one or two drinks/day)? Yes (+3) No (0)	
7. Do air pollution warnings occur where you live? Yes (–4) No (+1)	
8. **a** Do you drink more than 16 ounces of coffee a day? Yes (–3) No (0) **b** Do you drink tea daily? Yes (+3) No (0)	
9. Do you take an aspirin a day? Yes (+4) No (0)	
10. Do you floss your teeth every day? Yes (+2) No (–4)	
11. Do you have a bowel movement less than once every two days? Yes (–4) No (0)	
12. Have you had a stroke or heart attack? Yes (–10) No (0)	
13. Do you try to get a sun tan? Yes (–4) No (+3)	
14. Are you more than 20 pounds overweight? Yes (–10) No (0)	
15. Do you live near enough to other family members (other than your spouse and dependent children) that you can and want to drop by spontaneously? Yes (+5) No (–4)	
16. Which statement is applicable to you? **a** "Stress eats away at me. I can't seem to shake it off." Yes (–7) **b** "I can shed stress." This might be by praying, exercising, meditating, finding humor in everyday life, or other means. Yes (+7)	
17. Did both of your parents either die before age 75 of nonaccidental causes or require daily assistance by the time they reached age 75? Yes (–10) No (0) Don't know (0)	
18. Did more than one of the following relatives live to at least age 90 in excellent health: parents, aunts/uncles, grandparents? Yes (+24) No (0) Don't know (0)	
19. **a** Are you a couch potato (do no regular aerobic or resistance exercise)? Yes (–7) **b** Do you exercise at least three times a week? Yes (+7)	
20. Do you take vitamin E (400–800 IU) and selenium (100–200 mcg) every day? Yes (+5) No (–3)	

Table 3.4 | **Will YOU Live to be 100? (Continued)**

SCORE

STEP 1: Add the negative and positive scores together. Example: −45 plus +30 = −15. Divide the preceding score by 5 (−15 divided by 5 = −3).

STEP 2: Add the negative or positive number to age 84 if you are a man or age 88 if you are a woman (example: −3 + 88 = 85) to get your estimated life span.

THE SCIENCE BEHIND THE QUIZ

Question 1 Cigarette smoke contains toxins that directly damage DNA, causing cancer and other diseases and accelerating aging.

Question 2 Charring food changes its proteins and amino acids into heterocyclic amines, which are potent mutagens that can alter your DNA.

Questions 3, 4 A high-fat diet, and especially a high-fat, high-protein diet, may increase your risk of cancer of the breast, uterus, prostate, colon, pancreas, and kidney. A diet rich in fruits and vegetables may lower the risk of heart disease and cancer.

Questions 5, 6 Excessive alcohol consumption can damage the liver and other organs, leading to accelerated aging and increased susceptibility to disease. Moderate consumption may lower the risk of heart disease.

Question 7 Certain air pollutants may cause cancer; many also contain oxidants that accelerate aging.

Question 8 Too much coffee predisposes the stomach to ulcers and chronic inflammation, which in turn raise the risk of heart disease. High coffee consumption may also indicate and exacerbate stress. Tea, on the other hand, is noted for its significant antioxidant content.

Question 9 Taking 81 milligrams of aspirin a day (the amount in one baby aspirin) has been shown to decrease the risk of heart disease, possibly because of its anticlotting effects.

Question 10 Research now shows that chronic gum disease can lead to the release of bacteria into the bloodstream, contributing to heart disease.

Question 11 Scientists believe that having at least one bowel movement every 20 hours decreases the incidence of colon cancer.

Question 12 A previous history of stroke and heart attack makes you more susceptible to future attacks.

Question 13 The ultraviolet in sunlight directly damage DNA, causing wrinkles and increasing the risk of skin cancer.

Question 14 Being obese increases the risk of various cancers, heart disease, and diabetes. The more overweight you are, the higher your risk of disease and death.

Questions 15, 16 People who do not belong to cohesive families have fewer coping resources and therefore have increased levels of social and psychological stress. Stress is associated with heart disease and some cancers.

Questions 17, 18 Studies show that genetics plays a significant role in the ability to reach extreme old age.

Question 19 Exercise leads to more efficient energy production in the cells and overall, less oxygen radical formation. Oxygen (or free) radicals are highly reactive molecules or atoms that damage cells and DNA, ultimately leading to aging.

Question 20 Vitamin E is a powerful antioxidant and has been shown to retard the progression of Alzheimer's, heart disease, and stroke. Selenium may prevent some types of cancer.

Figure 3.2 | The Rectangular Survival Curve

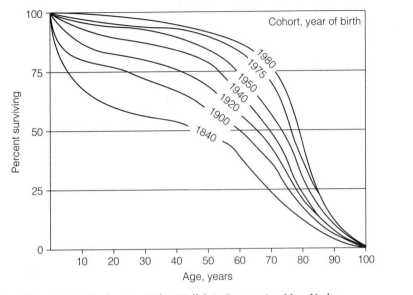

Adapted from H. Katchadourian, *Fifty: Midlife in Perspective*, New York:
W. H. Freeman, 1987. Reprinted by permission.

Rectangular Survival Curve　As described earlier, there has been a dramatic increase in human life expectancy over the past century in the United States as well as in other developed countries. However, human life span (maximum human longevity) has remained relatively constant over time as well as across cultures. In ancient times, a few people lived to very old ages, but the chances of approaching maximum human longevity are greater now than they were in the past. In modern times, especially in developed countries, more and more people are living closer to the maximum human life span.

As hygienic conditions improve, as disease-related causes of death are able to be prevented or at least delayed, and if more people have lifestyles that include healthy diet and exercise, life expectancy will continue to increase gradually and will more closely approach life span. As this occurs, the survival curve will take on a more rectangular shape. The term **compression of mortality** (Fries, 1995; 1997) refers to a phenomenon whereby a greater proportion of deaths will occur during a very narrow time period toward the upper limit of the human life span. In other words, more and more people will live closer to the maximum life span, with the resultant **rectangular survival curve** shown in Figure 3.2.

Quality of Life　With the trend toward compression of mortality, people have raised concerns about the quality of life in the final years. Will the final years be characterized by disability, dependency, and disease or by independence and robust health (Fries, 1997; Schneider, 1997)? In other words, will compression of mortality be accompanied by a corresponding compression of morbidity? **Compression of morbidity** means that illness and extreme disability will occur only in a narrow period of time immediately prior to death. To the extent that the onset of disease can be delayed and compressed into a short interval of time late in life, the quality of life should remain high until very close to its end.

In summary, a statement such as "People live longer now than they ever have" is somewhat misleading. In developed countries, life expectancies have been increasing gradually, largely because of improved sanitary conditions and medical advances that prevent or effectively treat diseases that occur at various points in the life span. However, maximum human longevity, or life span, has changed very little over time. The rectangular survival curve signifies that a larger and larger proportion of people will live closer to the maximum life span in contrast to earlier times when very few people lived that long. However, maximum human longevity, or life span, will probably not change until the key to the aging process is discovered (Hayflick, 1994; Olshansky, Hayflick, & Carnes, 2002). Meanwhile, a more realistic goal is to increase the quality of the years that we have left.

THE BIOLOGICAL AGING PROCESS

What is biological aging? Would it happen no matter where or how a person lives, or does it occur earlier under some circumstances than others? Even though the incidence of certain diseases increases with age, most researchers believe that aging is not the same as disease and should be distinguished from it.

Primary and Secondary Aging

A distinction is often drawn between two categories of biological aging: primary aging and secondary aging. **Primary aging** refers to the unavoidable (inevitable) biological processes that are sure to affect all members of a species. Thus, primary aging is considered to be universal, although there are individual differences in the rate at which it occurs. The effects of primary aging may not become apparent for many years, but primary aging processes are set in motion early in life and progress gradually over time. In addition to being inevitable and universal, primary aging is generally considered to be intrinsic, which means that it is internally generated and determined by factors within the organism rather than by outside forces. Some scientists use the term *senescence* to mean primary aging (Busse, 1995).

Secondary aging refers to processes that are experienced by most, but not necessarily all, members of a species. Thus, secondary aging is neither inevitable nor universal. Unlike primary aging, secondary aging is associated with defects and disabilities that result from hostile environmental influences or specific sources of trauma or disease (Busse, 1995). In short, secondary aging is considered to be a function of disease, disuse, and abuse. Disease can accelerate aging. Disuse, such as lack of exercise, can result in deterioration of the body or the mind. Abuse can result from smoking, excessive consumption of alcohol, poor nutrition, or overexposure to the sun or loud noise.

Table 3.5 | Theories of Biological Aging

Programmed Theories	Stochastic Theories
Time clock theory	Wear and tear theory
Immune theory	Rate of living theory
Evolutionary theory	Stress theory
Order-to-disorder theory	Cross-linking theory
	Free radical theory
	Error theory

The distinction between primary and secondary aging is not universally accepted (Busse, 1995), nor is it always possible to differentiate between them. Even so, a conceptual distinction between primary and secondary processes heightens people's awareness that they may be able to exert control over some aspects of their lives. At the same time, however, it is conceivable that primary aging renders individuals more vulnerable to sources of damage that are usually associated with secondary aging. Although some theorists consider deterioration from disease to be separate from primary aging, it is possible that primary aging simply renders individuals less able to cope with the stressors of disease processes.

Theories of Biological Aging

An extensive literature describes the molecular, biochemical, and cellular changes associated with biological aging (Turker, 1996), and more than 300 theories of biological aging have been proposed (Cristofalo, Tresini, Francis, & Volker, 1999). As yet, no single theory has proved definitive, but a number of them hold promise, either individually or in combination.

Theories of biological aging have been grouped into two general categories: programmed theories and stochastic theories (Cristofalo et al., 1999). **Programmed theories of biological aging** postulate that aging is a function of a genetically based program that directs the aging process. Programmed theories are more closely related to the idea of primary aging rather than secondary aging. In contrast, **stochastic theories of biological aging** focus on factors, both internal and external to the organism, believed to result in random damage that determines the rate of biological aging. Stochastic theories are more closely related to secondary aging rather than primary aging. Not every biological theory of aging falls into one category or the other, and some biological theories have both programmed and stochastic aspects (Cristofalo et al., 1999). However, some of the more prevalent theories appear in Table 3.5 under each of the two categories.

Programmed Theories In general, programmed theories postulate that longevity is written into the genetic code of the species (Hayflick, 1994).

Some programmed theories deal with aging on the cellular level, while others hypothesize that other systems show senescence in a predetermined way.

Hayflick proposed a *time-clock theory* based on some early research on cells that were removed from a variety of tissues from several different species. He found that when these cells were grown in culture outside the organism, they divided a limited number of times. The number of times the cells divided before they stopped appeared to be unique to the species from which they were drawn. For example, cells from a human infant doubled approximately 50 times, whereas cells from a mouse (life span of only 3 years) doubled only 10–15 times. The fact that the cells drawn from species with greater longevities divided more times before they stopped seemed to suggest that the life span of a particular species is controlled by a genetically determined time-clock that operates at the cellular level.

Hayflick also found that even within the human species the number of cell divisions can vary. With regard to age, cells from infants and young children divided more times than cells from older adults, presumably because cells from the older organisms have already used up part of their program. In addition, Hayflick acquired cells from children with Down syndrome, a genetic abnormality associated with shorter than average life expectancy and from children with progeria, a rare genetic abnormality characterized by premature aging and extremely reduced life expectancy. When grown in culture, cells taken from these two groups divided fewer times than cells taken from genetically normal individuals of the same age (Hayflick, 1995). This seemed to suggest that aging is controlled by a program that operates at the cellular level, and as the program progresses over time, fewer cell divisions remain. However, we still do not know exactly what determines the number of times cells divide, nor is it certain that cells grown in culture behave the same as cells that remain within the organism. Furthermore, not all researchers have been able to repeat Hayflick's finding that cells from younger organisms double more times than cells from older organisms. Cristofalo et al. (1999) found no relationship between the chronological age of 42 healthy adults and the number of times their cells doubled, so it is conceivable that the number of cell doublings is related to health more than it is to age. Even so, Hayflick's intriguing research on cells opened the door to thinking about programmed theories of aging.

Recent research on cellular aging has implicated **telomeres**, which are the protective caps at the tail ends of the chromosomes located in each cell. Each time a cell divides, the telomeres lose some of their length until they become so short that cell division is no longer possible (Cristofalo et al., 1999). There is some suggestion that length of the telomeres determines cell longevity and perhaps indirectly the longevity of the organism (Hayflick, 1995). Researchers are trying to determine whether supplying normal cells with an enzyme called telomerase will rebuild the telomeres and thereby rejuvenate older cells so that they can continue to divide.

Another theory in the program category is *immune theory*. The immune system defends the body against the invasion of foreign substances by controlling the production of antibodies whose job it is to circulate and deactivate substances that are not recognized as self. According to immune theory, the immune system

Children with a rare genetic disorder, progeria, experience premature aging and reduced life expectancy.

is programmed to maintain its efficiency for a certain amount of time, after which it starts to decline. The effect of this decline may be that the immune system fails to produce antibodies in a sufficient amount needed to protect against foreign invading substances. Another possibility is that decline in the immune system results in the production of antibodies that are of inferior quality and therefore prone to make mistakes such as attacking and destroying normal cells. Weakened immune system functioning has been linked to age-related diseases such as cancer. However, it is premature to conclude that decline in the immune system is the cause rather than the result of normal aging (Hayflick, 1994).

While some theories postulate specific programs at the cellular level or programs associated with the immune system, other theories hypothesize more general kinds of programs. According to the *evolutionary theory* of biological aging, members of a species are genetically programmed to bear and rear their young. Once they reproduce and raise their offspring to independence, they serve no further purpose in perpetuating the species. Nonetheless, they may have some energy left over and this allows them to coast along for some time. As excess energy is used up, however, they become more susceptible to disease. In describing the evolutionary perspective, Hayflick (1994) likens the years beyond reproduction and raising of offspring to the ticking of a watch after the warrantee period is over. Not every watch self-destructs on the warrantee expiration date, but a gradual aging process does lead to a final breakdown, at which point the watch stops running. Hayflick suggests that rather than asking, "Why do we age?", a better question would be, "How do we manage to live as long as we do?"

Another programmed theory of biological aging is the *order-to-disorder theory*, which is a variation on the evolutionary perspective. According to this theory, an organism's energy and activity are directed toward the goals of reaching sexual maturation and reproducing. To accomplish these goals, the organism's tissues and organs must be arranged in a highly orderly fashion. However, maintaining this order requires a great deal of energy and cannot continue indefinitely. Once sexual maturation is attained, energy begins to dissipate and the order and efficiency of the biological system breaks down. Although disorder is assumed to play a role in the aging process, it may not occur at the same time or progress at the same rate in all cells. This may explain why some tissues and organs age faster than others even within the same individual, and also why the rate of aging varies from one individual to another.

Stemming from the evolutionary premise that members of a species are programmed to survive to the point of sexual maturation, one avenue of research has included efforts to postpone reproductive maturity. The reasoning is that perhaps harmful mutated genes are suppressed to a point just beyond reproductive maturity, after which they can no longer be restrained. Delaying reproductive maturity could prevent these harmful genes from switching on, thereby delaying the onset of aging (Hayflick, 1994).

Stochastic Theories   According to stochastic theories, we age because our vital systems are damaged by random events that occur during the process of living. When the damage accumulates to a high enough level, we can no longer function efficiently and eventually life becomes impossible to sustain. Support for stochastic theories comes from the fact that aging occurs at different rates even among individuals whose genetic makeup is the same. For example, even though identical twins have exactly the same genetic makeup, rarely do both members of a pair live exactly the same amount of time. Findings that certain environmental factors are associated with accelerated aging and shortened longevity have also been used as evidence for stochastic rather than programmed aging (Cristofalo et al., 1999).

According to the *wear-and-tear theory*, some aspects of living lead to a more rapid build-up of damage. The *rate-of-living theory* is a variant of the concept of wear and tear, the main premise being that we begin life with a fixed amount of stored physiological energy. If we expend this energy quickly, aging begins early and proceeds rapidly. However, we can retard the aging process if we conserve energy and use it up slowly. Hayflick's (1994) analogy is that of a car that starts out with 5,000 gallons of gasoline. If this car gets 20 miles to the gallon on a smooth and level highway and with light traffic, it can travel a total of 100,000 miles. If driven 100 miles a week, it will run for close to 20 years before it stops. However, if the same car is driven 1,000 miles per week, its energy will be used up more rapidly and it will stop running sooner. Also, if the car is driven under challenging conditions, such as on steep hills and in heavy traffic, it will get fewer miles to the gallon so it will stop running sooner. On this basis, one might suppose that a person whose life is less physically demanding will incur less wear and tear, and his or her aging will progress more slowly. In fact, however, there is little scientific evidence that individuals who work in physically strenuous jobs show signs of aging any earlier than those who work in jobs that are not physically demanding (Hayflick, 1994; 1995).

But life can be demanding in ways that are not physical. For example, we may be able to conserve energy and age more slowly if we limit the amount of stress in our lives, or at least control the way we react to it. The two main regulatory systems in the body for responding to stress are the sympathetic nervous system (SNS) and the neuroendocrine hypothalamic-pituitary-adrenal (HPA) axis (Finch & Seeman, 1999). According to the *stress theory* of aging, the physiological activation triggered by stress results in the secretion of stress-related hormones called glucocorticoids (GC). In young organisms, the HPA axis is resilient, meaning that it quickly returns to a normal level of functioning following exposure to stress. In older organisms, the HPA axis is less resilient, so it takes longer to return to a normal level after exposure to stress. This delay in return to a normal level means that older organisms have prolonged exposure to the GC hormones secreted by the HPA axis in response to stress. There is evidence that prolonged exposure to heightened HPA activation and the resulting secretion of GC increases the risk of high blood pressure (hypertension) and cardiovascular disease. In fact, prolonged exposure to the GC associated with the physiological response to stress can damage the biological system and possibly accelerate the aging process (Landsfield, 1995).

To illustrate the different ways young and older adults react under stressful conditions, Finch and Seeman (1999) describe a study that employed a driving simulation test. On this test, young (ages 30–39) and older (ages 70–79) participants responded to potentially dangerous situations similar to those frequently encountered in real-world driving. Participants' hormone (GC) levels were measured prior to the test (baseline) and again at several times up to two hours after they had completed the test. The GC levels of the younger participants returned to baseline levels well before the two hours had elapsed, evidence that the HPA axis is quite resilient at younger ages. In contrast, the GC levels of the older participants were still elevated after two hours, a sign of less resiliency. Even so, there was considerable variability within the older group—older adults in poor health had less HPA resiliency than did older adults in good health. The GC levels of the less healthy older participants, many of whom suffered from diabetes (discussed later on) and high blood pressure, remained elevated for much longer than did the GC levels of the healthy older participants. These findings are intriguing, but further research is needed to clarify whether a decline in stress-regulating mechanisms is a cause of aging, or whether the aging process somehow reduces the efficiency of stress-regulating mechanisms, thus rendering older organisms more vulnerable to diseases that could reduce their longevity.

In sum, compared to young organisms, older organisms have had greater exposure to the GC hormones activated in response to stress. First, they have lived longer, so older organisms have had more opportunities than young organisms to be exposed to stress. Second, each exposure is magnified in older adulthood if physiological responses to stress are exaggerated and prolonged. Of course, even among older adults there are individual differences. Undoubtedly, some adults react more extremely to stress than others do.

© PhotoDisc

Social embeddedness is associated with feelings of control and may help individuals cope effectively with stress.

There is no simple answer to how neuroendocrine functioning can be regulated or what can be done to counteract the risk of prolonged exposure to neuroendocrine reactivity. However, several avenues are being investigated (Finch & Seeman, 1999). First, regular exercise for older adults seems to be a positive factor in improved endocrine regulation. Second, dietary regulation may have a protective effect. Restricted diets often result in lowered blood glucose, which may offset the negative effects of exposure to stress-related hormones. Finally, social and psychological factors may play a role in neuroendocrine activity. For many years, investigators have hypothesized that being embedded in a social network, or at least having a person in whom to confide, is beneficial for psychological well-being (Lowenthal & Haven, 1968). Also, feelings of well-being and personal control have been associated with less exaggerated neuroendocrine responses to stress. It is conceivable that wear and tear from exposure to high neuroendocrine levels accumulates more readily in people who have weak social bonds and low feelings of personal control. At the present time, we cannot make cause-and-effect statements. It is possible that social bonds instill feelings of personal control, which allow individuals to cope with stress more effectively. It is also conceivable that certain individuals possess a quality that allows them to form social bonds, to have feelings of control, and to cope with stress.

Damage to the biological system from prolonged exposure to stress-related hormones is the main premise of the stress theory of aging. However, different theories point to the buildup of other damaging substances or waste products that disrupt physiological functioning, resulting in aging and ultimately death. For example, *lipofuscin* is a substance that accumulates in brain and heart muscle cells. Although there is evidence for a build-up of lipofuscin with age, it has not been established whether, or even how, lipofuscin interferes with functioning.

Collagen is a common protein that forms a structure that surrounds and supports tendons, ligaments, bone, cartilage, and skin. Collagen consists of parallel molecules held together by rungs, or cross-links, much like those in a ladder. When neighboring molecules are joined by a small number of cross-links, they remain pliable. With aging, however, the number of cross-links increases and the ladders become less pliable. Age-related changes in the skin are a visible example of cross-linking. In young adults, the skin is soft and pliable, but with increasing age, the skin becomes less soft and pliable, presumably because of the increase in cross-links. The *cross-linking theory* of aging postulates that as collagen becomes more cross-linked, metabolic processes are affected because the passage of nutrients and waste products into and out of cells is obstructed. As with lipofuscin, there is little question that cross-linking increases with age. What has not been conclusively established is whether or how cross-linking actually blocks metabolic processes. In other words, we still do not know whether cross-linking is a cause, or simply a by-product, of the aging process (Hayflick, 1994).

Another stochastic theory of aging, *free radical theory,* focuses on the role of unstable molecular fragments, or free radicals, which are formed as a by-product of the body's normal process of metabolism. Because of their instability, free radicals unite with any molecules that happen their way, with the result that those molecules are prevented from functioning normally. Free radicals can damage proteins, fats, and lipids, and they have been implicated in the production of cross-links and the formation of age pigments often seen on older adults' skin. Free radicals have also been associated with changes in the brain that are characteristic of dementia, as well as with cardiovascular disease, cancer, and even the formation of cataracts on the corneas of the older eye (Rowe & Kahn, 1998). One theory is that the body does not have a fully effective mechanism for counteracting the damage caused by free radicals, so damage accumulates until it begins to interfere with functioning. However, an alternative possibility is that damage from free radicals accumulates because the body's natural defenses become less efficient with increasing age.

Some studies have demonstrated that antioxidants (including vitamins E and C and beta-carotene) serve to chemically inhibit the formation of free radicals, or at least compromise their ability to unite with surrounding susceptible molecules (Rowe & Kahn, 1998). Consumption of antioxidants has been associated with lowered incidence of cardiovascular disease and cancer, both of which are age-related diseases. There are some reports that animals fed antioxidants live longer on average compared to control animals not fed extra antioxidants. However, it has not yet been demonstrated that antioxidants actually increase the maximum longevity (life span) of a species (Hayflick, 1994). In sum, there is evidence that lipofuscin, collagen, cross-linking, and free radicals accumulate in the body with increasing age. The question remains, do these substances actually cause aging? Olshansky, Hayflick, and Carnes (2002) express concern about an anti-aging industry that advertises the use of antioxidant products and dietary supplements to slow down aging. They contend that antioxidants occur naturally in the body and in fruits and vegetables, and they warn that taking supplements could be harmful because we need some free radicals for certain necessary steps in internal biochemical reactions.

The role of diet in the aging process and longevity has intrigued researchers for decades. In an early study (McCay, Crowell, & Maynard, 1935), rats fed a severely reduced number of calories lived longer than rats allowed a normal caloric intake. In recent years, caloric restriction has received renewed attention. As long as they are given sufficient protein, fat, vitamins, and minerals for adequate issue and organ functioning, rats that consume 50 percent fewer calories and weigh 50 percent less than normally-fed control rats seem to have a lower incidence of cancer, a disease that becomes more prevalent in later life. Also, older rats fed restricted but nutritionally sound diets have the sleek appearance of younger rats and their average longevity is higher than that of older rats on unrestricted diets. Thus, as long as nutritional needs are met, caloric restriction may be the key to extended youthfulness and greater average longevity.

Several hypotheses have been suggested to explain the positive effects of caloric restriction in rodents (Weindruch, 1996). Caloric restriction may slow the rate of cell division in many tissues, thus reducing the chances of uncontrolled cell division, which is characteristic of late-life cancers. Also, caloric restriction is associated with lower blood glucose levels, which reduce the chances of damage from the buildup of sugar on long-lived proteins. Additionally, caloric restriction may limit the formation of free radicals. At present, there is no definite answer to the question of why caloric restriction seems to slow down aging in rodents. It may simply delay the onset of disease. Also, while average longevity is increased, it has not yet been demonstrated that caloric restriction raises the maximum life span of the species.

Recently, studies of caloric restriction have been extended to monkeys. Preliminary results are encouraging, but considerable time will be needed to assess the effects of restriction because the life span of moneys is much longer than that of rodents. Furthermore, it remains to be seen whether caloric restriction is beneficial for humans. Thus far, research on humans has been limited to the study of economically underprivileged individuals whose low-calorie diets often lack the proper nutrients. However, there is encouraging evidence from the greater than average longevity of individuals who live on the Japanese island of Okinawa, whose diets are low in calories but high in nutrients. In addition, there seems to be a lower incidence of some forms of cancer in people with reduced caloric intake. Weindruch (1996) recommends that people adhere to diets that reduce the levels of blood glucose and cholesterol. He also recommends that people strive to weigh 10 percent to 25 percent less than their natural "set point," which is not easy to determine. Certainly obesity is a risk factor that can shorten life. At present, however, questions remain about the benefits of caloric restriction for normal-weight humans.

If caloric restriction does prove to be beneficial for humans, at what point in life should it begin (Weindruch, 1996)? Severe caloric restriction could be harmful for children's development, and in adolescence and young adulthood, it could interfere with fertility. In research on rodents, restricting caloric intake starting in middle age has been effective in reducing the incidence of cancer and thus extending average longevity, but it is too soon to tell whether this will apply to humans.

The *error theory* of biological aging postulates that when errors are made at the cellular level, faulty molecules are produced. Errors can result from internal factors related to the organism's metabolic processes or they may be caused by external environmental factors such as radiation. Cells have protective mechanisms for repairing errors, but these mechanisms may not be able to keep up with all the damage created by faulty molecules. Over time, unrepaired damage builds up, eventually resulting in metabolic failure and ultimately death (Turker, 1996). There is evidence that cell repair processes are more efficient in animal species with greater longevities than they are in species with shorter longevities. The shorter-lived species may have less efficient mechanisms for repairing damage, so damage accumulates more readily, resulting in earlier death (Turker, 1996). We still have much to learn about how errors are repaired, but this theory is a promising approach to understanding biological aging processes (Hayflick, 1994).

In summary, the science of biological aging is relatively young and numerous theories have been proposed as to why it occurs. At present there is no definitive answer, but ongoing research should help clarify this highly complex process. It would be premature to predict which one or combination of theories will ultimately hold the key to biological aging. Although theories have been separated into programmed and stochastic categories, keep in mind that genetic programming could render organisms either more or less vulnerable to damage from internal and external sources. Thus, we need to consider both the programming and stochastic aspects of biological aging.

INDIVIDUAL DIFFERENCES IN LONGEVITY

The upper limit of human life span is approximately 120 years, but we know that few people live to that age. Indeed, there is great individual variability in longevity. Accidental deaths are one reason for the failure to attain maximum human longevity, but what other factors can predict how long a particular individual will live?

Nature and Nurture

Some people live closer than others to the maximum human longevity, and a relatively small proportion of individuals in the human population live into extreme old age with little evidence of disease or disability. These individuals have captured the attention of researchers and the popular media. Weiss (1997) offers the following examples: An 85-year-old California man who holds the world record for his age in the sport of competitive pole vaulting; a 93-year-old pilot who delivers newspapers to rural subscribers in California by dropping copies from a small aircraft; a 102-year-old religious Sister who retired from teaching at the age of 96 and has since become active in making pottery. By studying these healthy, long-lived individuals, perhaps we can discover the secret to living long, high-quality lives.

Who among us will have the good fortune to remain healthy and vigorous into the ninth decade or later? To answer this question, scientists are investigating factors related to both nature and nurture. Nature refers to heredity, or genetic makeup. The number of genes that underlie the aging process is not known (Turker, 1996), although heredity does seem to be a factor in longevity. Most people who live beyond age 70 have at least one parent or grandparent who lived into the 70s. Individuals who live into their 90s are likely to have at least one very long-lived parent. Furthermore, age of the mother's death seems to be a better predictor of a person's longevity than age of the father's death (Hayflick, 1994). Identical twins have exactly the same genetic makeup and tend to be more similar in longevity compared to fraternal twins, who are no more genetically related than siblings (Hayflick, 1994).

Although genetic makeup undoubtedly plays a role in longevity, it cannot fully account for the rate at which people age and how long they live. Nurture (environmental influences) must also be taken into consideration. Examples of nurture range from the quality of air a person breathes, a person's diet and exercise habits, a person's educational and work history, the level of stress in the environment, and the health care available to factors such as a person's marital status and social relationships. In their book on how to age successfully, Rowe and Kahn (1998) contend that the as we grow older, genetics are likely to become less important, but where and how we live become more important.

Even so, it is difficult to separate the effects of nature and nurture in the study of longevity. Unless identical twins are separated at birth and reared in completely different environments, they not only have the same genetic makeup, but they also were exposed to similar environmental influences in their early years. In most cases, both members of the pair were reared in the same household so they have common cultural backgrounds and child-rearing influences. Also, they were brought up under similar economic circumstances and had similar dietary regimens and health care. Despite their identical genetic makeup and the similarities in their early environment, identical twins do not necessarily age in a completely parallel fashion, nor do they live exactly the same amount of time. Aging and longevity are probably based on a complex mix of genetic and environmental factors that undoubtedly interact with one another (Turker, 1996).

It is virtually impossible to have complete control over the influence of nurture on humans, but some researchers have taken advantage of naturally occurring circumstances to study it. The Nun Study, a longitudinal research program under the direction of University of Kentucky epidemiologist Dr. David Snowdon, has been following more than 500 School Sisters of Notre Dame who reside in religious communities across the United States (Snowdon, 1997). These Sisters, who ranged from 75 to 102 years of age as of 1997, agreed to take periodic test batteries and donate their brains to science after they die. The older Sisters in this study have similar educational backgrounds and all of them worked throughout their adult lives in teaching and service careers. All lived for decades in religious communities and they had similar dietary and exercise habits. They never married or had children, nor did any of them indulge in habits such as smoking or drinking alcoholic beverages. In short, the influences of nurture from early adulthood when they entered the religious order have been very much the same for these Sisters. Even so, the variability among them is striking. Some older Sisters have remained healthy and active, both physically and cognitively, well beyond their ninth decade. Others are confined to wheelchairs or suffer from cognitive impairments due to strokes or dementia. The individual differences among these Sisters in their later years suggests that nature, or more likely the interaction between nature and nurture, plays a role in health and longevity. Keep in mind, however, that the influences of nurture could well have varied considerably prior to the Sisters' joining the religious order. Thus, the early influences of nurture cannot be ruled out as a reason for the late-life variability in their health and longevity.

The Sisters in the Nun Study lived in similar environments for a long time. Another way to evaluate the influence of nurture is to study individuals who are similar in a number of ways but live in different environments. In one such study, Pruchno and Rose (2000) followed the health status and mortality rate of 158 European American Jewish older adults over a 12-month period of time. Approximately half of these individuals resided in an assisted living facility and the other half resided in a nursing home. As described in Chapter 10, assisted living facilities provide services for people who need help with personal care such as dressing and bathing but do not require nursing care, whereas nursing homes offer a full array of both personal and health care services. In Pruchno and Rose's study, each facility had its own staff and managing administrator, but the two facilities were located within the same city block and both had the same executive director and board of directors. Pruchno and Rose purposely selected high-functioning nursing home residents and low-functioning assisted living residents so that study participants from the two facilities were matched at the outset of the study with regard to mobility, cognitive functioning, level of depression, and subjective feelings about health. In short, all the participants would have qualified for entrance into either facility. Pruchno and Rose's main question was whether type of living environment would be associated with rate of morbidity and mortality. Specifically, they set out to determine whether there would be a more drastic decline in health or a greater increase in mortality for those living in the assisted living environment that provides fewer services than a nursing home does.

At the end of the 12 months, the patterns of morbidity and mortality were very similar for the assisted living and nursing home participants, leading these investigators to conclude that high-functioning nursing home residents would likely fare just as well in assisted living facilities, which are less costly than nursing homes to operate and allow older residents to have greater independence. Whether the results would be the same for samples with different ethnic and religious backgrounds remains to be determined.

In addition to living environments, marital status has also been investigated with regard to both health and longevity. Marital status is a social factor that most would consider an aspect of nurture. Schone and Weinick (1998) inspected self-reported health habits from the National Medical Expenditure Survey (NMES), which was administered in 1987 to a nationally representative sample of 14,000 households in the United States. For their study, Schone and Weinick selected 4,443 men and women from the sample who were ages 65 and older, who lived independently in the community, and who were either married or widowed.

They found that for these older adults, marriage was clearly associated with preventive health behaviors. Relative to widowed older adults, married older adults were more likely to engage in healthy habits such as physical activity, eating breakfast, wearing seatbelts, and abstaining from smoking. However, the association between being married and engaging in healthy habits was stronger for the older men than it was for the older women. Schone and Weinick speculate that women may value health more than men do, so they may take the lead in monitoring or encouraging their husbands to engage in healthy behaviors. Schone and Weinick also found that individuals who were African American, who were lower in economic status, or who had fewer than 12 years of education were less likely to engage in healthy behaviors relative to individuals from other racial/ethnic groups and individuals with more education and higher economic status. In addition, they found that older adults with fewer social contacts were less likely to have healthy habits than individuals with a greater number of social contacts. Widowed women often have more social contacts than widowed men, which could explain why they are more likely to engage in healthy behaviors than widowed men are. For women, social contacts rather than marriage may be associated with healthy behaviors.

In another study on the relationship between marital status and longevity, Tucker, Wingard, Friedman, and Schwartz (1996) examined data from 1,077 male and female participants in the Terman Life-Cycle Longitudinal Study that was initiated in 1921. Those selected to participate in the Terman Study were intelligent, educated, primarily European American (99 percent), middle-class children. Tucker et al. set out to assess the relationship between marital history at midlife (in 1950) and mortality four decades later (as of 1991). Participants were placed into one of four categories based on their marital status as of the year 1950: (1) consistently married (married with no prior marital breakups); (2) inconsistently married (married, but with a prior marital breakup); (3) separated or divorced; (4) never married, or single.

Tucker et al. found that, overall, individuals who were married as of the year 1950 ended up living longer than those who were separated or divorced as of 1950. This lends support to the hypothesis that when it comes to longevity, marriage is indeed a protective factor. However, several of Tucker et al.'s findings indicate that we must exercise caution before we draw conclusions about the positive effect of marriage on longevity. First, individuals who were single as of midlife (1950) had no greater mortality risk than did those who were consistently married as of 1950. For the select sample of participants in the Terman Study, the status of remaining single may have been one of choice and not one due to exclusion from marital opportunities because of physical or mental difficulties.

Second, particularly for men but to a lesser extent for women, individuals who had experienced a marital breakup by midlife (inconsistently married) had a higher mortality risk than did individuals who had married only once (consistently married). Tucker et al. speculate that marital breakup may have long-term negative effects that are not completely reduced by remarriage. In addition, they point out that certain other factors may be associated with marital inconsistency. For example, individuals who are not consistently married may be less conscientious about healthy habits and thus have a higher risk of mortality. In sum, when studying the association between marriage and longevity, it may be important to look at marital history rather than simply at current marital status. Tucker et al.'s finding of higher mortality risk among the inconsistently married and their failure to find higher mortality risk among the never-married (singles) suggest that marriage may not be protective in and of itself. Rather, factors such as educational opportunities, personality, and lifestyle habits could underlie both marital status/marital history and longevity.

Individuals who participated in the Terman Study were born around 1910 and they were selected on the basis of high intellectual ability in childhood. They came from very homogeneous ethnic and socioeconomic backgrounds. Whether the findings from this sample can be generalized to samples with greater diversity, or to samples from different birth cohorts, cannot be determined at this time. In any case, Tucker et al.'s findings serve to caution us against drawing cause-and-effect conclusions about the relationship between organismic variables such as marital status and mortality and/or health.

Can Social Scientists Predict Longevity?

With such widely varying individual differences in human longevity, it is no wonder that social scientists are interested in predicting who will live a long time and who will not. Accurate prediction is a first step toward possible control through interventions that might enable more people to live closer to maximum human longevity.

Tests of cognitive ability and in some cases self-report measures of health and well-being have been used to detect whether the end of life is near. One of the earliest of such studies was conducted by Kleemeier (1962), who used an early version of the Wechsler Adult Intelligence Scale (discussed in more detail in Chapter 6) to test 13 elderly men on four occasions over 12 years. During the 12-year interval, the scores of these men declined. However, when Kleemeier looked back, he noted that the decline was much steeper for the four men who were deceased at the end of the 12-year period than it was for the nine men who survived to the end of the 12 years. The steeper decline of the deceased individuals became known as **terminal drop**. Subsequently, Kleemeier followed a sample of 70 elderly men, testing their intellectual ability at two different times. At a later third point, approximately half of the 70 men were deceased. When Kleemeier inspected the scores that these men had earned at the two points of testing, he found that the men who were deceased at Time 3 had shown a steeper drop in scores between Time 1 and Time 2 compared to the men who were still living at Time 3. Kleemeier's research on terminal drop has had considerable influence on those who conduct aging research

Kleemeier used a longitudinal design to test and retest the cognitive ability of the same people, so he was able to observe whether there was decline in scores from one time to the next and eventually to determine whether the extent of the decline was related to survival. In a study conducted by Riegel, Riegel, and Meyer (1967), 380 German men and women (ages 55 to 75) were tested twice (first in 1956 and again in 1961) on a German form of the Wechsler Adult Intelligence Scale. In 1966, 10 years after the study was initiated, those who had been willing to return in 1961 to be retested were more likely to be surviving than were those who had refused to be retested in 1961. Terminal drop cannot be examined here, but perhaps those who refused to be retested felt they were not at their best and therefore did not return. In any case, Riegel et al.'s data indicated that willingness to return for a retest was a powerful predictor of survival.

Most investigators only have access to scores from one time of testing, so they are not able to determine how much a person's score may have dropped from one time to the next. Even so, when a test score is much lower than might be expected on the basis of an individual's educational and professional background, it is often assumed that a drop has already occurred.

Maier and Smith (1999) inspected cross-sectional data from a battery of tests administered to a sample of 516 individuals (ages 70–103) as part of the Berlin Aging Study in Germany. The battery was administered to individuals only one time, between 1990 and 1993. By 1996 (3 to 6 years after the tests were given), 50 percent of the individuals were deceased. Maier and Smith were aware that chronological age itself is associated with greater risk of mortality, so they made separate calculations for two groups of participants, those ages 70–84 and those ages 85–103. For both groups, low scores on tests of intellectual functioning were strongly associated with high risk of mortality 3 to 6 years later (as of 1996). To a lesser but still significant extent, subjective feelings of dissatisfaction with aging were also associated with elevated mortality risk. Thus, psychological predictors of mortality in old age were not limited to cognitive functioning, but also included self-evaluations of personal well-being.

Similar findings were reported by Menec, Chipperfield, and Perry (1999), who inspected data from 1,406 older (ages 65–74, 75–84, and 85+) residents of Manitoba who participated in a longitudinal study conducted by the Canadian government. In one part of the survey, participants rated their health on a five-point scale from "bad" to "excellent." Older adults who rated their health as "bad" were more than twice as likely to die within the 3-year period following the initial survey compared to older adults who had rated their health as "excellent." The association between this measure of self-perceived health and mortality risk was significant even when information about the number of participants' physicians visits, hospitalizations, and disease diagnoses was taken into account. Clearly, additional research is needed to clarify what factors underlie the relationship between self-perceived health and mortality.

Some recent findings from the Nun Study that was described earlier indicate it may be possible to predict longevity on the basis of both cognitive and emotional measures made much earlier in life. Approximately 180 of the Sisters who entered several convents between 1931 and 1943 were asked to write an autobiography, which was then preserved in the archives of the convent. The Sisters wrote these autobiographies when they were approximately 22 years of age. All of them were born in the United States and were English speaking, and most had a high school diploma. Therefore, their cultural and educational backgrounds were similar. These authenticated handwritten autobiographies were made available to the Nun Study investigators, who analyzed them for grammatical structure and content. In 1991, the Sisters who had written their autobiographies as young adults ranged in age from 75 to 95. By the end of the follow-up period in 2000, 76 Sisters (42 percent) were deceased but 104 Sisters (58 percent) were still living. Not only was the level of linguistic ability evident in the autobiographies written six decades earlier positively related to survival, but so was emotional content (Danner, Snowdon, & Friesen, 2001). Sisters whose autobiographies contained more positive expressions of emotion (happiness, interest, love, hope, gratefulness, contentment, amusement) were more likely to have survived compared to Sisters whose autobiographies expressed more negative expressions of emotion (sadness, fear, confusion, shame, hopelessness, anger, disgust). These investigators speculate that individual differences in the emotional content of the autobiographies may reflect life-long patterns of emotional response to events. It would be premature to draw conclusions about cause-and-effect relationships, but these findings suggest that it would be worthwhile to undertake further investigation of early emotional well-being and longevity.

Researchers have employed similar strategies to determine what measures predict an individual's risk for morbidity (disease) rather than mortality (death). Rubin et al. (1998) investigated whether performance on cognitive ability tests could help detect the early stages of senile dementia of the Alzheimer's type (AD). (The most common form of dementia in older adults, AD, is discussed in greater detail in Chapter 11.) The main symptoms of AD are difficulties with memory, reasoning, and problem solving. Would decline over time on tests of cognitive ability signify the onset of AD, or would such decline simply represent a mild form of age-related memory loss unlikely to become debilitating later? Rubin et al. (1998) followed adults who were ages 62 to 83 at the outset over a 15-year time span, periodically administering a series of cognitive tests. Within 12 years, 59 percent of the individuals in the study were diagnosed with AD, but the other 41 percent were still experiencing relatively mild age-related memory loss. The most valuable index for predicting which individuals would eventually be diagnosed with AD was decline in scores on the Logical Memory Test. On this test, which measures the ability to recall the text of a paragraph that is read aloud by the examiner, there was a steep decline over time in individuals who were eventually diagnosed with AD. Scores on the Logical Memory Test did not decline as much for those who were not later diagnosed with AD.

The studies just described are retrospective. Participants were tested, sometimes on several occasions, but only at a later time did the outcome for each participant become apparent. Once they knew what the outcome was (either morbidity or mortality), investigators could look back to see whether decline in cognitive test scores, self-report ratings, or indexes of emotional well-being were any different for those who became ill or died compared to those who remained healthy or survived. Eventually, the findings of retrospective studies may make it possible to determine whether a low score or some critical amount of decline in test scores or self-report ratings signals impending mortality or morbidity. In other words, the goal is to predict which individuals are at risk so that it will be possible to intervene to postpone mortality or delay the onset of disease.

Maximizing Longevity

From the beginning of time, people have searched for ways to retard the aging process and extend longevity. Some people have traveled all over the world to spas and clinics that advertise treatments "guaranteed" to restore youth and prolong life. In the late 20th century, people of affluence traveled to Rumania to receive special vitamin injections, to Switzerland for injections of cells from a lamb fetus, and to London for injections of genetic material and enzymes from fetal cells (Woodruff-Pak, 1988). Many who sought these treatments reported that the effort and expense were worthwhile, but there is little scientific evidence that such treatments actually prolong youth or extend life (Woodruff-Pak, 1988).

However, some lifestyle practices do hold promise for maximizing longevity. First, abstention from smoking decreases the risk of cancer and heart disease. Individuals who give up smoking enjoy an immediate benefit in reducing the risk of heart disease (Rowe & Kahn, 1998). Cessation from smoking appears to have less immediate benefits in reducing the risk of cancer and other lung diseases (Rowe & Kahn, 1998).

Modifications in diet such as reducing the intake of fat and sugar can also reduce the risk of heart disease and possibly some forms of cancer. In addition, sedentary living has become a public health issue and daily physical activity reduces health risks in older adulthood. Exercise often prevents or at least minimizes the effects of circulatory diseases and it contributes to the maintenance of bone density in middle-aged and older adults.

In a survey of 327 independent community-living Canadian women ages 70 and older, Cousins (2000) found that most of them recognized the potential health benefits from activities such as walking and swimming. Even so, many of these women did not engage in sufficient physical activity. Many were fearful that muscle strength and flexibility exercises would do them harm. Clearly, those in charge of exercise programs must address such fears and be willing to customize exercise programs to fit the needs of individual participants.

In an article entitled, "Postponement of aging," Svanborg (1996) points out that in addition to adequate medical care and access to physical and intellectual stimulation, social factors are also important. In older adulthood, health and vitality tend to be preserved if individuals remain emotionally engaged and socially integrated. Rowe and Kahn (1998) also emphasize the importance of close relationships with others and of participating in regular activities that make life meaningful and exciting.

As mentioned earlier, Perls and his colleagues at Harvard University Medical School developed a Longevity Quiz for people who want to estimate what their individual longevities are likely to be (see Table 3.4). Note that the items on this quiz tap family background, lifestyle habits, and social factors.

PHYSICAL CHANGES AND DISEASE

Physical changes commonly occur over the course of adulthood, although there is considerable variation in the extent and rate at which they happen. Also, although a distinction is made between aging and disease, there is little question that the frequency of certain diseases increases with age. Today, the diseases associated with aging are mostly of the chronic type rather than the acute infectious type. Now we will look at some of the most prominent physical changes that take place as people age, as well as the most frequent chronic diseases. The changes and diseases mentioned are by no means exhaustive, but they are the more common ones found in older adulthood.

Body Systems

Changes occur in various body systems, but even within the same person, physical changes may be more noticeable in some parts of the body than in others. Also, certain diseases occur more frequently in older adulthood. Some diseases are associated with pain, disability, or limitations in functioning even in the early stages. Others have no noticeable symptoms until they are advanced, at which point they can be more difficult to treat.

Some physical changes hold more meaning than others for how aging individuals feel about themselves as well as how people view them. Other physical changes are important because they affect how older adults function, especially under demanding and stressful conditions.

Skin and Hair   Visible signs of aging in the texture and appearance of the skin and hair are among the first to be noticed. With increasing age, the skin becomes drier, and it begins to sag and show wrinkles. Thinning and graying of hair and, for men, loss of hair, become more prevalent. Perhaps because these changes are often the first ones to become evident to others, they seem to be associated with age-based and gender-based beliefs and stereotypes.

In a classic article, Sontag (1972) argued that in American society there is a *double standard of aging* whereby visible signs of aging are viewed more negatively in women than they are in men. Facial wrinkles are considered something to be avoided at all costs by women, but in men such wrinkles are often viewed as a sign of "character." Similarly, gray hair is considered unattractive in women, whereas in men it is seen as a sign of distinction and charisma. Furthermore, men are especially biased in favor of youth and harsh in their judgments about signs of aging (Kogan & Mills, 1992). Many years after Sontag wrote her article, Harris (1994) conducted a survey of adults ages 18 to 80 (69 percent European American, 19 percent Hispanic American, 6 percent Native American, and the remaining 6 percent of Asian American, African American, or mixed ethnic background) to learn more about their attitudes toward visible signs of aging. The 269 survey participants read a scenario in which a male or female protagonist (target) was described as having gray hair, sagging skin, and facial wrinkles. The target was described either as making use of age concealment techniques (such as coloring his or her hair, getting a facelift, or using wrinkle cream) or as refusing to use age concealment techniques. First, participants made judgments about the target. Afterward, they were asked how important they considered their own appearance to be and whether they would use age concealment techniques to make themselves look younger.

Not surprisingly, survey participants thought the target's physical signs of aging were unattractive with one exception: The male protagonist's facial wrinkles were not viewed negatively. Apparently, the double standard of aging described by Sontag in 1972 is alive and well. What is surprising, however, is that even though the survey participants considered physical signs of aging to be unattractive, they did not have a favorable view of targets who used age concealment techniques. They were especially disapproving of male targets who attempted to conceal their wrinkles and gray hair. The fact that the female target's use of age concealment techniques met with less disapproval suggests that the participants considered it more acceptable for women than for men to combat the signs of aging.

In addition to the double standard her study participants used to judge male and female targets, Harris found one other type of double standard: While study participants did not generally approve of the targets' attempts to conceal signs of aging, they felt that it would be acceptable if they themselves used such techniques. Apparently, people are more lenient in judging their own use of age concealment techniques than they are of others who attempt to cover up the signs of aging.

The Musculoskeletal System and Body Fat   In addition to changes in the hair and skin, muscle mass and strength gradually decrease with age, and older adults often take longer than young adults do to recover from exertion (Tonna, 1995b). Under ordinary conditions, older adults are likely to function just as well as young and middle-aged adults. However, when circumstances require the use of that extra capacity that most people hold in reserve but don't usually need, age-related differences often become apparent. The extra capacity needed when stressful or demanding situations require more than the normal capacity is called **reserve capacity**. In the musculoskeletal as well as other organ systems, there is a decrease in the level of the reserve capacity with increasing age.

With increasing age, joints show degenerative changes. Arthritis is a condition caused by degeneration of the joints that usually causes pain and often loss of movement. The two most frequent forms are *rheumatoid arthritis* and *osteoarthritis,* and for reasons not completely understood more women than men are affected. Rheumatoid arthritis (RA) is an autoimmune disease that often begins with inflammation and swelling of the small joints of the hands and feet and is associated with stiffness as well as general fatigue and weight loss. Some RA sufferers have periods of relative remission, but the disease is usually progressive and eventually affects not only the joints but other organs in the body as well. Over time, RA can lead to irreversible joint deformities and difficulties with walking and other normal activities (Badley & Rothman, 1996). RA typically appears in young or middle adulthood. However, some older adults are long-term RA sufferers and occasionally RA can develop in older adulthood (Badley & Rothman, 1996).

Osteoarthritis (OA) is the more common form of degenerative joint disease and in most instances is a milder condition than RA. Typically, OA is confined to the weight-bearing joints such as the knees, hips, and spine, but it can also affect fingers, wrists, and elbows (Tonna, 1995a). OA can result from injury but most often it is just a function of degeneration from wear and

Figure 3.3 | Loss of bone density and cartilage can result in compression of the spine. As a result, older adults lose some height and many develop a rounded, stooped posture.

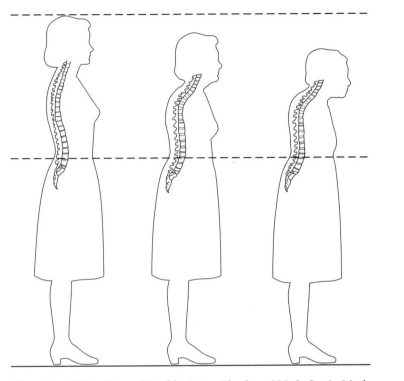

From Ebersole and Hess, *Toward Healthy Aging* 5th ed., p. 395, St. Louis: Mosby, 1998. Reprinted by permission of Elsevier.

tear over time. Some people are more predisposed than others to developing OA, but OA affects nearly half of the age 65+ group (Rowe & Kahn, 1998) and more than 80 percent of Americans ages 75+ (Solomon, 1999). Osteoarthritis begins with pain and stiffness and if untreated it can limit mobility and cause considerable disability (Tonna, 1995a). OA is rarely fatal on its own (Solomon, 1999), but it can reduce the quality of life of those affected. Fortunately, advances in surgical techniques, including hip and other joint replacement, together with appropriate use of medication, physical therapy, and exercise can allow older adults with OA to lead relatively pain-free and active lives (Rowe & Kahn, 1998).

With increasing age, the skeleton also becomes less movable and less able to sustain stress. From late middle-age to older adulthood, loss of bone density in the vertebrae can lead to decreasing physical stature. Between the ages of 55 and 75, men can lose up to an inch and women up to two inches in height (Kausler & Kausler, 1996). Along with shortened stature, a rounding

Figure 3.4   The thinner and less dense osteoporotic bone tissue is more vulnerable to fractures compared to normal bone tissue.

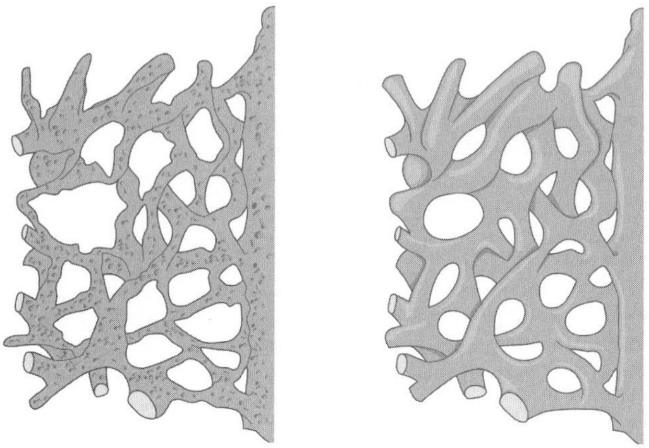

Osteoporotic bone tissue   Normal bone tissue

Cavanaugh & Blanchard-Fields (4th ed). Belmont, CA: Wadsworth/Thomson Learning.

of the back and stooped posture are frequently observed, especially in older women.

Osteoporosis is a metabolic disease that causes loss of bone mass that is much more extensive than the loss that occurs with normal aging. Osteoporosis is four times more prevalent in women than men, although it can occur in men older than age 55. Postmenopausal women, especially those of northern European extraction and slight build, are most at risk (Barzel, 1995). The extreme loss of bone density can result in fractures of the vertebrae, hips, wrists, and ankles when there is slight or even no apparent trauma. These fractures can be extremely painful and sometimes result in long periods of immobility. In its earliest asymptomatic stages, osteoporosis can be detected with scan technology for bone density. Hormone replacement therapy (HRT) may slow the progression of osteoporosis in some postmenopausal women. However, HRT is associated with an increased risk of breast cancer (Rowe & Kahn, 1998). Furthermore, recent findings have called into question what were once considered to be additional protective effects of HRT against heart disease and Alzheimer's disease. Each woman must determine whether HRT is the best course of action based on her own individual risk factors. For osteoporosis, other medications can be prescribed that are specifically targeted to the control of bone loss. In addition, intake of calcium and vitamin D together with a well-managed regular exercise program and abstention from smoking are important for maintaining bone density.

Proportion of body fat increases from young adulthood through late middle age. On average, sedentary men have body fat content of 17 percent in their 20s, which increases to 29 percent in their 60s. Sedentary women have a body fat content of 24 percent in their 20s, which increases to 38 percent in their 60s. Beyond age 60, however, body fat content declines (Masoro, 1995).

© Chuck Savage/Corbis

Engaging in exercise has many benefits, one of which is maintaining respiratory capacity.

There is some evidence that the regional distribution of fat (specifically, greater abdominal fat) is more important than absolute amount of body fat in predicting such serious diseases as Type II adult-onset diabetes mellitus, coronary heart disease, and stroke (Masoro, 1995). These diseases, which will be described shortly, do not always have obvious symptoms in the early stages, but medical screening can detect risk factors so steps can be taken to prevent these conditions, or at least minimize the possibility of irreversible damage or death.

Respiratory and Cardiovascular Functioning   The respiratory and cardiovascular systems become less efficient with advancing age. Again, the concept of reserve capacity applies because older adults are most likely to notice changes in functioning when conditions are stressful (Rowe & Kahn, 1998). With regard to the respiratory system, a decrease in lung elasticity results in smaller lung volume (Cherniack & Altose, 1996). The smaller reserve capacity resulting from this reduced volume may limit lengthy participation in strenuous exercise. However, normal age-related changes in lung capacity do not prevent older adults from engaging in some level of exercise. Exercise programs tailored to older individuals' capacities can help maintain respiratory capacity.

Sullivan (1995) provides an excellent review of the cardiovascular system, which consists of the heart and all the blood vessels throughout the body. Arteries are the relatively thick-walled tubes that carry blood away from the heart to a branching network of vessels that carry the blood to tissues throughout the body. The arteries terminate in extremely small thin-walled vessels called capillaries, which transfer nutrients and waste products between the blood and surrounding tissues. Eventually, the capillaries join together and meet in larger vessels called veins, which collect the blood and return it to the heart, which in turn moves the blood through the system. Over time, the walls of the arteries become less elastic, the heart valves become less flexible, and the maximum heart rate declines. As a result of these changes, blood pressure often increases. Despite some loss in reserve capacity, however, the cardiovascular system can continue to perform very well in older adulthood.

Diseases of the cardiovascular system become more frequent with age and affect approximately one-third of the U.S. population ages 65 and over (Rowe & Kahn, 1998). *Atherosclerosis* is a major problem associated with both increasing age and genetic background. With atherosclerosis, a buildup of a substance called *plaque* causes a narrowing of the arterial walls, which leads to restriction in blood flow. Early in the disease, there may be no noticeable symptoms but later on symptoms appear under stressful conditions and eventually even at rest. *Hypertension* is the term used when blood pressure is elevated to a danger zone, beyond what is typical with increasing age. *Aneurysms*, which are associated with hypertension, are weaknesses in the arterial walls that lead to bulging and possible rupture. *Stroke* is a general term that refers to a condition in which blood flow to the brain is disrupted, resulting in temporary or permanent damage depending upon which specific part of the brain is affected. Over time, hypertension can cause damage to the walls of the arteries and increase the risk of heart attacks, aneurysms, and strokes. Diseases of the veins also become more frequent with age and the usual feature is a backflow of blood that is supposed to be directed toward the heart. *Phlebitis* is the formation of clots in the veins, which can cause pain and inflammation and can be life threatening if large clots break free and drift to the lungs after passing through the right side of the heart. Lack of regular physical activity that serves to promote circulation can sometimes be a factor in causing these problems. Diseases of the heart itself can result from damage to the valves or arterial problems that reduce the flow of blood, which can cause pain and sometimes damage to the heart muscle. In the United States, hypertension and heart disease are frequent conditions in adults in the 65+ age group.

Another disease that affects the vascular system is *diabetes mellitus*, a chronic condition caused by the body's inability to create or effectively use its own insulin. Insulin is a hormone that converts food into glucose, which the body needs for energy. Without sufficient insulin, the level of glucose, or sugar, in the blood becomes too high. If the high level of blood sugar remains uncontrolled, blood vessels can be permanently damaged, resulting in complications such as blindness and arterial disease in the heart and peripheral vessels as well (National Academy on an Aging Society, 2000). Type I (insulin-dependent) diabetes is usually diagnosed in childhood, while Type II (noninsulin-dependent) diabetes is most often diagnosed in middle age or older adulthood. To some extent, Type II diabetes is hereditary but losing excess weight and increasing exercise can reduce the risk. Once diagnosed, Type II diabetes can sometimes be controlled through changes in diet and physical activity. However, medication may also be needed and eventually insulin therapy often becomes necessary. Type II diabetes is a major health problem that is costly to manage (Sinclair, 1995), but left untreated, complications can result in disability and death.

Figure 3.5

Axons and dentrites allow neurons to communicate over synapses. Neurons in the brains of rats housed in stimulating and complex environments show more dentritic branching than do neurons in the brains of rats housed in unstimulating environments.

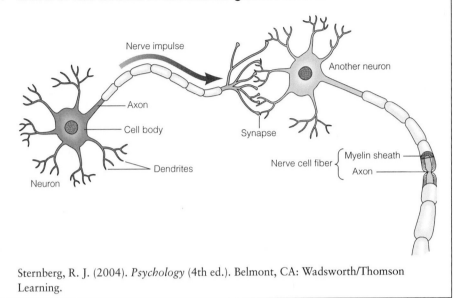

Sternberg, R. J. (2004). *Psychology* (4th ed.). Belmont, CA: Wadsworth/Thomson Learning.

Individuals with this disease must be motivated to follow the necessary diet, exercise, and medication regimen. If diabetes is controlled, people who have it are able to lead active lives.

Central Nervous System Functioning   The central nervous system is made up of billions of nerve cells, or *neurons*. A neuron consists of a cell body, an axon that transmits messages, and dendrites that branch out to receive the messages from the axons of other neurons. The gap between the axon terminal of one neuron and the dendrites of another neuron is called a *synapse*. A nerve impulse must cross the synapse in order for neurons to transmit messages to one another. Chemicals called neurotransmitters mediate contact, or act as chemical messengers at the synapses to help transfer information between neurons (Kausler & Kausler, 1996).

Over the adult life span, some neurons are lost. Neurons do not regenerate, but fortunately, we have more neurons than we need to maintain adequate functioning. Strokes, which were mentioned earlier, can cause damage or loss of neurons in the brain. However, the relatively minor loss of neurons during the course of normal aging does not seem to have an appreciable effect on brain functioning. Of course, with diseases such as Alzheimer's and Parkinson's disease, or in the case of strokes, there can be extensive damage and loss of neurons in the cerebral cortex, often with accompanying difficulties in physical and/or cognitive functioning. Chapter 11 discusses Alzheimer's disease and Parkinson's disease. Age-related changes in the level of neurotransmitters in the cerebral cortex and other areas of the brain can affect arousal and sleep, sense of balance and equilibrium, movement, and memory functioning (Kausler & Kausler, 1996). Also, the density of the dendritic connections between neurons is an important factor in brain functioning.

What effect does the environment have on neurological functioning? Studies have compared the brains of old rats housed in complex toy-filled group environments with the brains of old rats housed in standard cages that offer minimal stimulation. On autopsy, rats who lived in the complex environments had more extensive dendritic branching of the neurons in several areas of the brain compared to rats housed in the standard unstimulating environment. This suggests that the density of the dendritic branches may be fostered by stimulation from the environment. This is important because it is possible that dendritic density compensates for whatever neuron loss may occur in old age (Black, Greenough, Anderson, & Isaacs, 1987).

It is much more difficult to conduct well-controlled research on the effects of environmental stimulation on the human brain. Nonetheless, there is reason to believe that both mental and physical exercise foster "neural plasticity" in the human brain in terms of maintaining or possibly increasing the density of dendritic branching. Engaging in both physically and intellectually challenging activities beginning in early adulthood and continuing into middle age and later may protect brain functioning in older adulthood. Although further research is needed, engaging in such activities could reduce the risk of Alzheimer's disease in later life.

Changes in the sensory organs (the eyes and ears, for example) and in how visual, auditory, and other kinds of sensory information is processed by the central nervous system are covered in Chapter 4.

Urinary and Bowel Functioning   Age-related changes in urinary and bowel functioning are not uncommon and in mild forms they do not affect everyday functioning to a large extent. Sometimes symptoms can be relieved through changes in dietary and exercise habits. However, urinary incontinence is a clinical disorder characterized by loss of bladder control to the point of presenting a hygienic or social problem (Engel, 1995). The incidence of urinary incontinence increases with age and may be as high as 30 percent among community-living older adults and 50 percent among nursing home residents. Urinary incontinence is more common among older women than among older men (Engel, 1995), most likely because of earlier childbearing as well as changes in the urinary tract that occur with women's loss of estrogen at menopause. However, men can develop difficulties with urination, most often due to the enlargement of the prostate gland, which is situated below the bladder and can press against the urethra. Bowel incontinence is less common than urinary incontinence but is more socially disruptive and more likely to lead to institutional living (Engel, 1995). Urinary and bowel incontinence can occur for a number of reasons, including changes in pelvic floor muscles or other structural changes. It can also occur when individuals have cognitive impairments or motor difficulties that interfere with toileting habits (see later section on Activities of Daily Living). Care for this includes the use of diapers, medications, and in some instances surgical intervention. Some cases of incontinence have been treated successfully using behavioral intervention techniques such as prompting individuals to use toilet facilities at regular intervals (Burgio & Burgio, 1991).

Sexual Functioning   Weg (1996) points to "a growing acceptance among health professionals, educators, and older people themselves that sexual interest, capacities, pleasures, and libido remain throughout the life span into the ninth and perhaps the tenth decades (p. 479)." Furthermore, earlier interest and enjoyment of sexual activity seem to be reliable predictors for later life.

Still, several factors must be taken into account when it comes to sexual functioning. Moderately good physical and psychological health are usually needed for continuing sexual interests and expression in older adulthood. Heart disease, strokes, diabetes, pelvic disorders, arthritis, and enlargement of the prostate gland may interfere with the desire and ability to participate in sexual activity (Weg, 1996). Medications, both prescription and over the counter, are sometimes used to treat chronic conditions that affect older adults' sexual desire and capabilities.

Normal age-related physical changes mean that the nature of sexual activity may vary from young to middle to older adulthood. The time it takes to become sexually aroused may increase with age, especially for older men. Furthermore, the refractory period prior to physiological readiness for sexual activity may be longer. However, unavailability of a partner is usually the most important barrier to intimate sexual relations in older adulthood. This might be more the case for older women, who are more likely than older men to be widowed and less likely than older men to remarry after they lose their spouses.

There is relatively limited information on the sexual functioning of gay older men, and even less is known about lesbian older women (Weg, 1996). What information is available seems to indicate that older gay partners maintain longer relationships than young gay partners do (Weg, 1996). Further study is long overdue regarding the sexual relationships as well as the social support systems among gay and lesbian older adults.

In sum, physical changes occur as people grow older, but under normal conditions most of them do not interfere with adequate functioning. In some instances, changes can be minimized with a healthy diet and exercise regimen. Some older adults are more prone than others to specific chronic diseases, possibly because of genetics. Proper screening for risk factors can lead to early diagnosis so that treatment can be implemented before extensive damage occurs. The symptoms and progression of a number of chronic diseases can be controlled with medication, surgery, and changes in lifestyle. Although there are more chronic diseases at later ages, many older adults function with little or no disability if they receive proper care and follow a recommended regimen of diet and exercise.

Leading Causes of Mortality

Morbidity and mortality are related, but they are not one and the same. For example, Type II diabetes mellitus will result in death if it goes untreated. However, if controlled with weight loss, proper diet, and/or administration of medication and insulin, individuals with this disease can live for many years.

Table 3.6 | Leading Causes of Death in the United States for All Races and Both Sexes, 65 Years of Age and Older

Rank	Cause	Percent of Total Deaths, Ages 65+
1	Heart disease	33.0
2	Malignant neoplasms (cancer)	21.8
3	Cerebrovascular disease (stroke)	8.2
4	Chronic respiratory (lung) disease	5.9
5	Influenza and pneumonia	3.3
6	Diabetes mellitus	2.9
7	Alzheimer's disease	2.7

Source: National Vital Statistics Report (2002).

But complications can develop, so even diseases that are treated may still cause death, or mortality, at some point. Now that we have covered some of the main sources of morbidity in older adulthood, what are the main causes of mortality?

In the United States, heart disease and cancer are the two leading causes of mortality in the total population of individuals age 65 and over. Note in Table 3.6 that Alzheimer's disease is ranked as the seventh cause of death in individuals ages 65+. However, Alzheimer's disease moves up to the fifth leading cause of death in individuals ages 85+.

When causes of mortality in individuals ages 65+ are broken down by race and sex, the two leading causes are identical for European American and African American men and women—heart disease and cancer. However, there is some variation among these groups in the next five most frequent causes of mortality. As Table 3.7 shows, Alzheimer's disease is a more frequent cause of death for European American women than it is for the other three groups. Also for African American men and women, diabetes mellitus is ranked higher (fifth for African American men and fourth for African American women) as a cause of death than it is for European American men and women, for whom it is ranked sixth and seventh, respectively. The higher rank of diabetes mellitus as a cause of death in African Americans may reflect the fact that for socioeconomic reasons, medical care is less available to African Americans as a group than it is to European Americans. The symptoms of diabetes do not always become obvious until it is advanced, and the management and treatment of the disease at that stage is costly, so economic factors could limit treatment.

Olshansky, Carnes, and Grahn (1998) contend that medical and biomedical interventions have succeeded in extending the lives of people who previously would not have survived. Modern medical science has been successful in preventing or treating health problems that in earlier times caused death well before old age. For example, screening for heart disease and treating it through

Table 3.7 | Leading Causes of Death in the United States by Race and Sex, 65 Years of Age and Older

Rank	European American Males	European American Females	African American Males	African American Females
1	Heart disease	Heart disease	Heart disease	Heart disease
2	Malignant neoplasms (cancer)	Malignant neoplasms (cancer)	Malignant neoplasms (cancer)	Malignant neoplasms (cancer)
3	Chronic lung disease	Cerebrovascular disease (stroke)	Cerebrovascular disease (stroke)	Cerebrovascular disease (stroke)
4	Cerebrovascular disease (stroke)	Chronic lung disease	Chronic lung disease	Diabetes mellitus
5	Influenza and pneumonia	Alzheimer's disease	Diabetes mellitus	Nephritis (kidney disease)
6	Diabetes mellitus	Influenza and pneumonia	Influenza and pneumonia	Influenza and pneumonia
7	Accidents	Diabetes mellitus	Nephritis (kidney disease)	Septicemia (infections of the bloodstream)

Source: National Vital Statistics Report (2002).

diet or surgery means that individuals who in earlier times may have suffered from fatal heart attacks and stokes in their 50s and 60s are now able to live into late old age. However, as people live longer, there is a higher incidence of diseases that are associated mainly with late old age (Solomon, 1999). These diseases occurred much less frequently in earlier generations; most people did not live long enough to get them (Olshanksy, Carnes, & Grahn, 1998). A good example is the increasing prevalence of Alzheimer's disease (AD), which Chapter 11 describes in greater detail. Even so, older adults of today and tomorrow have a better chance of enjoying productive and independent lives than their parents and grandparents did.

EVERYDAY FUNCTIONING AND HEALTH CARE

How do the physical changes and chronic diseases that occur more frequently with increasing age affect how older adults function in their everyday lives? In 1996, 27 percent of older (65+) men and women assessed their health as only fair or poor. However, older African Americans (42 percent) and older Hispanic Americans (35 percent) were more likely to rate their health as only fair or poor than were older European Americans (26 percent) (A Profile of Older Americans: 2000). What kinds of care do older adults need to ensure that their lives have the highest possible quality?

Activities of Daily Living and Instrumental Activities of Daily Living

In evaluations of how well older adults are able to function, a distinction is made between **activities of daily living (ADL)** and **instrumental activities of daily living (IADL)**. ADL refers to the basic personal care tasks necessary for self-maintenance. These include eating, dressing, bathing, toileting, transferring into and out of a bed or chair, and getting around the house (Fillenbaum, 1995). Ability to perform all or most of these functions is necessary if older adults are to live independently in the community. ADL assessments are often used to determine disability and possible need for health care services.

IADL refers to the more complex activities required for carrying out the business of daily life. These include taking medication, preparing meals, managing personal finances, doing housework, using the telephone, shopping, and otherwise being able to get around the community (Lawton & Brody, 1969). Some older adults need help with instrumental activities to continue living in private homes or apartments.

Certain physical changes and age-related diseases can limit older adults in either or both kinds of activity, IADL and ADL. Such limitations occur more frequently in the oldest-old (85+) age group than at earlier points of older adulthood. For example, severe arthritis and osteoporosis can affect mobility and can even make it difficult for those afflicted to bathe and dress themselves. Strokes can affect ADL and in some cases IADL as well. Limitations on activities because of chronic conditions increase with age. In 1997, 30 percent of young-old (65–74) adults reported having a limitation caused by a chronic condition, while 50 percent of those 75 years of age and older reported limitations due to chronic conditions (A Profile of Older Americans: 2000). Of those age 80 and older, 28 percent have difficulty with ADLs and 40 percent with IADLs. These percentages are double what is found in the population ages 65+ in total (A Profile of Older Americans: 2000).

Compared to older men, older women experience more days per year when activities are restricted due to illness or injury. Also, older women are more likely than older men to have mobility and self-care limitations. In the young-old (65–74) age group,15 percent of women have trouble getting around or taking care of themselves compared with 12 percent of men. In the 75+ age group, 34 percent of women experience difficulties with mobility and self-care compared with only 24 percent of the men (Crispell & Frey, 1993). This gender gap cannot be attributed wholly to the larger proportion of women than men in the older adult age groups. The higher proportion of women with restrictions is more likely related to the fact that women are more likely than men to suffer from chronic conditions such as arthritis and osteoporosis. These diseases do not lead to immediate death but often cause mild to severe disability. It is interesting to note that women visit doctors more frequently but they live longer than men do. Perhaps woman are especially sensitive to health-related concerns. However, it is also likely that the kinds of chronic conditions from which women tend to suffer disproportionately cause sufficient pain that medical intervention is sought. Diseases such as hypertension, which affect many older men, have fewer symptoms but are more deadly.

Despite these statistics on restrictions in activities, remember that even though approximately 38 percent of older adults who live in the community experience temporary or permanent limitations of varying severity, the other 62 percent have no limitations in carrying out their daily activities (Crispell & Frey, 1993).

Medication

A small proportion of individuals remain free of disease-related symptoms into very late old age (Svanborg, 1996), and in rare instances death is assumed to occur from old age. In general, however, disease goes hand in hand with the aging process, and the majority of older adults have at least one chronic condition. Fortunately, chronic diseases can often be treated and controlled so that older adults can continue to lead active and independent lives.

One way physical changes or diseases can be prevented or controlled is with medication. Today, more and more drugs are available for such purposes and physicians are prescribing them. Approximately 34 percent of older adults take three or more prescribed drugs for chronic health problems such as diabetes, high blood pressure (hypertension), and arthritis. It is not unusual for older adults to be on as many as eight medications (Park, Morrell, Frieske, & Kincaid, 1992).

Unfortunately, older adults do not always take their medications exactly as directed, or prescribed. For example, hypertension, a major health problem and the number one cause of mortality in those ages 65 and older, can often be managed successfully if individuals adhere strictly to a prescribed medication regimen. Morrell, Park, Kidder, and Martin (1997) followed older adults for two months and recorded how closely they adhered to antihypertensive medication prescriptions. They found that individuals in the old-old age category (75–84) did not adhere as strictly to the medication regimen as did those in the young-old (65–74) age category. There could be several reasons for the old-old adults' failure to adhere strictly to the prescribed medication regimen. Their nonadherence may be related to their beliefs about medication and illness, their failure to understand the importance of taking the medicine, the possibility they experience unpleasant side effects with the medication, and the complexity of the medication regimen. With regard to complexity, adults in the old-old age group often take several prescription medications for more than one chronic condition. They may need the assistance of charts and containers for keeping track of pills to be taken at various times during the day (see Chapter 5 for a discussion of memory mnemonics).

Many older adults with several chronic conditions obtain prescriptions from more than one physician. In some instances, one medication interferes with the effects of another, or a combination of medications can actually cause a potentially harmful drug interaction. The chances that this will happen are greatly reduced if all prescriptions are filled by one pharmacy that monitors potential drug interactions. Of course, over-the-counter medication can also interact with prescription medication. Therefore, older adults should provide the pharmacist with a list of any medications they take.

Today, there are many effective medications on the market that can control chronic health conditions such as arthritis, making it possible for older adults to live with less pain and more independence than would be possible otherwise. Furthermore, medications that control cardiovascular disease and diabetes enable older adults to avoid hospitalization. Unfortunately, soaring costs mean that many older adults with chronic conditions who could benefit from prescription medication cannot afford to purchase it. Prescription medication has become a key aspect of health care for older adults, and recent government legislation may help make it more affordable.

In sum, there are two important concerns regarding older adults and medication. One is that they adhere strictly to the prescribed regimen, taking medications exactly as prescribed. The second is that new and effective medications are so costly that not all older adults can afford to purchase them. In many instances, the cost of medication is less than the cost of the hospitalization that can result when a chronic disease is not treated.

Medicare

In the United States, older adults may have more guaranteed access to group health insurance coverage than any other age group (Kane & Friedman, 1996). The main source of health insurance for older Americans (65+) is **Medicare,** which is a federal program that was initiated in 1965. Medicare has two components: Medicare Part A (hospital insurance) and Medicare Part B (medical insurance). If they have worked for the required number of quarters (3-month periods) in most jobs, Americans ages 65 and older are eligible for Medicare Part A without paying any premium. Medicare Part A covers hospital costs as well as brief nursing home stays or home health care for a limited period of time following a hospital stay. Medicare Part B, for which older adults pay a premium, covers a portion of physicians' fees, laboratory tests, services such as physical therapy, and some medical equipment.

Although some might consider older Americans privileged with regard to health-related services, Medicare does not cover all health care. Medicare is intended mainly for acute health care needs, and for the most part, it does not cover preventive care or the kinds of long-term care that many older adults need. For example, Medicare covers short stays in a nursing home if such care is needed immediately following a hospital stay of at least three days. However, older adults who need nursing home care beyond that period of time must pay their own expenses. As of 1995, the annual charge for nursing home care ranged from $36,000 in Florida to $50,000 in New York (Quadagno, 2002).

Until recently, Medicare did not cover the cost of prescription medications unless the medications were directly related to a recent hospital stay. However, government legislation that was just passed will add an optional prescription medicine benefit. Medicare recipients who pay an extra premium will be able to purchase prescribed medications at a reduced cost. Private insurance companies offer long-term-care policies that may cover the cost of extended nursing home stays, home health care, and at least part of the cost of prescription medications. However, such policies are expensive, especially if purchased late in life. Understanding which services are covered by a particular policy can be confusing, and older consumers must determine the coverage that they think will best suit their circumstances and needs.

Even for services that Medicare covers, deductibles and co-payments can be costly for older adults living on fixed incomes. Many private insurance companies offer *Medi-gap* policies to cover the cost of deductibles and co-payments, but not all older adults can afford such policies. Furthermore, understanding exactly what Medi-gap insurance policies cover can be a daunting task. Many unsuspecting older adults have become victims of scams related to the purchase of Medi-gap policies that may not deliver the benefits that they thought were covered.

Medicaid

The second main source of health care coverage available to older Americans comes from **Medicaid**, which is a federal program administered by individual states, each of which sets its own rules for eligibility. Unlike Medicare, Medicaid is *means tested*; to qualify for coverage, individuals must fall below a certain income level and can own only limited assets (savings and personal property). As mentioned earlier, if older adults need nursing home care beyond the short stay covered by Medicare, they must pay for it themselves. After they "spend down" enough to sufficiently deplete their assets, they can qualify for Medicaid coverage for continued nursing home care. Such spending down may not take long, given the high monthly cost of nursing home care.

For older adults, access to health care takes on greater importance. On average, individuals in the oldest-old (85+) age group need more health-care services than those in the young-old (65–74) or the old-old (75–84) age groups. Because the most rapidly growing segment of the U.S. population is the 85+ group, an important concern is whether the availability of the appropriate health care services will be sufficient to meet the demand.

REVISITING THE SELECTIVE OPTIMIZATION WITH COMPENSATION AND ECOLOGICAL MODELS

With increasing age, biological functions progress in the decremental direction. However, this does not mean that older adults cannot lead lives that are active and satisfying. First, there are large individual differences in the rate at which biological functioning declines. Also, the degree to which decline affects everyday life can vary widely.

According to the Selective Optimization with Compensation (SOC) Model (Baltes & Baltes, 1990), one strategy older adults can use to maintain optimal functioning is to focus on the aspects of functioning that are most important and expend effort to maintain them. If some aspects of functioning decline, then it may be necessary to compensate by putting more effort into aspects that can be maintained or possibly improved. The trick is to capitalize on the physical strengths that remain by doing whatever is necessary to control lifestyle habits of diet, exercise, and exposure to stress. The earlier in life this is done, the better the chances for deriving long-term benefits.

Biological aging can also be conceptualized using the Ecological Model (Lawton, 1989; Lawton & Nahemow, 1973). The decline in biological reserve capacity with increasing age means more attention must be paid to the environmental conditions in which older adults must function. When environmental conditions offer moderate challenge, young and older adults may function at a similar level. When there is too much environmental challenge, adaptation may be more difficult for the older biological system than it is for the young system. Environments with some, but not too many, demands allow older adults to achieve the highest level of adaptation possible. A proper match between biological competence and environmental press becomes more important with increasing age because of reductions in reserve capacity. Conditions that are too demanding for the reserve capacity that is available may accelerate biological aging.

KEY POINTS

- Longevity refers to the length and duration of life. Two aspects of longevity are life expectancy and life span.
- Life expectancy is the average number of years individuals in a particular birth cohort can be expected to live based on current information on mortality. Life span refers to the maximum longevity, or the extreme upper limit of time that members of a species can live.
- As life expectancy approaches life span, the survival curve takes on a more and more rectangular shape.
- Morbidity refers to illness and disease, and mortality refers to death. These two terms are related but they are not the same.
- Primary aging refers to the unavoidable (inevitable) biological processes that affect all members of a species. Secondary aging refers to biological processes due to disease, disuse, and abuse.
- Biological theories of aging are often categorized as programmed or stochastic. Programmatic theories focus on genetic blueprints of various species. Stochastic theories focus on random events that occur as a function of living.
- Scientists have studied the influences of nature and nurture on individual longevity. They have also tried to determine whether cognitive test scores, health self-ratings, and emotional outlook can predict longevity.
- With increasing age, changes occur in various body systems, but within the same person, physical changes may be more noticeable in some parts of the body than in others. Visible signs such as gray hair and wrinkles may have considerable psychological meaning.
- Certain chronic diseases occur more frequently in older adulthood, but aging does not automatically mean disease. Age-related diseases such as osteoarthritis are associated with pain and some disability even in the early stages, but often cardiovascular diseases have no noticeable symptoms until they are advanced.
- A distinction is made between activities of daily living (ADL) and instrumental activities of daily living (IADL). ADL refers to the basic personal care tasks required for self-maintenance, while IADL includes more complex activities required for carrying out the business of daily life.

- Physical changes and age-related diseases may limit how older adults function in either or both kinds of activity, but limitations are more frequent in the oldest-old (85+) age group than at earlier points of older adulthood. Older women experience more days per year on which activities are restricted due to illness or injury than do older men.
- A small proportion of individuals remain free of disease-related symptoms into very late old age, but most older adults have at least one chronic condition. However, chronic diseases can often be treated and controlled so that older adults are able to lead active and independent lives.
- Medication can often prevent or control diseases and many older adults take several prescription drugs for chronic health conditions. Older adults do not always take their medications exactly as directed, or prescribed.
- Medicare, a federal health insurance program for most Americans ages 65+, is focused more on acute care than preventive care. Medicare should be supplemented by private health insurance, but this can be costly.
- Medicaid is a state/federal program that covers medical expenses, but people must fall below a certain income level and own limited assets (savings and personal property)to qualify for coverage.

KEY TERMS

activities of daily living (ADL)   16

centenarian   83

compression of morbidity   88

compression of mortality   87

instrumental activities of daily living (IADL)   116

life expectancy   79

life span   83

longevity   79

Medicaid   119

Medicare   118

morbidity   79

mortality   79

primary aging   88

programmed theories of biological aging   89

rectangular survival curve   87

reserve capacity   106

secondary aging   88

stochastic theories of biological aging   89

telomeres   90

terminal drop   101

To learn more about the issues discussed in this chapter, point your browser to http://www.infotrac-college.com and use the passcode from the InfoTrac College Edition card that came with your book. InfoTrac College Edition gives you access to complete articles from many different journals.

Sensation, Perception, and Attention

4

For a number of years, Helen, who just celebrated her 70th birthday, has been meeting with her friends on a regular basis. They sit around a table and play cards while they catch up on all the happenings in their families. Lately, Helen has noticed she has trouble hearing, especially if the friend doing the talking is sitting on either side of her so Helen cannot see her face. She often has to ask to have things repeated. Also, Helen has noticed she has trouble concentrating on the card game when there is conversation going on. Sometimes she wishes she could ask her friends to stop talking while she figures out what cards to play.

SENSORY PROCESSES

To adapt to and interact with the environment, we must be able to take in, or register, what is going on around us. For this purpose we depend upon our eyes, ears, nose, and other sensory organs, through which we experience our initial contact with stimulus events and objects in our environment (Kausler, 1991). Our senses include taste, smell, touch, vision, and hearing. Many researchers who study aging have noted the importance of sensory processes, especially vision and hearing. According to the **common cause hypothesis**, the link between sensory processes and cognitive functioning becomes stronger in older adulthood than it was earlier in life (Baltes & Lindenberger, 1997). Although age-related differences in cognitive functioning may not be fully explained by age-related declines in sensory processes (Anstey, Luszcz, & Sanchez, 2001), there is little question that having good sensory capabilities is related to good memory and verbal abilities (Schneider & Pichora-Fuller, 2000). Also, for older adults, having good sensory capabilities, particularly vision and hearing, is associated with being able to perform self-care activities (for example, bathing, dressing, and grooming), being able to do household chores and go shopping (Marsiske, Klumb, & Baltes, 1997), and being able to take part in social activities.

Once the sensory organs register information, it can be passed along to the central nervous system for higher-level, perceptual processing, which entails interpreting what the information means and making decisions about how to respond. Often, there is more information in our environment than we can possibly register, let alone process, at any given time. Attention has to do with exactly what information we will process from the large array of stimuli that impinge upon our senses.

We begin this chapter by describing several important concepts identified with sensory processes. Following that, we will discuss higher-order, perceptual processing that occurs once information has been registered by the sensory organs. Next, we will focus on attention. Finally, we will conclude with what is known about age-related differences in sensation, perception, and attention in the individual sensory modalities, particularly vision and hearing.

Threshold and Sensitivity

Sensory organs need a certain intensity of stimulation before they record, or register, the presence of a signal, or stimulus. Psychologists use the term **threshold** to refer to the minimum amount of stimulation a sensory organ must receive before the presence of a particular stimulus is registered. The term **sensitivity** refers to the capability of the biological system to respond to stimulation.

Sensitivity is the inverse of threshold (Gilmore, 1996), which means that the greater the sensitivity to a particular type of stimulation, the lower the threshold will be. Thus, individuals with a high level of sensitivity will have a low threshold because they need only a low intensity of stimulation before they register its presence. In contrast, individuals with a low level of sensitivity will have a high threshold because the intensity of the stimulation will have to be stronger before they register its presence.

Absolute Threshold

Absolute threshold is a term psychologists use to refer to the intensity of stimulation needed in order for a stimulus to be detected 50 percent of the time when it is present. An auditory example can illustrate this concept. Let's suppose that an individual is fitted with headphones, seated in a soundproof booth, and instructed to press a key each time a particular tone is heard. The tone is presented numerous times at varying levels of loudness, or intensity. At low levels of intensity, the individual will not hear the tone, so he or she will not press the key. As the decibels (dB, which is a measure of the intensity of an auditory stimulus) of the tone gradually increase, eventually the individual will register its presence by pressing the key. Absolute threshold is the specific level of intensity the tone must reach before the individual registers its presence (by pressing the key) on half of the occasions when it is presented. For example, if the tone is presented 10 times at the same level of intensity, the individual will register its presence on five occasions.

For auditory thresholds, qualities other than intensity can influence an individual's threshold. For example, a threshold may vary depending upon the frequency, or pitch, of the tone (high or low). For most older adults, thresholds are lower for low-pitched tones than they are for high-pitched tones. In the case of visual stimuli, color can affect threshold. An individual may be able to identify one color more readily than another. Older adults have lower thresholds (are more sensitive) to red, orange, and yellow than they are to blue, green, and purple. Similarly, thresholds can vary for specific odors and tastes and for specific kinds of tactile stimulation.

Difference Threshold

Difference threshold refers to how large the difference between a pair of similar stimuli must be in order for the difference between them to be noticed. Again, let's use an auditory example. Two tones are presented, both having the same intensity. Can the individual sense whether there is any difference in pitch between the two tones? The more sensitive the individual, the greater the likelihood of sensing a difference between two tones that are only slightly different in pitch. The less sensitive the individual, the greater the difference between the tones will have to be before any difference in pitch will be noticed. Less research has been conducted on age and difference thresholds than on age and absolute thresholds. Undoubtedly, age-related differences in sensitivity to small differences between two stimuli will depend upon the specific qualities of the stimulus pair.

Signal Detection

Determining thresholds does not take into account the decisional processes that can enter into an individual's success or failure to register the presence of a stimulus. Assume for a moment that two individuals, Paul and Juan, are instructed to press a key when they hear a tone. Paul presses the key when he has even a slight suspicion the tone has been sounded. Juan is more cautious—he will press the key only when he is certain the tone has actually been sounded.

The **signal detection model** of determining threshold takes into account not only sensitivity but also the individual's decisional criteria (Green & Swets, 1966). Paul, the less cautious decision maker, will have more *hits* (saying "yes" when the tone is actually present than Juan will. However, Paul will also have a considerable number of *false alarms* (saying "yes" when the tone is not present). Juan, the more cautious, conservative decision maker, will have fewer hits, but he will also have fewer false alarms.

The signal detection model is important in the study of aging because older adults tend to be more cautious than young adults (Botwinick, 1984). In general, older adults have fewer false alarms (saying "yes" when a stimulus is not present) compared with young adults. By the same token, however, the more cautious older adults will have more *misses* (saying "no" when the stimulus is present) compared with young adults. Older adults' higher decisional criteria could result in an underestimate of their actual sensitivity.

In sum, older adults' cautiousness can inflate estimates of age-related differences in sensory processes. However, even when age-related differences in decisional criteria are taken into account, there is evidence for some age-related increase in sensory thresholds. Age-related changes in the structure of sensory organs affect sensitivity to stimulation. Such changes, particularly in the eye and ear, will be described in detail later in this chapter. In any case, if the sensory organs register information, then it is passed along to the central nervous system in the brain for higher-level, perceptual processing.

PERCEPTUAL PROCESSES

As mentioned earlier, sensation is related to the initial registration of physical stimulation by the sense organs and perception refers to the subsequent interpretation of the stimuli at the central level (in the brain). Depending on how stimuli are interpreted, decisions will be made about how to respond. Usually responses are visible, but it is difficult to observe what takes place in the brain between the onset of a stimulus and the initiation of a response.

Speed of Response and Reaction Time

In the laboratory, speed is often measured by how much time elapses between the onset of a stimulus (for example, a light or a tone) and the initiation of a response. Why are older adults usually slower to respond than young adults are? One suggestion has been that older adults respond more slowly because there is an age-related increase in sensory threshold (Botwinick, 1984). If older adults have higher sensory thresholds than young adults do, then the light or tone would effectively be weaker for the older adults. Responses to a weak stimulus are generally slower than responses to a strong one. In an early laboratory study, Botwinick (1971) made certain that the stimuli used would have the same functional intensity for young and older adults. Even when the intensity of the stimuli was matched for the two age groups, however, the older adults responded more slowly than the young adults did. Thus, age-related slowing cannot be solely attributed to older adults' higher sensory thresholds.

Reaction time is the interval that elapses between the onset of a stimulus (a light, a tone) and the completion of a motor response (Cerella, 1995; Salthouse, 1996a). In a controlled laboratory setting, reaction time can be measured by presenting a visual stimulus such as a light, or an auditory stimulus such as a tone. Individuals are instructed to make a motor response such as pressing a key as soon as they see the light or hear the tone. In some instances, individuals may be instructed to give a vocal response (such as "yes") to register the presence of a stimulus (Salthouse, 1996a). Reaction time tasks fall into several categories: simple, choice, and complex.

In a simple reaction time task, one stimulus is presented and there is only one possible response. For example, in a laboratory situation, individuals might be instructed to be on the lookout for the appearance of a cursor on a monitor. As soon as they see it, they are instructed to respond verbally ("yes") or make a motor response such as pressing a key.

In a choice reaction time task, individuals are on the lookout for two different signals, or stimuli, each of which calls for a different response. For example, in the laboratory, they might be told to press the key on the left when they see a red light and the key on the right when they see a green light. Or they might be instructed to press the key on the left when they hear a high tone and the key on the right when they hear a low tone. On choice reaction time tasks, there is usually more age-related slowing than there is on simple reaction time tasks.

Complex reaction time tasks are extensions of choice reaction time tasks because there are more than two stimuli, and each requires a different response or combination of responses. In a laboratory example of a complex reaction time task, one of three different shapes (a square, a circle, or a triangle) might appear on a screen. Each shape calls for a different response, such as pressing a key on the top, middle, or bottom row of a keyboard, respectively.

It is more complicated to study reaction time outside the laboratory because in the real world, situations are not as easily controlled as they are in a laboratory. Driving is a real-world skill most of us have, and it calls for simple, choice, and complex reaction time. In a simple reaction time situation, you spot a pedestrian in a crosswalk so you respond by stepping on the brake, or you hear an ambulance siren and you respond by pulling over to the curb. In a choice reaction time situation, you are driving along at 25 mph and you approach an intersection with a light. If the light turns red, the appropriate response would be to step on the brake. If the light is green, then you would keep your foot on the gas pedal and proceed through the intersection. In a complex reaction time situation, you are driving on a highway and you see an object in the distance that appears to be road debris. You must evaluate the spatial placement of the debris as well as its likely composition (metal or cardboard).

When deciding how to respond, you must take into account not only the placement and composition of the road debris, but also the surrounding traffic conditions. Your response could be to step on the brake before reaching the object, to swerve to the left or right, or just to drive right over the debris.

Reaction time has two components: premotor time (PMT) and motor time (MT) (Botwinick, 1984). PMT is the time that elapses between the onset of a stimulus and the initiation of a motor response. MT is the time needed from the initiation to the completion of the motor response. If an individual is instructed to listen for a tone and to press a key as soon as it is heard, PMT would be the time elapsing between the onset of the tone and the initiation of a muscle response in the forearm. The PMT component is difficult to observe directly because it consists mainly of the time taken for the brain to process information. MT is the time that elapses between the initial muscle activation and the actual lifting of the finger to press the key. MT can be measured using electromyographic recordings of muscle-action potentials (Kausler, 1991). Approximately 84 percent of total reaction time is estimated to be attributable to PMT, while the remaining 16 percent of reaction time is attributable to MT (Botwinick, 1984). The relatively large proportion of time devoted to PMT suggests that reaction time is largely a function of central processing in the brain.

We know that slower reaction times seem to be an inevitable consequence of normal aging (Kausler & Kausler, 1996), but why is the study of age-related differences in reaction time so important? Slowing has both theoretical and practical significance. From a theoretical point of view, reaction time has been used to assess the organization and efficiency of the central nervous system (Cerella, 1995). Speed of response, even on simple reaction time tasks, could be an indicator of brain functioning (Salthouse, 1996a). From a practical point of view, slowing is an important factor for driving and other aspects of everyday functioning, especially when it comes to safety. The older adult who is slow to enter a revolving door at the entrance to a hotel or public building is at risk for sustaining physical injury. The older pedestrian who is slow to respond to a "Walk" sign at an intersection may not make it across a busy street before the sign turns to "Don't Walk." Fatal injuries have resulted when impatient drivers do not realize that older pedestrians may need extra time.

Age-Complexity Hypothesis

In general, the complexity of a task affects how quickly people respond. The more complex the task, the slower the response will be. Task complexity can also affect how much slower older adults are compared to young adults. With simple reaction time tasks, the difference between young and older adults' speed of response is usually small. As tasks increase in complexity, the gap between young and older adults' speed of response becomes more pronounced (Kausler, 1991; Salthouse, 1991; Salthouse, 1996a, b). As Figure 4.1 illustrates, older adults become disproportionately slow relative to young adults as the complexity of the task increases.

This phenomenon, termed the *age-complexity effect,* or **age-complexity hypothesis** (Salthouse, 1991), means that older adults will be at a greater disadvantage relative to young adults as task complexity increases. On reaction

Figure 4.1 | Hypothetical Comparison of Young and Older Adults' Speed of Response on Simple, Choice, and Complex Reaction Time Tasks

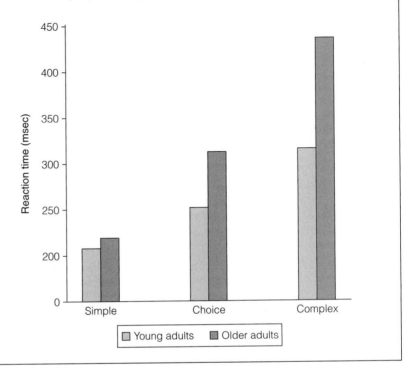

time tasks, the difference between young and older adults' speed of response becomes larger as tasks go from simple to choice to complex. Compared with simple reaction time tasks, choice and especially complex reaction time tasks require more extensive processing at the central level (Cerella, 1995). Thus, researchers conclude that the differences seen between young and older adults' reaction time is related to age-related differences at the level of central processing.

Some researchers have proposed that older adults' decline in speed on reaction time tasks can be attributed to only one factor: a generalized slowing in cognitive processing. Other researchers contend that slowing is one of many factors that play a role in the age-related differences found on various cognitive tasks (Cerella, 1994; Fisk & Fisher, 1994; McDowd & Shaw, 2000). Whether slowing can completely explain age-related differences on all cognitive tasks (reaction time, perceptual processing, memory, and so on) has been a subject of considerable debate (Salthouse, 1996b; Schulz, 1994).

Stimulus Persistence Theory

In an early article published in the *American Psychologist*, Birren (1974) proposed that the tendency toward slowness with advancing age reflects a basic change in the speed with which the central nervous system processes information. **Stimulus persistence theory** (SPT) is one theoretical model that attempts to explain why central slowing occurs (Botwinick, 1984; Gilmore, 1996). According to SPT, a stimulus registered by a sensory organ takes longer to be processed and cleared through the nervous system of an older adult than it does through the nervous system of a young adult. If a second stimulus were to follow quickly, then older adults would be less efficient at processing it because they are still trying to clear the first stimulus through the system. For this reason, older adults have greater difficulty than young adults do when they are required to process a series of stimuli presented at a rapid rate. Older adults need more time between stimuli than young adults do.

To build a case for stimulus persistence as an explanation for age-related slowing, Botwinick (1984) described a phenomenon that occurs when stimuli are presented one right after the other (sequentially). When individuals view a sequential series of light pulses at a low rate, they report seeing separate pulses of light. As the rate of the light pulses increases, they eventually report seeing only one continuous light. In other words, when the rate of presentation is sufficiently fast, the individual pulses of light are perceived as one blended light. The critical flicker fusion (CFF) threshold is the pulse rate at which this fusion occurs (Gilmore, 1996). A number of studies have reported an age-related decline in the CFF threshold (Kline & Scialfa, 1997). This means that at a relatively high pulsing rate, young adults are still able to distinguish the separate pulses of a flickering light, but older adults see only one continuous light. According to stimulus persistence theory, older adults no longer perceive the individual light pulses because there is a backup in central nervous system processing. Because of this backup, sequential stimuli blend together and are perceived as one continuous stimulus.

This fusion phenomenon is not confined to vision. When individuals hear a series of clicks one right after the other, they report hearing individual clicks. As the rate of the clicks increases, they report hearing one continuous sound. As with vision, older adults seem to have a lower threshold for auditory fusion. Thus, when the click rate is relatively high, young adults still distinguish the individual clicks, whereas older adults report hearing one continuous sound.

The stimulus persistence model is an intriguing way to conceptualize age-related differences in perceptual processing. Unfortunately, it has not been successful in accounting for all of the research findings on age and perceptual processing (see Botwinick, 1984). Also, the specific mechanism that mediates the slower processing is yet to be specified clearly. Even so, the studies conducted to test this model made it clear that older adults will surely benefit when the information they must process is not presented too quickly.

Moderating Age-Related Slowing

In general, older adults do not respond as quickly as young adults do. But what factors might moderate age-related slowing? First, older adults who engage in regular exercise seem to react more quickly compared to older adults who are not physically active. In one study (Hawkins, Kramer, & Capaldi, 1992), older adults who participated in a 10-week aerobic exercise program showed greater improvement in their speed of performance compared to an older control group who did

© PhotoDisc

Older adults who exercise regularly have faster reaction times compared to older adults who are sedentary.

not participate in an exercise program. However, not all studies have found that short-term exercise results in faster responding (Blumenthal & Madden, 1988; Madden, Blumenthal, Allen, & Emery, 1989). Extended periods of training, long-term habits of physical activity, and general physical fitness are likely to be the most effective means of increasing older adults' speed of processing (Blumenthal & Madden, 1988; Madden, Blumenthal, Allen, & Emery, 1989).

Second, older adults are often able to increase their speed of responding when they are given opportunities to practice (Kausler, 1991). The positive effect of practice on older adults' speed of responding is important from a practical point of view. However, young adults are also able to increase their speed of responding when they practice. Therefore, the difference between young and older adults' speed of responding cannot be attributed simply to older adults' lack of experience on a particular task. Age-related differences in speed of responding are not likely to disappear when young and older adults are both given opportunities for practice, especially when tasks are very complex. Still, practice is important for older adults' real-world functioning.

ATTENTION

Our senses are bombarded by many more stimuli than we can register, let alone process in a meaningful way. The human organism can only register and process some of those stimuli at any given time (Kausler, 1991; Madden & Allen, 1996). Fortunately, attention processes allow us to direct our efforts to processing some portion of the stimulation we receive.

A number of questions have been asked about attention and aging. Do older adults have the same amount of attentional resources, or attentional capacity, as young adults do? How many stimuli can young and older adults process at the same time? Are there differences in the strategies young and older adults use to select which stimuli will be processed? How do young and older adults deal with stimuli that are unimportant (irrelevant) and may be distracting when they are trying to process stimuli that are important (relevant) for the task at hand?

Most studies on attention and aging have been cross-sectional, so there is a confounding of cohort and age (see Chapter 2 for a discussion of the cross-sectional method). Also, cross-sectional comparisons of young and older adults do not always yield identical findings on all kinds of attention tasks (Hartley, 1995; Madden & Allen, 1996). The information that follows describes what is known about age-related differences and similarities in attention.

Theoretical Models

First, three theoretical models about age and attention will be examined. Then three different kinds of attention will be described, with some general findings about the capabilities of young versus older adults on each.

The Reduced Attentional Resources/Capacity Model   The **reduced attentional resources/capacity model** postulates that, compared to young adults, older adults have fewer attentional resources available for carrying out cognitive tasks (Craik & Byrd, 1982). That is, the quantity of processing resources, or the amount of attentional capacity, declines with increasing age (Salthouse, 1991). On simple tasks, older adults do not experience difficulty because their attentional resources are sufficient. However, the processing resources needed for more complex tasks may exceed older adults' resources, or capacity, thus rendering them less efficient and/or less accurate than young adults, whose resources/capacity are sufficient to handle the demands of complex tasks. Thus, increasing the complexity of a task may not make any noticeable difference in young adults' efficiency or accuracy.

The reduced attentional resources/capacity model is related to the age-complexity hypothesis described earlier. The greater the complexity of a task, the more attentional resources will be required. Older adults' attentional resources have limitations so their performance will suffer when they are required to perform complex tasks.

The reduced attentional resources/capacity model has generated a great deal of research, described later in the section on divided attention. However, a criticism of this model has been its lack of clarity about how resources or capacity should be defined and measured (Salthouse, 1991). Some researchers have expressed concern that the reduced attentional resources/capacity explanation of age-related differences in perceptual processing is somewhat circular. If indeed there is an age-related decline in attentional resources, further research is needed to specify the mechanism(s) by which resource limitations affect attention (McDowd, 1997).

The Inhibitory Deficit Model   A second theoretical model researchers have proposed is the **inhibitory deficit model** (Hasher & Zacks, 1988), which postulates that aging is associated with a decrease in the ability to ignore irrelevant stimuli (that is, stimuli that are not important for performing a particular task, sometimes called *distractors*) and to focus attention on relevant stimuli (that is, stimuli important for performing the task, sometimes called *targets*). If attention to distractors is not suppressed, or inhibited, then some portion of attentional capacity will be wasted processing information that is not important, and too little attentional capacity will remain for processing the important target stimuli.

May and Hasher (1998) found that inhibitory efficiency changes over the course of the day. At times of peak circadian arousal, people are at their highest level of efficiency, and they possess an optimal level of control over distracting thoughts that could interfere with their performance on attention tasks. This *synchrony effect* means that age-related differences could be magnified if one age group is tested at a peak arousal time and the other is not. May and Hasher (1998) suggest that testing young adults at nonoptimal times could serve as a model for both predicting and understanding how older adults function.

As with the reduced resources/capacity model, the inhibitory deficit model is related to the age-complexity hypothesis. The sources of distraction are likely to be more extensive in complex attention tasks than they are in simple ones, so the performance of older adults will suffer more than that of young adults as task complexity increases.

The inhibitory deficit model has generated a great deal of research, described in the section on selective attention. However, this model is not without its critics. One problem has been the lack of clear agreement on how to define inhibitory mechanisms (McDowd, 1997). Also, the model's predictions about age-related differences are not always accurate (Tun & Wingfield, 1997). Some types of inhibitory functioning seem more immune than others to the effects of aging. Nonetheless, the inhibitory deficit model has been an important framework for organizing research on aging and cognitive processes, including attention (McDowd, 1997).

The Frontal Lobe Model   A third theoretical model proposed to explain age-related decline on some attentional tasks postulates that the frontal lobes are more susceptible than other regions of the brain to the effects of normal aging (Arbuckle & Gold, 1993; Hartley, 1993; Kramer, Humphrey, Larish, Logan, & Strayer, 1994). The **frontal lobe model** has received support from cognitive neuroscience research that uses neuroimaging techniques such as positron emission tomagraphy (PET) scans (Hartley, 1995). PET scans can measure cerebral blood flow and metabolic activity in various regions of the brain when individuals are in a resting state and when they are performing various tasks (Madden & Allen, 1996).

Two different neural systems appear to play a role in attentional functioning. One system is located in the frontal area of the cortex and the other is located in the occipital and parietal areas of the cortex. Figure 4.2 shows the location of these areas.

Figure 4.2 | Two Views of the Human Brain. The frontal lobes are responsible for planning, decision-making, and inhibitory functioning. The frontal lobes connect to the basal ganglia and thalamus, which lie below the hemispheres of the cerebrum.

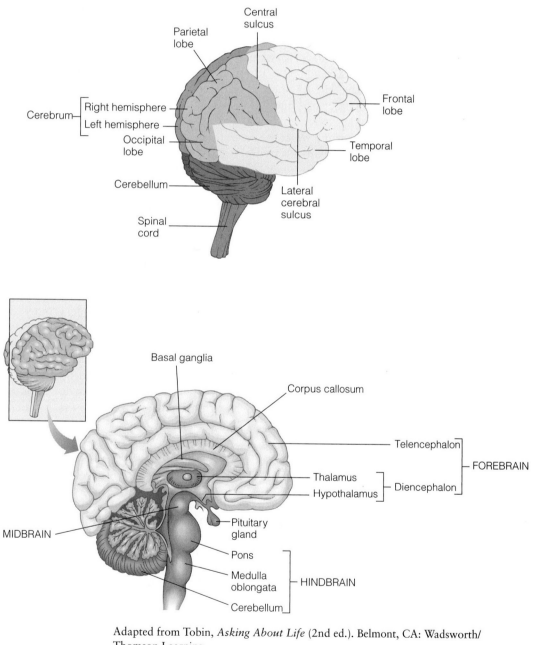

Adapted from Tobin, *Asking About Life* (2nd ed.). Belmont, CA: Wadsworth/ Thomson Learning.

Reductions in cerebral blood flow seem to occur earlier and to be more pronounced in the frontal lobe area than in other regions of the brain. Also, there is evidence that age-related loss of neural tissue is more prominent in the frontal area and the regions to which it connects, specifically the basal ganglia and thalamus (Kramer et al., 1994). Loss of neural tissue appears to be smaller, or nonexistent, in the posterior cortical and midbrain areas (Arbuckle & Gold, 1993; Kramer et al., 1994).

The frontal lobes are responsible for executive functions such as decision making, planning, and coordinating the processing of multiple streams of items, initiating and stopping behaviors, and impulse control (Kramer et al., 1994). Patients with known frontal lobe damage have difficulty shifting from one type of response to another. For example, if they are instructed to sort cards on the basis of the color of the object pictured on each card, they have difficulty if they are then instructed to switch and sort cards on the basis of the shape of the object pictured on each card. Such individuals often perseverate, meaning that they revert back to sorting the cards based on color.

The frontal lobe model predicts that age-related differences in attention will be most pronounced on tasks that depend heavily on frontal lobe functioning. Kramer et al. (1994) administered a battery of tests to young and older adults to determine whether age-related deficits would indeed be greatest on the two tests requiring the inhibitory functioning generally associated with frontal lobe processing—card sorting and stopping. On the card-sorting task, older adults made more perseverative errors than did young adults when they were required to shift to a new criterion for sorting the cards. On the stopping task, older adults were slower to react to an occasional signal to abort, or stop, the responses they were making to a visual display. In contrast, age-related differences were smaller on tests of spatial attention, which do not call for frontal lobe processing—for example, responding quickly to a visual display in which a target letter is surrounded by distractor letters. Kramer et al.'s findings are consistent with the frontal lobe model of attention and aging.

Arbuckle and Gold (1993) point out that perseveration can appear in speech patterns, specifically in "off-target verbosity," which has been detected more often in older adults than in young adults. Off-target verbosity is characterized by speech that is lacking in focus or coherence, and it could be related to difficulty inhibiting task-irrelevant thoughts, possibly stemming from a decrement in frontal lobe functioning. However, note that older adults display more off-target verbosity when answering personal questions than they do when answering factual questions (James, Burke, Austin, & Hulme, 1998). Table 4.1 gives an example of responses both low and high in off-target verbosity.

Although such findings are important, it may be premature to conclude that the frontal lobe model can explain all age-related inhibitory difficulties (for example, see McDowd & Shaw, 2000). Perhaps inhibitory mechanisms are not located exclusively in the frontal lobes. They may be located in other areas of the brain as well. With normal aging, the integrity of inhibitory mechanisms may simply decrease at different rates in different areas of the brain (Kramer et al., 1994).

Table 4.1	Examples from Arbuckle and Gold (1993) in Answer to the Question, "How Much Education Did You Get?"

Low off-target verbosity: *"I finished high school and then a bit of college."*

High off-target verbosity: *"Well, let's see. I went to school in ___ where, uh, uh, I grew up in ____. Back in those days, why, they didn't have the big high schools that they have now. When I went back there a few years ago in . . . uh, I don't remember exactly when it was. I think it was the summer of 1980 or maybe it was 1981. I went for my brother's 50th anniversary and I didn't recognize the place at all. We went to a small school, the only school in town. It was the only place to go. All the children were in one room. The school only went to grade 9 or uh, uh, I think it was . . . was it grade 9? No, it was only grade 8 because ___(neighbor's daughter) left to go to nursing school and she had to go to ___ to finish Grade 9. She never finished nursing anyway. She got married but it didn't last long."*

Attention Tasks

Tasks of attention fall into three basic categories: sustained attention, divided attention, and selective attention (Kausler, 1994).

Sustained Attention   Sustained attention, or **vigilance**, requires being able to monitor a situation and remain ready to detect any change that may occur in a pattern of stimuli that is usually stable and unchanging (Kausler, 1991). On a classic visual vigilance task called the Mackworth Clock Test (Kausler, 1991; Madden & Allen, 1996), individuals monitor the pointer on a clocklike device. The pointer moves in discrete steps much like a second hand on a clock, but individuals must remain ready to detect an occasional two-step jump. In an auditory vigilance task, individuals could be required to monitor a series of high-pitched clicks while remaining ready to detect an occasional low-pitched click. An example of a real-world vigilance task would be an automobile driver who is ready to detect a potential problem (such as a deer running across the road) while traveling on a monotonous stretch of highway (Kausler, 1991). In the workplace, a quality control manager stands ready to detect a defective product while inspecting a steady stream of that product, or perhaps the manager monitors a piece of equipment for any cue that signals malfunction (Kausler, 1991).

Over extended durations, simple vigilance tasks can lead to fatigue and ultimately a decline in accuracy. However, the accuracy of older adults does not seem to suffer any more than that of young adults (Kline & Scialfa, 1997). Studies using the Mackworth Clock Test report a high level of accuracy in the first 15-minute segment of an hour, with a gradual decline in accuracy over the next three 15-minute time segments. However, this decline does not seem to be any more pronounced for older individuals than for young ones (Madden & Allen, 1996).

Vigilance tasks can be simple or complex. A simple vigilance task involves readiness to detect only one type of change (for example, a jump in the second hand of a clock, one type of defect in a product, or one type of signal that equipment is malfunctioning). Simple vigilance tasks do not make excessive cognitive demands, and age-related differences on such tasks are usually small or nonexistent. In fact, there is some evidence that older adults are less prone than young adults to having task-unrelated thoughts, or mind wandering, while performing simple vigilance tasks (Giambra, 1989).

Vigilance tasks are more complex when the quality of the monitored stimuli is physically degraded in some way. For example, individuals may be required to monitor a screen and hit a key whenever the digit "5" appears. The complexity of this simple vigilance task increases when digits that appear on the screen are blurred. In all likelihood, the vigilance of both young and older adults will suffer under such conditions. However, degradation of the monitored stimuli often has a greater negative effect on older adults than it does on young adults (Kausler, 1991).

Vigilance tasks are also more complex when people are required to retain information in memory while keeping track of stimulus changes (Kausler, 1991; Rogers & Fisk, 2001). For example, an individual may be required to monitor a screen for a sequence of numbers (for example, 5, 2, 8) as opposed to the simpler task of monitoring the screen for a single number such as 5. Young and older adults will both have greater difficulty monitoring for a three-digit sequence than they will for a single digit. However, the increase in complexity will have a greater negative effect on the performance of older adults than it will on that of young adults.

Some have attributed the greater difficulty older adults experience when vigilance tasks involve degraded stimuli or increased memory demands to the likelihood that complex tasks require more attentional resources. Young adults may have sufficient attentional resources to handle the greater demands of tasks with degraded stimuli or memory requirements. Older adults may not have the additional attentional resources necessary, so their performance suffers more than that of young adults.

In general, both young and older adults benefit from practice on vigilance tasks (Rogers & Fisk, 2001). Not surprisingly, however, young adults seem better able to maintain a high level of accuracy when changes in the stimuli being monitored occur at a high rate (Kausler, 1991).

Divided Attention   **Divided attention** is required when attention must be paid to more than one thing at a time, or when two or more stimulus inputs must be processed concurrently. In some dual-task situations, two inputs are both presented to the same sense (visual or auditory). In other dual-task situations, one input is presented to one sense (visual) but the other is presented to a different sense (auditory).

In a dual processing task performed in a laboratory, individuals might be required to monitor a screen and respond when a particular geometric form appears. At the same time, they are also required to respond whenever a tone is sounded. The speed and accuracy of their responses when they are required to perform only one of these tasks can be compared with the speed and accuracy of their responses when they must perform both tasks concurrently.

Researchers have used dual attention tasks to determine the extent of age-related decline in processing resources, or capacity. A study by Somberg and Salthouse (1982) demonstrated that young and older adults are equally capable of dividing their attention between more than one task if the tasks are relatively undemanding and do not exceed their processing resources. As tasks become more demanding, however, the *cost* of dividing attention between more than one of them is greater for older adults than it is for young adults (Somberg & Salthouse, 1982). Cost is measured by comparing how well a task is performed by itself relative to how well it is performed when a second task must be performed at the same time. Young adults may have sufficient attentional resources to perform both tasks with little cost. However, dual-task demands may exceed the processing capacity of older adults, whose performance will begin to suffer by becoming slower or less accurate. Again, however, there are no agreed-upon definitions for capacity and resources. Thus, there is a risk of circularity when these terms are used to explain age-related differences on divided-attention tasks.

An alternative to the attentional resource model is the theory that when individuals are required to perform more than one task or activity at the same time, there may be a structural bottleneck at the central level of processing in the brain (Pashler, 1994). This bottleneck makes it difficult to attend to one task without temporarily suspending attention to the other, with the result that there is slowing down when two tasks must be performed at the same time (Ruthruff, Pashler, & Klaassen, 2001). As yet, however, it is not clear how any structural limitations associated with this bottleneck differ for young and older adults.

Some tasks require a great deal of attention at first, but with practice they come to require much less attention. Driving is a real-world case in point. When we are learning to drive, we devote considerable attentional resources to familiarizing ourselves with how to operate the car and follow the rules of the road. With practice, driving comes to require less effort and it demands fewer attentional resources. In fact, when the weather is good and traffic is light, most of us have little difficulty driving while listening to the radio or talking with a passenger (Kausler & Kausler, 1996). A contemporary example is the common practice of driving and having a conversation on a cell phone.

When the weather is inclement or traffic is heavy, we must allocate more attentional resources to our driving. Under such demanding conditions, driving while listening to the radio or talking on a cell phone may begin to exceed our attentional capacity. When this happens, the risk of accidents increases. This principle holds true for young and older adults alike. However, attentional capacity may be exceeded at an earlier point for older adults. Young drivers might have little difficulty listening to the radio or conversing with a passenger when it is raining lightly or when traffic conditions are only moderately heavy. Older drivers might find it necessary to turn off the radio or cease talking with passengers under these conditions. In one study (McKnight & McKnight, 1993), young, middle-aged, and older participants viewed videos of traffic situations that called for them to respond by manipulating simulated vehicle controls.

Many of us talk on a cell phone while we drive. In heavy traffic and bad weather conditions, dividing attention between driving and talking on the phone can be hazardous because it exceeds our attentional capacity.

At the same time, some of the study participants engaged in distracting activities such as talking on a cell phone, while others had no distractions. For the oldest group of study participants (ages 50–80), failure to make the appropriate response on the simulated controls was significantly more likely if they were also talking on a cell phone than it was when there were no distractions.

An intriguing study conducted in Finland assessed the strategies used by young (average age 37) and older (average age 68) drivers, mostly men, all of whom owned cars with manual gears (Hakamies-Blomqvist, Mynttinen, Backman, & Mikkonen, 1999). All study participants were allowed to practice driving a 1987 Audi test car that had manual gears and was fitted with seven hidden sensors that could record the driver's use of the car's controls. After practicing, they drove this car under normal traffic conditions along a previously planned route. The young and older drivers who came to the study with more everyday driving experience tended to use the car's controls in a more parallel manner, meaning that they operated four or more controls simultaneously. The young and older drivers who had less everyday driving experience did not use as many controls at the same time. Rather, they operated the controls in a more serial manner, favoring the use of only three controls at a time. In addition to driving experience, age also made a difference. The older drivers used car controls in a more serial manner, while the young drivers used car controls in a more parallel manner.

In sum, drivers with less experience and older drivers were more likely to use the car controls in a serial rather than a parallel manner. Perhaps the serial strategy lowered the demands on their attentional capacity. Hakamies-Blomqvist et al. (1999) point out that the serial strategy is likely to work well when traffic conditions are not too demanding. When driving conditions are complex, however, a serial strategy could increase the risk of accidents because it is more time-consuming than the parallel strategy. Perhaps this is a factor in the increased number of traffic accidents involving older adults when driving conditions are demanding.

As with vigilance tasks, practice on divided attention tasks is beneficial for both young and older adults. In the real world, experience is important for perfecting skills, or developing expertise. Older adults may be capable of performing several tasks at the same time if they have developed expertise in carrying out those tasks (Rybash, Hoyer, & Roodin, 1986). This was illustrated in Hakamies-Blomqvist et al.'s (1999) driving study, which showed that a greater amount of everyday driving practice was associated with greater likelihood of the drivers' using a parallel strategy to operate the car's controls.

Selective Attention   Of all the information, or stimulation, that impinges upon us, we must often focus our attentional resources on what is important, or relevant, to the task at hand. We must not allow ourselves to be distracted by unimportant, or irrelevant, information. **Selective attention** is required when we must pay attention to some information while ignoring other information.

Many real-world situations call for selective attention. For instance, a college student must try to study for an exam while fellow dormitory residents are having a loud party down the hall (Kausler & Kausler, 1996). If the student wants to pass the course, the material in the textbook is the relevant, or target, stimulus. The party noise represents irrelevant, distracting stimulation. In this situation, the relevant and irrelevant stimuli are presented to different senses (vision and hearing). The student must attend selectively to the relevant visual stimulus of what appears in the textbook, while suppressing the urge to pay attention to the distracting auditory stimulus, party noise. In other instances, relevant and irrelevant stimuli may impinge upon the same sense. In an auditory example, the college student must focus attention on tape-recorded lecture notes (relevant stimulus) while trying to ignore party noise (irrelevant stimuli). Another example would be that of the individual who tries to focus on a restaurant companion's dinner conversation (relevant stimulus) while attempting to "tune out" the conversations going on at other tables (irrelevant stimuli). The use of the World Wide Web calls for visual selective attention. Many Web sites place patterned backgrounds behind text and include unnecessary and distracting graphics and animation (Rogers & Fisk, 2001).

Older adults are likely to experience more difficulty than young adults do in selectively attending to relevant information and ignoring irrelevant information. The inhibitory deficit model, described earlier in this chapter, offers one explanation for this. According to this model, older adults have special difficulty focusing on relevant stimuli and suppressing, or inhibiting, the distracting influence of irrelevant stimuli. Inefficient inhibition may allow irrelevant stimuli to intrude, which could slow down processing or result in errors when relevant stimuli are being processed. An early version of this notion, proposed by Layton

(1975), was that aging is characterized by a decline in the ability to suppress what he referred to as *perceptual noise*. Of course, the reduced resources/capacity model comes into play as well. Particularly for older adults, being susceptible to interference from the irrelevant, or distracting, elements of a situation could mean that insufficient resources remain available for processing the relevant elements.

Tasks that require visual search are often used to evaluate selective attention for visual information. In a real-world example, Jane goes to a large and unfamiliar grocery store to purchase Brand Y whipping cream, which she has been told is best for a recipe she plans to try. The store manager tells her that dairy products are located on Aisle 3. In this example, Brand Y whipping cream is the target item, and all other brands and types of cream are distractor items. When Jane arrives at Aisle 3, she finds two entire shelves with various brands and types of cream. Jane must scan all of the containers in order to locate the target item, Brand Y whipping cream. Of course, the search would be easier if Jane knew that in the store's display of dairy products, Brand Y is always placed above all the other brands of cream. Additionally, the search would be easier if Jane had been told that Brand Y whipping cream is the only one packaged in a red-and-white checkered container.

In visual search tasks, the measure of performance is usually the amount of time it takes to locate a target item that is placed among distractor items. The search will take a fair amount of time if individuals must scan all of the distractor items to locate the target item. However, the search will be quicker if there is spatial precuing, which is prior information on where the target item will be located among the distractor items. The search will be also be quicker if individuals know ahead of time that the target item has certain distinguishing physical characteristics such as color or shape. When they are given precuing about the spatial location or physical characteristics of a target item, older adults are only slightly, and often not at all, slower than young adults in locating it (Hartley, 1995). Age-related differences in the speed of search will be much less pronounced if the target item always appears in the same location and has distinctive physical characteristics. If there is no precuing about where the target item will be located or about any novel or distinctive characteristics, visual search will be slower for both young and older adults. However, older adults will be at a greater disadvantage and they will be even slower than young adults. In sum, in visually complex situations when distractor stimuli must be visually scanned and target objects have no outstanding physical characteristics, older adults will have more difficulty than young adults.

Negative priming is a phenomenon that some researchers consider to be evidence for inhibitory processes (Madden & Allen, 1996). To illustrate a test of negative priming, individuals could be asked to look at letters that are printed in either red or green ink. Over a series of trials, individuals are instructed to name the red (target) letters as quickly as possible and to ignore the green (distractor) letters. Individuals are often slower to name a red target letter if that same letter served as a green distractor letter on the immediately preceding trial. Presumably, the reason for this slowing is that individuals actively suppressed their attention to that letter on the preceding trial. When the distractor letter now becomes the target letter, their inhibition lingers and they are slower

Figure 4.3 | Example of a Stroop Color–Word Test

to name it. In studies using not only letters, but also words and pictures as target and distractor stimuli, the magnitude of this slowing, called negative priming, is greater for young adults than it is for older adults. The conclusion researchers have drawn is that older adults did not inhibit the letters when they were distractors to the same extent that young adults did.

Another example of a visual selective attention task is the Stroop Color-Word test (Stroop, 1935). On this test, the name of a color (for example, white) is typed in an opposing color of ink (for example, black). The task is to name the color of the ink ("black"), while ignoring the fact that the letters typed in black ink spell the word "white." To accomplish this task, individuals must focus their attention on the color of the letters while suppressing a natural tendency to read the name of the word. What makes this task especially difficult is the virtual impossibility of completely ignoring the irrelevant stimulus (typed name of the color), which is embedded in the relevant stimulus (the color of the type). The Stroop Color-Word test is difficult for people of all ages, but it is especially challenging for older adults.

To summarize what is known about age-related differences in selective attention, older adults find it more difficult than young adults do to ignore irrelevant, or distracting stimuli, and to focus their attention on relevant stimuli. One hypothesis is that age-related differences on tests of selective attention stem from inhibitory deficit. But whether there is one general inhibitory process or whether different situations call for specific kinds of inhibitory processes is yet to be determined (McDowd, 1997). Also, the inhibitory deficit model cannot explain why age-related differences are not always found on tests of selective attention (McDowd, 1997). Furthermore, it is not clear what kinds of training might be effective for reversing, or at least reducing, age-related deficits on selective attention tasks (Kramer et al., 1994). In any case, older adults are often more susceptible to interference from distracting stimuli when environments are complex, so distracting stimuli should be kept to a minimum.

THE SENSES: A CLOSER LOOK

Now that we have covered some of the basic principles of sensation, perception, and attention, it is time to describe the age-related differences/changes for specific sensory modalities. Age-related differences/changes in sensory capabilities usually occur gradually from middle adulthood on. Although there are individual differences, older adults are often less sensitive, and have higher thresholds than do young adults, for registering information through their sensory modalities. However, some age-related differences/changes occur at the perceptual level and indicate age-related differences/changes in the higher-order central processing that takes place in the brain.

Smell and Taste

The majority of older adults experience some loss in smell and taste sensitivity. Such losses become apparent at around age 60 and tend to progress with increasing age (Schiffman, 1996). Loss of sensitivity to odors can stem from anatomical and physiological changes in the olfactory system that are associated with normal aging, but losses could also be caused by smoking, diseases, and use of some medications (Schiffman, 1996). The sense of smell can serve as a warning signal, so loss in smell sensitivity could represent a risk that smoke, gas leaks, or food spoilage will not be readily detected. Loss of taste sensitivity seems to be associated more with medications and medical conditions than it is with anatomical and biological losses associated with normal aging. When older adults have no diseases and take no medications, only minimal increases have been noted in their thresholds for salty, sweet, sour, and bitter tastes (Schiffman, 1996). Alterations in smell and taste sensitivity, which are related, can affect older adults' appetite because food loses its appeal. Nutritional deficiencies resulting from poor eating habits can have a negative effect on older adults' general health and relatedly, on their psychological well-being.

Touch, Proprioception, and Pain

The sense of touch includes tactile sensations related to pressure and temperature. The sense of proprioception refers to an awareness of the position and movement of the body and limbs in space (Weisenberger, 1996). The senses of touch and proprioception are mediated by various sensory structures as well as by higher-order perceptual processes, both of which are susceptible to the effects of aging (Weisenberger, 1996). Older adults have higher thresholds than young adults do for detecting vibration and thermal (hot, cold) stimulation. In addition, older adults have a higher threshold for detecting limb movements and changes in limb position, especially for the lower extremities such as knees, hips, and ankles (Weisenberger, 1996). With regard to postural control, older adults do not seem to differ from young adults in their ability to maintain balance under low-stress conditions. They may be able to compensate for proprioceptive losses by selectively using cues from other sensory sources. However, there may be difficulty with balance when cues from other senses, especially vision, are limited (Weisenberger, 1996). With age, there is an increasing risk of falls from loss of balance, perhaps more so for women than for men. Falls in older adulthood can result in hip fractures, which necessitate hospitalization and the need for rehabilitative services. Older adults' mobility and independence are compromised when they experience falls or even when they are afraid they will fall (Vercruyssen, 1997).

With age-related changes in vision, older adults begin
to have difficulty reading small print.

With regard to pain, experimental studies have not uniformly found that
older adults are any less sensitive, or that their pain threshold is any higher, compared with young adults (Harkins & Scott, 1996; Weisenberger, 1996).
However, Harkins and Scott (1996) point out the difficulties encountered when
attempting to assess whether older adults experience pain. First, older adults
may be suffering from one or more health problems (for example, osteoarthritis, osteoporosis, or diabetes) that predispose them to chronic pain. Pain from
these sources may interact with pain from more acute conditions. Second, the
functional consequences of pain may be different for young and older adults.
Older adults who experience pain from one or more chronic conditions may
have less reserve capacity for coping with stress from additional sources of
acute pain compared with young adults who are otherwise in relatively good
health. Third, it is difficult to assess pain in older adults with dementia, who are
limited in their ability to report the nature and the extent of any pain they are
experiencing. (See Chapter 11 for further discussion of dementia.) Finally, older
adults may have a different criterion than do young adults for reporting the
point at which they feel pain.

Vision and hearing have received the most extensive and detailed attention
from researchers in the psychology of aging. The following sections describe the
age-related differences/changes that occur in the anatomical structures of the eye

Figure 4.4 | The Human Eye

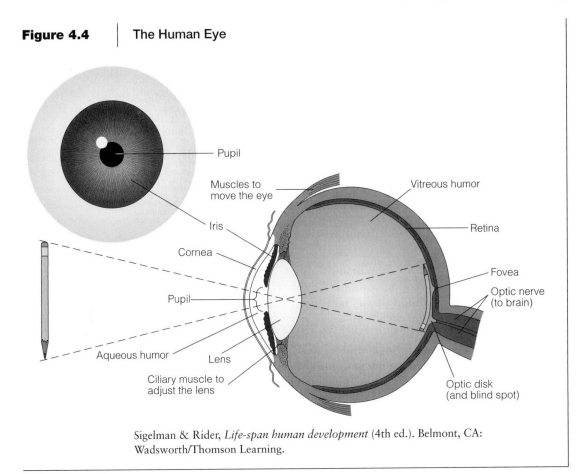

Sigelman & Rider, *Life-span human development* (4th ed.). Belmont, CA:
Wadsworth/Thomson Learning.

and ear, as well as the age-related differences/changes that seem to take place in
visual and auditory perception.

Vision

In general, there is some decline in visual capability, often beginning in the 30s.
This decline is gradual, and usually it is not noticeable until the decade of the
40s or later. Beginning in their 40s, many people start to notice that newspaper
print seems light and faded and numbers in the telephone book appear to be
very small and difficult to decipher. Furthermore, driving at night may seem
more effortful.

Structure of the Eye   Some of the visual changes that occur with aging can be
traced to age-related changes in the specific anatomical structures of the eye.
      The cornea, the refractive surface of the eye that also serves a protective
function, undergoes modest age-related changes. There is a slight age-related

decrease in sensitivity to mechanical stimulation, which means that older adults may not be quite as sensitive in detecting the presence of a foreign body in the eye. Also, there is slight decline in refractive power due to a loss of luster on the corneal surface. In addition, the thickness and curvature of the cornea may change, which may create a need for new corrective lenses. In most cases, however, age-related changes in the cornea are not large and do not have a substantial effect on visual functioning (Kline & Scialfa, 1996).

The aqueous humor is the fluid-filled chamber that lies between the cornea and the lens. It serves as a conduit through which nutrients are carried in to the lens and metabolic waste products are carried out. If the outflow of the fluid is impeded, there could be an increase in pressure. **Glaucoma** is a disease associated with elevated pressure in the aqueous humor. The onset of age-related glaucoma is often gradual. Initially, it may affect peripheral (side) vision rather than central vision. Over time, however, central vision may be affected as well. In its early stages, glaucoma can be treated with medication but more advanced cases require surgery (Roberts, 1995). Regular opthamologic checkups are the best means of detecting glaucoma at its earliest stages. If untreated, the prolonged elevation in pressure characteristic of glaucoma can cause irreversible damage to the nerve cells in the retina.

The pupil is the opening of the eye surrounded by the iris, and it controls the amount of light that enters the eye and ultimately reaches the retina. In general, the diameter of the pupil decreases with age (Kline & Scialfa, 1997), so less light is admitted into the older eye than into the young eye. Under the identical level of illumination, there is a linear decrease from age 20 to age 60 in the amount of light reaching the retina (Botwinick, 1984). This means that with increasing age, higher levels of illumination will be needed.

In addition to having a smaller diameter in older adulthood, the pupil becomes less able to adjust its size in response to changing levels of light. Especially at low levels of illumination, the older eye is not as sensitive as the young eye is and this undoubtedly contributes to the difficulties older drivers experience with night-time driving. In older adulthood, pupillary adjustment takes longer after exposure to the glare from the bright headlights of passing cars. During this prolonged period of adjustment, visual sensitivity is reduced.

The lens of the eye transmits light. It also changes in shape and thus refractive power. Changes in refractive power, called accommodation, allow the eye to focus on both near and far objects. In older adulthood, the lens increases in size and thickness and it decreases in flexibility (Kline & Scialfa, 1996). These changes make it difficult for the older eye to focus on near objects. This farsightedness is termed **presbyopia**. Presbyopia is different from myopia, or nearsightedness, which makes it difficult for the eye to focus on objects that are far away rather than near. Beginning in middle age, many individuals who never wore glasses before find that they need them for reading. Those who already wear corrective optical lenses for distance vision often find they need bifocal lenses that will correct for both distance and close-up vision. However, bifocals do not provide an equal degree of correction over the entire visual field. Many bifocal wearers have poorer visual acuity for peripheral images on the side of their visual field than they do for images in their central field of vision (Kline

& Scialfa, 1997). Thus, they are less aware of visual stimuli on either side as opposed to visual stimuli that are directly in front of them. Among the implications for driving is that older adults may be less ready than young adults are to detect when cars are passing them.

In addition to becoming larger and less flexible, the lens tends to become yellow with age. Less light can pass through a yellow lens than through a clear lens, which is one more reason a room that might seem bright enough to the young eye seems dim to the older eye. Furthermore, the yellowing of the lens is associated with a modest decline in the ability to discriminate between some colors with short wavelengths (Kline & Scialfa, 1997). Older adults have difficulty discriminating between various shades of blue, violet, and green. However, the ability to discriminate shades of red and yellow is usually maintained.

With increasing age, the formation of **senile cataracts** becomes more prevalent. Cataracts are areas of cloudiness or opacity in the lens. Not all older adults develop cataracts, but cataracts are common, affecting approximately 46 percent of people ages 75 to 85 (Roberts, 1995). Cataracts can develop in the center or on the side of the lens. If the cataract is located on the side, or peripheral area, of the lens, then vision under bright levels of illumination might not be affected but vision under dim conditions will be. Cataracts have the effect of scattering light, which causes increased susceptibility to glare. Although older adults require higher levels of illumination, the source of the lighting is particularly important. Indirect lighting is preferable for limiting glare. Surgery to remove cataracts has a high rate of success, but it is performed only when the cataract is sufficiently developed to significantly interfere with visual functioning. Many older adults have to cope with the milder effects of cataracts until such time when they become candidates for surgery.

Occasional changes in the vitreous humor may result in detachment from the retina, but this is not a major source of age-related visual change. Ultimately, images must be focused on the retina. With age, the number of retinal ganglion cell axons declines (Kline & Scialfa, 1997), and changes in blood vessels that nourish the retina can result in retinal damage. Two diseases, **macular degeneration** and **diabetic retinopathy**, are both associated with irreversible loss of nerve cells in the retina. Such loss leads to visual distortion or actual loss of vision. The macula, located in the central area of the retina near the fovea, consists of a high concentration of receptor cells. The macula is highly susceptible to the metabolic and circulatory insufficiencies that become more likely in older adulthood (Roberts, 1995). Atrophy, or degeneration, of these receptor cells affects vision for fine detail, resulting in difficulties with activities such as reading and driving. However, individuals with macular degeneration may still possess sufficient visual capability to move about and take care of themselves (Kausler & Kausler, 1996). Diabetic retinopathy is a complication of long-term diabetes whereby changes in the structure and function of blood vessels damage receptor cells in the retina (Kline & Scialfa, 1996). Often, the extent of such damage can be controlled through proper monitoring of blood sugar levels. Macular degeneration and diabetic retinopathy are not inevitable with increasing age, but they do become more prevalent, and the consequences of both are serious.

Visual Perception   Not all age-related changes in vision can be traced to changes in the structure of the eye. Vision is also a function of central processing in the brain. As mentioned previously, age-related changes in the visual field are characterized by greater decline in sensitivity to peripheral targets than to central targets (Kline & Scialfa, 1997). Age-related decline in peripheral sensitivity may be due, at least in part, to distortions created by the optical corrective lenses commonly worn by older adults. However, higher-order, central processing in the brain may also play a role.

Older adults often have more difficulty than young adults do when quickly changing visual stimuli must be processed. As described earlier, age-related differences in critical flicker frequency (CFF) threshold mean that the older eye may perceive a pulsing visual stimulus as being continuous. Also, older adults find it especially difficult to attend selectively to a visual target stimulus that is embedded in a background of visual distractors.

Perception of motion and depth are additional aspects of visual functioning most likely related to central processing. Age-related decline in motion perception is associated with a decreased ability to respond appropriately or accurately to moving objects (Gilmore, 1996; Kline & Scialfa, 1997). Motion perception is a critical skill in driving performance. Compared to young adults, older adults are less sensitive to differences in velocity. Also, older adults tend to overestimate the velocity, or speed, of slow-moving vehicles (Gilmore, 1996), which means that older drivers anticipate that slow-moving vehicles will arrive more quickly than they actually do. This may be one reason older drivers wait before turning into traffic while impatient young drivers honk their horns because they think there is plenty of time to make the turn (Gilmore, 1996). Overestimating the speed of moving vehicles seems to be more characteristic of elderly women. Elderly men are similar to young adults in their accuracy of estimating the speed of moving vehicles (Gilmore, 1996; Kline & Scialfa, 1997).

Depth perception involves being able to use visual cues to determine which of several objects in the environment is closest and which is farthest away. Decline in depth perception becomes apparent in the 50s, with further modest decline through the 70s (Kausler & Kausler, 1996). With regard to driving, poor depth perception can make parallel parking difficult because the driver must judge the distance between the car he or she is trying to park and the adjacent cars (Kausler & Kausler, 1996).

The **Useful Field of View (UFOV)** is an index of visual functioning used by some researchers who study visual aging. UFOV is the visual area over which target stimuli can be recognized and localized without the person having to make any eye or head movements (Kline & Scialfa, 1996). UFOV is one way to measure the amount of information that can be processed during a brief glance (Rogers, 1997), and it can be affected by factors such as number of competing attentional demands and the distinctness of the visual stimuli (Ball & Owsley, 1991). There are considerable individual differences among older adults, but in general UFOV is more restricted in older adults than it is in young adults. However, UFOV can be increased with practice (Kline & Scialfa, 1997) and training (Ball, Beard, Roenker, Miller, & Griggs, 1988).

Figure 4.5

The Human Ear. Hearing problems can result from conductive loss in the outer ear and middle ear, but sensorineural hearing loss stems from damage to hair cells in the cochlea and degeneration of neurons in the auditory nerve.

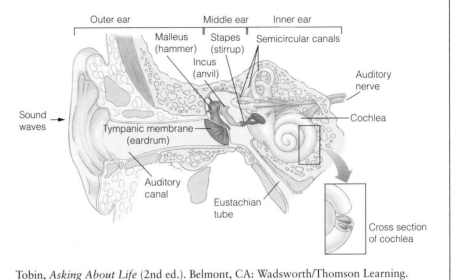

Tobin, *Asking About Life* (2nd ed.). Belmont, CA: Wadsworth/Thomson Learning.

Among older drivers, UFOV scores are a significant predictor of road test performance and crash frequency (Ball & Rebok, 1994), perhaps even more so than measures of reaction time and visual acuity (Carr, Jackson, Madden, & Cohen, 1992). Older drivers with low UFOV scores are more likely than those with high UFOV scores to report that they purposely avoid difficult driving situations (Ball et al., 1998). Limitations in UFOV may be an important reason many older drivers voluntarily limit their exposure to difficult conditions when there is rain or heavy traffic.

Hearing

Hearing loss is among the most common chronic conditions affecting older adults. Of adults over the age of 65, one source estimates that 29 percent have hearing impairments (A Profile of Older Americans, 1996), while another source estimates that 39 percent of the U.S. population over 65 experience some difficulty with hearing (Gordon-Salant, 1996). Older adults are more likely than young adults to report problems with everyday tasks that involve hearing, and hearing difficulties are associated with poor physical health and reduced levels of psychosocial functioning (Strawbridge, Wallhagen, Shema, & Kaplan, 2000). Hearing loss is negatively associated with quality of life during the retirement years—satisfaction with retirement is lower for people with hearing loss than for those without it (National Academy on an Aging Society, 1999).

Hearing consists of peripheral and central systems. The peripheral system includes the outer, middle, and inner ear. Sounds are registered by the peripheral system and carried by the auditory nerve to the central system located in the brainstem, midbrain, and cortex, where they are processed and interpreted.

Structure of the Ear   Auditory stimuli must be sufficiently loud, or intense, to be registered by the peripheral system. Impairments of a mechanical, or conductive, nature can impede the passing of sound waves through the outer or middle ear and can contribute to age-related hearing loss. Changes in the auditory canal, including the presence of impacted wax, can result in conductive hearing loss. With increasing age, the ear drum becomes stiffer, thinner, and less elastic and thus less easily displaced as a function of sound intensity (Kline & Scialfa, 1997).

In the middle ear, three tiny bones, or *ossicles* (hammer, anvil, and stirrup), transmit acoustic energy to the inner ear by creating mechanical vibrations at the entrance to the fluid-filled inner ear, or cochlea. Over time, calcification can lead to decreased mobility of the ossicles, which leads to further conductive hearing loss. Conductive loss resulting from age-related changes in the outer and middle ear usually affects all frequencies (high- and low-pitched) to a similar degree.

The inner ear consists of two structures. The semicircular canals control the sense of balance and the cochlea is associated with hearing. The cochlea is a fluid-filled chamber with a membrane (basilar membrane) running down the center. Mechanical vibrations created by the ossicles of the middle ear set the cochlear fluid in motion, and this motion bends the hair cells on the basilar membrane. This bending of the hair cells converts sound waves into neural energy by stimulating the release of neurotransmitter substances at the base of the hair cells, thus initiating nerve impulses that will be transmitted to the brain (Gordon-Salant, 1996). Any damage to the delicate hair cells on the basilar membrane will result in sensorineural hearing loss. Such damage can result from abuse such as exposure to loud noise, or from illness, but some degeneration of the hair cells may occur simply with aging. The hair cells located in the basal region of the basilar membrane are resonant to high-frequency tones, and it is in this basal region that hair cells show the most pronounced degeneration in older adults. Accordingly, older adults become less sensitive to high-frequency sounds such as high-pitched doorbells and smoke alarms, birds' chirping, cats' meowing, the sizzle of frying bacon, and the high notes on a piano keyboard (Slawinsi, Hartel, & Kline, 1993).

Auditory Perception   Signals from the cochlea are transmitted via the auditory nerve to the brain stem and ultimately to the cortex. Neurons in the auditory nerve may undergo some degree of age-related degeneration, which could distort auditory signals (Gordon-Salant, 1996). The central auditory system consists of neurons in the brain stem, mid-brain, and auditory (temporal) cortex, where complex acoustic information is translated into meaningful signals. Although there is considerable individual variability, there is evidence for age-related decline in the ability to process auditory information at the central level (Gordon-Salant, 1996).

The term **presbycusis** refers to a pattern of hearing loss associated with aging. Presbycusis is characterized by an increased threshold (that is, a decreased sensitivity) to high-frequency tones. Diminished sensitivity to high-frequency tones can begin in the 30s, but usually it does not become noticeable until the 40s, 50s, or sometimes later. As this high-frequency loss progresses, it begins to affect speech sounds that fall into the high-frequency range. Thus, older adults have increased thresholds for high-frequency consonants (for example, k, s, sh, f, t, th). With regard to speech perception, older adults have difficulty discriminating between words with high-frequency consonants (for example, "fit" and "sit").

Some of the difficulty with speech perception can be attributed to the decreased sensitivity to high-frequency speech sounds. However, older adults often comment, "I hear it but I cannot understand it," a phenomenon termed **phonemic regression**. Thus, older adults' understanding of speech or other complex signals is poorer than it should be based solely on their sensitivity to pure tones alone (Tun & Wingfield, 1997). Some increase in loudness, or intensity, can be helpful for older adults who experience difficulty with speech perception. However, increasing the intensity does not usually eliminate the difficulty with understanding speech. In fact, speaking too loudly may actually be detrimental. Rather than a speaker's raising his or her voice to a high level in an attempt to help the older listener, it is usually preferable to speak somewhat more slowly and to substitute key words that have fewer high-frequency consonants. Not speaking too quickly and being selective about words with high-frequency consonants are especially important in telephone conversations because many telephones do not transmit a high-quality signal.

Older adults with presbycusis have special difficulty understanding speech in noisy conditions. Even when young and older adults are matched for their sensitivity to pure tones and for their ability to understand speech in quiet conditions, older adults tend to experience greater difficulty than young adults do with understanding speech against a background of noise or "babble" from numerous other talkers (Schneider & Pichora-Fuller, 2000; Tun & Wingfield, 1997). This difficulty is compounded when the speech they are trying to understand is rapid, or time-compressed (Tun, 1998).

Tun and Wingfield (1999) compared young and older listeners, all selected for excellent pure tone hearing relative to their age peers. These young and older listeners, who were equivalent in pure tone hearing ability, were instructed to report the content of short target sentences, which were presented against a background of noise. The noise was either low or high in intensity, and it was generated from one other speaker, two other speakers, multiple-talker babble from 20 speakers, or white noise. Not surprisingly, the performance of both young and older listeners suffered under high-intensity noise. However, Tun and Wingfield found that despite their excellent pure tone hearing acuity, the older listeners were less accurate and slower to respond compared to the young listeners. In fact, the young listeners were able to withstand the interfering effects when the noise came from only one speaker. In contrast, the older listeners were negatively affected by noise even when it came from only one speaker. This finding has practical importance. Everyday situations often require people to comprehend what a speaker is saying when there is a single competing source of background noise from a radio or television. Older adults are likely to have greater difficulty than young adults under such conditions.

In summary, presbycusis is associated with peripheral hearing loss, stemming mainly from sensorineural loss in the inner ear. However, it also involves loss in the ability to process complex auditory information (such as speech) at the central level. Age-related changes in attentional capacity, as well as in certain aspects of the memory system (discussed in more detail in Chapter 5), could all contribute to decrements in processing auditory information. Age-related slowing means that older adults will be especially disadvantaged when they must report the content of rapid (time-compressed) spoken language (Wingfield, 1996). Older adults benefit greatly when they are given sufficient time to process auditory information.

There are gender differences in the prevalence of presbycusis. The decrease in sensitivity to high-frequency sounds begins earlier and progresses more rapidly for men, although the exact reason for this gender difference is not clear. Between the ages of 45 and 64, the proportion of men with presbycusis becomes notably greater than the proportion of women so affected (National Academy on an Aging Society, 1999). Also, again for reasons not completely understood, European Americans are more likely than African Americans to experience this type of hearing loss. Furthermore, the gap between these two groups widens in older adulthood (National Academy on an Aging Society, 1999).

Even though presbycusis is a commonly reported problem among older adults (Corso, 1995; Strawbridge et al., 2000), not all older adults suffer from hearing difficulties. Thus, presbycusis is not an inevitable consequence of the aging process. What, then, is the cause of presbycusis? One hypothesis is that it results from the accumulated effects of exposure to environmental noise from traffic or disturbances in the workplace (Gordon-Salant, 1996). Cross-cultural comparisons have found that age-related hearing loss is less prevalent in individuals who live in relatively noise-free nonindustrialized societies (for example, the Maaban tribe in Africa) compared to individuals in noisy industrialized countries such as the United States (Gordon-Salant, 1996). Within the United States, the prevalence of hearing loss has been increasing over the past three decades (Strawbridge et al., 2000). However, the rate of occurrence is higher among those who worked in occupations such as farming, machine operations and repair, and transportation as opposed to those who worked in administrative and professional occupations that probably involve less noise exposure (National Academy on an Aging Society, 1999). If noise exposure is indeed the source of presbycusis, then future cohorts of older adults may have an even higher incidence because of having attended rock concerts in their younger years.

Although noise probably contributes to presbycusis, there is no proof that presbycusis is attributable entirely to noise exposure. Other factors being investigated in connection with age-related hearing loss include diet, medications, alcohol consumption, smoking, hypertension, and genetic influences. As yet, cause-and-effect relationships between presbycusis and each of these factors have not been clearly established. Presbycusis may be attributable, at least in part, to intrinsic, age-related deterioration of the auditory system. It has even been suggested that presbycusis renders older adults more vulnerable to noise-induced hearing loss. If so, then avoiding exposure to noise would seem especially important for older listeners (Kline & Scialfa, 1997).

Hearing Aids   Hearing aids can be fitted to one ear (monaural) or both ears (binaural) to increase, or amplify, sound. The degree of amplification must be sufficient so that auditory signals will cross the individual's hearing threshold. At the same time, the intensity of the signals should not be so great as to become uncomfortably loud. It is important for a hearing aid to be tailored to the individual user's profile of hearing loss. For example, someone with a hearing loss in the high-frequency range should wear a hearing aid that amplifies high-frequency signals but not low-frequency signals.

Among people in the U.S. population with hearing loss, those ages 65 and over are more likely than young and middle-aged adults to wear hearing aids. Even so, it has been estimated that two out of three older (65+) individuals with hearing loss do not use a hearing aid (National Academy of an Aging Society, 1999). It has also been estimated that only about one-fourth of older adults who might benefit from a hearing aid actually own one (Schneider & Pichora-Fuller, 2000).

What are the barriers to hearing aid use? In a survey of 2,300 hearing-impaired individuals over 50 (National Academy of an Aging Society, 1999), the reason given by more than half of the respondents was cost. However, approximately 20 percent also reported concerns related to vanity and fear that wearing a hearing aid carries a stigma. Another common reason was that the individuals in the survey did not think their hearing was poor enough to necessitate the use of a hearing aid, and many did not believe that a hearing aid would help with their particular problem.

Under noisy conditions, hearing aids may have only limited usefulness in helping older adults to understand speech (Gordon-Salant, 1996). Approximately one-third of the older adults who have a hearing aid have difficulties in everyday situations in which they must attend to a number of signals (for example, group conversations) or when there is background noise (Schneider & Pichora-Fuller, 2000). Hearing aids may not solve difficulties with speech perception that are related to processing information at the central level. In addition, some hearing aids whistle or make other noises that annoy people. Recent advances in the development of digital hearing aids have incorporated noise-reduction circuitry that selectively reduces the amplification of noise (Gordon-Salant, 1996). However, digital hearing aids are very costly. There is little question that many older adults could derive some benefit from a hearing aid even if their hearing difficulties are not completely alleviated. Those who decide to try hearing aids should be encouraged to receive audiological counseling or to take part in an aural rehabilitation program to ensure that they make the most effective use of the device (Gordon-Salant, 1996).

Some older adults may consider a decline in hearing acuity as a threat to their self-image and therefore may be reluctant to acknowledge any difficulties with communication. Perhaps they fear that wearing a hearing aid will confirm to others that they are not competent (Ryan, Hummert, & Anas, 1997). Reluctance to deal with hearing difficulties often creates more difficulties than it solves. A strategy of smiling and nodding even when the listener does not understand what someone else is saying may backfire. Older adults who use this strategy to cover up hearing difficulties are likely to respond inappropriately at some point during a conversation. When that happens, they may create an impression that they lack competence even if they do not. As the baby boom generation moves into older adulthood and an even larger proportion of the population experiences age-related hearing difficulties, there may be less hesitancy to acknowledge hearing difficulties and more attempts to do whatever is necessary to maximize auditory functioning.

Using Visual Cues   Visual cues, which a listener can derive from reading a speaker's lips or observing a speaker's facial expressions or body language, provide additional information about the speaker's communication. Older adult listeners may use visual cues to compensate for degraded auditory signals. Every effort should be made to face older adult listeners who have presbycusis so that they can make maximum use of visual cues.

Visual alerting signals can be attached to safety devices when individuals have hearing difficulties. For example, some smoke alarm systems set off flashing lights in addition to auditory signals (Gordon-Salant, 1996). Strobe lights that flash when telephones or doorbells ring can be installed. Many movies and television programs have a captioning option for the benefit of individuals with hearing difficulties.

Bottom-Up and Top-Down Strategies in Language Processing   Listeners use a combination of **bottom-up and top-down strategies in language processing.** (Tun & Wingfield, 1997; Wingfield, Prentice, Koh, & Little, 2000). A bottom-up processing strategy calls for registering the details of the sensory-perceptual input. A top-down processing strategy uses contextual information about the semantic (word meaning) and syntactic (grammatical) structure of language as well as its prosodic features (intonation, stress, and timing). Older adults with presbycusis lose some efficiency in bottom-up processing, particularly when auditory signals fall into the high-frequency range. However, they may be able to compensate for limitations in bottom-up processing by relying more heavily on top-down processing. Top-down processing is based on the fact that spoken language has excess information, or redundancy, which allows listeners to use contextual cues to fill in the details of a speaker's message. For example, speakers of a particular language understand that some words are more probable than others in the context of a particular message. If the speaker says, "I want to ___ down," the older individual with presbycusis may not be able to distinguish whether the missed word is "sit" or "fit" purely on the basis of bottom-up processing. However, the older listener who is familiar with language probabilities can make an educated guess that the missed word is more likely to be "sit" than "fit." Listeners can use top-down processing more readily when speakers (a) talk at a normal rate, (b) use sentences that are not too long or too grammatically complex, and (c) use normal prosodic features (intonation, stress, and timing) in their speech (Wingfield & Stine-Morrow, 2000). When speech is time compressed (fast), when spoken phrases are long and grammatically complex, when pauses occur in the middle rather than at the end of sentences, and when stress and intonation patterns are exaggerated, older adults may have difficulty using top-down processing to compensate for a less-than-perfect bottom-up input.

Communicating with Older Adults   How do people communicate with older adults? Rubin and Brown (1975) asked young adult undergraduates to explain the rules and objectives of a simple game to a theoretical listener represented by a photograph of a child, a young-adult age-peer, a middle-aged adult, or an older adult. The undergraduates' explanations, as measured by the number of words they used, were less complex when they thought the listener was a young child or an older adult than it was when they thought the listener was a young adult or middle-aged adult. The undergraduates were not given any information about the "listener's" hearing or cognitive abilities. Yet, they spontaneously simplified their speech when they thought they were communicating with a young child or an older adult.

Elderspeak is a term that refers to a particular style of speaking often used by those who communicate with older adults (Kemper, 1994). It bears some similarities to the *motherese* adults use when they speak to infants and young children. Elderspeak is characterized by short sentences, simplified grammar, and exaggerated pitch and intonation (Kemper & Harden, 1999). Kemper (1994) analyzed 10-minute speech samples from service providers and caregivers as they communicated with groups of young or older adults. Both service providers and caregivers were more likely to use elderspeak when addressing groups of older adults than they were when they addressed groups of young adults. When speaking to the older groups, they were more likely to reduce the length and grammatical complexity of what they said, to use simpler words and more repetitions, and to speak more slowly.

Kemper and Harden (1999) conducted a series of experiments to determine more precisely which components of elderspeak are beneficial for older adults and which ones may not be beneficial and may even be perceived as unnecessarily condescending, or patronizing. Young and older adult study participants watched a videotape of a speaker describing a route that was also traced on a map. Afterward, study participants were given their own map and told to reproduce the route as accurately as possible. In addition, they were asked how competent they felt in the communication situation by rating whether they agreed with statements such as, "The speaker was hard to understand" and "I lost track of what was said." Kemper and Harden found that the videotaped speaker's use of semantic elaboration (repeating and expanding upon the map directions) was highly beneficial for the older adults' performance. In fact, when the speaker used semantic elaborations while giving directions, the older adults performed just as accurately as the young adults did. Moreover, the older participants reported that they felt that they had fewer communication difficulties when the speaker used semantic elaboration. When the speaker reduced the grammatical complexity of the directions, the older adults performed more accurately, although they did not feel, subjectively, that there was any improvement in their communication difficulties.

In a second experiment, Kemper and Harden manipulated two different aspects of the speaker's speech: grammatical complexity (the number of subordinated and embedded clauses) and length of utterance (short or long). This time, reduced grammatical complexity was beneficial for older adults' performance as well as for their subjectively perceived communication problems.

However, shortening the length of the speaker's utterances had no effect on the older adults' performance, and in fact it increased their perceived communication difficulties. That is, when the speaker's directions were divided into short two- and five-word sentences, older adults felt that their comprehension was impaired.

In a third experiment, Kemper and Harden found that exaggerated prosody (slow rate of speaking, many pauses, and exaggerated vocal pitch) did not benefit older adults' performance, nor was it helpful for their subjective perception of their own communicative competence. Furthermore, older adults had a lower opinion of the speaker's competence when the speaker used exaggerated rather than normal prosody when giving the directions. Apparently, being spoken to in short, simple, phrases with exaggerated pitch does nothing to enhance older adults' self-image, nor does it make them confident in the speaker's capabilities.

Ryan and her colleagues point out that conversational partners who assume that older adults are incompetent and dependent tend to use patronizing communication (Ryan, Hummert, & Boich, 1995). Features of patronizing communication include the use of overly simple grammar, short utterances, and the exaggerated prosody often found in elderspeak. In addition, patronizing communication may include exaggerated gestures and terms of endearment (such as "honey" and "dear"). They contend that this form of communication can lead to the **Communication Predicament of Aging Model,** which appears in Figure 4.6.

According to this model, people hold stereotyped expectancies that older adults have a hearing deficit and also that they are emotionally unstable, dependent, and suffering from general cognitive incompetence. When communicating with older adults, people modify their speech patterns to fit these assumptions. Modifications include speaking in a louder than normal level of intensity, using exaggerated nonverbal gestures, and using terms of endearment (for example, "good girl"). Ryan et al. (1995) consider these modifications to be overaccommodative and as such they impose unnecessary constraints on communication. When overaccommodative speech is used, both the speaker and the older adult listener may find the exchange to be unsatisfactory and may avoid communicating with one another on future occasions.

Ryan, Bourhis, and Knops (1991) asked healthy community-living adults of widely ranging ages to read a script of a conversation between a middle-aged female nurse and a 76-year-old nursing home resident who was described as either alert or forgetful. The conversational script was either neutral (the nurse tells the resident, "It is time to take your pills. Here's your glass of water, but take your time.") or patronizing ("I'm here to give you your pills. Be a good girl and take them right now."). Even though the scripts were written, study participants still rated the patronizing script as louder, more shrill, and as having more exaggerated intonation than the neutral script. Regardless of whether they were told the older nursing home resident was alert or forgetful, participants formed an unfavorable impression of the patronizing nurse. They viewed her as less competent, less respectful, and less benevolent than the neutral nurse. Furthermore, study participants thought that the resident spoken to by the patronizing nurse was more helpless and more frustrated than the resident

Figure 4.6 | The Communication Predicament of Aging Model

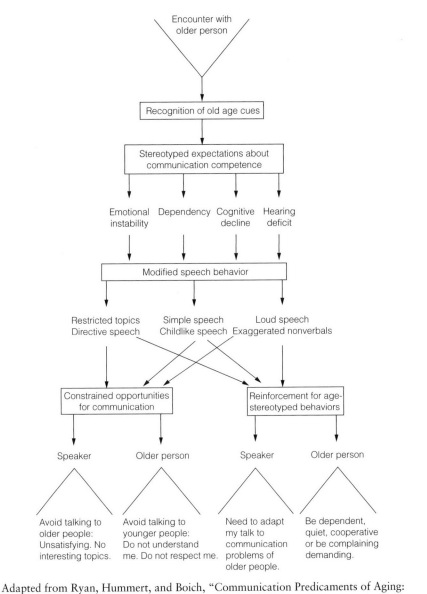

Adapted from Ryan, Hummert, and Boich, "Communication Predicaments of Aging: Patronizing behavior toward older adults," *Journal of Language and Social Psychology,* 14, p. 144–146, Figure 1, 1995. Reprinted by permission of Sage Publications, Inc.

spoken to by the neutral nurse. Clearly, the manner in which the nurse communicated with the older resident made a difference in participants' impression of both the nurse and the nursing home resident.

Ryan, Hamilton, and Kwong See (1994) asked young and older adults to listen to one of two versions of a brief tape-recording of a caregiver trying to convince a nursing home resident to come to the dining area for a meal. In the neutral version, the caregiver says, "Mrs. Fields, I've been searching everywhere for you. It's time to go to the dining room for supper." In the patronizing version (baby talk), the caregiver says, "There you are, Maggie. Come on, sweetie. It's time to go to the dining room for supper, remember?" The young and older participants both thought the caregiver who used baby talk was less respectful and less competent than the caregiver who used a neutral style of communicating. Also, participants thought that the older resident would be less satisfied with the baby talk than with the neutral interaction.

However, do all older adults view patronizing communication as negative and insulting? O'Connor and Rigby (1996) recruited older adult study participants from both a senior citizen activity center and a nursing home. Participants were told to imagine they were attending an entertainment event. During the intermission, another person comes over and asks if they would like some refreshments. In the neutral scenario, the person says, "I came over to see whether you are enjoying the show and to ask whether you would like some dessert." In the patronizing scenario, the person says, "I've brought some COFFEE and a plate of GOODIES for you dear. I hope you're COMFY and ENJOYING the SHOW." Even though the scripts were written, study participants thought the patronizing scenario would be louder and more shrill compared to the neutral scenario. However, the nursing home participants, who were chronologically older and lower in self-reported functional health than the activity center participants, did not react as negatively to the patronizing scenario as the activity center participants did. Furthermore, study participants with a high need for succorance—who seemed to have a high need for love and reassurance and endorsed statements such as, "I like to be with protective and sympathetic people"—were more likely to feel that the patronizing communication was warm than did study participants with a low need for succorance. Also, study participants who rated themselves high in self-esteem (who endorsed statements such as, "I feel I am a person of worth") reacted less negatively to the patronizing communication than did participants who rated themselves low in self-esteem. O'Connor and Rigby's findings suggest that there are individual differences in older adults' reactions to patronizing communication. Reactions to patronizing communications must be viewed within the context of people's needs and feelings of self-esteem. Furthermore, cultural differences could play a role in how older adults react to such communications. The exact nature of any such cultural differences awaits further investigation.

REVISITING THE SELECTIVE OPTIMIZATION WITH COMPENSATION AND ECOLOGICAL MODELS

In almost no other area of aging and older adulthood are these two theoretical models more relevant than they are when it comes to sensory and perceptual processes. With regard to the Selective Optimization with Compensation (SOC) Model (Baltes & Baltes, 1990), visual capabilities will be optimized if older adults have access to medical screening for diabetes, glaucoma, and cataracts.

Prosthetic devices such as reading glasses or bifocals can help older adults compensate for presbyopia. Older adults may need to be selective about the visual conditions under which they must function. For example, many limit their own nighttime driving and drive only when weather conditions are good and traffic conditions are light. In many communities, courses are available to teach older adults (ages 55+) how to improve their driving skills. Some insurance companies reward successful completion of such courses with a reduction in auto insurance premiums. With regard to audition, older adults may compensate for hearing loss by using hearing aids tailored to their individual needs and by using visual cues to make up for the auditory cues they miss.

The Ecological Model (Lawton, 1989; Lawton & Nahemow, 1973) is useful for defining an appropriate match between older adults' sensory and perceptual capabilities and the level of sensory and perceptual challenge to which they can adapt. Individuals with no sensory or perceptual difficulties will adapt well in a broad range of environments. In contrast, individuals with sensory and perceptual difficulties adapt best to environments that are more specifically tailored to their capabilities. Age-related changes in visual functioning call for environmental modifications that reduce visual challenge, or press. Ensuring adequate levels of illumination from light sources that prevent glare, as well as minimizing drastic changes in level of illumination, are beneficial. Exiting from a brightly lit room into a dimly lit space requires a period of dark adaptation, during which time the probability of falls may increase. Halls in apartment buildings or assisted living facilities should not be lit dimly to save on energy costs.

To maximize chances for adaptation, demand for close work should be kept to a minimum. Thus, forms and pamphlets intended for older adults should not be printed with reduced-size letters or numbers to save costs. More and more publishers are responding to the older population's need for large print, and many public libraries and bookstores have entire sections of large-print books. Signs posted in areas frequented by older adults should have large letters or numbers printed on a plain and clearly contrasting background. For example, black letters printed against a plain white background are better than blue letters against a light violet background or a background with a design.

Older adults with macular degeneration adapt best in environments with greatly reduced visual press. As the disease progresses, they will need assistance with activities such as cooking, reading mail, and writing checks. Older adults who must give up driving because of macular degeneration, or just because of normal age-related changes in visual capabilities, will adapt best in environments that provide transportation support such as van service or access to public transportation.

Individuals with reduced auditory competence will adapt best in listening environments with a reduced level of auditory press. The level of challenge can be kept to a minimum if speakers do not talk too quietly or too quickly and also if they limit their use of high-frequency consonants. In addition, there should be minimal background noise and reverberation to ensure that the level of auditory challenge is within the adaptation range of the older listener.

KEY POINTS

- The senses include taste, smell, touch, vision, and hearing.
- Sensory threshold refers to the minimum amount of stimulation a sensory organ must receive before the presence of a particular stimulus is registered. Sensitivity is the inverse of threshold. The greater the individual's sensitivity to a particular type of stimulation, the lower that individual's threshold will be.
- The signal detection model of determining sensory threshold takes into account not only sensitivity but also the individual's decisional response criteria (that is, level of cautiousness). Older adults are often more cautious than young adults are.
- Sensation refers to the initial registration of physical stimulation by the sense organs, while perception refers to the subsequent processing and interpretation of the stimuli at the central level (that is, in the brain). Depending on how stimuli are processed and interpreted, decisions will be made about how to respond.
- On reaction time tasks, older adults are usually slower than young adults, and this is more true on complex tasks than it is on simple ones.
- The nervous system of an older adult takes longer to process information than does the nervous system of a young adult. If stimuli follow one another very quickly, the older adult's nervous system is less efficient at processing the successive stimuli because the previous ones have not been cleared through the system.
- Older adults may have less attentional resources/capacity compared to young adults. Also, they may have greater difficulty ignoring distracting stimuli and focusing on relevant stimuli. Finally, age-related loss of blood flow in the frontal lobes of the cerebral cortex could explain why age-related deficits are often found on attention tasks that call for inhibition of responses or the ability to shift from one response to another.
- Older adults often have difficulty on divided attention tasks where attention must be paid to more than one thing at a time. Also, they have difficulty on selective attention tasks, on which they are required to focus their attention on relevant information and ignore irrelevant distracting information.
- Age-related changes in vision include a need for more illumination as well as changes in color vision and an increasing incidence of presbyopia. Disease-related problems with the retina can result in partial or complete blindness. Often there are ways to minimize the effects of such visual changes.
- Age-related changes in hearing include an increasing incidence of presbycusis, which affects high-frequency tones and the ability to understand speech. However, there are ways to minimize the effects of these auditory changes.
- Those who communicate with older adults often use "elderspeak," some aspects of which can be beneficial. However, a stereotype that older adults are not competent has been associated with patronizing speech, which can lead to the Communication Predicament of Aging Model, with the end result that some older adults may withdraw from communicating.

KEY TERMS

To learn more about the issues discussed in this chapter, point your browser to http://www.infotrac-college.com and use the passcode from the InfoTrac College Edition card that came with your book. InfoTrac College Edition gives you access to complete articles from many different journals.

Memory

5

Dorothy is 65 years old and has always taken great pride in her memory. She remembers events and experiences from her adolescent and young adult years as if they had happened yesterday. It amazes her that she can sit down at her friend's piano and play pieces that she learned as a teenager but has not practiced for years. Dorothy is known among her friends for her excellent memory for word definitions. To keep this up, she works the daily crossword puzzle in the newspaper, although lately Dorothy has noticed it takes her a little longer to come up with the necessary words. She also finds it somewhat disturbing when someone she knows greets her at the grocery store and the person's name does not come to her immediately. Recently, Dorothy has noticed a tendency to misplace things such as her reading glasses or car keys. To deal with this, she has started wearing her glasses around her neck and she is careful to put her car keys down in the same place as soon as she comes home so she will not have to look all over for them when she wants to go out again.

THE DEVELOPMENTAL STUDY OF MEMORY AND AGE

Memory is essential if we are to make immediate and subsequent use of the information in our environment. Functioning in academic settings and in everyday life would be difficult if not impossible without the ability to remember. Memory failures can cause inconvenience (for example, forgetting to buy an item at the grocery store), embarrassment (inability to remember another person's name), and even danger (forgetting to turn off a burner on the stove). Also, memory is related to a sense of self. People are heavily defined by their memories. Perhaps for this reason many individuals, and especially older adults, feel threatened when they experience lapses in memory.

Concerns About Memory and Aging

The topic of aging and memory has captured the interest of both scientists and nonscientists. Older adults often comment that their memory is not as good as it used to be. Many claim to have increased difficulty finding words, remembering names, and recalling where they put things such as their glasses or keys. The phrase "senior moment" jokingly refers to the often embarrassing lapses in memory that are thought to occur more frequently with increasing age.

On a more serious note, older adults and their families often worry that memory failures herald the onset of Alzheimer's disease. It is true that memory impairment is an essential feature of Alzheimer's disease as well as other forms of dementia (see Chapter 11 for more detailed description of dementia). However, Kral (1962) coined the term "benign senescent forgetfulness" to describe the difficulty some older adults have with remembering nonessential details or parts of past experiences. More recently, the terms "age-associated memory impairment" and "age-related memory decline" refer to mild forms of memory loss that can occur with the aging process (Butler, Lewis, & Sunderland, 1998). Actually, memory loss that occurs with aging is not always easy to differentiate from mild dementia (Skoog, Blennow, & Marcusson, 1996). However, mild dementia usually becomes more severe over time and eventually leads to a clinical diagnosis of Alzheimer's disease or other type of dementia (Butler et al., 1998).

A number of concerns have been raised by those who study aging and memory (often referred to as "memory aging"). What kinds of age-related changes or differences occur as a function of aging? Many normal, healthy older adults experience changes in certain types of memory functioning, and age-related differences are found on some memory tasks. However, age-related differences or changes are not the rule for every aspect of memory functioning. The fact that certain types of memory hold up or even improve with age suggests that some memory structures and processes are more vulnerable than others are to the effects of aging.

Methods of Studying Memory and Aging

In longitudinal studies on memory and age, individuals from a particular cohort are followed over time. Longitudinal studies, especially those that continue for a long time, make it possible to determine which memory functions decline and which are maintained as we grow older. The findings of longitudinal studies are highly informative about the patterns of change and maintenance that can be anticipated in normal memory aging.

However, the majority of developmental studies on memory aging are cross-sectional, with samples of young and older adults tested during the same period of time. The chief advantage of cross-sectional research is that we can make immediate comparisons between young and older adults' performance on memory tests. Still, any differences between the scores of young and older adults cannot be solely attributable to age because participants in cross-sectional studies differ not only in chronological age but also in generation, or cohort membership (see Chapter 2 for more detailed discussion of cross-sectional and longitudinal research). Thus, memory scores could be associated with differences in cohort factors such as educational background and experience.

In cross-sectional studies on memory, age-related differences that favor young adults may be especially pronounced when young adult university students are compared with older adults who have no more than a high school education. To limit the educational disparity between age groups, some researchers have compared young adult university students with older adult university alumni. This approach does not guarantee that the two age groups received the identical educational experience because teaching methods and standards may differ for the two cohorts. Also, the memory demands of academic courses are ongoing for the young adult college students, while older adult university graduates are less likely to be actively involved in formal educational pursuits when the research is being conducted.

Despite these potential limitations, comparing young adult university students with older adult alumni adds to the internal validity of a memory study because the two age groups have similar educational backgrounds. At the same time, however, the older adult university alumni may be not be highly representative of their cohort. For this reason, the findings obtained with older adult university alumni may not generalize to the broader older adult population. This means that the external validity of the study may be limited. (See Chapter 2 for more detailed discussion of internal and external validity.) Even so, being able to generalize the results obtained from one sample of older adults to a broader segment of the older population may not be the chief concern of a particular memory researcher. If the purpose of a study is to isolate how the aging process influences memory, then the external validity that would result from comparing representative samples of young and older adults may be less important than the greater internal validity that would result from testing samples of young and older adults who are matched as closely as possible on variables related to memory. Support for a hypothesis of age decrement for a particular type of memory functioning is more legitimate if older university alumni perform more poorly than young college students than it would be if the older adults who performed more poorly also had less education than the young adults. In sum, sampling older adults who are positively selected for a high level of education decreases the likelihood that performance differences will favor young adults. If young adults are still superior to a positively selected sample of older adults, it is more plausible to conclude that there is age-related decline for that type of memory. Thus, a positively selected older group can be appropriate when tests are made for age decrement in memory processes.

THE INFORMATION PROCESSING MODEL

Conceptualizing memory using an information-processing framework became popular in the 1960s when computers were being introduced on a large scale to college and university campuses. An early but influential information processing model (Atkinson & Shiffrin, 1968) conceptualized memory in terms of memory stores.

The Sensory Store

To be processed, information must be registered initially by the sensory store, which holds a momentary perceptual trace—visual (iconic) or auditory (echoic)—for as little as a fraction of a second. The sensory store is sometimes referred to as "preperceptual" because of its fleeting nature (Botwinick, 1984). One hypothesis has been that the sensory store is even more fleeting in older adults than it is in young adults. If so, information would dissipate more quickly, and thus be lost more readily, from the sensory store for older adults than it would for young adults. Once information fades away, it will not be passed along to subsequent memory stores.

Because the sensory store holds information so briefly, it has proven difficult to compare young and older adults. Some investigations have found modest age-related differences, but it is doubtful that such small differences in the sensory store of young and older adults can account for the age-related differences found on other tests of memory (Botwinick, 1984).

Figure 5.1 | Sensory, Short-Term, and Long-Term Memory Stores

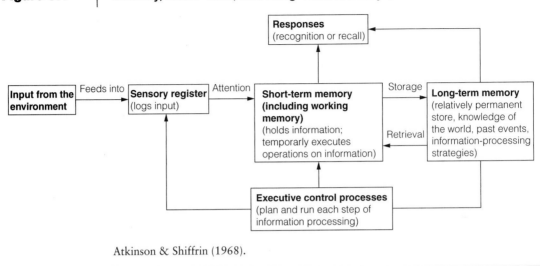

Atkinson & Shiffrin (1968).

The Short-Term Store

Assuming information is registered by the sensory store and does not fade away too quickly, it is entered into the **short-term memory store**, where it will be held for a longer, though still limited, amount of time (up to 30 seconds). Not only does the short-term store hold information for a relatively brief time, but it also has a limited capacity as far as how many items of information can be held at any given time. If the capacity of the short-term store is exceeded, some of the items of information being held there will be displaced as additional items are entered. If items are displaced before they are passed along to the long-term store, they will very likely be lost.

Just exactly how much information can be retained in the short-term store, also referred to as short-term memory? G. A. Miller (1956) referred to the capacity of short-term memory as "the magic number seven plus or minus two." However, Miller proposed that this limited capacity (five to nine units) can be expanded if individual items of information are "chunked" into meaningful units. Thus, a 10-digit telephone number can be reduced to six units if the three digits in the area code are chunked into one unit and the three digits in the exchange are chunked into another unit. The resulting six units (the area code, the exchange, and the four digits unique to that telephone number) are maintained by control processes that oversee exactly how the information is handled during its stay in the short-term store. One type of control process consists of rehearsal using rote repetition—repeating units of information over and over to oneself. Another type of control process consists of coding items of information into meaningful units (such as chunking individual numbers into an area code). Control processes take up space in the limited-capacity short-term store. However, a control process that involves coding would likely take up more space than one that simply involves rote repetition (Ellis & Hunt, 1993).

Figure 5.2 | The Working Memory System

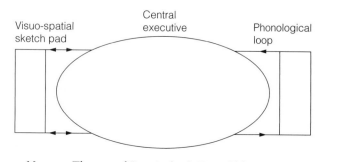

From *Human Memory: Theory and Practice* by A. D. Baddeley, Boston: Allyn and
Bacon, 1990. Reprinted by permission.

A more recent concept related to short-term memory is called **working
memory** (Baddeley, 1986). As with short-term memory, working memory is
limited in capacity and holds information temporarily. However, working
memory contains space in which information is not only held, but also worked
on, or processed. Baddeley (1986; 1990) proposed that working memory consists of a central executive and two storage/work space subsystems: the phonological loop and the visuo-spatial sketch pad (see Figure 5.2).

The central executive is the decision-making mechanism that selects and
controls which information will be temporarily held and/or processed by each
of the two subsystems (Ellis & Hunt, 1993). Speech-based information, such as
remembering a string of spoken numbers, is allocated to the phonological loop,
where it is stored or manipulated as necessary. For example, if someone tells you
a telephone number, you may rehearse it in the phonological loop until you can
press all the buttons on the phone pad, or perhaps you rehearse it until you can
code the phone number into a smaller number of meaningful units. Similarly,
visual and spatial information, such as remembering the location of objects in
a spatial array, is allocated to the visuo-spatial sketch pad, where images are held
temporarily and manipulated as necessary. Given the limitations in working
memory capacity, it might be possible to process more information at any given
time if some of it is speech-based (phonological) and some of it is visual or spatial (visuo-spatial) than would be the case if the information were all one or the
other. In any case, the total amount of capacity, or space, in working memory
is thought to be reduced in older adulthood.

Some researchers conceptualize short-term memory as consisting of two
components, primary memory and working memory, both of which have a
limited capacity and hold information for a limited time (Cherry & Smith,
1998). Primary memory is viewed as a passive receptacle, which holds information in the same form in which it was entered into the short-term store. In
contrast, working memory not only holds information but also actively
processes and manipulates it. Thus, working memory is similar to a "mental
scratch pad" because mental operations are performed on incoming information.

For example, in a test of primary memory, individuals would be instructed to listen to a string of digits (5, 4, 8, 9) and immediately afterward to repeat them back in the same order. In a test of working memory, individuals would be instructed to listen to a string of digits (5, 4, 8, 9) and immediately afterward repeat the digits back in the reverse order (9, 8, 4, 5).

In general, primary memory holds up well with increasing age. Young and older adults perform at a similar level when memory tasks require the passive holding of information for a brief time as long as there is no interruption between the time the information is registered and the time it must be remembered. For example, young and older adults are comparable in their ability to look up a telephone number and remember it long enough to punch in the numbers immediately afterward. However, age-related decrements become apparent when information in the short-term store must be actively processed and reorganized (Craik, 1994). Such reorganization requires working memory, and the more complex the mental manipulations that must be performed, the more difficulty older adults will experience relative to young adults. For example, a requirement to repeat a string of digits (5, 4, 8, 9) backwards after subtracting "2" from each (7, 6, 2, 3) calls for more complex mental manipulations than a requirement to simply repeat digits back in the reverse order (9, 8, 4, 5). Ability for these more complex manipulations shows a greater decrease with age than does ability for simpler manipulations.

To summarize, there are minimal age-related differences in the sensory memory store. Similarly, there is little or no age-related decline in short-term primary memory, which holds information passively. However, there is age-related decline in short-term working memory. When material must be manipulated, as in working memory, older adults usually have more difficulty than young adults do. The more complex the manipulations required, the greater the age-related decline likely to be found.

The Long-Term Store

Long-term memory is what most people think of when they refer to "memory." According to the information processing model, items of information entered into the **long-term memory store** remain there well beyond 30 seconds. In fact, information can be maintained in the long-term store for weeks, months, or years. In addition, the capacity of the long-term store appears to be unlimited. In general, we are consciously aware of information in our short-term store. In contrast, the information in our long-term store does not remain in our conscious awareness at all times. Rather, items are retrieved out of the long-term store on an as-needed basis.

Not all memories in the long-term store are alike. Some researchers (Smith, 1996; Cherry & Smith, 1998) conceptualize long-term memories as falling into three categories: procedural memory, semantic memory, and episodic memory (see Table 5.1).

Procedural Memory   **Procedural memory** makes it possible to acquire skills that are usually demonstrated indirectly by action (Bäckman, Small, & Wahlin, 2001). Examples are motor skills such as knowing how to ride a bicycle,

Table 5.1 | Long-Term Memory Categories, Examples, and Age-Related Effects

Long-Term Memory Category	Examples	Age-Related Effects
Procedural	Driving, typing, bicycle riding	Very little or none
Semantic	Word meanings, knowledge	Very little or none
Episodic	Specific events and experiences	Age-related decline

drive a car, play Ping-Pong, play a musical instrument, or type on a keyboard. Such skills are learned, or acquired, gradually with practice over a long time. Once acquired, they are readily available without much deliberate recollection. It is almost as if these skills become "automatic," so that even after a long lapse, we can perform them with little conscious effort or awareness. Even if you have not driven a car, played Ping-Pong, or typed for many years, for example, you will be able to take up these activities easily, although at first, performing tasks that call for skills not used for a long time may not be completely error-free.

Not all procedural memories are for motor skills. Abilities such as reading and understanding language are often considered examples of procedural memory. Learning a language requires effort and practice, but later on we read and engage in conversations without much thought.

In general, age-related differences in procedural memory appear to be small or nonexistent. Older adults may be somewhat slower than young adults in recovering procedural memories from storage, but given a little additional time, they are just as capable as young adults of doing so. However, some recent research has found that skills that call for complex mental manipulations in working memory (such as reading inverted sentences) or skills that call for very rapid responses do show some age-related decline (Bäckman et al., 2001).

Semantic Memory   Semantic memory (also called generic memory) is akin to general knowledge, or world knowledge. Information in semantic memory is well-learned and has been in the long-term store for a considerable time. Such information is remembered without regard to when or where it was learned. That is, no specific time or place can be identified as to when semantic information was placed into the long-term store. Examples of semantic memory are knowing your mother's maiden name and knowing the name of the first U.S. president. Older adults do not differ from young adults as far as the content and organization of the linguistic knowledge in their semantic store (Light, 1991; Wingfield, 1995). Both are equally likely to know that an apple is a kind of fruit and a cat is a kind of animal. Furthermore, young and older adults both associate the same words with one another ("up/down" and "baby/cries").

Although linguistic knowledge is preserved with age, word-finding problems are a common complaint among older adults. Compared to young adults, older adults are more likely to report tip-of-the-tongue (TOT) experiences, where they

Some skills stay with us throughout our lives even if we have not used them for a long time.

temporarily cannot retrieve familiar words (Kemper, 1995). In one study (Burke, MacKay, Worthley, & Wade, 1991), young, middle-aged, and older adults kept a diary over four weeks in which they recorded naturally-occurring TOTs. Most of the TOTs reported were for infrequent words in the language and proper names. During the one-month interval, older adults reported more TOTs than young and middle-aged adults did, and most of the older adults' TOTs were for names of acquaintances who had not been contacted recently. However, when they are allowed sufficient time and when they make an effort, older adults are usually successful in gaining access to the blocked word or name (Kausler, 1994).

In sum, older adults may be somewhat slower than young adults to retrieve semantic memories from long-term storage. Ultimately, however, they are usually just as capable as young adults of doing so and there is every reason to assume that semantic memory remains intact in older adults (Craik, 1994).

Episodic Memory   **Episodic memory** refers to memory for events and experiences that occurred at a specific place or time. A good example of episodic memory would be the ability to remember which words were on a list that was shown to you an hour, a day, or a week ago when you were in a class.

Table 5.2 shows a list of 15 words that individuals might be instructed to study for some period of time such as 60 seconds. Later, they will be asked to say or write down as many as they can remember. This is a test of episodic memory because the words that individuals must remember are those that they viewed on a list shown at a specific time.

Most likely, episodic memory will be better for the words on the list shown in Table 5.2 if individuals use an organizational strategy when they study it.

Table 5.2	A Sample of 15 Words Used to Test Long-Term Episodic Memory

Pear	Milk	Apple
Oak	Pine	Birch
Shoe	Hat	Gloves
Cat	Dog	Horse
Train	Car	Bus

One strategy would be to organize the list items according to categories that are based on semantic knowledge (word items on the list in Table 5.2 are food, trees, clothing, animals, or means of transportation). Thus, semantic memory, or knowledge, can be helpful in situations that call for episodic memory.

Episodic memory is not limited to lists of words. Sometimes we must remember locations, such as where we put our keys or glasses, or where we parked our car at the mall. Older adults often remark that forgetting of this type is particularly bothersome and stressful. In a controlled laboratory study, Cherry and Jones (1999) instructed young and older research participants to view 36 small, colorful pieces of dollhouse furniture, which were placed on a flat surface. Participants were told that after the items were removed, they would be asked to reconstruct the arrangement as best they could by placing each item back in its correct location. Half the young and half the older adults viewed the furniture items on a background that consisted of a schematic six-room floor plan. That is, typical living room items (couch, coffee table, fireplace) were placed in one room, nursery items (high chair, playpen, hobby horse) in another room, and so on. The other half of the young and older adults viewed the same items, but without the schematic floor plan background. Overall, the young adults replaced more items in correct locations than the older adults did, so there were age-related differences in memory for the spatial location of the items. However, the organizational structure provided by the schematic floor plan was helpful for both young and older adults. Supplying meaningful organizational cues that could be used to associate items with one another resulted in improved spatial memory for both age groups.

Another type of episodic memory that plays an important role in the daily lives of both young and older adults is memory for actions and activities. Examples are remembering whether you took your medicine, turned off the oven, paid a bill, mailed a letter, or locked the front door when you left the house. Memory for actions and activities differs from memory for a list of words because when we perform actions and activities, we do not usually make a deliberate attempt to remember them. Even though memory for actions and activities may not be intentional, it is still considered episodic because such memories are for specific actions or activities performed at a specific time and place.

Some older adults report that they have difficulty remembering whether they actually performed actions such as turning off the oven or locking the door or whether they only thought about performing them. But do older adults actually have more difficulty with this distinction than young adults do? To answer this question, researchers have conducted laboratory studies in which the nature and the duration of a series of activities can be controlled. In some studies, activities involve motor movements such as putting rubber bands on a tube. In other studies, the activities are more cognitive, such as solving word puzzles or arithmetic problems. In general, individuals of all ages have more accurate memory for motor activities than they do for cognitive activities. Overall, however, there are age-related differences in activity memory. In summarizing the findings of laboratory studies on activity memory, Kausler (1994) concludes that young adults recall a greater proportion (about 75 percent) of the activities they performed, whereas older adults recall a smaller proportion (about 60 percent).

Is memory better for activities or tasks that are difficult, or is it better for activities and tasks that are easy? One study (Earles & Kersten, 1998) found that level of task difficulty had the opposite effect on young and older adults. Young adults remembered difficult tasks better than easy tasks, whereas older adults remembered easy tasks better than difficult ones. Difficult tasks may create anxiety for older adults, and anxiety may hinder their memory. Clearly, further research is needed to establish the source of age-related differences in memory for actions and activities and why there is an age-related reversal in memory for difficult and easy tasks.

Noncontent Attributes of Episodic Memory

Some aspects of episodic memory are considered to be noncontent attributes of the particular episode or event that has occurred. Noncontent attributes supplement information in the episode, but in most instances there is no conscious intention or effort to remember them (Kausler & Kausler, 1996). Examples of noncontent attributes are remembering where, when, or from whom an item of information was acquired (source memory), remembering whether one event occurred more recently than another (temporal memory), and remembering how frequently a specific event occurred (frequency-of-occurrence memory).

Source Memory   Source memory is remembering where, when, or from whom an item of information was acquired. You heard that a movie playing at local theaters is excellent, but where did you obtain this information—from a television show, a radio program, the local newspaper, or a magazine you read in the waiting room of a doctor's office? You heard that an acquaintance is ill, but who told you this? At a party, you are introduced to somebody you remember having met before, but you cannot remember where. Somebody told you a funny joke, but who? Embarrassment will certainly follow if you repeat the joke to the person who originally told it to you. All of these are examples of source memories.

In the laboratory, source memory has been investigated by presenting items of factual information from more than one source. For instance, half of the items are presented using an overhead projector, while the other half of the items are read aloud. Later, study participants must identify the source by which they were exposed to each item. Another example is having half the items read by one investigator and the other half by a second investigator. On a subsequent test, are young adults more accurate than older adults in identifying which investigator read each fact? While older adults are somewhat less proficient in source memory, the difference between young and older adults is relatively small (Kausler, 1994). Very poor source memory may indicate problems with frontal lobe functioning of the brain (Kausler, 1994).

Temporal Memory   Events occur within a context of time, and **temporal memory** is another noncontent attribute of episodic memory. How good is memory for when events occurred or the order in which they occurred? Which day of the week did you do your grocery shopping, put gasoline in your car, get a haircut? Can you remember which of these events occurred earlier and which happened later? Temporal memory has been tested in controlled laboratory studies by showing study participants a lengthy series of words or by having them perform a series of actions (for example, raise your right arm, point to your nose, and so on). Later, study participants are asked which of two words or actions appeared more recently in the series or which action they performed first. In some studies, participants must reconstruct the order in which words or actions occurred. When the reconstructed order is compared with the actual order, there is clear evidence for an age-related deficit in temporal memory. Patients who suffer from pathology in the frontal lobes of the cortex have been found to exhibit special difficulties when performing temporal memory tasks (Schacter, 1987). Possibly, age-related deficits in temporal memory are related to some deterioration in the frontal lobe area of the brain which may occur as a function of the aging process (Kausler, 1994). However, the exact reason for the age-related deficit in temporal memory awaits further investigation.

Frequency-of-Occurrence Memory   Another noncontent attribute is the frequency with which events have occurred. How many times have you heard, seen, done, or otherwise experienced a particular event? In the past six months, how many times have you rented movies to view on home video? How many times have you attended movies in the theater? In general, individuals are accurate when they make relative frequency judgments (for example, in the past six months, I viewed movies on home video more often than I saw movies in the theater). They are somewhat less accurate when they are required to make absolute frequency judgments (in the past six months, I have rented movies exactly 15 times and I have gone to the movie theater exactly 10 times).

In controlled laboratory investigations of **frequency-of-occurrence memory**, a common method is to present a long series of word items. Some words occur only once in the series, while others occur two, three, or more times. Later, study participants are asked which of two word items occurred more frequently (relative judgments), or they are asked how many times one particular word occurred (absolute judgments). Presumably, frequency-of occurrence is a noncontent attribute of information that is acquired incidentally rather than intentionally since no conscious effort is made to remember how often something has happened. Nonetheless, people are usually accurate in their memory for frequency-of occurrence.

Hasher and Zacks (1979) distinguished between information we make a conscious and intentional effort to remember as opposed to information we remember incidentally, or "automatically," without any conscious effort. Presumably, conscious effort takes up space in working memory. The capacity of working memory may diminish with age, which could explain why older adults often do less well than young adults do on tasks that require effort. In contrast, incidental, automatic memory may bypass working memory (Kausler, 1994), so there should be little or no age-related decline on tasks that call for automatic processing.

Initially, the idea that some kinds of memory are incidental and automatic was tested by focusing on noncontent attributes such as frequency of occurrence. In early studies, frequency-of-occurrence memory seemed to be immune to decline with normal aging (Kausler & Kausler, 1996). The somewhat circular conclusion drawn was that frequency-of-occurrence memory is automatic, and because automatic memory does not use up any working memory capacity, no age-related deficit should be found in frequency-of-occurrence memory. Indeed, age-related deficits are not usually found when frequency judgments are relative (that is, which of two words occurred more frequently on a long list of words?).

Although frequency judgments were originally presumed to be automatic and therefore unrelated to age, further studies found modest age-related deficits when frequency judgments are absolute (that is, exactly how many times did a specific word appear on a long list of words?). This called into question the idea that frequency-of-occurrence memory is truly automatic (Kausler, 1991). Additionally, age-related deficits have been found for source memory and temporal memory, both of which were initially thought to be automatic rather than effortful. Furthermore, when research participants are specifically instructed to remember noncontent attributes of episodic events (such as their source, timing, or frequency), their memory for these attributes often improves. This suggests that memory for noncontent attributes may not be completely automatic and therefore may be susceptible to the reduced working memory capacity in older adults (Kausler, 1994).

Stages of Processing in Episodic Memory

Three stages of processing are thought to take place in episodic memory: encoding, storage, and retrieval. **Encoding** is related to input, or placing memory traces into the long-term store. **Storage** refers to retaining memory traces in the long-term store. **Retrieval** is related to output, or recovering memory traces from the long-term store when they are needed. Which stages of processing are vulnerable and which may be immune to the effects of aging?

Encoding   As items of information are encoded, or prepared for entry into the long-term store, memory traces must be established. The quality of these traces depends upon how the information was encoded. Encoding can be *rote* or it can be *elaborative*. With rote encoding, the individual might simply repeat, or rehearse, the items over and over again until they are placed into storage. Traces formed with rote encoding probably lack the unique characteristics that make items of information memorable because simple repetition does not involve the effort that would be required to process the meaningful characteristics of the information.

In contrast, elaborative encoding entails processing the unique, meaningful characteristics of the items so that their traces are more distinctive. Elaborative encoding can be verbal or visual. With verbal encoding, the individual could organize items of information into meaningful categories. For example, the 15 items in Table 5.2 fall into one of five categories—food, trees, clothing, animals, and means of transportation. By making the effort to categorize the items on the list, the individual would be forced to think about their meaning. With visual encoding, the individual could use imagery to try to remember items of information. For example, to remember the items of clothing in Table 5.2, it might be helpful to visually imagine getting dressed to go out in the morning, putting on shoes, a hat, and gloves. The distinctive memory traces that result from either verbal or visual encoding will probably be more accessible, or easier to get out of storage, later compared to traces formed by simply repeating items over and over again.

Why do older adults usually remember fewer items than young adults do after they study a list such as the one in Table 5.2? One hypothesis is that older adults are less likely than young adults to use elaborative encoding. Instead of categorizing the items on Table 5.2 or forming visual images that link several of them together, older adults may simply repeat each one several times ("shoe, shoe, shoe"). Rote rehearsal is less likely than elaborative encoding to result in distinctive memory traces that will be easy to access later. In sum, when older adults are free to use whatever encoding strategy they wish to, they are less likely than young adults to encode information elaboratively and they are more likely to use rote encoding. Does this mean older adults are unable to encode information elaboratively?

Inability to encode information elaboratively is termed **mediation deficiency**. However, being able to encode elaboratively but failing to do so spontaneously is termed **production deficiency**. Studies have shown that older adults may not take the initiative to encode elaboratively. However, when given structure and guidance, usually with specific instructions on how to do so, they are capable of using elaborative encoding strategies and at the same time of improving their memory scores. Thus, older adults have a production deficiency rather than mediation deficiency. It is possible that young adults are more accustomed to encoding information elaboratively because they must do so to do well in school. Most older adults are not students, so they may be less accustomed to using elaborative encoding and they may need to be instructed to do so. An additional consideration is that compared to rote encoding, elaborative encoding requires more cognitive effort, or uses more cognitive resources. Some researchers have proposed that with aging, cognitive resources are reduced. This might explain why older adults do not expend effort on elaborative encoding unless they are prodded to do so (see Light, 1991).

Storage The long-term store is conceptualized as a bin, or storage space, where memory traces are kept for a long time, often permanently. Presumably, the capacity of the long-term store is unlimited and the normal aging process does not affect the sturdiness of the storage bin. Once memory traces are entered into storage, they should be maintained there. Thus, with normal aging, there is little reason to believe that memory traces will be lost from the long-term store. However, memory traces will be most accessible if they are placed into the long-term store in an organized fashion.

Before we proceed to discuss retrieval, let's use a computer software analogy. Assume for a moment that you have numerous documents you wish to store on the hard drive of your computer. Also assume that your computer has ample storage space, so storing a large number of documents presents no problem because your hard drive will never be filled to capacity. Furthermore, unless you are unfortunate enough to have the hard drive on your computer "crash," you can be fairly confident that your documents will not be lost from storage and that any document placed into storage will remain there intact and undamaged. Nonetheless, if you intend to store numerous documents on your hard drive, you must assign a name to each document that describes what it contains. If the name you give the document is only generally descriptive, then you may be forced to retrieve many documents before locating the one you want. The more documents you store on your hard drive and the less specific their names, the more time consuming it will be to find the one you need.

The ease with which a document can be located in storage will be determined not only by the way the documents are named but also by how they are organized on your hard drive. You may discover that creating folders on your hard drive to hold documents related to the same course, or to the same project, will expedite your search for a particular document when you need it.

Retrieval After individuals study a list of items such as those in Table 5.2, how well can they retrieve them from storage? To make this determination, several different kinds of memory test can be used: recall, cued recall, or recognition. On a **recall** test, individuals study a list of items and afterward are told to say or write down as many as they can remember. On a **cued recall** test, individuals study a list of items and afterward are told to say or write down as many as they can remember, but they are supplied with hints, or cues, to guide their retrieval. On a cued recall test for items on Table 5.2, they might be asked, "What foods were on the list?", "What trees were on the list?", and so on.

A **recognition** test could take two forms. One would consist of a series of multiple-choice items. Individuals might be presented with two items (milk, juice) and asked to select the one that appeared on the list they just studied. Another test of recognition would display items one at a time. Individuals would be instructed to respond "yes" or "no" to each one, depending on whether or not they remember its having been on the list they studied. Of the 30 or 45 items displayed, only 15 items would actually be from the list they studied.

Regardless of age, most people remember, or retrieve, the smallest number of items on recall tests and the largest number of items on recognition tests. The number of items retrieved on cued recall tests falls in between.

Figure 5.3   Hypothetical Percentage Correct for Young and Older Adults on a Test of Recall, Cued Recall, and Recognition

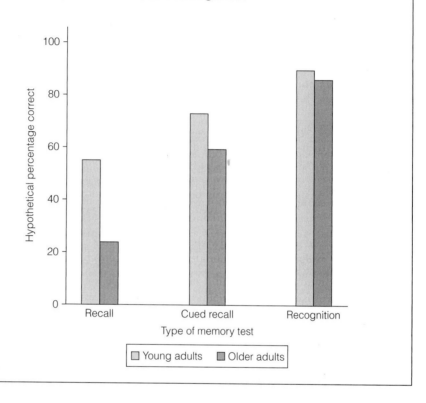

Is there an interaction between age and type of memory test? Yes, the type of memory test makes a bigger difference for the scores of older adults than it does for the scores of young adults. The scores of young and older adults show the greatest discrepancy on a recall test, with older adults recalling fewer items. On a cued recall test, there is less discrepancy in the scores of young and older adults, although older adults may not recall quite as many items as young adults do. On a recognition test, there is very little and perhaps no difference in the scores of young and older adults (see Figure 5.3).

Researchers have long sought to determine whether the source of age-related decrement in episodic memory is at the stage of encoding or whether it occurs during retrieval. Recent thinking is that encoding and retrieval cannot always be differentiated into separate and distinct processes. Cognitive resources are necessary for encoding and retrieval, and if the later years bring a reduction in cognitive resources, older adults will be at a disadvantage for both.

One theory is that retrieval is the attempt to recreate the original pattern, or context, that was present when information was encoded (Craik, 1994). If so, then the greater the similarity between the context at times of encoding and retrieval, the more environmental support will be available to aid remembering. According to the *encoding specificity* principle (Tulving & Thomson, 1973), memory will be best when the same information is available at the time of encoding (the encoding context) and at the time of retrieval (the retrieval context). In other words, memory performance will be optimal when encoding and retrieval conditions are compatible (Kausler, 1994). On recognition tests, the items present at the time of encoding are actually present at the time of retrieval. The presence of the same items at the time of retrieval reinstates the encoding context, creating a great deal of environmental support for retrieval. Individuals of all ages benefit from environmental support to aid the retrieval of information that was encoded earlier, although this support may be especially beneficial for older adults.

Unlike recognition tests, recall tests do not reinstate the encoding context, so recall tests do not offer environmental support that would aid in the retrieval of previously encoded items. To reinstate the encoding context, individuals will have to engage in "self-initiated" processing, which requires the use of cognitive resources. Self-initiated processing seems to be more difficult for older adults, and perhaps for this reason, age-related decrements are most apparent when self-initiated processing is necessary. If older adults have reduced cognitive resources compared to young adults, they will experience greater difficulty on memory tests that call for extensive effortful self-initiated processing.

Are all older adults equally vulnerable to memory difficulties when there is little environmental support for retrieval? Craik, Byrd, and Swanson (1987) compared the scores of four different groups of people who took memory tests under four different conditions of support. Three of the groups consisted of older adults with an average age of 74. The "Old 3" group was low in socioeconomic level, verbal ability, and community social activity. The "Old 2" group was low in socioeconomic level and verbal ability, but they were socially active volunteers in the community. The "Old 1" group was high in socioeconomic level, verbal ability, and social activity. The fourth group consisted of young adult college students who were high in both verbal ability and social activity.

Participants from all four groups studied a list of 10 words (for example "lark"), with words presented at the rate of one every three seconds. Participants in a high-support condition (cued-cued) received cues for each word both at the time of encoding ("A type of bird: lark") and at the time of retrieval ("A type of bird?____"). Participants in the no-support, free learning-free recall condition (free-free) viewed the 10 words without any cues and then tried to recall them without any cues. Participants in the two intermediate-support conditions (cued-free and free-cued) were given cues either at the time of encoding or at the time of retrieval, but not both. Not surprisingly, the combined performance of the four groups was highest in the cued-cued condition and lowest in the free-free condition. However, the availability of cues at time of encoding and/or retrieval had a different effect on the three old groups, particularly when their scores were compared to those of the young group. With high support (cued-cued), the Old 2 and Old 1 groups recalled just as many words as the young group did, but the Old 3 group lagged behind. To bolster their memory performance at all, the investigators needed to give the Old 3 group support both at the time of encoding and at the time of retrieval, and even then the Old 3 group did not reach the level of the other groups. Thus, intermediate support did not help the Old 3

Figure 5.4

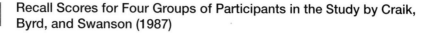

Recall Scores for Four Groups of Participants in the Study by Craik, Byrd, and Swanson (1987)

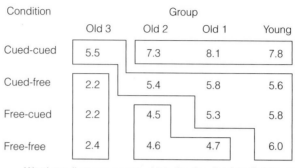

Condition	Group			
	Old 3	Old 2	Old 1	Young
Cued-cued	5.5	7.3	8.1	7.8
Cued-free	2.2	5.4	5.8	5.6
Free-cued	2.2	4.5	5.3	5.8
Free-free	2.4	4.6	4.7	6.0

Word recall scores grouped into four levels of performance.

From Craik, Byrd, and Swanson, "Patterns of memory loss in three elderly samples," *Psychology and Aging, 2,* 79–86, 1987. Copyright © 1987 American Psychological Association. Reprinted by permission.

group, but it did help the Old 2 group and it was especially beneficial for the Old 1 group. In fact, the scores of the Old 1 group were at the same level as the scores of the young group regardless of whether cues were given at the time of encoding or retrieval. These findings, shown in Figure 5.4, illustrate that the greater the environmental support (thus, the less the need for self-initiated processing), the closer older adults' memory performance will be to that of young adults. But just as important, the higher the older adults' level of cognitive and social functioning, the closer their episodic memory performance will be to that of young adults.

REMOTE MEMORY

We assume that the long-term memory store can hold information for a lengthy time, perhaps permanently. Even so, a distinction is sometimes made between long-term memory and very long-term, or remote, memory. There are many anecdotal reports of older adults' outstanding memory for information from long ago even though their memory for more recent episodic information is less accurate. Older adults themselves often claim that their memory for very dated information is excellent despite difficulties remembering what happened the day before. Ribot's Law (1882), which states that information is forgotten in the reverse order in which it was acquired, has become a stereotype regarding the pattern of age-related memory decline (Erber, 2001).

Researchers have investigated whether very dated information is spared despite the age-related decline that is often found for memory of more recent episodic information. Studies have tested **remote memory** for informational facts as well as memory for personal, autobiographical information that goes back decades (Erber, 2001).

Factual Information

Remote memory for factual information includes memory for long-ago political and sports events as well as memory for movies, television shows, and songs that were popular decades earlier. In general, it is difficult to assess remote memory for factual information because exposure to such information took place in the real world and not under strictly controlled laboratory conditions. It cannot be certain that all individuals in a particular age cohort received the same exposure to specific facts earlier in their lives. For example, older adults who were avid moviegoers in previous decades may have excellent memory for the popular movie stars from earlier times. Older adults who had little interest or opportunity to see movies during that time naturally would not have had direct exposure to such information in prior decades. Similarly, it is difficult to determine whether older adults obtained factual knowledge from direct experience with episodes and events when they actually happened, or whether they simply read or heard about these things years later.

Studies conducted on memory for the names and faces of high school classmates (Bahrick, Bahrick, & Wittlinger, 1975) and for the names of streets in a college town that alumni have not visited for many decades since graduating (Bahrick, 1979) indicate a fairly rapid rate of forgetting within 4 to 6 years after the information was acquired. After that, however, forgetting levels off, and 20 to 40 percent of the information is retained. Thus, this type of information is not immune to forgetting. Still, it is remarkable that the portion of information that is retained holds up into late adulthood without any further loss (Kausler, 1994).

Autobiographical Information

Autobiographical information includes memory for the details of personal events such as proms or weddings that took place decades ago. Older adults often say that they have very clear memories of such events, but it is not always possible to check the accuracy of their memories. Aunt Alice may remember that the menu at her wedding dinner 50 years earlier included beef tenderloin. However, if the information could be checked, it might be discovered that her wedding dinner actually was chicken. Each time we retrieve our memories of events and experiences that are meaningful to us, we may embellish them. Over time, our memories may come to represent what we believe rather than what actually happened.

The Reminiscence Bump

Despite the difficulties in studying remote memory, both scientists and nonscientists have been intrigued by the possibility that memories for events and experiences that occurred during a particular period of a person's life might be considered more important and perceived as more vivid than memories from other periods. Some research findings indicate that older adults' strongest and most vivid memories are for events and experiences that occurred between the ages of 10 and 30. This phenomenon, termed the **reminiscence bump** (Jansari & Parkin, 1996), seems to hold for both factual and personal information.

The period from ages 10 to 30 is the time during which older adults saw their favorite films, read their favorite books, listened to their favorite music, and considered world events to be most important. Older adults judge their memories from this period to be more important and more vivid than memories from other periods of their lives (Rubin, Rahhal, & Poon, 1998). Rubin et al. (1998) demonstrated that older adults were most accurate in their answers to multiple-choice questions about Academy Awards, the World Series, and current events that occurred during this period in their lives compared to other periods. Moreover, they found the same reminiscence bump when they tested a different sample of older adults 10 years after they tested the first sample. This means that the reminiscence bump phenomenon is not confined to one cohort of older adults. Other researchers have also reported evidence for a reminiscence bump in older adults. When adults in their 30s are told to recall memories from any time period in their lives, they are more likely to report recent memories than they are to report more remote ones. In contrast, older adults told to recall memories from any period in their lives show a preference for old memories over newer ones (Jansari & Parkin, 1996).

Several explanations have been suggested for the reminiscence bump phenomenon (Rubin et al., 1998). One is that older individuals have the most vivid memories for events that occurred from late childhood to early adulthood because during this particular span of life there is rapid change, which is followed by a period of relative stability. Rapid change may foster elaborative encoding of novel events, which will then be retrieved on a regular basis in the more stable period that follows. Another possibility is that the period from age 10 to young adulthood is an especially important one for developing a sense of identity. During this time, novel and varied social contacts lend themselves to the formation of vivid memories. It is also possible that many cognitive abilities, including memory, reach a peak during this time span. The reminiscence bump may simply reflect the high quality of the memory traces that people encode during this period compared to traces they encode later on in their lives.

In sum, there is much interest in remote memory. It is difficult to test how accurate such memories are, but based on what is known and what older adults say, memory for very dated events and experiences is relatively well-maintained over a long time. There is some evidence that memories are most vivid for the age period between 10 and 30. Further research replicating the stronger and more vivid recall of events that occurred during the late childhood and young adult years should bolster our confidence that the reminiscence bump is truly a robust phenomenon.

MEMORY IN EVERYDAY LIFE

Thus far, we have focused on retrospective memory, which is memory for information acquired in the past or for events that occurred in the past. However, sometimes we must remember to do something in the future. Also, there are many things we make a deliberate effort to remember, but sometimes past experiences affect our behavior even though we are not consciously aware of it.

Such memories are implicit rather than explicit, and these two types of memory may be associated with different parts of the brain. People who experience difficulties with everyday memory can be trained in techniques that will help them improve their performance. Finally, everyday functioning depends heavily upon discourse memory, which is the ability to remember language materials that we have either read or heard.

Prospective Memory

Prospective memory is remembering to perform some action at a designated future point; this type of memory plays an important role in everyday life. For example, we must remember to stop at the grocery store for milk and eggs on the way home from work. We must remember to pay bills, mail letters, make phone calls, schedule appointments with doctors and dentists, and make dates with friends. And of course we must remember to keep those appointments and dates. We try to remember to send birthday cards to friends and relatives, or at least to call them on special occasions. The term *absentmindedness* is often used to refer to prospective memory failures (Kausler & Kausler, 1996). Some prospective memory failures, such as forgetting to turn off burners when we finish cooking or forgetting to take medications at the scheduled times, can have serious consequences. Prospective memory is important for people of all ages, but it seems to be particularly crucial in determining older adults' ability to maintain their independence.

Although there is ample evidence for age-related decrement in retrospective memory for episodes and events, research on age and prospective memory is relatively recent and the findings have been mixed. Some studies report older adults' prospective memory is equivalent or even superior to that of young adults, while other studies have found evidence for age-related decline. Ability level, often measured by level of education or scores on a vocabulary test, is an important factor, especially for older adults (Cherry & LeComte, 1999). Educated older adults with high verbal ability perform similarly to young adults on tests of prospective memory. In contrast, less educated older adults with low verbal ability often perform less well than young adults do.

How is prospective memory measured? The tasks used to test prospective memory vary considerably across studies, which could be another reason for the contradictory findings as far as age-related differences. Prospective memory tasks can be performed in a controlled laboratory setting or in a naturalistic setting outside the laboratory. Also, prospective memory tasks can be event-based or they can be time-based (Einstein & McDaniel, 1990).

Event-Based Tasks   In event-based prospective memory tasks, individuals must remember to perform a particular action in response to a specific external cue. One example of a laboratory event-based prospective memory task would be requiring individuals to remember to press a certain key on a computer keyboard when a particular symbol appears on the screen. An example of a naturalistic event-based prospective memory task would be using a calendar as the external cue for which activities are scheduled or which appointments must be kept on a given day. Of course, this would assume that detailed reminders have been noted on a calendar that is readily available. Event-based prospective memory tasks tend to show little, if any, age-related decline as long as these tasks do not have to be performed against a background of many other activities. In fact, older adults often perform better than young adults do.

Time-Based Tasks   In time-based prospective memory tasks, individuals must remember to perform an action at some point without the benefit of any external physical cues. One example of a laboratory time-based prospective memory task would be requiring study participants to make a note of what time it is when they complete a series of questionnaires or tasks. In the laboratory, time-based tasks are more likely than event-based tasks to show age-related differences. Indeed, age-related decrement has been noted not only between the young adults in their 20s and older adults in their 60s, but also between older adults in their 60s and older adults in their 80s (Rendell & Thomson, 1999). Thus, the ability to perform time-based tasks in a controlled laboratory setting seems to decline increasingly with age. The most likely reason is that time-based tasks provide less environmental support and require more self-initiated processing, which seems to be more difficult for older adults than it is for younger adults.

In everyday life, a naturalistic time-based prospective memory task would be remembering to attend a meeting or keep an appointment on a certain date and time when there is no physical reminder. Researchers have tested time-based prospective memory in naturalistic settings by instructing individuals to carry out specific tasks at prescribed times within their daily lives. For example, young and older adults have been asked to make phone calls to the researcher or leave messages on the researcher's voice mail at designated times, or to mail postcards to the researcher on certain days. In these studies, older adults perform better than young adults, who more often neglect to make phone calls or mail postcards when they are supposed to. In other studies, the performance of young and older adults has been equivalent. Why do older adults often perform just as well and sometimes even better than young adults do in naturalistic time-based studies, given the age-related decrement found on laboratory time-based tasks? One possibility is that prospective memory is influenced by motivational factors. If individuals want to remember something, they will find a way to do it. For tasks performed in a naturalistic setting, older adults may feel more pressure to comply and they may be more motivated to conform to task demands (Kausler, 1994).

However, motivation may not wholly explain why older adults do as well or better than young adults under these circumstances. Rendell and Thomson (1999) point out that naturalistic time-based prospective memory tasks can be integrated into people's everyday lives. More specifically, there are opportunities to use conjunction cues to connect the requirements of the prospective memory task with daily activities carried out in a familiar environment. The more routine the activities of daily life, the easier it may be to integrate the requirements of a prospective memory task. Older adults may have a more routine pattern of daily activities than young adults do. If so, it could be easier for older adults to integrate a time-based prospective memory task into their daily routine using conjunction cues to connect the prospective memory task with regular events that occur during their day.

An important factor to consider is that most of the prospective memory tasks studied thus far have provided clear advanced notice of what is required. With regard to real-world prospective memory tasks, individuals know ahead of time that certain errands must be run or certain medications must be taken, and they can prepare a strategy for embedding these tasks into their daily routine. Less is known about prospective memory tasks that crop up unexpectedly and may be difficult to integrate into the daily routine. Further study is needed to determine the relative performance of young and older adults on crop-up as opposed to routine prospective memory tasks (Rendell & Thomson, 1999).

Another factor to consider is the content requirements of prospective memory tasks. It is one thing to remember to stop at the grocery store on the way home from work, but it is just as important to remember what you need to buy. It is one thing to remember you have a medical appointment, but it may also be important to remember that on the morning of the appointment you must skip breakfast or you must remember to bring your medical insurance card. This aspect of prospective memory also awaits further study.

Finally, actions are not always performed immediately after the intention to do them is retrieved. In the real world, there may be a delay between the time we remember to perform a prospective memory task and the time when we are actually able to execute it. Such a delay may be brief. For example, it may occur to you when you get out of bed in the morning that you must remember to take your medication right before you eat breakfast. But will you remember to actually do it 15 minutes later when you reach the kitchen and sit down to eat? In other situations, delays can be lengthy. It may occur to you at 3:00 p.m. that you need to stop at the grocery store on the way home from work, but will you remember to actually do it at 5:00 p.m. when you are driving home? Einstein, McDaniel, Manzi, Cochran, and Baker (2000) found that in laboratory-based studies, there was age-related decline in time-based prospective memory even when delays were brief.

Even so, there is reason to believe that in the real world, prospective memory holds up quite well with age. Older adults seem capable of accurate and reliable performance of tasks such as remembering to keep appointments and take medications (Rendell & Thomson, 1999). However, external cues may become more necessary as prospective memory requirements become more demanding. Remembering to take medications on a prescribed schedule is an especially important prospective memory task in the lives of many older adults. Medication regimens can be complex, especially for individuals in the old-old (75–84) and oldest-old (85+) age groups. If several medications must be taken on varying schedules (for example, take a blue pill at 8:00 a.m., a yellow pill at noon, an orange pill at 4:00 p.m., and another blue pill at 6:00 p.m.), then it will surely become necessary to use an external cue such as a container with compartments for the different pills with times they must be taken. Of course, in order for such a container to be an effective external cue, older adults must remember to load it with the appropriate medications at the same time each morning.

Furthermore, they must remember to take the pill container with them if they plan to be out during the day.

Up to this point, the focus of this chapter has been on explicit memory, which involves the conscious and deliberate recollection of information or events. For prospective memory, people make an effort to remember to carry out certain tasks and activities. For both semantic and episodic memory, traces were encoded previously, and deliberate attempts are made later on to search the memory store to retrieve them. For procedural memory (such as remembering how to ride a bicycle), traces were also encoded consciously at some earlier time. However, procedural memory differs from semantic and episodic memory in that retrieval of traces from the memory store requires little or no conscious effort. Thus, procedural memory bears some resemblance to implicit memory, described in the next section.

Implicit Memory

Implicit memory is memory without any deliberate recollection (Howard, 1996; Zacks, Hasher, & Li, 2000). Thus, individuals may be exposed to stimulus materials that they have no conscious intention to remember. They are unaware that any memory traces were encoded. However, implicit memory is inferred when prior exposure to stimulus materials has an effect on subsequent test performance or on some other kind of behavior even without the individual's realizing it.

How can implicit memory be measured? In tests of implicit memory for words (Howard, 1996), individuals are shown a series of word fragments, each with a blank space for a missing letter. They are instructed to fill in the blank space with a letter that will make the fragment into an actual word. For example, the word fragment s_ap can be made into a word by inserting the letter "l," "n," or "o." Let's assume that one person selects the letter "o," to create the word "soap." On a subsequent task administered later, this same individual is shown a series of four-letter items and instructed to press a key on the left side of a keyboard if the string of letters spells a word and a key on the right side of the keyboard if the string of letters does not spell a word. Implicit memory is inferred if the individual reacts more quickly to the word "soap" than to the words "slap" or "snap." A quicker reaction to "soap" indicates implicit memory for this word, undoubtedly gleaned from the previous word fragment task. Yet, the individual was not consciously aware of encoding "soap" during the word fragment task. In fact, even if the individual reacts more quickly to "soap," than to "slap" or "snap," there is often no awareness of why this occurred.

In another test of implicit memory, individuals are shown a list of words, one of which is rather unusual (for example, "abode"). They are instructed to study the word list and later they are asked to recall and then recognize as many of the words as they can. These are tests of explicit memory, and let us assume that one individual fails to recall the word "abode" and also fails to recognize that it was on the list of words studied previously. On a subsequent word fragment completion task, this individual is presented with "abo_ _" and asked to fill in two letters that will make it spell a word. The word "about" is much more common than the word "abode," so the expectation is that the letters "u" and "t" will be chosen. If the letters "d" and "e" are chosen, then memory for the word "abode" must have been primed by prior exposure even though the individual was unable to recall or even recognize this word on tests of explicit memory and remains unaware that he or she had seen this word on the earlier list.

Especially intriguing to researchers is that older adults often perform well on tests of implicit memory even when age-related decrements are found on tests of explicit memory. Thus, older adults' behavior can be influenced by stimuli in their environment, even though they may not be consciously aware of seeing or hearing these stimuli. When age-related decrements in implicit memory are found, they are generally of a much smaller magnitude than age-related decrements in explicit memory. In other words, there is a dissociation between implicit and explicit memory (Howard, 1996). Such a dissociation is often seen with normal aging, but even for older adults with Alzheimer's disease or other types of dementia, implicit memory holds up better than explicit memory does. Explicit and implicit memory processing may occur in different areas of the brain. If so, then selective preservation of implicit memory may indicate that brain functioning is maintained better in some parts of the brain than in others. What is the relationship between memory and brain functioning, particularly when it comes to aging? The following section briefly reviews what is known about memory, brain functioning, and aging.

Memory and the Brain

Neuropsychology is the study of brain-behavior relationships, and neuropsychologists evaluate how impairments in various areas of the brain affect memory functioning. They often serve on diagnostic teams formed to evaluate whether memory impairment is indicative of organic brain deterioration associated with Alzheimer's disease or some other type of dementia, whether memory difficulties signify depression, or whether memory problems are simply part of normal aging. (Chapter 11 describes dementia and depression in older adulthood.) Neuropsychologists use psychological tests to assess cognitive functioning, including memory. In the past, few such tests were developed specifically for older adults, but in recent years more test instruments with age-appropriate norms are available for assessing older adults. Thus, it is increasingly possible to differentiate cognitive functioning typical of normal aging from that typical of dementia or depression.

A relatively recent field of study, cognitive neuroscience, combines experimental cognitive psychology (laboratory studies of memory) and neuroscience (studies of brain structure and function). **Neuroimaging** techniques, such as magnetic resonance imaging (MRI) and positron emission tomography (PET), are used to measure brain activation while individuals are engaged in various kinds of memory tasks. Such techniques show which parts of the brain are most active while memory tasks are being performed. However, neuroimaging is costly, so it has not been used routinely to study memory in normal older adults.

On the basis of studies that have used neuroimaging technology, including studies of individuals with known brain lesions, the present thinking is that the

Figure 5.5   The frontal lobes and temporal lobes, as well as the hippocampus located in the central portion of the brain closest to the temporal lobes, play a major role in conscious memory. Subcortical structures may be more important for unconscious memory.

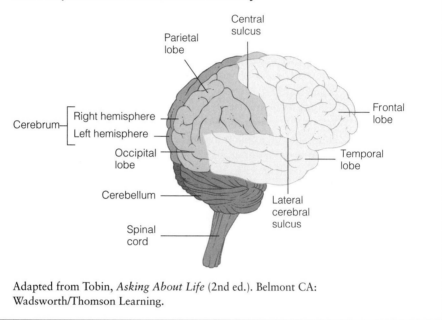

Adapted from Tobin, *Asking About Life* (2nd ed.). Belmont CA: Wadsworth/Thomson Learning.

frontal and temporal areas of the cerebral cortex play a major role in conscious memory. The frontal area seems to be the primary center for working memory, whereas the temporal lobe area (including the hippocampus) is the primary center for long-term episodic memory (West, 1996; Woodruff-Pak & Papka, 1999). Further research is needed to clarify whether patterns of cortical activity differ in young and older adults as they engage in working memory and long-term episodic memory tasks. It is possible that structural and functional changes in different areas of the aging brain are related to specific types of memory decrement even in older adults who are free of dementia or other pathological conditions (West, 1996).

There is evidence that implicit (unconscious) memory is associated more with subcortical structures. The possibility that different areas of the brain are involved with implicit as opposed to explicit memory may explain the dissociation between implicit and explicit memory that has been found in normal older adults and older adults with some pathological conditions.

Memory Training

Older adults often complain that their memory is not as good as it once was. However, they can learn to use strategies that will help improve their everyday memory functioning and at the same time bolster their feelings of competence and self-worth. These strategies generally include mnemonics, the term used for techniques people use to improve their memory.

Table 5.3	Classification of Memory Mnemonic Techniques with Examples of Each	

	Explicit	Implicit
External	Calendars, lists, and notes	Puzzles, maps
Internal	Verbal associations Visual imagery	Spaced retrieval

Camp et al., 1993.

Camp et al. (1993) classify mnemonic techniques along two dimensions: explicit/implicit and external/internal. The explicit/implicit dimension is related to whether the individual is consciously aware of using a mnemonic technique. An explicit mnemonic requires conscious awareness and effort, whereas an implicit mnemonic does not. The external/internal dimension is related to whether a mnemonic technique calls for external aids such as a list or calendar, or whether it relies on internal mental activity such as categorizing information or forming mental imagery. Combining these two dimensions, mnemonic techniques can fall into one of four categories (see Table 5.3).

Most mnemonic techniques that people use are of the explicit/external variety. These involve making a conscious effort to maintain or improve memory by using external cues. Examples of **explicit external mnemonics** are writing reminders on calendars, making lists or notes, using cooking timers, and putting items in a noticeable place. (B. F. Skinner spoke of hanging his umbrella on the front doorknob so that he would be reminded to take it to work.) Many older adults use calendars, lists, notes, and other devices to ensure that they keep appointments, run errands, purchase items, and take medications on the prescribed schedule. Explicit/external mnemonics are especially useful in aiding prospective memory (Lovelace & Twohig, 1990). Apparently, older adults employ explicit external mnemonics effectively because many of them report that memory failures do not seriously hamper their daily functioning (Lovelace & Twohig, 1990). However, adults of all ages use explicit external mnemonics, as evidenced by the popularity of appointment books and more recently of hand-held computers for recording daily agendas, appointments, and phone numbers.

Explicit internal mnemonics are often taught in memory training classes, where people are instructed to form verbal associations and use visual imagery. To remember names, people can make up verbal rhymes to associate names and faces (for example, "Matt is fat;" "Nan is tan"). To remember what items to buy at the store, they can compose a story with all the items in it. Another verbal mnemonic would be to organize items into categories (fruits, spices, dairy products). The acronyms used by many organizations are short-cuts but also serve as a verbal mnemonic (for example, CONA stands for the

This shopper uses a list so that she will not forget to purchase all the items she needs.

Committee on Aging sponsored by the American Psychological Association, or APA).

Visual imagery can be used to mentally retrace one's steps when trying to remember where something was placed (Now, where did I set down my keys when I came home?) or where something was lost (Where was I when I last wore that black sweater that I cannot find?). Visual imagery can be used to remember a recipe that is not written down by visualizing the steps you have followed previously when baking that favorite cake.

The *method of loci* is an old form of visual mnemonic that Roman orators used when they delivered speeches. It involves taking a mental walk through a familiar area such as one's home and mentally placing items that must be remembered in various rooms or locations. Using the method of loci to remember grocery items, one can imagine eggs splattered on the front porch of ones' home, loaves of bread stuffed into the front hall closet, and so on. When at the grocery store, one would simply take a mental walk through one's home to be reminded of which items to purchase.

A large regional mall in Florida frequented by many older adults uses a combination of cues to ensure that customers remember where they parked their cars. Each entrance to the mall is identified with a different species (alligator, seahorse, and so on). At the "alligator" entrance, there is a large figure of an alligator in addition to the name "Alligator" written in green letters. As shoppers step through the alligator entrance, a loudspeaker announces, "This is the alligator entrance." These cues promote both verbal and visual processing, but it is up to the shopper how to use these cues. The cues can be converted to an external explicit mnemonic if the shopper chooses to make a physical note to be stored in a wallet or purse. Alternatively, the shopper can process cues rotely simply by repeating "alligator" over and over again. A more effective, elaborative way to process the cues might be to imagine oneself being chased into the mall by a hungry alligator.

Older adults show less preference for explicit internal aids than they do for explicit external aids (Lovelace & Twohig, 1990). Using explicit internal aids requires a great deal of cognitive effort, although the effort may be worthwhile if external cues cannot be used. For example, when you are being introduced to someone, you may not be able to write down that person's name. Perhaps you can use an explicit internal mnemonic to associate the person's name and face until such time you can write the name down. As described in the earlier discussion of production deficit, older adults may not make spontaneous use of explicit internal mnemonics. However, they can do so when they are encouraged to and given the structure and guidance with memory training.

A question of practical importance in training older adults to use explicit internal mnemonics is whether any immediate positive effects will endure. Here the findings have been mixed (see Cherry & Smith, 1998). According to some reports, the benefit of formal memory training lasts for six months or longer. However, other reports about the long-term maintenance of training effects are less positive. Conclusive statements about the long-term effectiveness of memory training are difficult to make because studies have varied so widely on a number of dimensions. First, the older adult samples in the various studies have differed considerably in the extent of their memory complaints, their motivation to improve, and their level of cognitive functioning at the outset. Second, studies have employed varied training activities as well as different measures of long-term effectiveness. Some periodically retest memory with the same tasks used during training, while others measure the effects of training using new tasks. In any case, Cherry and Smith (1998) recommend that memory training interventions include follow-up to evaluate whether individuals are continuing to use what they learned in earlier training sessions. Also, it is a good policy to offer periodic post-training sessions to refresh and encourage older adults to keep using what they have learned.

In general, mnemonics are devices we use consciously to improve memory. However, mnemonics can also be implicit, or unconscious. Being exposed to an external cue may eventually aid our memory even though we may remain unaware of any connection. One example of an **implicit external mnemonic** is putting together a puzzle of a city map just for fun. Later, you may visit that city and feel a sense of familiarity even though you never made a conscious effort to memorize the layout of the streets or locations of the landmarks when you worked on the map puzzle. Yet by putting together the puzzle, you internalized a cognitive imprint of where things are. Implicit external mnemonics are not usually taught in memory training classes, but they may be helpful for older adults who suffer from cognitive impairment (Camp et al., 1993).

Implicit internal mnemonics make use of unconscious learning that is automatic (requires little or no conscious effort) and does not involve external cues. One type of implicit internal mnemonic is *spaced retrieval*, a method in which successive attempts are made to expand the interval over which information can be recalled (Camp et al., 1993). Individuals are exposed to information and their memory is tested after a set time. If they do not remember the information, they are given feedback about the correct answer and then tested after a shorter interval. Gradually, the interval between feedback and testing is expanded until the information is retained over a longer and longer time. In some instances, implicit internal aids are effective with older adults who suffer from dementia and do not seem able to benefit from explicit mnemonic techniques (see Cherry & Smith, 1998).

In sum, many older adults use explicit external mnemonics effectively. The strategies taught in standard memory training classes are mainly of the explicit internal variety. Training older adults to use these strategies seems to be helpful, but the long-term effects need further study. Implicit memory may be preserved better than explicit memory in normal older adults and may even be spared in older adults with dementia. Thus, interventions of a more implicit nature may be effective when explicit interventions are not.

Discourse Memory

After reading a brief article or listening to a conversation, how much do we remember? Memory for extended language materials, called **discourse memory**, is crucial for everyday functioning. Not surprisingly, memory for spoken language is often impaired when older adults have hearing loss (see Chapter 4 for a discussion of hearing), and memory for spoken and written materials may be negatively affected when older adults suffer from dementia or other neurological disorders. However, what is known about discourse memory in older adults who have no serious sensory or cognitive impairments?

In one study (Wingfield, Tun, & Rosen, 1995), young and older adults listened to tape recordings of spoken paragraph-length passages. Some passages were interrupted, or segmented, by the speaker at natural syntactic boundaries (that is, after sentences or major clauses). Other passages were segmented randomly at linguistically inappropriate intervals that did not occur at natural breaks in sentences or clauses. Not surprisingly, both age groups made more errors in recalling randomly segmented material than they did when material was segmented at natural boundaries. Moreover, age-related differences in recall were small when spoken materials were segmented at natural boundaries. However, older adults were at a greater disadvantage than young adults when they had to recall randomly segmented materials. Older adults may rely especially on their preserved knowledge of language structure to help them compensate for age-related decline in the ability to recall spoken discourse. When natural language cues are taken away, older adults are prevented from using this knowledge to bolster their recall of spoken discourse.

Researchers have used off-line and on-line methods to measure memory for written discourse, or text materials. With the more commonly used off-line technique (Stine, Soederberg, & Morrow, 1996), young and older adults read text materials and afterward take a memory test on what they just read. In general, older adults do not recall as much information from the written text as young adults do. However, age-related differences are smaller when the older adult sample is highly educated.

Fewer studies have used on-line techniques to measure discourse processing. With this approach, young and older adults either read text materials or listen to them being spoken. Measures are made as they are reading or listening. On-line measures make it possible for researchers to compare the strategies used by young and older adults while they are actually processing discourse materials. Stine-Morrow, Loveless, and Soederberg (1996) allowed young and older adults to pace themselves while reading passages on a computer screen; they were told they would be asked to recall the passages immediately afterward. Then Stine-Morrow et al. selected those young adults and older adults who had achieved good recall for the passages and compared the strategies they used. They found age-related differences in how reading time had been allocated. The young adults were more likely than older adults to devote extra time to infrequent words and new concepts when these first occurred in the passage. The older adults allocated their time more evenly as they progressed through the passage.

In some on-line studies of text processing, eye movements are tracked as discourse materials are processed. In the future, more researchers may study brain activation patterns (using the MRI and PET scans mentioned earlier) as individuals process discourse materials (Kemper & Mitzner, 2001). Such investigations should further our understanding of how young and older adults allocate their cognitive resources as they process both written text and spoken language.

Another aspect of discourse memory is how well young and older adults remember general themes, or ideas, from stories and narratives and also how well they remember precise details. Both age groups generally have better recall for themes than they do for details, which suggests that priority is given to ideas. Young and older adults usually have a similar level of memory for general themes, but older adults remember fewer details than young adults do. Age-related decrement in memory for discourse details becomes more noticeable when the capacity of working memory, or processing load, is strained (Stine et al., 1996). Processing load becomes strained when the familiarity of the material decreases, the grammatical complexity of the material increases, and the speed at which materials must be processed increases. However, an interesting contrast is that, when asked to describe various episodes and events that they themselves have experienced, the narratives of older adults are often more detailed that those of young adults (Kemper, 1995). Thus, while there is age-related decline in memory for the details of a story individuals have heard or read, some language skills actually increase with age (Kemper, 1995).

In sum, age-related decline has been noted when off-line measures are used to evaluate discourse memory. The decline is more pronounced when older adults are less educated and when they are prevented from using natural language features to help them remember. Further research using on-line measures as individuals process discourse materials should be helpful in determining the reason for age-related differences. Most people, especially older adults, are more likely to remember the theme than the details of discourse materials. Nonetheless, older adults often give more detailed narratives when describing episodes or events that they themselves have experienced.

KNOWLEDGE AND BELIEFS ABOUT MEMORY

What do people believe about memory in general and what do they know about their own memory system? Additionally, what do they think of their own memory capabilities? Memory is an important part of self-image, and self-evaluations about memory are often associated with emotional responses. For example, we may feel proud when we can remember something and embarrassed when we cannot. Complaints about memory are common among older adults, and the beliefs they hold about their own memory capabilities could affect their actual memory performance. Moreover, in some cultures people hold stereotypes about memory and age. How do such stereotypes influence the judgments people make about the competence of a young or older adult who forgets? Ultimately, stereotyped expectations about age and forgetfulness could influence how older adults feel about their memory and could even affect their actual memory capabilities.

Metamemory

If asked, most people would say that multiple-choice tests are easier than essay tests, and they would estimate that a highly associated word-pair such as "up-down" would be easier to remember than an unrelated word-pair such as "bus-knee." Most people would also agree that making a list helps them remember what they need at the grocery store. **Metamemory** refers to an inherent understanding about how the memory system works. Metamemory probably influences memory monitoring, which is more directly related to self-knowledge about one's own memory contents and processes (Light, 1991).

Researchers have questioned whether young and older adults differ in their beliefs, perceptions, and knowledge about how the memory system works. If older adults have a less accurate understanding, they may fail to engage in encoding or retrieval strategies that would help them remember. If they are deficient in monitoring their own memory processing, they might fail to use their cognitive resources when memory situations call for them.

Older adults are not as adept as young adults are in gauging their readiness for taking a memory test. For example, Murphy, Sanders, Gabriesheski, and Schmitt (1981) found that older adults did not take all the time allowed for studying materials on which they knew they would be tested later. Yet, their memory scores on such tests were lower than the scores of young adults.

When the older adults were then required to study the materials for additional time, they improved their scores to the level attained by the young adults. When left to their own devices, older adults may not realistically assess how much time they would have to study to obtain the best possible memory score (Kausler, 1994). However, despite older adults' lesser ability to gauge their test readiness, they are similar to young adults in their knowledge of how memory works and their beliefs about which memory tasks would be easy and which would be difficult (Light, 1991).

Memory Self-Efficacy

Bandura (1977, p. 191) defined self-efficacy as the conviction that one can successfully execute the behavior required to produce an outcome. **Memory self-efficacy** is related to metamemory and memory monitoring, but it refers specifically to a self-evaluative system of beliefs and judgments regarding one's own memory competence and confidence in one's own memory abilities (Berry, 1999). Berry, West, and Dennehy (1989) devised a Memory Self-Efficacy Questionnaire (MSEQ) to measure individual differences in this variable. For example, individuals rate how confident they would be (10 to 100 percent, in increments of 10) that if someone were to read them a list of 12 items two times, they would be able to remember a specific number of items (for example, 4, 6, 8, 10, or all 12).

West, Welch, and Thorn (2001) examined the effect of setting goals on memory self-efficacy and actual memory performance. On an initial baseline list-learning trial, young and older adults studied a 24-item shopping list and then recalled as many items as they could. Following the baseline trial, but before the next list-learning trial, some participants were asked to set a goal that they would consider difficult but not impossible to achieve. For example, the goal for an upcoming trial might be, "I will work to remember 7 out of every 10 items, or 70 percent." The rest of the participants, the control group, were not asked to set a goal prior to any of the trials. West et al. found that goal setting had a positive effect on feelings of memory self-efficacy and also on actual memory performance. However, the benefits of goal setting were somewhat greater for the young adults than they were for the older adults. Thus, while goal setting seems to be a positive strategy, the fact that older adults did not benefit as much from it as did young adults raises some question about whether age-related differences in memory can be totally explained by older adults' lower self-efficacy.

In another study, Riggs, Lachman, and Wingfield (1997) classified older adults into one of two categories based on their responses to a self-report inventory regarding beliefs about control over their own cognitive performance. Half the sample was classified as *internal* to reflect their strong belief that they could exert control over their own cognitive performance. The other half was classified as *external* because of their weak belief that they had any power to impact their cognitive performance. Then all participants listened to tape-recorded passages of meaningful spoken prose. They were told to listen to only as many words as they thought they would be able to recall with 100 percent accuracy. At that point, they were to stop the tape and recall as many words as they could from the segment they had selected. Allowing participants to stop the tape at points of their own choosing gave them personal control over the size of the segments they would attempt to recall. Riggs et al. found that recall was higher when the selected segments were smaller. They also found that the internals often chose segments that were well within their capacity for accurate recall. In contrast, the externals tended to choose segments that were longer than their capacity for accurate recall. Thus, the internals were better able to gauge their own capabilities and thus to exert the control necessary to achieve the best performance outcome possible. These findings remind us that there are individual differences among older adults concerning feelings of personal control over performance outcomes. Those who feel they have control may be more apt to expend cognitive effort to make effective use of their working memory capacity. It would seem that older adults stand to profit from memory training that devotes some attention to developing their sense of internal control over cognitive performance and their feelings of self-efficacy in memory-related situations.

Only further research will establish more clearly how memory self-efficacy and feelings of personal control are related to actual level of memory performance and whether a change in one will change the other. Assessing self-efficacy and feelings of control in young and older individuals who perform well as opposed to poorly on memory tasks should result in a more complete picture. Meantime, the search continues for the reasons age-related decrement is so often found on memory tasks.

Memory Self-Evaluations

A great deal of information about age-related differences in memory self-evaluation comes from responses to self-report questionnaires on which young and older adults rate their own memory (Cordoni, 1981; Erber, Szuchman, & Rothberg, 1992). However, in some studies, young and older adults keep diaries in which they record each time they forget something (Cavanaugh, Grady, & Perlmutter, 1983). With both self-report ratings and diary keeping, older adults typically report experiencing everyday forgetting more frequently than young adults do. This finding substantiates older adults' complaints that their memory is not as good as it once was. However, most studies have been cross-sectional so they did not follow the same individuals from their young to older adult years and therefore they do not measure individual changes in memory over a long time.

It may seem surprising that older adults' complaints about their memory do not always reflect their actual performance on objective memory tests. Sometimes older adults report memory difficulties, yet they perform well on objective memory tests. In longitudinal studies that follow older adults over several years, changes in objective memory performance do not necessarily correlate with self-reports of decline. There could be several explanations for why memory complaint and memory performance do not always coincide. One is that some older adults may sense a decline from an earlier level memory functioning even though their objective performance remains within a normal range. Another is that older adults' memory complaints may reflect depression, sadness, or other emotional difficulties having to do with health problems or general feelings of inadequacy.

Verhaeghen, Geraerts, and Marcoen (2000) investigated the relationship between memory complaints, coping behavior, and feelings of well-being among older adults in Belgium. Study participants rated themselves on an abbreviated version of the Metamemory in Adulthood (MIA) Questionnaire (Dixon, Hultsch, & Hertzog, 1988), which is a self-report instrument that measures people's beliefs about their own memory. Based on sophisticated statistical analyses of the older adults' responses on the MIA, Verhaeghen et al. proposed a theoretical model whereby memory complaints set in motion an appraisal mechanism that leads to heightened anxiety and concern about memory. This anxiety and concern motivates individuals to employ instrumental and/or cognitive coping strategies. Instrumental strategies include using memory mnemonics such as making lists or forming visual imagery. Cognitive strategies involve making social comparisons ("At my age, everyone experiences memory troubles from time to time"). Ultimately, these coping strategies lead to feelings of well-being. However, Verhaeghen et al. made an interesting discovery when they evaluated individual differences among their older participants. Those who had feelings of internal control about their memory ability (who felt that they could act effectively to change it) were more likely to implement coping behaviors in response to perceived memory difficulties than those who felt they had little control. Because coping behaviors seem to be the key to feelings of well-being, Verhaeghen et al. recommend that a basic component of any memory training program for older adults should be fostering feelings of internal control.

However, not all self-evaluation studies have found that older adults suffer inordinately when they experience everyday memory failures. Erber, Szuchman, and Rothberg (1992) asked young and older adults to rate how much discomfort and annoyance they would feel at experiencing eight different kinds of memory lapses. One week later, these same individuals rated how frequently they actually do experience each of these same types of memory failure. Older adults reported a higher frequency of forgetting than did young adults. Yet older adults reported feeling less annoyance and less discomfort with these lapses in comparison to young adults. Older adults may acknowledge that their memory has deteriorated with age, but often neither they nor their spouses believe this represents any particular handicap in everyday life (Sunderland, Watts, Baddeley, & Harris, 1986).

Stereotypes About Memory and Aging

What do most people believe about memory and aging? According to a variety of research studies, people think forgetting increases with age, and they expect older adults to be forgetful (Bieman-Copland & Ryan, 1998; Heckhausen, Dixon, & Baltes, 1989; Ryan, 1992; Ryan & Kwong See, 1993). In one study (Erber & Danker, 1995), participants (labeled "perceivers") who were employees of a large company were told to imagine themselves as a manager of a hypothetical company that was under pressure to cut costs. In that role they had to assess a supposed subordinate employee (labeled "target"), who was described as having memory difficulties that were creating problems for the company. The perceivers predicted that these memory difficulties were more likely to continue when they were told the target employee was age 62 rather than age 32, and they were more likely to believe that the 32-year-old target's memory difficulties would simply resolve themselves.

Kwong See, Hoffman, and Wood (2001) asked an important question in the real-world context of a courtroom, where juries often make their decisions based upon the testimony of eyewitnesses: Are older eyewitnesses perceived through stereotypes about old age? Young adult undergraduates at a Canadian university gave higher honesty ratings to a female witness described as 82 years of age than they did to a female witness described as 28 years of age. Even so, the older witness was rated as less competent than the young witness was. These researchers concluded that an association between incompetence and old age may compromise the believability of older witnesses.

But are older adults themselves affected by stereotypes about aging that are either positive or negative? There is evidence that they may well be. A study by Levy (1996) suggests that subliminal activation of positive or negative self-stereotypes about old age can actually influence older adults' memory performance. Older adults took a battery of memory tests, which served as a baseline measure of their memory performance. Then they were given a 10-minute implicit priming task designed to expose them to self-stereotypes about aging without their awareness. Participants were told that their motor and attention skills were being measured and that they should press a key to indicate where on the screen they saw a flash of light. In actuality, the light flashes consisted of words designed to activate either negative (decline, dependent, senile, misplaces, dementia, forgets, confused, and so on) or positive (wise, alert, sage, learned, advice, creative, insightful, and so on) stereotypes of old age. However, the words were flashed so quickly that participants were not consciously aware of seeing anything other than flashes of light. Following this priming task, participants took another battery of memory tests. The astounding finding was that older participants who had been implicitly primed with positive words improved in their memory performance. In contrast, those implicitly primed with the negative words did worse. Apparently, the priming activated self-stereotypes, which in turn seemed to affect actual memory performance. When Levy repeated this procedure on a sample of young participants, the implicit priming task had no effect on their actual memory performance. She concluded that implicit priming of self-stereotypes is effective only when the stereotype is relevant to an individual's self-image.

However, different cultures may have different views about aging, and older adults may be debilitated in memory functioning only when they are expected to have poor memory according to a cultural stereotype. Levy and Langer (1994) investigated whether negative aging stereotypes, which may contribute to age-related decrement in memory performance, are more characteristic of some cultures than of others. They recruited young and older study participants from the following three groups: (1) American hearing individuals from the Boston area; (2) American deaf individuals from the Boston area who were members of a deaf organization; (3) Chinese hearing individuals who lived in the Bejing area and were either employed by or retired from the same factory. Levy and Langer hypothesized that a negative age stereotype would be strongest in the American hearing culture and weakest in the Chinese hearing culture, which has a long tradition of honoring its elderly population. Because the American deaf culture lies outside the mainstream, Levy and Langer anticipated there might be a more positive view of aging than would be found in mainstream American hearing culture. Indeed, on a measure of attitude toward aging, the American hearing sample was least positive, the Chinese sample was most positive, and the American deaf culture fell in between. When Levy and Langer administered a series of explicit memory tests, they found that the young samples from the three cultures all performed at a similar level. However, the old Chinese and old American deaf samples outperformed the old American hearing sample. In fact, the old Chinese sample performed just as well on the memory tests as the young Chinese sample did. Levy and Langer concluded that negative stereotypes about cognitive aging contribute to a self-fulfilling prophecy of actual age-related decline in memory. Because the Chinese culture is less likely to hold negative age stereotypes, there may be fewer negative expectations interfering with older Chinese adults' memory performance.

Levy and Langer's (1994) interpretation is appealing, but the findings of other studies are not so clear-cut. Yoon, Hasher, Feinberg, Rahhal, and Winocur (2000) compared the memory performance of young and older adults living in Toronto, Ontario. Half the young and half the older adults were English-speaking Canadians, and the other half in each age group were Cantonese-speaking Chinese individuals who had lived in Canada for less than 5 years. The English- and Cantonese-speaking individuals were matched for socioeconomic factors and self-rated health. Presumably, however, the Cantonese-speaking individuals have a more positive view of aging. Nonetheless, the young adults in both cultural groups outperformed the older comparison group on all four of the memory tests administered. On two of the memory tests, there was no difference in the performance of the two older groups. In sum, these findings do not agree with those of Levy and Langer, who found that memory is maintained better in older Chinese adults. Further investigation is warranted to determine whether and how cultural views about aging influence the memory capabilities of older members.

Attributions for Memory Failure

Studies conducted mainly in American culture indicate that adults of all ages use an age-based double standard when giving reasons, or making causal attributions, for another person's forgetful behavior (Erber, 1989; Erber, Szuchman, & Rothberg, 1990a, 1990b; Erber & Rothberg, 1991). Memory failures are considered more serious and are attributed more to internal stable factors (such as poor memory ability or mental difficulty) when the forgetful individual is old. The identical failures are considered less serious and are attributed more to internal unstable factors (such as lack of effort or lack of attention) when the forgetful individual is young.

Internal stable factors are considered less controllable than internal unstable factors, and behaviors considered less controllable usually engender greater sympathy (Weiner, 1993). Thus, it is not surprising that people have more sympathy for older adults' memory failures than they do for the same failures in young adults. In one study (Erber, Szuchman, & Prager, 1997), young adults were especially sympathetic toward a forgetful older woman whose lifestyle was stereotypically old—she did not work or drive and she ate in restaurants with Early Bird specials. In another study (Erber, Szuchman, & Prager, 2001), young and older adults both thought a store manager would be more likely to believe an older shopper than a young shopper who claimed she forgot to pay for some merchandise before leaving the store. They also thought the manager would be more sympathetic toward the older shopper. Greater sympathy may stem from the higher internal stable attributions for the older shopper's forgetting.

In sum, people use an age-based double standard when making attributions for the memory failures of others. They think an older person forgets because of poor memory ability and mental difficulty but a young person forgets because of lack of effort and attention. Whether this same age-based double standard would be found in other cultures has yet to be determined.

INDIVIDUAL DIFFERENCES IN MEMORY AMONG OLDER ADULTS

Studies that compare the average performance of young adults as a group versus the average performance of older adults as a group often report older adults perform more poorly, particularly on episodic memory tasks. But there are individual differences in memory functioning within the older adult age group.

A number of variables are related to older adults' memory performance (Bäckman, Small, Wahlin & Larsson, 2000; Bäckman, Small & Wahlin, 2001). First, specific chronological age plays a role, with gradual deterioration in memory functioning from the young-old (mid-60s) to the oldest-old (85+) years. Second, while the reasons are not clear, women seem to hold the advantage over men on tests of episodic memory (Bäckman et al., 2001). In addition to chronological age and gender, level of education, lifestyle, and health are associated with episodic memory performance.

Education and Lifestyles Factors

Highly educated older adults perform better on memory tests than do older adults with less education. In addition, lifestyle factors are associated with memory functioning, and older adults who lead active lives—visiting friends, attending parties and meetings, and shopping and preparing meals—usually perform better on memory tests than do older adults who are less active. (Chapter 6 discusses the cognitive performance/activity level relationship in detail.) However, note that a causal relationship between activity level and memory has not been clearly established, so no firm conclusions can be drawn about whether high activity causes good memory or whether individuals with good memory functioning are more active. Furthermore, older adults with more education are likely to be more economically advantaged and therefore have more opportunities to participate in social and other kinds of activities. To the extent that level of education and lifestyle may differ for various ethnic groups, then memory functioning may differ as well. With regard to two other lifestyle factors, the use of alcohol and tobacco, reports have been mixed in determining any link with memory performance. Some researchers have reported small negative associations, others have found no association, and a few have even reported positive associations (see Bäckman et al., 2001).

Health Factors

Health factors have an increasingly important influence on memory functioning, particularly in very late older adulthood (Bäckman et al., 2000; 2001). In fact, for very old individuals who are in optimal physical health, level of education seems to play a less important role in memory functioning (Bäckman et al., 2000). Perhaps those who reach late adulthood with no health difficulties are a highly select group regardless of educational attainment.

Age is associated with increased prevalence of diseases that can affect cognitive functioning, including memory (Bäckman et al., 2000). Older adults with circulatory problems such as hypertension and coronary heart disease perform less well on memory tests than older adults who are free of such health issues. In extreme cases, circulatory problems can result in strokes, which are often associated with cognitive decline. However, even in the absence of diagnosable strokes, less severe abnormalities in circulatory functioning are associated with deficits in memory functioning.

Diabetes mellitus becomes more prevalent in old age and has been associated with deficits in cognitive functioning, especially when the disease is of long duration. Older adults who are not diagnosed with diabetes but have subclinical problems with glucose tolerance also show cognitive deficits, although these are not as great as those found in diabetic older adults (Bäckman et al., 2000). Memory deficits have also been found in older adults who take certain medications and in those with abnormal thyroid functioning and vitamin deficiencies. To the extent there may be a higher rate of such medical difficulties in some ethnic groups than in others, cognitive deficits may be more prevalent in some subgroups of older adults than in others.

Clearly, pronounced memory difficulties are the hallmark of dementia (see Chapter 11 for descriptions of Alzheimer's disease and vascular dementia). Researchers who want to study memory in normal aging often attempt to screen study participants for dementia. However, screening does not always eliminate older adults who are in the earliest stages before dementia has been diagnosed clinically. Thus, some studies may inadvertently include older adults with early dementia whose low memory scores inflate what appear to be age-related differences.

Also associated with memory difficulties is depression (discussed in greater detail in Chapter 11), which is among the most frequent of the emotional, or affective, disorders experienced by the older adult population. Compared to happy older adults, older adults who are depressed complain more about memory difficulties. However, the findings have been mixed about whether depression has a detrimental effect on the actual scores earned on memory tests (Bäckman et al., 2000). Most likely, severely depressed older adults perform more poorly on memory tests than mildly depressed older adults do. Also, depressed older adults have greater difficulty with demanding memory tasks that require elaborate encoding strategies and offer minimal cues when information must be retrieved from storage.

In sum, individual differences in both physical and mental health are an important consideration when it comes to memory functioning in older adulthood. Older individuals who are in good physical and mental health are likely to have fewer memory difficulties than older individuals with health problems.

REVISITING THE SELECTIVE OPTIMIZATION WITH COMPENSATION AND ECOLOGICAL MODELS

Normal aging does not mean decline in all kinds of memory. Rather, age-related decline has been found on some but not all types of memory tasks. Procedural memory is well-maintained with age, as is semantic memory. Thus, memory for how to do things and memory for general information remain intact, but there is some degree of age-related decline on tasks involving short-term working memory and episodic long-term memory. What does this mean in the framework of the Selective Optimization with Compensation (SOC) Model (Baltes & Baltes, 1990), and the Ecological Model (Lawton, 1989; Lawton & Nahemow, 1973)?

With regard to the SOC model, note that well-maintained memory skills can compensate for memory skills that are maintained less well. Semantic memory for word associations and definitions can be helpful for remembering what occurred in specific episodes. Older adults may benefit from training in how to exert control over their own memory functioning by making effective use of explicit external mnemonics such as lists, calendars, and pill organizers. Memory training can also provide tips on how to use explicit internal mnemonics. Successful aging is not the absence of psychological change. Rather, it is better viewed in terms of how older adults deal with change, or how they compensate for change using skills that are retained.

With regard to the Ecological Model, it is important to acknowledge that environmental factors play a role in older adults' memory functioning. For older adults whose memory abilities show signs of decline, the challenge, or press, of the environment may need to be reduced with regard to memory demands. Older adults may need more environmental support to encode and retrieve information. The posting of calendars and activity schedules in many older adult living facilities provide such cues. Also, older adults may need more time to retrieve information from their memory store, so situations that call for quick responses to memory demands should be minimized. Even so, environments should not be devoid of memory demands, as too few memory demands can be detrimental for older adults' cognitive functioning. Opportunities to exercise memory skills as well as physical skills may be especially important for the maintenance of memory functioning.

KEY POINTS

- Using the information-processing model of memory, there are age-related differences in working memory and long-term memory.
- Of the three types of long-term memory, procedural and semantic long-term memory are relatively spared with increasing age. However, there is age-related decrement on episodic memory.
- Of the noncontent attributes of episodic memory, memory for frequency of occurrence holds up well with age when judgments are relative rather than absolute. However, memory for the source of episodic memories holds up less well and the temporal aspects of episodic memory show the greatest age-related deficit.
- Three stages of processing take place in long-term memory episodic memory: encoding, storage, and retrieval. Older adults encode more rotely and less elaboratively than young adults do. However, this is a production deficit because older adults are able to encode more elaborately when they are instructed and encouraged to do so.
- Tests of recall offer the least retrieval support and tests of recognition the most retrieval support, with cued recall falling in between. Age-related differences are greatest on tests of recall and smallest on tests of recognition.
- Remote memories are difficult to test, but they seem to hold up well with age. There is some evidence for a "reminiscence bump" whereby older adults have the best memory for events that happened between the ages of 10 and 30.
- Prospective memory, or remembering to do things in the future, holds up well with age, especially if such memory is event-based rather than time-based.
- Implicit memory (memory without any deliberate recollection) holds up well with age, whereas explicit memory (conscious intentional memory) shows age-related decline.
- Explicit and implicit memory processing may occur in different areas of the brain. The frontal area is the main locus for explicit working memory and the temporal lobe area, including the hippocampus, is the main locus for episodic long-term memory. Implicit memory is associated more with subcortical structures.
- Older adults use explicit external mnemonics to help them remember. Memory training often involves instruction in using explicit internal mnemonics, for which considerable cognitive effort is necessary. Implicit mnemonics may be helpful to older adults who are unable to use explicit ones.
- In discourse memory, older adults recall fewer details when off-line measures are used, but the decline is smaller when older adults are more educated and when they are able to use natural language characteristics to help them remember. More research using on-line measures should help determine whether young and older adults process discourse materials any differently.
- Metamemory is understanding how the memory system functions. Age-related differences in metamemory may account for some, but not all, age-related differences on memory tests.

- Older adults often complain about their memory, but sometimes those who complain perform well on memory tests. Some researchers believe that positive or negative self-stereotypes about old age can actually affect older adults' memory performance.
- In general, people in mainstream American culture hold a stereotype that memory declines with age. They attribute older adults' memory failures more to internal stable causes such as poor memory ability and mental difficulty, while they attribute young adults' memory failures more to internal unstable causes such as lack of effort and lack of attention.
- There are individual differences in memory functioning within the older adult age group. Memory functioning is higher in the young-old than it is in the oldest-old. It is higher in older adults with more education, more active lifestyles, and better physical and mental health.

KEY TERMS

cued recall   177

discourse memory   192

encoding   175

episodic memory   171

explicit external mnemonics   189

explicit internal mnemonics   189

frequency-of-occurrence memory   174

implicit external mnemonics   191

implicit internal mnemonics   192

implicit memory   186

long-term memory store   169

mediation deficiency   176

memory self-efficacy   195

metamemory   194

neuroimaging   187

neuropsychology   187

procedural memory   169

production deficiency   176

prospective memory   183

recall   177

recognition   177

reminiscence bump   181

remote memory   180

retrieval   175

semantic memory   170

short-term memory store   167

source memory   173

storage   175

temporal memory   174

working memory   167

To learn more about the issues discussed in this chapter, point your browser to http://www.infotrac-college.com and use the passcode from the InfoTrac College Edition card that came with your book. InfoTrac College Edition gives you access to complete articles from many different journals.

Intellectual Functioning

6

Views of Intelligence
Fluid Versus Crystallized Abilities
Mechanics Versus Pragmatics of Intelligence

The Psychometric Approach to Intelligence
Brief History of the Test Movement
Psychometric Tests and Aging Research
Intelligence Quotient (IQ)
Cultural Diversity

Does Intelligence Decline with Age?
The Classic Aging Pattern
The Lifespan Developmental Perspective

Maximizing Intellectual Functioning in Older Adulthood
Testing the Limits
Intervention
Compensation
Optimally Exercised Versus Unexercised Abilities

Individual Differences Among Older Adult Test Takers
Factors Related to Maintenance of Intellectual Functioning
Mental Activity and Intellectual Functioning

Everyday Intelligence and Competence
Conceptions of Intelligence Across the Adult Life Span
Cognitive Competence and Psychometric Scores
Encapsulation
Competence in Daily Life

Revisiting the Selective Optimization with Compensation and Ecological Models

Key Points

Key Terms

John is 61 years old and has been an executive at the same company for more than 20 years. He knows that he does not always complete tasks as quickly as some of his younger co-workers do, but he thinks that his expertise in the operations of the company makes up for the fact that it takes him a little longer to learn some of the new technologies. John is planning to retire from full-time employment within the next several years. After he retires, he intends to keep his mind active by consulting part time for other companies and participating in intellectually challenging activities such as playing bridge and chess. John hopes that keeping busy with activities that require him to think will ward off the mental slowness that plagues many seniors.

VIEWS OF INTELLIGENCE

What is intelligence? There is no single answer to this question. The term "intelligence" is used frequently, but intelligence is not easy to define. Generally, however, there is some consensus that individuals with more intelligence seem to learn new things more easily, to have better memories, and to have a more extensive store of knowledge than do individuals with less intelligence (Kausler & Kausler, 1996).

A long-debated question is whether intelligence is one single ability or whether it consists of multiple abilities. An early conception was that intelligence could be defined as one broad, general ability factor referred to as "g" (Spearman, 1927). The "g" factor was thought to underlie more specific ("s") factors that represent the abilities needed for particular verbal, mathematical, and logical reasoning tasks. It was assumed individuals high in "g" would do well, whereas those low in "g" would do poorly on tests of more specific abilities.

However, a more recent view is that intelligence is not a single unitary factor. Rather, it encompasses many different kinds of abilities. Thurstone (1938) proposed that intelligence is made up of the following separate and distinct components, or "primary mental abilities": verbal meaning, number (arithmetic), word fluency, inductive reasoning, spatial orientation, memory, and perceptual speed. Gardner (1983, 1999) proposed eight distinct intelligences (see Table 6.1). A given individual may be stronger in some intelligences than in others.

Rather than thinking in terms of separate and distinct intelligences, Sternberg (1985) emphasizes three components of intelligence that work together: *contextual, experiential,* and *information processing.* With regard to the contextual component, Sternberg argues that the definition of intelligence can vary not only from one culture to another, but also from one period of history to another and from one stage of the life span to another. Thus, what is considered "intelligent" will depend upon the particular culture, the time in history, and the age of the person being evaluated. The second component of intelligence, experiential, means that experience must be taken into account when evaluating intelligence. The way a person approaches a novel task must be evaluated differently from the approach taken to a familiar task, which should be carried out more efficiently than a novel task. For this reason, when a particular task is used to assess intelligence, it is important to know how much prior experience the test taker has had on this or similar tasks. The third

Table 6.1 | Gardner's Eight Intelligences
(after Gardner, 1983, 1999)

Type of Intelligence	Examples
Linguistic intelligence	Reading comprehension, writing, understanding spoken words, vocabulary
Logical-mathematical intelligence	Abstract thinking, reasoning skills, and solving mathematical problems
Spatial intelligence	Ability to understand relationships between objects, to get from one place to another, to read a map, to pack suitcases into a car
Musical intelligence	Sensitivity to sound patterns, ability to compose or play a musical instrument or to appreciate musical structure
Bodily-kinesthetic intelligence	Skills at dancing, athletics, eye-hand coordination, body control
Interpersonal intelligence	Social skills, sensitivity to other people's behavior, motives, or emotions
Intrapersonal intelligence	Self-understanding, understanding one's own feelings and inner life
Naturalistic intelligence	Understanding patterns in the natural world of plants and animals

Adapted partly from Sternberg (2004) and Sigelman and Rider (2003).

component of intelligence, information processing, focuses on the cognitive aspects of intelligent behavior. These include being able to identify a problem and then deploy a strategy to solve it. In this regard, it is important to look not only at how efficiently the problem is solved but also at what processes a person uses to arrive at the correct solution.

A number of questions have been raised with regard to the aging process. Does intelligence mean the same thing (does it represent the same "construct") in older adults as it does in young adults? In addition, what is the developmental course, or trajectory, of intellectual functioning over the adult life span? Does it decline, does it stay the same, or does it improve? If there is age-related decline in intellectual functioning, which abilities are most vulnerable and which are preserved? Are some older adults more vulnerable than others are to age-related decline in intellectual abilities? If age-related decline does occur, can it be reversed? Finally, are there similarities between the intellectual abilities measured by intelligence tests and the intellectual abilities needed for functioning in a job or profession, or even for carrying out the tasks of daily life?

Figure 6.1 | Developmental Course (Trajectory) of Fluid Abilities (Mechanics of Intelligence) and Crystallized Abilities (Pragmatics of Intelligence)

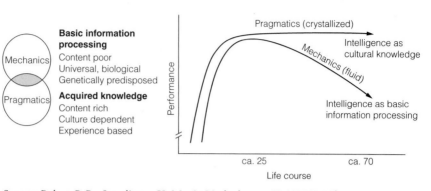

Source: Baltes, P. B., Staudinger, U. M., & Lindenberger, U. (1999). Lifespan psychology: Theory and application to intellectual functioning. *Annual Review of Psychology, 50,* 471–507. With permission from the *Annual Review of Psychology,* volume 50 © 1999 by Annual Reviews. www.AnnualReviews.org.

Fluid Versus Crystallized Abilities

A view that has been prominent in the study of adulthood and aging is that intelligence can be divided into two general categories, fluid intelligence and crystallized intelligence (Cattell, 1963; Horn & Cattell, 1967). **Fluid intelligence (Gf)** is "raw" intelligence, meaning that it is largely a function of the integrity of the central nervous system and is relatively independent of social influences and culturally based learning experiences. It is reflected in abilities such as numerical reasoning and logic. Gf is thought to decline from young to older adulthood.

In contrast, **crystallized intelligence (Gc)** is intelligence that is a function of education, experience, and exposure to a specific cultural environment. Gc is reflected in verbal and informational abilities that were learned in school or acquired from exposure to a particular culture. Gc is thought to be maintained or to increase somewhat from young to older adulthood.

Mechanics Versus Pragmatics of Intelligence

Baltes and his colleagues (Baltes, 1993; Baltes, Dittmann-Kohli, & Dixon, 1984) proposed a dual-process model of intelligence that builds upon the fluid-crystallized distinction. The dual-process model consists of the mechanics and the pragmatics of intelligence. The **mechanics of intelligence** are similar to fluid intelligence (Gf) and include basic operations such as perceptual processing of sensory input, comparing and categorizing information, and carrying out basic memory functions. As with Gf, the mechanics of intelligence are assumed to be genetically and biologically controlled and to depend on basic, physiologically determined brain functioning. The mechanics of intelligence have been likened to the hardware of the mind (Baltes, 1993) and they generally show gradual age-related decline.

The **pragmatics of intelligence** are similar to crystallized intelligence (Gc) and have been likened to the software of the mind (Baltes, 1993). The pragmatics of intelligence include culturally based factual and procedural knowledge. Specific examples are skills in reading and writing, comprehension of language, and skills in both social and professional domains. With increasing age, there are more opportunities for exposure to sources of pragmatic knowledge. The dual-process model emphasizes the possibilities for age-related cognitive growth in pragmatic intelligence and the idea that strong pragmatic abilities can compensate for age-related decline in the mechanics of intelligence.

Figure 6.1 shows a diagram of the developmental course, or trajectory, of fluid abilities (mechanics of intelligence) and of crystallized abilities (pragmatics of intelligence). Note that crystallized abilities (pragmatics) are maintained and may even increase slightly over the adult life span. In contrast, fluid abilities (mechanics) show gradual decline from a peak reached in early adulthood.

THE PSYCHOMETRIC APPROACH TO INTELLIGENCE

The psychometric approach to intelligence emphasizes quantitative measurement. When constructed, psychometric tests are administered to a large representative sample of individuals drawn from the same population for whom the tests are intended. On the basis of the scores earned by this *standardization sample,* test norms are established. Ultimately, the scores earned by an individual test taker can be compared to the test norms derived from the standardization sample. In other words, the individual test taker's score is evaluated in the context of scores earned by the larger, representative sample from the same population.

Note that test norms are appropriately used only when the individual test taker is a member of the same population as the standardization sample. For this reason, norms established on a standardization sample of English-speaking Americans should not be applied to individuals whose native language is not English or to individuals with a different cultural background. Similarly, norms established on young adults cannot be applied to test takers from other age groups.

Test norms must be re-established periodically because over time, the abilities of a population could shift. A standardization sample tested today may attain higher scores on some tests of intellectual ability in comparison to a standardization sample tested 10 or 20 years ago. The possibility that scores attained by members of a standardization sample could be higher now than scores from a standardization sample tested at an earlier point in time has been called the **Flynn effect** (Flynn, 1999).

Brief History of the Test Movement

Before we proceed with further discussion of psychometric intelligence as it relates to older adulthood, a brief history of the test movement is in order. The test movement, which marked the beginning of psychometric testing, began early in the 20th century and eventually came to play a highly influential role in the field of psychology. The basic premise was that tests could be constructed to render a quantitative measure of intelligence. These tests could be administered to individuals, whose scores could be compared with scores attained by a large sample of individuals from the same population.

The test movement had its beginnings in France at the turn of the 20th century when school officials in Paris wanted to develop a test to distinguish between low-achieving Parisian schoolchildren who were lacking ability as opposed to simply lacking motivation. The French government commissioned a psychologist named Binet to develop such a test. In 1905, Binet and Simon constructed the first version of what we now refer to as an intelligence test. This test would serve as a model for many psychometric intelligence tests developed later.

In 1916, a modified version of Binet and Simon's test was devised by Lewis Terman of Stanford University and introduced in the United States. The Stanford-Binet Test was suitable for children as young as age 2 up to adolescents ages 16–18. As with the original Binet test, the Stanford-Binet test consisted of items that tapped the kinds of skills expected to be mastered at various stages of children's and adolescents' formal schooling. Thus, it is not surprising that the scores on this test were fairly successful in predicting academic performance.

Interest in extending intelligence testing to adults led to the construction of the Army Alpha Test, which was developed in 1917 chiefly for the purpose of personnel evaluation and selection of individuals recruited into the U.S. armed forces. The Army Alpha Test could be administered to large groups of individuals at the same time. Items on this test measured abilities in the following eight categories: ability to follow directions, common sense (practical judgment), arithmetic reasoning, number series completion, knowledge of antonyms and synonyms, sentence rearrangement, verbal analogies, and general information. (See Salthouse, 1991, for a more comprehensive discussion of the Army Alpha Test and sample items from each ability category.) Scores on the Army Alpha Ability Test were used to guide decisions about military job assignments and to select the recruits most likely to succeed in officer training and other military training programs. The Army Alpha Test was suitable for testing literate adults. An additional version of the test, the Army Beta, consisted of nonverbal items and was intended for those who could not read (Salthouse, 1991). Interestingly, analyses of the Army Alpha Test scores earned by approximately 15,000 officers indicated a steady decline from the middle 20s through the middle 60s. Subsequently, Jones and Conrad (1933) administered the Army Alpha Test to nonmilitary individuals who lived in New England. They too found that between the ages of 19 and 60, average scores on the test declined. However, this age trend depended upon the type of ability tested. There were only small age-related differences on items that tested arithmetic reasoning, but there was considerable age-related decline on items that tested number series and verbal analogies.

In 1939, Dr. David Wechsler, a psychologist at Bellevue Hospital in New York City, introduced the first individually administered adult intelligence test, the Wechsler-Bellevue. This test was intended to measure the intellectual abilities of adults up to the age of 60. Subsequent revisions of this test, referred to as the Wechsler Adult Intelligence Scale (WAIS), were intended for test takers into their 70s and beyond. (Further details on the WAIS appear in the next section.) Interest in measuring intelligence beyond childhood and into the adult years had truly taken hold in the United States.

Psychometric Tests and Aging Research

Two psychometric intelligence tests have been used frequently in the study of aging and older adulthood: the Primary Mental Abilities (PMA) test and the WAIS. The PMA test can be administered on a group basis, while the WAIS is administered individually.

The Primary Mental Abilities Test   The PMA test (Thurstone & Thurstone, 1947) is based on Thurstone's (1938) factors of intelligence and has been used in a number of studies to measure adult intellectual abilities. Thurstone (1938) proposed that intelligence consists of seven components, each representing an independent factor. Five of these factors—verbal meaning, number, word fluency, inductive reasoning, and spatial orientation—are considered to have the greatest importance in measuring intellectual ability across the adult life span and form the basis of the test used by Schaie and his colleagues in the Seattle Longitudinal Study (SLS). Table 6.2 lists the factors with a brief description of each one (see Schaie, 1989).

The Wechsler Adult Intelligence Scale   The WAIS has been used for many decades to study adult intelligence. In addition, it has been used in clinical settings to assess skills and abilities. The WAIS consists of 11 subtests that fall into two categories: verbal (6 subtests) and performance (5 subtests). Over the years, the WAIS has been revised several times. The most recent version, the WAIS-III (Wechsler, 1997), includes several additional optional subtests. Unlike the PMA, each subtest in the WAIS taps a mixture of cognitive abilities rather than a separate and distinct cognitive factor (see Schulz & Salthouse, 1999, pp. 139–140). Figure 6.2 lists the basic WAIS subtests with an example of the kind of item found on each.

Of the six verbal subtests, four (vocabulary, information, comprehension, and similarities) measure some aspect of verbal ability. The remaining two (arithmetic and digit span) measure numerical ability. In varying degrees, items on the verbal subtests call for the use of stored information acquired from formal education and cultural exposure. On the whole, the verbal subtests tap crystallized abilities, or the pragmatics of intelligence. However, the correspondence is approximate because the digit span subtest taps memory, and the similarities subtest requires reasoning.

The performance subtests tap fluid abilities, or the mechanics of intelligence. In general, the performance subtests call for the solution of novel problems. Most have time limits, and bonus points are awarded for rapid responses. Of the five performance subtests, four (object assembly, picture completion, picture arrangement, and block design) test spatial abilities. Digit symbol is a test of perceptual-motor speed.

On each WAIS subtest, a raw score is calculated based on the number of points earned. The subtests vary in the maximum number of points, so the raw score on each subtest is converted to a scaled score ranging from 0 to 19 with an average of 10. The scaled scores on the six verbal subtests are then added together to obtain a total verbal score. Similarly, the scaled scores on the five performance subtests are added to obtain a total performance score.

Table 6.2 | The Five Primary Mental Abilities (PMA) Factors

Verbal Meaning (V):
Ability to recognize and understand words (passive vocabulary).
Test taker must match each test word with another word from a multiple-choice list that has the closest meaning (synonym).
V is considered a crystallized ability that is acquired and maintained by exposure to formal schooling and culturally determined experiences.

Number (N):
Ability to apply numerical concepts.
Test taker must solve arithmetic problems involving addition and other operations.
N is considered a crystallized ability that is acquired and maintained by exposure to formal schooling and culturally determined experiences.

Word Fluency (W):
Ability to retrieve words from long-term memory using a lexical rule (active vocabulary).
Test taker must write down in a short period of time as many words as he or she can think of that begin with a certain letter.
W is considered partly crystallized, but involves an aspect of fluid intelligence as well.

Inductive Reasoning (R):
Ability to identify regularities and infer rules.
Test taker must complete a letter-series task by choosing which of several letter sequences does not belong: ABCD, WXYZ, BFLK, JKLM.
R is considered a fluid ability since it involves novel problem solving.

Spatial Orientation (S):
Ability to rotate objects mentally in two-dimensional space.
Test taker is shown a geometric form and must select from several choices how that form would look when rotated.
S is considered to be a fluid ability because it involves novel problem solving.

Psychologists have used several different methods to study aging and intellectual functioning. The cross-sectional, longitudinal, and time lag methods of conducting research were detailed in Chapter 2. In cross-sectional studies, there is a comparison of the test scores earned by adults from different age groups, all of whom took the test at approximately the same time. Cross-sectional studies measure whether there are age-related differences in the scaled scores on individual WAIS subtests, on the combined verbal subtests, or on the combined performance subtests.

| **Figure 6.2** | **WAIS Subtests with Sample Item from Each One** |

Verbal Subtests

Vocabulary	Test taker must give oral definitions of words.	For example, "What is the meaning of the word 'persistent'?"
Information	Test taker must answer questions about general information and facts about geography, authors, etc.	For example, "How many miles is it from Kansas City to Washington, DC?"
Comprehension	Test taker must answer questions that require common sense judgments and reasoning.	For example, "Why do people put money into banks?"
Similarities	Test taker must explain the way in which two items are alike.	For example, "In what way are a policeman and firefighter alike?"
Arithmetic	Test taker must solve word problems without using paper and pencil.	For example, "If the price of an item is $30, how much will it cost with a 10 percent discount?"
Digit Span	Test taker must listen to and repeat back a series of orally presented digits in the same order (digits forward). Then test taker listens to a series of orally presented digits and repeats them in the reverse order (digits backward).	For example, "Repeat these numbers: 64395." For example, "Repeat these numbers backward: 58624."

Performance Subtests

| *Picture Completion* | Test taker must identify the element that is missing from each of a series of pictures. | For example, "What is missing from this picture?"

 |
| *Digit Symbol* | Test taker is given a key consisting of digits, each paired with a symbol. The test taker must then write the symbol associated with each digit in a blank box below the digit. Score is based on number of correct digit-symbol substitutions completed within a specific number of seconds. | For example, "Using the key on the left, write the correct symbol below each number without skipping any."

 |

(Continued)

Figure 6.2 | WAIS Subtests with Sample Item from Each One (Continued)

Block Design   Test taker must arrange a number of one-inch red and white cubes to match a design pictured in a diagram.

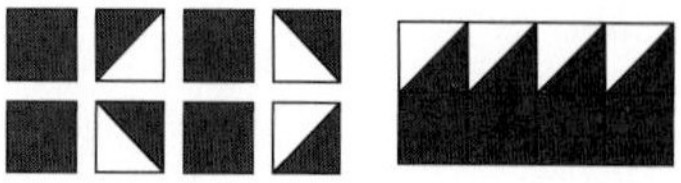

Picture Arrangement   Test taker must arrange series of pictures that are presented in a mixed-up order into a sequence that conveys a meaningful story.

For example, "Arrange these pictures in an order that tells a story."

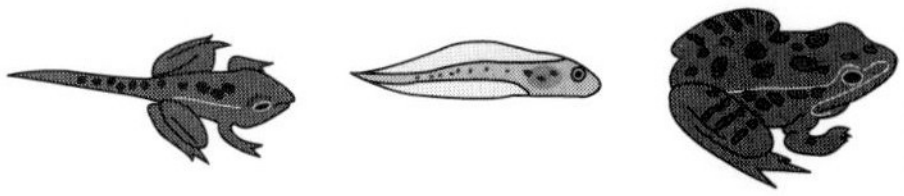

Object Assembly   Test taker must arrange pieces of a puzzle to make a complete meaningful whole, as in a jigsaw puzzle.

For example, "Put these pieces together to make something."

In longitudinal studies, the same individuals are followed and retested several times. Longitudinal comparisons indicate whether there is age-related change within the same individual (that is, intraindividual variability). Longitudinal comparisons of WAIS scaled scores make it possible to assess whether the abilities tapped by the individual subtests, the combined verbal subtests, or the combined performance subtests increase, decline, or remain stable with increasing age.

Time-lag studies on intellectual functioning assess whether there is any difference in the scores attained by individuals of a particular chronological age who take the test at different points in time. For example, one group of 60-year-olds may take a test in 1990 while a different group of 60-year-olds take the same test in 2000. Both groups are the same age, but they differ with regard to the time they took the test (1990 and 2000, respectively) and also with regard to their cohort membership (born in 1930 and 1940, respectively). The time-lag method is useful in establishing whether there are population shifts in abilities, as described earlier with the Flynn effect.

Intelligence Quotient (IQ)

Invariably, discussions of intelligence touch upon the concept of **intelligence quotient (IQ)**. IQ is related, but not identical, to an individual's score on an intelligence test. The way IQ is determined for adults who take the WAIS differs from the way IQ is determined for children who take the Stanford-Binet Test of Intelligence.

Binet's original test and the American version, the Stanford-Binet, were composed of age-graded items that tapped abilities such as counting, reading words, identifying items, and repeating numbers and sentences from memory.

An item intended for eight-year-old children was expected to be passed by most eight-year-old children but by very few six-year-old children. However, an eight-year-old child with below-average intelligence would not be able to pass all of the eight-year-old items. In contrast, an eight-year-old child of above-average intelligence would not only pass all the eight-year-old items, but also would pass some of the items intended for nine- or even ten-year-old children. Built into the test was the assumption that older children would be capable of responding correctly to more items than would younger children. Thus, the number of items answered correctly could be used as an index of mental age (MA). Whether a child of a particular chronological age (CA) was below average, average, or above average in intelligence was expressed with a ratio: MA/CA X100. With this ratio, a child of average intelligence would receive an IQ of 100, a child of below-average intelligence less than 100, and a child of above-average intelligence more than 100.

Unlike the Stanford-Binet intelligence test, the WAIS is not made up of age-graded items, although the items on each WAIS subtest progress from easy to difficult. Rather than defining IQ as the ratio MA/CA X 100, the WAIS uses a deviation IQ to reflect the relative standing of the individual test taker compared to others the same age. In other words, the deviation IQ reflects how the score of an individual test taker compares with the scores of age peers included in the standardization sample.

On the WAIS, a test taker can receive a verbal IQ, a performance IQ, and a full-scale IQ. To obtain a verbal IQ, the sum of the test taker's scaled scores on the six verbal subtests is entered into the verbal IQ table in the WAIS Manual that corresponds to the test taker's chronological age. To obtain a performance IQ, the sum of the test taker's scaled scores on the five performance subtests is entered into the performance IQ table that corresponds to the test taker's chronological age. To obtain a full-scale IQ, the sum of the scaled scores on all 11 subtests is entered into the full-scale IQ table that corresponds to the test taker's chronological age. The IQ scores obtained from these tables are based on the scores earned on the 6 verbal, the 5 performance, or all 11 subtests by the age-appropriate standardization sample. These IQ scores reflect whether the individual test taker is average, above average, or below average, compared to his or her age peers as far as verbal, performance, or total abilities.

The average score earned by the standardization sample in each age group is set at 100. If the number of points that a test taker earns equals the average number earned by age peers in the standardization sample, then the IQ of the test taker is 100. Higher or lower IQs reflect how much, and in which direction, the individual test taker's score differs (deviates) from the average score of age peers in the standardization sample. If the test taker's score is lower than the average score earned by age peers in the standardization sample, then IQ will be less than 100. Alternatively, if the test taker's score is higher than the average score earned by age peers in the standardization sample, then IQ will be greater than 100.

The standard deviation (SD) is a measure of how much individuals in each age group vary around the mean, or average, test score. The bell-shaped curve in Figure 6.3 shows a normal distribution of test scores. In a normal, bell-shaped distribution, 68 percent of the test scores fall between one SD below the mean

Figure 6.3

A Bell-Shaped Normal Curve with a Mean of 100 and a Standard Deviation of 15

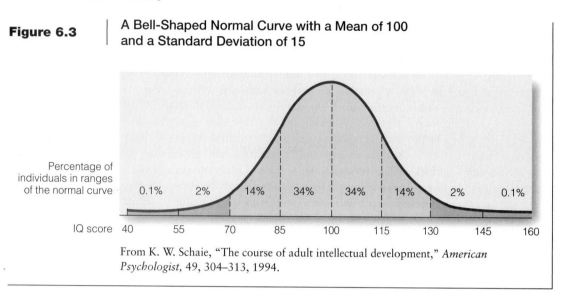

From K. W. Schaie, "The course of adult intellectual development," *American Psychologist,* 49, 304–313, 1994.

and one SD above the mean. If the mean of the normal distribution is 100 and the SD is 15, then 68 percent of the scores earned by individuals in any given age group will fall between 85 and 115.

Cultural Diversity

Psychometric intelligence tests and the concept of IQ have not been without controversy for two reasons. First, it is not always acknowledged that psychometric tests are only meaningful if test takers are members of the population on whom the test was standardized in the first place. Scores on psychometric intelligence tests are of questionable value when the cultural background and experience of the test taker differs from that of the standardization sample. Relatedly, test takers who interpret psychometric test questions as they are expected to by those who devised the scoring system are rewarded with more points than test takers whose answers do not agree with the scoring system. Yet a test taker who earns fewer points may be giving an answer that would be considered "intelligent" in the context of his or her own culture. Cross-cultural comparisons are often used to illustrate this point. Segall, Dasen, Berry, and Poortinga (1999) describe the findings of research conducted in various regions of Africa indicating that children in those cultures are considered intelligent not only if they have cognitive skills such as a good memory, but also if they have manual dexterity and perhaps most important, if they have social skills including cooperation and obedience in carrying out tasks that serve the family and the community.

Second, psychometric tests are only one way to measure intellectual functioning. Some have questioned whether the scores on such tests have ecological validity as a measure of a person's ability to function in the real world (see Chapter 2 for further discussion of ecological validity). Even within the United States, psychometric tests may have greater ecological validity for some groups than for others.

Table 6.3	Four Phases of the Socio-Cultural Process Model of Perspectives on Intelligence over the Adult Years

Phase I: Overriding perspective is that there is a decline in intelligence beyond the 20s. Main theme is identifying what is assumed to be a steep and inevitable age-related decline. Most research cross-sectional.

Phase II: Overriding perspective is that intelligence is not just one entity. Rather, it consists of subcomponents that can either remain stable or decline with age. Greater awareness that age is confounded with cohort in cross-sectional studies.

Phase III: Overriding perspective is a focus on intraindividual variability in intellectual functioning. Also, new interest in how experience (practice, training) can modify intellectual abilities.

Phase IV: Overriding perspective is that there is a need to explore new ways of defining and measuring intelligence. Definitions of intelligence are expanded to include qualitative as well as quantitative aspects of functioning.

Adapted from Woodruff-Pak (1988, 1989).

DOES INTELLIGENCE DECLINE WITH AGE?

The question of whether intelligence declines with age can be approached using what Woodruff-Pak (1988, 1989) referred to as **Socio-Cultural Process Model.** This model offers a framework we can use to follow the evolution of perspectives on aging and intelligence. According to the Socio-Cultural Process Model, research on aging and intelligence is influenced by the dominant perspective during the time studies are conducted. The Socio-Cultural Process Model divides these perspectives into four phases (see Table 6.3) that follow one another in chronological order. Entry into a new phase does not mean that perspectives of earlier phases are completely abandoned, but the perspective of the most recent phase exerts the main influence on which aspects of intellectual development receive the most attention (Schaie, 1996). This chapter focuses on studies closely related to perspectives in Phases I, II, and III. Studies related to Phase IV are covered in Chapter 7.

Phase I extended from the early 1900s, when intelligence tests were introduced in the United States, through the 1950s. During this time span, adult intelligence tests such as the Army Alpha Test and the WAIS were gaining widespread acceptance. Most studies on adult intelligence were cross-sectional, comparing young and older adults at a particular point in time (see Chapter 2 for more detailed discussion of the cross-sectional method). These studies usually demonstrated that older-adult test takers earned lower scores than young adult test takers did. This contributed to the dominant Phase 1 perspective that the peak of intellectual functioning is attained in young adulthood followed by inevitable decline. Research conducted during Phase I focused on finding the point at which the decline began and determining how steep the decline would be.

By the 1960s, the Phase I perspective of decline began to shift, signaling entry into Phase II. Two perspectives dominated in Phase II of the Socio-Cultural Process Model: (1) Intelligence is not just one entity, but rather it consists of individual abilities that vary in their developmental trajectories, and (2) the method used to study age and intellectual abilities makes a difference when assessing the extent of age-related decline. What was previously attributed to age could actually be a function of cohort membership.

With regard to the first Phase II perspective, heated controversy erupted in the 1970s about the developmental course of intellectual abilities from young to older adulthood. One side argued that there is an age deficit in intellectual abilities (Horn & Donaldson, 1976). This argument represents the decline perspective dominant during Phase I. The opposite side of the controversy argued that the age-deficit view of intelligence can only be described as the "myth of the twilight years" (Baltes & Schaie, 1974). The "myth of decline" contenders asserted that intelligence does not decline with age and in fact it may increase. The debate between the proponents of "age deficit" and "myth of decline" opened the door to closer scrutiny of the developmental course of individual intellectual abilities. This is described further in the section on the classic aging pattern.

With regard to the second Phase II perspective, that the method of studying aging and intellectual abilities has an influence on the findings, Woodruff-Pak (1988) cites an early longitudinal study conducted by Owens (1953). Owens located 127 young men who had taken the Army Alpha Test in 1919 at the beginning of their freshman year at Iowa State University. Thirty-one years later, these men, now middle aged, were retested. Owens found a gain in their total scores over the 31-year period. This result contrasted sharply with the Phase I perspective of age-related decline in intellectual functioning, which had been based primarily on cross-sectional research.

Those who still clung to a decline perspective maintained that Owens's sample was a select group—college students who undoubtedly possessed a high level of ability at the outset and had the advantage of completing four years of college education after taking the test the first time. However, they acknowledged that intellectual decline may be less extensive or may occur later when there is a high initial level of ability. Indeed, there is considerable evidence that older adults who are more educated show less age-related decline in intellectual abilities compared to older adults who are less educated. (See Kausler, 1991, pp. 671–672 for a concise review indicating that age-related differences in intelligence test scores are reduced and sometimes even eliminated when level of education is equivalent for young and older age groups.)

On the other hand, the decline supporters also pointed out that Owens's positive findings may have been inflated due to selective attrition, meaning that of the initial group, only the most able members may have returned 30 years later to be tested again. Indeed, selective attrition can result in an overly rosy picture of intellectual functioning because individuals who earned low scores on the earlier test may be unavailable for retesting later. (Chapter 2 discusses the phenomenon of selective attrition in longitudinal studies.) According to Woodruff-Pak (1988), Owens demonstrated that the initial scores of his retested group

Figure 6.4 | Longitudinal Estimates of Mean T Scores for Single Markers of the Primary Mental Abilities

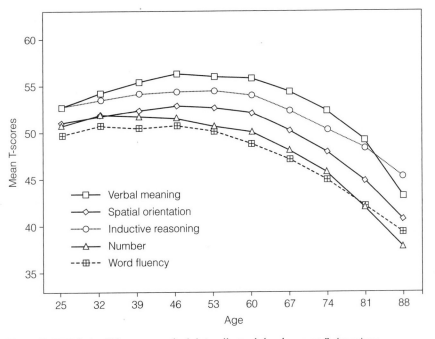

From K. W. Schaie, "The course of adult intellectual development," *American Psychologist,* 49, 304–313, 1994. Copyright © 1994 American Psychological Association. Reprinted by permission.

were unrelated to how much gain there was over the 30 years. Even so, it is not entirely clear whether the retested group may have been positively selected in some way compared to the group who did not return for retesting.

However, recent large-scale longitudinal studies have reported that decline in intellectual abilities is much less extensive and occurs at a much later point than was previously thought on the basis of cross-sectional studies (Schaie, 1996). Findings from the SLS indicate that community-living older adults show very little decline in fluid abilities until their mid-60s. Decline in crystallized abilities occurs much later, often not becoming apparent until the mid-70s (Schaie, 1996). By age 67, most SLS participants showed decline on at least one ability, but by age 88, none of the participants had declined on all five of the abilities that were tested (Schaie, 1989).

Figure 6.4 shows data from the SLS on tests of five primary mental abilities (Schaie, 1994). The curves in this figure were constructed from longitudinal gradients which represent scores earned at 7-year intervals by individuals ranging from 25 to 88 years of age. It is apparent that average scores increase or remain stable until the late 30s or early 40s. Any increases are followed by stability until the mid-50s or early 60s. In the late 60s, some decrement occurs over the 7-year interval, although it is modest until the mid-70s (Schaie, 1996). The decline in scores in these longitudinal gradients occurs later and is less extensive than would most likely be found with a cross-sectional method of research. Not shown in Figure 6.4 are the gender differences in patterns of decline. Women decline earlier on abilities considered to be fluid, whereas men decline earlier on abilities considered to be crystallized (Schaie, 1989, 1990; Schaie & Willis, 1996).

The decline supporters did not emphasize an important point that is now acknowledged more readily: The cross-sectional research method, which formed the main basis for the Phase I decline perspective, confounds two factors: (1) chronological age and (2) cohort, or generation to which study participants belong. It is not possible to determine whether any age differences found between young and older adults are due to their chronological age or to their cohort, or generational, experiences.

It is important to understand that differences between cohorts, sometimes called cohort trends, can be either positive or negative. Cohort trends can occur due to shifts in educational emphasis or for other reasons that are difficult to determine (Schaie, 1996), and such trends affect developmental comparisons. A **positive cohort trend** means that the present-day young adult cohort has a higher level of ability than an older-adult cohort had back in their young adult years. The Flynn effect, mentioned earlier, is an example of this phenomenon. With a positive cohort trend, even if members of an older cohort have not experienced any age-related decline in a particular ability, they still perform at a lower level compared to members of a young adult cohort (Schaie, 1996; Schaie & Willis, 1996). To illustrate, age-related differences are often found on tests of fluid ability. Even though fluid abilities are assumed to reflect the integrity of the central nervous system, it is conceivable that young adults have an advantage over older adults because of their exposure to newly developed technologies. To the extent that a young cohort's technological exposure helps on tests of fluid ability, then the young cohort may score higher than the old cohort would have scored even when young. This positive cohort trend could result in an inordinately negative picture of age-related decline on a particular intellectual ability.

In the case of a **negative cohort trend**, the present-day young adult cohort would have less ability than an older cohort had when young. To illustrate, when older adults were young, their numerical ability may have been higher than the numerical ability of young adults today. Perhaps the older adults' numerical ability was higher because there were no calculators or computers to help them solve arithmetic problems so they had more practice on this kind of task. With such a negative cohort trend, young and older cohorts in a cross-sectional research study might perform at the same level on a test of numerical ability, and thus it may appear that numerical ability remains stable over the adult life span. However, if the old cohort had started out in young adulthood at a higher level, then there may actually be age-related decline in numerical ability.

Clearly, using the cross-sectional method for studying age and intellectual abilities has disadvantages, one of which is difficulty in evaluating the possibility of positive and negative cohort trends. Despite the drawbacks, however, cross-sectional studies are useful for assessing age-related differences in intellectual abilities in the "here and now" with relative efficiency. Even so, cross-sectional research is limited because it cannot answer questions about the developmental course of intellectual abilities within individuals. How do intellectual abilities change over time in any given person, and why do some people change more than others do? Longitudinal research is needed to answer these questions, assuming that selective attrition does not result in inordinate positive bias.

Overall, Phase II of the Socio-Cultural Process Model brought greater awareness that cross-sectional studies would result in a more pessimistic picture of age-related decline in intellectual abilities than longitudinal studies would. Also, Phase II brought a heightened appreciation of the variation in the developmental trajectories of specific abilities over the adult life span. Some abilities decline, some remain stable, and some increase. Before we turn our attention to Phase III of the Socio-Cultural Process Model, the section that follows describes what has been termed the **classic aging pattern** (Botwinick, 1984), which is just another way to describe the developmental course of different types of intellectual ability.

The Classic Aging Pattern

The majority of studies on intellectual functioning over the adult years have found age-related decline in some abilities but not in others. Scores on the WAIS subtests are often used to illustrate the classic aging pattern. In this pattern, scores on the verbal subtests are relatively maintained into older adulthood. Therefore, verbal abilities are **age–insensitive abilities.** In contrast, scores on the performance subtests usually show age-related decline, so performance abilities are **age–sensitive abilities.** Note that "age-insensitivity" and "age-sensitivity" refer to scaled scores and not directly to IQ (which is simply an individual's comparison with age peers).

The most age-insensitive verbal subtests on the WAIS are information, vocabulary, and comprehension (Botwinick, 1984). In general, scores on these subtests hold up well with age and in some instances even increase from young to middle to older adulthood. The abilities tapped by these subtests are honed from formal education and cultural exposure and they fall into the crystallized category (Cattell, 1963; Horn & Cattell, 1967), or the pragmatics of intelligence (Baltes, 1987, 1993).

Among the most age-sensitive subtests on the WAIS are digit symbol, picture arrangement, and block design (Botwinick, 1984), all of which are performance subtests. On average, older adults' scores are lower on these subtests compared to the scores of young adults. Each of these subtests calls for the solution of unfamiliar problems in new ways. As such, they tap fluid abilities, or the mechanics of intelligence, which are assumed to reflect the integrity of central nervous system functioning. The WAIS performance subtests also have time limits or allow bonus points for speed. Because there is some slowing down of responses with increasing age (see Chapter 4 for more discussion of slowing), older adults are at a disadvantage when there are time requirements (Schaie, 1996).

The Lifespan Developmental Perspective

Once again let's turn our attention to the lifespan developmental perspective proposed formally by Baltes (1987) and introduced in Chapter 2. This perspective can be applied to many aspects of development, but it is especially relevant to intellectual abilities. Table 2.1 summarizes the key propositions of the lifespan developmental perspective, but they are listed here in abbreviated form they as they apply to intellectual development.

- Intellectual development occurs over the entire life span.
- Intellectual development is embedded in a historical and sociocultural context unique to each cohort group.
- Intellectual development is multidimensional, multidirectional, and multicausal.
- The study of intellectual development is enhanced by a multidisciplinary approach.
- Intellectual development includes both gains and losses over the life span (although the proportion of gains to losses may fluctuate from young to middle to older adulthood).
- Intellectual development is plastic, meaning that it can be modified with practice or training.

The influence of the lifespan developmental perspective is apparent in Phase II of Woodruff-Pak's (1988, 1989) Socio-Cultural Process Model. The proposition that development is embedded in historical context is evident in the heightened concern with the method used to study the developmental course of intellectual abilities. Researchers were becoming increasingly aware that intellectual abilities are a function not only of age, but also of cohort membership and time of measurement. (See Chapter 2 for further discussion of the roles of age, cohort membership, and time of measurement in developmental research.)

The proposition that development is multidimensional, multidirectional, and multicausal is reflected in the Phase II emphasis on the importance of studying the developmental course of individual abilities and the recognition that specific abilities may be influenced by different sets of factors. The classic aging pattern illustrates the life-span developmental proposition that while aging may entail losses, it may also entail stability and gains.

MAXIMIZING INTELLECTUAL FUNCTIONING IN OLDER ADULTHOOD

The lifespan developmental perspective is apparent in Phase II of the Socio-Cultural Process Model, and it also serves as a bridge between Phase II and Phase III. In Phase III, researchers were beginning to entertain the possibility that intellectual abilities are not written in stone. They were acknowledging that there is plasticity, another key proposition of the lifespan developmental perspective. Abilities can fluctuate over various occasions even within the same individual (intraindividual variability). In addition, abilities can be modified through practice and training.

Testing the Limits

Testing the limits refers to a strategy for investigating both the range and limits of cognitive reserve capacity (Kliegl, Smith, & Baltes, 1989). Researchers who recommend this strategy believe that measuring an intellectual ability on a single occasion does not provide a true picture of the highest possible level of functioning. Even under normal conditions, there is intraindividual (within-individual) variability in level of performance because an individual's scores can fluctuate across occasions of testing. Scores fall within a range, the upper limit of which would be considered the best estimate of that individual's true competence. True competence, which represents the upper limit of cognitive reserve capacity, may be underestimated if a score from only one testing occasion is used. It can only be determined with repeated testing.

Intervention

Not only can intellectual abilities fluctuate across occasions of testing, but there also is reason to believe that abilities can be modified by practice and possibly more so by interventions that entail training. The view that intellectual abilities can be modified is based on the premise of plasticity, one of the key propositions of the lifespan developmental perspective. The idea of plasticity represents an optimistic stance with regard to intellectual functioning in older adulthood. It is especially appealing with respect to fluid abilities, which show greater age-related decline compared to the better-maintained crystallized abilities.

Much of the work on cognitive training studies has been conducted as part of the Adult Development and Enrichment Project (ADEPT) (Baltes & Willis, 1982; Schaie, 1996) as well as the ongoing Seattle Longitudinal Study (SLS) (Schaie, 1996). Most training studies use pretest/post-test designs. Initially, a pretest, or baseline, assessment is made of older adults' abilities. The baseline assessment is followed by up to five hours of training on test-taking strategies, either on an individual or small group basis. On the whole, the effects of training are positive. Older adults who receive training improve their scores on tests of inductive reasoning and spatial abilities, both of which typically show age-related decline. These positive training results have been replicated by researchers in Germany as well in the United States, and the effects of such training have been shown to last for periods of up to seven years (Schaie, 1996).

Although training interventions do yield improved scores on ability tests, several questions remain. First, do training interventions have lasting effects in helping older adults maintain their higher scores on tests that measure these abilities? Thus far, follow-up studies have found that older adults who participate in training sessions on inductive reasoning and spatial abilities are less likely to show decline on inductive reasoning and spatial abilities tests compared to older adults who received no training (Schaie, 1996). Even so, periodic "booster" sessions are recommended to limit any age-related decline that might otherwise occur later (Schaie & Willis, 1996).

Second, does training have a positive effect only on the ability tests on which specific training was given? Or do the positive effects of training generalize to a broader array of abilities that may be similar but not identical? The answer to this question has been mixed and further research is needed.

Third, would similar kinds of training be effective for older minority groups within the United States and for older populations in cultures outside the United States other than in Germany (Schaie, 1996)? Replicating training studies on more diverse samples would make it possible to determine whether or not the positive effects of training generalize to a broader segment of the older adult population. Despite these caveats, there is reason to think that age-related decline in intellectual abilities is not inevitable, and that periodic training holds promise for the maintenance of such abilities (Schaie, 1996).

Although community-living older adults are able to improve their intellectual abilities with training, a question remains as to the meaning of positive training effects from a developmental point of view (Botwinick, 1984). Some have argued that older adults are at a relative disadvantage on certain ability tests because they have had less exposure than young adults to the kind of formal education that would prepare them for such tests. Furthermore, older adults' lifestyle might not call for the use of such abilities as much as young adults' lifestyle does. The fact that older adults benefit from training suggests that the age-related decline found in some types of intellectual abilities can be attributed to lack of experience. If so, practice and training should help older adults more than it does young adults. To test this idea, some researchers have given practice trials to both young and older adults on tests of fluid ability to determine whether practice is more beneficial for older adults. In one such study (Erber, 1976), young and older adults were given a series of practice trials on a digit symbol substitution task similar to the WAIS digit symbol subtest, on which older adults generally perform more poorly than young adults do. Both age groups showed approximately the same level of improvement over trials. The older adults improved with practice, but they started out and ended up at a lower level than the young adults did. The fact that both age groups improved to the same degree and a gap in performance between young and older adults remained even after a series of practice trials suggests that lack of experience cannot completely account for older adults' poorer performance on this task.

Compensation

The life span developmental proposition of multidirectionality states that abilities can show both gains and losses over the life span. However, as described in Chapter 2 and illustrated in Figure 2.1, the proportion of gains and losses fluctuates over the life span (Baltes, 1987). Early in life and through young adulthood, the proportion of gains in intellectual abilities is greater than the proportion of losses. In midlife, the proportion of gains and losses is equivalent. In older adulthood, the proportion of losses outstrips the proportion of gains. Despite the greater proportion of losses in older adulthood, however, gains may be used to offset them. For example, gains in crystallized abilities may

Figure 6.5 | Developmental Functions of Unexercised and Optimally Exercised Cognitive Abilities over the Life Span

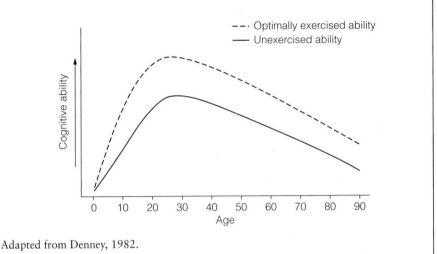

Adapted from Denney, 1982.

compensate for losses in fluid abilities. Similarly, gains in the pragmatics of intelligence may compensate for any losses that older adults experience in the mechanics of intelligence.

Optimally Exercised Versus Unexercised Abilities

Denney (1982) proposed a theoretical framework for considering cognitive development over the life span. In this framework, cognitive abilities fall into one of two categories: (1) untrained, unpracticed, or **unexercised abilities** and (2) **optimally exercised abilities**. The developmental course of unexercised abilities should indicate a normal, healthy individual's capability at various ages, assuming there has been no ability-specific training or practice. In other words, the level of the unexercised abilities reflects the individual's biological potential under normal environmental conditions. In contrast, the developmental course of optimally exercised abilities reflects the maximum ability attainable by a normal, healthy individual who has had opportunities for ability-specific training or practice. Figure 6.5 illustrates the developmental course for unexercised abilities and optimally exercised abilities. Note that at all ages, optimally exercised abilities are superior to unexercised abilities. However, the relative superiority of the optimally exercised abilities is slightly greater in late adolescence and young adulthood, suggesting that practice and training have the strongest positive impact during that period of development. Note that both the optimally exercised and unexercised abilities reach a peak in late adolescence or young adulthood, after which both gradually decline.

However, optimally exercised abilities retain their superiority over unexercised abilities even into older adulthood.

The distinction between fluid and crystallized abilities has been made on the basis of biological versus experiential factors, respectively. In the earlier discussion of the classic aging pattern shown on the WAIS subtests, performance abilities were referred to as fluid, whereas verbal abilities were referred to as crystallized. Denney's framework distinguishes between categories of ability on the basis of exercise, or practice, rather than on the basis of biological versus experiential influences. In American culture, verbal abilities may be practiced more than performance abilities are. Denney's model allows for the possibility that some cultures could call for more extensive exercise of performance abilities than of verbal abilities.

INDIVIDUAL DIFFERENCES AMONG OLDER ADULT TEST TAKERS

Thus far, the focus of this chapter has been on older adults as a group, or on how the intellectual abilities of older adults as a group compare to the intellectual abilities of young adults as a group. However, members of any age group vary on most dimensions, including intellectual abilities. In fact, the degree of variation among older adults is usually greater than the degree of variation among young adults. This means that among members of the older-adult age group, there are considerable individual differences in level of intellectual abilities as measured by scores on intelligence tests. Some older adults perform poorly on such tests, while others earn high scores. Indeed, the scores of some older adults surpass the scores that average young adults earn.

Factors Related to Maintenance of Intellectual Functioning

Maintenance of intellectual functioning in older adulthood is associated with the absence of severe sensory deficits in vision and hearing (Lindenberger & Baltes, 1994). As described in Chapter 4, the link between sensory and intellectual functioning becomes stronger in older adulthood, a phenomenon referred to in Chapter 4 as the common cause hypothesis (Baltes & Lindenberger, 1997).

Longitudinal research has been valuable in efforts to specify variables that are associated with the maintenance of intellectual abilities over time. This information could be highly useful in determining what can be done to minimize the risk of age-related decline in intellectual abilities. Based on findings from the SLS, Schaie (1994, 1996) reported that the following factors are associated with reduced risk of age-related decline in intellectual abilities:

- Absence of cardiovascular and other chronic diseases. Additionally, maintenance of high levels of perceptual processing speed into old age.
- Above-average level of education; an occupational history of high-complexity jobs that do not simply involve routine tasks; above-average income.

- A flexible as opposed to a rigid personality style, as measured by self-reported attitudes as well as by tests that measure flexibility on psychomotor tasks.
- A high level of satisfaction with one's accomplishments in midlife and early older adulthood.
- Membership in an intact family; marriage to a spouse who is well-educated and high in intelligence.
- Engagement in activities such as extensive reading, travel, attendance at cultural events; pursuit of continuing education activities; participation in clubs and professional associations.

Clearly, these factors overlap. Older adults who held high-level, complex jobs often have relatively high incomes in retirement. Those with high incomes are more likely than those with low incomes to live in stimulating environments that offer opportunities for exposure to cultural and educational resources. Thus, it cannot be concluded with certainty that any one factor listed above is a direct cause of a high level of intellectual functioning. Individuals who engage in behaviors known to maintain health and delay the onset of chronic disease and sensory deficits may be the same individuals who have a high level of intellectual functioning. Good health may make it possible for individuals to engage in activities that foster the maintenance of intellectual functioning.

Mental Activity and Intellectual Functioning

What is the relationship between people's mental activities and their level of intellectual functioning? Do older individuals who engage in cognitively challenging activities—for example, reading, attending cultural events, completing crossword puzzles, and playing bridge—have a higher level of intellectual functioning compared to older individuals who do not? The answer to this question appears to be yes.

The **disuse hypothesis of cognitive aging** postulates that skills and abilities get rusty when they are not used on a regular basis. Through disuse, these skills and abilities suffer from decline (see Kausler, 1982; Salthouse, 1991). The cautionary advice, "Use it or lose it!," is frequently given to older adults who are concerned about keeping up their intellectual abilities (Rowe & Kahn, 1998). The corollary to the disuse hypothesis is that practicing cognitive skills can reverse any decline that has taken place or possibly prevent it from occurring in the first place. The **engagement hypothesis** refers to the idea that participation in novel and challenging intellectual tasks is a way to prevent decline in intellectual functioning. Several studies have attempted to determine the accuracy of the disuse and engagement ideas.

The Victoria Longitudinal Study   As part of the Victoria Longitudinal Study (VLS), Canadian researchers tested a large sample of healthy, community-dwelling men and women between the ages of 55 and 86 (Hultsch, Hertzog,

Engaging in complex mentally challenging activities is associated with the maintenance of intellectual abilities in older adulthood.

Small, & Dixon, 1999). At the outset, study participants completed a self-report questionnaire on how frequently they engage in physical activities (such as walking and jogging), self-maintenance activities (such as meal preparation), social activities (such as visiting friends), hobbies and home maintenance activities, and novel information processing activities (such as learning a new language or playing bridge). A significant positive relationship was found between engagement in novel information processing activities and level of verbal intelligence (for example, vocabulary, verbal fluency, and reading comprehension). Individuals who engaged frequently in novel information-processing activities tended to have higher levels of verbal intelligence than did individuals who did not participate in such activities.

However, the question both researchers and nonscientists ask is whether engaging in challenging activities is the key to maintaining a high level of intellectual functioning in older adulthood. By exercising their minds through participation in complex and demanding cognitive activities, can older adults prevent decline in their own intellectual functioning? Extent of engaging in challenging activities and level of intellectual functioning are both organismic variables (see Chapter 2 for further discussion of organismic variables), so finding a positive relationship between them does not allow us to draw conclusions about cause and effect. Even though there is a positive relationship between level of engagement in challenging activities and level of intellectual functioning, we cannot conclude with certainty that engaging in challenging activities actually causes the maintenance of intellectual functioning.

One way to investigate the cause-and-effect question is to follow the same individuals, keeping track of their cognitive activity level and measuring their intellectual abilities at several points over time. We cannot determine whether a high level of cognitive activity causes high intellectual abilities by examining concurrent relationships between cognitive activity level and intellectual ability. However, if the same people are followed and tested several times, sophisticated statistical analyses can estimate whether decline in one of these variables is a precursor to subsequent decline in the other (Schaie & Willis, 1996). That is, does detection of decline in cognitive activity precede detection of decline in intellectual functioning that occurs later? A decline in cognitive activity that occurs before any decline in intellectual functioning would suggest that decline in cognitive activity plays a role in causing intellectual decline.

Participants in the VLS were highly educated men and women and most had high levels of professional and semi-professional occupational attainment. Over six years, these individuals were tested several times on a variety of cognitive measures. Each time they were tested, they also reported their level of participation in mentally challenging activities. By the end of the 6th year, the sample size had dwindled from 487 participants to only 250 participants, although the smaller sample was reasonably representative of the original sample. Statistical analyses did show a relationship between change in level of mentally challenging activities (such as reading novels and playing bridge) and change in level of intellectual functioning. Although this relationship suggests that engaging in mentally challenging activities may have buffered individuals against decline in intellectual functioning. Hultsch et al. (1999) were unable to rule out the possibility that changes in intellectual functioning may have resulted in reduced engagement in mentally challenging activities. In other words, the onset of cognitive decline could limit participation in mentally challenging activities rather than the other way around. Thus, Hultsch et al. questioned the strength of any evidence for an engagement hypothesis, wherein participation in novel and challenging intellectual tasks would actually prevent decline in intellectual functioning.

The Canadian Veterans Study   Other researchers have made stronger claims that an engaged lifestyle has a causal effect on intellectual functioning. Pushkar et al. (1999) used archival data from the Canadian Veterans Study, in which a large sample of working-class men were followed longitudinally. The men in the Canadian Veterans Study lived independently in the community, but their overall health was not as high as the health of the VLS participants. On the basis of statistical analyses, Pushkar et al. were able to show that decreases in cognitive activity were a precursor to cognitive decline. Accordingly, they concluded that across the adult life span, a cognitively active lifestyle does have a small but significant effect on level of verbal ability, and thus that there is some support for the engagement hypothesis.

Note that not only did the study samples differ in the VLS and Canadian Veterans Study, but so did the measures used to determine level of cognitive activity. Hultsch et al. (1999) measured level of engagement in activity strictly in terms of self-reported participation in intellectual activities. In contrast, Pushkar et al. (1999) had a broader definition of an engaged lifestyle that included participation in intellectual activities plus variables related to socio-economic status (SES). High SES is associated with a high level of education and also with complex, challenging work careers. Pushkar et al. contended that educational background and job history provide a context for a cognitively challenging environment over the adult life span. The contrasting conclusions as to cause and effect in these two studies is not surprising given the different participant samples and different ways of defining cognitive activity.

Leisure Activities and Cognitive Functioning   Schooler and Mulatu (2001) investigated the relationship between engagement in complex leisure activities and level of intellectual functioning among a sample consisting mainly of European American men and women (ages 41 to 88) who had participated in a national survey conducted 20 years earlier. When these individuals were located again, approximately 42 percent were gainfully employed and the rest were retired. Schooler and Mulatu's index of participation in complex cognitive leisure activities was based on the following:

1.   Number of books read in past six months
2.   Number of magazines read regularly, as well as the magazines' intellectual level
3.   Frequency of visits to institutions of fine art, as well as concerts and plays within the past six months
4.   Number of special interests and hobbies and amount of time spent on them per month

For those still working for pay as well as those who were retired, there was moderate evidence that participating in complex leisure activities leads to an increase in intellectual functioning. However, Schooler and Mulatu acknowledge that a high level of intellectual functioning could lead to a high level of environmental complexity, which in turn could raise the level of intellectual functioning. They acknowledge that it is not possible to rule out uncontrolled factors that might influence both participation in complex leisure activities and the level of intellectual functioning.

Despite the mixed findings as to cause and effect, there is a positive association between participating in complex and stimulating cognitive activities and intellectual functioning. Thus, it seems reasonable to recommend that adults of all ages engage in intellectually stimulating activities. They should "take on and solve difficult and challenging problems at work and in their everyday lives" (Hertzog, Hultsch, & Dixon, 1999, p. 533). Schooler and Mulatu (2001) maintain that even into old age, participating in complex leisure activities could build a capacity to deal with the intellectual challenges found in complex environments. Rowe and Kahn (1998) strongly recommend intellectual engagement as an important aspect of successful aging. However, it is premature to conclude that engaging in challenging intellectual activities is guaranteed to prevent cognitive decline in old age. Clear identification of the specific antecedent variables that account for the individual differences in older adults' intellectual functioning awaits further research.

EVERYDAY INTELLIGENCE AND COMPETENCE

As described previously, psychometric tests were devised originally to evaluate the likelihood of a child's success in school. Accordingly, items on these tests tapped skills and abilities that were expected to be mastered at various academic levels. In fact, psychometric tests have proven useful for decisions about whether to admit children, adolescents, and young adults to special schools, colleges, and universities. For such purposes, the predictive value of psychometric tests, while not perfect, is often significant. Children and young adults spend a good part of their daily lives in school, so psychometric tests represent a measure of their everyday intellectual functioning.

For adults, psychometric tests serve two important functions. First, they are useful for predicting success in jobs that require educationally based knowledge and skills. With some exceptions, recent laws have abolished mandatory retirement at a set chronological age. This means that workers cannot be forced to retire simply on the basis of age. In the future, employers may make greater use of psychometric tests to evaluate whether workers (regardless of their age) are capable of carrying out the complex tasks necessary for some jobs (Salthouse & Maurer, 1996). Second, psychometric tests have been useful for clinical assessments of neuropsychological status in the older adult population (Botwinick, 1984; Schaie, 1996; Schaie & Willis, 1996). Tests such as the WAIS tap a broad array of abilities, and the scores of an older adult test taker can be evaluated in comparison to the scores attained by others the same age.

Even so, the meaning of psychometric tests for older adults has been called into question. Are psychometric test scores the best or only way to measure intellectual functioning in older adulthood? Most older adults are not full-time students, and many completed their formal education in the distant past. Thus, the ecological validity of psychometric intelligence tests for older adults has been criticized (see Chapter 2 for further discussion of ecological validity). Put simply, psychometric intelligence tests may not measure the kinds of intellectual abilities that older adults need to function well in the real world.

This criticism has led some researchers to consider the possibility that intelligent behavior may not take exactly the same form across the adult life span. In other words, intelligence may be qualitatively different at different points in the life span. The overriding perspective in Phase IV of Woodruff-Pak's (1988, 1989) Socio-Cultural Process Model emphasizes the need for exploring new ways to conceptualize and measure intelligence that go beyond quantitative scores on psychometric tests. The Phase IV perspective has resulted in some new insights about the purpose, meaning, and function of cognition. This expanded view of intelligence has led to interest in studying wisdom, creativity, and everyday problem solving in a social context. Chapter 7 covers these topics.

Table 6.4 | Three Factors Underlying Adults' Conceptions of Exceptional Intelligence, with Examples of Representative Behaviors for Each

Interest in and Ability to Deal with Novelty
Is able to analyze topics in new and original ways
Is interested in gaining knowledge and learning new things
Is open-minded to new ideas and trends
Is able to learn and reason with new kinds of concepts

Everyday Competence
Displays good common sense
Acts in a mature manner
Acts responsibly
Is interested in family and home life

Verbal Competence
Displays the knowledge to speak intelligently
Displays good vocabulary
Is able to draw conclusions from information given
Is verbally fluent

Source: Berg and Sternberg (1992).

Conceptions of Intelligence Across the Adult Life Span

We know something about how psychologists define intelligence. But how is intelligence viewed by people who are not psychologists and have little or no familiarity with psychometric intelligence tests? How do such individuals conceptualize intelligent behavior for a young, middle-aged, and older adult? And does the view that individuals have about the nature of intelligence agree with the lifespan developmental perspective that intelligence is characterized by multidirectionality and plasticity?

To answer these questions, Berg and Sternberg (1992) asked adults of widely ranging ages (17 to 83) to generate examples of behavior that they would consider to be "intelligent" for a 30-year-old, a 50-year-old, or a 70-year-old. Using statistical analyses, Berg and Sternberg determined that the examples given could be categorized on the basis of three factors, which appear in Table 6.4.

Next, Berg and Sternberg found a new sample of individuals, also of various ages, and asked them to describe an "exceptionally intelligent person" age 30, 50, or 70. Their conception of what would be considered "exceptionally intelligent" differed for the 30-, 50-, and 70-year old. "Interest in and ability to deal with novelty" was an important factor for the exceptionally intelligent

30-year-old, but this factor was less important for the exceptionally intelligent 50-year-old and 70-year-old. In contrast, two factors, "everyday competence" and "verbal competence," were considered more important for the exceptionally intelligent 50-year-old and 70-year-old than they were for the exceptionally intelligent 30-year-old.

"Interest in and ability to deal with novelty" is closely related to fluid intelligence (mechanics of intelligence), whereas "everyday competence" and "verbal competence" are closely related to crystallized intelligence (pragmatics of intelligence). In short, these individuals' conception of intelligence over the adult life span was consistent with the classic aging pattern (maintenance of stored information over the adult years but age-related decline in abstract problem-solving abilities) seen on psychometric intelligence tests such as the WAIS.

The majority of Berg and Sternberg's study participants believed that intellectual abilities can either increase or decrease over the adult life span, and 90 percent of them believed that the level of intellectual functioning can be improved with practice and training. Furthermore, most were of the opinion that reading, education, experience, and contact with stimulating people would be associated with increases in intelligence, whereas illness, lack of mental stimulation, or lack of interest in learning would be associated with decreases in intelligence. Overall, then, the ideas these individuals had about intelligence were consistent with the lifespan developmental perspectives of multidirectionality and plasticity. Furthermore, their belief that participating in stimulating activities and social interactions would be associated with increases in intelligence is consistent with the engagement hypothesis, which has been of such interest to aging researchers. For the most part, Berg and Sternberg's study participants were middle-class European Americans. Extending this type of research to a more diverse sample of the U.S. population and other countries would be a way to test the generality of these findings.

Cognitive Competence and Psychometric Scores

As described earlier, cross-sectional studies on psychometric abilities generally find age-related decrements from the decade of the 20s through the decade of the 70s, particularly on tests of fluid ability. In general, however, adults in their 60s and 70s are not less competent than adults in their 20s and 30s. Indeed, many older adults hold responsible and demanding leadership positions.

Salthouse (1990) described the findings of several studies that reported age-related differences in cognitive abilities as measured by psychometric tests, but no age-related differences in cognitive competence outside the psychometric testing situation. In one study, young (21–42) and older (60–79) university faculty members with similar professional specializations took psychometric tests. The scores of the young faculty were higher than the scores of the older faculty. Yet the older faculty members were just as successful as the younger faculty members in their chosen fields. In another study, older business executives earned lower scores than young business executives did on a battery of complex neuropsychological tests. Yet the older executives held high-level managerial positions that called for complex judgments and decisions. Salthouse (1990)

speculates that psychometric tests are more rigorous and demanding and therefore more sensitive to even a slight decrement as opposed to the less stringent
assessments of everyday competence. He offers the analogy that standards for
ranking professional race car drivers are more stringent, or strict, compared to
standards for a passing score on a test for obtaining a driver's license. Indeed,
most real-world situations call for an evaluation of whether a person can function under normal conditions and not whether a person can function at the maximum level under highly demanding conditions.

As described earlier, a key proposition of the lifespan developmental perspective is that individuals experience both gains and losses over the life span. A
corollary of that proposition is that over the adult years, the proportion of gains
and losses can shift (Baltes, 1987). In the later years, the proportion of losses may
be greater than the proportion of gains. Nonetheless, older adults can use abilities that have improved to compensate for any losses. By taking advantage of the
cognitive abilities they have honed (see the section that follows on encapsulation),
older adults can maintain, or possibly even increase, their overall level of competence. This may account for older adults' high level of success in work-related
situations even when their scores on psychometric tests show some loss.
Additionally, competence in work-related situations is often a function not only
of cognitive abilities, but also of interpersonal abilities. The social and interpersonal aspects of cognitive functioning are covered in more detail in Chapter 7.

Encapsulation

According to the **Encapsulation Model** (Rybash, Hoyer, & Roodin, 1986), as
individuals grow older, their knowledge becomes channeled into, or encapsulated within, specific domains. In other words, over the adult years, individuals
are transformed from generalists into specialists by accumulating, organizing,
accessing, and applying knowledge in specific chosen areas. Older adults concentrate on fewer areas, or domains, of intellectual functioning than young
adults do, but they become more efficient at acquiring knowledge related to their
specialized domains. At the same time, older adults become less efficient in
acquiring knowledge that is not related to these specialized, encapsulated
domains.

The Encapsulation Model may explain, at least in part, what appears to be
contradictory evidence: There is age-related decline in speed and efficiency on
fluid psychometric ability tests that require the solution of novel problems. Yet
older adults often function at a high level when their thinking and problem-
solving abilities are assessed within specialized domains of expertise for which
they have learned to use their knowledge and experience.

Competence in Daily Life

There is no simple definition of competence in daily life, but most of us would
probably agree that it entails responding effectively to whatever tasks and
demands are necessary (Schaie & Willis, 1996). To some extent, the tasks and
demands of daily life depend upon an individual's age or stage of life. In young

© PhotoDisc

The expertise required for some specialized skills
and abilities takes years to develop.

adulthood, tasks and demands revolve around school, jobs, and parenting.
Older adults' lifestyles are more diverse, so the tasks and demands of their
daily lives are more variable (Schaie & Willis, 1996). Some older adults enroll
in academic programs, although the student role is less normative in older
adulthood than it is in young adulthood. Some older adults work full time or
part time, but many are retired from paid employment. Some older adults are
involved in parenting roles, although this too is less normative in older adulthood than it is in young or middle adulthood.

For a considerable portion of older adults, competence means being able
to perform the tasks required to meet the demands of living independently. In
the United States, the old-old (75–84) and oldest-old (85+) age groups are
growing at a rapid rate. The majority of adults ages 75 and over live in the
community and many (especially women) live alone. Often their main concern
is to continue living independently. The two domains of competence associated
with an independent lifestyle are caring for oneself and managing one's property (Willis, 1996). As Chapter 4 describes in detail, visual and auditory acuity
play a role when it comes to competence in these domains (Marsiske, Klumb,
& Baltes, 1997). In addition to adequate sensory functioning, what other abilities are required for meeting the challenges of daily living? Are the abilities

Table 6.5 | IADL Categories and Sample Tasks

IADL Category	Sample Tasks
Managing medications	Determining how many doses of cough medicine that can be taken in a 24-hour period
	Completing a patient medical history form
Managing finances	Comparing medigap insurance policies
	Completing an income tax form
Shopping for necessities	Ordering merchandise from a catalog
	Comparing brands of a product
Using the telephone	Determining amount to pay for a phone bill
	Determining emergency phone information
Meal preparation and nutrition	Evaluating nutritional information on a food label
	Following recipe directions
Housekeeping	Reading instructions for operating a household appliance
	Comprehending appliance warrantee
Transportation	Computing taxi rates
	Reading a bus schedule

Adapted from Willis (1996).

needed to maintain independent living related to the abilities measured by psychometric intelligence tests?

Activities of Daily Living and Instrumental Activities of Daily Living   With regard to competence in daily life, a distinction is made between activities of daily living (ADL) and instrumental activities of daily living (IADL), two terms that were introduced in Chapter 3. The ADL category includes basic personal care tasks that are necessary for self-maintenance (for example, bathing, dressing, eating, walking, getting to the toilet, transferring from a bed to a chair). ADL assessments are often made to determine disability and the need for health care services.

The IADL category includes higher-order tasks that are necessary for carrying out the business of daily life, including the management of one's property (Schaie & Willis, 1999). Competence on IADL tasks includes (1) taking medications properly (that is, medication adherence); (2) managing personal finances; (3) shopping for necessities; (4) using the telephone; (5) preparing meals; (6) performing housekeeping tasks; and (7) transporting oneself outside the home (Schaie & Willis, 1996, 1999). Table 6.5 lists these seven IADL categories with task examples for each.

Impairment in the ability to perform IADL tasks can occur in the early stages of Alzheimer's disease or other types of dementia (see Chapter 11 for further discussion of dementia). However, not all older adults who experience difficulty with IADL tasks are victims of dementia. For sociocultural or other reasons, some individuals may have been functioning at a marginal level for most of their adult lives. Normative age-related changes resulting in further decline may place them at risk in terms of competence to perform IADL tasks (Willis, 1996).

Willis and her colleagues examined the relationship between abilities measured by psychometric tests and competence in daily living. To measure competence in daily living, they devised an Everyday Problems Test (EPT) that included written tasks in each of the seven IADL categories. For managing medications, one task on the EPT was to read a medicine bottle label. For managing finances, one task was to fill out a Medicare form. One shopping task was to fill out a mail-order catalogue form. One telephone task was to select the appropriate emergency phone listing from several possibilities. One meal preparation task was to read a nutrition label. One housekeeping task was to read instructions for use of a household appliance. One transportation task was to read a bus schedule. The older adults' scores on the written EPT tasks were positively related to their psychometric test scores. However, the relationship was somewhat stronger for psychometric tests of fluid abilities than it was for psychometric tests of crystallized abilities (Marsiske & Willis, 1995).

Instead of relying on written materials, Diehl, Willis, and Schaie (1995) decided to use behavioral observations to measure competence in daily living. Older adults were observed in their homes as they performed tasks related to medication adherence (for example, loading a pill reminder device), telephone usage (for example, activating call forwarding on a telephone), and meal preparation (for example, following instructions for use of a microwave oven). Strong positive relationships were found between these behavioral observations and the scores the older adults earned on the written EPT. As with the written EPT, behavioral observations of everyday tasks were positively related to psychometric test scores. Also as with the written EPT, the level of observed behaviors had a stronger positive relationship with scores on psychometric test of fluid abilities as opposed to crystallized abilities. In sum, the ability to carry out the tasks of daily life is positively correlated with psychometric test scores, especially those that tap fluid abilities. The better the ability to carry out such tasks, the higher the scores on psychometric tests of fluid ability.

Allaire and Marsiske (1999) tested a large group of community-living older adults ranging from 60 to 92 years of age. Their sample was composed of approximately two-thirds European American individuals and one-third African Americans, although the African American participants were underrepresented at the later points of the age distribution. Allaire and Marsiske administered traditional psychometric tests of inductive reasoning (fluid intelligence) and knowledge (crystallized intelligence). Inductive reasoning was measured using letter sets and numbers series tests. For example, participants chose which of five letter sets had a different pattern from the other four (for example, ABCD,

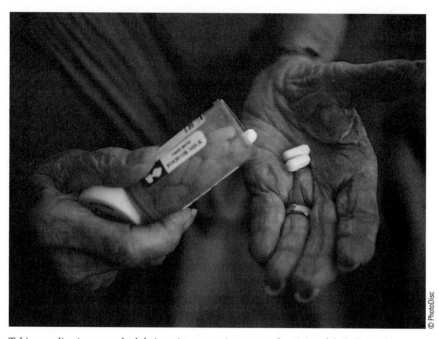

Taking medications on schedule is an important instrumental activity of daily living for many older adults.

LMNO, QRST, EFGH, QXYZ), and which number would come next in a series (for example, 2, 4, 6, 8, 10). Knowledge was measured with a verbal meanings test: for each word, participants selected the correct synonym from a list of five choices.

In addition to the psychometric measures, Allaire and Marsiske devised a written Everyday Cognition Battery (ECB) with items that tested inductive reasoning and knowledge in three domains of daily functioning: medication use, financial planning, and food preparation/nutrition. In the inductive reasoning section of the ECB, participants were given printed information they could use to answer questions in each of the three domains of daily functioning. For example, for the food preparation/nutrition domain, they received "nutrition labels" for two different brands of chili and they had to select the brand best suited for someone on a low-fat diet.

On the knowledge section of the ECB, participants were given multiple-choice questions in each of the three domains. One question in the food preparation/ nutrition domain was, "The expiration date, or "use by" date on a product means: (a) the last date the food should be used; (b) last day the product can be expected to be at its peak quality; (c) the date the food was processed or packaged; (d) none of the above.

Allaire and Marsiske found that scores on the ECB inductive reasoning and knowledge items were highly correlated with scores on the psychometric tests of inductive reasoning and knowledge, respectively. Individuals who scored high on the everyday cognition battery also scored high on the analogous psychometric test. Furthermore, Allaire and Marsiske obtained evidence for the classic aging pattern on both the psychometric and the everyday tests. Scores on the psychometric and everyday inductive reasoning tests, both of which measure fluid ability, showed age-related decline over the age range of 60 to 92. In contrast, scores on the psychometric and everyday knowledge tests, both of which measure crystallized ability, remained stable over that age range.

Clearly, the research findings just described illustrate that there is overlap between psychometric test scores and everyday competence. However, note that both the EPT and the ECB measure potential competence on IADL-related tasks. They do not measure how well older adults would actually perform such tasks if this became necessary in their daily lives. Also, keep in mind that everyday competence is defined by the cultural context in which one lives. Each culture is likely to have its own conception of competence in daily living. In some cultural contexts, competence in daily living may not call for the ability to follow a medication regimen or to understand the meaning of expiration dates on packaged food. Finally, most studies that have compared psychometric and everyday abilities have collected data at only one time. Longitudinal studies in which the same individuals are followed and tested at several points in time are really needed to determine whether there is intraindividual (within-person) change in patterns of performance on traditional psychometric and/or everyday measures. This information would also make it possible to evaluate whether change on one type of measure precedes change on the other.

Legal Considerations   Assessment of competence is sometimes necessary for the purpose of legal judgments (Schaie & Willis, 1996, 1999). **Legal guardianship** refers to "care and protection by someone who is empowered to make decisions in the interest of the individual concerning everyday matters such as living arrangements, health care, and provision of other basic needs" (Grisso, 1986, p. 268). Legal judgments about the need for guardianship are not usually based on assessments of competence in an absolute sense. Rather, a determination of a person's competence is made within the context of a specific living environment (Grisso, 1986). This means that consideration is given to whether a particular living situation meets an older individual's essential needs for survival or whether the older individual is endangering himself or herself or others in a particular living situation (Schaie & Willis, 1999). Competence may be deemed sufficient if the older adult's capabilities are in line with the resources available in the environment (Schaie & Willis, 1999).

Legal conservatorship refers to "management of an incompetent person's estate and financial transactions" (Grisso, 1986, p. 268). Each state within the United States has laws regarding the conditions under which either a guardian or conservator can be assigned to individuals who are deemed incompetent to care for themselves or to manage their own property and financial affairs, respectively.

Legal definitions of incapacity and incompetence focus on extremes, and the decision to assign a guardian or conservator generally requires indisputable evidence of dysfunctional behavior and inability to solve problems or make decisions (Schaie & Willis, 1999). In some cases, there is little question that older adults are suffering from Alzheimer's disease or other types of dementia that render them unable to care for themselves physically or to make decisions. (See Chapter 11 for further discussion of dementia.) However, the need for legal action, especially conservatorship, is not always clear. Consider Maria, a middle-aged woman whose 75-year-old widowed father is living independently and seems to be in good health. Maria discovers her father has been writing checks to charities that may or may not be legitimate. She also finds out that her father wrote a check for a sizeable amount of money to a very exclusive shop that specializes in fancy cocktail dresses. When Maria asks her father about this, he tells her that the check was for a new dress for a young woman who has worked for several months at the reception desk in his apartment building. This young woman is very pleasant and on several occasions she has gotten his groceries when he was unable to get to the store because of bad weather. Maria is beginning to worry that her father is becoming susceptible to scam artists, and she is not sure whether he is still competent to handle his own finances.

In many instances, family members have concerns about the competence of an older relative who makes decisions they do not consider to be financially prudent. However, it is not always a simple matter to determine whether an older adult is incompetent and requires a conservator. The older adult may simply be exercising his or her freedom to spend money as he or she wishes. Clearly, issues regarding determinations of competence point to the intersect between psychology and the legal system.

REVISITING THE SELECTIVE OPTIMIZATION WITH COMPENSATION AND ECOLOGICAL MODELS

Once again it is time to revisit the two theoretical frameworks introduced in the first chapter of this book: The Selective Optimization with Compensation (SOC) Model (Baltes & Baltes, 1990) and the Ecological Model (Lawton, 1989; Lawton & Nahemow, 1973). Each provides a framework within which to evaluate what is known and to ascertain what still needs to be investigated with regard to aging and intellectual abilities.

Normal aging is often associated with decline in some aspects of intellectual ability. Developmental studies have reported evidence for age-related decline in fluid abilities, but crystallized abilities are usually maintained and in some instances even improved over the adult lifespan. According to the SOC Model, the pragmatics of intelligence, which are akin to crystallized abilities, can be used to compensate for any decline in the mechanics of intelligence, which are akin to fluid abilities. Also according to the SOC Model, older adults can cope with losses by becoming more selective and concentrating on the domains of intellectual functioning that are most important to them. Even with some loss in fluid abilities, especially those that call for speed of processing, older adults may compensate by making use of their expertise in specific domains of functioning. A recommendation based on the SOC model would be that older adults not spread themselves too thin. Rather, they might do well to concentrate their efforts on the domains in which they are motivated to maintain a high level of functioning. In selected domains, efforts at maintaining a high level of functioning can be deployed through participation in challenging activities. Older adults who are successful at investing their efforts and energies in this way have been referred to as "resource rich" (Baltes & Lang, 1997). Longitudinal research that follows the same individuals could be highly informative as to just exactly how "resource rich" older adults manage to buffer themselves against loss over time.

According to the Ecological Model, the potential for adaptation is related to the interaction between the intellectual challenge, or press, of the environment and the intellectual competence of the individual. From this perspective, optimal adaptation will occur if the intellectual press of the environment is tailored to a person's level of intellectual competence. Individuals will experience difficulty adapting to environments with too much press for their level of ability. Indeed, older adults whose intellectual abilities are overwhelmed in a highly demanding environment could become vulnerable in terms of confusion, mental stress, or even physical peril. Under such circumstances, level of adaptation is likely to improve with the introduction of environmental supports that reduce the level of intellectual press. Such supports could include availability of guided instruction or providing help with solving the problems required for optimal daily functioning. At the same time, keep in mind that adaptation is optimal when the environment poses some degree of intellectual challenge. An environment with too few intellectual demands, one in which opportunities for intellectual stimulation are severely limited, could have a detrimental effect on adaptation. Thus, it is important that environments provide opportunities for the exercise of intellectual abilities.

KEY POINTS

- Researchers often conceptualize intellectual abilities as falling into two categories: fluid and crystallized. Fluid abilities (Gf) are "raw" intelligence, largely a function of the integrity of the central nervous system and relatively independent both of social influences and specific culturally based learning experiences. Crystallized abilities (Gc) are a function of education, experience, and exposure to a specific cultural environment.
- Gf is reflected in abilities such as numerical reasoning and logic, which usually decline from young to older adulthood. Gc is reflected in verbal and informational abilities, which are usually maintained or increase somewhat from young to older adulthood.
- The dual-process model (Baltes, 1993) includes the mechanics and the pragmatics of intelligence. The mechanics of intelligence are analogous to fluid intelligence (Gf) and have been likened to the hardware of the mind. As with Gf, the mechanics of intelligence are assumed to be genetically and biologically controlled and to be dependent upon basic, physiologically determined, brain functioning. The mechanics of intelligence generally show gradual age-related decline.

- The pragmatics of intelligence are analogous to crystallized intelligence (Gc) and have been likened to the software of the mind. As with Gc, the pragmatics of intelligence include culturally based factual and procedural knowledge. With increasing age, there are more opportunities for exposure to sources of pragmatic knowledge, thus offering possibilities for age-related cognitive growth.

- Psychometric intelligence is measured by the number of points earned on intelligence tests. These scores are quantitative.

- In order to be meaningful, psychometric tests of intelligence must be limited to individuals who are members of the population on whom the test was standardized in the first place. Scores on psychometric tests are of questionable value when the cultural background and experience of the test taker differs from that of the individuals in the standardization sample.

- Two psychometric tests used frequently to study aging and intellectual abilities are the Primary Mental Abilities (PMA) Test and the Wechsler Adult Intelligence Scale (WAIS).

- The classic aging pattern is a phenomenon whereby scores on the verbal subtests on a test such as the WAIS are maintained with increasing age, whereas scores on the performance subtests show age-related decline.

- With the cross-sectional method, scores earned by young adults are compared with scores earned by older adults to determine whether there are age-related differences in psychometric abilities. With the longitudinal method, the same individuals are followed over time to determine whether there are age-related changes in the scores earned at various times of testing. The time-lag method can determine whether there are positive or negative cohort effects for people of a given age.

- Longitudinal studies generally find that age-related decline in intellectual abilities occurs much later and appears to be much smaller than is typically found in cross-sectional studies.

- Intelligence quotient (IQ) on a psychometric test such as the WAIS represents a comparison with age peers. The concept of IQ is of limited value in cross-sectional developmental studies, which involve comparisons of people from different age groups. For developmental comparisons, scaled scores are appropriate.

- Despite age-related losses in some abilities, abilities that are maintained or improved may compensate for those that decline. The idea that gains can be used to offset losses is an important tenet of the SOC Model.

- Positive relationships have been found between older adults' performance on everyday reasoning tasks and their fluid abilities as measured by psychometric tests.

- A positive relationship exists between maintenance of intellectual functioning and good sensory functioning, good health, high educational level, high-level job history, flexibility of personality, membership in an intact family, and engagement in challenging cognitive activities. However, cause-and-effect relationships are difficult to determine.

- In late adulthood, competence is often measured by how well individuals can perform activities of daily living (ADL) and instrumental activities of daily living (IADL).
- Legal definitions of incapacity and incompetence are needed when decisions must be made about whether to assign a guardian or conservator to a person who shows evidence of dysfunctional behavior and inability to solve problems or make decisions.

KEY TERMS

age-insensitive abilities   223

age-sensitive abilities   223

classic aging pattern   223

crystallized intelligence (Gc)   210

disuse hypothesis of cognitive aging   229

Encapsulation Model   236

engagement hypothesis   229

fluid intelligence (Gf)   210

Flynn effect   211

intelligence quotient (IQ)   216

intraindividual variability   216

legal conservatorship   241

legal guardianship   241

mechanics of intelligence   210

negative cohort trend   222

optimally exercised abilities   227

positive cohort trend   222

pragmatics of intelligence   211

Socio-Cultural Process Model   219

testing the limits   225

unexercised abilities   227

To learn more about the issues discussed in this chapter, point your browser to http://www.infotrac-college.com and use the passcode from the InfoTrac College Edition card that came with your book. InfoTrac College Edition gives you access to complete articles from many different journals.

Cognition and Problem Solving in the Everyday World

7

At age 73, Carlos thinks he is much better at solving problems than he was when he was younger. He remembers how unsure of himself he used to feel, but also how he would usually rush to judgment before considering all aspects of a problem. Carlos is very close to his adolescent grandson Pablo, who often confides his problems to Carlos. Recently, Pablo asked for advice on how to handle an incident that came up in school where two of his good friends got into a heated argument. Carlos tells Pablo to try to see the situation from the perspective of each friend, to think carefully before taking sides, and to find out what else was going on that may have triggered the argument. Carlos thinks about times in his own life when he acted too hastily before thinking a situation through, and he wishes he'd always been such a reasonable problem solver.

STAGES OF COGNITIVE DEVELOPMENT

Many older adults claim their memory is not as good as it once was (Erber, Szuchman, & Rothberg, 1992). In contrast, however, they feel their problem-solving skills have improved with age. In one study (Williams, Denney, & Schadler, 1983), more than three-quarters of the older men and women who were interviewed stated that their ability to think, reason, and solve problems had gotten better over the years. This perception contrasts sharply with the age-related decline found on some of the psychometric intelligence tests described in Chapter 6, especially those that tap fluid abilities such as spatial reasoning and psychomotor speed.

Perhaps the reason older adults' believe that their problem-solving abilities have improved even though they show decline on psychometric intelligence tests is that some of the problems they confront in everyday life differ from those on psychometric tests. For example, there may be more than one solution to some of the problems encountered in real life, whereas for most problems on psychometric intelligence tests there is only one correct answer. Are there differences in the way young and older adults approach everyday problems and in the actual solutions they reach? Some situations call for processing social information. For example, we form impressions about other people and we make judgments about their behavior. Are the factors that enter into such impressions and judgments any different for young and older adults?

At various stages of life, individuals may have different reasons, or motivations, for using their cognitive capabilities. As a first step in approaching the topic of cognition and problem solving in the everyday world, we will begin by discussing theories that view cognition as having distinct purposes and taking different forms at each stage of the life span.

Schaie's Stage Model of Cognitive/Intellectual Development

Schaie (1977–1978) proposed a theoretical model that postulates we use our cognitive/intellectual capabilities for purposes with the most meaning, or relevance, for us at our particular stage of life. Schaie proposed four sequential stages of development, each associated with a different motivation for using cognitive processes (see Table 7.1).

In the **acquisitive stage**, which occurs in the childhood and adolescent years, individuals try to gain as much information and knowledge and as many skills

Table 7.1 | Cognitive Processes in Four Sequential Stages of the Life Span

Age/Stage	Description of Stage	Motivation for Cognitive Processes
Childhood/adolescence	Acquisitive	Broad acquisition of knowledge. "What should I know?"
Young adulthood	Achieving	Apply knowledge to achieving long-term goals. "How should I use what I know?"
Middle adulthood	Responsible/ Executive	Use knowledge to take care of others and/or for leadership roles. "How can I help?"
Older adulthood	Reintegrative	Selective use of knowledge for meaningful purposes. "Why should I know?"

Source: Schaie (1977–1978).

as they possibly can to prepare themselves for participation in society. The main concern during this stage of cognitive development is "What should I know?"

In the **achieving stage,** which occurs in the young adult years, individuals shift from the broad acquisition of knowledge for its own sake to a focus on applying the knowledge they have gained. Their main goal at this time is to establish themselves as independent, competent members of society. The knowledge they have accumulated will help them make decisions that will assist them in achieving long-term goals in the domains of career and marriage. At this stage, the main concern is "How should I use what I know?"

In the **responsible/executive stage,** identified with middle adulthood, individuals apply their knowledge and skills to situations related to care and concern for others. During this time, they are establishing and raising families, which means taking on responsibility for a spouse and possibly offspring. At this time of life, many become homeowners and/or parents of school-aged children, thus assuming responsibilities for the community. In the work domain, many middle-aged individuals are in charge of directing and supervising others.

Later in middle age, some individuals take on executive responsibilities, holding leadership positions in jobs (head of department, president, CEO) or in the community (homeowner or condominium association board member, member of a parent-teachers association). In some cases, executive positions that began in midlife continue into older adulthood. For example, some retired executives lend their expertise as professional consultants (Schaie & Willis, 2000). However, this practice depends upon cultural values and needs, including

Figure 7.1 | Revised Cognitive Stage Model

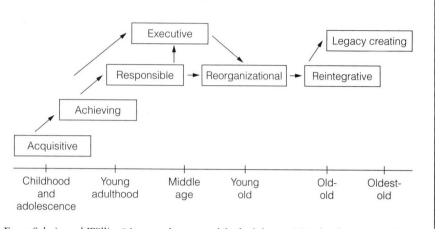

From Schaie and Willis, "A stage theory model of adult cognitive development revis-ited," in Rubinstein, Moss, and Kleban (eds.) *The Many Dimensions of Aging,* pp. 175–193, New York: Springer Publishing Co., 2000.

respect for the knowledge of the older generation and the perceived usefulness of their knowledge.

In the **reintegrative stage,** associated with older adulthood, individuals become more selective about how they expend their cognitive efforts. At this stage, they are less motivated to acquire large amounts of new information and the central question becomes, "Why should I know?" Many older adults want to avoid "wasting time" on tasks and pursuits that have little meaning for them (Schaie & Willis, 2000). It is not clear whether their selectivity stems from basic biological and neurological change that causes limitations in cognitive functioning, or whether it is simply a reaction to reduced responsibility for others and the recognition that the future is less distant.

Schaie & Willis (2000) expanded the period of older adulthood to include a **reorganizational stage** that comes just before the reintegrative stage and a **legacy-creating stage** that overlaps with or comes after the reintegrative stage (see Figure 7.1). The reorganizational stage is identified with the young-old years (ages 65–74), which in American society are generally associated with retirement from paid work and an end to responsibilities for offspring, who are now fully grown and independent adults. At this time, young-old individuals apply their cognitive competence to two tasks: (1) restructuring their lives for the years of retirement and (2) planning for a time when they may have to give up some of their independence. The first and most immediate task, restructur-ing their lives, entails creating a routine of meaningful pursuits to replace the work and family responsibilities of middle adulthood. Time must be restructured around volunteer and leisure activities. The second task, planning for possible dependence, may involve contemplating or actually making changes in living situations. Older adults may sell the large family home and move into an apartment or retirement community, or they may make long-distance moves to locales with milder weather or greater proximity to other family members.

In terms of financial arrangements, wills and trusts may be written and attention may be given to advanced medical directives. (See Chapter 10 for a more detailed description of living wills and durable power of attorney for health care.)

Note that the reorganizational tasks just described apply best to upper-middle-class European Americans and that there is diversity even within the American culture. For example, some young-old adults take on the role of surrogate parents to their grandchildren because of family crises such as the divorce, illness, or drug addiction of their adult children (Quadagno, 2002). Under these circumstances, there will not be much time for leisure pursuits or volunteer work. In some Native American tribes, it is customary for grandparents to rear grandchildren for the first few years of their lives, or at least care for them and impart Native American customs during the summer school holidays (Quadagno, 2002). With regard to plans for future dependence, young-old African American and Hispanic American women are more likely than young-old European American women to live with relatives other than a spouse (Quadagno, 2002), so there may be less need to make plans for changing their living situation.

Overlapping with or following the reintegrative stage is a final legacy-creating stage, identified mainly with the old-old (75–84) and oldest-old (85+) years. During this stage, older adults expend cognitive effort anticipating the end of life. It is not uncommon for them to reminisce about their past, or engage in life review, which Chapter 8 describes in greater detail. Some older adults write autobiographies, but many direct their efforts toward recording an oral history, devising a family tree, or leaving a legacy of carefully labeled family pictures and heirlooms. They may distribute possessions to relatives or friends or at least prepare instructions for how such items should be distributed upon their death. Many make final revisions to wills and concrete funeral arrangements.

In sum, Schaie's model offers a framework for considering how people use cognitive abilities at different stages of life. The exact chronological age when stages occur, and indeed whether all stages actually occur for every individual, may depend upon factors such as health, socioeconomic status, and cultural background. Nonetheless, the reasons for using cognitive processes may change over the life span. Cognitive efforts will be directed toward meeting challenges and accomplishing goals that are most important at a particular stage of life.

Postformal Thought

Jean Piaget, a Swiss physician and psychologist, put forth a theory of cognitive development that has been highly influential in the field of developmental psychology (Piaget, 1952). According to Piaget's theory, every member of the human species progresses through a universal set of cognitive stages that occur in a fixed, or invariant, sequence. The first, sensorimotor, stage (birth to age 2) culminates in a toddler's becoming capable of cognitive representation of objects and object permanence. Just because an object is out of sight does not mean it is out of mind. In the second, preoperational, stage (ages 2 to 7), children acquire spoken language and skills at solving problems that involve objects directly in front of them. In the third, concrete operational, stage (ages 7 to 11), children become capable of mental manipulation of objects and they can sort objects into categories. In the fourth and final **formal operations** stage, beginning at approximately age 11 and extending into adulthood, most individuals become able to use reasoning abilities to reach logical solutions to abstract problems. Through scientific deductive reasoning, they can generate and test hypotheses and systematically eliminate all but the correct solution to a problem.

Although Piaget's theory has had a major influence on our understanding of human development, one criticism has been that the proposed transitions from one stage to the next are not always consistent, nor do the stages occur in the same order for everyone. Also, not all adolescents, or even all adults for that matter, use a logical scientific approach to solve problems. Furthermore, individuals who use a logical scientific approach to solve one kind of problem do not necessarily use that approach to solve other kinds of problems. Whether individuals use a logical approach may depend on how familiar they are with a particular type of problem and what their past experience has been in similar situations. For example, formal logical reasoning is useful for solving a real-world physical problem such as why a car breaks down, and an experienced auto mechanic should be successful at eliminating all possible causes except the one that is actually creating the problem. However, the same individual who uses formal reasoning to solve a car repair problem may not be able to use it to determine why a recipe failed (Why did that cake I baked come out of the oven only one inch high?). In other words, people seem to use formal operations in some domains but not others.

Formal reasoning is often beneficial on psychometric tests, especially those that measure fluid abilities (see Chapter 6). Many items on tests of fluid ability call for abstract problem solving and the correct answer is determined through logical deduction. Older adults tend to perform less well than young adults on such tests. However, not all problems occurring in everyday life lend themselves to formal logical solutions, and some real-world problems have more than one possible solution (Sinnott, 1996). For example, what is the best way to resolve an argument between two good friends? What is the best way to approach your boss to request a pay increase? Solving these types of problems calls for thought processes that are quite different from those used to solve formal logical problems.

Some researchers have proposed that Piaget's theory be extended to an additional stage of development characterized by **postformal thinking**. In contrast to formal thinking, postformal thinking calls for tolerance of ambiguity. Postformal thinkers are flexible and open to more than one possible solution to a problem. The relativistic, or dialectical, nature of postformal thinking, differs from the formal logical thinking required on tests of psychometric intelligence for which there is only one correct answer to a question.

Postformal thought serves an important purpose in many real-life situations. Sinnott (1996) considers it a form of adaptive intelligence because in life, there is often more than one "truth" about an event or a relationship. In social situations, it may be necessary to shift perspectives, at least for the moment, to see things from another person's point of view. For example, for a marriage to be successful, each member of a couple must attempt to see reality from the other's perspective. Ultimately, the couple may have to create a shared reality by compromising on what is right or true. Politics is another domain in which taking different perspectives is useful. The effective politician must be able to grasp the various concerns and points of view of his or her constituents.

Studying postformal thinking is no simple task. It is difficult to measure with the kinds of quantitative tests that have been used to measure formal reasoning (Berg & Klaczynski, 1996), and constructing paper-and-pencil tests has met with only limited success (Sinnott, 1996). More often, postformal thinking is assessed by analyzing the structure and content of verbal responses people give in answer to open-ended questions.

Despite the difficulties in measuring it, postformal thinking is now recognized as a legitimate type of cognition that has very different qualities compared to the cognition used to solve logical problems. Whether postformal thinking constitutes a stage that emerges more fully in older adulthood, and indeed whether most older adults engage in this type of thinking under the appropriate conditions, remains to be determined. The perspective-taking aspect of postformal thinking is closely related to the concept of wisdom, which we will now consider.

WISDOM

First, what is the definition of **wisdom**? More pointedly, what properties of thought, judgment, and advice are considered wise? Similarly, what are the characteristics of wise individuals? Second, is wisdom related to age? Are older adults more likely to possess wisdom compared to people in other age groups?

Definition of Wisdom

Wisdom is a multidimensional concept that is not easy to define. Long before psychologists began to study wisdom, philosophers such as Plato and Aristotle had conceptions of wisdom (Sternberg & Lubart, 2001). For psychologists, the words "wisdom" and "wise" imply elevated forms of behavior, and to display wisdom is to behave in admirable, moral ways (Birren & Fisher, 1990; Birren & Schroots, 1996). Baltes and his colleagues (Baltes & Staudinger, 1995; Smith & Baltes, 1990; Smith, Staudinger, & Baltes, 1994) define wisdom as expert knowledge in the fundamental pragmatics of life.

In general, wisdom encompasses cognitive aspects—expert factual and procedural knowledge. In most people's minds, wisdom is associated with intelligence (Sternberg & Lubart, 2001). However, Birren and Fisher (1990) contend that wisdom is not so much how much information you have. Rather, it is knowing what you do and do not have and being able to make good use of whatever you do have. The wise individual uses the knowledge that he or she has accumulated to interpret and solve problems and dilemmas that have elements of uncertainty. Many of these problems and dilemmas are of a social and interpersonal nature (Baltes & Staudinger, 1995).

An important aspect of wisdom is "problem finding," which means being able to ask appropriate questions when problems are undefined and situations are uncertain (Arlin, 1990). The wise individual demonstrates exceptional insight into life problems and can give good advice about how to deal with important but difficult situations (Smith & Baltes, 1990). The wise individual also recognizes that human nature and life itself have limitations (Taranto, 1989).

Wisdom calls for a balance between reflection and action. Birren and Fisher (1990) contend that youth may have the capacity to be wise but often they are too impelled to action to demonstrate it. Acting rashly is the antithesis of wisdom, while rational reflection on the consequences of actions is the hallmark of wisdom. Even so, excessive caution does not fit the conception of wisdom. The wise person weighs what is known and what is not known about a situation and then carefully chooses what action to take (Birren & Fisher, 1990).

Wisdom also requires a balance between cognition and emotion. When confronting problems, the wise person remains calm and to some degree detached while considering what action to take. A wise person understands that a reflective state of mind makes it more likely that alternative solutions to a problem will be generated (Birren & Fisher, 1990). In other words, a person must remain sufficiently impartial so that all aspects of a problem can be considered before a conclusion is reached and any action taken.

Wisdom bears a distinct similarity to postformal thinking in that it calls for an appreciation that truth is not absolute and may differ depending upon the perspective one takes (Sternberg & Lubart, 2001). A wise person can integrate opposite points of view or at least consider multiple aspects of complex and uncertain situations while maintaining some level of objectivity. In short, the wise individual thinks before acting and does not allow decisions to be dominated by personal preferences or emotions such as anger or fear.

Relationship Between Wisdom and Age

Wisdom is often considered the pinnacle of successful human development (Ardelt, 2000). A common assumption is that time is needed for people to acquire the necessary experience that makes wisdom attainable (Birren & Fisher, 1990; Birren & Schroots, 1996). For this reason, it is commonly thought that older adults are more likely than young adults to be wise because they have had time to gain experience from many years of living.

However, not all investigators have found wisdom is a necessary corollary of age. Ardelt (2000) reported that even among a homogeneous sample of healthy, educated, financially well-off, European American older women in the longitudinal Berkeley Guidance Study, there was considerable variation in degree of wisdom. Not surprisingly, those rated higher on cognitive, reflective, and emotional indicators of wisdom by clinically trained interviewers also rated themselves higher in life satisfaction. Clearly, wisdom is a positive factor in aging, but age does not automatically lead to wisdom.

One method psychologists have used to investigate age and wisdom is to present young and older adults with a hypothetical dilemma being faced by a

Some professions require expert factual and procedural knowledge and exceptional insight.

fictitious person (labeled "target") and to ask them how they think the dilemma should be resolved and what advice they would give. In most cases, there is no single "correct" solution to the dilemma, but some kinds of advice are considered wiser than others. One study by Smith and Baltes (1990) investigated the judgments made by individuals from various adult age groups with regard to several dilemmas involving the relationship between work and family. Study participants were young (ages 25–35), middle-aged (ages 40–50), and older (ages 60–81) adults recruited through advertisements in Berlin newspapers. Participants from all three age groups were highly educated professional German nationals who spoke English fluently. They read several scenarios, each one describing a young or older fictitious target person who is faced with a dilemma about future life planning and must decide what to do. Two examples follow:

> Michael, a 28-year-old mechanic with two preschool-aged children, has just learned that the factory in which he is working will close in 3 months. At present, there is no possibility for further employment in this area. His wife has recently returned to her well-paid nursing career. Michael is considering the following options: He can plan to move to another city to seek employment, or he can plan to take full responsibility for child-care and household tasks. Formulate a plan that details what Michael should do and should consider in the next 3 to 5 years. What extra pieces of information are needed?

Joyce, a 60-year-old widow, recently completed a degree in business management and opened her own business. She has been looking forward to this challenge. She has just heard that her son has been left with two small children to care for. Joyce is considering the following options: She could plan to give up her business and live with her son, or she could plan to arrange for financial assistance for her son to cover child-care costs. Formulate a plan that details what Joyce should do and should consider in the next 3 to 5 years. What extra pieces of information are needed?

After reading each dilemma, participants were instructed to think aloud as they formulated a plan of action for the target person. Their responses, or the advice they would give to the target, were evaluated by trained raters on five dimensions of wisdom:

1. General and specific factual knowledge about the matters involved
2. General and specific procedural knowledge about what strategies can be used to deal with the problem, with an understanding of the costs and benefits of each one
3. Knowledge about the past, current, and future life contexts in which an individual's problem may be embedded
4. Relativism, including the understanding that not everyone holds the same values, goals, and priorities
5. Recognition of uncertainty, with an understanding that no solution is perfect and that there are inherent uncertainties in life

To attain a high wisdom rating, a study participant's plan of action would need to have many components. It would have to:

1. Clearly define and discuss many aspects of the problem faced by the target
2. Give advice that is not one-sided but offers several alternatives about what the target could do, with the positive and negative aspects of each alternative for the target
3. Discuss the short-term and long-term goals for each alternative
4. Recognize that all strategies hold some uncertainly and evaluate the risk of using each one
5. Suggest that the alternative selected be monitored and revised if necessary

Only 5 percent of the responses given by the study participants received high wisdom ratings, but this small proportion of wise responses was evenly distributed over young, middle-aged, and older participants. Thus, the older participants' responses were no wiser, but neither was there any evidence for age-related decline on this type of cognition.

Specific experiences (as opposed to chronological age or membership in a particular generation, or cohort) may determine an individual's degree of wisdom. For the dilemma faced by the young target (Michael), the responses that the young and middle-aged participants gave received higher wisdom ratings than those given by the older participants. For the dilemma faced by the older target (Joyce), the responses of the older participants were rated the same or higher than those given by the young and middle-aged participants.

Perhaps participants identified more closely with targets of similar age since their responses to the similar-age targets seemed to show special insight.

Smith, Staudinger, and Baltes (1994) conducted a study in which the responses that clinical psychologists gave to life planning dilemmas were rated high in wisdom. Baltes, Staudinger, Maercker, and Smith (1995) conducted another study in which one group of participants consisted of highly educated older clinical psychologists (average age of 66 years) recruited through an advertisement in a professional newsletter. However, the main focus was on a second group, which consisted of individuals who had been nominated as "wise" by top newspaper, radio, and television journalists in Berlin. None of these wisdom nominees (whose average age was 64 years) were psychologists, but Baltes and his colleagues wanted to determine how their responses would compare to the responses of the clinical psychologists. Wisdom was assessed on the basis of the advice participants claimed that they would give to a fictitious target in dilemmas such as that of the 60-year-old widow who must decide between giving her son money for child care or giving up her new business to take care of her grandchildren. Participants' responses were evaluated on the five dimensions of wisdom by a panel of raters (whose average age was 49), which included teachers, journalists, librarians, economists, a theologian-minister, and a physicist.

Clinical psychologists are professionally trained to help clients solve real-life dilemmas, so it was not surprising that their responses received high wisdom ratings. Interestingly, though, the responses given by the wisdom nominees were rated as highly as those of the clinical psychologists. Despite their lack of formal training in how to help others solve dilemmas, the wisdom nominees were considered just as wise as the clinical psychologists. Even so, there were some differences between these two groups. The responses of the clinical psychologists were rated higher on the factual knowledge dimension, while the responses of the wisdom nominees were rated higher on the relativism dimension, which included an understanding that not everyone holds the same values, goals, and priorities. Clearly, we have much to learn about how the wisdom nominees acquired their ability.

In sum, the studies just described found no evidence for any age-related decline in the cognitive skills necessary to give advice that is considered wise. However, there was little support for the commonly held assumption that older adults are wiser than young adults. Some older adults are wise, but old age does not guarantee wisdom. One researcher (Meacham, 1990) contends that increasing age could actually limit a person's chances of achieving wisdom. Meacham's reasoning is that wisdom involves a balance between knowing and doubting. As people accumulate power, information, experience, and success, they may become overly confident in what they know and more set in their opinions, which Meacham considers the antithesis of wisdom. With less knowledge, there is less likelihood of overconfidence and of having set opinions. From this perspective, Meacham believes that young adults have a greater chance of achieving wisdom, and older adults might have more to overcome.

REAL-WORLD INTELLIGENCE AND PROBLEM SOLVING

In the academic arena, and on most psychometric tests of intelligence, solving problems depends on formal, factual knowledge and the ability to think logically (Sternberg, Wagner, & Okagaki, 1993). Sternberg, Wagner, Williams, and Horvath (1995) point out that in most cases, academic problems (1) are formulated by others, (2) have little intrinsic interest for problem solvers and are usually unrelated to their ordinary experience, (3) provide all the necessary information from the beginning, and (4) are well-defined and have only one correct solution and one method of obtaining it.

Even when educational level is held as constant as possible, young adults usually perform at the highest level on such problems, with a steady decline in performance from middle to older adulthood. However, the ability to solve academic problems does not always go hand in hand with the ability to solve problems outside the academic context. Sternberg and his colleagues contend that individuals who earn high scores on psychometric tests and/or achieve success in academic pursuits are not necessarily the ones who are most successful in real-world contexts such as work. Similarly, individuals who do not earn high scores on psychometric tests or did not achieve outstanding grades in school are sometimes highly successful in their careers. The problems encountered in some aspects of the working world, and in other real-world situations as well, may differ substantially from the problems that must be solved on exams in an academic context.

Practical Intelligence

Most of us distinguish between academic and practical intelligence. Academic intelligence is often referred to as "book smarts" and practical intelligence as "street smarts" (Sternberg et al., 1995). As opposed to academic problems, the problems faced in the real world are often (1) unformulated and poorly defined, (2) of great personal interest and highly relevant to everyday experience, (3) lacking in specific information necessary for solution, and (4) characterized by multiple "correct" solutions, each with assets and liabilities, as well as by multiple methods that can be used to pick a solution (Sternberg et al., 1995).

The distinction between academic and practical intelligence is similar to the distinction between **formal knowledge** and **tacit knowledge** (Sternberg et al., 1995). Formal knowledge is often measured by psychometric intelligence tests and reflected in the grades earned in academic courses. Tacit knowledge is closely associated with practical intelligence and has the following characteristics (Sternberg et al., 1995; Sternberg & Lubart, 2001):

- It has to do with "knowing how" (procedural knowledge) rather than just "knowing that" (declarative knowledge). Thus, tacit knowledge implies action. For example, what does an employee have to do to get along with his or her superior in the workplace? What does an insurance salesperson have to do to complete a sale?
- It has a practical use in attaining valued goals. For example, in the world of work, knowing how to make subordinates feel valued or knowing how to make a sale has practical use for those aspiring to be successful managers or

salespeople, respectively. However, such knowledge would have little practical value for people who do not strive for success as managers or salespeople.

- It is acquired with little help from others and little environmental support. Tacit knowledge is not written, nor is it articulated explicitly. Rather, it must be inferred from actions or indirect statements. For example, to advance in a company, a new employee might have to observe how other employees behave and what rewards they are given.

Sternberg and his colleagues have investigated tacit knowledge mainly in the context of work, including success in academic jobs. To measure tacit knowledge, they ask research participants to read vignettes describing problems that could actually arise in the workplace. Afterward, participants select what they perceive to be the best solution from a number of possible alternatives, which successful managers and professionals have ordered by rank. Study participants who choose the highly ranked solutions earn more points for having tacit knowledge than do those who choose the lower-ranked solutions. The findings of these studies indicate that tacit knowledge scores do not necessarily correlate with the scores these participants earn on psychometric intelligence tests. Also, unlike the age-related decline frequently found on psychometric tests of fluid ability, tacit knowledge often increases with both age and experience. When older adults claim that their problem-solving abilities have gotten better over time (Williams et al., 1983), perhaps (without realizing it) they are referring to improvements in tacit knowledge.

For older adults, tacit knowledge could be especially useful in selecting and also in adapting to a new living environment. How does an older adult determine what is the best time to sell the big family home and move to an environment that offers more support? How does an older adult who moves into an assisted living facility "learn the ropes" that will allow a relatively smooth transition to the new environment? How does a resident in an assisted living facility use tacit knowledge to get along with fellow residents and ensure that his or her needs are met in a timely manner by busy staff members? Tacit knowledge could make an important difference in how quickly, and ultimately in how well, the older individual is able to construct a comfortable niche in such an environment. It is very likely that tacit knowledge plays a role in successful aging.

Creative Intelligence

Sternberg (1996) distinguishes among three components of successful intelligence: analytic, practical, and creative. Analytic intelligence is closely related to academic intelligence and is often measured by the psychometric intelligence tests discussed in Chapter 6. However, analytic intelligence can be applied to problems outside the academic arena, such as figuring out what kind of car or house offers the desired features but is still within one's budget. The practical component of intelligence includes tacit knowledge, described in the preceding section. Practical intelligence is useful in knowing how to get what one wants in the real world.

Figure 7.2 | Sternberg's Triarchic Theory of Intelligence

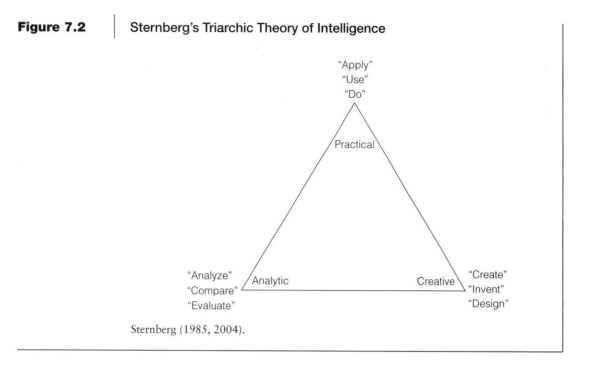

Sternberg (1985, 2004).

The third component, creative intelligence, is somewhat elusive and difficult to measure, but it taps an aspect of intelligence that seems to lie outside the abilities measured by psychometric tests or used in practical situations. In general, creative intelligence connotes divergent thinking, or the ability to generate many answers to a question and to find novel insightful solutions to a problem. One way of measuring creative intelligence is to see how many uses a person can name for an object such as a brick or a ballpoint pen. This differs from the convergent thought typical of analytic intelligence, where the emphasis is on finding one correct solution to a problem.

Does creativity increase, decrease, or remain stable over the adult years? To make this determination, some investigators have attempted to chart the work produced over the adult life span of individuals who are recognized as creative geniuses in various fields (Simonton, 1997). Deterioration in physical health and vigor can have a negative effect on creative contributions. Even so, Simonton (1990) points out that many individuals with creative genius have been successful in surmounting obstacles and have been able to continue their creative productivity. For example, the artist Renoir dealt with rheumatism by painting with the brush tied to his hand. Some creative individuals adapt to altered physical conditions by enlisting help from others. For example, older Renaissance artists often employed apprentices to perform mundane tasks such as preparing materials. Also, many older illustrious scientists have a team of research assistants to facilitate their work (Simonton, 1990).

Lehman (1953) investigated the relationship between age and the production of highly creative works in various academic fields. Overall, he found

Figure 7.3

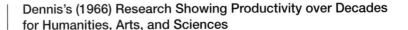

Dennis's (1966) Research Showing Productivity over Decades for Humanities, Arts, and Sciences

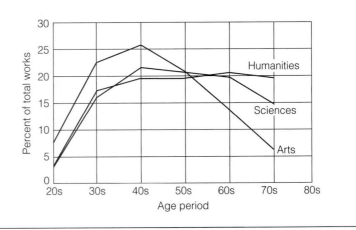

that creative output peaks in the decade of the 30s, followed by steady decline. (see Figure 7.3). However, Dennis (1966) studied the output of creative people in the arts, sciences, and humanities and found that the age of peak productivity depends upon the specific field of achievement. For the humanities, productivity tends to remain stable over the adult life span, whereas productivity tends to fall off in the decade of the 60s in the sciences and even earlier in the arts (see Figure 7.3).

In many academic fields, creativity peaks in mid-life (Simonton, 1997). But the age at which a peak occurs may depend upon the age when a career is launched (Simonton, 1990, 1998). Individuals who enter a career in mid-life or later often have a later peak of productivity and a higher rate of output in the older adult years. Indeed, there are numerous examples of artistic, literary, scientific, and other kinds of creative accomplishments in older adulthood. For instance, the classical composer Anton Bruckner did not embark on a creative career as a symphonic composer until mid-life. He composed his first symphony at age 42, his first "unquestioned masterpiece" at age 50, and his ninth symphony at age 70 (Simonton, 1998).

Note that the quantity of output, or productivity, is not necessarily the same as the quality of creative work. However, the **constant-probability-of-success model of creativity** is based on the premise that during the course of a career, the point of maximum creativity often coincides with the point of maximum productivity (Simonton, 1990, 1998). If this model is correct, then individuals who generate the largest number of works (high productivity) have the greatest chance of generating a masterpiece (high creativity). If the ratio of major creative works to the total number of works produced remains constant over the adult life span, then the likelihood of a "creative hit" in any given age period would depend upon how many works are produced during that time. Individuals who make the greatest number of creative contributions will produce

© Rob Lewine/Corbis

Artistic creativity can continue well into the older adult years.

many minor works as well. As overall productivity falls off with increasing age, the number of creative works may fall off proportionately. However, there is some evidence that those who are most productive in their early years continue to be productive in their later years (Simonton, 1990, 1998).

Simonton (1990) refers to the **swan-song phenomenon**, which is a resurgence in creative output stemming from a final burst in creative activity in the sixth and seventh decades that follows a post-peak decline in the rate of creative contributions (Simonton, 1990). The swan-song peak of last works may not be as high as the peak achieved in mid-life, but the work is often outstanding in its simplicity and elegance. Simonton (1998) contends that the swan-song phenomenon "enables the greatest creators to end their career trajectories with a bang, not a whimper" (p. 14). Evidence for the swan-song phenomenon has been demonstrated most pointedly for classical composers such as Beethoven, Brahms, Handel, and Strauss (Simonton, 1990). However, it may hold for visual artists, writers, and scientists as well.

Lubart and Sternberg (1998) point out that the creative works of musicians, artists, and writers tend to take different forms and focus on different content over the life span. In general, the creative works produced in older adulthood show a simplicity of style and may represent a summing up or integration of ideas. Late-life creative works in fields such as basic science, social science, and philosophy often consist of memoirs, historical analyses, or observations made over a period of time (Lubart & Sternberg, 1998). The content of older adults' creative work focuses more on the subjective interpretation of experiences than it does on an objective listing of experiences. Also, the themes of aging and death are more prominent in the creative works of older adults than they are in the creative works of younger adults.

Abstract Versus Practical Problem Solving

Denney and Palmer (1981) asked men and women 20 to 79 years of age to perform problem-solving tasks that were both abstract and practical. For the abstract task, which was similar to academic problem solving, participants were shown an array of 42 pictures of common objects such as a lamp, shoe, tree, and apple. They were instructed to figure out which of the 42 pictures the investigator was thinking of, asking as few yes/no questions as possible. The fewer questions people asked to discover the answer, the better their performance would be. To this end, **constraint-seeking questions** ("Is the object on the left side of the array?"), which would eliminate more than one item, are more efficient than **hypothesis-testing questions** ("Is the object the lamp?"), which would only eliminate one item. With increasing age, participants asked fewer constraint-seeking questions and more hypothesis-testing questions. Not surprisingly, then, there was an age-related increase in the number of questions asked before a correct solution was attained and thus an age-related decrease in level of performance.

In addition to the abstract tasks, Denney and Palmer presented the same participants with several practical problems. Here's an example of one:

> Let's say one evening you go to the refrigerator and you notice that it is not cold inside, but rather, it's warm. What would you do?

Several independent raters judged the quality of the responses people gave to each practical problem. In the refrigerator example, one point was given for no solution, two points for a solution that involved reliance on others (such as calling a repair person), three points for a solution that involved some self-action (such as making sure the refrigerator was plugged in or checking the circuit breakers), and four points for more than one solution that included at least one self-action (checking the circuit breakers and calling a repair person if that does not solve the problem).

In contrast to the steady linear age-related decline found with abstract problem solving, the solutions for the practical problems showed a different pattern. Performance increased from young to middle adulthood, reaching a peak in the 40–50-year-old age range. There was some decrease in level of performance beyond the age of 50, but the decline was less steep than it was for the abstract problems. Thus, problem-solving abilities hold up better across the adult years, and there is less decline in older adulthood when individuals can use real-life experience or expertise. Abstract and unfamiliar problems do not lend themselves as readily to the use of past experience. Perhaps older adults who say that their problem-solving abilities have improved with age are referring to practical rather than abstract problems.

Interpersonal Problem Solving

Unlike the warm refrigerator problem, some practical problems are of a more interpersonal nature. Interpersonal problems are less likely to have one simple answer, and the best solutions may be relativistic, which means that they show some recognition that the problem can be approached from more than one perspective and that no single solution will please everyone.

Collins, Luszcz, Lawson, and Keeves (1997) interviewed 64 Australian women, who ranged in age from 65 to 90. Half of the women lived independently in the Adelaide community and the other half lived in group nursing hostels in the same general vicinity. Older residents of Australian nursing hostels are more physically and mentally competent than residents of Australian nursing homes, but Collins et al. screened the nursing hostel sample for neurological and psychiatric disorders to ensure that their study participants had an adequate level of cognitive competence.

Collins et al. devised two pairs of problems. The problems within each pair were similar, but one was set in a community-living context, while the other was set in a nursing hostel context. The researchers anticipated that participants would offer the best solution for the problem that took place in the familiar environmental context rather than the unfamiliar one. The following problem descriptions were adapted from Collins et al.:

> 1. Let's say an elderly couple who moved into the house that adjoins yours watches television and listens to music till late at night. They are both hard of hearing, so the noise is very loud and it keeps you awake. (OR: Let's say you have moved into a new room in the hostel in which you live. The new room is located next to the social lounge, where residents watch TV, play cards, and chat until late at night because they have difficulty sleeping.) You have hesitated to say anything because you get on well with the couple (residents) and you can sympathize with their plight, but you are suffering from loss of sleep. What can you do?

> 2. Let's say you are a member of a neighborhood watch committee. (OR: Let's say you are a member of a hostel social committee.) You feel uncomfortable attending meetings because you are continually in conflict with a highly opinionated committee member who disapproves of your suggestions. You have hesitated to say anything because you realize the other member has some good ideas and also is very popular with the other residents. You are becoming increasingly apprehensive about attending meetings. What can you do?

Although all of the study participants were older adults, Collins et al. still found that chronological age was negatively associated with the quality of problem solving. Thus, the older the participants' chronological age, the less ideal the solutions they offered in terms of taking more than one perspective. Contrary to what Collins et al. predicted, the problem context (community versus nursing hostel), and whether it was familiar or unfamiliar, offered neither an advantage or disadvantage for either group. Interestingly, many nursing hostel residents said that they would ask staff members to intervene to assist them in solving the problems that took place in the nursing hostel. In contrast, very few community-living residents said that they would ask staff members to help them solve problems in the nursing hostel. This suggests that the nursing hostel residents were less capable than the community-living residents of tackling interpersonal problem solving, perhaps because they are accustomed to living in a less complex environment compared to the community-living sample.

In this study, the community-living participants were more relativistic in their problem solutions than the nursing hostel participants were. However, Collins et al. point out that, compared to the older nursing hostel group, the older community-living group was somewhat younger chronologically. Also, they were more engaged in everyday problem-solving activities and had a higher sense of perceived control than the nursing hostel residents did. Even so, caution must be exercised prior to concluding that the more independent living environment is a direct cause of more relativistic problem solving. It is possible that the community-living group was not familiar with the social standards, expectations, and living conditions that exist in nursing hostels. Nursing hostel residents have come to depend upon caregivers for meal preparation and activities, so perhaps it is not surprising that they said they would seek the help of caregivers in solving interpersonal problems. In any case, this study offers some insight into how older adults might approach interpersonal problems that could occur both in the community and in group living situations.

DECISION MAKING

In the everyday world, we must often make decisions. What role does age play in the information-seeking and reasoning processes used? Do adults of all ages take the same amount of time to make a decision, and is the final decision any different for young and older adults?

Decision Making in a Health Context

In modern medical practice, it is becoming the norm for patients to play a role along with physicians in decisions about treatment interventions. The sharing of responsibility between physicians and patients contrasts with the older and more traditional practice of treatment decisions being made solely by the physician. Being allowed to take part in treatment decisions seems to have overall beneficial effects for patients (Zwahr, Park, & Shifren, 1999).

In general, health problems become more prevalent in older adulthood, so as people grow older, they must often make more decisions regarding their health and physical well-being. Some decisions may be related to specific medical conditions for which more than one treatment is available. In selecting a treatment option, various factors must be weighed regarding potential risks and benefits. There have been several recent studies on the young and older adults' medical decision-making processes.

Menopause   Women frequently become involved in decision making regarding the effects of menopause. What factors play a role in the final decision about what, if any, medical intervention should be chosen? Zwahr et al. (1999) investigated this question in a study that included 102 community-dwelling women between the ages of 20 and 79. Women in the various age groups included (20–29, 30–39, 40–49, 50–59, 60–69, 70–79) were similar in level of perceived health as well as in level of education (high school graduates or the equivalent) and in vocabulary test scores. However, some age-related decrements were found on measures of cognitive ability such as memory for sentences read aloud, memory for written text, abstract reasoning, and perceptual speed measured by how quickly participants could determine whether two strings of letters were the same or different. Age-related differences in cognitive abilities could be an important factor in the medical decision-making process, which usually calls for the ability to understand and remember information about various medical treatments.

Study participants read a scenario describing a 56-year-old woman (target) with postmenopausal symptoms such as insomnia, heart palpitations, hot flashes, and mood swings that caused her to visit her doctor. The scenario included a brief medical history, which would have potential relevance for treatment options: The target used to smoke but has given it up, she has experienced recent weight loss and recurrent urinary tract infections, and her mother has been diagnosed with osteoporosis. After reading the scenario, participants were given written information about estrogen replacement therapy (ERT), which is one way to treat the symptoms of menopause. (Recent research findings have resulted in a more conservative use of ERT.) They were instructed to imagine themselves as this 56-year-old woman with the same symptoms and medical history, and to decide what, if any, medical intervention they would choose to alleviate menopausal symptoms.

Zwahr et al. found age-related differences in the decision-making process in the number of treatment options participants recognized, the number of comparisons they made between treatment options, and the quality of the explanation given for their final decision. Statistical analyses revealed that age did not contribute directly to any of these decision variables. Rather, level of cognitive ability was the basic contributor, and age contributed only indirectly through its relationship to cognitive abilities.

Cancer   Diagnoses of cancer are not uncommon in middle-aged and older adults and often there is more than one treatment alternative. For men diagnosed with prostate cancer, various treatments are available, each having potential side effects and long-term survival statistics (Mazur & Merz, 1995). When men are given information on prostate cancer prior to being screened for it, they take a more active role along with their physicians if a diagnosis is made (Davison, Kirk, Degner, & Hassard, 1999).

For women diagnosed with breast cancer, various treatment options are also available. Meyer, Russo, and Talbot (1995) conducted a study on the decision-making processes women use when choosing a breast cancer treatment. In the first part of the study, 94 women (ages 18 to 88) read an authentic case history in which a lump was discovered in a woman's breast. Various treatment options were described, each one justified by some data and expert opinions. Very few of the study participants had personal experience with benign breast lumps or breast cancer, and less than half had close friends or relatives with breast cancer.

After reading the scenario, participants wrote down the factors that would influence their treatment decision and stated their reasons for selecting the treatment option they chose. In this type of problem-solving situation, decision-making strategies can be *bottom up* or *top down* (Sinnott, 1989), terms introduced in Chapter 4 to describe how listeners process spoken language. In that context, bottom up referred to processing the details of a spoken message, while top down referred to using previously-learned rules of spoken language to fill in the gaps when details of a conversation are missed. In the present decision-making context, a **bottom-up processing strategy** would involve collecting and integrating new information. This strategy is sometimes described as "youthful" because it is assumed that young adults lack the necessary knowledge so they must gather it from scratch and integrate it. In contrast, a **top-down processing strategy** relies on prior knowledge and experience and is considered less cognitively demanding because it does not call for acquiring and integrating new information. The top-down strategy can be effective if the information already in storage is accurate and relevant to the decision at hand. However, it is often preferable to collect some new information and integrate it with what is already in the knowledge store. Striking a balance between the bottom-up and top-down strategies is viewed as a "mature" style of problem solving, or decision making (Sinnott, 1989).

In their study, Meyer et al. found that the younger women relied more than the older women did on bottom-up processing, seeking additional information and making more comparisons between treatment options before reaching a final decision. The older women made their final decisions more quickly and sought less additional information prior to reaching a decision, indicating they relied more on top-down processing. The older women thought decisions should be made quickly because they felt it was important to get treatment as soon as possible before the cancer had time to spread. However, Meyer et al. contend that reliance on top-down processing could also be a way to compensate for reduced cognitive capacity because cognitive demands are lower if no new information is sought or integrated.

In a second part of their study, Meyer et al. surveyed young, middle-aged, and older women who had been diagnosed with breast cancer within the previous 3 years and had been involved in making a decision about their own treatment. The findings of this survey coincided with the findings from the first part of the study in which participants read a case scenario. Compared to the young and middle-aged patients, the older patients took less time to make a treatment decision. Also, more older patients than young patients said that they did not seek further information or opinions about treatment options because they felt that time was of the essence to prevent the cancer from spreading.

In sum, the older women in both parts of Meyer et al.'s study sought less information than younger women did before making a treatment decision about breast cancer. When the older women did intend to seek additional information, their plans were less systematic than those of the younger women, and the older women made treatment decisions more quickly. Meyer et al. hypothesize that the older women's poorer recall of treatment information, their less systematic analysis of the treatment options available, and their quicker decisions could reflect their attempts to use their cognitive resources efficiently. In some sense, the older adults' quicker decisions suggest less tolerance for ambiguity and a greater need to reduce uncertainty.

In this study, the quality of the decisions about breast cancer treatment did not differ for the young and older women. However, Meyer et al. maintain that this may not be true for all health problems. In some instances, the quality of a treatment decision could be tied more closely to the decision-making strategy. They recommend that health-care providers encourage older adults to consider an array of treatment alternatives and offer them assistance in locating accurate sources of information that will help them in their final decision.

Meyer et al. caution that their findings are based on the responses of older adults of average verbal ability in rural Pennsylvania. Individuals who have higher verbal ability and/or reside in urban areas might be more proactive in seeking information before making a decision. Note also that older adults of lower socioeconomic status may have less access to health-care services and fewer treatment options available.

In another study on decisions about cancer treatment, Turk-Charles, Meyerowitz, and Gatz (1997) examined how patients seek information not only from medical sources but from nonmedical sources as well. They recruited men and women from an outpatient oncology clinic. These individuals, most of whom were European Americans, ranged from 18 to 81 years of age, and all of them had been diagnosed and treated for various types of cancer within the past 3 years. Contrary to the findings of Meyer et al., there were no age-related differences in these patients' inclination to seek information about their diagnosis. However, the young and older patients obtained the bulk of their information from different sources. Compared to the young patients, the older patients sought a smaller portion of their information from the medical establishment (doctors and nurses) and a larger portion from nonmedical sources (newspapers, television, friends).

There are several possible explanations for the older patients' tendency to rely more on nonmedical information sources. First, older adults may have more friends with similar diagnoses with whom they can consult. Discussing an illness with a friend or reading about it in the media may give older adults a greater sense of control, which could help them cope with the illness. Second, older adults may feel more deference toward health professionals and they may think it would be impolite to ask for additional information. Health professionals should be aware that older adults may be reluctant to ask for information unless they are encouraged to do so.

Long-Term Care   As discussed earlier in this chapter, many older adults plan for a time when they may experience some loss of independence (Schaie & Willis, 2000). Indeed, as more people live into the oldest-old (85+) years, they may need extra services if they are to remain in their homes. Some may require care that can only be offered in assisted living facilities or nursing homes. To fill the potential need for services and care, many companies are offering long-term-care insurance policies. In exchange for a yearly premium, such policies offer benefits for nursing home stays. Some cover the expense of assisted living facilities, or even home health-care benefits if older adults want to live in their own homes but need help to do so. Long-term-care insurance policies vary widely both in price and in the specific benefits offered. Whether to purchase a long-term-care policy, and if so which one, is a decision being faced by more and more middle-aged and older adults in the United States. Assuming that detailed information about various policies is available, a decision about which one to purchase could be based on an objective cost/benefit comparison. However, policy benefits should be tailored to the potential needs of the individual, so each person must take into account his or her personal future health risks and projected financial situation. Social factors that are less clearly defined also enter into the decision. For example, will family members be available if care and assistance become necessary? Not only is the decision about long-term-care insurance related to the individual's projected health, financial status, and personal family situation, but the decision should also take into account the financial soundness of the company selling the policy. As such, some aspects of the decision to purchase long-term-care insurance fall into the consumer category, which the following section discusses further.

Decision Making in a Consumer Context

In addition to health-related decisions, people make decisions about items or services to purchase. Some consumer choices are relatively minor. For example, is it better to buy a small box of cereal or a large box of cereal? This decision could be made on the basis of an objective calculation of cost per ounce, although factors such as the number of cereal eaters in the household probably deserve consideration.

Other consumer decisions are more important purely from a monetary standpoint. For example, a decision about what kind of car to purchase is usually not made casually. The discerning consumer decides about this type of investment only after considerable thought about cost, quality, and potential satisfaction with a product that will be used for years. Are these decision processes any different for young and older adults?

Johnson (1990) examined the decision-making processes of 36 young adult college students and 36 older retirees about which of six cars they would purchase. In this study, comparative information on the cars (fuel economy, riding comfort, maintenance cost, safety record, styling, purchase price, resale value) could be accessed via computer. Thus, Johnson was able to trace the information search strategies that study participants used as they were trying to reach a decision.

Johnson's young and older study participants took approximately the same amount of time to reach a final decision about which car to purchase. However, based on the study participants' patterns of accessing the computer-based information, Johnson was able to determine that the older participants viewed fewer pieces of information about the cars but spent more time on each one. In contrast, the young college students, who had less experience than the older retirees with car buying, viewed more pieces of information but spent less time than the older retirees did on each one. Johnson concluded that compared to the young college students, the older adults had a greater tendency to use **noncompensatory decision rules**. This means that the older adults eliminated alternatives after an incomplete search, thereby reducing the cognitive processing demands of the task. In contrast, the young adults made greater use of **compensatory decision rules,** which entail summing, weighing, and averaging all possible alternatives prior to making a decision. Clearly, compensatory decision rules pose heavier cognitive processing demands than do noncompensatory decision rules. Johnson hypothesized that tasks such as purchasing a car may only be moderately difficult for young adults but could present a cognitive challenge for older adults.

Evaluating political candidates is not exactly the same as making decisions about consumer purchases. Nonetheless, voters engage in decision making about whether a candidate running for office represents their interests and points of view. Riggle and Johnson (1996) investigated the strategies used by younger (ages 18–35) and older (ages 50–85) adults to evaluate political candidates. As in the car purchasing situation, the older adults accessed less information and took longer to examine it than the young adults did. However, unlike the car selection situation, the older adults took a longer time overall than the young adults did to reach a final decision. Perhaps older adults are more careful in their decisions about political candidates than they are when purchasing a car. In any case, further study is certainly needed to clarify why older adults took longer than young adults did to reach a final decision about a political candidate but not about purchasing a car.

Decision Making in a Legal Context

In civil trials, the lawyer for the plaintiff and the lawyer for the defendant present evidence. After both sides have argued their case, jurors are required to make a decision about the liability of the defendant that is consistent with the evidence and also with legal principles. If the defendant is found liable, a further decision must be made about how the defendant will compensate the plaintiff.

Fitzgerald (2000) used a mock jury trial format to compare the decision-making processes of young adult college students and university staff members (ages 19 to 35) and older adults (ages 55 to 75) who were recruited through newspaper advertisements and from senior centers and apartment buildings. The young and older study participants (mock jurors) had similar levels of education, and the two age groups were similarly diverse with regard to ethnic background and socioeconomic status.

Fitzgerald's mock jurors viewed one of two versions of a two-hour video that conveyed a complex civil trial in which four plaintiffs were claiming that a large corporation (the defendant) had allowed a chemical to leach into the local groundwater. Information in the video favored the plaintiffs, who varied in the extent of the injuries they were claiming (exposure to illnesses such as cancer and economic damages from tainted farm property and polluted water supply).

The two versions of the video were identical except for the timing of the judge's instructions to the mock jurors explaining legal concepts such as "liability" and "compensatory damages." Half the mock jurors in each age group heard the judge's instructions at the standard time, right after the opening arguments and evidence were presented. The other half of the mock jurors in each age group were "preinstructed." That is, they heard the judge's instructions before the opening arguments and liability evidence were presented. After viewing the video, the individual mock jurors were asked to decide about the liability of the corporation. Afterward, they made a decision regarding compensation awards if they had found in favor of the plaintiff(s).

Mock jurors in both age groups benefited from preinstruction in that they were able to give more detailed and more cohesive accounts of the evidence that was presented. However, for some aspects of their decisions, the older mock jurors especially benefited from preinstruction. When asked to explain how they reached their liability decision, the preinstructed older mock jurors gave more probative statements than evaluative statements. In jury decision making, probative statements are based on evidence and thus considered more appropriate than evaluative statements. In contrast, older jurors instructed at the standard time gave more evaluative statements (expressions of opinion about witnesses, attorneys, or plaintiffs). Moreover, compared to the older mock jurors given standard instructions, the preinstructed older mock jurors were better able to make the appropriate distinctions between the most injured and least injured plaintiffs with regard to compensation awards. One explanation for the positive effect of preinstruction on older jurors is that older adults depend more than young adults do on being able to use knowledge structures as a scaffold upon which to organize incoming information (Bransford & Johnson, 1972). With instructions given before incoming information, a scaffolding structure is in place to guide top-down processing and thus minimize cognitive demands.

In sum, much remains to be understood about the decision-making strategies used by young and older adults on juries as well as in other contexts. At present, it seems clear that providing structure is especially helpful to older adults. Also, older adults may need some encouragement to consider the full array of alternatives before making a final decision.

SOCIAL COGNITION

Social cognition has to do with how people process social information. Such processing is influenced by their cognitive representations, or **schemas**. Individuals have schemas about themselves, and Chapter 8 covers the topic of self-concept (how schemas about the self are formed, maintained, and revised). However, social cognition also deals with how individuals form impressions of other people, as well as how they appraise social dilemmas. Individuals have schemas about other people and about everyday situations and events (Blanchard-Fields, 1999; Blanchard-Fields & Abeles, 1996). These schemas may influence how they interpret the behavior of others and how they evaluate social dilemmas. Those who study age and social cognition have asked the following questions:

- Are there age-related differences in the pre-existing schemas people have about others?
- How do young and older adults integrate inconsistent, or contradictory, information into their already-existing schemas?
- What inferences, causal judgments, or attributions do individuals make to explain why a social dilemma occurred and also how it should be resolved?

- Do individuals attend to one aspect of a situation more than they do to another? If so, does a person's age or perhaps a person's generation, or cohort, play a role in how social situations are interpreted?
- How do emotional factors affect young and older adults' judgments about the behavior of others and about how social dilemmas should be resolved?

Impression Formation

Individuals (labeled "perceivers") construct mental representations, or form impressions, of other people (labeled "targets") whom they encounter in everyday life. The impressions they form guide their social interactions and can influence their adaptation to the social world.

Two types of cognitive operation can be used to form impressions about targets (Cuddy & Fiske, 2002; Hess, 1999). **Category-based operations** rely on previously formed cognitive representations, or schemas. Thus, once a target is identified as a member of a certain category (for example, college professor), perceivers base their impression of that target using a previously formed schema about the characteristics of college professors (for example, scholarly, absent-minded, and so on). Category-based operations are similar to the top-down processing described earlier. The advantage of category-based operations is that they are efficient and place minimal demand on a perceiver's cognitive resources. A potential disadvantage is that a schema that was useful in the past may not be appropriate in a new situation. When perceivers rely exclusively on category-based operations, they may pay less attention to detailed information about a specific target or situation.

In contrast to category-based operations, **piecemeal operations** are similar to bottom-up processing. Perceivers construct a unique and possibly a more accurate representation of a target by integrating individual pieces of information about the target (such as physical characteristics, specific behaviors, stated likes and dislikes, motivations, and goals). Piecemeal operations require active processing of detailed information, so they consume more cognitive resources than category-based operations do. If there are age-related limitations in cognitive resources, then older perceivers may be less likely than young perceivers to use piecemeal operations when forming impressions, and they may rely more on category-based operations. As well, however, older adults may have less need to use piecemeal operations because many of them come to social situations with considerable experience and extensive knowledge, both of which could influence the judgments they make about others. During the impression-formation process, older adults may rely more on information that has been useful in the past.

Some behaviors are high in **trait diagnosticity** (Hess, 1999; Hess & Auman, 2001), which means that these behaviors seem to be especially informative when perceivers must make inferences about a target's traits. Behaviors that are high in trait diagnosticity are associated exclusively with a specific characteristic. In contrast, behaviors that are not high in trait diagnosticity carry less information about whether a target possesses a particular trait. With regard to the trait of competence, positive behaviors are more diagnostic than negative behaviors (Hess & Auman, 2001). For example, getting good grades in calculus (a positive behavior) is high in diagnosticity for inferring that an individual has mathematical competence. Thus, perceivers would categorize students who make "A's" in a calculus course as being high in mathematical ability. On the other hand, a poor grade in calculus (a negative behavior) is not high in diagnosticity for inferring poor mathematical competence. Perceivers may surmise that a student earned the poor grade because he or she did not study enough.

With regard to the trait of morality, however, it appears that negative behaviors are more diagnostic than positive behaviors (Hess & Auman, 2001). For example, perceivers categorize targets who steal money as dishonest, so stealing (a negative behavior) is high in diagnosticity for inferring the trait of dishonesty. In contrast, honest acts are not high in trait diagnosticity for honesty, possibly because a target's motivation for performing such acts is not always clear. For example, a target may behave in an honest way simply because he or she fears the consequences of stealing. However, research on age and trait diagnosticity has been conducted mainly in the United States, and the trait diagnosticity of specific behaviors reflects cultural norms. Behaviors high in trait diagnosticity in one culture may not be high in a different culture or society.

In their investigations on impression formation, Hess and his colleagues demonstrated that with increasing age, perceivers place greater emphasis on the diagnostic value of a target's behaviors. After reading brief descriptions of targets that included information about behaviors high in trait diagnosticity, older perceivers were more likely than young adult perceivers to maintain the impression they formed even when they were later given additional information about the target that was low in trait diagnosticity. Similarly, older perceivers were more likely than young perceivers to change their initial impression if later they were given information about the target that was high in trait diagnosticity (Hess, Bolstad, Woodburn, & Auman, 1999).

The greater weight older perceivers place on information that is high in trait diagnosticity seems to hold regardless of a target's age or whether the target's behavior is positive (getting A's) or negative (stealing) (Hess & Auman, 2001). Interestingly, however, older perceivers' heavier reliance on information high in trait diagnositicity is more evident in their impressions of a target's morality than it is in their impressions of a target's competence (Hess et al., 1999). Perhaps older perceivers place greater importance on morality, whereas competence is more important to young perceivers (Hess & Auman, 2001).

In any case, older perceivers' reliance on information high in trait diagnosticity may signify an age-related increase in social expertise, as evidenced by their ability to discriminate between aspects of a target's behavior that are more informative (high in diagnosticity) as opposed to less informative (low in diagnosticity) when making inferences about certain traits. Hess and Auman (2001) contend that this ability signifies an age-related increase in adaptive functioning in the society or culture in which perceivers live.

Causal Attributions

How do individuals interpret the social events they encounter in everyday life? Do young and older perceivers make similar causal attributions to explain why such events occurred? These questions are significant because causal attributions provide insight into perceivers' construction of social reality and their reasoning about social dilemmas. Understanding how young versus older perceivers evaluate others (targets), and what attributions they make for the cause of a target's social dilemma, provides important clues about the strategies they themselves might invoke in real-life social situations.

A number of factors are related to the appraisals perceivers make of social dilemmas. One is the social knowledge, or schema, the perceiver brings to the situation. Such a schema has probably been shaped by prior encounters in similar situations, and the nature and extent of prior experience could be a function of a perceiver's chronological age or cohort membership. Specific values may play a more prominent role in the development of some cohorts than in others. Finally, a schema is influenced by the culture, or society, in which perceivers live.

A popular approach researchers have taken to investigate social reasoning is to present perceivers with a brief sketch, or vignette, about a target who faces a dilemma or has experienced a particular social outcome. Perceivers are instructed to make causal attributions for what caused the dilemma or outcome. Blanchard-Fields (1996) offers the following example:

> Allen had been dating Barbara for over a year. At Barbara's suggestion, they moved in together. Everyone kept asking when they were going to get married. Allen found it extremely uncomfortable to live with Barbara and not be married to her. Even though Barbara disagreed, Allen kept bringing up the issue of marriage. Eventually, they broke up.

Causal attributions for this negative outcome could be dispositional, situational, or interactive. **Dispositional attributions** would place responsibility for the breakup entirely on the personal characteristics of the main character, Allen (for example, that he was impatient or rigid), or possibly on Barbara (for example, that she was immature or lacked commitment to Allen). Alternatively, **situational attributions** would place responsibility for the breakup on external extenuating circumstances such as the reaction of families, friends, or society in general to Allen and Barbara's living together without marriage, or even to the idea that the time was not right or the union was not destined to take place. **Interactive attributions** would take both dispositional and situational factors into account rather than attributing the outcome entirely to one or the other. Thus, perceivers would attribute the breakup to Allen's and possibly to Barbara's personal characteristics combined with external extenuating circumstances. Interactive attributions represent a more compromising, dialectical view, and they seem to be more common in Asian cultures than in Western cultures (Peng & Nisbett, 1999). Even within Western culture, however, age or cohort membership could make a difference in the type of attributions people make. For example, today's older adult cohort is less likely than today's young adult cohort to have lived as couples without marriage, and the different experiences of these age/cohort groups might contribute to their attributions.

One hypothesis about age-related attributional differences is that young perceivers focus either on dispositional factors or on situational factors in an all-or-none manner, whereas older perceivers are more likely to attribute the outcome of an event to a combination of factors. The reasoning is that with greater maturity, interactive attributions become more prevalent because older adults are more likely to perceive and coordinate multiple perspectives, a process similar to the perspective-taking aspect of postformal thinking or perhaps to wisdom.

But do older adults really make more interactive attributions than young adults do? Blanchard-Fields (1994) found that compared to young adults, older adults make higher interactive attributions (thinking an outcome is caused both by the main character and the situation) when vignettes have to do with relationships (such as an adult son moving out when his parents asked him to pay rent) but not when vignettes have to do with achievement (such as a student who did not study and failed her college courses). Yet, even though Blanchard-Fields's (1996) scenario about Allen and Barbara described a relationship outcome, older perceivers were more likely than young perceivers to attribute the couple's breakup to something about Allen, which is dispositional. Thus, no set rule can be used to predict when older adults will make more interactive attributions than young or middle-aged adults do. It seems likely that the specific nature of the event and whether the outcome is positive or negative both play a role in the attributions made by young and older perceivers. Most certainly, age-related and/or cohort-related differences in cognitive schemas can surface when attributions are made for specific dilemmas. This could explain why older adults make higher interactive attributions for some outcomes than they do for others. In addition, the age of the character in the vignette, as well as the relevance of the character's outcome to the life of the perceiver, could be important factors in the attributions that are made (Blanchard-Fields, Baldi, & Stein, 1999).

In attribution studies conducted with young adults (most often college students), researchers have found evidence for what is termed a *correspondence bias*, also referred to as the **fundamental attribution error** (Gilbert & Malone, 1995; Jones, 1979; Ross, 1977). When making attributions for social outcomes involving others (targets), young adult perceivers tend to overemphasize dispositional factors and to underemphasize the possible influence of situational factors. In other words, social outcomes are attributed to the target's characteristics, and little consideration is given to situational factors that could be operating. This bias is especially apparent when the outcome of an event is negative rather than positive and also when there is ambiguity about the possible role of dispositional and situational factors (Blanchard-Fields, 1994). For example, a perceiver might be told that a student failed an exam, but little or no information is given about the content of the course, the skill of the teacher, or about events such as the student being in a minor car accident right before taking the exam.

Note that the fundamental attribution error has been demonstrated mainly in individualistic cultures in North America and Europe. It is less frequent in the more collectivist East Asian cultures, many of which foster a strong belief that dispositions are malleable and individuals should always be considered within the context of their particular situation (Choi, Nisbett, & Norenzayan, 1999).

Although the fundamental attribution error is found when young perceivers make attributions for the negative outcomes of others (targets), it is not usually found when young perceivers make attributions for their own outcomes. For example, when asked why a target received a poor grade in a course, young perceivers usually attribute this negative outcome to a dispositional factor such as the target's poor ability. However, when making attributions for their own negative outcomes, young perceivers do not show the same bias. They think their own poor grades are the result of situational factors, such as not enough time to study or an unfair exam.

Blanchard-Fields and her colleagues investigated whether middle-aged and older perceivers would also make the fundamental attribution error. In one study (Blanchard-Fields, 1994), young, middle-aged, and older adult perceivers read brief vignettes, each describing a hypothetical scenario in which a target experiences either a negative or a positive social outcome in a relationship situation or an achievement situation. In all of the vignettes, the factors that actually caused the event outcome were ambiguous. When the outcome was negative, the older perceivers had an even greater tendency than the young and middle-aged perceivers did to commit the fundamental attribution error by overattributing the target's negative outcome to dispositional factors.

Blanchard-Fields et al. (1999) found that the age of the target described in their vignettes had an effect on perceivers' attributions for the event described. Perceivers of all ages made higher dispositional attributions for young targets, whereas they made higher situational attributions for old targets. Additionally, dispositional attributions were higher if the event took place in a work context, whereas situational attributions were higher if the event took place in a family context.

In sum, conclusions about age-related differences in causal attributions must be qualified by the context in which attributions are made (relationship, family, achievement, work), by whether the outcome is positive or negative, and by the age of the target in the vignette. In some cases, older perceivers make higher interactive attributions than do perceivers from other adult age groups. In other cases, older perceivers show a more exaggerated fundamental attribution error than do young and middle-aged perceivers. Further research in this intriguing area of study should clarify the conditions associated with age-related similarities and age-related differences in causal attributions.

Moral Reasoning

In many situations encountered in the context of work, family, and community, we find ourselves making judgments about the "rightness" or "wrongness" of the actions taken or choices made by others (Pratt & Norris, 1994). For example, if an individual steals, many of us would consider it wrong and we would have a low opinion of that individual's morality. But are there some circumstances in which stealing would not be considered wrong or as signifying immorality? Consider the following scenario, which was one of several hypothetical dilemmas used by Kohlberg (1969) to study moral reasoning:

> A druggist insists on charging a premium amount for a medication that will save a woman's life. The woman's husband is unable to borrow enough money to purchase the medication, so he breaks into the pharmacy and steals the medicine.

What kind of moral reasoning do individuals use to determine whether it was right or wrong for the husband to behave the way he did? Based on responses to the medication scenario as well as other scenarios describing hypothetical moral dilemmas, Kohlberg (1969) proposed a cognitive-developmental perspective of moral reasoning, or moral maturity. This perspective has three levels, each of which is divided further into several stages. On the basis of their responses to the moral dilemmas, individuals can be assigned scores to indicate their level/stage of moral maturity.

- Level 1: Preconventional Morality (the childhood years from ages 4–10)—moral judgments are made with an eye to obtaining a reward or avoiding punishment.
- Level 2: Conventional Morality (commencing some time after the age of 10)—moral judgments are made on the basis of pleasing others, being "nice," "good," doing one's duty and what is expected, and maintaining the social order.
- Level 3: Postconventional Morality—morality becomes fully internalized. Moral judgments are based on abstract ethical principles as opposed to concrete rules. There is recognition that conflict may exist between the laws and expectations of society and universal ethical principles such as justice, compassion, and equality. Level 3 often begins in adolescence or young adulthood, but it is not necessarily reached by everyone.

Kohlberg's ideas are widely respected, but his levels and the stages within each one were devised within Western culture and they may not account for culturally based differences in moral values. Also, his studies were conducted chiefly with boys and men. Even within Western culture, there may be gender-related differences in thinking about moral conflict, and Gilligan (1982) questioned whether Kohlberg's levels and stages are applicable to women. For example, men might think in terms of justice, whereas women might focus on the preservation and enhancement of relationships (Pratt & Norris, 1994). However, studies that have included both men and women have not always found gender-related differences in moral development.

Chap (1986) conducted a cross-sectional study in which a group of young/early middle-aged (ages 30–49) and older (ages 63–85) men and woman from the metropolitan Washington, DC, area were presented with several moral dilemmas. The content of some of the dilemmas was age appropriate for the young group, while the content of other dilemmas was age appropriate for the

Table 7.2 | Four Levels of Moral Perspective Taking

Level 1
Only a single point of view is considered, with no acknowledgment that other points of view could or do exist.

Level 2
Several points of view are acknowledged, but no attempt is made to reconcile them, or to recommend that one character in the dilemma try to understand another character's point of view.

Level 3
Two or more points of view are considered, and it is recommended that one character in the dilemma try to understand the another's point of view (but not vice versa).

Level 4
Two or more points of view are considered, as in Level 3, but there is acknowledgment of reciprocity between the competing points of view.

Source: Adapted from Chap (1986).

older group. Here are examples of the young-appropriate and old-appropriate dilemmas used by Chap (1986):

- *Age appropriate for the young/early middle-aged group:* A woman considers lying in a child custody hearing about her husband's suitability as a parent to ensure that she will gain custody.
- *Age appropriate for the old group:* A 70-year-old elderly man living on a fixed income occasionally shoplifts a few dollars' worth of food to make ends meet.

Based on their open-ended responses, participants received a score for their level of moral maturity based on Kohlberg's theory. When these scores were adjusted for years of education, neither gender nor age differences were found. However, the age appropriateness of the dilemma was significant. Participants received higher moral maturity scores for their responses to dilemmas that were relevant for their own age group.

In addition to level of moral maturity, Chap investigated **moral perspective taking**, which is the inclination to consider a moral dilemma from various perspectives. Table 7.2 describes Chap's four levels of moral perspective taking. At the lowest level, responses focus on one point of view and discount all others. At the highest level, responses show recognition that several points of view can be reconciled with one another.

Chap found that the men and women in the study did not differ in their level of perspective taking. However, the average level of perspective taking was lower for the older group than it was for the young/early middle-aged group. Thus, the older group was less likely than the young/early middle-aged group to consider the perspective of all the characters involved in a moral dilemma. Rather, the older adults were more likely to voice the opinion that there was only one correct point of view. This seems counter to the idea that postformal thinking increases with age.

To determine whether the level/stage of moral maturity and perspective taking remain constant over time, or whether there would be a regression to a lower level, Pratt, Diessner, Pratt, Hunsberger, and Pancer (1996) conducted a longitudinal study following 28 middle-aged (ages 35–54) and 36 older (ages 64–80) adults over 4 years. At the outset of the study and again 4 years later, participants read descriptions of moral dilemmas. At both times, these researchers used the same measures as Chap (1986) did to assess their study participants' level of moral maturity and level of moral perspective taking.

Pratt et al.'s longitudinal results reflected Chap's cross-sectional findings. Over the 4-year period, the level/stage of moral development did not change for either age group. However, there were small changes in the older group's level of perspective taking. Both age groups started out with an average of 2.5 on the 4-level perspective-taking scale. By the end of the study, the middle-aged group's average perspective-taking level remained unchanged, but the older group's level had declined to an average of 2.0. Because Pratt et al.'s study participants were relatively well-educated residents of a moderate-sized metropolitan area in Eastern Canada, they were not broadly representative of the general population of North American adults. However, even within this relatively select sample, Pratt et al. found that what they called "resource" variables (level of education, self-reported health at the study's start, and perceived social support from others) protected against decline in both moral level/stage and moral perspective taking. In both age groups, participants who had the highest level of education, considered themselves most healthy, and reported having the greatest access to social support from others were the ones most likely to maintain their moral stage/level over the 4-year interval. With regard to perspective taking, the resource variables also served a protective function, although over the 4 years there was still some decline in the older group in this aspect of moral development. Perhaps the decline in perspective taking reflects a strategic attempt on the part of the older study participants to minimize cognitive overload as they deliberate about moral issues.

Collaboration in Reasoning and Problem Solving

Collaborative cognitive activities are those in which more than one individual performs a common task with a common goal (Dixon, 1999). By its very nature, collaborative cognition, or problem solving, encompasses a social element. One example of collaborative cognition is an older adult couple who help each other to reminisce about a wonderful vacation they took in the past. Each member of the pair may remember different details about the trip, but the details recalled by one may compensate for those forgotten by the other. Together, the couple re-creates a more complete picture of this event than would be possible for one of them alone.

Two heads are better than one when trying to re-create the details about a special occasion.

Just as two scientists often collaborate to find a solution to an abstract problem in a research laboratory, two or more individuals may collaborate to find optimal solutions to the logistical problems of everyday life. Consider a married couple, Martha and Jack. Martha has been a homemaker throughout her 40-year marriage to Jack. She has had complete charge of shopping, cooking, and other household chores, while Jack held a full-time job. Their collaboration has been based on a strict division of labor. Recently, Jack retired and now he wants to become involved in the shopping and household tasks. Martha and Jack will need to restructure their daily lives, forging a mutually agreeable solution as to who will do what. In this example, the collaborators are a married couple. However, collaborative problem solving is not limited to marital relationships or to just two people working together.

Researchers in aging have a great deal of interest in the utility of collaboration when real-life decisions are necessary (Dixon & Gould, 1996, 1998). When faced with solving a real-life problem, how extensively do older adults collaborate, or even just consult, with others? The problems they face could range from selecting a shade of "off-white" paint for a room in the house to decisions about distributing possessions to friends or relatives when they downsize from a large home and move to an apartment or assisted living facility. Clearly, some decisions have more social and emotional implications than others do, yet all of them still involve choices.

Compared to those who make decisions without consulting anyone else, those who seek advice, support, and validation from others tend to think about their problems in more complex ways. Also, they tend to be more satisfied and to have more confidence in the solutions they reach (see Pratt & Norris, 1999). Thus, collaboration, or consultation, is associated with increased quality of reasoning about everyday problems and dilemmas. Perhaps collaboration compensates for an individual's age-related decline in such abilities.

As described previously, Pratt et al.'s (1996) study found that social-cognitive support offers some protection against age-related decline in the perspective-taking aspect of moral reasoning. Perhaps consulting with others about difficult decisions fosters a more complex level of thinking that encourages consideration of multiple perspectives of a problem. However, the inclination to consult with others prior to making decisions could also be related to personality. Individuals who are highly authoritarian may view the moral world in more simplistic terms, and they may not consider the opinions of others to be important. Such individuals are less likely to reach out to others for advice or support, and they are more likely to make decisions on their own. Much remains to be understood about the conditions under which consultation works best. Some kinds of problem solving may benefit from collaboration more than others. Also, some individuals may be more open than others to using such opportunities.

Emotion and Cognition

Until recently, researchers viewed emotion and cognition as two separate domains. In fact, Blanchard-Fields (1997) points out that when these two domains were viewed together, emotion was often considered a nuisance factor that got in the way of evaluating whether there was age-related decline in cognition. For example, there have been hypotheses that age-related decline on cognitive tasks simply reflects a level of emotional arousal that is either too high (high anxiety) or too low (low motivation).

A more recent perspective is that emotion and cognition are interrelated (Labouvie-Vief & Diehl, 2000). The influence these domains have on one another may depend upon cultural background, age, and cohort factors such as level of education and values. The relationship between emotion and cognition has special relevance when social information is processed because social goals, values, and belief systems influence the interpretation of social information.

Social cognition research has been conducted mainly with young adult college students, but investigations are being extended to other age groups. Blanchard-Fields and her colleagues (Blanchard-Fields & Norris, 1994; Blanchard-Fields, Jahnke, & Camp, 1995) have conducted studies on what strategies individuals from various age groups say they themselves would use to resolve dilemmas described in vignettes. In some cases, study participants were asked to select one strategy from a menu of alternative strategies. In other cases, participants gave open-ended responses describing what they would do if faced with the dilemma presented.

Some of the dilemmas used in these studies were rated previously as low in emotional significance, while others were rated as high in emotional significance.

Dilemmas low in emotional significance described instrumental problems that often occur in everyday life. For example, study participants were asked what they would do if they found they had purchased merchandise that was defective (a consumer-oriented problem) or if they had a landlord who refused to make needed repairs (a home-management problem). Dilemmas high in emotional significance were more interpersonal. For example, participants were asked how they would handle conflicts with co-workers, friends, or family members. The solutions they gave for dealing with the dilemmas fell into the following categories:

- **Problem-focused strategies**—taking direct action to control, or "fix," the problem
- **Cognitive-analytic strategies**—efforts to solve the problem by thinking it through
- **Passive-dependent strategies**—attempts to withdraw from the situation
- **Avoidant strategies**—denial of the problem, often by attempting to reinterpret its meaning

For dilemmas low in emotional significance, participants of all ages most frequently endorsed problem-focused action strategies. In fact, in the consumer domain, middle-aged and older adults were even more likely than adolescents and young adults were to say they would use problem-focused strategies such as taking defective merchandise back to the store. Additionally, middle-aged and older adults engaged in extensive cognitive-analytic analyses of the situation, thus demonstrating they were capable of using complex strategies most likely honed from years of experience.

For dilemmas high in emotional significance, problem-focused strategies were less likely to be endorsed by participants of all ages, but this was especially true for older adults. Thus, older participants were even less likely than young ones to say they would take an action such as confronting the interpersonal situation directly. While older participants did not abandon problem-focused strategies altogether, they were more likely than young or even middle-aged participants to endorse passive-dependent and avoidant strategies, indicating they were less willing to confront such dilemmas head on. The fact that older adults were more willing to avoid, or passively accept, an interpersonal dilemma could mean that as a result of life experience, they are more accepting of ambiguity and uncertainty in emotionally laden situations (Blanchard-Fields, 1997). Another interpretation of their tendency to use passive-dependent and avoidant strategies in emotionally laden situations is that older adults show more emotional control by avoiding conflict, stressors, and negativity when relating to others (Magai & Passman, 1997).

Labouvie-Vief (1997, 1999) contends that older adults are less likely than young adults to engage in impulsive behavior such as hostile acting out or turning against others. In contrast, they tend to reinterpret negative situations, avoid conflict, and accept negative events. When older adults use these strategies, it may appear that they are flexible and that their behavior is well-regulated. However, these strategies may simply be a way to screen out negative experience, thereby reducing the complexity of any emotional conflict they must handle

(Labouvie-Vief, 1999). Older adults may adapt to restrictions in cognitive and emotional resources by becoming less confrontational and more self-protective, and this well-controlled behavior may help them to maintain a sense of well-being.

Up to this point, most of the research conducted on emotion and aging has been cross-sectional, so the young and older adult research participants have come from different generations, or cohorts. Older adults' tendency to avoid the negative aspects of interpersonal relationships could be partly attributable to the possibility that they were socialized with stricter rules of emotional regulation (Labouvie-Vief, 1999). There is a clear need for longitudinal studies that follow the same people over time to determine whether there are any age-related changes in emotional regulation.

REVISITING THE SELECTIVE OPTIMIZATION WITH COMPENSATION AND ECOLOGICAL MODELS

The Selective Optimization with Compensation (SOC) Model (Baltes & Baltes, 1990) is useful as a framework within which to consider how older adults use cognitive processes in the everyday world and what strategies they employ when solving problems, making creative contributions, making decisions, and forming impressions. It is important to recognize that older adults may direct their cognitive efforts toward concerns that have the most meaning for their particular stage of life. Problems in everyday life often have more than one possible solution. Because of their experience, older adults may consider a problem from several different perspectives before reaching a solution. When making decisions, older adults rely more heavily than young adults do on top-down, or category-based, processing as opposed to bottom-up, or piecemeal, processing. This may reflect a way of compensating for limitations in cognitive capability. However, because of their accumulated wealth of experience, older adults may be less dependent than young adults are on the piecemeal processing of new details. Given their expertise in some areas of decision making and impression formation, top-down strategies may serve them well, limiting their need to "reinvent the wheel" each time a new problem must be resolved or a new decision made. In their creative endeavors, older adults may place greater value on the simplification and synthesis of ideas as opposed to making complex, novel contributions.

The Ecological Model (Lawton, 1989; Lawton & Nahemow, 1973) can be viewed as a framework for considering which environments are likely to foster the highest level of adaptive functioning for older adults. If older adults tend to make final decisions without considering all of the alternatives, then their functioning might be most adaptive when an array of alternatives is introduced in a structured and organized manner. To adapt to new environments, older adults may need to use tacit knowledge gathered from the actions and indirect statements of others. If older adults are hesitant to confront highly emotional situations head on, then their level of adaptive functioning may be highest when they are in a supportive environment where they are not forced to do so.

KEY POINTS

- There may be different motivations for using cognitive capabilities at different stages of life. The acquisitive, achieving, responsible/executive stages describe the reasons in childhood/adolescence, young adulthood, and middle adulthood, respectively. In older adulthood, motivations are reorganizational, reintegrative, and legacy creating.

- Postformal reasoning requires perspective taking and is well-suited for real-life problems that have more than one correct solution. Interpersonal problems and moral dilemmas often benefit from postformal reasoning. Many older adults think postformally but there are mixed findings about whether older adults make more use of this type of thinking than young adults do.

- Wisdom has not been easy to define, but it is considered an admirable characteristic associated with perspective taking, knowing what and knowing how, knowing what one does not know, and maintaining a balance between reflection and action. Studies show that some older adults are wise, but old age does not guarantee wisdom.

- Practical intelligence calls for tacit knowledge, which requires "knowing how" rather than "knowing what." Tacit knowledge is acquired with little help from others and must be inferred from actions and indirect statements. It has been studied mainly in the context of work but it could help older adults adapt to new environments.

- Some creative contributions peak in mid-life, but there may be a resurgence later. Creative works of older musicians, artists, and writers show a simplicity of style and integration of ideas and often emphasize subjective experience.

- Real-world problem solving shows less age-related decline than abstract problem solving. Real-world decisions are made in health, consumer, and legal contexts. Older adults weigh fewer alternatives than young adults do before reaching a decision. Also, older adults use top-down strategies more, while young adults use bottom-up strategies more.

- When forming impressions about the traits of other people, older adults rely more than young adults do on information that has high trait-diagnosticity. There could be an age-related increase in social expertise such that older adults have a heightened ability to discriminate between aspects of behavior that are more informative as opposed to less informative about a trait.

- Causal attributions for a social outcome of another person can be dispositional, situational, or interactive. Whether there are age-related differences in a particular kind of causal attribution depends upon a number of factors, including the nature of the context in which the outcome occurs.

- For dilemmas that are not emotional, such as what to do if a defective item is purchased, adults of all ages usually say they would use a problem-focused strategy to confront the situation directly. When dilemmas are emotionally laden, involving interpersonal dilemmas, older adults are more likely than young adults to say they would avoid or passively accept the situation. Similarly, older adults are more likely than young adults to reinterpret negative situations, to avoid conflict, and to accept negative events.

KEY TERMS

acquisitive stage   248

achieving stage   249

avoidant strategies   282

bottom-up processing strategy   267

category-based operations   272

cognitive-analytic strategies   282

collaborative cognitive activities   279

compensatory decision rules   270

constant-probability-of-success
model of creativity   261

constraint-seeking questions   263

dispositional attributions   274

formal knowledge   258

formal operations   252

fundamental attribution error   275

hypothesis-testing questions   263

interactive attributions   274

legacy-creating stage   250

moral perspective taking   278

noncompensatory decision rules   269

passive-dependent strategies   282

piecemeal operations   272

postformal thinking   252

problem-focused strategies   282

reintegrative stage   250

reorganizational stage   250

responsible/executive stage   249

schemas   271

situational attributions   274

swan-song phenomenon   262

tacit knowledge   258

top-down processing strategy   267

trait diagnosticity   272

wisdom   253

To learn more about the issues discussed in this chapter, point your browser to http://www.infotrac-college.com and use the passcode from the InfoTrac College Edition card that came with your book. InfoTrac College Edition gives you access to complete articles from many different journals.

Personality and Coping

8

Paulina looks back over her life and reminisces about what a social butterfly she used to be when she was in her 20s. Back then, she was constantly on the go with her friends, and she went to several parties each week. At age 78, Paulina still enjoys social gatherings more than most people her age, but one party a month is enough to satisfy her. Still, she finds herself drawn to situations where she will be spending time with good friends and family members rather than situations in which she is likely to be alone. Paulina has noticed that some people her age seem happier and more satisfied with their lives than others do. She thinks the key to happiness and satisfaction in older adulthood is to have realistic expectations, to concentrate on those aspects of life that you can control, but to change the way you think about things you cannot do anything about.

STUDYING PERSONALITY IN AGING AND OLDER ADULTHOOD

Most of us make judgments about what other people are like by how they behave. For example, a person who is friendly and approachable would probably be viewed as outgoing, or extraverted, whereas a person who is quiet and shy would not. Ideally, the inferences we make about someone's personality are based on observations of their behavior on a number of occasions and not on behavior that occurs only one time.

Although we often judge the personality of other people based on their behavior, another aspect of personality is how we view ourselves. What is important to us, what is distasteful to us, what opinions do we have about various issues? In short, what is our own theory about who we are? In some instances, the way others view us corresponds with how we view our inner self. However, there are exceptions. For example, a person who is viewed as hard nosed by others because of his or her behavior as a manager at work may perceive him- or herself as tender hearted and as showing concern for employees by being strict.

In sum, personality is a complex concept, or construct, with many different aspects (Hall, Lindzey, & Campbell, 1998). It has to do with how we view others, how they view us, and how we view ourselves. As such, personality directly relates to behavior because the way people act conveys information about what they are like. However, personality also has an inner aspect because it relates to how we see ourselves, and our inner thoughts and feelings are not always reflected in our immediate behavior.

Approaches to Investigating Personality

What approaches are used to investigate personality in the field of aging and older adulthood? As discussed in Chapter 2, one way to study the developmental aspects of personality is to use a cross-sectional research design, which compares the personality characteristics of individuals in two or more age groups. The advantage of cross-sectional studies is that all research participants are tested or interviewed at one specific time, so information can be obtained quickly and efficiently. The disadvantage is that any age-related differences found could stem not only from chronological age, but also from diverse factors that may have affected the personality of individuals from different generations, or cohorts.

To illustrate, if we compare 20-year-olds with 70-year-olds, we may find that the two age groups differ in some aspects of personality. These differences could be associated with their differing chronological ages. However, differences could also be a function of the fact that the 20- and 70-year-olds come from different cohorts and have been not been exposed to the same influences at crucial points during their development. For example, age-related differences in personality could stem from the enduring influence of childrearing philosophies and practices that were prevalent when members of the two cohorts were growing up. Perhaps 70-year-olds as a group are more socially inhibited because of their stricter upbringing, while 20-year-olds as a group are more impulsive due to their more permissive upbringing.

Another way to study the developmental aspects of personality is to use a longitudinal research design, which follows a sample of individuals over time and assesses whether personality remains stable or whether it changes as they grow older. The advantage of the longitudinal design is that it can detect changes within the individual. The disadvantage of longitudinal studies is that they take a long time to complete—from several months to years—and some study participants do not come back time after time. Selective attrition means that the participants who drop out of the study may have different personality characteristics compared with those who remain. For example, individuals who drop out may be less dependable than those willing to be retested. Those who remain in the study may not only be more dependable, but they may also be more well-adjusted than those who are unwilling or unable to return. Some of us have had opportunities to conduct informal longitudinal research when we attend high school or college reunions in the years after we graduate. Which of our former classmates attend these reunions? Do the classmates who attend seem the same or different compared to how we remember them from high school?

To study the personality characteristics of only one age group, we can use a time-lag design, which tests people of one specific chronological age (or age group) at different points in time. For example, in the year 2000, we could administer a personality questionnaire to a sample of 75-year-olds, who were born in 1925. We could compare their responses with the responses of a sample of 75-year-olds tested in 1980, who were born in 1905. Perhaps the responses of the 75-year-olds from these two cohorts will be similar. If so, then any conclusions we draw about the personality characteristics of 75-year-olds will not be limited to only one cohort group. However, if we find differences, can these be attributed to the fact that the two groups of 75-year-olds come from different cohorts (born in 1905 versus 1925) or to the fact that the two groups were tested at different times (1980 and 2000)? One possible time effect might be that societal pressures were not as great in 2000, thus making it more acceptable for 75-year-olds to express their feelings and ideas in 2000 than it was for 75-year-olds to do so in 1980.

Personality over the Adult Years

The concept of personality implies that an individual's behavior will be stable across a variety of situations and also that the individual's inner self will remain relatively constant from day to day. Even so, is there any evidence that personality undergoes change with increasing age? Are some aspects of personality more dominant at one stage of life than they are at another, and are certain personality characteristics more descriptive of older adults than they are of other age groups? Fleeson and Heckhausen (1997) suggest that early adulthood is a time of exploration, striving for growth, self-actualization, and mastery of new roles. Middle adulthood is a time of productivity and gains in the ability to competently and confidently deal with the world through experience. In older adulthood, there is less striving for competency and a greater tendency to reflect, hopefully with satisfaction and contentment, on what has been accomplished in life.

Although some aspects of personality may be more common, or normative, for a particular age group, it is generally recognized that no two people are exactly alike. Within any age group, there are individual differences in personality characteristics. For example, some people are more contemplative and thoughtful while others are more impatient, daring, and willing to take risks. A fundamental question posed by those who study personality and aging is, "What are the personality characteristics of individuals who age most successfully?" How individuals cope with the challenges encountered over the course of adulthood and individual differences in the ability to maintain a positive outlook or achieve happiness are of great interest to personality and aging researchers.

HOW IS PERSONALITY MEASURED?

As we set out to study personality, how do we measure it? One way would be to ask individuals to describe themselves. A less direct approach would be to ask them to respond to ambiguous visual or verbal stimuli, with the hope that what they say will tell us something about what they are like. Still another approach would be to observe how individuals behave either in completely naturalistic settings or under more carefully controlled conditions. Regardless of how personality is measured, the instrument used should be both reliable and valid (see Chapter 2 for detailed explanation of these concepts). Now let's take a closer look at these three ways of measuring personality.

Self-Report Questionnaires

Personality inventories are self-report measures consisting of questions meant to be answered based on test takers' personal evaluations of themselves. On some self-report questionnaires, test takers are instructed to agree or disagree with a series of statements related to personality characteristics. For example, "I always want to be with other people and I never want to be alone" would be a statement with which an outgoing person would agree but a shy person may not. On some self-report questionnaires, test takers are given a list of traits (for example, "talkative" or "quiet") and told to check the ones that describe them or rate how much each trait describes them (such as not at all, a little, or very much). Some personality inventories have norms that have been established on the basis of the responses given by a large sample of individuals who completed the inventory previously. Responses of an individual test taker can be compared with those of the larger standardization sample.

Self-report questionnaires can be written or conducted orally. An advantage of written self-report inventories is that they can be given to large numbers of people. A possible disadvantage is that self-disclosure is required, so a test taker's responses may not be totally candid, or honest. Unbeknown to the test taker, some personality inventories include "lie scales" and "social desirability scales." If a test taker receives a high score on a lie scale (giving responses that are untrue for most people) or on a social desirability scale (giving responses he or she thinks are expected or that appear to be socially acceptable), then a red flag is raised about whether the test is a valid measure of personality for that particular individual.

Another way to gather self-report information on personality is to conduct open-ended interviews. An advantage of this technique is that information may come to light that would not be revealed in a person's answers to the predetermined set of questions found in most written self-report measures. A disadvantage is that responses to open-ended interviews can be difficult to quantify. Responses must be evaluated by more than one objective rater, who must agree on how to interpret or rate them.

Projective Techniques

With projective techniques, inferences are made about personality on the basis of a test taker's responses to ambiguous stimuli. The Thematic Apperception Test (TAT) is a projective measure that some studies on aging and older adulthood have used. It consists of pictures of characters who appear to be involved in ambiguous social interactions. Test takers tell a brief story about what has gone on and what will happen to the characters in the picture. Other examples of projective techniques are word association and sentence completion tests. Asking a test taker to say the first word that comes to mind in response to another word or to complete a phrase may uncover something about his or her personality. The advantage of projective techniques is that in responding to ambiguous stimuli, individuals may reveal feelings, thoughts, and thus aspects of their personality that they would be unwilling or unable to express directly on personality inventories or even in open-ended interviews. A disadvantage is that the responses individuals give on projective tests may be difficult to interpret.

Behavioral Observation

Another way to evaluate personality is to observe how people behave. We could rate the behavior of others on various scales or use behavior checklists to record how many times specific behaviors occur. We could demonstrate the necessary inter-rater reliability if two or more observers make the same ratings or have the same behavioral records.

Most often, we observe behavior in naturalistic settings. For example, we may want to determine which residents of an assisted living facility (ALF) are friendly (see Chapter 10 for a discussion of ALFs). To accomplish this, we could arrange for two observers to visit the ALF at several times during the day for a week to keep tabs on a sample of residents. Residents who exhibit behaviors such as smiling, eye contact, and talking to or touching others would probably be considered more friendly than those who do not display these behaviors. However, not all residents may exhibit the behaviors of interest when observers are visiting the ALF. To supplement the information gathered by the observers who visit periodically, we could ask AFL staff members to rate whether various residents show friendly behavior. Staff members will not be as objective as observers sent in from the outside, but they spend more hours per day with the residents and have more exposure to them. An advantage of this approach is that observations are made in a real-life, naturalistic setting. A disadvantage is that it is not possible to hold all aspects of the environment constant so that every resident can be observed under the same conditions. Also, as already mentioned, there is no guarantee that the behaviors of interest will occur while individuals are being observed.

Behavior can also be observed under more controlled conditions. For example, after signing a consent form (see Chapter 2 for a discussion of consent forms), individuals could be asked to sit in a room equipped with a one-way mirror so that they can be observed but cannot see who is watching them. A stooge (that is, a person trained by a researcher to follow a specific script) could enter the room and ask these individuals a series of questions in a set tone of voice. The verbal responses and body language of each individual can be recorded on videotape and later evaluated by raters, who must agree on what they observe. One possible drawback in this situation is that individuals' behavior may be affected by the knowledge they are being observed.

In sum, personality can be measured in a number of different ways, each having advantages and disadvantages. Those who study personality over the adult life span must take into consideration which approach is best suited to their goals when they investigate personality and aging.

NORMATIVE MODELS OF PERSONALITY

Do people change or do they remain the same over time? Are there universal (normative) changes in personality as we progress through adulthood, or do our personalities remain stable throughout our adult lives? There is more than one school of thought on this issue. Initially, we will focus on stage theories of personality, which emphasize changes that are expected to occur over the course of adult development. Then we will turn to research that emphasizes the stability of personality traits over the adult life span. Finally, we will look at how personality development is viewed by nonprofessional (lay) people who do not conduct scientific studies but are natural observers of others as well as of themselves.

Stage Models

Some theorists view personality as something that unfolds over time and takes different forms as individuals progress through their adult years. Personality development is thought to proceed in stages. There is a noticeable shift between stages, and each one is qualitatively different from the others. At each stage, certain qualities, or traits, are thought to predominate, or there may be a focus on coping with specific personal concerns. Stages are often linked to a chronological age range, and personality is thought to develop over the course of age, time, and experience.

Sigmund Freud (1856–1939) was a prominent stage theorist who lived most of his life in Vienna, where he attended medical school and specialized in neurology and nervous disorders (Hall et al., 1998). Based chiefly on case histories, Freud proposed a psychoanalytic theory that emphasized the role of unconscious biological instincts in motivating behavior. According to Freud's theory, personality development proceeds in a series of psychosexual stages that begin in infancy and extend through adolescence. However, Freud emphasized the importance of early childhood experiences in the formation of the basic structure of personality (Hall et al., 1998). Carl Jung and Erik Erikson were both trained in the Freudian tradition and like Freud, both are stage theorists. But each later one went his own way to develop a theory that extended beyond adolescence and throughout the adult years. Also, while Jung and Erikson acknowledged the importance of biological factors, both of them placed more emphasis than Freud did on the influences of the environment and society.

Carl Jung   Carl Jung was a young psychiatrist in Switzerland when he traveled to Vienna in 1907 to study with Freud. However, by 1916, Jung had developed his own theory of personality. Jung believed that throughout adulthood and into old age, we continue to grow toward the realization of our potential by balancing various aspects of our personality in response both to our inner needs and the demands of the external environment (Hall et al., 1998). Jung theorized that at different points in the adult life span the balance can shift, with some aspects of the self receding into the background and others coming to the forefront. While Jung believed that biological and social needs are primary in the first half of life, he thought that cultural and spiritual needs become more important in the second half (Stevens, 1994).

Jung viewed adult development in terms of two dimensions of personality: introversion/extraversion and masculinity/femininity. He believed that a person's position on either of these dimensions was not fixed, but rather that placement between the two poles of each dimension could shift at different stages of development.

With regard to introversion/extraversion, Jung thought that in young adulthood the emphasis is on meeting the demands of the external world and expanding the social environment. Important tasks at this stage of life include finding a mate and a vocation, both of which are more attainable if the outgoing aspects of personality predominate. Thus, in young adulthood, the extravertive aspects of personality are pushed to the forefront while the inner (introverted) aspects are suppressed. By middle adulthood, the social world is not expanding so rapidly, and there is less pressure to meet the demands of the external world and more time to devote to the inner self. Accordingly, there is a greater balance between the external and internal aspects of the personality. In older adulthood, the demands of the external social world are reduced even further, leaving more time for reflection on the inner self. The balance now shifts more toward the intro-version pole of the dimension.

Jung's idea of a shift toward introversion in older adulthood is supported by some of the findings of an ambitious research project known as the Kansas City Study of Adult Life. The Kansas City Study was conducted by members of the Committee on Human Development at the University of Chicago, who investigated personality from early middle age into older adulthood (Neugarten, Havinghurst, & Tobin, 1968). The Kansas City Study, so named because its participants were community-living residents of that Midwestern city, included 700 men and women ranging from 40 to 70 years of age. Among other measures, participants were given the projective Thematic Apperception Test (TAT), and on the basis of the stories they told about characters pictured in ambiguous social situations, the Kansas City Study researchers detected age-related differences in personality. In the stories told by those in their early 40s, the characters possessed boundless energy to meet and actively master the demands of the outer world and they were rewarded for boldness and risk taking. In contrast, in the stories told by those in their 50s, 60s, and 70s, the characters were more reflective and less willing to deal with challenging situations or to make emotional investments in other people. Neugarten and her colleagues characterized the older adults' stories as indicating a move from the active mastery typical in the 40s to more passive mastery and a greater preoccupation with inner life, which they referred to as *increased interiority*. The increased interiority beginning in the decade of the 50s concurred with Jung's hypothesis that introversion tends to predominate in later adulthood and formed the basis for what became known as disengagement theory, which Chapter 9 will describe.

Jung also contended that every individual's personality has both masculine and feminine aspects, and these can co-exist and even complement one another. He thought that in young adulthood, the same-sex tendencies predominate. That is, the masculine aspects predominate in young men, whereas the feminine aspects predominate in young women. Beginning in middle age but more so in older adulthood when there is less pressure to fulfill culturally prescribed sex roles, the suppressed aspect is freer to emerge. Accordingly, men become more accepting of their nurturing (feminine) side and women of their assertive (masculine) side. This idea was reflected in the TAT stories told by the Kansas City Study participants. Compared to the stories told by the middle-aged men, those told by the older men indicated they were more receptive to their nurturing and sensual feelings. Compared to the stories told by the middle-aged women, those told by the older women indicated they were more receptive to their aggressive and self-centered impulses. In keeping with Jung's theory, older adults become more tolerant and accepting of opposite-sex tendencies that were suppressed at earlier stages of adulthood.

The same pattern of sex differences found in the Kansas City Study has also been found in various geographical areas and subcultures within the United States (for example, in rural Florida among both European American and African American ethnic groups) as well as in Israel, Asia, and Africa (Gutmann, 1977). Regardless of their ethnic background, older men are more tolerant than younger men are of their domestic interests and they focus less on competitiveness.

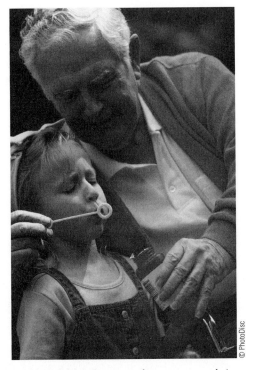

In older adulthood, men are freer to express their nurturing side than they were when they were younger.

In contrast, older women are more domineering and less submissive compared to their younger counterparts (Gutmann, 1977). The fact that there are similar sex differences cross-culturally suggests that these may truly be developmental.

Erik Erikson   Erik Erikson is one of the most prominent stage theorists in the field of adult development and aging. Erikson acknowledged the contribution of biological factors and inner psychological processes to personality development but like Jung, he placed greater emphasis than Freud did on the influence of cultural and social forces. Erikson thought that society had an expansive rather than a restrictive influence on development and that social institutions such as school and marriage play a positive role in psychosocial development.

According to Erikson's theory, development unfolds in a sequence of eight psychosocial stages, which span from infancy to old age. Each stage revolves around a different crisis, or challenge, that is the central concern for that particular developmental period. The challenge of each developmental stage can be resolved positively or negatively. If the challenge is resolved positively, then the self is strengthened, the social world expands, and the individual has a good chance of resolving the next stage positively. If the challenge is resolved negatively, then the development of the individual's personality suffers because a

Table 8.1 | Erikson's Eight Stages of Psychosocial Development

Stage/Age Range	Psychosocial Challenge
I. Infancy (birth to age 1)	Trust versus mistrust
II. Early childhood (ages 1–3)	Autonomy versus shame and doubt
III. Childhood (ages 3–6)	Initiative versus guilt
IV. School age (ages 6–12)	Industry versus inferiority
V. Adolescence (teens)	Identity versus role confusion
VI. Young adulthood (20–40)	Intimacy versus isolation
VII. Middle adulthood (40–65)	Generativity versus stagnation
VIII. Late adulthood (65 and older)	Ego integrity versus despair

positive resolution of the stages that follow will be more difficult to achieve. Thus, Erikson believed in the sequential interdependence of the stages, meaning that how the challenge of an earlier stage is resolved will affect how positively or negatively subsequent stages are resolved.

Erikson's last three stages cover young, middle, and older adulthood, respectively. In the sixth stage, the main challenge is **intimacy versus isolation,** and young adults who resolve this challenge positively are successful in developing close give-and-take relationships with others. Erikson believed that to truly know oneself, there must be mutual verification with a partner. While intimate relationships are important well into older adulthood, the ability to form a close relationship with another person may develop in young adulthood. Young adults who resolve this challenge positively are graced with the virtue of love.

In the seventh stage, the main challenge is **generativity versus stagnation.** Middle-aged adults who resolve this challenge positively are able to take responsibility for others and feel they are making a contribution to the next generation. They become graced with the virtue of care and concern for others. In middle age, many adults lose their parents, and in some sense they become the barrier to death for the next generation. That is, they become the protectors rather than the protectees. Failure to resolve this challenge positively can result in the feeling that life has little value or meaning, which can lead to a sense of boredom and a tendency toward self-indulgence. Rather than being concerned with the care of others, stagnated middle-aged adults may take on youthful habits to defend against thoughts of aging and death. This behavior fits what has been popularly referred to as the *mid-life crisis* (Levinson, 1978), which is often identified with middle-aged men who are dissatisfied, feel they are running out of time to accomplish anything worthwhile, and yearn to return to the freedom of their adolescent years and to start over again making different choices.

In the eighth and final stage, the main challenge is **ego integrity versus despair.** Older adults who resolve this challenge positively feel that their lives have consistency, coherence, and purpose. Ego integrity is associated with contentment and satisfaction with the life one has led despite its imperfections, and older adults with ego integrity are graced with the virtue of wisdom. If the challenge of the eighth stage is not resolved positively, then older individuals will feel despair and disappointment with their lives. They may dwell on all the roads not taken.

Erikson's psychosocial theory was not based on empirical data from large numbers of individuals and for this reason there has been criticism. In recent years, however, several researchers have conducted empirical studies to test the assumptions of Erikson's stage theory. One assumption is that there is sequential interdependence among the stages. If sequential interdependence exists, then individuals who resolve the challenge of middle adulthood positively (that is, feel generative) are likely to resolve the challenge of older adulthood positively (that is, achieve ego integrity). In contrast, individuals who are stagnated in middle age are apt to be despairing in older adulthood. Hannah, Domino, Figueredo, and Hendrickson (1996) interviewed 520 healthy, relatively well-educated men and women between the ages of 55 and 84. For these individuals, a positive resolution in the final stage (ego integrity) was tied to a positive resolution in earlier stages, particularly the immediately preceding one (generativity rather than stagnation).

Another assumption of Erikson's theory is that each stage of development is characterized by a unique, central challenge. If this assumption is accurate, then concern with a particular challenge should reach a peak in the designated stage and decline in subsequent stages. McAdams, de St. Aubin, and Logan (1993) used self-report measures on a sample of 152 young (ages 22–27), middle-aged (ages 37–42), and older (ages 67–72) adults to test the hypothesis that concern for others (generativity) would be relatively low in young adulthood, would rise to a peak in midlife, but then decline in the later years. In keeping with this prediction, the young adults did not show a high level of concern about caring for or making creative contributions to others. On the contrary, they were more concerned with figuring out what to do with their lives, making their own jobs more interesting, enjoying life, and keeping up with current events. However, as predicted by Erikson's theory, the middle-aged adults had more generative concerns than the young adults did. These were indicated by their expressing the desire to be a positive role model for younger people, to help their children work through difficult situations, and to provide for others to the best of their ability.

McAdams et al. were able to demonstrate the predicted increase in concern with generativity in midlife, but did they find that the generative peak in middle adulthood was followed by a dip in generative concern in the older adult group? Contrary to what was expected, the older adults in this study were just as concerned with generativity as the middle-aged adults were. The older group's generative concerns were apparent in statements indicating that they considered it important to "counsel a daughter who was recently let go from a job," "help a daughter with her sick child," and "help as a volunteer at a nonprofit organization" (McAdams et al., 1993, p. 228). McAdams et al. used a cross-sectional design (described earlier), so the findings may have been influenced by cohort effects. Perhaps more important, however, is that the older study participants ranged from 67 to 72 years of age, which falls into the young-old age range (see Chapter 1 for a definition of young-old). Even though Erikson associated the challenge of generativity versus stagnation with middle age, concern with this challenge may last longer because today, people remain healthy and continue to actively participate in society to later ages. If the participants in McAdams et al.'s study had been in the old-old or oldest-old age categories (that is, 75 and over), perhaps the predicted decline in generative concerns would have been seen.

McAdams's Life Story Model   According to McAdams (1996), individuals construct a personal myth to make sense of their lives. This myth is actually a **life story** that integrates a reconstructed past with a perceived present and an anticipated future. As such, it allows people to feel that their lives have unity and purpose.

The life stories that individuals construct reflect the values of the culture in which they live. In Western cultures, young adults enter the workplace, begin raising families, establish themselves in the community, and commit themselves to social roles such as worker, parent, and so on. Over time, they refine the plot of their life story, and by middle adulthood they become concerned with integrating and balancing the various themes in the life story. Middle-aged individuals are often considered to be in the prime of their lives, but the themes of their life stories indicate increasing concern with mortality and what will survive them after death. As part of their life story, middle-aged individuals start to fashion a generativity script, which guides how they define themselves and what gifts they want to leave for the generations that follow. In the decades of the 40s, 50s, and 60s, individuals concentrate not only on integrating the beginning and middle of the life story narrative, but also on creating an appropriate and satisfying ending. Ideally, this ending will tie together the various threads of the story so it has continuity and purpose. Further, a "good" ending will make it possible for individuals to attain a kind of symbolic immortality, or legacy of the self, which will live on after their death (McAdams, 1996). McAdams's idea of a good ending bears some similarity to Erikson's conception of ego integrity.

Peck's Necessary Adjustments in Older Adulthood   Robert Peck (1968) described three adjustments that must occur in older adulthood. Success in making these adjustments will result in positive growth, leading to what Erikson called ego integrity. In contrast, failure to make these adjustments could result in what Erikson called despair.

The first of Peck's necessary adjustments in older adulthood is **ego differentiation versus work-role preoccupation.** In late adulthood, individuals may need to reappraise and redefine their personal self-worth. Retirement from work is approaching or has already occurred, so older individuals must learn to define their self-worth outside the workplace. That is, they cannot remain preoccupied with their work role, and the structure and meaning of their lives is best defined by interests other than work. They must ask themselves, "Am I a worthwhile person only if I can perform a full-time job, or can I be worthwhile in other ways?" A well-adjusted older adult, one with ego differentiation, will have a varied set of roles and a complex sense of identity and self-worth that does not depend completely upon the work career.

Peck's second necessary adjustment in older adulthood is **body transcendence versus body preoccupation.** Late adulthood often brings some physical decline, and aches and pains may prevent older adults from engaging in the same activities they did in their younger years. In addition, there may be physical changes of a cosmetic nature, such as increased wrinkles. To adjust positively, older adults must rise above physical discomfort and avoid placing too much importance on cosmetic changes. They must find ways to enjoy life with reduced physical capabilities and less physical perfection.

Peck's third necessary adjustment in older adulthood, **ego transcendence versus ego preoccupation,** has to do with adapting to the prospect that life is finite and that the focus must be on future generations and not on preoccupation with one's own needs. The older adult who makes this adjustment will feel that he or she has achieved something of lasting meaning. This meaning could come from the knowledge that children have been raised, strong personal relationships have been formed, and meaningful contributions have been made to society. This adjustment bears some similarity to Erikson's idea of generativity, although Peck emphasizes achievements that have been attained already rather than achievements that are occurring on an ongoing basis. Ultimately, the individual with ego transcendence is likely to have what Erikson referred to as ego integrity.

Life Review   The idea that older adults "live in the past" is almost part of a folklore about aging (Cohen & Taylor, 1998). Many older adults claim that they remember things that happened a long time ago with a clarity that eludes them when they try to remember what happened a day or a week ago (Erber, 1995). The act of reminiscence involves evoking personal memories from the past, possibly in a somewhat reconstructed form that is not always completely objective. Reminiscence is not necessarily confined to the older adult age group, but older adults seem to engage in it more than younger age groups do (Cohen & Taylor, 1998). Young adults may be less concerned with life review because they do not feel they have limitations in time left to live.

Some years ago such reminiscence, or **life review,** was considered an idle pursuit, best discouraged in the elderly. However, Butler (1963) was one of the first to contend that life review is an active and important part of the aging process that older adults use to integrate who they are now (present) and who they were before (past). If older adults' life review is positive, then they come to accept their lives as having meaning. Thus, life review enables older adults to achieve what Erikson called ego integrity, which goes hand in hand with positive adjustment in the final stage of life. However, if life review does not result in an integration of the present and past, then older adults may wish they could do things over again. This could lead to feelings of despair because most older adults realize that time is running out.

The idea that life review can play a significant role in successful aging is acknowledged by professionals who work with older adults. Life-story discussion groups are popular with community-living older adults, and reminiscence therapy is often recommended for nursing home residents. In one study (Haight, Michel, & Hendrix, 1998), 256 older adults who had been recently admitted to 1 of 12 different nursing homes were randomly assigned to a six-week program that entailed one of two different interventions, either reminiscence or friendly visits. Half of the residents met individually for six weeks with a trained therapeutic listener who encouraged them to reminisce about various facets of their lives. The other half of the residents received friendly visits from the same listeners that lasted the same amount of time as was spent with residents who were encouraged to reminisce. However, the residents assigned to the friendly visit group were discouraged from reminiscing, and the topics of conversation during the friendly visits focused on health, the weather, television shows, and current events. Compared with residents who got friendly visits, residents who were encouraged to reminisce derived greater benefit both immediately and one year later, as indicated by their lower degree of depression, hopelessness, and despair and their higher degree of ego integrity, life satisfaction, and psychological well-being. Thus, life review, or reminiscence therapy, may be an effective preventive intervention for elderly individuals who are at risk for depression.

When studied more closely, however, reminiscence can take several different forms, some of which may be more beneficial than others. Wong and Watt (1991) interviewed over 400 older adults, half of whom lived in the community and the other half in retirement and nursing homes. Through a careful screening procedure, these older adults were categorized as either "successful agers" (meaning that they were superior in physical and mental well-being) or "unsuccessful agers" (meaning that they were less healthy and had a low sense of well-being). The successful and unsuccessful agers were asked to review their past and identify one or two events that had shaped their lives significantly. Wong and Watt analyzed the content of these reviews and found differences in the memories of the successful and unsuccessful agers. Compared to the reviews of the unsuccessful agers, those of the successful agers had more integrative and instrumental themes. Integrative reminiscences indicate that the individual feels at peace about the way past conflicts were resolved. An example of an integrative reminiscence given by one of Wong and Watt's successful agers was, "I resented my parents' divorce when I was a young adult but in time I came to understand why they did not get along and I was able to maintain a relationship with both of them." Instrumental reminiscences show that the individual has been able to draw on past experience to reach a positive resolution of more recent problems. An example of an instrumental reminiscence given by one of Wong and Watt's successful agers was, "During the Great Depression, life was very hard and we had very little money. We learned to survive by budgeting and doing without many things. That experience helped me when I retired and had to adapt to living on a pension." In contrast, the reviews of the unsuccessful agers contained more obsessive themes that indicated persistent unresolved feelings such as guilt. An example of an obsessive reminiscence given by one of the unsuccessful agers was, "My husband died while I was out shopping. He fell and I was not there to help him and I still cannot forgive myself."

In Wong and Watt's study, participants were not randomly assigned to the successful ager versus the unsuccessful ager groups, so care must be taken not to draw conclusions about cause-and-effect relationships between type of reminiscence and success in aging. Even so, the fact that certain types of reminiscence seem to be associated with successful aging suggests it may be best to encourage integrative and instrumental reminiscences but discourage those that stir up obsessive feelings of guilt.

In sum, stage models conceptualize personality or specific personality processes as emerging as an outcome of age, stage, or time. Specific aspects of personality or personality processes such as life review may slip into the background or they may become more dominant as individuals move from early adulthood toward old age.

Personality Dimensions and Traits

Rather than emphasizing that personality evolves in various stages over the adult life span, some theorists focus on whether personality dimensions and personality traits stay the same or whether they change over time (Berry & Jobe, 2002). Dimensions are broad categories of personality such as neuroticism and extraversion. Each personality dimension includes a constellation of personality characteristics, or traits. For example, someone high on the neuroticism dimension would probably be anxious and hostile, while someone high on the extraversion dimension would probably be warm and sociable. Are personality dimensions consistent across adulthood? Also, are some personality traits more likely to be found in older adults than they are in young adults, or do they stay the same over time?

The Baltimore Longitudinal Study   An ideal way to examine whether personality remains stable or whether it changes over the adult life span would be to follow the same individuals over time. Researchers Costa and McCrae did just that as part of the Baltimore Longitudinal Study (BLS), in which a large initial sample of men and women ranging from the 20s to the 80s completed two well-established self-report personality inventories, the Cattell 16PF and the Guilford-Zimmerman Temperament Survey.

By analyzing the responses that study participants gave on the self-report measures, these researchers derived a model for the structure of personality that consists of five dimensions, or factors: neuroticism, extraversion, openness to experience, agreeableness, and conscientiousness (NEO-AC). Based on their **Five-Factor Model (FFM) of Personality,** Costa and McCrae (1991, 1992) developed a self-report questionnaire called the Revised NEO Personality Inventory (NEO-PI-R), which consists of 240 items, or statements, that are intended to measure the traits that make up each of the five factors. Test takers rate each statement on a 5-point scale from strongly disagree to strongly agree. Each personality factor is measured using several scales, listed in Table 8.2 (McCrae & Costa, 1997). High scores on these scales would result in a high score on that personality factor. The NEO-PI-R has been translated into several languages and used to study whether the Five-Factor Model is found in other cultures. An abbreviated version of the NEO-PI-R called the NEO-FFI consists of only 60 items.

As the BLS participants were followed longitudinally and retested, their personality structure remained stable. The same five personality dimensions continued to fit their responses on the self-report measures. Not only was there

Table 8.2 | The Big Five Personality Factors

Personality Factor	Scales
Neuroticism (N)	Anxiety, angry hostility, depression, self-consciousness, impulsiveness, vulnerability
Extraversion (E)	Warmth, gregariousness, assertiveness, activity, excitement-seeking, positive emotions
Openness to Experience (O)	Fantasy, aesthetics, feelings, actions, ideas, values
Agreeableness (A)	Trust, straightforwardness, altruism, compliance, modesty, tender-mindedness
Conscientiousness (C)	Competence, order, dutifulness, achievement-striving, self-discipline, deliberation

Adapted from McCrae and Costa (1997).

consistency in the dimensions over time, but there was relative stability in the specific traits associated with each personality dimension. When the BLS participants were tested repeatedly in subsequent years, they retained their approximate rank order compared to others their age on the dimensions as well as the traits. In other words, individuals who scored high on the neuroticism, extraversion, or other dimensions relative to the rest of their age peers at one point in time tended to score high on these dimensions relative to their age peers at subsequent points in time. Clearly, over long periods there is some shifting of personality traits so that some change occurs (Kogan, 1990). However, evidence from a large number of longitudinal studies indicates a remarkable level of consistency in the rank order of traits, particularly in late middle-aged and older adults who have been followed over 6-year periods (Roberts & DelVecchio, 2000).

What does being high on the various personality dimensions mean in terms of life satisfaction and feelings of well-being? High scores on some dimensions are associated with positive affect and feelings of well-being, while high scores on other dimensions are not (McCrae & Costa, 1991). Most notably, being high on the extraversion dimension is associated with positive affect and feelings of well-being, while being high on the neuroticism dimension is associated with negative affect and a lower degree of well-being. For the other three dimensions, the association with affect and well-being is mixed. Being high on the openness to experience dimension is associated with both positive and negative affect, with no overall effect on level of well-being. Being high on the agreeableness and conscientiousness dimensions is associated more with positive than with negative affect, and there is a weak positive association with feelings of well-being.

Silver, Bubrick, Jilinskaia, and Perls (1998) conducted a study on 23 New England centenarians ages 100 to 110, the majority (85 percent) of whom were females. The centenarians all completed the 60-item Five-Factor Inventory (NEO-FFI). The main finding was that the centenarians were relatively low on the neuroticism dimension. Neuroticism is associated with poor ability to handle stress, so being low on this dimension would seem to indicate better ability to manage stress. It seems likely that neuroticism is negatively associated with longevity, but it would be premature to draw conclusions about a cause-and-effect relationship.

Those who support the dimensional continuity model contend that personality functions jointly with age to influence outcomes at various stages of development. Theorists such as Costa and McCrae contend that the choices we make at various transition points are related to where we fall on the five personality dimensions of neuroticism, extraversion, openness to experience, agreeableness, and conscientiousness. The level of adaptation we experience at various points in our lives is best viewed within a framework of relatively stable personality dimensions. A positive outcome (such as adjustment to the circumstances in which we find ourselves) could be a function of the roles and relationships we select, which is influenced by where we fall on the personality dimensions. The following questions, posed by McCrae and Costa (1982), are quite different from the questions that stage model theorists might ask:

- "How do the lives of those high in extraversion differ from the lives of those low in extraversion?"
- "What aspects of life are influenced by openness to experience?"
- "What role does personality play in adapting to stressful life events?"

With regard to the last question, those working within a dimensional continuity framework are not likely to use the term *mid-life crisis*. Rather, they would consider some individuals, notably those high in neuroticism, to be more crisis prone than others. Moreover, they might speculate that an individual who experiences a crisis in middle-adulthood most likely experienced crises earlier in life as well, although the exact nature of a particular crisis might depend upon the individual's age and stage of life.

Cross-Cultural Comparisons   McCrae and Costa (1991) acknowledge the importance of considering biological, historical, and cultural influences on personality dimensions, so it is particularly noteworthy that the five-factor model seems to generalize across cultures (McCrae, 2002). When translated versions of the NEO-PI-R were administered to over 7,000 individuals from diverse cultures, McCrae and Costa (1997) found that the five-factor dimensional structure demonstrated in English-speaking samples was also found with samples from Germany, Portugal, Israel, China, and Japan. Furthermore, the traits included in each of the five personality dimensions were very much the same in American, German, Italian, Portuguese, Croatian, and Korean study samples (McCrae et al., 1999). This suggests that there is not only a common overall personality structure across cultures in terms of dimensions, but also cross-cultural similarity in terms of the specific traits that define the dimensions.

Cross-Sectional Studies   The dimensional continuity model emphasizes stability in personality dimensions over time. But does this mean that personality is written in stone and that people do not change at all throughout adulthood? Most of the information we have on this question is based on cross-sectional studies, in which people of various ages were all tested at the same time. McCrae et al. (1999) found that between young and middle adulthood, there is a pattern of decrease on the neuroticism, extraversion, and openness-to-experience dimensions and increase on the agreeableness and conscientiousness dimensions. Similar decreases and increases on these dimensions have been reported when translated versions of the NEO-PI-R self-report questionnaire are given to German, Italian, Portuguese, Croatian, and Korean samples. Helson, Kwan, John, and Jones (2002) summarized the findings of cross-sectional studies conducted in the United States and countries such as Turkey, South Korea, and Poland. They concluded that older adults have higher scores than younger adults on traits related to conscientiousness and agreeableness, whereas older adults have lower scores than younger adults on traits related to neuroticism, extraversion, and openness to experience. This cross-cultural similarity could be interpreted as evidence for universal maturational changes in personality.

Age and cohort cannot be separated in cross-sectional studies, so it will be important to conduct longitudinal studies that follow the same individuals over time, plotting small changes in personality traits. It is entirely possible that personality dimensions remain stable over time in terms of rank-order. Thus, a person who falls on the high end of the extraversion dimension at one age may also fall at the high end later on compared to others of the same age. However, average scores on the extraversion scale may decline for everyone at later ages. If so, a person's score on a dimension or the separate traits within it could decline, but that person could still remain at the high end of the extraversion dimension compared to others the same age. Questions of stability and change in personality will probably be prominent on the agendas of developmental researchers for some time to come (Ryff, Kwan, & Singer, 2001).

Lay Views of Personality

Another way to study personality is to investigate how individuals who are not research scientists conceptualize it. Do these lay individuals view themselves as having stayed the same or as having changed over time? In their opinion, do the personalities of other people stay the same or do they change over time?

People's Views of Their Own Personality   Many older adults feel a strong sense of continuity. Troll and Skaff (1997) interviewed 150 individuals ages 85 and older, and most of them felt that they were basically the same as they had always been.

Most individuals have perceptions about what they were like in the past and what they are like at the present time, but what do they think they will be like in the future? Fleeson and Heckhausen (1997) tested adults ranging from 26 to 64 years of age using a short self-report inventory that measured Costa and McCrae's five dimensions of personality (NEO-AC). Participants rated how much they thought each item on the inventory would describe what they were like in the past when they were age 20–25, what they are like now, and what they anticipate they will be like at a future point when they reach the ages of 65–70. Responses showed evidence for both stability and variability in participants' perceptions of their own personality over time.

There was a moderate degree of stability across the three time periods as far as participants' rank-ordering of their personalities on all five personality dimensions. For example, those who rated themselves high in present level of extraversion and agreeableness tended to rate themselves high on these two dimensions both retrospectively (in the past) and prospectively (in the future). At the same time, there were some changes in the exact level of some ratings over the three points in time. On average, participants' ratings were lower for extraversion but higher for agreeableness. These findings on how individuals view themselves match those obtained on the cross-sectional studies described in the previous section.

Perceptions of the Personality Traits of Others   What perceptions do people have of older adults as a group? Despite evidence for stability in personality dimensions and associated personality traits over the adult life span (McCrae & Costa, 1982), do lay individuals associate certain personality traits with older adulthood? Are some traits viewed as either increasing with age or decreasing with age?

Heckhausen, Dixon, and Baltes (1989) asked young, middle-aged and older adult residents of Berlin, Germany to rate the desirability of 358 characteristics, or traits, and also to estimate the rise and fall of each one over the adult years. Participants from all three age groups showed considerable agreement in their beliefs about age-related change in these traits over the course of adult development. In general, they viewed development as multidirectional, with both gains and losses over the adult life span. Gains were defined as an increase over the adult life span in desirable traits such as wise, responsible, and level headed. Losses were defined as an increase over the adult life span in undesirable traits such as weak, dependent, and stubborn. Overall, expected gains outnumbered expected losses. However, the proportion of expected gains decreased somewhat with increasing age. Thus, the proportion of gains was smaller in later adulthood than it was in early adulthood.

In a similar study examining trait desirability and age, Heckhausen and Krueger (1993) selected 10 desirable traits and 10 undesirable traits for each of five personality dimensions that overlapped somewhat with the dimensions in Costa and McCrae's model. Table 8.3 shows the five personality dimensions with an example of a desirable trait and an undesirable trait for each. Young, middle-aged, and older adult men and women, also residents of Berlin, Germany, rated each trait on the following scales: (a) its degree of desirability, (b) whether it increases during seven decades of adulthood (20s, 30s, 40s, 50s, 60s, 70s, 80s), and (c) whether it decreases during the seven decades of adulthood. In addition, they rated the perceived controllability of each attribute ("How much can one control the modification of the attribute?"). In one session, participants rated themselves on the traits. In another session, they rated what they thought was true for most other people.

| **Table 8.3** | Personality Factors with Examples of Desirable and Undesirable Traits |

Personality Factor	Desirable Trait	Undesirable Trait
Extraversion	Assertive	Inhibited
Agreeableness	Affectionate	Quarrelsome
Conscientiousness	Dependable	Irresponsible
Emotional stability	Self-controlled	Nervous
Intellectual functioning	Knowledgeable	Naive

Heckhausen and Krueger (1993).

In general, Heckhausen and Krueger's participants were optimistic about adult development in that they expected gains would outnumber losses. Again, gains were defined as increases in desirable traits and decreases in undesirable traits. Losses were defined as decreases in desirable traits and increases in undesirable traits. However, the age-related curves for the expected gains and losses showed a gradual shift so that the predominance of expected gains was greater for early adulthood than it was for late adulthood. Even so, most participants thought that it would be possible to control, or modify, undesirable traits.

For both expected developmental change and perceived controllability, Heckhausen and Krueger found a high degree of agreement between what individuals thought would be true for themselves and what they thought would be true for other people. For instance, if they thought they themselves would become more dependable with increasing age, they believed the same would be true for most other people. Despite this general level of agreement, however, there was some evidence of self-enhancement among the middle-aged and older participants. Most of them expected that increases in desirable attributes would be greater for themselves than for other people. They anticipated that increases in undesirable attributes would be smaller for themselves than for others. These findings indicate that individuals are more optimistic about their own future personality traits than they are about how their age peers will fare.

Hummert, Garstka, Shaner, and Strahm (1994) asked young, middle-aged, and older adults to list the traits they would consider to be typical of older adults. Table 8.4 lists 20 traits that were named by at least 20 percent of the adults in at least one age group or at least 10 percent of the adults in all three age groups. Although the older adult group listed fewer traits compared with the young and middle-aged groups, there was considerable overlap in the traits generated by the three age groups. Some of the traits were positive (for example, trustworthy), while others were negative (for example, depressed).

In another study, Slotterback (1996) posed an important question: Are the perceptions that young adults have about older adults' personality traits related to older adults' chronological age or are they related to older adults' generation,

Table 8.4 | Traits Descriptive of a Typical Elderly Adult Named Most Frequently by Young, Middle-Aged, and Elderly Adults*

Age Group Trait	Young (n = 40)	Middle-Aged (n = 40)	Elderly (n = 40)	Trait Valence
Conservative	7.5	20.0	2.5	Positive
Depressed	12.5	20.0	7.5	Negative
Determined	2.5	20.0	17.5	Positive
Eager to learn and experience	0.0	17.5	25.0	Positive
Sense of humor	12.5	15.0	12.5	Positive
Health-conscious	15.0	45.0	30.0	Positive
Independent	5.0	25.0	22.5	Positive
Likes social activities	25.0	20.0	17.5	Positive
Move after retirement	22.5	10.0	2.5	Positive
Politically aware and active	22.5	17.5	17.5	Positive
Pursues a hobby	30.0	30.0	27.5	Positive
Religious	12.5	32.5	20.0	Positive
Scared of becoming sick and incompetent	0.0	35.0	52.5	Negative
Successful	12.5	25.0	5.0	Positive
Timid	5.0	27.5	7.5	Negative
Tired	25.0	17.5	2.5	Negative
Travels often	10.0	20.0	32.5	Positive
Trustworthy	2.5	20.0	5.0	Positive
Well-groomed	5.0	17.5	20.0	Positive
Worried about finances	7.5	5.0	35.0	Negative

*Named by 20 percent or more of informants in at least one age group or 10 percent or more informants in all three age groups.

Hummert, Garstka, Shaner, and Strahm (1994).

or cohort? To investigate this issue, Slotterback (1996) asked young adult college students to rate a hypothetical individual (a target) whom they were told was either 22, 41, or 69 years old. The scales on which the target was rated were based on Costa and McCrae's five personality dimensions: neuroticism, extraversion, openness to experience, conscientiousness, and agreeableness. Each student rated one target at one point in time (present, past, or future). Thus, some students were instructed to rate what the target is like at the present time. ("Think about a typical 22- [41-, or 69-] year-old today. What kind of personality does that person have?") Some were instructed to project what they thought the 22-year-old target would be like in the future. ("Think about a typical 22-year-old today who will become a 41-year-old [or a 69-year-old] adult in the future. What will that person be like?") Some were instructed to rate what they thought the 41-year-old target was like in the past at age 22 or what the 41-year-old target would be like in the future at age 69. Finally, some students were instructed to rate what they thought the 69-year-old target was like in the past (at age 22 or at age 41).

Based on their ratings of what the young (22), middle-aged (41), or old (69) target is like at the present time, students thought that two personality dimensions, openness to experience and conscientiousness, decrease with increasing age. Interestingly, however, the students' ratings indicated that they thought today's generation of older adults had always been less open to experience even when they were young adults. Furthermore, although they believed that conscientiousness decreases with age, the students thought that the present generation of older adults is more conscientious compared with the present generation of young adults. Slotterback's findings serve to remind us that our perceptions of other people's personality characteristics may be influenced not only by their chronological age but also by the generation, or cohort, to which they belong.

Stereotypes About Older Adults   Stereotypes are ideas that we hold in our heads about categories of people. With age stereotypes, we make assumptions about people on the basis of their chronological age. Using age stereotypes can lighten the load of processing a large amount of complex information about older adults. However, a potentially negative consequence is that age stereotypes can interfere with our ability to make judgments about a specific older adult as a unique individual (Hummert, 1999).

The stereotypes that young adults have about older adults are shaped by the information to which they are exposed. One way information is conveyed is through written materials. Whitbourne and Hulicka (1990) explored how older adults are depicted in undergraduate psychology textbooks and found that they were often described as unable or unwilling to change.

Even very brief exposure to written information can influence young adults' views of older adults. Guo, Erber, and Szuchman (1999) asked young adults to read one of two short but authoritative articles about memory and age. One article stated that memory declines with age, whereas the other article declared that memory remains constant with age. Afterward, all of the young adults read the same brief vignette that described an older adult who experiences memory failures. Compared to the young adults who read the article that stated memory stays constant with age, the young adults who read the article that stated memory declines with age were more likely to attribute the older person's memory failures to lack of ability.

Sometimes age stereotypes exist in our minds but not in our conscious awareness. However, when these unconscious stereotypes are activated, or primed, they can influence our behavior even without our realizing it. An example of such priming was reported by Perdue and Gurtman (1990), who found that young adult college students were more efficient at remembering the trait "forgetful" after it was presented in association with the age label "old" rather than with the age label "young." Bargh, Chen, and Burrows (1996) asked young adult college students to unscramble 30 different five-word sets by constructing grammatically correct sentences using four of the five words from each set. The word sets unscrambled by half the students contained words stereotypically associated with older adults (for example, forgetful, conservative, withdrawn, dependent) that were drawn from prior studies on stereotypes about the elderly. This unscrambling task was intended to prime age stereotypes. The word sets unscrambled by the other half of the students contained neutral words unrelated to an elderly stereotype (for example, thirsty, clean, private) to ensure that this task would not prime age stereotypes. After the students completed the unscrambling task, Bargh et al. timed how long it took them to walk down a corridor from the laboratory to the elevator. Students in the elderly-prime condition walked more slowly than students in the neutral-prime condition did. After ruling out the possibility that the elderly-primed students' slower walking speed was induced by a sad mood resulting from exposure to the negative prime words they received, Bargh et al. concluded that slow walking was consistent with the activation of an elderly stereotype. As is typical with implicit priming, the students were unaware that the prime words had affected them in any way, or even that the words they had unscrambled were related to an elderly stereotype. Bargh et al. concluded that the slower walking of the students exposed to elderly-stereotypic words indicated that they had an unconscious age stereotype, which when primed without their awareness, influenced their behavior.

The view of older adulthood as a time of irreversible decline is consistent with a conceptualization of aging as a process of physical deterioration (Hess & Blanchard-Fields, 1996). Stereotypes about older adults often include negative views of aging as a time of failing mental powers and competency (Tuckman & Lorge, 1953). Traits such as absent minded, forgetful, obstinate, and depressed are thought to have their onset in late middle-age (Heckhausen & Baltes, 1991). Furthermore, older adults are often viewed as overcautious and dependent (Heckhausen et al., 1989). Such negative views about aging may even be harbored by older adults, which could explain why many of them insist that they feel younger than they are and why they often think they compare favorably to others the same age. Surprisingly, evidence for negative age stereotypes has been found in Thailand, a country known for its tradition of respect for the elderly. Compared to young adult students from the United States, young adult students from a rural area of Northern Thailand generated proportionately more negative adjectives to describe the elderly (Sharps, Price-Sharps, & Hanson, 1998).

However, the idea that stereotypes of older adults are uniformly negative may be overly simplistic. As mentioned earlier, Heckhausen et al. (1989) asked young, middle-aged, and older adults to estimate the expected age of onset for 358 traits. Of the traits thought to have a late onset (age 55 or later) and believed to remain stable into very late old age, some were undesirable (bitter, forgetful), but others were desirable (dignified, wise). Also, Hummert (1990) reported that young adult college students hold multiple stereotypes about older adults, some negative and some positive. The students did not view negative stereotypes such as "inflexible senior citizen" (which includes traits such as "set in ways" and "old-fashioned") as any more typical of the elderly than they did positive stereotypes such as "perfect grandparent" (which includes traits such as "generous" and "loving"). Hummert's findings contradict the idea that stereotypes of older adults are uniformly negative, although she noted that negative stereotypes were somewhat more frequent in the young students' perceptions of the old-old age group (75 and over) than they were of the young-old age group (65 to 74). Perhaps negative age stereotypes are more likely to be activated in response to the over-75 age group. Kite and Johnson (1988) analyzed data from numerous studies on stereotypes about older adults and concluded that people may hold negative views about older adults as an abstract group, but they are not negative when asked what they think of specific older individuals about whom they have some information.

In sum, people have certain perceptions and stereotypes about what personality traits are typical of the present generation of older adults. These perceptions and stereotypes include both negative and positive views of what older adults are like. Whether these views will be the same when today's young and middle-aged adults enter their older-adult years remains to be seen. Regardless of the generation to which they belong, however, not all older adults are the same, so we now turn our attention to individual differences among older adults rather than what they have in common.

INDIVIDUAL DIFFERENCES IN COPING AND ADJUSTMENT

Instead of studying what is typical of most older adults, some investigators focus on how they differ. The study of individual differences in personality is often coupled with an interest in which older adults experience a high level of satisfaction and a high degree of psychological well-being (Ryff et al., 2001). How can we distinguish between older adults who are more satisfied and those who are less satisfied with their lives? What are the characteristics of those who have a high sense of well-being? A high sense of life satisfaction and well-being is usually associated with self-acceptance, positive relations with others, autonomy, feelings of environmental mastery, purpose in life, and personal growth (Ryff, 1989).

Closely tied to the idea of well-being is the concept of coping. How do individuals handle the events and challenges that take place over the life course? Effective coping strategies become increasingly important in dealing with the changes and losses that could occur in late adulthood. Physical changes and health-related concerns become more frequent, as do social changes related to retirement and living arrangements (discussed in more detail in Chapter 10). What strategies do older adults use to cope with the stress that may surround such changes? Are some coping strategies more likely than others to maximize the chances of successful aging? We will approach these questions first by introducing the idea of self-concept, which is related to our ideas and beliefs about who we are. Then we will discuss feelings of personal control.

Self-Concept

Self-concept is the image we have of ourselves. All of us have ideas about who we are, and researchers often refer to these ideas as schemas. Our schemas play a part in how we define ourselves and determine what information we attend to most and also how we process that information (Hooker, 1992).

Figure 8.1 | The Dynamic Self-Concept

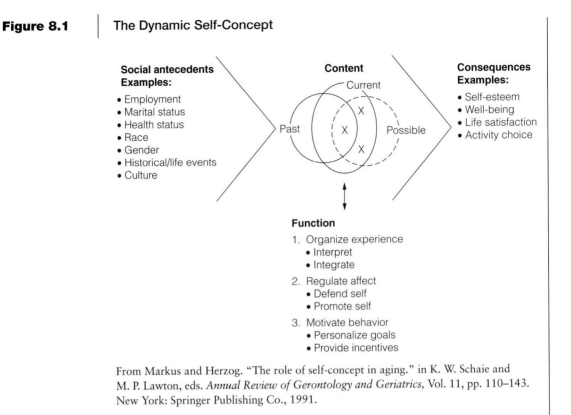

From Markus and Herzog. "The role of self-concept in aging." in K. W. Schaie and M. P. Lawton, eds. *Annual Review of Gerontology and Geriatrics*, Vol. 11, pp. 110–143. New York: Springer Publishing Co., 1991.

The self-concept is not just one general image. Rather, most of us have a collection of schemas that are related to different areas of our self-image. Researchers refer to these areas as domains. For example, an individual might have a schema about his or her physical appearance (physical domain) and a schema about his or her intellectual capability (intellectual domain). The domains that are most important for a particular individual's self-concept indicate what he or she considers meaningful (Markus & Herzog, 1991).

Theorists have emphasized the importance of self-concept for the aging process. The schemas that make up our self-concept play a role in regulating our behavior and guiding the decisions we make. The content, organization, and functioning of these schemas may hold the key to how individuals negotiate life events and navigate the changes that occur as they move from young to middle to older adulthood (Cross & Markus, 1991; Markus & Herzog, 1991). In short, studying self-schemas could provide insight into why some people successfully maintain a positive outlook and high levels of life satisfaction even when they face negative events.

Self-concept is what we think about ourselves, and **self-esteem** refers to the affective, or evaluative, aspect of the self-concept. Some consider self-esteem to be an actual personality trait that may or may not remain stable throughout life (Giarrusso & Bengston, 1996). A person with high self-esteem perceives him- or

Even after they officially retire, many teachers continue to identify with their profession, which is an important part of their self-concept.

herself as having worth, whereas a person with low self-esteem does not. Self-esteem is shaped by a combination of objective information and the opinions of others. However, it is also a function of how the individual processes social information and interprets social experiences. As with self-concept, self-esteem occurs in different domains. An individual may have high self-esteem in one domain ("I feel good about my appearance") but low self-esteem in another ("I feel bad that I cannot understand computers"). People often evaluate themselves in comparison to others, so self-esteem can change from high to low depending upon the group with which one compares oneself (Baron & Byrn, 2000).

As individuals grow older, some aspects of their past self-concept may continue to define who they are. For example, retired teachers or retired lawyers may continue to identify with their respective professions, which remain an important part of their self-concept even after they are formally retired. Compared with young adults, older adults place greater importance on what they were in the past.

People often use past self-schemas as a standard for judging whether they have changed in positive or negative ways (Markus & Nurius, 1986). However, past self-schemas are not always completely objective—they may be influenced by social stereotypes. In one study (Woodruff & Birren, 1972), middle-aged adults who had completed a self-report test on personal adjustment when they were college students were contacted 25 years later and asked to recall how adjusted they had been as young adults. Most of them thought that they were not very well-adjusted in their young adult student years. However, their scores on the test completed 25 years earlier indicated their level of adjustment was much higher than they remembered it to be. The fact that they thought their personal adjustment in young adulthood was lower than it actually was (based on their test scores) may have been influenced by a stereotype that young adults are not well-adjusted.

Possible Selves   Not only do we have self-schemas about our past and present (current) selves, but we also have self-schemas about what we may be like in the future. These **possible selves** include our schemas about what we would like to become (hoped-for selves) as well as about what we do not want to become (feared selves) (Cross & Markus, 1991; Markus & Herzog, 1991). Examples of hoped-for possible selves might be the rich self, the attractive self, the independent self, or the healthy self. Feared possible selves might be the poor self, the unattractive self, the dependent self, or the unhealthy self.

The possible selves of adults over the age of 60 often have less to do with occupation and career and more to do with leisure pursuits and physical functioning (Cross & Markus, 1991). Health in particular becomes a more and more important aspect of the self over the adult life span. In comparison with the hoped-for selves of young adult college students, the hoped-for selves of older adults are more invested in health (Hooker, 1992). Not surprisingly, concern with attaining healthy selves actually begins to gain importance in mid-life, with middle-aged adults reporting more feared selves than hoped-for selves regarding health (Hooker & Kaus, 1994).

Individuals have possible selves well into the advanced older adult years. Smith and Freund (2002) studied transcripts of interviews conducted over 4 years in which individuals ranging from 70 to 103 years expressed their personal hopes and fears for the future. Even the oldest members in their sample showed evidence of dynamic possible selves with images that were added and deleted over time. Possible selves, both hoped for and feared, continue into very old age.

Possible selves are not just idle fantasies. Rather, they motivate us to set and achieve goals to fulfill our hoped-for possible selves and avoid our feared possible selves. Possible selves serve to regulate the way we behave. For instance, possible selves can motivate us to eat nutritious meals and get sufficient exercise, both of which protect our health. To illustrate, 65-year-old Margarita notices that she has gained weight and is not as trim and fit as she used to be. On a recent visit to her doctor, she was warned that the extra weight could lead to elevated blood cholesterol and related health problems. Margarita has a hoped-for self of being trim and fit and attractive. At the same time, she has a feared self of becoming someone with health problems that require a daily regimen of medication and that might eventually make her dependent upon others for her care. Margarita's hoped-for possible self and her feared possible self may motivate her to change her eating habits and increase her level of exercise.

Different individuals define possible selves differently. For example, two individuals may have a hoped-for possible self of being a successful writer. John defines this hoped-for self as being the author of a novel that makes it onto the best-seller list, while Maury defines this hoped-for self as having a letter to the editor published in the local newspaper.

What happens if the behaviors motivated by our possible selves do not have the desired effect within some reasonable period of time? Despite Margarita's efforts to follow a strict diet and exercise regimen, she has yet to reach the goal she set of a 15-pound weight loss. Despite the time John spends writing a novel followed by weeks of travel on a publicity tour, the novel has not sold enough copies to be included on the best-seller list. A prolonged discrepancy between the hoped-for possible self and the present self can lead to feelings of anxiety, discouragement, or depression. Avoiding or at least minimizing such negative feelings means that the gap between the hoped-for possible self and present self will have to be narrowed. Strategies to narrow this gap may call for redefining the possible self.

One strategy that can be used to close the gap is to completely eliminate the hoped-for self from the self-schema repertoire. For Margarita, this would mean giving up all hope of becoming trim and fit. Accordingly, she might cease all efforts to stick to her diet and exercise program. This course of action (or inaction) might alleviate her feelings of discouragement for a while, but such a strategy carries risks. In the long run, her complete surrender of the trim and fit hoped-for self may increase her chances of realizing her feared possible self of being unhealthy. In the case of John, giving up the successful author hoped-for self may temporarily alleviate his feelings of anxiety and depression. Ultimately, however, this could increase the chances that John will realize a feared possible self of being a failure.

Another strategy for closing the gap between a hoped-for possible self and a present self is to readjust the hoped-for self. Instead of completely surrendering her goal of a trim and fit possible self, Margarita could simply redefine it. She could readjust her hoped-for self of being 15 pounds lighter to one of being 5 pounds lighter. If Margarita redefines her definition of trim and fit, she is more likely to be satisfied with small progress toward her goal. By achieving even small progress, she is more likely to remain motivated to continue gradually striving toward her trim and fit possible self and avoiding her feared unhealthy possible self. As for as John, perhaps his possible self of being a successful author could be redefined as having a book that receives at least a few good reviews.

Closing an overwhelming gap between a desired possible self and a present self may call for adjusting not only self-schemas but also social comparison. Consider Manuel, a 67-year-old man with a possible self of being a fast jogger. If Manuel compares his jogging speed with the jogging speed of others his age, he may find that he is fairly proficient. In fact, he may even be motivated to pursue efforts to increase his jogging speed so that he is a little better than his age peers. However, if Manuel compares his jogging speed with that of the average 35-year-old, he may become discouraged and give up his goal of being a fast jogger. In other words, "I want to be a fast jogger for my age" may be a strategy for adjusting a possible self-schema so that it feels within reach. Once Manuel achieves his goal of being a fast jogger for his age, perhaps he can gradually increase his standards by comparing his jogging speed to that of the average 60-year-old. Now let's look at two theoretical models that further describe adjustments to self-concept in older adulthood.

Assimilation, Accommodation, and Immunization (AAI) Model   The AAI Model (Brandtstädter & Greve, 1994; Brandtstädter, 1999) outlines three adaptive and self-protective coping strategies, or processes, that individuals can use to maintain personal continuity and integrity of the self. These are not unique to older adulthood, but they are useful for understanding how older adults may cope with age-related discrepancies between actual and desired selves. All three processes—assimilation, accommodation, and immunization—can occur at the same time. However, the relative prominence of each will depend upon the specific situation at hand.

Assimilation has been termed *tenacious goal pursuit* (Brandtstädter & Renner, 1990; Brandtstädter, 1999), and it is often the first process to be activated when individuals detect a gap between hoped-for goals and actual circumstances. Assimilative processes typically involve intentional actions or efforts to transform actual situations into situations that are closer to ideal. In early adulthood, assimilative efforts often focus on goals that extend well into the future. For example, many young adults work at a succession of jobs with a goal to establish their identity in a career. Assimilative efforts can also be preventive, corrective, or compensatory. In late adulthood, assimilative efforts are directed more toward maintaining resources and avoiding mismatches between skills and demands. For instance, one goal that becomes especially important in later life is minimizing health risks (Hooker, 1992). Assimilative efforts can include modification of eating and exercise habits. A related goal that has high priority for many older adults is maintaining a competent and independent level of functioning. For some older adults, being able to continue living in the home where they have lived for years or decades is very important. They may cope with changes in their physical capabilities by taking assimilative actions such as installing grab bars in the bathroom, strobe lights on telephones, and emergency call buttons in each room.

Assimilative actions are often the first line of defense when there is a gap between what is desired and what actually exists at a particular time. However, sometimes it becomes apparent that even with assimilative efforts, a goal is not readily attainable. At this point, **accommodation** may be activated. Accommodative processes are characterized as *flexible goal adjustment* (Brandtstädter & Renner, 1990) and usually they are unintentional. Accommodative processes involve re-evaluating and adjusting personal goals and preferences in accordance with situational and personal limitations.

Rather than making persistent but futile attempts to pursue previously set goals, individuals can use accommodative strategies to redefine their goals. By gradually modifying aspects of their self-concept, individuals can attain a closer match between their aspirations and the personal and environmental resources that are available. Accommodative coping strategies often take on greater importance in older adulthood when there is more need to adjust ambitions and preferences in accordance with situational constraints (Brandtstädter, 1999; Brandtstädter, Wentura, & Greve, 1993; Heckhausen & Schulz, 1995). Examples of accommodative processes include revising one's goals and aspirations and changing one's standards of self-evaluation. Surprisingly, a number of studies have reported very little age-related decline in life satisfaction or feelings of well-being despite the losses that often occur in older adulthood. Perhaps accommodative strategies buffer older adults against such losses, allowing them to maintain the integrity of their self-concepts and therefore their feelings of life satisfaction (Brandtstädter & Renner, 1990; Brandtstädter & Greve, 1994).

How well accommodative processes actually do help an older individual to achieve a sense of well-being might depend on the complexity of the self-concept and on cultural expectations. Accommodative strategies are usually more effective when an individual's self-concept is complex and includes a number of personally meaningful aspects. Modifying a single aspect of a multifaceted self-concept might be less emotionally traumatic than modifying a single aspect upon which the self-concept is entirely dependent. For example, one of Peck's (1968) necessary adjustments in older adulthood described earlier in this chapter was ego-differentiation versus work-role preoccupation. Peck contended that the chances of achieving positive adjustment in late life would be enhanced if individuals did not invest themselves totally in the work role, which is vulnerable to loss through retirement, but instead defined themselves in other ways. Indeed, employees who derive their self-concept solely from their work role often experience greater anxiety about retiring than do those with interests outside of work (Cross & Markus, 1991). Sociocultural context must also be taken into account when considering how well accommodative processes work (Brandtstädter, 1999). A culture that worships youth may make few allowances for older adults who try to rescale their goals and performance standards. A culture that is less strongly youth oriented may be more accepting of flexible goals and standards for different age groups.

In any given situation, both assimilation and accommodation may play a role. To illustrate the interplay between these two processes, consider Helen, an 80-year-old widow. An important part of Helen's self-concept is that she continue to live in the single-family home where she and her husband spent their married years and brought up their children. Helen has made assimilative efforts to safeguard this goal even though she suffers from arthritis and no longer drives. She has had modifications made to her bathroom and kitchen to ensure safety and convenience, and she has friends who drive her to the grocery store and a transportation service that takes her to medical appointments. Despite these assimilative efforts, however, Helen's life is becoming more and more difficult. Even with grab bars in the bathroom, she is beginning to feel less confident about taking a bath or shower without slipping. Even with modifications in the kitchen, she finds that cooking is becoming more difficult because of her arthritis. Several times she has been horrified to discover that she forgot to turn off a burner on the stove. When the weather is rainy or cold, her friends cannot drive her to the grocery store, and the transportation service she enlisted to take her to appointments is not always reliable. In short, Helen is beginning to realize there is a widening gap between her cherished ideal of remaining in her own home and the actual reality of doing so.

How can Helen cope with the distinct possibility that she might have to give up the aspect of her self-concept that she is a person who can continue living as she always did? Can she give up her home and move to a more supportive group retirement home and still maintain her self-concept of being an independent person who makes choices about living arrangements? Helen could use accommodative coping strategies, one of which might be to downgrade the quality of life in her own home. For example, she could focus on the fact that things in her home are always needing repairs and she could convince herself that getting good service people is more difficult than it used to be. Another strategy might be to make a positive adjustment to her thoughts about living in a group retirement home, which previously she might have found threatening to her self-concept of independence. For example, Helen could focus on the fact that many group retirement homes have individual apartments and allow residents to bring their own furniture.

Those who value assimilative coping strategies might be critical of accommodative strategies, perhaps seeing them as giving up or lowering goals. However, Brandtstädter (1999) argues that continued use of assimilative strategies to reach goals that are clearly not attainable can lead to frustration and can have negative emotional effects. Accommodative strategies maintain an individual's positive self-image and protect against depression in the face of irreversible and uncontrollable decline or loss. In fact, accommodative processes can be used to redefine goals so that the individual can direct assimilative actions toward more realistic aspects of living. For example, if Helen readjusts her idea of independence, she might feel free to direct her assimilative efforts toward maintaining as much independence as possible in a group retirement home.

The third process in the AAI Model, **immunization**, protects against threats to the self-concept that are central to an individual's identity (Brandtstädter, 1999). As with accommodative processes, immunizing processes are unintentional. However, immunizing processes call for tactics that help shield people from information that may conflict with the definitions they have of themselves, thus allowing them to preserve their personal self-worth in the face of evidence that could destroy it. To illustrate how immunizing processes operate, consider Peter, who is retired and prides himself on being an excellent golfer. Peter's golf scores, and the fact that he has won or come close to winning almost every golf tournament he has entered, are easily assimilated into his self-concept of being an excellent golfer and in fact have strengthened it. He practices almost every day (assimilative action) to maintain his status as a good golfer. Unfortunately, this season Peter's scores have been disappointing and so far he has not won any tournaments. This information is threatening because being an excellent golfer is a crucial aspect of Peter's self-concept.

Immunizing processes offer a line of defense against information that conflicts with this highly valued aspect of Peter's self-concept and can take various forms. Peter could attribute his poor scores to substandard maintenance of the golf course, to the fact that he needs a new set of golf clubs, to his recent sleeping problems, or to the loud conversations of the other members of the foursome that distract him from his game. In some sense, these immunizing processes are rationalizations, but they help Peter preserve the continuity of his self-concept and prevent his self-esteem from plummeting. Of course, immunizing strategies cannot serve a protective purpose forever. If Peter continues to get poor golf scores, his self-concept of being an excellent golfer will become increasingly difficult to maintain. At some point, the immunizing processes could actually represent denial of reality. For some period of time, however, immunizing processes can protect against information that threatens Peter's self-concept and self-esteem, allowing him the opportunity to take stock of the situation. He may decide to engage in further assimilative actions to improve his golf game (for example, canceling other activities to focus on taking lessons from a new golf pro). If these assimilative actions do not help, eventually Peter will be forced to adjust his standards as to what golf scores will lead to personal satisfaction. Gradually, he may modify the importance of being a good golfer and focus on other aspects of his self-concept.

Multiple Threshold Model of Identity and Physical Aging   The physical aging process can challenge a person's sense of identity. To explain how physical changes can affect self-concept, Whitbourne (1999) proposed a **multiple threshold model of identity and physical aging.** The term *threshold* refers to the point at which the individual recognizes that he or she has changed in a particular aspect of physical functioning. Once the threshold is crossed, the individual realizes there is a decline in functioning and feels a need to adapt his or her self-concept, or identity (such as admitting "I am getting old."). The term *multiple* refers to the fact that physical aging can occur in a number of bodily systems, each with its own threshold. Thus, it is possible to consider oneself old in one area but young in another. For example, at age 74, Dave is experiencing increasing difficulty with walking because of arthritis. At some point, his mobility threshold will be crossed and Dave will find it necessary to integrate this change into his self-concept (such as admitting "I am not such a good walker now."). However, Dave may not be experiencing any noticeable changes in vision and hearing so he will not need to make adjustments to his self-concept for sensory capability. He may not feel any different in this area of functioning from how he did as a young or middle-aged adult.

Not surprisingly, the ease with which age-related changes are integrated into the self-concept may depend on the importance of a particular area of functioning for an individual's identity. If Dave values taking long walks, it may be especially challenging for him to integrate age-related changes that affect his mobility. However, integrating age-related changes in mobility may be somewhat easier for a person who has a sedentary lifestyle and whose identity depends largely on being able to read books and attend movies and concerts.

Personal Control

The concept of personal control has intrigued psychologists for some time. Feelings of personal control relate to the perception that one governs what happens in one's own life. Personal control can be considered on a general level or within more specific domains. For example, one can feel a sense of personal control physically, socially, cognitively, and so on.

Internal Versus External Control   According to Rotter (1966), personal control varies along an internal-external dimension. Individuals with an **internal locus of control** feel that they have a great deal of personal control over what happens to them. They believe that experiencing positive outcomes and avoiding negative outcomes are contingent upon their own efforts, actions, and behavior.

In contrast, individuals with an **external locus of control** feel that their own efforts, actions, and behavior have little to do with what happens to them. They believe that positive and negative outcomes are determined by chance or other outside forces. Rotter (1966) devised an Internal-External (I-E) Locus of Control Scale on which individuals read pairs of statements and select the statement from each pair that best describes their personality. For example, one statement in a pair would indicate feelings of internal control ("When I make plans, I am almost certain that I can make them work"), while the other statement in the pair would indicate feelings of external control ("It is not always wise to plan too far ahead because many things turn out to be a matter of good or bad fortune anyhow").

A central question in the study of aging and older adulthood is whether the sense of personal control changes over the adult life span. A common belief is that individuals become less internal and more external in their locus of control as they move from young to older adulthood (Gatz & Karel, 1993). The idea that there is an age-related decrease in internal control is based on the assumption that many events that occur more frequently in older adulthood (for example, loss of loved ones, loss of the work role, illness) do not seem to be within the realm of personal control. The results of some early research studies did indicate that, compared with young adults, older adults feel less able to control the course of their lives (Pratt & Norris, 1994). However, other studies have called into question the idea that older adults have decreased feelings of internal control compared to young adults.

Gatz and Karel (1993) analyzed the responses of individuals from four generations (grandchildren, children, parents, grandparents) who participated in a study on locus of control that was conducted over 20 years, from 1971 to 1991. Participants were given several pairs of statements from Rotter's I-E Locus of Control Scale and asked to select the statement from each pair that would best describe them. Out of 1,267 participants, 560 participated at four different times of measurement, so the study yielded both cross-sectional and longitudinal information.

In the cross-sectional analysis on the responses of the 1,267 individuals who were tested only once, individuals from all four generations were similar in their feelings of internal control. In the longitudinal analysis on the responses of the 560 individuals who participated at all four times of measurement, there was a small but significant trend toward increased internal control over the 20-year period. Gatz and Karel speculate that the increase in feelings of internal control in individuals who were followed longitudinally could represent a time of measurement effect rather than a developmental (age) effect. Specifically, sociocultural changes that took place during the 20 years might have encouraged greater autonomy and fostered a spirit of self-improvement, resulting in greater feelings of internal control. In any case, Gatz and Karel found no evidence that internal control declines with age either in the cross-sectional or longitudinal part of their study.

In another study on locus of control, Rhee and Gatz (1993) asked young adult college students and older adult university alumni to rate themselves on an adapted version of Rotter's I-E scale. Compared with the young adult college students, the older adults had a higher degree of internal control. Once again, the assumption that older adults have a lower sense of personal control was not borne out in the self-ratings of the two age groups. Then Rhee and Gatz asked the same young and older adults to designate ratings on the Rotter I-E Scale that they thought would represent the beliefs of the opposite age group. Interestingly, the young college students perceived the older adults as being more external than older adults' actual self-ratings had indicated. The older adults thought that the young college students were more internal than the young students' actual self-ratings reflected. In sum, the beliefs that individuals held about their own personal control did not agree with beliefs that others from a different age group had about them. Young adults may assume older adults are externally controlled, but older adults do not actually view themselves that way.

Ultimately, however, older adults' feelings about whether they have internal personal control over what happens to them could be influenced by how others view them (Rodin & Langer, 1980). Labeling older adults as "helpless" or "senile" could have a negative effect on their feelings of personal control. This can be a vicious circle—if older adults feel that they have little or no control, then they may lose their motivation to engage in behaviors that actually could affect what happens to them.

It is generally believed that older adults who live in institutions such as nursing homes have very little control over their environment. If so, then what would happen if nursing home residents were given an opportunity to exert control over their environment? In one study (Schulz, 1976), older adult nursing home residents were visited by college students. One group of residents was allowed to control the frequency and duration of the visits. A second group of residents also received visits from the college students, but they had no choice about the frequency or duration of the visits. Even when Schulz controlled for the number, duration, and quality of the visits received by the nursing home residents in the two groups, he found that the positive impact of the college students' visits on the residents' well-being was greater when the residents were allowed to control the visits.

In a classic study (Langer & Rodin, 1976), one group of nursing home residents received a communication that emphasized they were responsible for themselves. In addition, the residents in this group were given a plant and told they were in charge of its care. A second group of nursing home residents received a communication that emphasized the staff was responsible for them. These residents were also given a plant but they were told the staff would care for it. Compared to the nursing home residents in the cared-for group, residents in the group told they were responsible for themselves and the care of the plant were more alert, participated more in activities, and had a higher general sense of well-being. The studies conducted by Schulz and by Langer and Rodin are clear in demonstrating that when individuals have little control over their environment, allowing them to control even a small aspect of it can benefit their psychological well-being.

Compared to older adults who reside in nursing homes, older adults who live in the community probably have more control over their environment.

Nonetheless, even community-living older adults can experience some decrease in control over what happens to them, especially with health-related events and losses. Thus, it seems reasonable to speculate that with increasing age, individuals will experience some drop in their level of life satisfaction and psychological well-being. Yet, studies with large international samples have found little evidence for any overall decline in life satisfaction with increasing age (Diener & Suh, 1997). In fact, level of life satisfaction seems to be stable across the adult years and well into older adulthood.

If life events that older adults confront—for example, illness, widowhood and loss of other close relationships, or loss of income through retirement—permit little personal control, how can we explain the maintained level of life satisfaction in late adulthood? It is likely that feelings of personal control are a great deal more complex than was previously thought. Such feelings may be derived not only from how much objective control individuals can actually exert but also from their expectations about personal control.

Although there may be an age-related decline in amount of personal control, Schulz and Hanusa (1980) argue that there may be a simultaneous decline in expectations for control. It is conceivable that feelings of well-being decline only when the actual level of control differs drastically from the level of control that is expected. A large discrepancy between actual and expected levels of control is most likely to occur when a change in the actual amount of control is so sudden that individuals do not have time to adjust their expectations.

For example, consider Raymond, a 79-year-old widower. Until several months ago, Raymond was living independently in his own condominium, cooking his own meals, and driving his own car. A sudden illness forced Raymond to spend some time in the hospital. When he returned home, he no longer felt strong enough to cook or drive himself. Raymond moved into an assisted living facility (ALF) where meals are served at certain times in a common dining room and transportation to medical appointments and stores is provided by a mini-van, but only by advance reservation. In a short time, Raymond experienced a significant decline in control over his environment, and his emotional outlook may suffer as well. In the early weeks of life in his new residence, Raymond's negative feelings may be especially intense, particularly if he compares the high level of control he had when he lived in his own condominium and drove his own car with the reduced amount of control he has now that he is living in the ALF. Eventually, however, he may adjust his expectancies. Perhaps he will begin to compare the level of control he has with the level of control most of the other ALF residents have. If the level of control he expects to have matches the level that is potentially available to him, then his negative feelings may give way to positive ones. In sum, feelings of personal control are not based solely on absolute and objective measures, and older adults can maintain a sense of personal control by adjusting their expectations.

The example of Raymond is not meant to negate the findings of Schulz (1976) or Langer and Rodin (1976), who demonstrated that nursing home residents showed a noticeable increase in positive affect when given an opportunity to exert control over a small facet of their environments. There is little question that Raymond has less freedom to exert personal control in the ALF than he had when he lived in his own condominium, but he may still be able to exert personal control over some aspects of his new environment.

Primary and Secondary Control   In addition to the concepts of internal and external locus of control, a recent model refers to primary control and secondary control. **Primary control processes** are actions and behaviors that influence, shape, or change the environment (Heckhausen & Schulz, 1995; Schulz & Heckhausen, 1996). Primary control processes drive individuals to adapt the environment to fit their needs and desires (Schulz & Heckhausen, 1996). As such, primary control processes are similar to the assimilative processes discussed earlier.

Behaviors and actions aimed at primary control may be applied to specific areas of functioning. For example, a person may engage in behaviors in an effort to attain primary control in the area of cognitive competence or social competence. A given individual may have a better chance of achieving primary control in one area than in another. One person might concentrate on mastering computer skills, while another might devote efforts to mastering social skills.

Efforts at primary control are not always successful. If too many attempts to achieve primary control end in failure, then the individual may become frustrated and discouraged and could begin to feel helpless and depressed. When attempts to achieve primary control meet with limited success or outright failure, **secondary control processes** often come into play. Unlike primary control processes, which are characterized by actions and behaviors directed at the external world, secondary control processes are related to internal resources (Heckhausen & Schulz, 1993). Secondary control processes are similar to accommodative processes in that they involve altering goals and expectations along with accepting existing realities that cannot be changed. For example, a person who tries to become an expert in computer skills on his or her own may become extremely frustrated if these attempts result in failures. A form of secondary control would be for this individual to lower the expectancies he or she had of being able to learn these skills without help. Secondary control processes buffer the individual against the negative effects of failure at achieving primary control. This buffering protects emotional well-being and self-esteem and enables the individual to remain sufficiently motivated to make further attempts at primary control in areas where efforts are more likely to be successful (Heckhausen & Schulz, 1995).

Heckhausen (1997) proposed a model that calls for **optimization of primary and secondary (OPS) control** over the adult life span. According to the OPS model, physical and cognitive losses may reduce the likelihood of achieving primary control in advanced old age. Thus, older adults become increasingly selective about where they place their efforts, and efforts at primary control include more compensatory strategies that require technical aids such as hearing aids and assistance from other people (Heckhausen & Schulz, 1993). To some degree, being selective in their efforts is adaptive since primary control

Figure 8.2   Availability and Use of Primary and Secondary Control over the Life Course

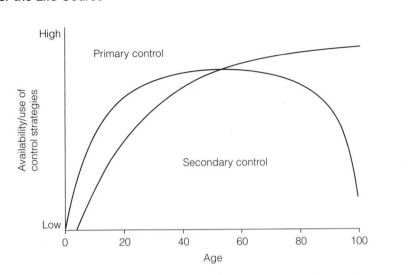

From Schulz and Heckhausen, "A life span model of successful aging." *American Psychologist*, 51, pp. 702–714, 1996. Copyright © 1996 American Psychological Association. Reprinted by permission.

efforts can be directed toward areas in which success is most attainable. However, if selection is too narrow, as can happen when individuals concentrate all their efforts at primary control in too few areas, they may limit their chance of success. Also, compensation can be dysfunctional when individuals prematurely adopt compensatory aids that result in greater dependency than is actually necessary. To achieve the best outcome in terms of primary control, people must monitor the areas they select and the compensatory strategies they adopt.

Figure 8.2 illustrates Schulz and Heckhausen's (1996) model in which primary and secondary control operate jointly to optimize development. It shows that the need for both primary and secondary control increases through early adulthood. With the approach of middle age and especially older adulthood, biological and social challenges may limit the broad use of primary control, and secondary control strategies take on greater importance. "As the ratio of gains to losses in primary control becomes less and less favorable, the individual increasingly resorts to secondary control processes" (Schulz & Heckhausen, 1996, p. 709). Also, as previously described, the number of areas in which primary control can be exerted gradually decreases as older adulthood approaches.

In sum, studies that have found life satisfaction does not significantly decline in older adulthood may simply reflect older adults' success in achieving a balance between primary and secondary control processes. Perhaps older adults cannot or do not wish to pursue the same goals, or at least as many goals, as they did in their younger years. Accordingly, they adjust their expectations and concentrate their efforts at primary control on goals that are age appropriate and likely to be attainable.

REVISITING THE SELECTIVE OPTIMIZATION WITH COMPENSATION AND ECOLOGICAL MODELS

Personality and coping in older adulthood can be viewed from the perspective of the SOC Model (Baltes & Baltes, 1990) and the Ecological Model (Lawton, 1989; Lawton & Nahemow, 1973), which were introduced in Chapter 1. According to the SOC model, selection, optimization, and compensation are necessary processes for realizing developmental goals. Stage theories imply that certain aspects of personality and personal issues are more dominant at some stages of adulthood than others, perhaps in keeping with society's expectations for people of different ages and at different stages of life. Individuals are likely to function optimally when they meet the challenges that are most compelling at their particular stage of life rather than attempting too many challenges at the same time. With regard to the idea that personality dimensions and traits are stable over the adult years, it is likely that individuals will be better able to meet some challenges than others, so those who struggle at one age and stage of life may not have to at other ages or stages of development. Even so, it may be possible to compensate for being low on some dimensions of personality by being high on others.

Also in keeping with the SOC Model, the balance between gains and losses may shift toward a greater proportion of losses in older adulthood (Baltes, 1987). When irreversible and uncontrollable losses occur, older adults may find it necessary to concentrate their efforts on goals that are most important to them. They may do this by giving up or adjusting aspects of their self-concept and concentrating their efforts on a select set of possible selves. Older adulthood may be a time when individuals must adjust the image they have of themselves and what they hope to become. Indeed, compared with young adults, older adults report having fewer possible selves but they are highly directed toward achieving the goals of their hoped-for possible selves and preventing their feared possible selves (Markus & Herzog, 1991).

The ecological model also provides a framework for considering personality and coping in older adulthood. Older adults adapt best in environments that permit them to realize their ideals of who they are and wish to become and also allow them sufficient opportunities to exert some level of personal control. To reduce the challenge of the environment so that it matches their level of competence more closely, older adults may engage in assimilative actions such as modifying a home. The closer the match between their ability to cope and the demands of the environment, the more likely they will be to enjoy a maximum level of adaptation. If assimilative actions do not modify the environment to a level that is adaptive, older adults may need to be in environments that are less challenging and more flexible to their needs.

KEY POINTS

- Personality development can be studied using the cross-sectional or longitudinal method. The time-lag method is used to study personality of individuals in one age group.
- Personality can be measured using self-reports, projective techniques, or behavioral observation.
- According to stage theorists, personality unfolds over time, taking on different forms or revolving around different issues or challenges as individuals progress through the adult years. Stages of personality development are usually linked to a chronological age range, and each stage is qualitatively different from the others. Personality is assumed to develop, or change, over the course of age, time, and experience.
- Other theorists emphasize the broad dimensions of personality, with a focus on whether these dimensions, or factors, remain stable or whether they change over time. Longitudinal research conducted in various cultures indicates continuity in personality dimensions in terms of people's rank-order over time relative to their age peers. However, age-related differences have been found in cross-sectional research. Compared to younger adults, older adults often have higher absolute scores on the dimensions of agreeableness and conscientiousness, but lower absolute scores on the dimensions of neuroticism, extraversion, and openness to experience.
- People associate various personality characteristics, or traits, with older adulthood. Some of these traits are negative, but some are positive.
- Self-concept is related to the image we have about ourselves. It consists of multiple cognitive schemas in any number of domains, and the aspects of the self-concept that are most important can regulate our decisions and behavior. Self-esteem refers to the affective, or evaluative, part of the self-concept. Self-concept has past, present, and future aspects. Our behavior is influenced by our future hoped-for and feared possible selves.
- Assimilation, accommodation, and immunization are three adaptive coping strategies that individuals use to maintain personal continuity and integrity of the self.
- Feelings of personal control are related to the perception that one governs what happens in one's own life. One conception is that personal control varies along an internal-external dimension. Studies have reported mixed findings about whether internal control declines and external control increases in older adulthood.
- When people want to maintain control over their lives, they make active efforts to do so. If efforts at active, primary control are not successful, they may call into play secondary control processes, which involve alterations in goals and expectations about things that cannot be changed through efforts

at primary control. Maintaining life satisfaction in older adulthood may reflect the fact that older adults have been successful in achieving a balance between primary and secondary control processes.

KEY TERMS

accommodation   315

assimilation   315

body transcendence versus body preoccupation   299

ego differentiation versus work-role preoccupation   298

ego integrity versus despair   296

ego transcendence versus ego preoccupation   299

external locus of control   319

Five-Factor Model (FFM) of Personality   301

generativity versus stagnation   296

immunization   317

internal locus of control   318

intimacy versus isolation   296

life review   299

life story   298

multiple threshold model of identity and physical aging   318

optimization of primary and secondary (OPS) control   322

possible selves   313

primary control processes   322

secondary control processes   322

self-concept   310

self-esteem   311

To learn more about the issues discussed in this chapter, point your browser to http://www.infotrac-college.com and use the passcode from the InfoTrac College Edition card that came with your book. InfoTrac College Edition gives you access to complete articles from many different journals.

Social Interaction and Social Ties

Ruth became a widow last year at the age of 76, and recently she moved from her house to an apartment about 8 miles from her daughter and son and their families. Ruth sees her adult children about once a week and she speaks to at least one of them on the phone almost every day. She is learning how to use e-mail to keep in touch with her grandchildren who are away at college. Ruth gave up her car when she moved to the apartment, but several friends in the building still drive and they usually ask her if she wants a lift when they go to the grocery store or the mall. Ruth reciprocates by watering their plants when they are out of town, occasionally baking them one of her "famous" coffee cakes, or just being there if they want to confide in her. Ruth knows she can ask her children to help her out if she ever becomes ill. However, for now she prefers to count on friends as long as she is sure she will be able to pay them back for their favors.

SOCIAL INTERACTION IN OLDER ADULTHOOD

Social interactions are an essential part of life, but do they differ in older adulthood from other points in adult life? How are social interactions related to older adults' level of adjustment and well-being, and what kinds of interactions buffer older adults against feelings of depression? Investigators have been very interested in the patterns of social interactions and social ties that are most likely to be associated with successful aging.

Early research focused primarily on the quantity of social interactions in older adulthood. Also, the emphasis was on the positive aspects of social interactions, which were considered to be the same as social support. More recently, those who study aging and older adulthood have acknowledged that social interactions are complex—they have rewarding aspects, but they can also be stressful. In short, it is important to evaluate not only the number of social interactions but also their quality. Both quantity and quality of social interactions may play a role in determining life satisfaction, well-being, and adaptation to stressful situations.

Another recent trend in studying social interactions is the greater acknowledgment that older adults actively shape their social environments. This contrasts with an earlier view that older adults are passive recipients of social attention. With whom do older adults choose to interact, and are some interactions more important than others?

It is generally recognized that the level of social interaction declines somewhat in older adulthood. Factors such as loss of a partner through widowhood, loss of the work role through retirement, loss of income through both widowhood and retirement, loss of a familiar environment because of relocation, and in some cases loss of health are all associated with reduced opportunities for social interaction. Several theories have offered perspectives on the meaning and implications of the apparent age-related decrease in social interactions. First we will describe early theories and then the more recent theoretical perspective that social interactions may fulfill different functions at various points in the adult life span.

Activity Theory

One early perspective about social interactions in older adulthood was **activity theory**. Its basic assumption was that older adults have the same social wants and needs as young and middle-aged adults. Although events such as retirement and widowhood (discussed in Chapters 10 and 12) could reduce the number of social interactions in later adulthood, this decrease was thought to be imposed upon older adults by external circumstances. According to activity theory, older adults strive to maintain their level of social interaction by substituting new roles when old roles are no longer available. For example, a man who retires from paid employment might become involved in volunteer work, or a woman who loses her husband might join a new social group. If older adults are successful in replacing social roles they have lost, they will have high life satisfaction, or high morale and feelings of well-being (Passuth & Bengston, 1988). On a practical level, activity theory justified the implementation of social programs targeted to the older adult population, which would provide opportunities for older adults to replace social roles lost due to circumstances beyond their control.

The premise that older adults seek new opportunities for social interaction seemed at odds with the common finding that older adults do not always take advantage of the social opportunities offered to them. For example, only 15 percent of the older-adult population visit senior centers that offer social programs (Carstensen, 1991). Most contemporary researchers do not subscribe to activity theory in its original form. Yet elements of activity theory are evident in popular media communications that urge retired older adults to remain engaged by doing volunteer work and participating in social groups.

Disengagement Theory

Disengagement theory originated from some early findings from the Kansas City Study on Adult Life that indicated that in late middle-age, people begin to show signs of withdrawal from social and emotional relationships. (See Chapter 8 for more description of this study.) According to disengagement theory, social and psychological withdrawal is a necessary component of successful aging. Older adults voluntarily withdraw from roles they played in middle age, possibly in preparation for the final withdrawal, death. At the same time, society withdraws from older adults by expecting them to step aside voluntarily to make room for the upcoming younger generation. Older adults who disengage meet with society's approval, so they experience a high level of life satisfaction. Based on disengagement theory, one might conclude that encouraging older adults to participate in social programs is contrary to what they want or need and could actually reduce their chances of attaining a positive state of well-being. In sum, disengagement theory proposed that older adults withdraw from society and society withdraws from older adults (Cumming & Henry, 1961), and the mutual withdrawal of older individuals and society from each other benefits them both (Passuth & Bengston, 1988).

The suggestion that older adults are willing to withdraw from society, and furthermore that they are happy and satisfied when they are allowed to do so, was highly controversial. It certainly conflicted with the activity theory's premise that older adults disengage only because of circumstances beyond their control. To be totally accurate, prior to disengagement theory, it had been assumed that a high level of activity and engagement was consistently positive for older adults. It was only after disengagement theory was introduced that researchers gave the label activity theory to this general assumption.

Figure 9.1 | Social Exchange Theory

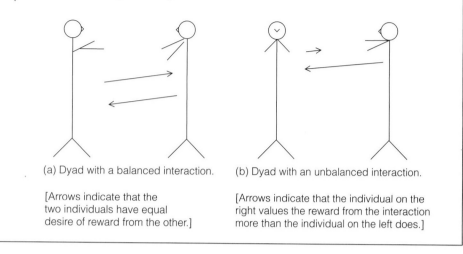

(a) Dyad with a balanced interaction.   (b) Dyad with an unbalanced interaction.

[Arrows indicate that the two individuals have equal desire of reward from the other.]   [Arrows indicate that the individual on the right values the reward from the interaction more than the individual on the left does.]

But is life satisfaction in older adulthood associated with a high level or a low level of social activity? For several decades after disengagement theory was proposed, a flurry of studies attempted to pit activity theory against disengagement theory in a contest to see which was correct. Over time, it became evident that neither theory by itself could explain all of the variations in older adults' level of social interaction or life satisfaction. In fact, subsequent findings from the Kansas City Study indicated that some older adults are satisfied with their lives only if they have a high level of activity, while others are satisfied with a lower level. By the 1980s, interest in pitting activity theory against disengagement theory had waned. Nonetheless, the activity theory/disengagement theory controversy laid the groundwork for more sophisticated ideas about the nature and role of social interactions in older adulthood.

Social Exchange Theory

According to **social exchange theory** (Dowd, 1975), social interactions are transactions between two or more people and these exchanges can have both rewards and costs. Seeking rewards in a social interaction often means incurring some costs, which may include unpleasantness experienced during the course of a social exchange, especially if the interaction is with someone who is not a close family member or friend. In general, individuals continue to interact only as long as the rewards in an exchange are perceived to be greater than the costs.

Consider a social interaction between two participants, or partners, often referred to as a dyad. According to social exchange theory, the interaction is balanced if both partners in the dyad have an equal desire for the reward offered by the other. However, if one partner values the reward from the exchange more than the other partner does, then the partner who places greater value on the reward is more dependent upon the exchange. The concept of power enters when there is imbalance in a social exchange. The less powerful partner is more in need of the exchange and therefore will feel obliged to comply with the demands of the more powerful partner. Over time, such compliance can become costly to the less powerful partner, who has less choice in the relationship. Older adults may engage in fewer social interactions with a more powerful partner if such interactions have greater costs than potential benefits. The more powerful partner may be another individual, but it could also be an institution in the broader social environment or society.

In nonindustrialized agricultural societies, older adults often held positions of power and privilege because they controlled property, often farmland, which generated resources needed by others. Older adults in industrialized societies have less status and power because property ownership is not as crucial (Cowgill, 1986; Cox, 1990). In the modern workplace, older adults may be less familiar than recent college graduates are with cutting-edge technology, so older workers may be at some disadvantage in employee-employer exchanges. Despite laws against age discrimination in the workplace, older workers may be forced into less prestigious job positions. Ultimately, they may comply with management's unspoken wish for their resignation (often in the guise of retirement, which is sometimes made more palatable with an exit bonus or the promise of an early pension). See Chapter 10 for additional discussion of the older worker, pensions, and retirement.

In 1975, Dowd contended that in American society, youth holds a low degree of power resources, but power increases through late middle age only to be followed by a sharp decrease in old age. However, Dowd predicted that in the future, older adults would experience less decline in power resources because they would be more educated, more knowledgeable about technology, and more independent financially. Indeed, there is good reason to believe that Dowd's earlier prediction is coming true.

Nonetheless, social exchange theory is useful for understanding social interactions in some contexts. For example, older residents of long-term care facilities such as nursing homes and assisted living facilities (described in Chapter 10) often experience difficulties negotiating with administrators and staff members to get what they need. To combat this power imbalance, many states have laws that require providing individuals admitted to nursing homes with a list of "Nursing Home Residents' Rights," which must also be posted in a prominent area that is easily accessible. The statements in Table 9.1 are adapted from Florida Statute 400.022 concerning nursing home residents' rights in the State of Florida.

In addition, most states in the United States have ombudsman programs. Ombudsmen are usually volunteers trained in how to resolve complaints about quality of care made by or on behalf of older adults who reside in nursing homes and assisted living facilities. Ombudsmen work to ensure that older adults who reside in such facilities receive the legal, financial, social, and rehabilitative services to which they are entitled. In some sense, their role is to maintain a balance

Table 9.1   Nursing Home Residents' Rights

Nursing home residents enter their new home losing none of the civil rights they were entitled to in the community. Additionally, state regulation requires nursing homes to assure residents special rights, including the following:

- civil and religious liberties, including independent personal decisions.
- private and uncensored communication, including mail, phone access, and visitation.
- reasonable access to health, social, and legal providers, and immediate access to any representative of federal and state government, including the Department of Children and Families, Agency for Health Care Administration, law enforcement, ombudsman, and the resident's personal physician.
- present grievances as well as organize and participate in resident groups.
- participate in social, religious, and community activities.
- manage their own financial affairs.
- be fully informed of the charges and services not covered by per diem rate.
- be adequately informed of their medical condition and proposed treatment.
- refuse medication or treatment and be informed of the consequences.
- receive adequate and appropriate health care and protective and support services.
- be given privacy in treatment and in caring for personal needs.
- be given courteous, fair, and dignified treatment.
- be assured freedom from mental and physical abuse, punishment, and seclusion.
- be transferred or discharged only for medical reasons or for the welfare of other residents, and only with advance notice of no less than 30 days.
- be given freedom of choice in selecting a personal physician, pharmaceutical supplier, and services.
- be allowed to retain and use personal clothing and possessions as space permits.
- be given copies of facility rules and regulations.
- receive notice before any room change is made.
- be fully informed of the nursing home's bed reservation policy in case of hospitalization.

Adapted from Florida Statute 400.022.

in the exchange relationships between residents and the staff and administrators in long-term care facilities.

Socioemotional Selectivity Theory

Socioemotional selectivity theory (SEST) is a life-span model that proposes that the reduced social activity often seen in old age reflects a lifelong selection process (Carstensen, 1991, 1995). That is, the number of individuals in a person's overall social network is smaller in older adulthood than it is in young adulthood. However, in older adulthood very close social relationships are maintained while more superficial ones are filtered out. The focus of SEST is on the adaptive aspect of age-related reductions in social interactions.

According to SEST (Carstensen, 1991), social interactions have three central goals, or functions: information acquisition, development and maintenance of identity, and emotional regulation. These functions motivate individuals to select the social partners with whom they will interact, but as described below, at different points of adulthood, some functions are more prominent than others.

Information Acquisition   Information acquisition is a prominent motive for social interactions early in life, a time when we are reaching out to meet new people. From the people we meet, we may ultimately select a life partner or spouse or form long-term friendships. Early in life we are likely to gather information about potential careers and interests we want to pursue in the future. Acquiring information usually calls for interactions with new people, or novel partners. In later adulthood, there is less need to acquire new information for future use.

Development and Maintenance of Identity   Social interactions help us mold how we perceive ourselves, to know who we are or who we want to be. Identity formation is an important challenge faced in adolescence and into young adulthood (Erikson, 1950). This challenge can be met by interacting with novel partners.

In older adulthood, there is less motivation to develop identity. Instead, older adults are motivated to preserve their self-concepts. Therefore, older adults may want to avoid social interactions with novel partners who could erode their self-concept. Instead, they may prefer to interact with familiar people who share some of the same history and on whom they can rely to affirm who they are (Carstensen, 1991).

Emotional Regulation   Social interactions, especially pleasant ones, fulfill emotional needs. According to SEST, emotional regulation, or emotional fulfillment, becomes more important in older adulthood. Older adults prefer to socialize with familiar partners because they place great importance on the positive emotions, or affect, that comes from intimate and gratifying social interactions. There is less guarantee of experiencing positive affect in interactions with novel partners.

More recently, Carstensen and her colleagues (Carstensen, Gross, & Fung, 1997; Carstensen, Isaacowitz, & Charles, 1999) have focused on only two categories of social motives: acquisition of information, or knowledge, and regulation of emotion. Figure 9.2 illustrates the importance of these two goals over the life span.

Also, rather than focusing exclusively on chronological age, these investigators emphasize that social goals are influenced by the perception of time (Carstensen et al., 1999). When time is perceived as open ended, or unlimited, then our main motivation for engaging in social interactions is acquiring information. In contrast, when time is perceived as limited, emotional regulation becomes the primary motive. Older adults may prefer interactions with emotionally meaningful and familiar social partners because they feel that the amount of time they have left is limited.

To test the importance of time as it relates to preferences for social partners, Fredrickson and Carstensen (1990) attempted to manipulate what they call

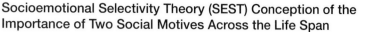

Figure 9.2 | Socioemotional Selectivity Theory (SEST) Conception of the Importance of Two Social Motives Across the Life Span

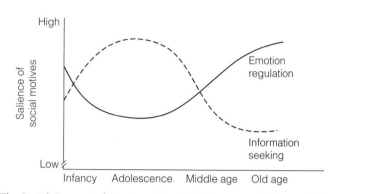

From "The Social Context of Emotion," by L. L. Carstensen, J. Gross, & H. Fung, *Annual Review of Geriatrics and Gerontology, 17,* p. 331. New York: Springer Publishing Co., 1997.

"anticipated endings." Initially, they instructed both young and older adults to imagine having 30 minutes of leisure time with no pressing commitments. Study participants were asked to select one of the following individuals with whom they would prefer to spend that time: (a) a family member (familiar partner), (b) a recent acquaintance with whom they seem to have much in common (novel partner with possibility for future contact), or (c) the author of a book they have read (novel partner with little possibility for future contact). Not surprisingly, 65 percent of the older adults chose the familiar partner whereas only 35 percent of the young adults did.

Next, the young adults were told to imagine that they were preparing for a cross-country move and would be leaving family and friends behind. Then they selected from the same choices described above the individual with whom they would choose to spend 30 minutes of leisure time. Under this time-limitation condition, the proportion of young adults who chose a familiar partner increased from 35 percent to 80 percent. Thus, when time limitations were explicitly stated, the young adults' pattern of preference for the familiar social partner was similar to that of the older adults. The same findings were reported in a parallel study conducted in Hong Kong (Fung, Carstensen, & Lutz, 1999) in which some participants were told to imagine they would be emigrating in the near future. Older Asians tended to select a familiar social partner whether or not they were told emigration was imminent, while young Asians showed the same pattern found with young Americans: When told their time was limited because they would be emigrating soon, they were much more likely to select the familiar social partner.

In another study, Fung et al.(1999) hypothetically extended the future rather than restricting it. Young study participants selected a novel partner for potential social interaction regardless of whether or not they were told to imagine that their physician had informed them that a medical breakthrough would add 20 years to their life. However, older participants told to imagine they had received this "life-extending" news were more likely to choose a novel social partner compared to older participants who were not given this information. Thus, the social preference of older adults given a reason to believe that their future would be extended was very similar to young adults' preference for a novel partner.

In sum, Carstensen and her colleagues contend that social preferences are related to the perception of time. Knowledge-based goals and novel social partners take precedence when time is viewed as unlimited. In contrast, emotional goals are more important when time is viewed as limited. Perception of time limitation is most likely to occur in older adulthood, when there is an impending long-distance move, or when there is terminal illness (Carstensen & Fredrickson, 1998). When emotional aspects of relationships have priority, people prefer to interact with familiar social partners, who are more likely than unfamiliar partners to provide positive emotional experiences and feelings of belonging.

Positive and Negative Aspects of Social Relationships

Most research has concentrated on the benefits of social interactions for older adults' health and well-being. Less attention has been paid to the potentially negative aspects of social interactions and social relationships (Lachman, 2003; Rook, 1997).

Rook (1984) asked 120 relatively healthy, independent widowed older women (ages 60 to 89) to identify the people to whom they could turn for socializing, confiding their personal problems, and help when they are ill (positive relationships). The same women also identified the people who cause them problems such as invading their privacy, taking advantage of them, breaking promises of help, and provoking conflicts or feelings of anger (negative relationships). Rook found that positive and negative social relationships were relatively independent. That is, women with many negative relationships did not necessarily have few positive ones, and women with very few negative relationships did not necessarily have many positive ones. Rook concluded that older women with problematic relationships do not necessarily lack social skills because they are just as likely as anyone else to have good relationships as well.

Ingersoll-Dayton, Morgan, and Antonucci (1997) investigated the link between positive and negative exchanges and both positive and negative emotions. Their respondents were drawn from a large national sample of 718 individuals ages 50 to 95 from a broad range of income levels. Individuals in the sample had an average age of 66; they were predominantly European American (89 percent), slightly more than half female (58 percent), and mostly not employed (64 percent). Approximately half were married, 29 percent were widowed, and 12 percent were separated, divorced, or never married. Respondents reported how many of the following stressful life events they had experienced within the past five years: death of a spouse; death of another family member or friend; illness or injury of a family member or friend; change of residence; having a family member reside in a nursing home; having a child leave home; retiring from work; experiencing a job change; being fired, laid off, or quitting work; being robbed or attacked. Based on the number of stressful life events endorsed, Ingersoll-Dayton et al. split their sample into a low-stress subgroup (experienced fewer than two life stressors) and a high-stress subgroup (experienced three or more life stressors).

To measure positive social exchanges, Ingersoll-Dayton et al. asked respondents to list the people in whom they confided about health issues and from whom they sought reassurance, respect, and care when they were upset or ill. As a measure of negative social exchanges, respondents listed the people in their social network who got on their nerves, did not understand them, or were too demanding. Respondents also completed self-report scales intended to measure positive affect (such as feeling excited, proud, pleased, on top of the world) as well as negative affect (such as feeling restless, lonely, bored, depressed, and upset).

Perhaps not surprisingly, positive exchanges were associated with feelings of well-being and negative social exchanges were associated with negative affect. Of particular importance, however, was that negative exchanges and negative affect were more closely related in the high-stress subgroup than they were in the low-stress subgroup. This means that older adults who are coping with multiple stressors seem to be particularly vulnerable to negative treatment from others. Another difference between the two subgroups was in the relationship between the positive and negative affect. For low-stress individuals, positive and negative affect were independent, so being high on the positive affect dimension did not necessarily mean being either high or low in negative affect. In contrast, high-stress individuals who were high in negative affect were low in positive affect. The different pattern of findings for the low-stress and high-stress subgroups points to the importance of considering the relationship between social exchanges and affect within the context of the stress individuals are already experiencing.

In another study, Okun and Keith (1998) investigated the relationship between positive and negative social exchanges and the extent to which each predict depressive symptoms in both young and older adults. Their sample consisted of a subset of respondents (452 younger adults ages 28–59; 849 older adults ages 60 and older) from a larger national survey. To be included in the data subset for this study, respondents had to have a living spouse, at least one child, and at least one other relative or friend. Positive social exchanges were measured by respondents' answers to two questions: how much the spouse, child, or other relative/friend makes them feel loved and cared for and also whether these people were willing to listen to them talk about their worries or problems. Negative social exchanges were measured by respondents' answers to questions about how often the same three sources make too many demands and are critical of what they do.

Okun and Keith found that positive social exchanges were inversely related to depressive symptoms. That is, the higher the frequency of positive exchanges, the lower the level of depressive symptoms. For the younger adults, the key source of positive social exchanges was usually the spouse, whereas older adults reported positive social exchanges with a broader range of sources including a spouse, children, and close friends. For older adults, limiting positive social exchanges to a spouse might prove to be maladaptive should they lose their only source of happiness through widowhood.

Okun and Keith found that for both young and older adults, positive and negative social exchange were inversely related, but only when both types of social exchange were with the same person (a spouse or one particular child or friend) rather than with different people (for example, a negative exchange with a spouse or friend and a positive social exchange with a child). In other words, if positive social exchanges with a specific individual are high, then negative social exchanges with that same individual tend to be low. Such an inverse relationship between the positive and negative exchanges was strongest when the source of both was a spouse rather than a child or friend.

Can the detrimental effects such as depression or sadness that result from negative social exchanges be buffered by positive social exchanges? Conceivably, positive and negative social exchanges could come from the same individual, or source. Alternatively, positive and negative social exchanges could have different sources. Okun and Keith found evidence for different-source buffering in the older adults. For example, positive social exchanges with adult children seemed to cushion older adults against the adverse depressive effects of negative social exchanges with a spouse or friend. Similarly, positive social exchanges with relatives and friends buffered older adults against the adverse effects of negative social exchanges with adult children. A different pattern was found for the younger adults, whose positive social exchanges with a relative or friend seemed to buffer them against negative social exchanges with the same individuals.

Why does same-source buffering work for younger adults but not for older adults? Okun and Keith point to socioemotional selectivity theory (SEST) as a possible explanation. As individuals age, they become more selective in their social relationships by seeking out social partners who will enhance their emotional well-being. On the whole, younger and older respondents both reported more positive than negative social exchanges. Nonetheless, the older adults reported fewer negative social exchanges with a spouse, children, relatives, and friends. It is possible that older adults are more likely than younger adults to choose social partners who provide them with uniformly positive rather than mixed social experiences.

The findings of these and other studies on the benefits and risks of positive and negative social exchange are complex. Undoubtedly, the results of specific studies are related to the personal characteristics of the respondents (Krause & Rook, 2003), the measures used to index positive and negative social exchanges, and the nature and specificity of the exchange source. Additional research is certainly warranted in this interesting and important area of research.

SOCIAL TIES IN OLDER ADULTHOOD

Social ties are an important factor in older adults' physical and psychological well-being (Fees, Martin, & Poon, 1999). Some relationships are closer and longer lasting than others. Many ties are with family members but some are with individuals outside the family.

Figure 9.3 | Three Concentric Circles Demonstrating a Person's Social Network

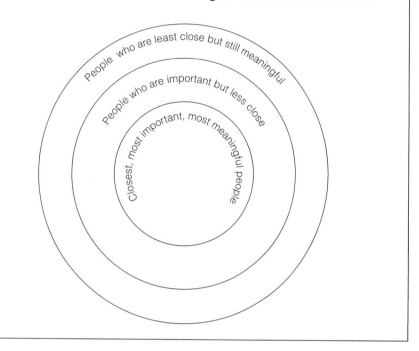

Social Convoys, Social Networks, and Reciprocity

According to the **convoy model** (Antonucci, Sherman, & Akiyama, 1996), individuals move through life both affecting and being affected by a constellation of other people who play a central role in their network of social relationships. The people in an individual's social convoy are often family members, but there may also be friends with whom there is close contact on a regular basis. Whether the people included in the social convoy are family or friends, they have an important influence on the individual's well-being.

The term **social network** refers to the structural characteristics of an individual's social ties, including the number, age, sex, relationship, and frequency of contact with people who are part of it (Antonucci et al., 1996). Some researchers study social networks by asking individuals to map their social ties onto a three-tier concentric-circle diagram. Individuals place those people whom they consider to be closest and most important to them in the innermost circle, those somewhat less close in the middle circle, and people whom they consider least close but still somewhat important in the outermost circle (Antonucci, 1986).

Members of a social network provide social support in various forms (Antonucci et al., 1996; Levitt, Weber, & Guacci, 1993). Some offer assistance when we are ill or help us when we encounter financial difficulties. Others are individuals in whom we can confide when we are upset or worried and who can replenish our feelings of control and self-worth (Krause & Borawski-Clark, 1994). Still others may just be individuals with whom we want to spend time

(Antonucci & Akiyama, 1987; Levitt et al., 1993). Social support in all of these forms can buffer individuals against the negative effects of stress (Antonucci et al., 1996).

Social exchanges that are balanced in terms of amount of support both provided and received are said to have **reciprocity**. In reciprocal social exchanges, each individual gives as much support as he or she receives. In contrast, nonreciprocal exchanges are those in which an individual gives more support than he or she receives, or conversely receives more support than he or she gives. One suggestion has been that we make deposits into a **support bank** by giving more support than we receive as long as we are able to do so. Later we may need more support than we can give, at which point we feel it is legitimate to make withdrawals from the support bank (Antonucci et al., 1996).

To test the idea of a support bank, Levitt et al. (1993) interviewed triads, or three generations, of women consisting of young adult daughters (university students), their mothers, and their grandmothers. Levitt et al. found that the women in the older (grandmother) generation reported giving less support than did women in the young adult and middle-aged (mother) generations. The grandmothers may have provided more support in the past, but now they are receiving more support than they are giving.

The triads of women interviewed by Levitt et al. (1993) were bicultural (English speaking or Spanish speaking). Members of each triad mapped the structure of their social networks onto a concentric three-circle diagram, placing those individuals to whom they felt most attached in the inner circle and those whom they considered to be less close but still important in the middle and outer circles. The participants indicated the extent to which each member of the network provided social support of various types (for example, giving reassurance, advice, care if they were ill, and so on). Across the two cultural groups and three generations, there was a considerable degree of similarity in network structure and type of support. Both English-speaking and Spanish-speaking participants placed primarily close family members in the inner circle and indicated that family members provided the greatest support.

However, there was some variation in network structure and function across the two cultural groups and three generations. Compared to the networks of the English-speaking triads, the networks of the Spanish-speaking triads were more family focused, with fewer friends included in their support networks. Also, while family members were the primary source of support for all three generations, there was an age-related shift in the proportion of family members versus friends. In both cultural groups, the proportion of friends in the network declined from the young to the middle to the older generation. Levitt et al. speculated that the more extensive friendship networks of young adults help them attain independence from their families so that they can establish intimate relationships that lead to new family structures through marriage and the birth of children. Later, family members are likely to become the primary source of support.

As far as the size of the social network in older adulthood, both chronological age and individual personality differences play a role. In a study conducted in Berlin, Germany, the size of the social networks reported by 156 individuals between the ages of 70 and 104 was negatively related to chronological age (Lang & Carstensen, 1994). That is, the older the person, the smaller the social network. Even into very late older adulthood, individuals maintain meaningful emotional ties with others, but they become more exclusive. The oldest members of the sample reported a decline in the number of social interactions, but this decline was due mainly to the more limited interactions with people who were not considered to be particularly close.

With regard to personality factors, Lang, Staudinger, and Carstensen (1998) found that even into the ninth decade of life, extraverts have larger social networks than introverts do. Similarly, individuals who are more open to experience have larger social networks than those who are less open. Thus, older adults who are outgoing, sociable, and have high tolerance for new experiences and unfamiliar situations are likely to maintain larger social networks than older adults who are less outgoing, less sociable, and less open to new experiences. Still, it is important to emphasize that older adults with a smaller social network are as emotionally close to those in it as are people with larger networks.

Older adults who have family members available to them have larger social networks and seem to enjoy greater feelings of social belonging. When a spouse and adult offspring are available, emotional closeness with other social partners may be less important. When a spouse and grown children are not available, however, older adults may seek support from sources such as other relatives or friends.

Family Relationships

Family is sometimes defined in terms of household members. The **nuclear family household** is common in urban American society; it consists of parents and their children who live under the same roof. For the parents, the nuclear family represents the **family of procreation.** For the children, the nuclear family represents the **family of origin.** Eventually, children grow up and many move out to form their own family of procreation.

The **extended family household,** which was common in rural areas especially in earlier decades, consists of members from more than two generations (grandparents, parents, children), all living under the same roof or in very close proximity. The extended family household could also include aunts, uncles, and cousins. Some extended families formed an economic unit, such as running the family farm. In the United States today, there are fewer multigenerational extended families who live under the same roof or work together. This has given rise to a common myth that older adults are isolated from and abandoned by their families (Bengston, Rosenthal, & Burton, 1996).

To determine the accuracy of this myth, Shanas (1979) conducted an extensive survey of older adults and found that most did not yearn to live under the same roof with adult children and grandchildren. Rather, many expressed a preference for **intimacy at a distance,** which means that they welcomed contact and involvement with family members but preferred to maintain their own households as long as they were physically and financially capable of doing so.

When family members live far apart, they remain in contact with frequent telephone conversations.

Over half the older adults in Shanas's survey lived within 10 minutes of at least one adult child and many had visited with an adult child in the week prior to the survey. In addition, many had frequent contact with siblings and other relatives either in the form of face-to-face visits or telephone conversations. Shanas concluded that older adults are not alienated or uninvolved with their families just because they do not live under the same roof. In fact, she concluded that the dominant family structure in the United States is the **modified extended family,** which consists of a broad kinship network including grandparents, parents, grandchildren, siblings, and even nephews, nieces, and other relatives by blood or marriage. Members of this family network have frequent contact and provide support for one another even though they do not live under the same roof or work together.

The **beanpole family structure** describes what families will be like in the future. Thanks to increases in life expectancy, more families will have four or even five living generations. However, each generation will have fewer members because the birthrate is lower today than it was in earlier decades.

The **blended family** is a term for families in which some members are unrelated by blood but nonetheless live together and share family responsibilities. Such families are usually the result of divorce and remarriage. One or both members of the remarried couple may bring children from a prior marriage into a newly formed (reconstituted) family.

Marital Relationships   The marital relationship is central to the lives of many adults. In older adulthood, more men than women are married because women tend to marry men who are older than they are and also because women have a higher life expectancy than men do. (See Chapter 3 for more detailed discussion of life expectancy.) Thus, women are more likely than men to lose a spouse through death (Chapter 10 discusses widowhood), and they are less likely than men to remarry.

What factors play a role in marital satisfaction? Reedy, Birren, and Schaie (1981) located 102 young, middle-aged, and older couples (ranging from 22 to 83 years of age), all of whom were described by others as happily married and also considered themselves to be happily married. Each member of the happily married couple rated a series of statements as to how important each was for the marriage. Compared with the young and middle-aged couples, the older couples considered emotional security ("I really feel I can trust my spouse") and loyalty ("The future will be perfect as long as we are together") to have greater importance, and sexual intimacy ("We try to please each other physically") to have less importance. Compared with the middle-aged and older couples, the young couples considered communication ("My spouse finds it easy to confide in me") to have greater importance. This study was cross-sectional, so the age of the married couples cannot be separated from the generation, or cohort, to which they belong. (See Chapter 2 for a discussion of cross-sectional research.) Also, the age of the couples could not be separated from the length of time they had been married. Perhaps the older couples placed less importance on communication because they had been married for so many years and took good communication for granted.

The **upswing hypothesis of marital satisfaction** refers to a phenomenon found to characterize marriages over the course of adulthood (Anderson, Russell, & Schumm, 1983). The level of marital satisfaction appears to be highest in the early years of marriage before the arrival of children. There is a dip in marital satisfaction in the ensuing years, during which childrearing and the establishment of careers are the main tasks. Later, marital satisfaction shows an increase, or upswing, although not to as high a level as in the early years of marriage. The upswing in marital satisfaction occurs at about the time children are launched and living independently. At this point, many couples are in good health and can enjoy more personal freedom.

The upswing hypothesis of marital satisfaction was derived from cross-sectional studies in which couples of various ages and number of years married were interviewed at the same time. Note that individuals who remain in the same marital relationship for a long period of time may represent a select subgroup whose marriages withstood stresses that caused other couples to separate or divorce. Although the divorce rate in the United States stabilized in the 1990s with approximately 50 percent of first marriages ending in divorce, this figure is higher than it was in the 1950s and 1960s. This means that in the coming years, long-lived marriages that have endured over the adult life span may be less common than they are now. Even so, what is the nature of the relationship of older married couples compared to that of middle-aged couples?

Levenson, Carstensen, and Gottman (1993) and Carstensen, Gottman, and Levenson (1995) studied middle-aged married couples (ages 40–50 and married at least 15 years) and older married couples (ages 60–70 and married at least 35 years). Of the 156 couples who participated in their studies, 155 were in first marriages and 149 had children. All of the couples resided in Berkeley,

Figure 9.4 | The Upswing Hypothesis of Marital Satisfaction

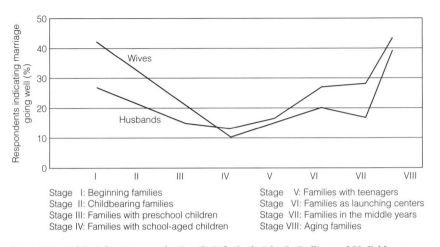

Stage I: Beginning families
Stage II: Childbearing families
Stage III: Families with preschool children
Stage IV: Families with school-aged children

Stage V: Families with teenagers
Stage VI: Families as launching centers
Stage VII: Families in the middle years
Stage VIII: Aging families

From "Marital Satisfaction over the Family Life Cycle," by B. Rollins and H. Feldman, 1970, *Journal of Marriage and the Family, 32*, p. 25.

California, and they were predominantly European American (85 percent), upper middle class, and well-educated. The middle-aged and older couples were similar in level of education and income. On average, couples in both age groups had married at about the same age, but the middle-aged couples had known each other somewhat longer before marriage and they had fewer children, both of which are probably typical for their cohort group.

Overall, the middle-aged and older couples were comparable in average level of marital satisfaction as determined by their answers to a self-report questionnaire administered at the beginning of the study. After completing the marital satisfaction questionnaire, the couples were asked to rate how much disagreement they had experienced in each of 10 areas of potential conflict. The greatest difference between the middle-aged and older couples was in the area of children, which ranked highest as a source of conflict for the middle-aged couples but only fourth in importance for the older couples. Older couples ranked children and grandchildren highest as a pleasurable and enjoyable topic of conversation, whereas middle-aged couples ranked this topic only third as a subject of enjoyable conversation. Middle-aged couples had children still living at home or who left home recently, so children may have been a more immediate source of conflict for them. Children of the older couples were grown and no longer living with them, which might explain why they were a more enjoyable topic of conversation.

Across the 10 areas of potential conflict, the older couples reported having fewer disagreements and greater pleasure in conversing about various topics than the middle-aged couples did. These findings bode well for long-term marriages. However, it is conceivable that couples who experience significant conflict in middle-age may simply not remain married. If so, then the older couples may represent a more positively selected group. Only longitudinal follow-up of middle-aged couples would make it possible to evaluate whether disagreement decreases and pleasure increases as middle-aged couples enter old age, or whether those who experience the greatest disagreement and the least pleasurable interactions in middle adulthood end up separating or divorcing.

Even though Levenson et al.'s (1993) and Carstensen et al.'s (1995) couples had been married for a number of years or decades, there was still considerable variation in their self-reports about marital satisfaction, which they completed at the beginning of the study. Thus, these investigators were able to divide both middle-aged and older couples into satisfied and dissatisfied subgroups. Not surprisingly, the couples in the dissatisfied subgroup reported greater disagreement than did the couples in the satisfied subgroup in almost all areas of potential conflict (for example, children, money, communication, sex, friends, and so on).

Among the dissatisfied couples, the wives reported more physical and psychological symptoms than the husbands did. Furthermore, for the wives but not the husbands, the number of symptoms reported was related to degree of marital dissatisfaction. For reasons not completely understood, being married seems to have a more uniformly positive influence on happiness and well-being for men than it does for women (Mroczek & Kolarz, 1998). In other words, men as a group are better off married, but women are better off only when happily married. Perhaps women have a greater need to feel emotionally important to their spouse, and women may be more likely than men to derive their feelings of self-worth from an interpersonal connection to the spouse (Tower & Kasl, 1996). When the spousal relationship is not fulfilling, women may suffer more than men. Also, there is some evidence that men are more likely than women to buffer themselves against health problems by withdrawing from conflict (Levenson et al., 1993).

In addition to collecting self-report data on marital satisfaction, Carstensen, Gottman, and Levenson (1995) made video recordings of the married couples as they interacted during the course of a 15-minute conversation about a problem that they claimed was causing continuing disagreement in their marriage. The feelings, or emotional affect, shown by the member of the pair who was speaking were rated by objective observers for verbal content, voice tone, context, facial expression, gestures, and body movement. Examples of positive affect included interest, affection, joy, humor, and validation (that is, acknowledgment of the partner's feelings). Examples of negative affect included anger, contempt, disgust, belligerence, defensiveness, fear/tension/worry, and sadness. Objective observers also rated the facial expression (positive, neutral, negative) of the member of the pair who was listening.

There were no differences in the middle-aged and older couples with regard to listener behaviors, but there were age-related differences in speaker behaviors. Compared with speakers in older couples, middle-aged speakers displayed more emotion, both positive (interest, humor) and negative (anger, disgust, belligerence, whining). The lesser degree of emotion expressed by the older speakers suggests that there is an age-related increase in emotional regulation, or control (Gross et al., 1997).

Gender differences were found for both listener and speaker behaviors in the middle-aged and older couples. As listeners, the husbands' facial expressions tended to be neutral whereas the wives' facial expressions showed more emotion, either positive or negative. As speakers, wives were more expressive than husbands. Compared to the husbands, the wives showed more positive emotions such as joy and more negative emotions such as anger and contempt. Overall, husbands were more emotionally restrained, and husbands in the dissatisfied couples were especially likely to avoid conflict.

The differences between satisfied couples and dissatisfied couples followed a similar pattern for the middle-aged and older couples. Not surprisingly, the facial expressions of listeners in the satisfied couples were more positive than the facial expressions of listeners in the dissatisfied couples. Speakers in the satisfied couples showed more positive emotion than did speakers in the dissatisfied couples. They were more humorous, more affectionate, and more validating than speakers in dissatisfied couples, who were more angry, contemptuous, sad, domineering, and belligerent. Also, among the satisfied couples, the husbands and wives expressed a similar level of emotions. However, among the dissatisfied couples, the wives were more emotional than their husbands were.

These findings illustrate that even after many years of marriage, some couples are happy and satisfied, which is indicated by their expressions of humor, affection, and validation even when they are discussing topics that have aroused marital conflict. On the other hand, even in marriages lasting more than 35 years, there can be dissatisfaction and negative emotions. However, the older couples showed less negative affect, less emotional intensity, and greater affection when trying to resolve conflicts than the middle-aged couples did. Although older couples expressed negative emotion, their negativity was mixed with affection even when they disagreed. In short, the dissatisfied older couples were more likely than the dissatisfied middle-aged couples to control the negative expression of emotion. In addition, the dissatisfied older couples showed less tendency than the dissatisfied middle-aged couples to engage in "negative start-up sequences," which are defined as responding to a spouse's neutral response with a response that expresses negative affect. Perhaps dissatisfied older couples have learned to leave well enough alone and to maintain neutrality by not escalating conflict as they interact.

Even in studies that do not involve married couples, there is evidence that older adults are more likely than younger adults to control their immediate feelings and reactions (Diehl, Coyle, & Labouvie-Vief, 1996) and to express emotion less intensely (Lawton, Kleban, Rajagopal, & Dean, 1992). In a study of community-living adults ranging from 19 to 96 years of age, Gross et al. (1997) found a consistent pattern of age-related increase in emotional regulation in European American, African American, and Asian American groups. In sum, with increasing age, negative emotions tend to decline and control over emotions seems to increase.

Most studies on couples have focused on older heterosexual married couples, and less is known about older gay (men) and lesbian (women) couples. Some older lesbian and gay couples practice serial monogamy by having one relationship at a time, each of limited duration. However, a number of gay and lesbian couples have long-term partnerships that last for decades (Hooyman & Kiyak, 2002; Kimmel, 1992), and it is not uncommon to see the word "companion" in published obituaries (Kimmel, 1992). Compared to young cohorts of gay and lesbian adults, older gay and lesbian adults probably experienced more discrimination earlier in life because American society was less accepting of same-sex relationships in the past. Even so, many older gay and lesbian couples are satisfied with their lives. Some have built "surrogate families" from a self-created network of friends who provide much of their social support (Hooyman & Kiyak, 2002; Kimmel, 1992). Older gay men are especially likely to derive social support from friends rather than from family ties (Dorfman et al., 1995). Even so, some maintain close relationships with members of their biological families, and family members often count on them for material and emotional support in times of emergency (Kimmel, 1992).

Intergenerational Relationships and Caregiving   Adult children maintain greater contact with their older mothers than they do with their older fathers, and this seems to be the case in European American as well as African American families (Spitze & Miner, 1992). Moreover, parent–adult child closeness seems to be strongest between mothers and daughters (Fingerman, 1996). Most often, women are the kinkeepers, meaning that they work harder than men do to keep the family in touch. Also, women are usually the primary caregivers and main providers of social support in intergenerational families (Bengston et al., 1996).

Even though contact is less frequent between mothers and sons than between mothers and daughters, the bond between older parents and their adult sons may be underrated (Bengston et al., 1996). One reason is that questionnaires used to assess older parent/adult child social support are often weighted with questions that apply to relationships between women (for example, serving a comforting role). With traditional gender roles in families becoming less rigid, men may now have more freedom to maintain an attachment to their family of origin and to play an important role in kinkeeping activities. The beanpole family structure means that families will have fewer children, and more will have only one child. When a man is a couple's sole offspring, he is often an important source of social support for his older parents. There is a clear need for more research on men's role in intergenerational family relationships because much of the information available now refers to mothers and daughters.

Close relationships generally imply family solidarity, which includes affection, contact, and mutual support. Even so, few relationships are without some interpersonal tension. The perceptions people have about older parent–adult child relationships may be overly rosy if family members are unwilling to acknowledge tension and conflict. Some studies have found that older adults are more reluctant than their adult children are to admit any tension exists in their relationships (Mancini & Bleiszner, 1989). This discrepancy between older parents' and adult children's tendency to report conflict has been attributed to the **intergenerational stake hypothesis** (Bengston & Kuypers, 1971), which proposes that older parents are invested in perceiving their offspring in a favorable light and therefore view their relationships with adult children as positive and highly compatible. Adult offspring wish to make their own mark on the world, and therefore they are motivated to perceive their parents as less compatible.

Fingerman (1996) used an open-ended interview technique to study 48 pairs, or dyads, of older mothers (average age 76) and their adult daughters (average age 44). Initially, each member of the dyad was interviewed individually about her relationship with the other. Several weeks later, mother and daughter were interviewed together. Fingerman's older mothers were all healthy, active, independent, educated, and financially comfortable, so any tensions they might report could not be attributed to stress due to poor health, educational deprivation, or financial problems. The older mothers and their adult daughters each considered the other to be an important part of her life, and both mothers and daughters generally expressed positive feelings about their relationship.

However, as predicted by the intergenerational stake hypothesis, the older mothers attributed greater positive emotional value to their daughters than their daughters did to them. For example, the older mothers tended to praise their daughters even when discussing their daughters' faults. Also, the older mothers were more likely to name the daughter as a preferred confidante and the person with whom they most enjoy spending time, whereas daughters were more likely to find their mothers intrusive. Perhaps the daughters' complaints about intrusiveness stemmed from their mothers' heavy investment in the relationship and need for closeness. The daughters felt their relationship with their mothers was separate and distinct from the relationship they had with their nuclear family of procreation (that is, spouse and offspring). In contrast, the older mothers felt that they were an integral part of their daughter's family of procreation. Most of the middle-aged daughters (40 out of 48) were married, but less than half (18 out of 48) of the older mothers were. Perhaps the older mothers needed to feel part of their daughters' family of procreation and because of this may have offered advice, which some daughters did not appreciate.

Another source of tension between Fingerman's older mothers and their daughters arose over the daughters' anxious concern for their mothers' well-being. Daughters expressed worry about their mothers' self-care (for example, refusing to go to the doctor or overexerting themselves). This concern may stem from the daughters' worry about whether they would be able to care for their mothers if their mothers' health should decline, especially since 27 of the 48 older mothers were widowed and two were divorced. Some of the older mothers found their daughters' anxious concern to be intrusive and a source of tension because most considered themselves healthy and independent.

The older parents in Fingerman's study were a narrowly selected group. Most of them (46 out of 48) were European Americans who were educated, financially secure, and healthy. Only further research can determine whether Fingerman's findings would apply to a broader segment of mother–daughter dyads from various ethnic and socioeconomic groups.

In another study on older parent–adult child relationships, Clarke, Preston, Raksin, and Bengston (1999) used data from a large mail survey in which older parents (average age of 62) and adult children (average age of 39) were asked to respond to the following open-ended question:

> No matter how well two people get along, there are times they disagree or get annoyed about something. In the last few years, what are some things on which you have differed, disagreed, or been disappointed about (even if not openly discussed) with your child (or parent)? [Clarke et al., 1999, p. 262]

Clarke et al.'s survey participants did not seem reluctant to acknowledge that tension existed and over two-thirds of the older parents and adult children willingly supplied examples of conflict. The fact that the older parents were just as likely as the adult children to acknowledge tension contradicts the intergenerational stake hypothesis, which theorizes that the parent generation will have a more positive view of their children than the children do of their parents. Perhaps Clarke et al.'s older participants were more comfortable airing their complaints about adult children in a mail survey than they would have been in face-to-face interviews. Also, the average age of Clarke et al.'s older survey respondents was only 62 as opposed to the average age of 76 in Fingerman's study. The intergenerational stake hypothesis may be less applicable in the early older adult years than it is later.

Research on intergenerational conflict often focuses on the frequency, intensity, and duration of interactions, but what, specifically, are the sources of tension or conflict between older parents and their adult children? Clarke et al. found conflict occurs in the following areas (with the percent of examples given by the total sample):

- Communication and interaction styles (for example, strained or nonexistent communication), type of communication (for example, yelling and criticism), lack of contact, or criticism of the relationship between older parents (32 percent)
- Habits and lifestyle choices (for example, disapproval of style of dress, hair style, educational or occupational choices, or use of alcohol) (32 percent)
- Childrearing practices and values (for example, decisions about having or spacing children, adult child's permissiveness with children, or grandparents' interference in disciplining grandchildren) (16 percent)
- Politics, religion, and ideology (for example, lack of religious beliefs, over-involvement in religion, or conflicting political views) (12 percent)
- Work habits (for example, lack of ambition) (6 percent)
- Household standards or maintenance (for example, cleanliness and upkeep) (2 percent)

Although intergenerational conflict can occur in a number of areas, most of the conflict reported by both older parents and adult children fell into the first two categories: communication/interaction styles and habits/lifestyle choices. The most frequently mentioned area of conflict for older parents was that of lifestyle choices (38 percent), followed by communication (25 percent). For adult children, the most frequently mentioned area of conflict was communication (34 percent), followed by lifestyle choices (30 percent).

Despite conflicts in some areas, many older parents and their children still maintain close relationships (Bengston et al., 1996). A challenge for future study is to develop greater understanding of the balance between conflict and solidarity in older parent–adult child relationships.

Relationships between older parents and their adult children can be reciprocal, with older parents providing support to their adult children and vice versa. By some measures, older parents are more likely to give help than they are to receive it (Spitze & Logan, 1992). However, as people live into the old-old (75 to 84) and oldest-old (85+) years, many need support from family members to continue living in the community. For example, older adults who give up driving because of a decline in sensory or perceptual capabilities may need help with transportation for shopping, doctors' appointments, and so on. Widowed older adults may need help with tasks that a spouse used to perform (for example, managing finances or food preparation). Those who lose a spouse may need emotional support, especially if close friends are no longer available because of death or relocation to places too distant to visit. Also, older family members with failing health may need assistance with personal care such as bathing and dressing.

When older adults do need care, who gives it? Men often help with tasks such as finances, whereas women help more with day-to-day tasks such as shopping, transporting to doctors' appointments, and providing emotional support. Middle-aged women have been labeled the **sandwich generation** because many are caught between competing intergenerational demands (Bengston et al., 1996). Not only do they provide care for their older parents, but many have obligations to a spouse and children still living at home. On the positive side, married middle-aged women with children may receive support from family members while they are giving support to their older parents. Many middle-aged married women who are caregivers for older parents get emotional support from their spouses, and this may buffer them against some of the negative effects of caregiving stress (Franks & Stephens, 1996). In contrast, single or divorced middle-aged daughters often bear responsibility for older parents by themselves, with little support from anyone else (Brody, Litvin, Albert, & Hoffman, 1994). Currently, less is known about unmarried middle-aged sons, although with the increasing beanpole family structure, adult sons may take a more active role in caring for older parents in the future. However, widowed older women may feel more comfortable having personal care provided by adult daughters than by adult sons (Bengston et al., 1996).

It is commonly assumed that caregiving for elderly parents places a burden on adult children, but in many instances adult children derive satisfaction from helping their elderly parents. Walker, Acock, Bowman, and Li (1996) followed 128 predominantly European American mother–daughter pairs over two years to determine whether there would be any patterns in the daughters' satisfaction or lack thereof with caregiving. The older mothers were at least age 65, single (widowed or divorced), and lived within 45 miles of their middle-aged daughters. The support the daughters gave to their mothers was mostly help with shopping, indoor maintenance, and food preparation and cleanup. The duration of caregiving was not a significant factor in daughters' satisfaction, but if the amount of care the mothers needed increased over time, the daughters' satisfaction declined. Thus, it is not the length of time care is needed, but rather the need to provide increasing levels of care that seems to erode the daughters' positive feelings.

Even so, the daughters' satisfaction remained relatively high over the duration of the study, which suggests that any costs the daughters incurred were

Middle-aged daughters are often the caregivers for their older parents.

largely offset by the rewarding aspects of their caregiving role. The older mothers in this study had some physical problems, but most were cognitively intact and none required extensive personal care. It is not clear whether the rewards of caregiving would still offset the costs if the mothers suffered from cognitive impairment or needed extensive personal care such as help getting dressed rather than help with errands and household chores.

What is the relationship between objective caregiver burden (for example, the number of hours per day or week spent helping an older parent) and a caregiver's subjective feelings about burden? Some middle-aged daughters provide very little help on an objective basis, but they still feel burdened with caregiving responsibilities. Other middle-aged daughters provide a great deal of help on an objective basis, but subjectively they do not feel burdened (Bengston et al., 1996). It is likely that the quality of a mother–daughter relationship moderates the middle-aged daughter's feelings of subjective burden. Compared with daughters who are not close to their mothers, daughters who have positive relationships and strong feelings of attachment are likely to feel less subjective burden even if they provide extensive care for their mothers (Cicirelli, 1993; Walker, Martin, & Jones, 1992).

Dilworth-Anderson, Williams, and Cooper (1999) studied how families provided care to 42 male and 160 female widowed African Americans with an average age of 74, the majority of whom had physical limitations and some

Stephanie L. Erber

With increasing life expectancy, people are spending more time as grandparents and many will become great-grandparents as well.

cognitive impairment. In approximately one-fourth of these African American families, the caregiving structure was individualistic, meaning that caregiving responsibilities fell to only one family member. In the other three-fourths of the families, the caregiving structure was collectivistic, meaning that caregiving responsibilities were shared by two or more caregivers. Not surprisingly, the collectivistic structure was more common when the older adult family member had greater caregiving needs and also when several adult children lived close by. Not all African American elderly adults have multiple caregivers, but Dilworth-Anderson et al. theorize that the collectivistic structure may stem from an African American cultural legacy of extended family caregiving. Additional studies are needed if we are to make accurate comparisons between families from various racial and ethnic groups with regard to an individualistic versus a collectivistic structure of caring for elderly family members.

Grandparenthood   With the increase in life expectancy, a large proportion of older adults are grandparents, and many will spend four or more decades in this role (Kivnick & Sinclair, 1996). However, in keeping with the beanpole family structure, grandparents in the future will probably have fewer grandchildren than grandparents had in the past. Even so, not only will they spend more years as grandparents, but also they are more likely to become great-grandparents.

The study of grandparenthood is complex because the grandparent role consists of several components: behavior, meaning, and satisfaction (Kivnick & Sinclair, 1996). The nature of the grandparent role can vary depending upon gender, socioeconomic status, marital status, ethnicity, age of the grandchildren, and the age and stage of life when grandparenthood actually begins. Grandparents who are chronologically younger may still have children living at home and many work full time outside the home. Under such circumstances, competing roles can limit the amount of time spent with grandchildren. Older grandparents are more likely to be retired and therefore may have more time to spend with grandchildren, but the nature of their activities with their grandchildren may depend upon their health. For example, grandparents must be in good health to take their grandchildren on trips to places such as Disney World. Relationships with grandchildren may also depend on how close they live. Grandparents who live within a mile of their grandchildren have more chances to see them than grandparents who live hundreds of miles away.

In an early study, Neugarten and Weinstein (1964) conducted interviews with 70 grandparent couples and identified five styles of grandparenting: formal, fun seeker, surrogate parent, reservoir of family wisdom, distant figure. More recently, Kivnick and Sinclair (1996) identified three grandparenting styles: remote, companionate, and involved. Remote grandparents are emotionally distant and formal. Many live far from their grandchildren, or they may be at the stage of life when they are busy with work or other interests. Companionate grandparents, probably the most common style in contemporary American society, engage in entertaining and pleasurable leisure activities with grandchildren (for example, playing games and baking cookies). In general, they avoid interfering in the discipline of grandchildren, leaving punishment to the child's parents. Perhaps this is a wise strategy, given the negative attitudes, particularly of middle-class European American mothers, toward grandparents who give unsolicited advice about childrearing (Norris & Tindale, 1994; Thomas, 1990). However, advice from grandparents may be more acceptable in African American and Asian American families, especially when the grandparents live in the same household (Norris & Tindale, 1994). Involved grandparents spend a great deal of time with grandchildren. In some instances, they care for their grandchildren while the parents work outside the home. With the increasing divorce rate, more parents of young children must work and some turn to grandparents to assist with child care. Involved grandparents may even function as surrogate parents if their adult children are deceased or otherwise unable to fulfill the parental role because of substance abuse or problems with mental or physical health. Under such circumstances, grandparents assume a role of authority in bringing up their grandchildren.

The relationship between grandparents and grandchildren is often influenced by the middle generation (Giarrusso & Silverstein, 1995). Parents (that is, adult children and/or their spouses) are often the ones who make opportunities available for grandparents and grandchildren to interact. If parents are close to grandparents, then grandchildren are likely to spend time with grandparents. Grandchildren tend to have a closer relationship with maternal grandparents simply because they see them more than they do paternal grandparents.

Disruption of the nuclear family through divorce can affect grandparents' involvement with their grandchildren. Grandparents on the familial side of the custodial parent usually see more of their grandchildren and may become closer than they were before the parents divorced. Sometimes divorced adult children move in with their older adult parents on a temporary or permanent basis, both for economic reasons and to provide additional family support for the grandchildren. In contrast, grandparents on the familial side of the noncustodial parent may see less of the grandchildren and may even lose contact with them altogether after their parents divorce. In some states in the United States, grandparents' rights legislation allows grandparents to go to court to secure the right to visit their grandchildren (Giarrusso & Silverstein, 1995). Even so, such litigious conditions could compromise relationships with grandchildren.

In blended families, grandparents not only have grandchildren who are related by blood, but they may acquire step grandchildren if their adult children remarry spouses with children from a previous marriage. With divorce and remarriage becoming so common, there is much to be learned about how grandparents successfully negotiate attachments and relationships with step grandchildren.

A grandparent's marital status may have some bearing on time spent with grandchildren. Widowed grandparents, particularly grandmothers, tend to spend more time with grandchildren than do married grandparents, who may have busier social lives that compete with the grandparent role. Divorce of a grandparent couple can affect relationships with adult children and grandchildren because one or the other of the divorced grandparent couple may spend less time with the grandchildren. If one or both of the divorced grandparents remarry, or if a widowed grandparent remarries, there may be less opportunity or interest in spending time with the grandchildren.

More is known about the care grandparents give to grandchildren than vice versa. Healthy, financially secure grandparents in the young-old age category probably provide more support to their adult children and grandchildren than they receive in return. Many of them are ready to provide assistance, both emotional and financial, during difficult times in the lives of their adult children and grandchildren (Norris & Tindale, 1994). In late older adulthood, grandparents may need care themselves. When this occurs, it is most likely provided by adult children. If grandchildren are old enough, they may simply "be there" to demonstrate love and concern (Norris & Tindale, 1994).

Fingerman (1998) contends that grandparents have unique relationships with individual grandchildren. She interviewed 91 grandparents, most of whom lived in a rural university town and had a total of 346 grandchildren. For the grandmothers in her study, the grandchildren seen most often were the ones who were the most emotionally meaningful. Most of the grandparents reported experiencing pride and feelings of well-being after spending time with these "special" grandchildren. In contrast, they felt a sense of fatigue after spending time with grandchildren whom they considered to be irritating or worrisome.

Research on grandparenthood has concentrated mainly on individual grandparents rather than the experience of grandparenthood for a couple (Norris & Tindale, 1994). Yet particularly in the middle-age and young-old years, many grandparents are married couples, and members of a couple may not always see eye to eye about which aspects of grandparenting are important. For example, grandfathers may think that helping with finances fulfills the grandparent role, whereas grandmothers may feel that physical nurturing of the grandchildren is essential.

Norris and Tindale (1994) describe several situations that can result in tension over an older couple's differing views of the grandparenting role. A newly retired grandfather may be counting the days until he and his wife can spend winters in a warmer climate. However, this means that the couple will be at a great distance from their grandchildren for that period of time. His wife may yearn for close contact with the grandchildren year-round and not be as enthusiastic as he is about spending so much time away from them. In another case, a new grandfather may be recently retired and excited about spending time nurturing his grandchildren, something he was not able to do when his children were growing up because he was working such long hours. He may feel that he and his wife should take an active role in helping an adult daughter or son take care of the grandchildren. However, his wife may be tired of the nurturing role and at this point in her life may want to pursue her interests in work or travel. A couple's differing views about grandparenthood and poor communication with one another or with adult children can lead to friction.

Much remains to be understood about the role of grandparents in ethnic minority groups. In urban African American families, grandmothers are often responsible for rearing grandchildren, especially if the grandchildren's mother is a single parent (Hooyman & Kiyak, 2002). Across all ethnic and economic groups, the number of children under 18 who live in grandparent-headed households is up 30 percent since 1990 (Reese, 2003).

Sibling Relationships   Sibling attachments and sibling rivalry exert strong socializing influences during the childhood years in the family of origin. However, as children grow into young adulthood, they usually establish their own households, and with marriage and the birth of children, the family of procreation becomes more dominant (Bengston et al., 1996). Any rivalry that existed between brothers and sisters in the family of origin may die down, but at the same time, young adult and middle-aged siblings often become less close as each becomes absorbed in raising children and establishing a career.

Geographical proximity is an important factor in the closeness of sibling ties (Connidis, 1994). Opportunities for career advancement may necessitate geographical relocation and physical separation from siblings. Those who relocate often have less contact with the family of origin. Many develop a surrogate family by forming a network of friends who live close by and share common interests.

However, there is an **hourglass effect in sibling relationships** over the life span (Norris & Tinsdale, 1994). Ties that were strong earlier in life when siblings lived under the same roof tend to weaken in young and middle adulthood, but they are often reactivated in the later years. The re-establishment of sibling ties in later adulthood can be attributed to several factors. One is more available free time once children in the nuclear family of procreation leave home. Another is that the friendship networks adults establish during their young and middle adult years often shrink due to geographical migration, divorce, and death.

One further factor contributing to increased closeness in later adulthood is that siblings who were scattered across geographical regions may return to the location of their family of origin when they retire. Sometimes sibling ties are revitalized in older adulthood simply because sources of conflict that interfered with their relationship earlier in life may no longer exist or may become less important (Bedford, 1989). For example, a spouse who interfered with a strong sibling relationship may cease to be an obstacle due to divorce or death. Conflicts between siblings sometimes arise over the need to share caregiving responsibilities for an elderly parent. This source of tension may be lessened when the elderly parent moves into a nursing home or is deceased. Finally, as people grow older, they often place greater value on memories of a common past that they can only share with siblings who grew up in the same family of origin (Cicirelli, 1995).

Compared to interactions with spouses and children, interactions with siblings are generally considered to be more voluntary (Bengston et al., 1996). Of particular interest to those who study sibling ties in the middle and older adult years is the nature of the support that siblings provide for one another in times of need (Connidis, 1994). Several theoretical models have been proposed for understanding late-life sibling ties. According to the **hierarchical-compensatory model** (Cantor, 1979), individuals have a hierarchy of relationships that they call upon when they need support. At the top of this hierarchy are a spouse and adult children, who are the first ones older adults turn to when support is necessary. When a spouse or adult children are not available because of divorce, death, or geographical distance, older adults compensate by turning to siblings, who are lower down in the hierarchy.

The hierarchical-compensatory model is frequently used to explain why sibling support tends to be stronger among older adults who are single, widowed, and childless than it is among older adults who are married and have adult children (Cicirelli, Coward, & Dwyer, 1992). In a Canadian survey of individuals ages 55 and over (Connidis, 1994), marital status was a significant predictor of sibling support. Compared with married respondents, those who were widowed were more likely to receive sibling support during an illness and more likely to expect that they would receive long-term support from siblings if needed. Furthermore, widowed and divorced respondents were more likely than married ones to say that a sibling could live with them if circumstances made it necessary. However, unless siblings have a reciprocal relationship whereby they help one another, support from a sibling is usually temporary (Cicirelli, 1995).

Do the number of siblings make a difference in the support an older brother or sister will receive in a time of need? Connidis (1994) found that receiving or expecting to receive support from siblings was related to family size. Compared to older adults with two or more siblings, those with only one sibling were less likely to have received support in a time of need and less likely to expect that sibling support would be available. It is not clear why having only one sibling should be a disadvantage because most often support is supplied by only one individual. But Connidis (1994) suggests that even though support is usually provided by only one sibling, that sibling's efforts may be the result of active

Sibling attachments often become closer in older adulthood, and usually
the bond between sisters is the strongest.

negotiation among all of the siblings, who reach an agreement over which one
will be responsible for helping a brother or sister in need.

In addition to number of siblings, sibling gender is a significant factor in the
level of support in a time of need. Of Connidis's (1994) respondents who had
two or more siblings, those with sisters were more likely to think they would
receive support during a crisis than were those who had only brothers. As mentioned previously, respondents with only one sibling were less likely to think they
would receive sibling support during a crisis than did those with two or more
siblings. However, those with only one sibling felt that their chances of receiving support were greater if that sibling was a sister rather than a brother. This
reinforces a common belief that women have stronger familial ties than men do.
Even though the family of procreation tends to become more important than the
family of origin in the young and middle-adult years, women remain closer
than men do to their family of origin and often they serve as kinkeepers. Men
may have a closer attachment to their wives' family of origin, including her siblings, than they have to their own family of origin (Bengston et al., 1996).
Longitudinal research studies following sibling attachments over time would be
of great value in aiding our understanding about family dynamics that influence
sibling support.

The hierarchical-compensatory model has not been very useful for explaining why sibling ties are often strong among never-married and childless older adults. A spouse or children were never part of their lives, so it is unlikely that single and childless older adults simply substitute sibling ties for ties that were lost. According to the **functional-specificity model** (Simons, 1983–1984), people have a variety of social relationships that are negotiated over time to serve certain functions. Rather than turning to siblings to compensate for ties they have lost, older adults who never married or have no children make greater efforts over their lifetime to nurture supportive ties and give-and-take relationships with siblings (Campbell, Connidis, & Davies, 1999; Connidis, 1994).

Analyses of sibling ties according to the hierarchical-compensatory and functional-specificity models do not always take into account all the variations in sibling relationships within families. Based on interviews of 89 European American late-life sibling dyads, Gold (1989) found their relationships fell into five categories, which fall on a continuum from a greater to a lesser degree of emotional closeness: intimate, congenial, loyal, apathetic, and hostile.

- *Intimate siblings* are highly devoted, share a relationship of mutual love and understanding, confiding their most personal thoughts and feelings and considering each other "best friends." Contact is frequent, including visits and telephone calls.
- *Congenial siblings* feel strong friendship and caring, but their emotional ties are not as deep except in times of crisis or stress. There may be weekly or monthly contact, but congenial siblings would name a spouse or child as the person to whom they feel closest.
- *Loyal siblings* have a bond based on shared family background and a strong sense of family obligation. There is little contact but they usually appear upon request at important family occasions like weddings, funerals, and holiday celebrations. They rarely exchange emotional support, but they would help in times of illness or financial difficulties.
- *Apathetic siblings* are not close and they are uninterested in taking any responsibility for one another. They do not attend family occasions and even if they live nearby, contact is rare. They may go for years without talking to each other because of indifference rather than anger or disagreement.
- *Hostile siblings* go out of their way to avoid one another. They feel disdain and anger and claim they would reject any requests for support. They are emotionally involved, but unfortunately in a negative way. Sometimes hostility stems from a dispute over an inheritance or envy from past sibling rivalry or parental favoritism.

Gold found that the gender composition of the sibling dyad rather than the gender of an individual sibling determined the closeness of a sibling relationship. Dyads that included a woman (either woman-woman or woman-man) clustered in the more positive categories, whereas male-male dyads tended to have less involvement

In a subsequent study, Gold (1990) compared information from interviews with 64 African American dyads with information obtained previously from the

89 European American sibling dyads. The two groups were similar in age (average age in the mid-70s) and level of education (at least some college), and individuals in both groups were healthy and considered themselves middle class or upper middle class. The European American dyads were distributed across all five categories: 14 percent intimate, 30 percent congenial, 34 percent loyal, 11 percent apathetic, and 11 percent hostile. In contrast, the African American dyads were distributed more heavily in the emotionally close categories: 20 percent intimate, 20 percent congenial, 55 percent loyal, 2 percent apathetic, and 3 percent hostile. Note that compared to the European American dyads, the African American dyads were more interested in providing support for each other. However, we cannot conclude that race causes closer sibling relationships because factors associated with race (such as religion) could be the basis for the difference between the two groups. The samples of dyads in Gold's studies were small, so her findings may not generalize to broader groups of older European American or African American siblings. Further research on late-life sibling relationships is of particular interest because the rate of divorce is increasing and married couples are having fewer children. In the future, siblings may be an even more important source of support for older adults than they are now.

While Gold's categorical scheme certainly affords some insight into sibling relationships, it may not capture the complexities that are based on a history of interactions between family members. Family dynamics do not necessarily cease when children grow up and physically leave the family of origin. For many siblings, getting together in late middle-age over shared concerns for aging parents may strengthen feelings of closeness (Bengston et al., 1996). However, if siblings harbor resentment over earlier conflicts that were never resolved, then negative feelings may flare up when they are forced to reunite later in life over caregiving for aging parents (Bengston et al., 1996; Connidis, 1994). In many cases, the sibling who lives closest is the one who shoulders the responsibility for the aging parent. This sibling may resent brothers and sisters who live far away and make no effort to help out with regular visits or financial contributions when these are needed. The resentment felt by the sibling with the caregiving responsibility may be especially intense if he or she feels that a brother or sister was always favored by the parent.

Nonfamilial Relationships

Not all close social ties are with family members. Most older adults have friends who are important to them and to whom they feel attached. Also, older adults who have lived in the same place for a long time maintain social ties in the community, where both friends and acquaintances are a meaningful part of their daily lives and often provide support.

Friends   When family members are available, friends usually make up a smaller proportion of older adults' social networks than they do in the social networks of young or even middle-aged adults (Levitt et al., 1993). In the old-old years and beyond (age 75 and over), involvement outside the family tends to decline (Field & Minkler, 1988). Nonetheless, friends who are familiar and close are likely to remain in the inner circle of an older adult's social network.

Close friends can be a significant source of emotional support even in late older adulthood. When family members are not available, friends are particularly important (Lang et al., 1998), but even when family members are available, friends can be a source of enjoyment and emotional fulfillment. They provide advice, moral support, and aid in times of need (Norris & Tindale, 1994). Being able to converse with friends of similar age about common physical problems such as arthritis, and feeling that friends understand the pain we are experiencing, can help to ease stress. Often, friends serve as "confidantes" to whom we can entrust our worries and on whom we can count for emotional support.

Friends are not bound to each other by duty or formal rules, as is generally the case with family members. Perhaps because friendship is voluntary, reciprocity in giving and receiving support is especially important (Rook, 1987). In fact, there may be greater reciprocity in interactions with friends than with adult children. However, in intimate long-term relationships, it is not usually expected that support given to a close friend will be repaid immediately (Norris & Tindale, 1994).

As mentioned previously, older adults often express a preference for intimacy at a distance with their adult children. However, many enjoy spending time with friends (Connidis, 1989). When help is needed, older adults may hesitate to impose on their busy children. Spending time with friends and feeling that they can reciprocate favors given by friends, even if not immediately, helps older adults maintain a feeling of independence. But older adults often hesitate to ask for help from their friends if they do not think they will be able to return the favor within a reasonable amount of time. If they know they cannot reciprocate, then it is unlikely they will be able to maintain an equitable social exchange relationship with their friends (Connidis, 1989). In critical situations such as serious illness, especially when help will be needed on a long-term basis, older adults often turn to adult children or other family members.

Friendship may be based on common interests or on a deep, long-term, emotionally meaningful bond (Kausler & Kausler, 1996). Interest-related friendships revolve around common hobbies such as playing bridge or golf. This type of friendship may decline in older adulthood when health problems or transportation difficulties limit opportunities for getting together to pursue these activities. In contrast, deep, long-term friendships involve a closer bond based on familiarity because of a similar background or a common history such as living in the same neighborhood for many years or raising children who went to the same school. Such friendships are more likely than interest-related friendships to be maintained in older adulthood (Fredrickson & Carstensen, 1990).

When older adults develop limitations in physical mobility or when they no longer have access to transportation, they often maintain emotionally intimate relationships with close friends via telephone (Fees et al., 1999). As mentioned earlier, in very old age, individuals often prefer to engage in social interactions with friends who are emotionally meaningful. Interactions with close friends of long duration contribute to their feelings of self-worth. Interest in reaching out to make new friends or initiate social exchanges with new acquaintances seems to decline in older adulthood (Carstensen, 1992). Particularly in the old-old and oldest-old years, individuals often prefer to spend time alone rather than participate in social interactions that are not deeply meaningful (Lang & Baltes, 1997).

Women are usually the main instigators and perpetuators of friendship. It is commonly believed that among married couples, husbands rely on their wives for planning social activities and cultivating a social network (Norris & Tindale, 1994). Until recently, women were more likely than men to have a domestic role and less likely than men to work full time. It will be interesting to see whether married women's entry into the workplace on a full-time basis will mean they have a less dominant role in organizing the social life in couple relationships. Of course, in older adulthood women are more likely than men to be widowed and they are less likely than men to remarry, so in later life women have more opportunities to spend time with friends.

Peripheral Social Relationships   Older adults tend to limit their social interchanges to individuals with whom they feel emotionally close, and in general, they are less interested than young adults are in socializing with unfamiliar individuals (Carstensen, 1992; Lang & Baltes, 1997). Even so, most older adults maintain some peripheral ties with people who are not intimate members of their social circle. These peripheral ties may be with individuals seen regularly but from whom extensive social support is not expected. For example, older adults who live in the community may have regular contact with those people working in the local pharmacy, grocery store, department store, hair salon, barber shop, restaurant, or doctor and dental offices. There are the passing "hellos" of neighbors out walking their dogs or working in their yards. Such contacts are not intimate but they hold some significance in older adults' daily lives.

Fingerman and Griffiths (1999) conducted a study on another type of peripheral tie—that represented by the exchange of greeting cards during the holiday season. These researchers surveyed 87 young, middle-aged, and older individuals who engaged in holiday greeting card exchanges. Of the three age groups who participated in the survey, the older group sent and received the greatest number of cards. Among the older survey participants, more women than men both sent and received greeting cards. Some of the cards were exchanged with individuals who had close emotional ties with the survey participants. However, survey participants in all three age groups also exchanged cards with people who were not central to their immediate day-to-day emotional support network and with whom social ties were peripheral. Individuals from all three age groups reported that the sending and receiving of holiday greeting cards contributed to a feeling of social embeddedness. But the meaning of the peripheral ties generated by the card exchange varied for individuals in the different age groups. Older adults were more likely to consider such ties a link to their personal past. In contrast, the young adults considered them to be an opportunity to build future relationships.

In sum, older adults have social ties both within and outside the family. Many have relationships with a spouse or partner, adult children, grandchildren and siblings. In addition, even in older adulthood people have social relationships outside the family. They often have close long-term friends who do favors that they can reciprocate. In the periphery of their social networks are people with whom they are familiar in their daily commerce or individuals they have not seen for a long time but with whom they maintain contact on a yearly basis.

ELDER ABUSE AND NEGLECT

Elder abuse is the darker side of social interactions. It refers to harmful behavior directed toward elderly persons by individuals whom the older individual trusts or depends upon for assistance. Outside a trusting relationship, the same actions and behaviors are often classified as crimes (McDonald, 1996). In most reported cases of elder abuse, the abusers are family members, but abuse can be committed by unrelated individuals such as lawyers, nurses, physicians, home-care providers, housekeepers, storekeepers, financial advisors, or even presumed friends (Quinn, 1995).

Elder abuse can take several forms, of which physical violence (for example, slapping, bruising, kicking, burning, or excessive restraining) is the most extreme and attracts the most attention from the media (Bengston et al., 1996). However, abuse can also be psychological or material (McDonald, 1996). Psychological abuse (for instance, name calling, humiliation, intimidation, yelling) involves intentionally inflicting mental anguish or provoking fear of violence or isolation in the older adult. Material abuse involves exploiting older adults' property or personal resources, such as taking their possessions or spending their money without their consent.

Incidences of material abuse are probably more common than reflected in formal reports (Bengston et al., 1996). Cultural norms affect definitions of material abuse. In some cultures, elders are expected to share their financial assets with the younger generation, while in others they are not (Quinn, 1995). Thus, what might be considered material abuse in one culture would not necessarily be interpreted as abusive in another.

Neglect generally refers to the failure of a caregiver to fulfill the older adult's needs (McDonald, 1996). Some examples of neglect are abandoning an older adult who cannot properly care for him- or herself, failing to provide proper food, or not furnishing access to health services that the older adult cannot obtain for him- or herself. Abuse and neglect are generally committed by others on the elderly victim, but some situations involve self-abuse and self-neglect. For example, an older man may live alone in a large house in obvious need of repair. When neighbors catch sight of him in his yard, they notice he looks disheveled and appears to be undernourished, but he is not willing to seek or accept any help. Not everyone agrees about whether self-abuse and self-neglect should be considered in the same category as abuse and neglect committed by someone an older adult trusts (McDonald, 1996; Quinn, 1995).

Abuse in Domestic Settings

Elder abuse and neglect have probably been occurring for many decades, but official recognition of the problem only began in the late 1970s (Quinn, 1995). Most reported incidents of abuse and neglect occur in domestic settings. Abusers tend to be family members, many of whom serve as caregivers for elderly individuals who suffer from dementia (Pillemer & Suitor, 1992) or physical impairments that limit their ability to take care of their everyday needs (Quinn, 1995). The typical victim of abuse is a woman age 75 or over (Quinn, 1995), although elderly men have been victims of abuse as well (Pillemer & Suitor, 1992).

The most common family abusers are spouses (Pillemer & Suitor, 1992), although abusers are often adult children, typically daughters (McDonald, 1996), perhaps because they serve as caregivers more often than sons do. Many spousal abusers suffer from poor health themselves, which creates additional stress in marital situations that are already less than ideal (Wolf, 1996). Too little relief from the burden of caregiving is also a factor.

In many cases, adult children or in-laws who abuse elderly family members have a history of mental instability and problems with substance abuse. These abusers often live in the same household with the older victim, and they may depend on the older adult victim for financial and/or emotional support. Their abusive behavior may stem from their own feelings of powerlessness (Quinn, 1995).

Abuse in domestic settings is not easy to document. Many victims of elder abuse suffer from cognitive difficulties and thus have limited capacity to report it. Victims who are cognitively capable of reporting abuse may hesitate to do so out of family loyalty, feelings of embarrassment, or fear that nursing home placement will be the only alternative. Based on the limited statistics that are available, the incidence of elder abuse in domestic settings seems to be increasing in the United States. In a large 1985–1986 survey conducted in the Boston area on a representative sample of 2,020 persons aged 65 and over, approximately 3 percent had experienced some type of abuse (2 percent physical and 1 percent verbal) (McDonald, 1996). Questions on material abuse were not included in the survey, so the overall rate of abuse was probably underestimated. Of the reported incidents, most of the abusers were spouses (58 percent), followed by adult children (24 percent). The elderly victims were men and women from all socioeconomic levels.

A more recent survey on elder abuse in the United States conducted by the National Resource Center reported an increase in substantiated reports of abuse in domestic settings: 117,000 in 1986; 128,000 in 1987; 140,000 in 1988, 211,000 in 1990, and 227,000 in 1991 (McDonald, 1996). However, these increases must be viewed with caution because the criteria for defining abuse fluctuated during the time period of the survey. In addition, greater sensitivity to the problem of elder abuse and more stringent rules about reporting it could make actual increases appear greater than they really are (McDonald, 1996). Even so, elder abuse is a serious problem. At present, each state in the United States has laws mandating that physicians, nurses, social workers, and law enforcement workers report any instances of suspected elder abuse and neglect (Quinn, 1995).

Pillemer and Suitor (1992) conducted an empirical investigation on feelings of violence and actual acts of violence committed by caregivers for elderly relatives diagnosed with Alzheimer's disease or other forms of dementia. Most of the 236 caregivers in this study were referred by dementia screening programs in major medical centers in the Northeastern United States. The majority of the caregivers (82 percent) were women, 51 percent were adult children, 32 percent were spouses, 15 percent were other relatives (siblings, grandchildren), and 2 percent were friends. These caregivers were relatively highly educated and largely European American (99 percent). Half of the caregivers lived with the elderly adult and half did not. Data were gathered using interviews in which questions on feelings of violence and actual violent acts were embedded in more neutral questions. The self-report interview technique has drawbacks for collecting data of such a sensitive nature, but it is one method for gathering information systematically. Other methods of gathering information on abuse, such as victims' reports and behavioral observations, are not as practical.

Pillemer and Suitor found the following factors were associated with caregivers' fears that they would become violent:

- Low self-esteem
- Living in the same household with the elderly care recipient
- Caring for an elderly relative who displays physically aggressive and disruptive behavior

The following two factors were associated with caregivers who admitted to engaging in violent acts toward an elderly care recipient:

- Violent behavior on the part of the elderly care recipient
- Being a spousal caregiver, which would of course be associated with living with the care recipient

Pillemer and Suitor stress the need for longitudinal studies to track the relationship between feelings of violence and acts of violence. Perhaps such studies could reveal what factors cause caregivers to cross the line from thoughts of violence to actually committing it.

Research on elder abuse and neglect has been conducted in countries besides the United States. A study on cognitive functioning and cognitive decline in Holland was able to identify a subsample of community-living Dutch older adults who reported being recent victims of verbal, physical, or financial mistreatment (Comjis, Penninx, Knipscheer, & van Tilburg, 1999). These victims had an average age of 76 and were evenly divided as to gender. The majority reported themselves to be in good or fair health but low in socioeconomic status. They were equally likely to be living alone or with a partner. Most of these individuals had not experienced severe abuse, but it is hardly surprising that they reported a higher level of psychological distress compared with a control sample of older adults matched on age, gender, self-reported health, socioeconomic status, and living situation who reported no incidents of mistreatment. Comjis et al. found that availability of social supports (for example, having good friends who provide emotional support) seemed to moderate the degree of psychological distress in individuals who reported abuse. This suggests that when it is not possible to deal directly with the source of mistreatment, having social support groups may buffer the distress of those who suffer from mild forms of mistreatment. Such groups might help victims of abuse to become more competent at managing their family situations.

Understanding why elder abuse occurs is essential if abusive situations are to be prevented (McDonald, 1996). The **situational model of elder abuse** views elder abuse as a response to a stressful situation (McDonald, 1996). Several situational factors have been linked to actual abuse or the potential for abuse in domestic settings. One factor is total dependency of an older adult who suffers from physical and/or cognitive incapacities on a single caregiver. Caregiver burden is especially heavy when no other family members are available to offer physical, emotional, or financial support. Long hours of taking care of a frail older adult with no relief can lead to social isolation, which can further increase a caregiver's level of stress. Another contributing factor is the unrealistic expectations a caregiver may have about the capabilities of the elderly care recipient. The caregiver may not understand why so much help is necessary. In trying to meet the needs of elderly recipients, caregivers may become exhausted, frustrated, and resentful. All of these stressors are risk factors for abuse.

The stress associated with family caregiving is a serious issue that has received much recent attention (Zarit, Johansson, & Jarrott, 1998). It is especially important to develop ways to alleviate caregiver stress because demand for caregiving is likely to increase in the future, given the numbers of individuals who are living into the old-old and oldest-old age ranges. Also, the beanpole family structure means that the typical family is becoming smaller, so there will be fewer family members to share in caregiving responsibilities. One resource that has proven helpful in reducing the stress and increasing the psychological well-being of family caregivers is the availability of adult day-care services (Zarit, Stephens, Townsend, & Greene, 1998). Family caregivers can take elderly relatives to centers that provide an appropriate level of care and activity while they themselves work at outside jobs or tend to personal matters.

Abuse in Institutional Settings

Compared to research on abuse in domestic family settings, fewer studies have been done on abuse and neglect in institutional settings (Quinn, 1995). Yet physical abuse (for instance, a staff member's rough treatment or excessive use of restraints on a nursing home resident) and verbal abuse (such as a staff member's yelling at a nursing home resident) does occur in institutional environments (Pillemer & Moore, 1989). There have been efforts to implement programs to prevent abuse in such settings. These programs often aim to increase nursing assistants' knowledge and motivation (Smyer, Brannon, & Cohn, 1992) and to help them recognize abuse and develop strategies for dealing with potentially abusive situations (Pillemer & Hudson, 1993). To protect the rights of institutional residents, the "Nursing Home Residents' Rights" (see Table 9.1) together with the ombudsman advocacy programs in most states provide some protection for elderly individuals who live in institutions.

Caregiver stress can occur in institutional settings as well as domestic settings, especially when the demands of the elderly residents' care are placed upon too few staff members. Many individuals employed in institutional settings are not highly paid and must hold second jobs to support their families financially. In a telephone survey of 577 nurses and nurses aids who worked in nursing homes, Pillemer and Bachman-Prehn (1991) found two factors that were significant predictors of reported incidences of physical and verbal abuse in institutional settings: level of staff-patient conflict and degree of staff "burnout." Providing staff members with educational and morale-building workshops, together with increased pay so that nursing home staff members do not need a second job, could help reduce institutional abuse.

Clearly, many factors play a part in domestic and institutional elder abuse and neglect. These include characteristics of the older adult, characteristics of the caregiver, and availability of social and material support to assist the caregiver. An additional factor with regard to abuse of the elderly is how older adults are viewed by society as a whole (McDonald, 1996). If older adults have low status in a society, they may be devalued. When this happens, abusers feel little remorse and do not fear punishment for their cruel treatment of victims. When societies discriminate against older adults, older adults themselves may have negative attitudes toward their own age group and may view abuse or neglect as deserved (McDonald, 1996). Reduction in abusive and neglectful treatment of the elderly calls for a multifaceted approach. Modification in society's views of the elderly would limit the acceptability of abusive or neglectful treatment. At the same time, there is a need for better methods of detecting abuse, improvement in enforcing laws that require the reporting of suspected abuse, and more services to relieve caregiver burden.

REVISITING THE SELECTIVE OPTIMIZATION WITH COMPENSATION AND ECOLOGICAL MODELS

Social interaction and social ties in older adulthood can be viewed from the perspective of the SOC (Baltes & Baltes, 1990) and Ecological Models (Lawton, 1989; Lawton & Nahemow, 1973), introduced in Chapter 1. According to the SOC model, selection, optimization, and compensation are necessary processes for realizing developmental goals. For social relationships, the socioemotional selectivity theory complements the SOC model by specifying the goals of social interactions that older adults select and the strategies they use to ensure that social interactions will optimize their needs (M. M. Baltes & Carstensen, 1996). Conceptualizing social ties as a network of close supportive social relationships can also be viewed in terms of SOC. A core of close others follow us throughout a large part of our lives. Over time, we may add or delete members of the social convoy, which often becomes smaller in older adulthood. Ideally, however, relationships with those who remain in the convoy (largely family members but some close friends as well) are just as close and provide social support, feelings of social embeddedness, and chances for positive social exchanges, all essential in optimizing older adults' feelings of life satisfaction and well-being.

The ecological model is also a framework for considering social interactions and social ties in older adulthood. Social interaction and ties represent one aspect of environmental press. Older adults adapt best when their environments allow sufficient opportunities for social interaction and access to social ties. However, chances for positive adaptation will be enhanced when the level of social press in their environment does not exceed older adults' wishes and needs. Older adults seek to maintain social ties that hold significance for them, but they weed out those with less importance. Chances for adaptive functioning are maximized when older adults have opportunities for meaningful social ties and positive interactions and when the likelihood of negative social exchange is minimized.

KEY POINTS

- Activity theory, disengagement theory, social exchange theory, and socioemotional selectivity theory all offer hypotheses about the ideal quantity and quality of social interactions in older adulthood.
- Social interactions can have negative as well as positive aspects, and older adults can experience both.
- Individuals move through life with a constellation of other people who play a central role in their network of social relationships. For older adults, this social convoy consists largely of family members, although long-term familiar friends are also included, especially if there are no grown children and few family members close by.
- The marital relationship is important, and older married couples tend to show more control of negative emotions than do middle-aged married couples, even when discussing topics on which they disagree.
- Older adults may not live under the same roof with adult children or other family members, but their relationships can still be close. Older mothers and their daughters are especially close, even though they may have areas of conflict.
- Many older adults are grandparents, but there is wide variability in how they play this role. Some see grandchildren occasionally, while others actually bring them up.
- Many older adults are closer to siblings than they were as middle-aged or young adults. Siblings, especially sisters, often provide support when their brothers and sisters need it.
- Older adults enjoy spending time with friends, but they prefer reciprocal relationships with them. If friends do favors for them, they want to pay them back. Older adults usually turn to family if long-term help is needed.
- Elder abuse and neglect can be physical, psychological, or material. It can occur in both domestic and institutional settings. It is difficult to study, but undoubtedly, many factors are related to its occurrence both in family and institutional settings.

KEY TERMS

 To learn more about the issues discussed in this chapter, point your browser to http://www.infotrac-college.com and use the passcode from the InfoTrac College Edition card that came with your book. InfoTrac College Edition gives you access to complete articles from many different journals.

Employment, Retirement, and Living Arrangements

10

Marvin just celebrated his 64th birthday, and his long-time dream has been to retire as soon as he turns 65 and move with his wife Ella to a retirement community in a warm climate. The one thing Marvin did not count on was that Ella would start working outside the home in her late 50s and would end up being dedicated to her career. Ella has no intention of retiring any time soon even though the two of them could afford to live comfortably on savings, Social Security, and the income from Marvin's company pension. Marvin still intends to retire in the coming year but he realizes that a long-distance move is not in the cards. Instead, his new plan is to play golf during the summer months with a group of retired cronies. In the winter he will volunteer at the local hospital. Marvin knows that many men his age are totally dependent on their wives for anything domestic. In all the years of his marriage, Marvin has never set foot in the kitchen, but now he thinks he might take up the challenge of learning how to cook.

EMPLOYMENT AND RETIREMENT

This chapter highlights aspects of living that have special significance for older adults in the United States: employment, retirement, and living arrangements. Some older adults work full time or part time, but those who retire from paid employment usually need to restructure their everyday activities. After retirement, there is greater freedom for those who want to relocate for reasons such as a better climate, but the majority of older adults continue to live in the same location. Many older adults remain in the same houses where they have always lived, but for some, a decline in physical capabilities dictates the need to live with or near adult children or siblings who can provide the necessary social and/or instrumental support. Older adults who need a more supportive living environment move into housing that is less physically demanding and offers meal service and in some instances assistance with personal care such as bathing, dressing, and following a prescribed regimen of medications.

Riley (1994) labeled the social structure of present-day American society as "age-differentiated," meaning that education is for youth and young adults, work is for the middle-age years, and leisure is confined to older adulthood (see Figure 10.1). Riley proposed that, ideally, society should have an age-integrated structure with greater balance among education, work, and leisure over the entire adult life span. Thus, all adults, regardless of age, would allocate some of their time to all three endeavors rather than spending all their time on only one.

The Older Employee

How can older employees be characterized? Do they perform their jobs as well as younger employees, and are their motivations for working and their attitudes toward work any different from those of younger employees? Is there age discrimination when it comes to hiring older adults and evaluating older workers?

How many older Americans continue to work at paid jobs? One way to answer this question is to look at statistics on the median age of retirement, which is the chronological age by which half of the population has left the

Figure 10.1 | An Age-Differentiated and Age-Integrated Social Structure

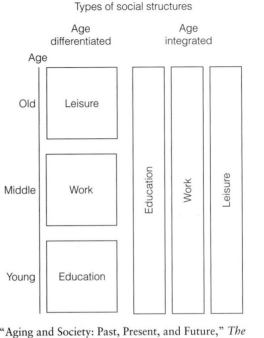

From M. W. Riley, "Aging and Society: Past, Present, and Future," *The Gerontologist*, 34, pp. 436–446.

paid labor force but half still remain. A younger median age of retirement indicates that individuals are leaving the work force early, while an older median age would indicate they are remaining in paid jobs longer. Most of the information we have is based on European American men. Less is known about women, and thus far little is known about African American, Asian American, Native American, or Hispanic American workers (Gendell & Siegel, 1996).

One factor that makes it difficult to determine age of retirement is that some workers exit from the labor force but later re-enter it to work at a different job. Under these circumstances, it is not easy to ascertain whether a specific exit from the labor force is the final one to be counted as retirement, or whether a specific exit simply represents a time gap between leaving an old job and starting a new one (Gendell & Siegel, 1996). Determining age at retirement is simpler when individuals have worked steadily prior to leaving the labor force than it is when they have experienced interruptions in their job history for either voluntary or involuntary reasons.

What we do know about workers in the United States is that the median age of retirement dropped from approximately 67 in 1950–1955 to approximately 63 in 1985–1990 (Gendell & Siegel, 1996). Thus, over a period of four decades, the trend was for workers to leave the paid labor force at younger ages.

The decline in median age of retirement was similar for European American and African American men, but the absolute age of exit from the labor force was somewhat lower for the African American men at various points of comparison (Gendell & Siegel, 1996). Statistics on median age of retirement are particularly sparse for African American women (Gendell & Siegel, 1996).

Following the drop from 1950 to 1990, the decline in median age of retirement leveled off in the early 1990s (Gendell & Siegel, 1996). As of the mid-1990s, experts disagreed about future trends. Some predicted that in the early 21st century, median retirement age would drop further, falling below 62, meaning that workers would be expected to leave positions of paid employment at even younger ages than they did previously. Others predicted the opposite trend, that the median age of retirement would increase early in the 21st century, meaning that workers would remain in the paid labor force to older ages than they had in prior years (Mergenhagen, 1994). The following arguments have been made in support of the latter prediction, which now seems the more likely scenario:

- Americans remain healthy later into older adulthood than was true in the past. Not only are many of them physically able to continue working longer, but also jobs are less physically demanding today than they were in the past. A large-scale national survey of men and women in their 60s indicated that in 1993, a lower percentage of 67-year-olds were unable to work compared with the percentage of 65-year-olds who were unable to work in 1982 (Crimmins, Reynolds, & Saito, 1999). This was true across racial and ethnic groups, although African Americans and individuals with less educational attainment were less healthy to begin with.
- In the United States, average life expectancy has been increasing, so workers who retire in their early 60s might live for 30 or more years after leaving the paid labor force. With so many years after retirement, they will have to accumulate enough economic resources during their working years to last for three decades. Yet, as of the 1990s, 40 percent of American workers between the ages of 51–60 did not expect to have any income when they retired other than payments from Social Security (a pension from the federal government discussed later). In addition, 20 percent had no assets such as a house, investments, and savings, and many had no health insurance. This means that older adults may have to continue working out of financial need (Sterns & Sterns, 1997).
- Mandatory retirement has been eliminated for most jobs, so individuals can no longer be forced to retire at a certain chronological age. Also, fewer corporations are likely to offer incentives for early retirement as they did in the past. At the same time, the age at which workers become eligible for full Social Security pension benefits is scheduled to increase from age 65 to 66 and then 67 in a phased-in process beginning after the year 2000. Also, recent legislation has eliminated restrictions in the amount of money that workers ages 65 and over will be able to earn without losing their Social Security benefits.

In sum, a number of factors lead to the prediction that individuals will continue to work to later ages than they did in the immediate past. Increased life expectancy, improvements in health, easing of physical requirements in the workplace, as well as economic incentives all point to the distinct possibility that more, rather than fewer, older adults will participate in the paid labor force. Thus, there is good reason to learn more about older employees.

Job Performance   Just how well do older employees perform in their jobs? Some common stereotypes are that older workers are less productive, less motivated, less receptive to innovations, and less able to learn, especially when it comes to new technologies (Czaja, 2001; Panek, 1997). Other stereotypes are that they are physically unable to do their jobs and that they have a high rate of accidents and absenteeism. In fact, the information we do have paints a very different picture. Older workers are less likely than younger workers are to be injured on the job. When injury or illness does occur, older workers may need more time than younger workers do to recover, but for male workers especially, avoidable absenteeism (being absent without prior approval) tends to decrease with age (Panek, 1997). Furthermore, most older workers express a high level of commitment to their jobs and have a great deal of emotional investment in the work role (Ekerdt, 1986).

There are relatively few well-controlled studies on age and job performance. Salthouse and Maurer (1996) point to some of the difficulties involved in making accurate comparisons between the job proficiency of young and older workers. First, only a limited number of occupations have been studied, and many of these have included small samples; therefore, they lack the sensitivity needed to detect whether there are any differences between young and older employees. Second, the test instruments used to measure job performance have not always been reliable or valid (Chapter 2 discusses the concepts of reliability and validity), and it is especially difficult to measure performance when jobs are complex. Third, samples of younger and older adults who work in a specific occupation may not be equivalent. Younger employees are often new to the job and may represent a broad segment of their age group. In contrast, older employees have often worked in the job for a longer time, so they are more likely to represent a select sample of individuals who have demonstrated competency over the years and thus have been retained in the occupation. Fourth, age comparisons between younger and older workers in a given occupation are meaningful only if both age groups have the same actual responsibilities. Young and older employees may have the same job title, but that does not necessarily mean that their job responsibilities are identical. Older employees often have more seniority, which means the tasks they perform may differ from those performed by younger workers.

Given these complexities, conflicting reports regarding the relationship between age and job performance should come as no surprise. Overall, there seems to be little connection between age and job performance (McEvoy & Cascio, 1989; Waldman & Avolio, 1986). However, the relationship between age and job performance may depend upon the specific type of job as well as the measures used to determine performance. Any analysis on the relationship between age and job performance must take into account the complexity of the job, the pace at which the job must be performed, and the past experience of those performing the job (Czaja, 2001).

Job performance is a function of both ability and experience (Salthouse & Maurer, 1996). Older employees may use accumulated knowledge and expertise to compensate for any age-related decline, particularly when it comes to speed of response. (See Chapter 4 for more detail on speed of performance and reaction time.) In a classic study that demonstrated just this point, Salthouse (1984) found that experienced older typists maintained the same level of speed and accuracy as young typists by placing greater reliance on anticipating forthcoming keystrokes. The same principle could apply to strokes on computer keyboards.

In recent years, computers and other technology have gained greater importance in occupational settings, and the effect this could have on older workers is only beginning to be examined (Czaja, 2001). In one study (Czaja & Sharit, 1993), women ranging in age from 25 to 70 performed three computer-based tasks: data entry, file maintenance, and inventory management. On all three tasks, the older women were slower than the younger ones. However, none of the study participants had much prior experience with computers, so the older participants would not have had time to gain whatever experience they might need to compensate for declines in speed. In a subsequent study (Czaja & Sharit, 1998), prior experience with computers was an important determinant in how older adults performed a data entry task. Additional research is needed, but it seems clear that older adults are receptive to using technology and capable of learning the necessary skills. However, they may need more training and practice to acquire these skills than young adults do (Czaja, 2001).

Job experience is generally a positive factor in the workplace, but with rapid changes in technology, some skills that employees have sharpened over the years may become obsolete. Thus, workers of all ages must remain open to regular retraining to update their skills. A common myth is that older workers are not as open as young workers to retraining and that they are less flexible and less willing to change their ways. In other words, "You can't teach an old dog new tricks." However, an important consideration is that older workers have probably been following a certain procedure for a longer time than younger workers have, so older workers may need to put forth greater effort to switch to new procedures. Even so, there is little reason to believe that older workers cannot be trained, although they often benefit more from training when there is less pressure and more time to learn (Panek, 1997). Training older workers is a good investment because they are often committed to their jobs and less likely than young workers are to switch companies.

To determine how older workers cope with any age-related losses and thus maintain their job performance, Abraham and Hansson (1995) developed a survey questionnaire based on Baltes and Baltes's (1990) Selective Optimization with Compensation (SOC) Model. A strategy of selection would involve restricting or narrowing the range of work activities to fewer domains, or aspects, of the job (for example, endorsing statements such as, "I now try to avoid spreading myself too thin" and "I now delegate low priority responsibilities to others"). A strategy of optimization would involve efforts to maximize one's work capabilities (for example, endorsing statements such as, "I am now more likely to participate in training to polish rusty skills and abilities"). Finally, a strategy of compensation would involve efforts to create a positive impression by downplaying deficiencies (for example, endorsing statements such as "I now try to perform my job in such a way that my weaker points are less visible") and efforts to present oneself in the most positive way possible (for example, endorsing statements such as, "I now try to make my accomplishments visible to my boss and co-workers"). Abraham and Hansson administered their survey to 224 workers, mostly European American men and women ranging in age from 40 to 69. Survey respondents worked in a broad range of jobs, including professional, managerial, and administrative/clerical, but the managerial positions included a higher proportion of men and the administrative/clerical positions included a higher proportion of women. As anticipated, the older respondents were more likely than the younger ones to endorse statements indicating they would use selection, optimization, and compensation strategies. In addition, there were gender differences. Selection strategies were more likely to be endorsed by men, more of whom held managerial positions in which this strategy might be more easily adopted. Optimization and compensation scores were more likely to be endorsed by women, fewer of whom worked in positions that would allow them to control which aspects of the job they would select. Abraham and Hansson emphasize that even though the older respondents were more likely than the younger ones to endorse the strategies described in the survey questionnaire, whether they would actually employ such strategies probably depends on situational factors. Workers with lower status in an organization may have less freedom to select which aspects of their jobs they will attend to. Furthermore, optimization and compensation strategies might be more acceptable and encouraged more in some organizational environments than in others.

Evaluation of Older Employees   Do supervisors use the same standards to evaluate older employees as they use to evaluate younger employees, and do factors other than actual job performance play a role in how older workers are evaluated? Evaluations of older workers may be positively influenced by the perception that they are loyal and reliable, and older workers may be given credit for past achievements and experience. Also, those who evaluate older workers may take into account the fact that older workers have lower rates of avoidable absenteeism and higher levels of job satisfaction compared with young workers (Rhodes, 1983). From years of experience, older workers may have more realistic expectations than younger workers do, and perhaps for that reason older workers often express greater satisfaction with their jobs (Ekerdt & DeViney, 1993). In one study (Erber & Szuchman, 2002), older adults were considered more disciplined, reliable, dependable, knowledgeable, and cheerful than young adults in the context of a volunteer work situation. Perceptions regarding their positive personal qualities could make up for the possibility that older workers take longer to complete a task. Overall, then, older workers may be judged by those who evaluate them to be just as valuable as young workers are. On the other hand, supervisors' appraisals of younger workers might be positively influenced by a belief that they will devote more years to the company and are better candidates for promotion than older workers are.

Another factor that can influence how older workers are evaluated is the age of co-workers in the same company or office. One or two older workers among a majority of younger co-workers might be evaluated more negatively than older workers whose co-workers are all about the same age as they are. Moreover, age differences between a supervisor and employee can influence how the older employee is evaluated (Cleveland & Shore, 1992). When they have limited information about employees who work for them, young supervisors are more likely to rate older employees less favorably than they do young employees (Finkelstein, Burke, & Raju, 1995; Lee & Clemons, 1985). On a more optimistic note, as the proportion of older workers increases, chronological age may become a less important factor for decision makers, and evaluations of job performance may be more heavily based on skills and productivity, as well they should.

Age Discrimination in Employment   Some years ago, mandatory retirement was the rule for most jobs and workers had to retire at a specific age, typically 65. Employers could refuse to hire anyone above a certain age, and they were permitted to demote or reduce the salaries of older workers. The 1967 enactment of the **Age Discrimination in Employment Act (ADEA),** which applies to companies with more than 20 employees, prohibited discrimination against workers aged 40 to 65 by making it illegal to use age in hiring decisions, or to terminate, demote, or reduce the salaries of older workers without showing good cause. The ADEA was amended in 1978 to include workers up to age 70 and again in 1986 to prohibit mandatory retirement altogether. However, one exception to the ADEA is that age can be used in employment decisions if it can be demonstrated that older employees would be not be capable of doing the job in a way that is reasonably necessary for the normal operations of the business (McCann & Giles, 2002). Not surprisingly, many employers attempt, successfully or unsuccessfully, to use this exception as the basis for their defense when older employees file charges of age discrimination (McCann & Giles, 2002). In 1990, a further amendment to the ADEA prohibited employers from treating older workers any differently from young workers when companies reduce their workforce, or downsize. In principle, the ADEA makes it illegal for employers to make work-related decisions on the basis of age stereotypes concerning abilities, physical status, or performance. Thus, employers need to keep accurate performance evaluation records of their employees. In turn, employees are well-advised to keep copies of their performance evaluations in the event they must show that they have been the subject of age discrimination.

Thanks to the ADEA, it is uncommon to find flagrant examples of age discrimination such as publishing job ads that specify age, telling job applicants that they are too old, or informing employees they are being terminated because of age. However, subtle forms of age discrimination persist, as evidenced by the large number of age discrimination cases that have resulted in employers' paying pretrial settlements to older workers (Lavelle, 1997). Between 1990 and 1993, there was a 26 percent increase in the number of age discrimination charges filed with federal and state agencies, and as of 1996, 30,600 cases had been filed (Sterns & Sterns, 1997). These figures suggest that not all older workers are leaving their jobs voluntarily and that many who want to work may be subject to subtle forms of age discrimination. The majority of discrimination complaints have been filed by workers at the managerial level (Lavelle, 1997), many of whom earn relatively high salaries. However, the courts have ruled it legal to terminate long-time (often older) workers if employers can show there are budgetary constraints. In one case, a large chain of discount stores dismissed middle-aged store managers who had been in charge of inventories. The company claimed this function could be performed more efficiently by electronic scanners at the checkout counter. Termination of these employees was rendered legal because the company demonstrated that the jobs of these managers had become obsolete.

Unfortunately, the ADEA has not been highly effective in ensuring that older adults will be hired or in guaranteeing that older workers will be treated fairly in the workplace (Quadagno & Hardy, 1996). In many instances, young job applicants are selected over older applicants with equivalent credentials. Some older job applicants try to increase their chances of being hired by attempting to hide their age. Interestingly, it is considered poor strategy for older job applicants to emphasize their experience, stability, loyalty, and maturity. While these qualities are positive, they are stereotypically associated with age (Lavelle, 1997).

Perry, Kulik, and Bourhis (1996) conducted a study on how job applicants are evaluated. Undergraduate business administration majors at a large university first read a description of what was considered to be either a young-type job (selling CDs and tapes) or an old-type job (selling stamps and coins). Then each participant viewed three videos in which an applicant had high, low, or average qualifications for the job. The focus of the study was on the applicant with average qualifications, who was always viewed last. For half the participants, the average applicant was a young adult, and for the other half the average applicant was an older adult. Three factors were found to be associated with discrimination against the older job applicant. First, student evaluators with a pre-existing bias against older workers, as indicated by their responses on a survey questionnaire administered one month earlier, gave the older average-qualified job applicant lower evaluations than did student evaluators who were not biased to begin with. Second, student evaluators gave higher evaluations when applicants were applying for an age-congruent job. Thus, the older applicant for the job selling CDs and tapes was viewed less favorably than the older applicant for the job selling stamps and coins. Third, compared with the student evaluators who were not distracted while making the evaluations, those who were distracted (by being told that after they evaluated the videos they would be asked to make a video of their own) tended to show age discrimination by giving lower evaluations to the older applicant than they did to the younger one. Presumably, student evaluators who were distracted had more on their minds and thus fewer cognitive resources to devote to processing detailed information about the applicant. Individuals with fewer cognitive resources often fall back on stereotypes rather than judging other people on an individual basis. In sum, young adult business majors, our future business leaders, may well show age discrimination in some employment selection situations.

With regard to treatment in the workplace, age discrimination can take the form of giving older employees fewer opportunities for training and fewer rewards for updating their skills, which could ultimately lead to their obsolescence (Avolio & Waldman, 1990). Erber and Danker (1995) asked employees of a large corporation to imagine themselves as managers in a hypothetical company, which was described to them as having either high or low pressure to downsize. In their hypothetical role as managers, study participants answered questions about how they would handle a situation in which a young or older employee is experiencing performance problems related to poor memory. When told that the company had high pressure to downsize, study participants had a greater expectation that the older worker's performance problems would continue to occur and they were less likely to recommend training opportunities when the employee was old rather than young. Given the importance of job training, this would represent an indirect form of age discrimination in the workplace.

Sterns and Sterns (1997) submit that subtle forms of age discrimination should be remedied by implementing affirmative action plans with the goal of increasing age diversity in the workplace. Under such plans, young and older job applicants would be evaluated using the same standards. However, if a young and an older applicant are equally qualified for the job, and if older employees are under-represented in the company or organization, then the older applicant would be selected. Still, not everyone agrees that adopting an age-based affirmative action policy is a preferred strategy to combat age discrimination in the workplace. Longman (1997) points out that age-based affirmative action programs could create resentment among young and even middle-aged adults, resulting in intergenerational conflict. Longman argues that two opposing philosophical viewpoints about older adults seem to exist in American society. According to one viewpoint, older Americans are entitled to special benefits solely on the basis of their age. Senior discounts offered by some merchants reflect this viewpoint, although some businesses use such discounts to bolster sales at slow times of the day or week. Another indication of this viewpoint is the conviction that older adults should be considered a special group that deserves entitlements. Therefore, there should be no reduction in benefits offered by federal programs such as Social Security (described later on) even for the well-to-do elderly. The contrasting viewpoint is that older adults are no different from any other age group and they should not be treated any differently. Those who support this viewpoint contend that older adults are healthier now than ever before and in most cases they are fully capable of working and otherwise contributing to society. While special benefits should be available for individuals who are frail or needy, such benefits should not be distributed solely on the basis of age.

Age discrimination is less glaring now than previously. However, if workers are to remain in the paid labor force to older ages out of economic necessity or desire, we must remain alert to the conditions under which it can occur.

Retirement

While some older adults continue to work full time, others have immediate plans to leave the paid labor force and enter into retirement. What does it mean to be retired and when do people decide to stop working? **Retirement** is a broad concept. At the level of society, retirement is a social institution with rules about when it is permissible for workers to leave the paid labor force. At the level of the individual, retirement represents a transition to a stage of life in which paid employment is no longer required (Atchley, 1996). However, when are individuals actually considered to be retired? Definitions vary, but factors used to define whether individuals are retired include reduced labor force participation, cessation of a career, receipt of income from pensions (periodic financial payments made to formerly employed individuals who meet certain eligibility rules, as discussed later), willingness to identify themselves as retired, or some combination of these factors (Ekerdt, 1995).

For people with a steady work history throughout their adult years, the transition to retirement is usually easy to identify, and such individuals have no difficulty in considering themselves as retired as soon as they stop working (Szinovacz & DeViney, 1999). In today's cohort of older adults, a work career with few disruptions is more typical for men than it is for women. Many older women did not participate in the labor force and if they did, they probably experienced periods of interruption to rear children or to care for elderly parents. Because older women's paid employment history has been more sporadic than the steady work history of older men, determining when women are retired is less clear-cut. With regard to race and ethnic background, it is more common for African American workers than it is for European American workers to exit the labor force for health reasons, although some prefer to identify themselves as retired rather than disabled (Szinovacz & DeViney, 1999). Also, compared to European American older workers, both African American and Hispanic American older workers are more vulnerable to involuntary job loss in the pre-retirement years (Flippen & Tienda, 2000). Once jobs are lost, it may be difficult to find new employment, especially if there is limited education and few job qualifications. After a prolonged period of joblessness, many individuals eventually refer to themselves as "retired." In sum, retirement can be ambiguous, particularly for women and minorities, because the boundary between work and nonwork is blurred due to movement in and out of the labor force (Flippen & Tienda, 2000).

Effects of Retirement   It is difficult to conduct well-controlled studies on the effects of retirement because retirement status (that is, being retired versus not retired) is not a true independent variable (see Chapter 2 for further discussion of independent variables and true experiments). This means that one cannot manipulate who remains in the workforce and who retires. For individuals who retire due to poor health or job loss through downsizing, retirement is not voluntary and could well be associated with negative outcomes in the physical or psychological domains. However, there is little evidence that voluntary retirement causes poor physical or mental health. When individuals choose to leave the workforce and when their departure is "on time," meaning that they discontinue paid employment at a stage of life that is typical in their culture, then retirement does not seem to have any detrimental physical or psychological effects.

To explore the social and psychological consequences of retirement, Reitzes, Mutran, and Fernandez (1996) conducted a two-year longitudinal study following 757 male and female workers (83 percent European American, ages 58–64) and testing their level of self-esteem and depression at six-month intervals. During the two-year interval, 299 of the workers made the transition to retirement and the rest continued to work full-time. For both groups, level of self-esteem remained relatively stable over time, but depression scores actually declined in the group that retired. Perhaps the retired individuals enjoyed some relief from work-related stress.

In a cross-sectional study of 1,339 individuals ages 55 and older who were all interviewed at approximately the same time, Herzog, House, and Morgan (1991) found that extent of labor force participation had little relationship to health and well-being in and of itself. What was important for study participants' health and well-being was whether their level of labor force participation (that is, full-time work, part-time work, or no work) reflected personal preference as opposed to constraints imposed by forces outside their own control. Those who chose whether to work and how much to work reported having better health and well-being compared with those who had little control over whether and how much they worked.

When they retire, older adults lose a role that once held a prominent place in their lives. For those with a strong commitment to the work role, can retirement trigger a "crisis" in identity, with negative effects on physical and mental well-being (Atchley, 1971)? Individuals who find social transitions difficult may experience anxiety surrounding the anticipation or actual event of retirement (Fletcher & Hansson, 1991). In general, however, loss of the work role does not result in an identity crisis. Most individuals are able to replace the work role and the social contacts they had at work. For the majority of older adults, the years before and after retirement are characterized by continuity (Atchley, 1971). Even so, the transition to retirement may be smoother if individuals can identify with their former occupations after they retire. For example, teachers may continue to identify themselves as members of that profession even when they no longer have a formal classroom.

How does retirement affect the marital relationship? Vinick and Ekerdt (1991) interviewed 92 couples aged 55 and over in which the women did not work and the men had been retired for 6–22 months. The majority of the men reported greater participation in household tasks, and most of the couples had increased the number of leisure activities they did together. Approximately half the women admitted to some feelings of impingement on their sphere of personal activity now that their husbands had retired, but most claimed they had adjusted to the situation. The majority of the couples did not consider the transition to retirement to be a "crisis," and their feelings about it were mainly positive. Today, more married women are participating in the paid workforce and wives are more likely to have full-time career paths similar to those of their husbands. There is some evidence that wives who continue to work after their husbands retire become dissatisfied if their husbands do not help with house-work even if their husbands did not help much before they retired. Dual-earner couples who time their retirements to coincide and who share household chores seem to have a high level of well-being (Quadagno, 2002).

Economics of Retirement   Retirement is considered a legitimate right earned through years of work. Even so, leaving the paid labor force means giving up a regular paycheck, so how do retired individuals pay their living expenses? Other than savings and investments accumulated during the working years, an impor-tant source of income for most retirees comes from pensions. Pensions are reg-ular payments, or benefits, that produce a steady income based on the retired worker's former participation in the paid labor force. Pension benefits can come from a public source such as the federal government or they can come from pri-vate employers or corporations.

In the United States, a federally sponsored public pension plan was estab-lished with the passing of the **Social Security** Act in 1935, during the years of the Great Depression. Older adults who had worked at paid jobs for a certain min-imum number of three-month periods (quarters) became eligible to receive monthly benefit payments from the government. These benefits would protect them from impoverishment. At the same time, the Social Security system would make it possible for more older workers to retire, thus making room for younger workers during a time of extreme job scarcity.

The Social Security system in the United States was modeled after the German retirement system devised by Otto von Bismarck in 1871, which des-ignated 65 as the age when retired workers could begin receiving pension ben-efits. Similarly, American workers were eligible for a monthly pension benefit from Social Security at age 65, with a dollar amount based on the salary they earned prior to retirement. Currently, those who have worked for the required number of quarters are eligible for full Social Security benefits when they are 65, but in the near future they will have to be 66 and then 67. Retired workers are eligible for reduced benefits at age 62, with a dollar amount approximately 20 percent less than they would receive if they waited until the age at which they would be entitled to the full benefit. On the other hand, monthly payments increase for workers who delay taking any benefits beyond the age of 65 (66 or 67 in the near future).

As mentioned in Chapter 1, the economic status of older Americans has improved over the years. In 1958, 22.4 percent of American households had incomes below the poverty level, but the comparable figure for Americans over age 65 was 35.2 percent. By 1990, 13.5 percent of the American population lived in poverty, but the rate of poverty for older adults was 12.5 percent (Hess & Markson, 1995). Decline in the rate of poverty for older adults can be traced at least in part to Social Security payments, which include yearly cost-of-living increases. Another factor contributing to the reduced proportion of older adults living in poverty was the introduction of Medicare, the federally sponsored health insurance program described in Chapter 3.

Although their economic well-being has improved in recent years, a con-siderable portion of retired older adults are not financially "comfortable"

(Hess & Markson, 1995). On average, African American and Hispanic American workers have lower salaries than do European American workers, and these lower salaries are reflected in lower Social Security benefits after they retire. Also, economic disadvantage is more common among the old-old (75+) age group than it is among the young-old (65–74) age group (Hess & Markson, 1995). Social Security benefits are paid monthly throughout older retired workers' lives, but these payments were intended to serve as a financial cushion and not as the sole source of income in retirement. A likely reason for the greater economic disadvantage of the old-old group is that savings accumulated during their working years to supplement Social Security become depleted after a decade of retirement. In addition to the age factor, there is a clear gender difference in rate of poverty among older adults. There is more poverty among older women than among older men. Sixty percent of Social Security beneficiaries are women, and more women than men rely on Social Security payments as their sole source of income. This may explain why three out of every four poor older adults are women, with poverty rates highest among women who are single and live alone (Smeedling, Estes, & Glasse, 1999).

With regard to married couples, the rule is that if one member of a married couple is eligible for Social Security benefits, the spouse is eligible for an additional 50 percent of that amount even if he or she never worked outside the home. For example, if Tomas receives a monthly benefit of $400, his wife Elena, always a homemaker, will receive $200. Together, they will receive a total of $600. If either Tomas or Elena dies, the benefit paid to the living member of the couple is reduced by one-third. Thus, Tomas or Elena will receive only $400 per month rather than the $600 they received as a couple. This reduction could cause financial hardship for a widowed older adult who relies solely on Society Security benefits for retirement income and who lives alone. Today, more women are entering the workforce and in the future there will be more dual-earner couples. Married women may qualify for higher Social Security benefits based on their own work history than they would have based on their status as a spouse. Even so, there will be a need to supplement Social Security benefits with other sources of income for both individuals and couples.

In addition to federally sponsored Social Security pension benefits, some retired employees receive benefits from pensions sponsored by the companies for which they worked. The specific details of such private pensions vary, but most fall into two basic categories: **defined benefit pension plans** (DB) and **defined contribution pension plans** (DC). In general, DB plans require that individuals work for a certain number of years for the company in order to be vested, or eligible to receive benefits when they retire. Also, in most DB plans, employees must reach a specific age before they can begin to receive benefits. The amount of the monthly benefit that retired workers receive from a DB pension plan is usually based on their salary in the latter years on the job. DB retirement plans generally pay benefits to retirees for the rest of the their lives and some offer periodic cost-of-living increases. Social Security is a DB pension plan, but the federal government sponsors it, rather than a private employer. With DB plans, the burden of paying pension benefits to retired employees falls squarely on the employer, or in the case of Social Security on the federal government. In recent years, many private companies are moving away from DB pension plans and are switching to defined contribution pension plans (Cutler, 1996).

Defined contribution (DC) pension plans place the burden of pension income in the retirement years squarely on the employee. Companies, or employers, make periodic contributions, usually a percentage of the employee's salary, into the employee's retirement account. Depending on the specific rules of the plan, the employee may or may not be required to match the employer's contribution. Regardless, contributions into the employee's retirement account accumulate and are taxed only when the employee begins to make withdrawals at any time after the age of 59 1/2. Withdrawals prior to 59 1/2 incur a 10 percent penalty over and above the taxes paid. Withdrawals must begin by the time the retired individual reaches the age of 70 1/2. In many DC plans, employees have some choice about how their own contributions, or even their employers' contributions, are invested. This means that employees with DC pension plans are responsible for investment decisions that will determine their standard of living in retirement. The earlier in their work careers they make wise investment decisions, the better their chances of accumulating sufficient funds for their retirement years (Cutler, 1996). Employees with DC pension plans are generally not required to remain with an employer for a long time to receive benefits in retirement. This makes DC pension plans more "portable" than DB pension plans because employees are entitled to the money that has accumulated even if they change employers. In sum, employees with DC retirement plans have some control over their income in retirement, but at the same time they have greater responsibility. To ensure that they will live comfortably in retirement, they will have to play an active role in financial planning during their working years.

Because they earned lower salaries during their working years, retired older women receive lower benefits than retired men do not only from Social Security but also from employer-sponsored DB and DC pension plans. In a recent study of full-time middle-aged employees who were enrolled in employer-sponsored (private) pension plans, anticipated pension wealth (an important factor in retirement income) was 76 percent greater for men than it was for women (Johnson, Sambamoorthi, & Crystal, 1999). Less than one-third of this gender gap could be explained by differences in level of education, demographics, or even by variation in the men and women's job characteristics. For the most part, the gender gap in anticipated pension wealth can be attributed to the fact that women had less advantaged employment situations in terms of wages, years on the job, and types of industries that employ women. Whether the gender gap in pension benefits will narrow in the future remains to be seen. Meanwhile, young women should be aware of the steps they must take to provide for their financial security in older adulthood.

As discussed earlier, there was a decline in median retirement age from the 1950s to the 1990s. This decline was most likely linked to economic factors because workers were confident that they would receive adequate pension benefits and in many cases health benefits from their companies once they left the paid workforce (Fronstin, 1999). However, there are signs that the era of early retirement is drawing to a close. As mentioned earlier, there is a phased increase in age of eligibility for full Social Security benefits—from 65 to 66 and then 67.

The financial incentives and continued health benefits offered by large corporations to encourage employees to retire in their 50s or early 60s are becoming less common. Furthermore, there is a trend for companies to hire workers on an hourly basis with no pension or health benefits at all, thus leaving workers on their own to make financial plans for retirement and to pay for their own health costs. These factors, combined with middle-aged workers' low level of savings and high level of debt, lead to the forecast that retirement age will increase and people will spend more years in the paid labor force.

The rules and regulations for pensions vary considerably even among developed nations. For example, in the United States, workers and their employers both contribute a percent of the worker's wages to the Social Security system, whereas this may not be the case in all industrialized countries. Also, a person's eligibility for retirement benefits from Social Security is tied to age and prior work history but not to financial need (although income taxes may have to be paid on some part of Social Security benefits depending upon total income). In fact, older adults in the United States can continue to work and still receive Social Security benefits. However, in some countries, any benefits received from the government are means tested, so older adults are eligible for payments only if they fall below a certain income level. For example, the pension program sponsored by the Australian government (described by Quadagno, 2002) is not linked to prior employment, but rather it is based on age, residency, and financial need. Older Australian residents can receive pension benefits if their income and assets fall below a certain level, so eligibility must be determined on a case-by-case basis. Each year, the criteria for eligibility is raised to a higher level, so fewer people qualify for payments.

In sum, public pensions from the government and private pensions, together with savings and assets, determine the standard of living of older adults once they retire. In the United States, Social Security provides a base for living expenses, but if older adults are to achieve a comfortable standard of living, Social Security benefits will need to be supplemented by private pensions, savings, or continued part-time or full-time work.

Retirement as a Process   Is retirement from paid employment a sudden event, or is it just the end point in a process that ulitmately leads to a decision to leave the paid workforce? Atchley (1994) proposed that retirement takes place in a series of phases. Not every individual goes through every phase, but this framework is a way to consider retirement as a process rather than a single event and to think about retirement as something beyond the simple cessation of paid labor.

In the preretirement phase, workers make remote and then more immediate plans for retirement. Once retirement actually occurs, some individuals experience a honeymoon phase, which is a period of euphoria and enthusiasm, typified by a high level of activity. In this phase, new retirees try to do everything they did not have time for when they were working. The honeymoon phase often entails fulfilling preretirement fantasies, a common example being travel. The honeymoon phase could be brief or it could go on for a year or more, but usually it does not continue indefinitely. How long it lasts may depend upon the

Figure 10.2 | Phases of Retirement

Prerertirement Phase	Honeymoon Phase	Disenchantment Phase	Reorientation Phase	Stability Phase	Termination Phase

Atchley, 1994.

health of the retiree and/or the retiree's spouse or upon financial resources. However, even with good health and sufficient finances, most retirees are unable to keep up the high level of activity of the honeymoon phase. When life starts to slow down, some (though not all) retirees enter into a disenchantment phase, in which they experience emotional let-down, boredom, or even depression. After some time, retirees enter a reorientation phase in which they take stock and begin to fashion a realistic structure for their daily lives. They come to realize that life may have its high points, but it cannot be exciting all the time. They develop new interests, pursue hobbies, visit with family and friends, or do volunteer work. Once they establish a satisfactory and comfortable routine, retirees enter the *stability phase*. Some, but not all, retirees enter a final termination phase. This can occur when individuals find that the retirement role no longer suits their needs. Some miss working and decide to re-enter the labor force. A newspaper feature in the *Miami Herald* (Greenberg, 1998) described a 91-year-old man who had always been restless and bored in retirement. He did not need the income, but when he was widowed for a second time, he applied for a job selling luggage at a local department store, giving his age as 66 to secure the job. By the time he was 93, he had won the honor of "sales star of the month" several times even though he worked only 16–20 hours per week. For this self-described "workaholic," work was the key to feeling happy and productive. Other individuals relinquish the retirement role because illness and disability prevent them from taking part in the daily activities of a retired lifestyle. Sadly, the retirement role is replaced by the sick role.

Retirement can be abrupt and unanticipated if a worker experiences sudden illness or loss of a job through corporate downsizing and is unable to find suitable employment elsewhere. However, many workers entertain thoughts about what their lives will be like in retirement for some period of time before they actually exit the paid labor force. One way to study preretirement thought processes more closely would be to ask middle-aged and older workers about their plans for retirement. Ekerdt, DeViney, and Kosloski (1996) developed a profile of retirement plans, or intentions, based on the responses given by 5,072 male and female, predominantly European American, workers (ages 51–61) to questions from the 1992 Health and Retirement Survey (HRS). All of these individuals worked at least 35 hours per week, and they were asked whether they planned to keep working, whether they would work fewer hours, whether they planned to stop working completely, or whether they would change jobs

Table 10.1   Categories of Survey Respondents' Retirement Plans

- *Retire completely:* 20% of the respondents said that by a certain age or date, they planned to stop working altogether.
- *Retire partially:* 20% of the respondents said that by a certain age or date, they planned to reduce their work efforts.
- *Change jobs:* 9% of the respondents said that by a certain age or date, they planned to continue working full time, either in a new job or in a self-employment context.
- *Never retire:* 7% of the respondents said that they would never stop working.
- *No plans:* more than 40% of the respondents stated they had no plans for retirement.

Ekerdt, DeViney, & Kosloski, 1996.

by a certain age or date. Survey respondents' plans fell into five categories, as Table 10.1 shows.

The older individuals in this sample were less likely than the younger ones to plan a job change, and the older individuals were also less likely than the younger ones to have no plans at all. Of the 20 percent of the respondents who planned to stop working altogether by a certain age or date, more were men than women, and many worked for companies that would pay them private pensions upon retirement. Also, the married respondents were more likely than the unmarried ones to have plans to retire completely, presumably because they anticipated that retirement would give them more time for companionship. Other investigators (Reitzes, Mutran, & Fernandez, 1998) have also reported that married workers are more likely than unmarried ones to engage in retirement planning and to retire earlier, especially if their level of marital satisfaction is high. Ekerdt et al. (1996) also found that self-employed respondents were more likely to favor reduced or partial employment, and most said they would work fewer hours in the same job rather than changing jobs. Women were more likely than men to say they would reduce their hours of employment or change jobs rather than stop working altogether, and more women than men had no set plans. It is probable that more men than women had jobs that guaranteed a private pension at a certain time or age. In short, men were more likely to know what their financial situation would be once they retired, so they were in a better position to make concrete plans.

Ekerdt and DeViney (1993) studied job attitudes over three years in a sample of 900 men from the Veterans Administration Normative Aging Longitudinal Study. These men ranged in age from 50 to 69 and they worked full time. However, all of them had a definite target date by which they planned to retire from their jobs. Regardless of their exact chronological ages, the closer these workers were to their retirement target date, the more likely they were to report their jobs were causing tension and fatigue. The inclination to view a job as more burdensome as the retirement target date draws closer suggests that workers engage in a preretirement "role-exit" process. That is, they gradually disengage psychologically from the work role in preparation for actual retirement.

Ekerdt and DeViney's study is correlational so no firm co... ...sions can be drawn about any cause-and-effect relationship between job att... ...les and the proximity of planned retirement. Nonetheless, the suggestion that o... ...r work-ers engage in a psychological role-exit process is intriguing because ...lder workers often express positive attitudes and high levels of satisfaction w... their jobs.

Ekerdt and DeViney were the first to study variation in job attitudes along the temporal dimension of time-left-to-work rather than exact chronological age. Their sample consisted entirely of men, so the findings cannot be generalized to women. Most women have experienced work interruptions over the adult life span, so their attitudes toward work and anticipation of retirement could well differ from those of men. Regardless of gender, it is doubtful that workers who hold less stable jobs would engage in the same role-exit process as did the employees in this study, most of whom had continuous work careers over many decades.

Life After Retirement   Workers may engage in a role-exit process to ease their transition into retirement (Ekerdt & DeViney, 1993), but how do they shape their lives once they leave positions of paid employment? Ekerdt (1986) describes a phenomenon he terms the **busy ethic.** The busy ethic is most appli-cable to retirees in the young-old age category (ages 65 to 74), many of whom are in good health. The term busy ethic stems from the work ethic philosophy, wherein work is considered virtuous and individuals are viewed positively if they are diligent and industrious. When relatives, friends, and former co-workers ask new retirees how they are managing to keep busy now that they no longer work, retirees often remark, "I am busier now than when I was working!" The things retirees do to keep busy include educational pursuits, projects such as quilting, playing cards, or taking up a musical instrument, maintenance activi-ties (household tasks, shopping, going to the doctor), socializing with family members and friends, and volunteer work. Ekerdt stresses that the specific activities in which retirees engage are not important. What is important is that they feel busy and also that other people think they are busy. Keeping a list of activities may help retirees feel or seem busy regardless of whether they actually do everything on the list.

Ekerdt suggests several reasons retirees have a busy ethic. First, an active lifestyle is socially desirable in American society and leisure unbalanced by work is considered self-indulgent. Since relaxation is guilt-free only when it is balanced by work, retirees may strive to feel busy to legitimize their leisure time. Second, the busy ethic may allow retirees to feel that their activities in retirement are not that different from those they performed at work. In other words, the busy ethic may narrow the psychological gap between work and retirement, making the transition to retirement less drastic. Feeling busy also may reinforce retirees' desire to maintain the same level of vigor they had when they were working and may calm their fears of becoming useless or obsolescent.

However, retirees' claims that they are busy may not be wholly attributable to their need to feel socially desirable or their fear of being seen as obsolescent.

Even after they retire from full-time employment, some older adults keep busy with part-time jobs and many contribute to the community by doing volunteer work.

Conceivably, age-related slowing down, even for those in good health, could affect older retirees' perceptions of how busy they are. Hence, a trip to the grocery store that young or middle-aged adults tack on at the end of an eight-hour workday may be perceived by the older retiree as a great deal of activity.

In any case, keeping active and busy in retirement is touted by the popular media as a necessary strategy for holding at bay the possibility of stagnation and decline. Articles in newspapers and magazines feature retired older adults who cheerfully compensate for the loss of the work role by joining the Peace Corps, climbing mountains, or volunteering their time for worthwhile causes. Many businesses that market products and services to retired American consumers convey the message that retirement is an active and engaged time of life and that keeping busy is therapeutic for both body and soul. The advertisements of investment firms often convey retirees as dynamic, energetic, intelligent consumers who are savvy enough to enlist the services of financial advisors to ensure their hard-earned savings will yield sufficient financial returns to allow travel, golf, and living in luxurious retirement communities with state-of-the-art recreational facilities.

One way older adults restructure their lives in retirement is to take advantage of the educational opportunities that are increasingly available for older adults. Some older adults have dreamed of completing an interrupted because of family responsibilities. The author has had several inter-their mid-70s enrolled in undergraduate psychology courses. The women in raised families and worked at paying jobs throughout their adult lives, a men some cases they cared for aging parents or spouses with debilitating illness. Now they were free to fulfill a long-held wish of completing the Bachelor of Arts degree.

Some universities permit older adults to sit in on, or audit, courses free of charge. Many older retirees take advantage of this opportunity to pursue knowledge without the specific intention of obtaining a course grade or official degree. They enjoy mingling with young adult students and taking part in campus life. Some universities have formed institutes for retired older adults, which provide opportunities for intellectual and social stimulation. To become members of such institutes, individuals pay a nominal fee. In exchange, they can attend lectures and take short continuing education courses. Institute members often have library privileges and opportunities to attend cultural events on campus.

Elderhostel is a program offering an extensive network of noncredit short courses and seminars held on campuses in various locations. Older adults live in college dormitories for a week or two while they take these courses. Elderhostel provides intellectual stimulation, socialization with age peers, and a chance to spend time in a new location.

The recent growth of technology has altered many aspects of everyday life, and it has created the need for education and training for people of all ages. Most adolescents and young adults learn computer skills in their high school and college years. But today's older adults were not exposed to computers during their years of formal education and most of them did not use computers at work. However, many retired older adults want to learn basic computer skills so they can take advantage of what computers have to offer. A popular use of computers is electronic mail (e-mail), which makes it easy to keep in touch with loved ones who live at great distances. Older adults also use computers to access the Internet for information about government agencies, health issues, or consumer products such as the ratings and price of new and used cars. They can also shop "online" for all manner of goods, from purchasing stocks and bonds to ordering groceries. Online shopping can be especially advantageous if older adults no longer drive. Older adults can combat loneliness and isolation by visiting chat rooms to take part in discussion groups with others who have common interests but live in distant parts of the country or world. There are many opportunities for computer training. Courses are sponsored by continuing education programs at community colleges. Short courses are often available in local public libraries and community centers, and some may be offered right on the premises of apartment buildings where older adults live.

Some older adults participated in volunteer activities even when they were employed in paid jobs, but after retirement they may increase the amount of time spent volunteering. Others take up volunteer work for the first time after they retire from paid employment. Older adults volunteer for religious organizations, schools, community centers, hospitals, and nursing homes, as well as advocacy and political groups. Some retired executives volunteer their services as consultants to business entrepreneurs both within and outside the United States. Older men's motivation for volunteer work is more often a substitution for the work role, while older women's motivation is more to serve in a helping role. However, this gender difference may change as more women enter the paid labor force and have professional career paths (Hooyman & Kiyak, 2002). In general, the number of individuals who participate in volunteer activities increases in times of economic growth, probably because people are more likely to reach out to help others when they feel secure economically and emotionally (Harootyan, 1996). Also, those with some college education are more likely to volunteer than are those with a high school education. This bodes well for the future of volunteerism because upcoming cohorts of older adults are more likely than previous ones to have attended college (Harootyan, 1996). Not only does volunteering benefit others, but it also is associated with high life satisfaction and high self-rated health for the volunteers themselves (Hooyman & Kiyak, 2002; Quadagno, 2002).

In sum, many avenues are available for structuring an enjoyable life in retirement. One decision older adults make around the time they retire is related to where they will live. As we will see, there are many options, some of which provide more physical and social support than others.

LIVING ARRANGEMENTS

There is a common belief that as soon as older adults retire, they pack up and move to distant locations to live out their "golden years" in the sun. The majority of older adults do not relocate across state lines, but those who do are often seeking milder climates and opportunities for year-round outdoor recreation. Such migration has stimulated economic expansion in states such as Florida and North Carolina, where booms in construction of retirement communities have had a significant impact on the local communities.

Litwak and Longino (1987) contend that long-distance migration can be separated into three stages. In the first stage, usually immediately following retirement, most older adults are in the young-old (65–74) age category. The majority are in good health, have intact marriages, and adequate financial resources. In this stage, they are eager to join with age peers in taking full advantage of the swimming pools, golf courses, and tennis courts available in many retirement communities. Such moves have been termed *amenity migration.*

In the second stage, older adults have reached their mid- or late 70s and some are beginning to experience moderate physical or cognitive difficulties. In addition, a number of them have had spouses die and some have seen their financial resources dwindle. At this point, there is a trend for migration to occur in the reverse direction—from the sun belt back to the frost belt. Some older adults return from distant locales to hometowns or places where they can count on informal care and support from family members, most often adult children (Stoller & Longino, 2001). This type of move has been characterized as one of *independence maintenance* because older adults often continue to live on their own, but they need some help to do so (Rowles & Ravdal, 2002).

Not all older adults reach a third stage, but those who do have more severe disabilities. They usually require more help than informal caregivers such as family members can give. Older adults who reach the third stage need a more supportive environment, such as an assisted living facility or nursing home (discussed shortly). For older adults who reach the third stage, these *dependency moves* are typically local and often they are involuntary (Rowles & Ravdal, 2002).

Although a portion of older adults make long-distance moves when they retire, most do not. The majority of older adults remain in their native geographical areas after they retire, and some continue to live in the same dwelling units where they have lived for years or decades. Others remain in the same locale, but for any number of reasons they eventually make some type of move. Such a move may be to **age-integrated housing,** which is for people of all ages, or it can be made to **age-segregated housing,** which caters to the older adult population.

Aging in Place

Individuals who remain in the same locale and continue to live in the same housing unit are said to be **aging in place.** Older adults who remain in homes where they have lived for many years may eventually need to make physical modifications to ensure ease and safety of bathing, cooking, climbing steps, and performing household chores. Such modifications include installing improved lighting and safety features in bathrooms and kitchens, mounting railings in stairwells, and placing ramps in entryways. In addition to physical modifications, another key to aging in place successfully is knowing when to enlist assistance with tasks such as transportation, shopping, housekeeping, and meal preparation.

In many cases, older couples manage to age in place if the capabilities of one member of the pair complement those of the other. For example, one member may still drive, while the other is perfectly capable of cooking and doing household chores. Together, the couple can fulfill their everyday needs, but either member alone would experience difficulties. The single older adult who ages in place may be able to count on neighbors or friends for help with transportation or shopping. However, these sources of support are not always reliable and may become less available if familiar people move away and the older adult is left behind in a deteriorating neighborhood (Thompson & Krause, 1998). Often, family members who live in the vicinity, particularly adult daughters, make it possible for older adults to age in place by helping with transportation, shopping, and social outings. Older adults who never married or have no adult children may get help from siblings, nieces, nephews, or long-time friends.

One option for older adults who live alone and have no family members nearby is to share their homes with unrelated individuals. Such sharing can be a source of additional income or could be provided in exchange for household repairs, assistance with personal care, or just for company and companionship. Some public agencies sponsor match-up programs where older adults may even receive monetary subsidies for taking in unrelated house mates (Pynoos & Golant, 1996). However, this type of living arrangement is not common and only a small proportion of match-ups seem to be successful on a long-term basis (Pynoos & Golant, 1996). Communal living is another option, particularly for single unrelated older women who would otherwise live alone. However, living with unrelated individuals does not appear to be widespread among community-living older adults.

When individuals want to age in place but have little access to informal help from relatives, neighbors, or friends, they may need to pay for supportive services. However, knowing how and where to purchase such services can be an overwhelming task. Medicare, the federally sponsored health insurance program, pays for some in-home health care services for older adults, but only for a limited time following a hospitalization or certain medical procedures (Pynoos & Golant, 1996). In recent years, there has been an increase in the number of private agencies that offer not only home health care but also assistance with transportation and housekeeping tasks such as meal preparation and cleanup and laundry. Workers from such agencies can transport older adults or accompany them on shopping trips or visits to doctors and dentists. However, these services are usually costly—many agencies charge by the hour and require a minimum number of hours.

Recent years have also brought an expansion of community-based day-care services for older adults. Some day-care centers are targeted to private-paying individuals or their families, while others are subsidized by local and state agencies and charge fees based on the older adult's financial means. With the support of day-care centers during part of the week, older adults may be able to continue living in their own homes or apartments. Day-care services can also be vital for employed relatives who provide informal care for older adults. They can be assured that their older family members are being served a nutritious meal, receiving medication on schedule, and having opportunities to socialize throughout the day. Some day-care centers even provide door-to-door transportation.

Some older adults want to continue living in their own homes but utilities, repairs, renovations, or property taxes are becoming too costly for their retirement budgets. Those who qualify financially may be eligible for federal programs that subsidize the cost of utilities, and some states and counties make allowances for property taxes. For homeowners over the age of 62 who have little or no mortgage debt remaining on their homes, some lenders offer reverse mortgages whereby homeowners sell the equity in the house to the bank or loan company in exchange for a lump sum payment or a monthly stipend while they are still living in the house (Hooyman & Kiyak, 2002). This concept is relatively new, and at the present time few older adults have or would consider a reverse mortgage. The current generation of older adults places a high value on outright ownership of property and many are reluctant to incur debt. Some have plans to leave their property to adult children, who may or may not want it. However, future cohorts of older adults may be more open to such a financial arrangement. The baby boomers (the large cohort of individuals born between 1946 and 1964) are rapidly approaching older adulthood, and they may feel less need to own a home free and clear of any mortgage. Also, there is a recent trend among middle-aged adults whose children have grown up and left home to seek housing that can be easily converted to their potential needs in later years. Such housing has features such as a master bedroom and bath on the first floor and doorways and halls wide enough to accommodate walkers or wheelchairs (Hooyman & Kiyak, 2002). The next decade or two may find that an even greater proportion of middle-aged adults have made specific plans to age in place safely and comfortably.

Age-Segregated Living Arrangements

Rather than making physical modifications to residences, bringing in services from outside agencies, or counting on informal support from neighbors, friends or relatives, some older adults cope with changing needs by moving to living environments that they hope will be easier to maintain, safer to navigate physically, or better suited to their social needs. Older adults who move from single-family homes can select housing alternatives that are either age integrated or age segregated.

Age-integrated apartments and condominiums have no specific age requirements, so residents can be any age. Compared to single family housing, age-integrated apartments and condominiums require less maintenance and frequently supply greater security. These buildings are often more convenient to public transportation, and they may offer opportunities for informal companionship and social participation on the premises. Even so, age-integrated apartments and condominiums are essentially independent living arrangements because the residents are responsible for their own transportation needs, housekeeping tasks, meal preparation, and social life. If they need help, older adults who live in age-integrated settings will need to enlist the support of family members, neighbors, or friends, or they will have to hire paid workers or meal delivery services. Some older adults move to small apartments ("granny flats" or "echo housing") that are attached or semi-attached to their relatives' main living quarters (Kendig & Pynoos, 1996). These individuals have access to support close by, but at the same time they can enjoy some privacy and independence.

Some older adults elect to move to housing environments that offer services such as group meals in a common dining room, planned in-house social activities or group social outings, and transportation (Silverstein & Zoblotsky, 1996). In most cases, these more supportive housing environments are age segregated, meaning that they are intended for individuals over a particular age, usually 62. Single older adults or even older couples may have health problems, physical disabilities, or sensory losses that make living in a single family home or other type of age-integrated housing difficult or unsafe. Some choose to move to more supportive age-segregated living environments because they are unable or unwilling to rely on adult children or other close relatives, yet they want to feel secure in knowing that immediate assistance is available in case of emergencies or perhaps on a regular basis (Pynoos & Golant, 1996).

In exchange for the services provided in age-segregated environments, older adults must be willing to make whatever compromises are necessary for living in a group situation with others their age. It is especially important that the characteristics of the living environment be congruent with, or match, the individual's personal preferences (Kahana, 1982). Older adults who are extravertive and enjoy being with other people are likely to adapt well to age-segregated

Table 10.2   Types of Housing on a Continuum Ranging from Independence to Dependence

Housing Type	Independent		Semi-Independent		Dependent	
Single-family home	X					
Apartment/condominium	X	X				
Granny flat, echo housing		X	X			
Retirement hotel		X	X			
Retirement community		X	X			
Adult congregate living facility			X	X		
Board and care home				X	X	
Assisted living facility				X		X
Nursing home					X	X

Adapted from Kendig & Pynoos, 1996.

living environments where residents eat one or more meals in a common dining area. While outgoing older adults may look forward to such meals as pleasurable social events, older adults who prefer time alone in a quiet environment may dread what they perceive as the social pressure of group dining. Such individuals might be happier if they remain in a private residence and pay for supportive services from an agency.

In general, age-segregated environments have more services on the premises than age-integrated environments do. Even so, age-segregated living environments vary in the extent of support provided. Table 10.2 shows an array of housing arrangements that range from totally independent (very little support) to highly dependent (extensive support). The sections that follow describe age-segregated living arrangements on a continuum from least to most supportive.

Retirement Hotels and Retirement Communities   Often located in urban areas, **retirement hotels** consist of individual rooms occupied primarily by single residents, most typically men from lower-income groups. Housekeeping services such as vacuuming and changing linens are provided, but meals are not usually served on the premises. Some residents keep hot plates, microwave ovens, or coffee makers in their rooms, but they eat most meals in nearby restaurants and cafeterias. With urban renewal and gentrification, many old retirement hotels have been torn down to make way for new luxury hotels or high-priced condominiums that are beyond the means of lower-income older adults. Inexpensive restaurants and cafeterias have been replaced by gourmet dining spots and upscale coffee shops. South Beach in Miami Beach, Florida, is an example of such a transformation. Less than 20 years ago, South Beach was lined with retirement hotels populated by older adults who were able to live with limited means.

Low-cost retirement hotels such as this one on Ocean Drive in South Beach, Florida (ca. 1991) have been replaced by upscale hotels and gourmet restaurants.

Today, most of these hotels have been renovated and are affordable only to affluent vacationers, as are the high-priced restaurants in the surrounding area.

Unlike retirement hotels, **retirement communities** tend to attract more affluent older adults and are inhabited by couples as well as single older adults. Some retirement communities are subsidized by government agencies or religious organizations, but many are not. The unsubsidized retirement communities attract the most affluent older adults because residents bear the total cost of living in them. Large retirement communities such as Sun City in Arizona resemble towns or villages, but other retirement communities are more similar to subdivisions. Many retirement communities are enclosed complexes accessible only through secured entry gates. Most feature a centrally located club-house, which is used for social activities and programs, as well as recreational facilities such as swimming pools, tennis courts, and in some instances even golf courses. Many retirement communities operate vans for transporting residents within the community if it is large or to points outside the community such as grocery stores and shopping malls. These vans may also be used for group outings to plays and concerts. In most instances, residents are responsible for their own housekeeping, meal preparation, and health care. However, retirement communities provide a relatively secure environment in which older adults can lead active lives with their age peers.

Despite the potential advantages, moving from a single-family home to a retirement community or other type of age-segregated housing can be stressful because older adults must leave a familiar environment and often they must dispose of possessions accumulated over decades (Quadagno, 2002). The chances of adjusting to a retirement community or other type of age-segregated living environment are usually better if older adults themselves, and not their adult children, make the final decision about such a move. Even so, some adaptation to the new living situation will be necessary and this may take more time for some older adults than for others.

Adult Congregate Living Facilities   Adult congregate living facilities are buildings that require residents to meet a minimum age requirement (often 62) and to be capable of living with relative independence. In most such facilities, single older adults or older couples live in a studio, one-bedroom, or two-bedroom apartment that is equipped with safety features such as grab bars in bathrooms and call buttons in case emergency assistance is needed. Individual apartments usually have modest kitchens, but many congregate living facilities serve at least one meal per day, usually dinner, in a common dining area. The cost of the meal service may be included in the monthly rent. In one such facility visited by the author, residents must notify the director if they plan to skip the evening meal. This notification policy serves as a check on each resident's well-being.

Many congregate facilities provide housekeeping services and most have an office staff. In addition to an on-site director, larger facilities may have other personnel such as an activities director. In some congregate facilities, a committee of residents plans activities and social programs in conjunction with a staff member, and there may be resident associations that communicate suggestions and concerns to the staff. Some residents still drive, but many adult congregate living facilities provide van or bus service for transporting residents to grocery stores and shopping malls, or for scheduled outings to concerts, plays, and sightseeing trips. Often residents can make appointments for transportation to doctor and dentist appointments.

Some apartment buildings were not specifically intended for older adults, but long-term tenants grow old over time. Owners or managers may choose to incorporate safety features or offer limited meal service on the premises. However, even when congregate living facilities are designed at the outset to be age segregated, residents' needs can change as time goes by. A cohort of tenants who move into a newly built age-segregated living environment may be healthy and may need only a minimal level of services. In fact, some facilities screen applicants to ensure the older tenants who move in will be able to function with relative independence. As tenants grow older, however, they often need more supportive services.

Lawton, Greenbaum, and Liebowitz (1980) described two different models for older adult housing: **constant housing and accommodating housing.** The constant housing model aims to preserve the original character of the tenants. Tenants may be relatively independent when they move in. Later, if they need more services than are available, they are forced to find alternative housing to secure the level of service they need, and a new cohort of relatively independent

In many adult congregate living facilities, an activities director and committee of older adult residents schedule outings and sight-seeing trips for all who want to participate.

tenants moves in to take their place. In contrast, accommodating housing is more flexible in providing additional services to meet the needs of an aging tenant population. In some cases, arrangements might be made to deliver meal trays to the apartments of residents who are unable to eat in the common dining area because of temporary illness or disability. Or a congregate housing facility that serves only dinner in the common dining area could begin to offer the option of breakfast and lunch as tenants become less capable of preparing meals in their own kitchens. Such flexibility may necessitate physical modifications to the facility because space may have to be added or existing space remodeled for a different use. For example, a large open lobby and lounge area may be converted into an additional common dining area with expanded kitchen facilities. Such physical modifications are easier to make in some congregate living facilities than in others, and accommodations are more feasible when plans for them are included in the original design. Most congregate facilities do not represent either an extreme constant model or an extreme accommodating model. Rather, many fall somewhere in between.

Board and Care Homes and Assisted Living Facilities   A trend in the past several decades in the United States is for older adults who have difficulty managing on their own to move into **board and care homes** (Quadagno, 2002). Most often these are small, privately run homes converted from single-family structures, and many of them serve three or four older adults or individuals of any age who are unable to live independently in the community. A large number of board and care residents are widowed European American women who have no children or any other close kin (Quadagno, 2002). The proprietors of board and care homes provide meals, supervision, and limited assistance with daily activities (Pynoos & Golant, 1996).

Residents of board and care homes tend to be somewhat older than residents of adult congregate living facilities and they usually have lower incomes. Board and care residents share a living room, dining room, kitchen, and bathroom, and many even share bedrooms. Thus, board and care homes have less privacy compared with adult congregate living facilities, in which residents usually have self-contained apartment units. Board and care homes are subject to the licensing regulations of the specific state in which they are located, but many of the smaller ones slip through the cracks and remain uninspected and unlicensed (Kendig & Pynoos, 1996; Quadagno, 2002).

In the United States, **assisted living facilities** are a rapidly growing type of supportive age-segregated living environment (Kendig & Pynoos, 1996). In general, assisted living facilities offer more supportive services than board and care homes do. Also, they are more upscale than board and care homes, mainly serving middle- and upper-income older adults (Pynoos & Golant, 1996). Most assisted living facilities have common dining and lounge areas, but individual residents or couples usually have private rooms with an adjoining bath or efficiency apartments with very limited kitchen facilities. Assisted living combines the privacy of individual apartments with provision of all three meals in a common dining area, housekeeping and laundry service, help with personal care such as bathing and dressing, and staff members to monitor residents' medication on a 24-hour basis. Many offer social programs and exercise classes on the premises, transportation to medical appointments, and occasional social outings.

Nursing Homes   Of all the age-segregated living environments, **nursing homes** provide the most support and they are the most closely regulated in terms of licensing requirements. Many nursing homes have a hospital-like atmosphere compared to assisted living facilities. In addition to meals and personal care, residents receive skilled nursing services around the clock if necessary, and some nursing homes offer several levels of such care. Nursing home residents tend to be physically frail and a high proportion of them also suffer from mental disorders, most commonly Alzheimer's disease and depression (described in Chapter 11). Most nursing home residents need help with activities of daily living (ADLs) such as eating, walking, transferring from a bed to a chair, dressing, bathing, and using a toilet.

In the United States today, nursing homes are an integral part of the managed health care continuum. As mentioned in Chapter 3, Medicare, the federally sponsored health insurance program for those age 65 and over, pays for a certain number of days in a certified nursing home if older adults need rehabilitation following a hospital stay. Some older adults who spend time in a nursing

Many assisted living facilities and nursing homes offer social programs and exercise classes on the premises for the benefit of all the residents.

home immediately following a hospital stay are eventually able to return to less supportive environments such as assisted living facilities, board and care homes, congregate living facilities, or even private homes or apartments. If nursing home care is needed beyond the number of days allowed by Medicare, older adults or their families must bear the expense.

Nursing homes are the most costly form of supportive living environment. Once older adults become personally responsible for payment, many expend their financial resources in a relatively short time. Medicaid, the federal-state-sponsored health insurance program for the economically disadvantaged, will cover nursing home costs once an older adult's savings or monthly income dip below the amount specified by the state in which the older adult lives. Considering the high cost of nursing home care, it is not surprising that Medicaid is the primary payer for nursing home care. In the case of married couples, Medicaid will allow a spouse who lives outside the nursing home to keep whatever income is in his or her own name up to a certain level. A spouse can also keep a house and car as well as savings and assets up to an amount set by each state. The spouse may not be forced into poverty, but in all likelihood his or her standard of living will be greatly reduced. To plan for the possibility that nursing home care will be needed someday, some older and even middle-aged adults purchase long-term-care insurance that will cover some part of the cost of the nursing home. Some policies also include health-care services in living environments other than nursing homes. The educated consumer will discover that long-term care insurance policies vary a great deal both in yearly premiums and in the potential benefits that will be paid.

In general, nursing homes are not a preferred living arrangement, but those who reside in them on a long-term basis usually do so out of necessity. They need the high level of support and the intensive services provided in such an environment. The "Eden Alternative" is a new concept whereby nursing home residents are encouraged to participate in activities such as caring for plants and pets and even volunteering to help in child-care centers that may be located in or near the building (Hooyman & Kiyak, 2002). Control over some part of their environment, if they are capable, will most likely enhance nursing home residents' quality of life.

Continuing Care Retirement Communities Continuing care retirement communities (CCRCs) offer living environments with various levels of support, ranging from independent (often congregate) living to assisted living to nursing home care. All three levels may be located in the same building, but more commonly they are situated in close proximity to one another. In most instances, older adults who move into CCRCs must initially qualify for the independent level. Residents pay an entrance fee that guarantees access to higher levels of care if necessary without their having to relocate. In addition, many CCRCs have monthly fees that remain the same regardless of the level of care the resident needs. CCRCs are a good option for couples because one member of the pair can get a higher level of care if necessary but still remain within close range of the other.

Some CCRCs are run by not-for-profit organizations, but others are run by large for-profit corporations. Particularly for the latter type of CCRC, entrance fees are often high, so residents are usually relatively affluent. By their very nature, CCRCs are accommodating housing environments because as competence declines or improves, residents have access to the level of support they need without having to leave the community. In some CCRCs, residents can get increased care while remaining in their own apartment unit. In others, residents who need more care while recovering from an illness or hospital stay move to the nursing unit or assisted living unit until they are strong enough to return to their own apartments.

In sum, many different living arrangements are available for older adults. A proper match between older adults' needs and preferences is likely to result in the best outcome for their level of functioning and satisfaction with life.

REVISITING THE SELECTIVE OPTIMIZATION WITH COMPENSATION AND ECOLOGICAL MODELS

Employment, retirement, and living arrangements are all aspects of life that can be viewed from the perspective of the SOC Model (Baltes and Baltes, 1990) and the Ecological Model (Lawton, 1989; Lawton & Nahemow, 1973) introduced in Chapter 1. Older workers may optimize their job performance when they compensate for age-related slowing by selecting and concentrating on aspects of their jobs for which they have acquired expertise. In terms of optimal job performance and job satisfaction, older workers will adapt best if their skills and ability levels match the demands of the work environment (Panek, 1997). The challenge of retirement lies in the older adult's success at shaping a life that offers an appropriate level of challenge.

No single living environment is ideal for all older adults. Rather, a living environment that matches an older adult's physical capabilities and social needs will maximize the likelihood of positive adaptation. To achieve optimal adaptation, older adults must select living environments that have sufficient support to compensate for age-related decline in physical capabilities. Environments should not be so demanding that accidents become likely or that the older adult's ability to get around as independently as possible is compromised. For example, a multi-story single family home may present an overwhelming challenge for the older adult with severe arthritis. For such an individual, a one-story residence or an apartment building with an elevator would be more appropriate.

Although some living environments may be too challenging, it is important that there be a sufficient level of challenge for a particular older adult's degree of competence. Older adults who are physically fit and able to participate in community-based activities may not find sufficient challenge in congregate living facilities with on-site meals and social programming. Similarly, older adults who still enjoy cooking and other housekeeping tasks might find too little challenge in an assisted living facility where meals and cleaning services are provided for residents. The better the match between the older adult's competence and the demands of the living environment, the higher the older adult's adaptation and sense of well-being is likely to be.

Most nursing home environments make minimal demands, but older adults who are low in competence may need a high level of technological and medical assistance. A nursing home environment enables residents to compensate for diminished capacity and to concentrate their efforts on a select number of activities that they are still able to perform. A good assisted living or nursing home environment provides physical and social stimulation to help residents optimize their functioning. Such environments offer sufficient challenge to be stimulating and allow older adults to function optimally with as much independence as possible.

KEY POINTS

- In general, age of retirement decreased from the 1950s to 1990s, but there is reason to believe that people will be remaining in the paid labor force to later ages in the near future.
- A number of factors make it difficult to compare young and older workers. In general, older workers have a high level of job commitment and many have developed expertise from years of experience.
- Overall, there is little connection between age and job performance, although older workers benefit more from training when there is less pressure and more time to learn.

- It is illegal to use age in hiring decisions, or to terminate, demote, or reduce the salaries of older workers without showing good cause. Even so, subtle forms of age discrimination still exist in the workplace.
- When workers retire voluntarily, there are no adverse effects on their physical or mental health. Most people adapt well to retirement, keeping very busy with hobbies, educational pursuits, volunteer work, and other activities.
- Most retired Americans receive monthly Social Security benefits from the federal government. Some receive additional benefits from private defined benefit or defined contribution pension plans. The latter are becoming more popular but require financial planning on the part of the worker.
- Some older adults relocate to retirement communities in warm climates, but most stay in the same area where they have always lived. Some age in place, meaning they continue to live in the same housing unit. Others relocate to more supportive living environments.
- Supportive living environments are more likely to be age segregated (for people over a certain age) rather than age integrated (for people of all ages). On a continuum from the least to the most supportive age-segregated living environments are retirement communities and retirement hotels, adult congregate living facilities, board and care homes and assisted living facilities, and nursing homes.

KEY TERMS

adult congregate living facilities   398

Age Discrimination in Employment Act (ADEA)   378

age-integrated housing   393

age-segregated housing   393

aging in place   393

assisted living facilities   400

board and care homes   400

busy ethic   389

constant housing and accommodating housing   398

continuing care retirement communities (CCRCs)   402

defined benefit pension plans   384

defined contribution pension plans   384

Elderhostel   391

nursing homes   400

retirement   381

retirement communities   397

retirement hotels   396

Social Security   383

To learn more about the issues discussed in this chapter, point your browser to http://www.infotrac-college.com and use the passcode from the InfoTrac College Edition card that came with your book. InfoTrac College Edition gives you access to complete articles from many different journals.

Mental Health Services, Psychopathology, and Therapy

11

Sidney just turned 67 and he has always had an active and busy life. He cannot imagine a time when he no longer has to wake up on schedule and get to the office five mornings a week. Lately, however, Sidney has been forgetting things he never had trouble remembering before. For example, he left the keys to his office at home, he missed an important meeting at work, and once he even forgot his long-time administrative assistant's name. After working a full day, Sidney never used to have difficulties with sleep, but lately he has been waking up at 3 a.m. and cannot get back to sleep. Sidney has experienced several traumatic events in the past six months. He lost his sister, who died suddenly of an aneurysm, and several of his closest friends moved to Florida. He does not know whether his forgetting and sleep problems could be due to these losses, or whether they are just part of getting older. He worries too that he might have the beginnings of Alzheimer's disease, which he has heard so much about in the news. Sidney does not like to admit to any weakness, but he hopes he can get up the courage to mention his forgetting and sleep problems to the doctor when he goes in for his next regular checkup.

OLDER ADULTS AND MENTAL HEALTH SERVICES

In large-scale surveys, a high proportion of older adults report being happy and satisfied with their lives (Hinrichsen & Dick-Siskin, 2000), and most have satisfying relationships with family and friends and can manage their lives effectively. The overall rate of mental disorders is not any higher, and by some measures it is even lower, in older adulthood than it is in young adulthood. In fact, most older adults cope amazingly well with the changes that occur in late life. Loss of a long-term marital partner often occurs in the older adult years, and the onset of health problems can bring physical limitations, particularly in the old-old (75–84 years) and even more so in the oldest-old (85+ years) age groups. Many older adults experience pain from arthritis and other physical problems, which may restrict their activities. Some older adults find that they can no longer live with complete independence and it may become increasingly difficult for them to maintain themselves in the familiar house or apartment where they have resided for years or decades. Some relocate to living situations that place them close to sources of help (see Chapter 10 for more on living arrangements) but far from familiar neighbors and friends. The fact that most older adults are able to adjust to these changes is a testament to their mental health.

At the same time, it is important to recognize that some older adults do need mental health services and a minority have diagnosable psychiatric disorders (Hinrichsen & Dick-Siskin, 2000). The American Psychological Association published an edited volume entitled *Emerging issues in mental health and aging* (Gatz, 1995) that reported the proceedings of a conference sponsored by the Coalition on Mental Health and Aging. In the preface of this volume, editor Dr. Margaret Gatz points out that the majority of older adults do not have mental disorders but "a significant portion do have serious mental health needs that have major effects on individuals, their families, and society" (p. xv). This chapter is about these older adults.

Rate of Mental Disorders Among Older Adults

What proportion of older adults do have mental disorders? Several decades ago, Dye (1978) estimated that the percentage ranged from 12 percent to 22 percent. More recent estimates range from 18 percent to 28 percent (Gatz, 1995; Gatz & Finkel, 1995; Gatz & Smyer, 1992, 2001). As far as actual numbers, one projection made in 1995 estimated that by the year 2000, approximately seven million older adults would have mental health problems that warrant professional mental health services (Gatz, 1995). However, the number of older adults with mental health problems could be even greater in the years beyond 2000 simply because the proportion and number of older Americans is increasing (Gatz, 1995). In 1995, one in eight Americans was over the age of 65, but members of the baby boom generation (born between 1946 and 1964) are set to enter older adulthood between the years of 2010 and 2030, at which time approximately one in five Americans will be over the age of 65. This translates into greater numbers and more older adults who are likely to need mental health services.

Not only will the number of older adults increase, but also a higher proportion of them may need mental health services for two reasons. First, members of the baby boom generation have already shown relatively high rates of depression, anxiety, and substance abuse, and their mental health problems are likely to follow them into old age (Gatz & Smyer, 2001). Second, more individuals are living into the oldest-old (85+) age range. As discussed later in this chapter, the incidence of dementia, one of the most prevalent mental disorders in the older adult population, escalates with increasing age. If no effective cure or preventive measures become available in the near future, the number of individuals with dementia will be higher than it is today.

Older Adults and the Mental Health System

More than two decades ago, Dye (1978) pointed out that even though 12 to 22 percent of older adults were suffering from psychological problems, only 2 percent of the clients receiving mental health services on an outpatient basis in the clinics or offices of private mental health practitioners fell into the older-adult age range. Moreover, a considerable proportion of older adults included in the 2 percent only received routine diagnostic assessment as opposed to any type of ongoing treatment.

With the recent focus on successful aging, the provision of mental health services for older adults is receiving more attention. Even so, the resources devoted to older adults still fall short of the estimated needs of this age group (Gatz, 1995; Gatz & Finkel, 1995). Furthermore, the mental health resources available to older adults may not be distributed equitably across all socioeconomic and ethnic groups in American society. Lower education and income levels are associated with higher incidence of mental health disorders in the older-adult age group (Gatz & Smyer, 2001). Yet individuals with little education and limited income have less access to services. Also, compared with older adults as a whole, older members of minority groups—for example, African

Americans, Hispanic Americans, Asian Americans and Native Americans—are especially underserved by the mental health system (Butler, Lewis, & Sunderland, 1998). This could be due to economics as well as to language and cultural barriers. These minority groups are not sufficiently represented among mental health workers, nor is the delivery of mental health services always tailored to the needs of specific minority groups (Butler et al., 1998).

Still, even European American older adults are underserved by the mental health system. A number of factors may be barriers to their receipt of mental health services. Some have to do with the nature of the health-care system, some to the attitudes and behavior of mental health professionals, and some to the attitudes and behavior of older adults themselves.

The Health-Care System   Policies for the delivery of mental health services generally reflect the policies and systems used to administer general health-care services. In the United States, the movement toward managed health care will probably become even more widespread in the future. This means that older adults with mental health problems are most likely to have their initial contact with nonspecialists. Gatz and Finkel (1995) estimate that only 32 percent of community-living older adults who need mental health care actually receive it from mental health professionals. Another 31 percent are treated mainly with medication by primary care physicians, while 37 percent receive no care at all. These statistics illustrate why it is important for primary care physicians to be sensitive to mental health problems and to recognize when mental health referrals are appropriate. Clearly, there is a need for training in gerontology and geriatrics for general medical personnel as well as mental health professionals who are expected to serve older adult clients (Gatz & Finkel, 1995).

Medicare, the federal government-sponsored health insurance program that covers a large proportion of adults ages 65 and over in the United States, is similar to most health insurance programs in covering more costs for inpatient hospital care than for outpatient community-based care. However, even for inpatient care, there is pressure to limit the length of hospital stays, including those for psychiatric diagnoses.

A deinstitutionalization movement that began in the 1960s has resulted in a drastic decline in admissions to mental institutions (Gatz & Smyer, 1992). Today, very few people are life-long or even long-term residents of mental institutions. Individuals with mental disorders may be hospitalized for a short time while they receive acute care. Many are discharged without an adequate plan for rehabilitation, which could partially explain the growing number of homeless individuals who populate the streets of major urban areas. Also, pressure for quick, cost-effective treatment often means greater reliance on medication and less emphasis on psychosocial therapy despite evidence of its effectiveness by itself or in combination with other treatments (Gatz & Finkel, 1995). Psychosocial therapy is free from the side effects that can occur with medication, and it can help patients develop skills for coping if problems recur in the future.

While mental institutions have been downsizing, the nursing home industry has been thriving. In recent years, there is an increasing trend for nursing homes to serve as outlets for acute care hospitals, which are under pressure from insurers to discharge elderly patients who may be in need of continued mental health services. To a large extent, nursing homes have replaced the old state and county institutions as the primary setting for older adults with mental disorders.

As described in Chapter 3, Medicaid is the joint federal and state program that pays for nursing home care for older Americans who have expended their financial resources down to a specified state-mandated level. Guidelines for Medicaid reimbursement to nursing homes limit the proportion of residents who have mental disorders as their primary diagnosis. For this reason, the actual percent of nursing home residents with mental disorders is difficult to determine (Gatz & Smyer, 1992). However, it is estimated that 50 percent of nursing home residents suffer from at least one form of mental disorder (Butler et al., 1998). Even so, active psychosocial treatment programs for mental disorders are generally less available in nursing homes than they might be in hospitals or institutions specifically devoted to the treatment of mental disorders. There is a great need for training programs for nursing home staff members who have daily contact with older residents. Foundations such as Robert Wood Johnson have responded to this need by funding programs for research and training in teaching nursing homes, which offer rotations for medical students as well as internships for psychology trainees.

Therapists   The number of psychologists who provide mental health services for older adults is not sufficient to meet the estimated need of individuals in this age group (Gatz & Finkel, 1995). In addition, only a small proportion of psychologists who do serve older adult clients have received specialized training in clinical geropsychology (James & Haley, 1995).

A number of recent plans have been implemented to remedy such training deficiencies. More internships that provide exposure to older adult patients are now available to clinical psychology graduate students. Also, psychologists with established clinical practices have opportunities for training in the specialized needs of older adult clients. Two divisions of the American Psychological Association (Division 20, Adult Development and Aging, and Division 12 Section II, Clinical Geropsychology) are cooperating in efforts to offer continuing education workshops to psychologists and other professionals who want to develop skills for effective work with older adults. The 1997–1998 President of the American Psychological Association (APA) published a booklet describing what practitioners should know about working with older adults (Abeles, 1997).

Therapists who are not trained in how to work with older clients may view mental and emotional difficulties as an inevitable outcome of old age. Those with limited exposure to older adults may assume that their efforts are better spent helping children and young adults, who they assume will reap the benefits of therapy over many more years of improved functioning. Yet, increases in life expectancy mean that more individuals will live well into older adulthood and are capable of enjoying a high quality of life for many years. Also, the positive effect that therapy can have on the health and emotional well-being of older adults often extends to family, friends, and the community.

Aside from lack of exposure and limited training, what are some other reasons therapists may be reluctant to work with older adults? Some considerations are practical. There have been fewer test norms available for assessing older adults, which makes it more challenging to interpret their test results. However, this situation is improving as more tests are developed with the elderly in mind. Also, older adults' problems often require more time to assess and treat than do the problems of young and middle-aged adults (Zarit & Haynie, 2000). Older adults often fatigue more easily than young adults do, so more sessions may be required for them to complete a battery of tests or possibly to benefit from therapeutic techniques. The greater expenditure of time needed to assess and treat older adult clients may not be reflected in reimbursement payments from insurance carriers, which could render practice with older adults less attractive.

Some therapists shy away from older clients for reasons other than practical ones. If therapists have had complicated relationships with their own parents, it may be difficult for them to avoid projecting their feelings onto older adult clients (Hinrichsen & Dick-Siskin, 2000). Also, working with older adults may raise therapists' own fears about the prospect of aging, and some of them could experience anxiety when dealing with issues of mortality and dependency (Knight, 1996). Furthermore, not all therapists are comfortable discussing issues related to sexuality with older adult clients. Yet issues of mortality, dependency, and sexuality are often of great concern to older adults who are adjusting to illness, decline in physical functioning, and loss of a longtime marital partner.

James and Haley (1995) conducted a survey in which 400 practicing clinical psychologists read a vignette that described symptoms of depression experienced by a younger (age 35) or older (age 70) individual (target person). The younger or older target person was also described either as being in good health or having congenital heart disease. There was evidence for age bias ("ageism"), with clinicians offering a poorer prognosis for the older target than for the younger target. However, evidence for health bias ("healthism") was even stronger. Compared with healthy targets, unhealthy targets were perceived as much less likely to benefit from therapy. Also, the clinicians reported that they would feel less comfortable treating targets who had health problems than those who did not. James and Haley concluded that older adults in poor health have double jeopardy with regard to receiving mental health services.

Assessing older adults' need for mental health services can be complex. Therapists who work with older adults must have basic knowledge about physical illnesses that commonly occur in older adulthood. Also, they must be familiar with the side effects of medications used to treat those illnesses, and in some instances they must be able to communicate effectively with the older adult client's physician (Knight, 1996). In addition to possible health problems, many older adults have experienced traumatic events such as hospitalization or bereavement. When developing treatment plans for older adult clients, Knight (1996) suggests that therapists make use of a decision tree, which is based on a biopsychosocial model that considers older clients' medical, social service, and psychological needs (see Figure 11.1).

Figure 11.1   Decision Tree for Assessment of Older Adults

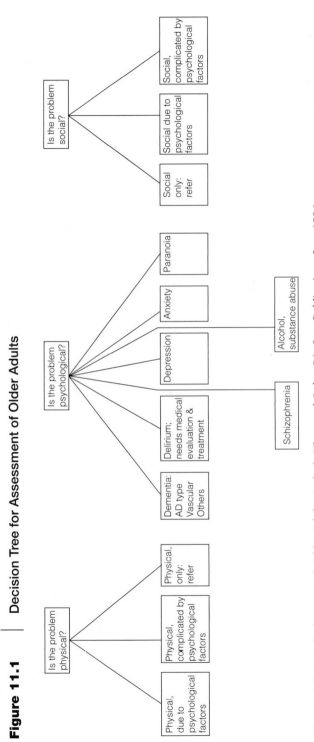

From Knight, *Psychotherapy with Older Adults*, 2nd ed., Thousand Oaks, CA: Sage Publications, Inc., 1996.

Ethics considerations are often more complicated when therapists treat older adult clients than when they treat young or middle-aged clients (Knight, 1996). Prior to treatment, clients must give informed consent. This could present some difficulty if the therapist suspects that a potential client is suffering from mild cognitive impairment or dementia (discussed later in this chapter), which could preclude a full understanding of what consent means. Cognitive capabilities could also be an important factor in determining whether older adults will derive any benefit from a particular type of therapeutic intervention.

It is not uncommon for older adults to be brought to a therapist by family members such as adult children. Under these circumstances, the therapist must be certain that the older adult has consented to therapy without undue pressure. It is important for the therapist to discuss with the older-adult client exactly what the therapy will entail, and there should be some agreement between the therapist and older-adult client about the goal of the therapy (Knight, 1996). In addition, the therapist must be aware of any difficulties the older client may have with vision or hearing that could affect communication. (See Chapter 4 for discussion of age-related changes in vision and hearing.) In sum, therapy that is tailored to the older adult's sensory and cognitive capabilities has the greatest chance of yielding a positive outcome.

Sometimes therapists are pressured by family members to report on an older client's progress. This is especially likely to happen when family members are paying for the service or providing transportation to the therapy sessions. In most cases, the therapist should only comply with such requests with the older client's consent or agreement. Therapists must be aware of current ethical standards and locally applicable laws on when it is appropriate to communicate with family members about the evaluation of the older adult client (Knight, personal communication).

In some instances, it may be appropriate for family members to attend some or all of the therapy sessions. When this occurs, the therapist must take special care to make eye contact with and direct comments to the older adult as well as to the other family member(s) so that the older adult will not feel that he or she is being ignored or discounted by the therapist (Hinrichsen & Dick-Siskin, 2000).

Older Adults   Older adults do not always make full use of the mental health services available to them for several reasons. First, psychotherapy is relatively costly, especially when retired older adults are living on fixed incomes. For many retirees, economic resources are stretched to the limit with payments for housing, food, and medication needs. In recent years, Medicare has increased coverage for outpatient mental health services. However, co-insurance payments may still be high for many older adults, especially those who are members of economically disadvantaged racial or ethnic groups.

However, even when older adults can afford mental health services, they do not always take advantage of the opportunity. Older adults who lived through the Great Depression may not see the value of monetary expenditures on mental health services (Zarit & Haynie, 2000). In addition, individuals who reached older adulthood in the 1980s and 1990s are often more hesitant compared to younger adults to acknowledge that they are having psychological problems

(Knight, 1996). Throughout their lifetime, these older adults were less exposed to information on mental health. They did not have the access so readily available today to radio and television programs that deal openly with mental health issues, and there were fewer references to mental health issues in newspapers and magazines. In other words, the older adults of today are less *psychologized* than young or even middle-aged adults are.

At the extreme end of the continuum, some individuals in the present older adult cohort fear that seeking mental health services will result in their being locked up in an asylum. In their view, a therapist is needed only if a person is crazy. A less extreme but perhaps more common point of view is that seeking mental health assistance is an admission of personal or moral failure (Hinrichsen & Dick-Siskin, 2000).

Today's older adults have been socialized to seek help for physical problems more than they have for mental health problems. In fact, their psychological problems may manifest themselves in bodily, or somatic, complaints. Also, many older adults have a long-term relationship with a medical doctor, and they are more comfortable going to a family physician with their problems than they would be visiting a mental health clinic. As the health-care system becomes more dominated by managed care, however, long-term relationships with familiar family physicians will become less and less common (Knight, 1996).

However, older adults are not necessarily opposed to mental health services. In a written survey conducted on over 500 well-educated older residents of an affluent retirement community in Florida, the majority of respondents acknowledged that "good psychological health is important for physical health," that "people should do things to improve their mental health," and that "people should seek professional help when they have problems" (Haley, Robb-Belcher, Becker, & Polivka, 1999). Despite their relative financial affluence, however, these survey participants were still concerned about the cost of such treatment, and most of them claimed they would seek mental health services only if problems were severe. Not surprisingly, their preference was to consult first with the family physician, and most said that they would prefer to use mental health services if these were on the same site where their family physician practiced.

Even when they are experiencing mental difficulties, some older adults deny they need help because they are motivated to maintain their independence and they think that seeking out mental health services means they are surrendering their personal freedom. But fear of losing their independence is not the only reason older adults do not seek outpatient mental health services. Another reason is that compared to young and middle-aged adults, many older adults are not as integrated into the social system. Older adults may be retired from the workforce, their social circle may be reduced by virtue of long-time friends' moving or passing away, and they may not live in close proximity to family members. When older adults are not socially embedded, there is little pressure for them to get help when they do have problems. In contrast, young and middle-aged adults who experience difficulties are more likely to be noticed. Their performance in the workplace can suffer and their employer may put them on notice. If their problems are affecting their school-age children, pressure may be placed on them to get help.

Undoubtedly, as older-adult cohorts become more educated and exposed to factual information about mental health, they will become more accepting of mental health services. Greater acceptance, combined with adequate insurance payments, should increase the likelihood that future cohorts of older adults will take advantage of mental health services when necessary.

PSYCHOPATHOLOGY

Most older adults are mentally healthy, but now we will focus on the portion of them who suffer from mental disorders. It is not easy to determine the incidence of mental disorders across the adult life span partly because most epidemiological studies have been cross-sectional (Gatz, Kasl-Godley, & Karel, 1996). Cross-sectional epidemiological studies evaluate the prevalence and features of mental disorders experienced by large numbers of young, middle-aged, and older adults at one specific time. (Chapter 2 discusses cross-sectional studies.) A cross-sectional study is guided by the version of the American Psychiatric Association's *Diagnostic and statistical manual of mental disorders* (DSM) that is in use when the study is conducted. Since 1980, the *Diagnostic and statistical manual* has been revised three times (DSM-III in 1980; DSM-III-R in 1987; and DSM-IV in 1994), and the nomenclature and diagnostic criteria for mental disorders varies across versions of the DSM. Therefore, it is difficult to compare epidemiological data obtained from cross-sectional studies conducted at different times using different versions of the DSM to define mental disorders.

The current version, **DSM-IV** (American Psychiatric Association, 1994), uses a classification system with the following five axes: (1) a list of clinical syndromes, (2) a list of developmental (mental retardation) and personality disorders, (3) a list of physical disorders/general medical conditions, (4) a checklist of psychosocial stressors, and (5) a Global Assessment of Functioning Scale. On Axis I, which is the focus here, no distinction is made between functional and organic disorders as was made in earlier versions of the DSM (Butler et al., 1998).

Although exact determinations of the prevalence of mental disorders in the older age group are difficult to make, there are estimates. For a combination of community-living and institutional populations ages 65+, one estimate is that 22 percent meet the criteria for some type of mental disorder when both emotional dysfunction and cognitive impairment are included (Gatz & Smyer, 1992, 2001). This figure is similar to the estimated rate of 17–22 percent for individuals age 18 and over who meet the criteria for mental disorder. Thus, the proportion of the population who suffer from mental disorders does not seem to vary greatly with age. However, different disorders may predominate at different points in the life span (Gatz et al., 1996).

Diathesis-Stress as a Developmental Model

The likelihood that a particular individual will suffer from a mental disorder can be viewed using a **diathesis-stress model.** Diathesis refers to an individual's level of vulnerability (for example, genetic propensities, acquired biological vulnerability, or psychological factors). Stress refers to the occurrence of negative events (for

Figure 11.2 | The Diathesis-Stress Model

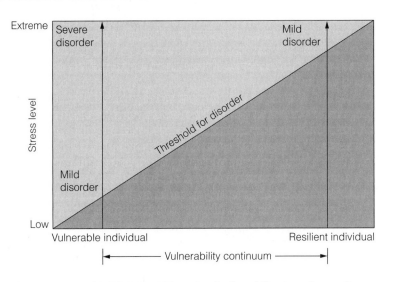

From R. E. Ingram and J. M. Price, "The role of vulnerability in understanding psychopathology," in Ingram and Price (eds.) *Vulnerability to Psychotherapy: Risk across the lifespan,* Guilford Publications, 2001.

example, loss of a loved one, loss of a job, stress in a particular living situation). The diathesis-stress model, illustrated in Figure 11.2, has been used as a framework for studying disorders such as depression (Monroe & Simons, 1991). In Figure 11.2, level of stress from low to high appears on the vertical axis of the graph. Diathesis, or vulnerability, is shown on the horizontal axis of the graph ranging from the most vulnerable individual (high diathesis) on the left to the most resilient individual (low diathesis) on the right. Individuals with high diathesis are sensitive to stressful conditions and succumb to a disorder even when the level of stress is not very high. Those with low diathesis can withstand higher levels of stress without succumbing to a disorder, and if they do succumb, the disorder may be relatively mild and may not last very long. Careful consideration of age-related and/or cohort-related differences in diathesis, as well as the likelihood of exposure to stress at different stages of development, could increase our understanding of why some types of mental disorder occur more frequently in the older adult age group (Gatz et al., 1996).

Several possible patterns can characterize the mental disorders seen in older adulthood (Gatz et al., 1996). First, disorders may be long-standing, beginning earlier in life and simply continuing into the older adult years. Second, disorders may have an initial onset early in life and may recur periodically over the life span and into old age. Third, mental disorders may occur for the first time in older adulthood. Finally, mental disorders may have existed earlier in life, but in later adulthood there is no evidence of psychopathology. It is possible that factors related to stress increase or decrease over the adult life span. However, the individual with a high diathesis would be especially vulnerable when stress does occur. It is also conceivable that an individual's diathesis can fluctuate over the adult years. Longitudinal studies following the same people over time would be ideal for ascertaining patterns of mental disorders without relying on retrospective self-reports about what individuals say they were like at earlier points in their lives. (Chapter 2 discusses the longitudinal method.)

A number of the mental disorders listed on Axis I of the DSM-IV are seen in adults of all ages, but the following sections describe those of the greatest concern for the older age group. First we will discuss depression, which is one of the most frequent mental disorders in older adulthood.

Depression

Depression is as an affective, or mood, disturbance. The psychological symptoms of depression include painful sadness, feelings of emptiness, irritability, generalized withdrawal of interest and pleasure in activities that were enjoyed previously, pessimism, diminished self-esteem and feelings of guilt, worthlessness, hopelessness, and helplessness. Depression can also be associated with bodily, or somatic, symptoms, such as feelings of fatigue and loss of energy, sleep difficulties, changes in appetite and weight, and bowel disturbance. Furthermore, depression can be accompanied by cognitive difficulties such as problems with attention, concentration, and memory, as well as a slowing down of speech, thought, and decision making.

Prevalence   Estimates of the prevalence of depression in community-living older adults have varied widely. A number of epidemiological studies report a lower incidence of major depressive disorders among older adults than among younger adults, with only 2.5 percent of the older adult population meeting the DSM-IV diagnostic criteria for depression (Gatz et al., 1996). However, the incidence of depression is higher when surveys define depression more broadly and make determinations of depression by asking participants to complete brief symptom checklists. In these broad surveys, as many as 27 percent of older adult respondents have reported at least some symptoms of depression (Koenig & Blazer, 1996). A panel on the diagnosis and treatment of depression that convened at a National Institutes of Health conference estimated that symptoms of depression occur in approximately 15 percent of community-living residents over the age of 65 but in up to 25 percent of older adult nursing home residents (Friedhoff, 1994).

When depression is defined broadly, the highest scores on symptom checklists are found among young adults and adults over the age of 75 (Blazer, Burchett, Service & George, 1991). In one cross-sectional study, Gatz and Hurwicz (1990) analyzed 548 community-living older adults' responses on the Center for Epidemiological Studies Depression Scale (CES-D), a self-report questionnaire used in many large-scale studies on depression. Depression scores declined from early adulthood to late middle age but then increased after the age of 75. However, the reason for depressive symptoms may differ for young adults and adults over the age of 75, who are more likely to be suffering from physical illness.

Depression has been differentiated into primary and secondary categories (Cohen, 1990). Primary depression occurs in the absence of physical disorders or drug side effects. Secondary depression either accompanies or can be traced to bodily illness or adverse reactions to medication. Studies that report low rates of depression among older adults usually limit the definition of depression to the primary category. Studies reporting higher rates of depression among older adults generally include both primary and secondary categories. Some of the symptoms commonly associated with depression in older adults are difficult to differentiate from symptoms of physical illness such as cancer and heart disease or from side effects of medications used to treat physical illness.

Depression is not a normal part of aging. However, it is one of the most frequent emotional disorders experienced by the older adult population (Wykle, Segall, & Nagley, 1992). In individuals over the age of 65, unipolar depressive disorder is more common than bipolar disorder, which is characterized by manic-depressive mood swings (Gatz et al., 1996). On the positive side, depression is one of the most treatable mental health problems experienced by older adults (Butler et al., 1998; Gatz & Hurwicz, 1990). Unfortunately, however, it is estimated that only 10 percent of depressed older adults receive treatment (Schneider, 1995).

Risk Factors   There are a number of risk factors for depression in older adulthood. One is being female. Overall, more women than men report symptoms of depression. However, this trend may be reversed after the age of 80, at which point the prevalence of depression appears to be higher in men (LaRue, Dessonville, & Jarvik, L. F., 1985). Another risk factor is chronic physical illness. Given their relatively high incidence of physical illness and use of medication, older adults are more at risk for secondary depression than any other age group (Cohen, 1990). As many as 50 percent of older adults with a chronic physical illness suffer from depression (Schneider, 1995). Depression often coexists with heart disease, stroke, cancer, diabetes, and painful conditions such as arthritis. However, it is not always clear whether depression is an outcome of physical illness or whether depression increases an older adult's vulnerability to physical illness.

Stressful events involving loss are another risk factor for depression. Aging may bring loss of physical vigor, loss of the work role and associated loss of income because of retirement, loss of community because of relocation, loss of loved ones (often a spouse), and a general reduction in social contacts. When social contacts are reduced, some older adults are hesitant to express feelings of anger for fear of alienating the few people left in their lives. Their angry feelings may be turned inward, which is another risk factor for depression (Cohen, 1990). Considering the losses and life changes that can occur in older adulthood, it is a testimony to older adults' strength and adaptability that only a minority become clinically depressed.

Another risk factor for depression is being the sole caregiver of a chronically ill family member. Many older adults, particularly women, care for spouses or other relatives who have physical illnesses or cognitive disorders such as dementia, which is described later in this chapter. Caregiver burden resulting from heavy responsibility and accompanying social isolation is a potential source of depression (Hinrichsen & Dick-Siskin, 2000).

With regard to caregiver burden, ethnic group membership may be an important factor. Thus far, most caregiver burden research has been conducted on European American caregivers whose family members have been diagnosed with dementia. Less is known about the effects of caregiving among African American, Hispanic American, Asian American, and Native American groups. Roth, Haley, Owen, Clay, and Goode (2001) followed African American and European American caregivers, all of whom had a family member diagnosed with dementia, most often Alzheimer's disease. At three different times over the two years of the study, caregivers from both ethnic groups completed self-report measures regarding their own depression and life satisfaction as well as their own physical health symptoms. For caregivers from both ethnic groups, physical symptoms increased over time. However, compared to the African American caregivers, the European American caregivers sustained higher levels of elevated depression and a greater decline in life satisfaction over time. The African American caregivers appeared to experience less psychological stress even though they had just as many physical symptoms as the European American caregivers did. Roth et al. speculate that the African American caregivers' psychological resiliency may be attributable to family role expectations, prior experience with stress, or stronger spiritual beliefs.

Aranda and Knight (1997) reviewed what is known about the stress, or burden, experienced by Hispanic American caregivers. However, it is important to recognize that caregivers from different ethnic groups minister to family members whose disabilities vary. For example, diabetes and diabetes-related complications, which result in visual impairment and amputation, are more prevalent among Hispanic Americans than among European Americans. Thus, Hispanic American caregivers are more often responsible for family members with diabetes, which tends to occur earlier in the adult life span compared to disorders such as Alzheimer's disease.

Much remains to be learned about the physical and mental health of older African American, Hispanic American, Asian American, and Native American caregivers. There is some evidence that family solidarity is stronger and family support systems are more readily available to moderate the effects of stressful life events in these groups than they are for European American caregivers. At the same time, however, socioeconomic factors may limit the access ethnic minority groups have to services that could alleviate any caregiving burden they do experience. There is a clear need for further research on the relative importance of family relationships and access to services for various racial and ethnic groups. Meanwhile, we should avoid generalizing the findings of studies that have been conducted on African Americans or Hispanic Americans who live in one geographic area to members of these ethnic groups from other parts of the country (Aranda & Knight, 1997).

Diagnosis and Treatment   Depression can be difficult to diagnose in the older adult population, and sometimes neither depressed older adults nor their families or health care workers recognize the symptoms. As described earlier, depression in older adults can co-exist with one or more physical illness, and the symptoms of depression may be interpreted as physical illness (Schneider, 1995). In fact, some older adults who seem to be in a state of vague physical decline may actually be suffering from depression (Cohen, 1990). There is a common assumption that fatigue, sleep problems, and feelings of sadness are simply a normal consequence of aging, but such symptoms may signify depression (LaRue et al., 1985). Additionally, it can be difficult to determine when older adults' grief reactions constitute a normal response to loss and at what point they are a sign of depression. For all of these reasons, depression may be *underdiagnosed,* and thus remain untreated, in the older adult population (LaRue et al., 1985).

Just as depression may be underdiagnosed in older adults, it may also be overdiagnosed. The term *overdiagnosis* refers to a readiness to diagnose depression when symptoms could actually stem from another source. Changes in appetite, bowel, and sleep habits can be part of the normal aging process, but many self-report depression scales include items that ask about somatic complaints. If a diagnosis of depression is based on the number of such items that are endorsed, then depression may be overdiagnosed in older adults.

In a 30-item Geriatric Depression Screening (GDS) scale developed specifically for older adult populations, the items de-emphasize bodily questions and focus on test takers' feelings (Yesavage, 1982–1983). Two examples of the "yes/no" questions on the GDS are as follows (a "yes" answer to the first question and a "no" answer to the second one would be counted toward an overall depression score):

- "Do you feel your situation is hopeless?"
- "Are you in good spirits most of the time?"

With regard to cognitive symptoms, older adults often complain about memory. Normal aging may be associated with some decline in memory functioning. However, depression may be overdiagnosed if older adults' memory complaints are always interpreted as a sign of depression. On the other hand, health-care workers untrained to work with older adults often assume that older adults who complain about memory are suffering from dementia (Knight, 1996). If cognitive symptoms are automatically considered a sign of dementia when they are actually a sign of depression, then depression is underdiagnosed and the appropriate treatment intervention will probably not occur. In sum, cognitive symptoms can signify more than one potential problem, so making a **differential diagnosis** (that is, determining the exact basis for a particular constellation of symptoms) can be challenging.

Those trained in evaluating older adults are often able to make the subtle distinction between depression and dementia. For example, depressed older adults may score better than older adults with dementia do when given multiple-choice memory tests that require a reduced level of cognitive effort. (See Chapter 5 for discussion of recognition and recall tests of memory.) Also, depressed older adults may be able to improve their scores on memory tests when given more time to respond, whereas older adults with dementia usually continue to perform poorly on memory tests even when they are allowed additional time. Differential diagnosis is even more complicated when older adults are suffering from a combination of depression and dementia. In some instances, depression has been known to herald the onset of dementia (Cohen, 1990; Gatz et al., 1996; Smyer & Qualls, 1999). In sum, therapists who work with older adults must consider multiple factors when making a diagnosis and planning appropriate treatment.

Once diagnosed accurately, how is depression treated? Treatment interventions for depression include drug therapy (often antidepressant medications) and electroconvulsive therapy (ECT). ECT ("shock therapy") is reserved for severe episodes of depression or cases in which drug therapy is not effective or cannot be administered because of co-existing medical conditions (King & Markus, 2000). For long-term maintenance of functioning, psychological therapies have proven useful, either alone or in combination with drug therapy. One psychological intervention that has shown promise for older adults suffering from depression is based on a cognitive-behavioral model (Dick, Gallagher-Thompson, & Thompson, 1999; King & Markus, 2000). Older adult clients are encouraged to identify which aspects of their lives they think can be changed. They are encouraged to keep track of the relationship between their behavior and their mood and also to avoid self-defeating thoughts and behavior. With cognitive-behavioral therapy, older adults are trained to take an active role in setting treatment goals, which include monitoring any negative patterns of thinking and making plans for how to handle future stressful events.

Suicide   Suicide is the voluntary termination of one's life, and it is considered a behavior rather than a mental disorder. However, suicide is often associated with mental illness. It can be viewed as a final act driven by intolerable psychological pain and feelings of hopelessness (Blazer & Koenig, 1996).

Suicidal ideas and/or actions often accompany severe depression (Duberstein & Conwell, 2000). Attempts to commit suicide may be direct, or there may just be a passive wish for death. With regard to direct attempts, gunshot wounds are the most common means used by older men, whereas drugs and poisons are the most common means used by older women. Less direct methods include refusal to seek advice for medical care or failure to follow a prescribed medical regimen for a serious medical condition (Blazer & Koenig, 1996; Cohen, 1990).

Reports of attempted suicide are less common in the older adult age group than in the young adult age group. In other words, older adults who set out to commit suicide are more likely than young adults are to complete the act. According to Conwell (1994), the rate of completed suicides for older people is more than twice that of the general population (26.5 per 100,000 in 80- to 84-year-olds, versus 12.4 per 100,000 for all age groups). Between 1974 and 1987, the suicide rate in the industrialized developed world increased at a faster pace among people ages 75+ than it did for any other age group (Blazer & Koenig, 1996). However, this increase was mainly for older European American men, who appear to be at the highest risk for completed suicide (Duberstein & Conwell, 2000). There is some evidence that suicide is less likely in older adults who practice religion, attend church frequently, and take an active role in church-related activities (Duberstein, Evinger, & Conwell, 2002).

Approximately three-fourths of older adults who commit suicide have paid a visit to a primary care physician in the month prior to taking their owns lives (Conwell, 1994). Such individuals were probably suffering from moderate to severe depression, but their depressive symptoms may have gone unrecognized and untreated. Many older adults, especially older men, do not report sadness or other symptoms, which makes it more difficult for health care providers to detect depression (Duberstein & Conwell, 2000). Allen-Burge, Storandt, Kinscherf, and Rubin (1994) asked 200 hospitalized geriatric psychiatric patients to complete self-report depression scales. Even though all of the study participants were being treated for depression, the male patients were less likely than the female patients to be identified as depressed on the basis of their responses to the depression scales. Yet older men are at greater risk for suicide compared to older women.

The lower rate of suicide among older women even though they are more likely than older men to be diagnosed with depression could be related to several factors. One is that throughout their adult years, women are more likely than men are to shift roles or hold more than one role at the same time. Shifting roles and holding multiple roles such as worker, parent, and homemaker may foster coping skills that buffer women against the potential peril of suicide (Kline, 1975). Another factor is that women are more likely than men to have a social network outside the marital relationship (Bengston, Rosenthal, & Burton, 1996), so women have more social resources at their disposal. When they are feeling downhearted, they are more apt than older men are to express their feelings and get emotional support from others. Perhaps older women's social resources and coping strategies prevent them from reaching the point of hopelessness that leads to suicide.

An additional factor that could play a role in suicide is that some of the physical illnesses older adults experience can cause extreme pain and accompanying feelings of helplessness and hopelessness. Under such circumstances, older adults may view suicide as a rational alternative to extreme suffering or a life of complete dependence upon others for physical care (Knight, 1996).

Anxiety Disorders

Compared with depression, anxiety has received less attention in the older adult population. Symptoms of anxiety include impairment in concentration, attention, and memory, dizziness, severe insomnia, and disabling fear (Schneider, 1995). **Anxiety disorders** include generalized anxiety disorder, phobic disorders, obsessive-compulsive disorder, and post-traumatic stress disorder (Schneider, 1995). Older adults may suffer from anxiety because of situational factors. However, anxiety may occur for no apparent reason; when it does, it can severely disable older adults who might otherwise function adequately (Schneider, 1995).

Factors associated with anxiety disorder include alcohol abuse and dependence (discussed later in this chapter), sedative or hypnotic abuse and dependence, chronic pain, sleep disorders, various medical illnesses, and the use of certain prescription medications (Schneider, 1995). However, diagnosing anxiety disorders in older adults can be particularly challenging. First, anxiety can coexist with depression (Gatz et al., 1996; Knight, 1996), and sometimes the symptoms of these two disorders overlap. As with depression, anxiety reactions can be associated with changes in cognitive functioning such as inability to concentrate or remember. Second, the symptoms of both anxiety and depression can mimic the symptoms of cardiovascular disease (heart attacks) as well as the symptoms of endocrine disorders (Schneider, 1995). Furthermore, symptoms of anxiety such as rapid heartbeat and intestinal cramps can be side effects of the medications some older adults take for other chronic health problems.

Anxiety disorders are less prevalent among older adults than they are among younger individuals (Gatz et al., 1996). At the same time, they are not uncommon in the older age group. Estimates of the combined prevalence of phobia, panic, and obsessive-compulsive disorders in people age 65+ have ranged from 5.5 percent (Schneider, 1995) to 18.6 percent (Butler et al., 1998). However, anxiety disorders, including phobias, often begin early in life. It has been estimated that only 3 percent of anxiety disorders have their initial onset after the age of 65 (Gatz et al., 1996).

Therapists who are unaccustomed to working with older adults might assume that certain behavioral manifestations of anxiety such as rambling speech and disorganized thinking are signs of dementia. Indeed, anxiety can occur with dementia (Schneider, 1995). A reduction in symptoms following relaxation exercises is one indication that an older adult's main problem is anxiety rather than dementia (Knight, 1996). For those with anxiety symptoms, psychosocial therapy and relaxation training exercises can help, and these interventions seem preferable to total reliance on prescriptions for tranquilizers.

In some instances, individuals who suffered from anxiety earlier in life show improvement in older adulthood. A decrease in anxiety symptoms can be viewed within the framework of the diathesis-stress model. Older adults may have fewer symptoms of anxiety if they have retired from work situations that previously aroused anxiety.

Hypochondriasis

Hypochondriasis is a somatoform disorder, meaning that it is associated with symptoms that suggest a physical disorder. Upon closer examination, however, the symptoms appear to be "psychologically rather than physically caused" (Butler et al., 1998, pp. 107–108). The diagnosis of hypochondriasis is usually made when physical findings are negative despite a patient's preoccupation with illness and anxious concern with bodily functions that intensifies in the presence of medical personnel. Individuals with hypochondriasis often resist any suggestion that their symptoms are related to emotional stress or psychological disorder. It is difficult to determine whether hypochondriasis reflects a longstanding personality dimension (Costa & McCrae, 1985) or whether it increases with age. Only long-term longitudinal studies that follow individuals over a number of decades can truly answer this question.

The symptoms of hypochondriasis and depression overlap in that some depressed individuals show signs of bodily preoccupation as well. In most instances, however, the depressed individual will not seek out help actively, whereas the individual with hypochondriasis will make frequent trips to the doctor (Butler et al., 1998).

There have been several interpretations of the underlying basis for hypochondriasis in older adulthood. One is that older adults are anxious about loss of social prestige and/or loss of financial security. This anxiety is shifted to heightened concern with bodily functioning. Another interpretation is that in American society, performance is highly valued but physical illness is generally an acceptable excuse for failure to perform. Also, older adults who claim physical illness are considered exempt from normal social responsibilities. Yet another interpretation of hypochondriasis is related to social isolation: Energy that older adults previously invested in social interactions is turned inward, resulting in an exaggerated focus on bodily processes (Cohen, 1990).

Because hypochondriasis can be a psychological defense against anxiety, it is generally not recommended that the older patient be reassured that his or her medical condition is normal. A good doctor-patient relationship and a doctor who is willing to acknowledge and understand the patient's worry can be helpful in reducing the patient's anxiety. Unfortunately, with the spread of managed care and associated constraints on physicians' time, it is becoming less likely that older adults will be visiting a familiar family doctor who provides emotional support.

As indicated earlier, today's older adult cohort may have been socialized to believe that physical complaints are the only legitimate excuse for failure. When today's young and middle-aged adults enter older adulthood, they may be more willing to attribute distress to emotional causes and seek the help they need. Perhaps the incidence of hypochondriasis will be lower in future older adult cohorts. Even so, keep in mind that physical health problems increase with age, and there is always some chance that older adults' complaints are based on real, perhaps undiagnosed, medical conditions (Butler et al., 1998).

Paranoid Disorders

In DSM-IV, a number of criteria are used to diagnose schizophrenia, which is a severe psychiatric disorder marked by disturbances in thought, perception, and attention. Most often, schizophrenia has its onset in early adulthood, although now it is recognized that it can occur for the first time in later life (Knight, 1996). The paranoid type of schizophrenia is characterized by delusions, hallucinations, and disorganization in speech and behavior (Meeks, 2000).

However, **paranoid disorders** can also occur in milder form, in which case they are considered a type of personality disorder (Axis II of DSM-IV). Mild paranoia may represent a lifelong pattern of long-standing duration or it may occur for the first time in older adulthood (Butler et al., 1998). Individuals with paranoid disorders tend to construct faulty explanations or interpretations of events. They are highly suspicious and distrustful of others even when there does not seem to be a realistic basis for suspicion or distrust.

In older adults, paranoia can occur in connection with a mood disorder such as depression or in connection with a cognitive disorder such as dementia. Paranoid thinking that occurs for the first time in older adulthood is often associated with sensory impairment (Knight, 1996), particularly in vision and hearing (discussed in Chapter 4). In such instances, paranoid thinking may simply be the older adult's attempt to fill in the blanks when trying to interpret an inaccurately perceived environment, as in the following example:

> Elsa, a 79-year-old widow, has been ill and unable to participate in any social events. For the first time in quite a while, she has decided to attend a special gathering at her church. As she enters the crowded social hall, Elsa observes several female acquaintances standing close together and engaged in animated conversation. They seem to be mumbling and she cannot decipher what they are saying even when she gets close. She concludes that they are purposely excluding her from their conversation and they may even be talking about her.

Paranoid thinking can also be associated with declines in cognitive functioning. An older adult who misplaces a pair of glasses or a wallet may accuse others of stealing those items. This accusation may be a defense against acknowledging problems with memory. Paranoid reactions may also be a defense against social losses and social isolation. For example, the older woman who does not receive any Mother's Day cards from her adult children may find it less threatening to conclude that someone is stealing her mail rather than admit to herself or others that her adult children have forgotten about her.

In some sense, paranoid reactions can be adaptive in that they protect the older adult from feelings of decline or failure. Unfortunately, paranoid reactions can alienate the people in the older adult's social support system. For example, a long-time live-in housekeeper might quit if accused of stealing. An adult daughter might become estranged from an older mother who accuses her of stealing money from the checking account that she has been helping her mother to balance.

Treating older adults who express paranoid ideas would involve correcting sensory or cognitive deficits to the extent possible and providing a friendly, familiar, structured environment. Small doses of tranquilizers are sometimes prescribed to reduce anxiety. However, Knight (1996) cautions that an older adult's suspicions should always be checked out before they are written off as paranoid thinking. In some cases, what seems to be paranoid thinking actually has some basis in reality. For example, an older nursing home resident accuses the staff of trying to poison him. Investigation of his complaint may reveal that the food served in this nursing home is unpalatable or spoiled. In a case cited by Drevenstedt and Russell (1986), an elderly woman confined to a nursing home complained that her nephew was stealing from her unoccupied home. Upon the elderly woman's death, it was discovered that the nephew assumed his aunt would never return from the nursing home and had been helping himself to her belongings without her permission. Unfortunately, it is not uncommon for older adults who live alone or are dependent upon others for care to become the victims of thieves or scam artists. Careful investigation of an older adult's complaint that a housekeeper is stealing silverware, jewelry, or money may verify that this has indeed been occurring. In such situations, the perpetrators may be counting on the likelihood that nobody will believe the older adult who makes such accusations.

Alcoholism

Alcohol-related disorders fall under the category of substance-related disorders on DSM-IV Axis I. Alcohol abuse is not always apparent in the older population, but chronic and acute alcoholism are not uncommon in this age group. Epidemiological surveys have estimated that between 2 percent and 10 percent of the older adult population living in the community have problems with alcohol, but the incidence is much higher for older adults in health-care settings. One estimate is that 21 percent of hospitalized adults ages 60 and over have a diagnosis of alcoholism and 14 percent of older adults treated in hospital emergency rooms have a drinking problem (Dupree & Schonfeld, 1999). Alcohol-related hospital care for older adults has been estimated to cost $60 billion annually (Dupree & Schonfeld, 1999; Tasker, 2003).

Most older adults do not readily admit to themselves or anyone else that they have a problem with alcohol, but drinking to cope with negative emotions places older adults at risk for becoming problem drinkers. Tasker (2003) describes a 72-year-old woman who remarried after her first husband died. After her second brief marriage ended in divorce, she began drinking, but her problem with alcohol was only discovered when she was hospitalized after a fall. In fact, many older adults are only identified as problem drinkers when they are being treated for other health problems. Even so, physicians are more likely to misdiagnose alcoholism in female patients than they are in male patients (Tasker, 2003).

Compared to younger adults with alcohol problems, older adults are less likely to get into fights or to have work-related problems because many are retired. However, the older drinker is more vulnerable to health problems and accidents such as falls (Gomberg, 1996). Alcohol consumption can be particularly detrimental when older adults have co-existing physical disorders such as heart problems or when they take medications that can exaggerate the effect of alcohol. It may take less alcohol for older adults to become intoxicated than it would for young adults (Zarit & Haynie, 2000).

Some older adults have a long-standing problem with alcohol, while others turn to alcohol late in life to alleviate depression or anxiety. A question often raised is whether older adults who live alone are more likely to be heavy drinkers than older adults who live with family members, the implication being that living alone is a risk factor for problem drinking. However, there is no clear evidence for a cause-and-effect relationship between living alone and problem drinking. First, more older women than older men live alone. Yet older women have a lower rate of alcoholism compared with older men (Gomberg, 1996). Second, living alone may be a consequence rather than a cause of problem drinking. An older adult with a history of alcohol abuse may have become alienated from family much earlier in life.

Some older adults have a long-standing drinking problem, but others turn to alcohol late in life to alleviate feelings of loneliness and depression.

What is the appropriate treatment for older drinkers? A good success rate has been reported for treatment programs that are supportive rather than confrontational (Dupree & Schonfeld, 1999). That is, trained staff help older clients to overcome depression and loneliness in an atmosphere of enhanced emotional support. Older clients are taught to identify high-risk situations for drinking and to rehearse coping skills they could use to control their drinking behavior. Such a treatment program might be most effective for late-onset drinkers who are highly motivated to recover (Woods, 1999). Many professionals view group therapy as preferable to individual treatment because many older adults have experienced loss and ordinarily they are isolated. However, there is some debate about whether group programs should cater specifically to older clients or whether clients should be of mixed ages (Lisansky-Gomberg, 2000). Older-adult membership in self-help groups such as Alcoholics Anonymous (AA) has increased, and AA has developed some special groups for older adults.

Delirium

Delirium falls under the category of cognitive disorders on Axis I of DSM-IV. It is an acute physiological brain dysfunction characterized by confusion, disorganized thinking, disturbance of consciousness, perceptual disturbances such as hallucinations, disturbances of the sleep-wake cycle, disorientation, and memory impairment (Zarit & Haynie, 2000). Individuals with delirium are generally not in contact with the immediate environment (Knight, 1996). For example, they may believe they are in a foreign country rather than in a hospital room.

Delirium usually develops over a short time, and it often occurs in older hospitalized patients following surgical procedures. However, delirium can also be associated with intoxication from alcohol as well as from sedative-hypnotic and antidepressant medications, anti-inflammatory medications, analgesics, antibiotics, anticonvulsants, antihypertensive and cardiovascular drugs, ulcer drugs, anticancer medications, or even over-the-counter medications. In addition, it can result from toxins produced by the body in response to renal, endocrine, metabolic, and infectious disorders. It can also be associated with malnutrition.

Before delirium can be treated, its cause must be identified. A stable environment and appropriate medications may be helpful. Some patients suffering from delirium are briefly restrained to prevent harm to themselves and others (Schneider, 1995), although there is a risk of increased confusion when physical restraints are used (Sullivan-Marx, 1995). If the condition underlying delirium is identified and treated immediately, most of the symptoms are reversed and the patient has an excellent chance of returning to a normal level of cognitive functioning. However, if delirium is mistaken for an untreatable dementia disorder and no efforts are made to alleviate the symptoms, then dysfunction may become permanent (Knight, 1996).

Dementia

Dementia, also listed under cognitive disorders on Axis I of DSM-IV, refers to a syndrome of global cognitive decline that most typically occurs for the first time in old age (Corey-Bloom, 2000; Skoog, Blennow, & Marcusson, 1996). The estimated prevalence of dementia in adults ages 65 and over ranges from 2 percent to 5 percent (Butler et al., 1998). Over the age of 85, the prevalence of dementia has been estimated at 30 percent (Schneider, 1995) or higher. Dementia is seen even more frequently among older adults who are institutionalized. Approximately 58 percent of institutionalized older adults have some form of dementia, possibly because dementia is often a major factor in decisions to place older adults in institutions (Skoog et al., 1996).

According to DSM-IV, dementia is characterized by deficits in memory, language, orientation, abstract thinking, reasoning, and problem solving. These deficits must represent a significant decline from a prior level of functioning and they must be severe enough to cause impairment in occupational and/or social domains. For a diagnosis of dementia to be made, the cognitive deficits cannot occur exclusively during the course of delirium, which is generally a temporary condition. Unlike patients with delirium, patients with dementia maintain a normal level of consciousness until late in the disorder, although there can be changes in personality and emotional responsiveness (Corey-Bloom, 2000).

Several instruments have been developed to measure cognitive impairment with the purpose of making an initial determination of possible dementia.

Table 11.1 | A Brief Mental Status Questionnaire (MSQ) Used to Screen for Dementia

	Number of Errors	Presumed Mental Status
1. Where are we now?		
2. Where is this place (located)?	0–2	Dementia absent/mild
3. What is today's date/day of month?	3–8	Moderate dementia
4. What month is it?	9–10	Severe dementia
5. What year is it?		
6. How old are you?		
7. What is your birthday?		
8. What year were you born?		
9. Who is the President of the United States?		
10. Who was President before him?		

Source: Kahn, Goldfarb, & Pollack (1964).

Brief mental status exams have been used to screen large populations or monitor the effectiveness of medications or other treatments. However, more extensive testing is necessary to make a determination of the reason for the cognitive decline or a clear diagnosis of dementia (Butler et al., 1998).

Table 11.1 shows an early form of a **Mental Status Questionnaire (MSQ)** along with suggested cut-off scores meant to identify the extent of the dementia (Kahn, Goldfarb, & Pollack, 1964).

The widely used **Mini-Mental State Examination (MMSE)** (Folstein, Folstein, & McHugh, 1975) includes items similar to those on the MSQ that test orientation (date, year, month, day of the week, season, current location [building], town/city, state). In addition, the MMSE tests the immediate recall of three unrelated words spoken by the tester and delayed recall of the three words later on in the testing session. Attention and calculation abilities are assessed by asking the testee to count backward from 100 by 7s or to spell a word backward. Language ability is assessed by asking the testee to repeat a sentence spoken by the tester, to read and follow an instruction, and to write a sentence. As a test of spatial ability, the testee is asked to copy a geometric figure.

With dementia, certain symptom patterns are common but no two patients are exactly alike. Some show signs of anxiety and depression, others show signs of paranoia and violent, angry behavior, and still others may simply withdraw. The clinical manifestations of dementia vary with the extent of the brain impairment, the rapidity of onset of the illness, the personality of the individual, and the nature of the living environment. In determining whether symptoms of cognitive impairment indicate a diagnosis of dementia, the clinician must take the individual's history into account. It is often helpful to interview a spouse or close family member or friend who can describe the individual's past interests and abilities and prior level of functioning.

In one case study (Corey-Bloom, 2000), a 67-year-old woman was brought to a clinic by her husband, who explained that his wife had owned and managed a successful interior design company for many years and she had been an avid golfer. Over the past six months, she had been having difficulty remembering appointments, orders, and even conversations with co-workers, and she had given up her European buying trips. Also, she had stopped playing golf because of difficulties keeping track of the score. This woman's history of being an active and competent individual, together with her relatively low score on a test of mental status, made dementia a likely diagnosis. A diagnosis of dementia would be less clear if the individual had always led a dependent life in an undemanding environment.

Among people age 60 and older, Alzheimer's disease (AD) is the most common form of dementia (Albert, 1995), and vascular dementia (VaD), is the second-most common form (Chui, 1995). AD and VaD are described in more detail in the sections that follow. However, dementia is associated with other conditions as well. Long-term alcohol abuse has been associated with dementia. Also, Parkinson's disease, which is a neurological syndrome characterized by tremors, muscle rigidity, slowness in initiating movement, and loss of motor dexterity, is associated with symptoms of dementia in some proportion of cases (Kaszniak, 1995).

Alzheimer's Disease   As described in a report from the National Institute on Aging (1998), **Alzheimer's disease (AD)** is an irreversible gradually progressive brain disorder that results in memory loss, loss in the ability to think, and changes in personality and behavior. The individual with AD often lives for 8 to 10 years after the diagnosis is made; however, the disease can last up to 20 years. The immediate cause of death is often pneumonia or some other infection brought on by the patient's lack of mobility in the final stages of the illness.

At any specific point in time, it can be difficult to differentiate AD from other types of dementia purely on the basis of behavioral symptoms. In some cases, laboratory tests can rule out secondary causes of dementia such as thyroid disorders, vitamin deficiency, or chronic infections. Visual imaging can identify treatable structural diseases such as hematomas and tumors (Skoog et al., 1996). The diagnosis of AD is becoming more accurate, but a conclusive diagnosis is only possible when pathologists examine characteristic features of the brain upon autopsy (NIA, 1998).

The losses experienced by AD victims are related to the death of brain cells (neurons) and the breakdown of connections between them (National Institute on Aging, 1998). In certain areas of the brain, there is extensive formation of neuritic plaques and neurofibrillary tangles. Plaques and tangles are also seen in the brains of very old individuals who have shown no behavioral evidence of dementia prior to death (Snowdon, 1997), but usually they are more extensive in the brains of AD victims (Skoog, et al., 1996). Also, there are large spaces, or vacuoles, in the brains of patients with advanced AD.

With regard to risk factors, women are more susceptible than men are to AD even when their greater longevity is taken into account (Corey-Bloom, 2000). There has been some speculation that highly educated people are more protected against dementia because they have more "brain reserve" in terms of brain volume or quantity of dendritic connections between neurons than do people with less education. However, this has not been proven scientifically, and more longitudinal studies that follow individuals over time as well as more sensitive measures of cognitive functioning are needed to address this question adequately.

Even though AD is not usually considered part of normal aging, the clearest risk factor for this disease is increasing age. The prevalence of AD doubles every five years beyond age 65, and it is estimated that nearly half of all people in the oldest-old (85+) age group have some symptoms of AD (NIA, 1998).

There has been some suggestion of a genetic risk factor for a rare form of familial AD. Familial AD is associated with specific mutations in genetic material and it usually has an earlier age of onset than nonfamilial AD does. However, the majority of AD victims have no obvious family history (Skoog et al., 1996). AD that is not clearly familial has a later onset and is thought to result from a series of pathological processes associated with age, possibly combined with a reduced reserve capacity (Skoog et al., 1996). More specific hypotheses about the causes of AD include aluminum toxicity and slow viruses, but these have not received definitive research support (Butler et al., 1998).

At present, it seems probable that AD results from a complex series of events in the brain that interact in different ways in different individuals to trigger the disease. However, a certain form of genetic material (the APOE epsilon4 allele) has been associated with an increased risk of AD in some individuals who have no family history of the disease (NIA, 1998).

With regard to the prevalence of AD in various racial and ethnic groups, an ongoing study is following approximately 1,000 older New Yorkers for up to five years to see if they develop AD (NIA, 1998). Of this sample, 22 percent are European American, 17 percent are African American, and 61 percent are Hispanic American. Thus far, researchers have found that having the APOE epsilon4 allele, which can be determined from a simple blood test, is associated with increased risk of AD in the European American group but not in the African American or Hispanic American groups. However, of the individuals without the APOE epsilon4 allele, African Americans had four times the risk and Hispanic Americans had two times the risk of European Americans of getting AD before the age of 90. Further investigation of why the risk of AD is higher in African American and Hispanic American populations who do not have the APOE epsilon4 allele may lead to some insight regarding what triggers AD.

Finding reliable biological markers that increase the risk of AD is important not only for understanding why the disease occurs, but also because it is best to diagnose the disease in its early stages. As medications become available, they are likely to be most effective when given earlier rather than later in the course of the disease. Also individuals who are diagnosed early have time to plan for their future care while they are still able to.

Families do not always recognize that a member is having memory problems, and even if they do, they may not bring their relative in for medical evaluation.

In a study of Japanese American men living in Hawaii, the family members of 191 men found to have dementia were interviewed. When the older man had mild dementia, over half of his family members failed to recognize any problem. Even when the older man had severe dementia, 13 percent of the families failed to recognize it. Of those who did realize there was a problem, less than half brought the older family member in for a medical evaluation (NIA, 1998). This study illustrates the difficulty of collecting accurate statistics on how many individuals from various racial and ethnic groups have AD.

According to the National Institute on Aging (1998) report, there is some evidence that women who take the hormone estrogen for longer than a year after menopause have a reduced risk of developing AD. However, more recent reports suggest the opposite—that women who take estrogen have an increased incidence of AD. Other studies have indicated a reduced incidence of AD among individuals who regularly take anti-inflammatory drugs such as ibuprofen (for example, Advil or Motrin), and that vitamin E or ginkgo biloba extracted from the leaves of the ginkgo tree slows down the progression of AD. But high doses of all these substances can have undesirable side effects, and it is not yet proven that any of them directly prevents AD or slows down its progression. These preliminary findings are hopeful, but the search continues for ways to reduce the risk of developing AD, or at least of moderating its symptoms.

AD usually has a gradual and insidious onset. Early in the course of the disorder, memory and intellectual problems may be difficult to differentiate from memory difficulties that can occur with normal aging. Language may be relatively normal, although conversational output may decline. Recent memory for names and conversations may be lost, but more remote memories are often retained. Later on, word-finding difficulties increase, verbal fluency is greatly reduced, and well-learned skills may be lost (Corey-Bloom, 2000). Although there may be some loss of judgment early in the course of the disease, interpersonal skills are usually preserved until much later (Corey-Bloom, 2000). Tuokko et al. (2003) reported the outcome of a five-year longitudinal study conducted in Canada (Canadian Study of Health and Aging) on large numbers of people ages 65+ whose cognitive measures at the beginning of the study indicated either no cognitive impairment (NCI) or cognitive impairment but no dementia (CIND). Those with CIND at the beginning of the study were more likely to be diagnosed with dementia five years later (47 percent) compared to those with NCI (15 percent). Still, further research is being conducted to differentiate between mild memory loss and memory loss that foreshadows AD.

AD is characterized by a steady progressive deterioration in cognitive functioning (Butler et al., 1998). Early on, the symptoms are often so vague that the precise onset of the disease can be difficult to pinpoint. Later, however, it becomes evident that the symptoms are not just signs of normal aging. The cognitive and behavioral symptoms of AD have been described as falling into three main stages, or phases (Schneck, Reisberg, & Ferris, 1982; Skoog et al., 1996).

In Phase I ("senescent forgetfulness phase"), the individual may complain and be anxious about misplacing items, forgetting appointments, and forgetting names. Difficulties are mainly with recalling new information, but there might also be slight impairment in language and concentration (Skoog et al., 1996).

Even so, many individuals continue to function at work and in social situations. Years ago, Kral (1962) used the term "benign senescent forgetfulness," to describe a static form of memory difficulty to be differentiated from "malignant" memory problems, which instead of remaining static would progress and develop into dementia. In Phase I, it can be difficult to differentiate benign senescent forgetfulness from malignant forgetfulness. More recently, a new category of memory problems has been termed "age-associated memory impairment" (AAMI), or just "age-related memory decline" (Butler et al., 1998). This category, which some consider to be intermediate between normal aging and dementia, includes an equal proportion of older men and women whose memory failures are of some concern but do not seem to be progressive as would be typical of dementia (see Knight, 1996; Woods, 1999). On the basis of research studies presently being conducted, it may eventually be possible to clearly distinguish between memory difficulties that signify Phase I of AD as opposed memory difficulties that signify AAMI.

In Phase II ("confusional phase"), cognitive impairment becomes more apparent and the older adult's spouse or close family members begin to suspect something is seriously wrong. Sometimes the beginning of this phase is marked by an episode in which the older adult gets lost while traveling to a location that ordinarily would have been reached with no difficulty.

In the confusional phase, the individual is often unable to remember entire recent events or experiences. For example, John complains to his wife Gert that it has been months since they saw a movie when in fact the two of them had gone to a movie the day before. This scenario is quite different from one in which John remembers attending a movie the day before but just forgets the title of the movie, the actor who played the main character, or the details of the plot. Memory for past events may seem relatively preserved, but a stringent test may reveal some memory loss for past information as well (for example, the name of the elementary or high school attended many years in the past). In Phase II, the individual begins to have problems with word finding and difficulties develop in work and social situations.

The person in the confusional phase often denies having any difficulties. Rather than expressing anxiety and concern, the individual who gets lost may not admit that a problem exists ("I got lost because of the construction on the roads."). Or consider a man who has always taken an active interest in current events. He appears to be engrossed in watching the early evening news on television, but when his wife asks him about it at the dinner table, he responds, "I am not interested in those things." When asked to recall the name of a childhood friend, his response might be, "That was so many years ago, how can I be expected to remember?" Such an individual may seem to be avoiding any recognition of intellectual decline, but occasionally anxiety and anger break through if he is confronted with too great a challenge.

In addition to denial, the individual in the confusional stage may show a decline in emotional responsiveness. There may be withdrawal from a job if he or she has not yet retired as well as withdrawal from demanding social interactions. Sometimes, the individual in this phase appears to be depressed. As mentioned previously, astute clinical skills are needed to make a differential

Individuals afflicted with Alzheimer's disease can become confused and lacking in emotional responsiveness. Eventually, they will need assistance with activities of daily living such as bathing, eating, and dressing.

diagnosis of depression versus dementia. Depression tends to have a more rapid onset, whereas AD comes on more gradually. Also, patients with depression are likely to complain about difficulty with concentration or poor appetite. In contrast, patients with AD are more likely to deny any symptoms. Depressed patients often complain about sleep disturbance, whereas AD patients rarely complain of insomnia even though their sleep patterns are often irregular.

In Phase III ("dementia phase"), mental and physical functions are severely impaired, and the individual will need assistance with activities of daily living such as bathing, dressing, eating, and toileting. There may be extreme confusion and disorientation, and in some cases the individual may mistake a spouse for a parent or a daughter for a sister (Schneck et al., 1982). There may be psychotic symptoms such as delusions, hallucinations, paranoid reactions, and, in some cases, severe agitation. As the phase progresses, the individual often becomes incontinent of urine and feces. At that point, many families decide to place the older adult in a nursing home.

Early in the dementia phase, individuals may be able to report the year, month, season, or even their location. As the dementia phase progresses, they become disoriented about time and place, and they often forget well-known information such as the name of a spouse. In this phase, some individuals remain motionless for long periods and become extremely withdrawn and uncommunicative. They appear to be suffering from severe depression, but they may also have episodes of severe anxiety and agitation, as well as psychotic-like experiences similar to those seen in patients with schizophrenia. Late in the dementia phase, a person with AD may not recognize him- or herself in the mirror and may be afraid of the reflection or talk to it as if it were another person.

Thus far, the approaches taken to treat AD consist of efforts to slow down the cognitive deterioration (Schneider, 1995). There is ongoing research to develop medications to alleviate the cognitive impairments associated with AD. Some have produced modest improvements but as yet there are no long-term effects. Antidepressant medications can be helpful for mood disturbances associated with AD, as are medications for treating behavioral disturbances such as agitation and hallucinations that often occur in the late stage.

Over the past two decades, AD has received a great deal of publicity, and this has been important in raising the level of research funding for this disorder. The more research that is conducted, the greater the chance that effective treatments will be developed or, better yet, that preventive measures will be discovered. Publicity has also resulted in increased awareness of the devastating effects that AD can have both on the victims and their families. At the same time, increased awareness may have created an unfounded fear that AD is an inevitable outcome of aging. While increased awareness may improve the chances that actual cases of AD will be diagnosed, there may also be a tendency for overdiagnosis (Gatz & Pearson, 1988). Lay individuals, as well as professionals who have not had experience with AD, may conclude prematurely that an older adult who experiences memory difficulties must certainly have AD (Knight, 1996). The assumption that an older adult has AD when he or she is suffering from a more treatable disorder such as depression could have adverse consequences—the older adult may not receive the proper treatment in a timely manner. Knight (1996) admonishes that heightened awareness of AD must be balanced with concern for accurate differential diagnosis. Even so, there is no doubt that AD is a major health problem, and as more people live into the oldest-old years, there will be increasing numbers of AD victims unless a way to cure or prevent the disease is found.

Vascular Dementia   **Vascular dementia (VaD),** the second most common form of dementia in older adults, is associated with disorders of the cerebrovascular system. VaD is associated with blockage of cerebral blood vessels, which can lead to focal destruction of brain tissue (Gatz et al., 1996). The term VaD is sometimes used interchangeably with the term **multi-infarct dementia (MID),** which is dementia stemming from multiple small or large brain infarcts, or strokes. However, VaD includes a broader category of dementias associated with a variety of vascular problems or with lesions in the subcortical white matter (Skoog et al., 1996). Thus, MID is only one type of VaD.

Patients with MID often have a history of stroke or hypertension (Skoog et al., 1996). Risk factors that increase a person's vulnerability to VaD as well as MID are advanced age, being male, being a smoker, and having hypertension, heart disease, or diabetes. Ethnic groups with higher rates of diabetes are more vulnerable to this type of dementia.

Computed tomography (CT) and magnetic resonance imaging (MRI) scans are sometimes used to differentiate MID from AD. CT scans can detect areas of cerebral degeneration (or atrophy) in the structure of the brain. MRI scans use magnetic fields to detect abnormalities in soft tissue. These scanning techniques can often detect small focal lesions in the brain, which suggest a diagnosis of MID. However, there is not always a strict one-to-one relationship between such lesions and behavioral symptoms.

In contrast to the gradual and insidious onset of AD, VaD, and MID come on more suddenly, or abruptly. Typically, the course of deterioration is stepwise and fluctuating as opposed to the slow but steady downhill progression seen with AD (Skoog et al., 1996). In sum, AD and VaD typically have different patterns of onset and course. However, the differential diagnosis of AD and VaD is not always straightforward because at any given time, the symptoms of the two disorders can overlap. There may be somewhat greater preservation of personality with VaD than with AD. Also, the severity of impairment is often greater with AD. However, it can be difficult to make exact comparisons between VaD and AD because patients with the two types of dementia may not be at the same stage of their illness.

Upon autopsy, VaD accounts for an estimated 20 percent of all dementia cases (Butler et al., 1998). However, approximately 10 percent of patients with dementia are diagnosed with a mixture of AD and VaD or MID (Corey-Bloom, 2000), which further complicates the task of differential diagnosis. It has even been suggested that some cases of dementia could result from a combination of AD and VaD, with neither sufficient by itself to produce dementia-like symptoms (Skoog et al., 1996).

Most scientists believe that dementia is not an inevitable consequence of old age. However, the prevalence of dementia does increase with age. Although there is some variation in the figures reported, one estimate is that by early in the 21st century, the number of individuals in the United States afflicted with probable AD may reach seven million (Corey-Bloom, 2000). AD as well as other types of dementia have had an enormous impact on the cost of health care and the need for social services. There is increasing recognition that family members who serve as caregivers for AD and other dementia victims are themselves vulnerable to mental health problems such as depression. Counseling, support groups, and relief in the form of day-care services for AD victims can alleviate caregiver burden to some extent. Hopefully, strategies that alleviate caregiver burden will not only minimize caregiver stress, but also will prolong the time that AD patients can remain in a home environment as opposed to needing institutionalization.

THERAPEUTIC INTERVENTIONS WITH OLDER ADULTS

A number of therapeutic interventions have been useful in treating older adults with mental disorders. Some have been employed with young and middle-aged adults as well, while others are uniquely tailored to problems found more frequently in older adulthood. The sampling of therapeutic techniques described here is not all-inclusive, but it represents an array of psychosocial approaches that have been used with older adults.

Environmental Design and Sensory Retraining

Modifying an older adult's physical environment can be therapeutic, particularly when physical and/or cognitive competence has declined to the point where opportunities for physical, cognitive, or social stimulation are limited (Erber, 1979). Older adults with dementia often live in institutional settings designed for older adults who have physical rather than cognitive impairments. Yet older adults with dementia can benefit from environments that enhance their level of independent functioning.

Gladwell (1997) described one residence designed to accommodate the needs of individuals with Alzheimer's disease (AD). It consisted of three houses, each with 10 bedrooms and adjoining private baths. The floor covering in the bedrooms differed from that in corridors and public rooms to give cues to prevent disorientation. The three houses were linked to a main building, and circular walkways throughout an accessible garden limited the chance that residents would reach dead ends or suffer anxiety from feeling lost. The landscaping in the garden had very few trees and shrubs because these cast shadows which upset people with AD, who might misperceive the shadows as people. A preliminary report indicates that AD patients appear to have a slower rate of deterioration in this type of setting than they would in traditionally designed nursing homes, possibly because they are able to remain more physically active and there are more opportunities to socialize with fellow residents. Also, family members and friends feel more comfortable visiting in this setting than they do in more traditional nursing homes. An added benefit is that the cost of care is lower in this type of setting than it would be in a traditional nursing home. Clearly, additional research is needed, but the preliminary positive findings should stimulate further efforts to design environments that foster the highest possible level of functioning in older adults who suffer from AD or other dementias.

Sensory retraining therapy (Richman, 1969) involves activities and exercises designed to stimulate kinesthetic and proprioceptive, tactile, olfactory, auditory, and visual receptors. In addition to encouraging older adults to recognize various stimuli, exercises have a perceptual-motor component as well (for example, catching a ball). The origins of sensory retraining derive from the field of early childhood education, where sensory contact and stimulation are considered essential for development. Sensory retraining therapy is well-suited for older adults with limited physical and cognitive capabilities, and it is often carried out with small groups of geriatric patients in institutional settings.

Behavioral Interventions

Behavioral interventions have been used to modify behaviors that have a negative effect on the quality of an older adult's life (Newton & Lazarus, 1992). Some behaviors frustrate caregivers and lead to institutional placement, but even if older adults already reside in an institutional setting, unacceptable behavior can have a negative impact on the way they are treated. For example, they may be excluded by fellow residents from social activities and responded to negatively by staff members. In some instances, their behavior may drive away family members who would otherwise visit them. Problem behaviors that have been responsive to behavioral intervention include incontinence, poor feeding behaviors, and wandering.

With **behavior therapy,** attempts are made to manipulate the environmental cues that prompt negative behaviors (stimulus-control techniques) or environmental consequences that reinforce unwanted behaviors. Prior to designing an intervention intended to shape new and more appropriate behaviors, it is important to gather information about the older adult's reinforcement history and analyze the reinforcement contingencies that already exist in the environment. Of course, the application of behavioral intervention is appropriate only when there is reason to believe that the older adult is capable of deriving some benefit from it.

Baltes and Zerbe (1976) used a behavioral intervention strategy to train nursing home residents to re-acquire and maintain self-feeding skills. After an initial (baseline) assessment of the feeding behavior of two different residents, they used stimulus control to exclude cues that were associated with dependent feeding behavior. For example, training procedures took place in the residents' rooms rather than in the dining room where they had always been fed by the nursing home staff. If the resident could not follow eating instructions, shaping procedures were used. Initially, the therapist placed her hand over the resident's hand to help guide the spoon to the resident's mouth. Residents were positively reinforced with sips of juice, milk, or coffee for approximations to independent eating behavior. In addition, residents were socially reinforced for their self-feeding behavior with praise, verbal interaction, patting, and stroking. Undesirable behaviors such as dumping food, eating with fingers, or refusing to pick up or hold eating utensils were followed by a time-out period, during which the therapist turned her back to the resident and took away the glass of juice, milk, or coffee. These techniques resulted in more self-feeding behaviors, thus illustrating that environmental conditions that foster dependent behavior can exaggerate aging losses, while conditions that encourage independent behavior can minimize losses. Of course, for treatment gains to be maintained, appropriate environmental contingencies must remain in place. Thus, caregivers themselves must be reinforced for consistent participation in behavioral intervention programs (Newton & Lazarus, 1992; Smyer, 1993).

In some instances, older adults can be trained to manage their own problems. For example, insomnia can be helped when older adults are taught how to regulate their sleep habits by eliminating daytime naps, going to sleep and getting up at the same time each day, and controlling the cues in their sleep environment by eliminating sleep-incompatible behaviors such as reading in bed (Puder, Lacks, Bertelson, & Storandt, 1983). Incontinence has also shown improvement when older adults are trained to use behavioral techniques such as self-monitoring and self-scheduled toileting (Burgio & Engel, 1990). Behavioral interventions hold great promise for boosting older adults' feelings of personal control and their self-esteem.

Reality Orientation and Reminiscence Therapy

Reality orientation (RO) therapy has been used to treat older adults with moderate to severe memory loss, confusion, and disorientation. It is often applied in living environments that might otherwise lack cues to help older adult residents stay oriented to time and place. RO programs have two components. One, which is found in many institutional settings, is a 24-hour program of environmental stimulation that includes bulletin boards posting information such as the day and date, scheduled activities, the next meal to be served, the next holiday to be celebrated, and so on. Obviously, the posted information must be kept up to date if this component of the RO program is to be effective.

A second component of RO, which is found less often than bulletin board postings, consists of classroom sessions in which several older adults meet with a staff leader to discuss topics relevant to the "here and now." The leader initiates a discussion on a particular topic and offers positive verbal feedback to older adults whose contributions indicate that they are oriented to the present time and place. There have been anecdotal reports that the classroom component lowers older adults' level of confusion, although this is not always substantiated by objective evidence. One criticism of the classroom component of RO is that people who reside in institutional settings may not want to be reminded of the here and now, and such reminding may not improve their emotional outlook (Schwenk, 1979).

Reminiscence therapy encourages older adults to think and talk about the past. As described in Chapter 8, life review, or reminiscence, is considered a naturally occurring, healthy phenomenon (Butler, 1963). Reminiscence therapy is a means of helping older adults to re-evaluate and integrate their experiences, which could alleviate feelings of depression and sadness. Ideally, reminiscence will result in a sense of continuity and self-worth. Reminiscence therapy conducted on a group basis could also help reduce older adults' feelings of loneliness and social isolation, particularly if group members have a common past. However, this type of therapy may not be appropriate for older people who focus on the past to avoid resolving issues that exist in the present (Newton & Lazarus, 1992).

One study (Baines, Saxby, & Ehlert, 1987) found that a combination of reminiscence therapy and reality orientation led to greater improvement in the cognitive and behavioral functioning of nursing home residents compared with either technique by itself. However, nursing home residents who participated in reality orientation therapy followed by reminiscence therapy seemed to benefit more on both cognitive and behavioral measures compared to residents who participated in these two therapies in the reverse order. Further research is needed, but these findings suggest it may be advisable to conduct reality orientation sessions to orient people to the present before involving them in remembering the past. It is unfortunate that the staff in many nursing homes and assisted living facilities are required to devote most of their time to caring for the physical needs of the residents. Many facilities do not have enough staff members to conduct therapy sessions.

Pet Therapy

Having even one confidante to whom one can tell one's deepest thoughts and fears has long been considered a buffer against the risk of depression (Lowenthal & Haven, 1968). Unfortunately, opportunities for social interaction with a confidante may diminish in older adulthood, but there is considerable interest in whether interactions with pets have beneficial effects on mental health. The application of pet therapy is not confined to older adults, but it may be an important source of support for individuals in this age group.

Research on pet therapy includes studies of naturally occurring pet ownership as well as studies in which pets are introduced into the environment as a therapeutic intervention. In most studies on naturally occurring pet ownership, participants live in the community and are capable of caring for a pet. There is some evidence that both mental or physical benefits are associated with pet ownership (Siegel, 1993), although this has not been found in every study (Tucker, Friedman, Tsai, & Martin, 1995).

In one study (Goldmeier, 1986), community-living older women either did or did not have a pet. Pet ownership was associated with higher morale, but only for older women who lived alone. Pet ownership made little difference for older women who lived with other people.

In another study (Fritz, Farver, Hart, & Kass, 1996), 244 men and women varied in age, but all of them identified themselves as caregivers for individuals with Alzheimer's disease. Approximately half had pet companions (dogs or cats) and the other half did not. Fritz et al. found that the men who were attached to their dogs scored higher on some measures of psychological health than did the men with no pets. The younger women in the sample (under age 40) who were attached to their cats scored higher than the younger women with no pets. However, the older women (over age 40) who were attached to dogs scored higher than the older women who were not attached to dogs. The authors concluded that attachment to pets may serve to moderate some of the psychological stress associated with caring for a cognitively impaired adult. However, the mixed outcome depending upon the caregiver's gender, age, and type of pet mirrors the diversity of findings from a variety of studies on the benefits of pet ownership.

It is difficult to evaluate the validity of studies on the effect of pet ownership (see Chapter 2 for a discussion of validity). These studies are usually not experimental and there may be a self-selection effect—people who are physically and mentally healthy may be more likely to own pets than those who are not. Thus, it may be best to assess the effect of pet ownership within the context of an individual older adult's larger environment and lifestyle.

Most studies on the effect pets have on older adults have been conducted in institutional environments such as nursing homes or assisted living facilities. In some instances, a dog or cat becomes a permanent resident of the facility. More often, however, **pet-facilitated therapy (PFT)** is an intervention whereby an animal is introduced into the environment for a limited time, during which residents can make whatever contact they wish (for example, petting the animal, talking to the animal, or just observing). In some instances, there have been

Introducing friendly pets like this Labrador retriever into nursing homes or assisted living facilities can lift the spirits of residents and staff alike.

opportunities to conduct real-world experiments on the effectiveness of PFT (Chapter 2 describes the experimental approach). A researcher who wants to conduct an experiment on the effectiveness of PFT could make baseline measures on residents who will participate in the study. These measures might include physiological indexes such as blood pressure, psychological indexes such as self-reports on morale and life satisfaction, or possibly behavioral measures such as amount of time spent smiling, laughing, or interacting with other residents or staff. Once the baseline measures are made, residents could be randomly assigned to an experimental group or a comparison (control) group. After a specified number of sessions during which residents in the experimental group have access to the pet, a set of post-intervention measures could be made. Residents assigned to the control group would not be given access to a pet. Ideally, however, they would be given opportunities to interact with each other and with the same individual who brings the pet to members of the experimental group. If there is greater improvement among older adults in the experimental group than among those in the control group, there can be some confidence in the internal validity of PFT (that is, that the pet is the factor causing the improvements observed in the experimental group rather than just the social interaction with other people). (See Chapter 2 for a description of internal validity.) Ethically, if positive effects are found for the experimental group, then members of the control group should be given opportunities to interact with pets at a later time.

Most studies on PFT have not included a control group such as the one just described. Also, allegations about the effectiveness of PFT are frequently based on clinical impressions. However, glowing anecdotal reports of improved morale and increased social interaction among nursing home residents following the introduction of a pet cannot be ignored. It is possible that pets elicit positive responses not only from the research participants (that is, the nursing home residents), but also from the researchers themselves, who tend to believe fervently in the benefit of PFT (Siegel, 1993). Also, introducing pets into an institutional environment may increase the morale of the staff, which could benefit the residents indirectly. Moreover, family members may find their visits more enjoyable when pets are present, and visitor enjoyment may have a positive effect on the residents themselves. As with any therapeutic intervention, it is important to follow up a positive outcome over time to see whether the initial beneficial effects of PFT (or any other type of therapy) are maintained.

PFT may not be the first line of therapy in the case of serious mental disorders. However, it could be beneficial for treating feelings of loneliness when older adults experience loss. Also, it may make institutional environments more stimulating and it may provide an incentive for family members to visit. As such, PFT could help to prevent more serious psychological problems.

Individual Psychotherapy

In the past, it was often assumed that supportive treatment was the only therapy older adults needed (Newton & Lazarus, 1992). With supportive therapy, the therapist would simply help the older adult to maintain self-esteem in the face of losses and physical impairments. However, other types of individual therapy have been used successfully with older adults. Insight-oriented therapy can be effective with psychologically healthier and more vigorous older adults who have the cognitive resources, the capacity for introspection, and the motivation for establishing a relationship with the therapist (Newton & Lazarus, 1992).

With psychodynamic approaches, the emphasis is on helping older adults develop a fuller understanding of psychological issues in relation to their individual personality structure, self-image, and earlier development. Brief psychodynamic approaches have been used successfully with some older adults as they deal with issues related to retirement, widowhood, or physical losses (Newton & Lazarus, 1992).

Cognitive-behavioral therapy, described earlier in the section on depression, helps older adults modify maladaptive thinking habits. This approach can be useful when depression or anxiety stem from feelings of incompetence and uselessness (Gallagher & Thompson, 1983). To benefit from cognitive-behavioral therapy, older adults must have a sufficiently high level of cognitive functioning so that they are capable of comprehending and remembering. Positive results have been reported mainly with middle-class and upper-class European Americans, but more information is needed on the effectiveness of this type of therapy for older adults from racial and ethnic minority groups (Dick et al., 1999).

Family Therapy

Even when older adults live alone, they are typically members of a broader family system. In some instances it may be effective for therapists to meet with older adults and other family members as well (Herr & Weakland, 1979).

A common source of conflict among family members is an older relative's apparent or actual need for assistance. For example, a married couple may disagree about how much care to provide for an older relative. Conflict can arise when one member of the couple feels that an older relative's needs are interfering with time available for other family members or perhaps that the older relative's demands for assistance are excessive. Care of an older parent often falls to one adult child, and this adult child may resent siblings who are perceived as shirking their responsibilities. In some cases, however, an adult child may feel driven to over serve an elderly parent because of a long-standing need for that parent's approval.

> John and Susan are in their early 60s. They enjoy traveling to new places, often combining their trips with visits to their grandchildren who live more than 1,000 miles away. Recently, Susan's mother, age 84, lost her husband. She lives alone in an apartment for senior citizens about 15 miles from John and Susan's home. Since her mother has become widowed, Susan feels responsible for taking her mother shopping, to doctor and hairdresser appointments, as well as out to dinner and to movies and shows. John is willing to take some responsibility for these things, but he would like to have more time for the travel they used to do. Susan feels she cannot leave town for any length of time because of her mother. Susan's brother and sister live nearby, but they have not volunteered to share the responsibilities for their mother on a regular basis and Susan is hesitant to ask them. John thinks that his mother-in-law is capable of arranging some of her own shopping, getting to some of her own appointments, and having some social life of her own. The situation is causing a great deal of family tension.

Perhaps John is correct that Susan's mother is capable of greater independence, but Susan may have a long-standing need for her mother's approval and so she does more than she really has to do. In other situations, conflict can occur when adult children detect clear signs of physical and/or cognitive decline in an older relative, but the older relative is adamant about maintaining his or her independence.

> Allison has been so busy that she has not had a chance to visit with her mother since her mother's 75th birthday party last month. After running an errand in her mother's neighborhood, she decided to stop by for a quick visit without calling first. When she arrived, she found newspapers piled high, the trash can in the kitchen filled to overflowing, the sink full of dirty dishes, the kitchen cupboards bare, and the refrigerator almost empty. Allison offered to help her mother clean the house and get groceries, but her mother insisted that she did not need help. She said that she intended to go to the grocery store the next day and she had every intention of cleaning the house herself when she got around to it.

Allison thinks that her elderly mother needs assistance with shopping, cooking, and household tasks, but her mother does not want to accept help. Perhaps her mother fears becoming a burden to her daughter and losing her independence. In any event, the reasons for any conflict could be addressed in family therapy.

Another situation with the potential for conflict occurs when a middle-aged child asks to return to the nest. Adult children who leave their parents' home but then return, sometimes many years later, are referred to as **boomerang kids.** This scenario is becoming more common given the realities of divorce and economic hardship (Stains, 2002). An older couple may disagree about whether to allow an adult child to move back in. If the adult child does move back, conflict can arise over expectations about daily responsibilities and financial contributions to the household or even how long this living arrangement should last. Such conflict may be intensified if the middle-aged child returns to the nest with adolescent children. In some cases, family therapy serves as a forum where the concerns of all parties can be addressed in a fair and equitable manner.

In sum, older adults and their families face many problems and concerns that could benefit from therapeutic intervention. To be effective, the intervention should be matched to the specific problem as well as to the needs and capabilities of the older adult.

REVISITING THE SELECTIVE OPTIMIZATION WITH COMPENSATION AND ECOLOGICAL MODELS

The majority of older adults maintain an adequate level of emotional well-being and a high level of life satisfaction. However, some older adults experience difficulties that range from mild to severe. How can such difficulties be understood, and hopefully minimized, from the perspective of the Selective Optimization with Compensation (SOC) model (Baltes & Baltes, 1990) and the Ecological Model (Lawton, 1989; Lawton & Nahemow, 1973)?

According to the SOC model, maintaining an optimal level of mental health would call for focusing selectively on the aspects of life that are most fulfilling and minimizing the importance of those aspects that are least fulfilling. The most and least fulfilling aspects might vary depending upon the individual. For one person, being near family members might have priority, but for another person, being near a religious congregation might be most important. For yet another person, ready access to cultural events might have priority. To maximize mental health and life satisfaction, each person must strive to optimize the chances of having access to what is most important. This should compensate for giving up things with lower priority.

The Ecological Model (Lawton, 1989; Lawton & Nahemow, 1973) is also applicable to mental health and mental disorders in older adulthood. The diathesis-stress model described in this chapter bears some similarity to the Ecological Model. Diathesis, or the individual's level of vulnerability, bears some similarity to the concept of competence. Stress, or the occurrence of negative events, bears some similarity to the concept of environmental press. In the Ecological Model framework, adaptation can be viewed as maintaining mental health or minimizing any disabling effects of mental disorder. As such, adaptation is most likely when there is a match between the individual's competence and the degree of challenge, or press, in the environment. The Ecological Model can be used more specifically when designing environments for older adults with Alzheimer's disease (AD). AD patients maintain the best possible level of functioning in environments with some but not too much press. The Ecological Model can also be helpful in understanding why older adults who may have suffered from mental difficulties such as depression and anxiety earlier in life sometimes show improvement in older adulthood. In older adulthood, the press of the environment may be better matched to the emotional competence of these individuals. For example, for individuals with a high level of anxiety, competing in the workplace may have been too demanding, whereas life in retirement is less so and thus their emotional health improves. Alternatively, the emotional health of an individual who thrives on work-related achievement might suffer if the environmental press is too low in retirement.

KEY POINTS

- Most older adults enjoy an adequate level of emotional well-being and have satisfying relationships. However, a proportion of them suffer from mental disorders.
- The rate of mental disorders does not seem to be any greater, and may even be lower, in older adulthood than it is in young adulthood. Even so, the number and proportion of older adults who will need mental health services is likely to increase in the future mainly because of increased life expectancy and cohort factors.
- Currently, older adults are underserved by the mental health system. Reasons for this may be related to aspects of the health-care system, to the attitudes of therapists, and to the attitudes of older adults.
- The diathesis-stress model can be used to conceptualize the likelihood that a mental disorder will occur. Diathesis refers to the individual's level of vulnerability, while stress refers to the occurrence of negative events. Those with higher diathesis might be at greater risk for mental disorders when there is stress than will those with lower diasthesis.
- Types of mental disorder in older adulthood include the following: depression, anxiety disorder, hypochondriasis, paranoid disorders, alcoholism, delirium, and dementia. Of these disorders, depression is one of the most common but also the most treatable.
- Delirium and dementia are disorders with cognitive symptoms, but it is important to distinguish between them. Delirium is an acute physiological brain dysfunction that usually develops over a short period of time and subsides when its cause is treated.
- Dementia refers to a syndrome of global cognitive decline that most typically occurs in old age and increases in likelihood from the young-old to the oldest-old years. Dementia involves deficits in cognitive functioning, including memory.
- Among older adults, Alzheimer's disease (AD) is the most common form of dementia, while vascular dementia (VaD) is the second-most common form.

The symptoms of AD and VaD can overlap, but the two types of dementia have different patterns of onset and course.

- AD is more common among women and comes on gradually, whereas VaD is more common among men and comes on more abruptly. With AD there is a steady downhill course, while the progression of VaD is more stepwise and fluctuating. In a number of cases, individuals can have a combination of AD and VaD.

- Various types of therapy have been used to help older adults with mental disorders. The main concern is that therapeutic intervention be appropriate both for the problem being treated and for the older adult's level of functioning. Compared with young and middle-aged adults, older adults are more likely to have co-existing physical and/or cognitive difficulties that could have a bearing on the effectiveness of therapeutic interventions.

KEY TERMS

Alzheimer's disease (AD)   431

anxiety disorders   423

behavior therapy   439

boomerang kids   445

cognitive-behavioral therapy   443

delirium   428

dementia   429

depression   418

diathesis-stress model   416

differential diagnosis   421

DSM-IV   416

hypochondriasis   424

Mental Status Questionnaire (MSQ)   430

Mini-Mental State Examination (MMSE)   430

multi-infarct dementia (MID)   436

paranoid disorders   425

pet-facilitated therapy (PFT)   441

reality orientation (RO)   440

reminiscence therapy   440

sensory retraining therapy   438

suicide   422

vascular dementia (VaD)   436

To learn more about the issues discussed in this chapter, point your browser to http://www.infotrac-college.com and use the passcode from the InfoTrac College Edition card that came with your book. InfoTrac College Edition gives you access to complete articles from many different journals.

Facing the End
and Looking
Toward the Future

12

Myra is 70 years old and six months ago she became a widow. Her husband Victor was ill for several years prior to his death and throughout that time Myra devoted herself to caring for him. Although Victor was bedridden the last few months of his life, he was mentally alert and able to have a say in his end-of-life care. Myra is thankful that Victor could remain at home thanks to a program called "hospice," which sent people to give Myra emotional support and help with Victor's care. Throughout their marriage, Victor was always in charge of the family finances and Myra never had to worry about paying bills or taking care of investments or insurance policies. Fortunately, before he died, Victor was able to teach Myra what she would need to know about these things. Now that she is a widow, Myra feels lonely and she realizes she must reinvent her life. Since Victor's funeral she has not heard from the couples with whom they used to socialize before Victor became ill. However, several widowed women in her apartment building have extended invitations to social activities. Myra is grateful she still has her health, and now that she has free time she thinks she will participate in a meaningful activity such as volunteer work at the nearby elementary school.

DEATH AND DYING

Death is the irreversible cessation of biological functioning. In the past, the moment of death was determined by signs such as lack of respiration, pulse, or response to stimulation as well as lowered body temperature. However, with modern life-support technology, it is more difficult to detect when the exact moment of death occurs (Corr, Nabe, & Corr, 2003).

Dying is defined as the period immediately preceding death when it becomes apparent that the individual is losing vital functions and is beyond successful medical intervention (Kastenbaum, 1996). In some cases, modern medical technology makes it difficult to determine when a person has begun dying (Kastenbaum, 1996). Also, surgery, new medications, and advances in organ donation techniques have extended the interval between onset of an illness and the actual event of death.

Thanks to advances in public health and sanitation, relatively few young people in the United States and other developed countries die from acute infectious diseases, and we take it for granted that most people will live long lives. Death is more common in old age, and in the United States, approximately 80 percent of all deaths occur after the age of 60 (Kastenbaum, 1999). Table 12.1 shows the number of deaths and death rates in the United States in the older adult age group. The number of deaths increases from the young-old (65–74) years to the old-old (75–84) years, but it tapers off in the oldest-old (85+) years, largely because there are fewer people in this age category. However, the rate of death rises from the young-old to the old-old years, with a dramatic increase in the oldest-old years. As discussed in Chapter 3, the leading causes of death among the population of older adults in the United States are chronic illnesses such as heart disease, cancer, and stroke.

Human development cannot be fully understood without attention to death and bereavement (Kastenbaum, 1999), and in older adulthood many people spend time anticipating the end of their own lives (Lawton, 2001). We will discuss death and dying first, followed by bereavement, which often follows the loss of a loved one.

Table 12.1	Number of Deaths and Death Rates (per 100,000) Ages 65 and Older, All Races, by Age and Sex: United States, 1999

	Number of Deaths			Death Rates		
	Both Sexes	Males	Females	Both Sexes	Males	Females
65–74 years	452,600	254,920	197,680	2,484.3	3,109.3	1,972.9
75–84 years	698,590	340,970	357,620	5,751.3	6,999.8	4,915.4
85 years and elder	646,141	209,989	436,152	15,476.1	16,931.3	14,861.1

Source: Corr, Nabe, and Corr, 4th ed.

The Dying Trajectory

The **dying trajectory** refers to the speed, or rate, of decline in functioning that precedes death. With a sudden trajectory, death of a healthy individual occurs instantaneously, as in fatal car accidents. In earlier times and in present-day societies with limited access to medical care and poor hygienic conditions, death can occur after a brief acute illness (Kastenbaum, 1996). At the opposite extreme, a slow and gradual trajectory is one in which death is certain to occur eventually but not immediately. For example, a person could be diagnosed with a long-term illness or condition with no known cure, but medical treatments could extend life for weeks, months, or years. Gradual dying trajectories are common in modern technologically advanced societies where medical treatments are available. Indeed, it can often be difficult to pin down the point when an individual enters a dying trajectory (Kastenbaum, 1996).

A gradual trajectory allows the dying individual time to resolve personal issues such as rifts with family members and to make decisions about the distribution of property to family members, friends, and charities. Additionally, if a decline in health progresses gradually, the individual can participate in decisions about end-of-life care (Lawton, 2001). For example, the dying individual can have a say in which type of medical intervention to choose to prolong life, and the informed patient can give some thought to weighing the quality against the quantity of life. In the case of Alzheimer's disease (discussed in Chapter 11), the dying trajectory can be gradual because individuals often live for more than a decade after this diagnosis is made. Tragically, however, individuals with Alzheimer's disease lose the cognitive capability that would enable them to prepare for death.

Advance Directives

Many people make plans about what will be done with their possessions when they are no longer living. A **will** is a formal document that states how individuals want their property to be distributed to heirs upon their death. It is not uncommon for people to put off drawing up a will, but at the time a will is drawn up, signed, and dated, the person must be of sound mind and not subject to undue influence. A will can be changed at any point before death so long

Figure 12.1 | Contrasting Dying Trajectories

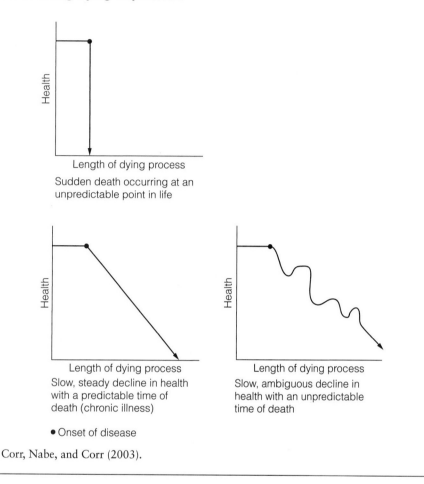

Length of dying process
Sudden death occurring at an
unpredictable point in life

Length of dying process
Slow, steady decline in health
with a predictable time of
death (chronic illness)

Length of dying process
Slow, ambiguous decline in
health with an unpredictable
time of death

• Onset of disease

Corr, Nabe, and Corr (2003).

as the person drawing it up remains of sound mind. The most recent version is used to determine the disposition of the deceased individual's property.

The signing of a will must be witnessed by the number of people required by state law, and witnesses cannot have any personal interest in the will. Depending upon the laws of the state in which a deceased person has lived, handwritten or unwitnessed ("holographic") wills may be accepted. However, it is highly advisable to seek professional legal assistance when making a will. Usually, a will names a personal representative, or executor, as the person responsible for carrying out the business of collecting the property of the deceased individual and notifying those who will receive it. If no executor is named, the court appoints an administrator. Individuals who die without a valid will are said to have died "intestate," or without a testament stating their wishes (Corr et al., 2003). Each state has laws governing how the property, or estate, of an intestate individual is to be distributed. This may not correspond with what the deceased individual would have wanted, which is why it is so important to have a will. Also, a will often specifies the type of funeral or memorial service the individual wishes to have and whether there is a preference for burial or cremation.

In addition to drawing up a will specifying how property should be distributed upon their death, individuals can also complete advance directives regarding their medical care in the event they lack the capacity to express their wishes at some time in the future. Although a will stating the deceased person's wishes for distribution of property must be made ahead of time, the term "advance directive" more commonly refers to the individual's wishes for his or her own end-of-life care.

The **living will** is an advance directive that first appeared in 1968, opening the way for public dialogue on end-of-life issues that previously were generally not discussed (Kastenbaum, 1999). This document instructs physicians and family members about a patient's wishes regarding the use of medical treatments that would artificially prolong the dying process if death is determined to be inevitable (Mishkin, Mezey, & Ramsey, 1995). Theoretically, a living will could request that life-prolonging measures be administered even if death is inevitable, but consent to withhold life-prolonging treatments is more typical. In most living wills, the preference is to withhold certain kinds of interventions ("artificial means" or "heroic measures") so that the dying process can take its own natural course. Also, living wills may give permission for medical personnel to administer "palliative" (pain-reducing) treatments even if such treatments hasten the actual moment of death (Corr et al., 2003).

Initially, there was no basis in law for the living will and many physicians and hospitals tended to shy away from it out of fear of malpractice lawsuits. In recent years, however, there is greater acceptance of the idea that a competent adult has the right to refuse medical treatment. Today, each state in the United States has procedures for creating a legally valid living will (Mishkin et al., 1995).

In 1991, federal legislation known as the **Patient Self-Determination Act (PSDA)** was enacted (Kastenbaum, 1999). The PSDA directs all health-care facilities (hospitals, nursing homes, health maintenance organizations) that receive funds from Medicare and Medicaid (two government health-care programs discussed in Chapter 3) to provide patients with information on advance directives that could be used in case a critical situation should arise. Individuals who do not already have an advance directive must be told about it so they can express their preference for accepting or refusing treatment. In addition, patients are asked to specify who will make medical decisions if they are not able to do so themselves. However, Kastenbaum (1999) points out that health-care organizations vary a great deal in how extensively they explain a patient's options. Some simply ask patients to endorse one of two statements such as "I want my life to be prolonged as long as possible, no matter what my quality of life" or "I do not want my life prolonged if I will be permanently unconscious." Unfortunately, not all people are competent to make this decision at the time they enter a hospital or nursing home. Clearly, it is preferable for people to understand and execute advance directives when they are of sound mind and before they are facing a medical crisis.

Efforts to educate community-living older adults about advance directives have not been very effective in boosting the number who actually execute them. In one study, Cicirelli (1997) asked 388 European American and African American adults ranging from 60 to 100 years of age about the end-of-life decision they would make if they faced a situation in which their quality of life was poor. Interestingly, even under dire circumstances, the majority of these older adults stated they would want to continue living for as long as possible, undergoing whatever treatments might extend their lives. Those most likely to favor maintaining life tended to be African American and to have lower socio-economic status (less education and lower occupational level) and stronger religious feelings. Also, they tended to have less fear of dying but greater fear of destruction of the body. In contrast, those more likely to favor ending their lives tended to be European American, to have higher socioeconomic status and weaker religious feelings, and to have more fear of the dying process but less fear of destruction of the body. In this and other studies (Smyer & Allen-Burge, 1999), many older adults express a preference for a family member, close friend, or even a physician, to make treatment decisions for them should they become incapacitated.

The **durable power of attorney in health-care matters** is another advance directive whereby the individual designates a trusted relative or friend to make health-care decisions on his or her behalf in the event of serious incapacitating physical illness or mental incapacity. Without this document, the medical system generally relies on relatives to make such decisions. However, the individual can use this document to specify in advance which of several family members should be the final decision maker. This can be crucial when relatives are likely to disagree about what medical decision should be made (Mishkin et al., 1995), or when the individual prefers a close friend or companion rather than a relative to make health-care decisions.

In sum, the will, living will, and durable power of attorney for health-care matters are documents that individuals can use to plan ahead for a time when they themselves are unable to make important decisions about their property or health care. It is advisable to give a relative or close companion the name of the lawyer who has a copy of the will. Also, a relative or good friend as well as a health-care provider should have copies of the living will and durable power of attorney for health-care matters because these documents serve no purpose if nobody knows where they are.

Anxiety About Death

It may seem paradoxical that older adults are closest to death, but as a group, they express less anxiety about, or fear of, death compared to middle-aged adults (Kastenbaum, 1999; Fortner, Neimeyer, & Rybarczyk, 2000). One possible reason for the higher anxiety among middle-aged adults is that many of them have children who are not fully launched into independent lives and they may also be involved in helping elderly parents. Anxiety about death could stem from concern about the well-being of those who would be left behind. In contrast, older adults are likely to have children who are fully

California Medical Association
DURABLE POWER OF ATTORNEY FOR HEALTH CARE DECISIONS
(California Probate Code Sections 4600-4753)

WARNING TO PERSON EXECUTING THIS DOCUMENT

This is an important legal document. Before executing this document, you should know these important facts:

This document gives the person you designate as your agent (the attorney-in-fact) the power to make health care decisions for you. Your agent must act consistently with your desires as stated in this document or otherwise made known.

Except as you otherwise specify in this document, this document gives your agent power to consent to your doctor not giving treatment or stopping treatment necessary to keep you alive.

Notwithstanding this document, you have the right to make medical and other health care decisions for yourself so long as you can give informed consent with respect to the particular decision. In addition, no treatment may be given to you over your objection, and health care necessary to keep you alive may not be stopped or withheld if you object at the time.

This document gives your agent authority to consent, to refuse to consent, or to withdraw consent to any care, treatment, service, or procedure to maintain, diagnose, or treat a physical or mental condition. This power is subject to any statement of your desires and any limitations that you include in this document. You may

state in this document any types of treatment that you do not desire. In addition, a court can take away the power of your agent to make health care decisions for you if your agent (1) authorizes anything that is illegal, (2) acts contrary to your known desires or (3) where your desires are not known, does anything that is clearly contrary to your best interests.

This power will exist for an indefinite period of time unless you limit its duration in this document.

You have the right to revoke the authority of your agent by notifying your agent or your treating doctor, hospital, or other health care provider orally or in writing of the revocation.

Your agent has the right to examine your medical records and to consent to their disclosure unless you limit this right in this document.

Unless you otherwise specify in this document, this document gives your agent the power after you die to (1) authorize an autopsy, (2) donate your body or parts thereof for transplant or therapeutic or educational or scientific purposes, and (3) direct the disposition of your remains.

If there is anything in this document that you do not understand, you should ask a lawyer to explain it to you.

1. CREATION OF DURABLE POWER OF ATTORNEY FOR HEALTH CARE

By this document I intend to create a durable power of attorney by appointing the person designated below to make health care decisions for me as allowed by Sections 4600 to 4753, inclusive, of the California Probate Code. This power of attorney shall not be affected by my subsequent incapacity. I hereby revoke any prior durable power of attorney for health care. I am a California resident who is at least 18 years old, of sound mind, and acting of my own free will.

2. APPOINTMENT OF HEALTH CARE AGENT

(Fill in below the name, address and telephone number of the person you wish to make health care decisions for you if you become incapacitated. You should make sure that this person agrees to accept this responsibility. The following may not serve as your agent: (1) your treating health care provider; (2) an operator of a community care facility or residential care facility for the elderly; or (3) an employee of your treating health care provider, a community care facility, or a residential care facility for the elderly, unless that employee is related to you by blood, marriage or adoption, or unless you are also an employee of the same treating provider or facility. If you are a conservatee under the Lanterman-Petris-Short Act (the law governing involuntary commitment to a mental health facility) and you wish to appoint your conservator as your agent, you must consult a lawyer, who must sign and attach a special declaration for this document to be valid.)

I, _____, hereby appoint:
                                    (insert your name)

Name _____

Address _____

Work Telephone (_____) _____   Home Telephone (_____) _____

as my agent (attorney-in-fact) to make health care decisions for me as authorized in this document. I understand that this power of attorney will be effective for an indefinite period of time unless I revoke it or limit its duration below.

(Optional) This power of attorney shall expire on the following date: _____.

© California Medical Association 1996 (revised)

Individuals can use this advance directive to designate a trusted friend or relative to make health care decisions on their behalf if they are unable to do so themselves.

grown, independent adults, and they may worry less about leaving their children to fend for themselves. However, some studies have found that older women are more anxious about death than older men are (Neimeyer & Fortner, 1995), perhaps because of their more nurturing role. Many older adults feel that they have had time to carry out whatever they planned to do in their lives (Kastenbaum, 1996) and hopefully they consider their lives to have had purpose and meaning.

Thorson and Powell (2000) point out that young adults think that they are immortal and they find it difficult to imagine there might not be a long future stretching out in front of them. In contrast, older adults are well aware that death is inevitable and some feel that the future does not hold as many possibilities as it did earlier in life. It is conceivable that older adults express less anxiety about death because they experience the death of friends and loved ones with increasing frequency as time goes by, so in some sense they have been socialized to the possibility of death. It is not uncommon for older adults to read the obituaries in local newspapers on a daily basis. Many older adults are not so much afraid of death as they are about the circumstances of dying. They wish to die with dignity.

Even so, among adults of any age, there are individual differences in death anxiety. Any conclusion that older adults are less anxious about death than middle-aged adults must be qualified by the ethnic and religious group to which they belong, by their individual coping styles and competencies, and by the environments in which they live (Neimeyer & Fortner, 1995). Cicirelli (2002) found no differences in the fear of death expressed by European American and African American Midwestern community-living adults over the age of 60. Based on a review of numerous studies on death anxiety in older adults, Fortner et al. (2000) concluded that older adults with strong religious beliefs (that is, intrinsic belief in God and belief in the afterlife) had less death anxiety than those with no strong religious beliefs. However, religious behaviors such as frequent church attendance were unrelated to level of death anxiety. Further studies of adults with various ethnic, racial, and religious backgrounds would do much to increase our understanding of death anxiety over the adult life span. One factor that does play a role is health. Older adults with more physical problems and those who live in institutional settings such as nursing homes express higher anxiety about death compared to those in better health who live in the community (Fortner et al., 2000). Perhaps older adults who are dependent upon others feel less in control of their environment and therefore have more anxiety about the circumstances surrounding their death (Cicirelli, 2002).

Stages of Death and Dying

In spite of its inevitability, death has been, and to some extent still is, a taboo topic in American society. In the 1960s, Elisabeth Kübler-Ross, a Swiss psychiatrist practicing at the University of Chicago Hospital, was approached by theology students who wanted to learn more about terminally ill patients. To humanize the dying process and counteract the tendency she saw in America to depersonalize dying persons, Kübler-Ross invited dying patients to come to a seminar and share their thoughts and feelings with the students. Based on interviews with over 200 patients, many of whom were diagnosed with terminal cancer, Kübler-Ross (1969, 1974) noted five stages in the dying process (shown in Table 12.2).

Of **Kübler-Ross's five stages of death and dying,** the first is denial, which often occurs when the individual is diagnosed with a terminal illness. The individual's initial reaction is often disbelief and a feeling that this diagnosis could not possibly be correct. According to Kübler-Ross, denial serves as a short-term buffer, which allows time for the individual to take in shocking news. As the realization begins to sink in that there is no mistake about the diagnosis, the individual may express anger and resentment that other people are healthy. In the bargaining stage, the individual attempts to strike a deal

Table 12.2 | Five Stages of Death and Dying

Stage	Example of a Dying Patient's Response
Denial	No, not me, it cannot be true.
Anger	Why me?
Bargaining	Maybe I will have more time if I pray and ask God nicely.
Depression	I am going to die and that is sad.
Acceptance	I am at peace and ready for death.

Adapted from Kübler-Ross (1969).

for more time or a second chance by promising to be on his or her best behavior, by strictly following a doctor's orders, or perhaps by praying. One phenomenon that may be related to this stage is the evidence for a dip in deaths prior to birthdays and major holidays followed by an increase afterward. In the next stage, depression, the individual feels a great sense of loss and sadness that his or her life is coming to an end. During this stage, there is a tendency to withdraw from emotional attachments to all but a few people with whom the dying individual has the most meaningful relationship. In the final stage, acceptance, the individual has reached a state of peace that the end is near.

Kübler-Ross's stages captured the attention of professionals who deal with death and dying and many adopted her ideas wholeheartedly. Eventually, however, some leveled criticism, contending that dying patients do not necessarily progress through the stages in an orderly manner and furthermore that not every dying individual goes through all of the stages Kübler-Ross described. For example, not all dying patients bargain for more time, nor do all of them reach the final stage of acceptance. Such criticism was not entirely fair because Kübler-Ross never insisted on hard and fast rules for her stages. In fact, she herself pointed out that some individuals remain in the stage of denial right up to the end. Reactions to dying vary considerably depending upon the specific illness and upon such factors as age, cultural background, religion, and the dying individual's social network (Kastenbaum, 1996). Also, there may be a series of overlapping reactions during the dying process (Wortman & Silver, 1990). In any case, Kübler-Ross's stages have been a major cornerstone in our thinking about the dying process, and it would be a mistake to underestimate her contribution to lifting some of the taboos about death and dying.

Not only do Kübler-Ross's stages apply to dying, but they also are helpful for understanding how people deal with the loss of a loved one. In fact, Kübler-Ross contended that an individual with a sudden dying trajectory obviously has not had time to work through the stages. However, the loved ones left behind may go through these stages as they deal with their loss. With a lengthier trajectory, close friends and relatives as well as the dying individual him- or herself may experience aspects of Kübler-Ross's stages. In some instances, Kübler-Ross's stages have also been applied to loss through circumstances other than death of a loved one. For example, married individuals who separate or divorce may experience feelings similar to those who have lost a loved one through death.

Care of the Dying Patient

In American society, most medical care is administered in traditional hospital settings, and approximately 50 percent of people who die do so in hospitals (Corr et al., 2003). Even so, the focus of traditional hospital care is on diagnostic testing and interventions aimed to extend life (Kastenbaum, 1999). Unfortunately, not all dying patients can benefit from the acute care provided in traditional hospital settings. Even when they cannot be cured, however, they may need pain-reducing (palliative) care.

Hospice care is an alternative to the acute medical intervention provided in traditional hospital settings. It is administered by a team of professionals including physicians, nurses, social workers, and counselors, but highly trained volunteers also play an important role. The aim of hospice care is to enhance the terminally ill patient's quality of life. Medication is administered as needed to control the patient's pain. In addition to palliative treatment, spiritual, psychological, and social support are provided not only for patients but for their families as well.

The hospice concept had its beginnings in care for the ill given by religious orders of nuns in Ireland and England. Today's hospice movement is attributed to Dr. Cicely Saunders, who founded St. Christopher's Hospice in southeast London in 1967 as a place to care for incurably ill patients (Corr et al., 2003). Initially, hospice care was provided on an in-patient basis in units located within a traditional hospital or in nearby buildings. The atmosphere of hospice units or buildings conveys a sense of warmth and comfort for patients and family members, who are encouraged to visit at any hour of the day or night. Later, hospice care was extended to terminally ill outpatients who wish to remain in their own homes.

The first hospital-based hospice in North America was established in 1975 as a palliative care unit in Royal Victoria Hospital in Montreal. In the United States, the first hospice program was established in 1974 in New Haven, Connecticut, as a community-based home-care program (Corr et al., 2003). Today, there are more than 2,000 hospice programs in North America (Hayslip, 1996). Starting in 1982, hospice care was approved as a benefit by Medicare, the federally sponsored health insurance program for older adults in the United States (Corr et al., 2003). To be eligible for hospice care, Medicare patients cannot be seeking cure-oriented treatment for a terminal illness. However, patients do have the right to withdraw from hospice care if they change their minds and decide to pursue life-prolonging measures (Corr et al., 2003).

In sum, hospice care for terminally ill patients and their families emphasizes quality of life over quantity of life. Dying persons are encouraged to make decisions for themselves until they are unable or unwilling to do so (Hayslip, 1996), and they are made as comfortable as possible. After the patient's death, hospice workers provide emotional support to family members.

A topic that has sparked heated controversy is euthanasia, a term that refers to a gentle and easy death, or more specifically to the means of inducing, or bringing about, a gentle and easy end to another person's life (Jecker, 1996). **Active euthanasia** is defined as taking action to induce a patient's death, such as administering a lethal injection. **Passive euthanasia** is defined as withholding action that would sustain a patient's life, such as failing to apply cardiopulmonary resuscitation after a heart attack (Jecker, 1996). Euthanasia is usually distinguished from **assisted suicide,** which involves providing a patient with the means (for example, supplying lethal medications) to end his or her own life (Jecker, 1996).

Some have argued that euthanasia and assisted suicide are compassionate when mentally competent patients who are experiencing severe pain make repeated requests that something be done to end their suffering. However, opponents of these practices argue that they violate the sanctity of human life and furthermore that it is not always possible to determine whether patients are mentally competent when they ask for help to end their lives. Because a patient's true wishes may not be known, critics warn that helping them end their lives may not be what they really want. Other arguments against euthanasia and assisted suicide are that it is difficult to decide how great a patient's pain and suffering should be before such practices are applied and also that it is not always known how soon death would occur naturally.

How are euthanasia and assisted suicide viewed from a legal standpoint? According to Quadagno (2002), in the year 2000, the Dutch parliament approved a bill allowing euthanasia and physician-assisted suicide, thus making Holland the first country to legalize these practices. Prior to that time, some Dutch physicians had quietly engaged in these practices when a patient had an incurable condition that was causing extreme suffering and when that patient initiated a request that his or her life be terminated after being told about all the medical options available (Jecker, 1996; Quadagno, 2002). In the United States, such practices are not supported by the American Medical Association. Even so, the state of Oregon allows physicians to prescribe, but not administer, lethal medication (assisted suicide) with the restriction that a terminally ill patient must be mentally competent and must request it repeatedly (Jecker, 1996). There is little doubt that ethical issues concerning euthanasia and assisted suicide will continue to be debated.

BEREAVEMENT AND LOSS

During the course of our lives, most of us will experience the loss of meaningful relationships. Such loss may occur in early childhood when a best friend moves to another neighborhood or city, or it may occur in adolescence or adulthood when a love relationship ends. Loss also occurs when someone we know dies.

Bereavement refers to both the situation and the long-term process of adjusting to the death of someone to whom a person feels close (Lund, 1996). The terms grief and mourning refer to specific aspects of the broader bereavement process (Lund, 1996). **Grief** is the affective, or emotional, response to bereavement, whereas **mourning** refers to culturally patterned ways of behaving and the rituals followed when there is a loss (Lund, 1996). Aspects of mourning include participating in funeral or memorial services as well as burials, abstaining from everyday routines for a specified time, dressing in certain kinds of clothing, and behaving in a way that is culturally acceptable for someone who has lost a loved one, especially a family member.

Bereavement due to the loss of a close family member or friend is not unique to older adulthood, but in modern societies it occurs more frequently in the later years. However, children and young adults may also go through a bereavement process when they lose an older family member. With the increase in life expectancy, it will not be unusual for children to experience bereavement with the death of a great grandparent.

Attitudes Toward Death

Most of us experience feelings of sadness and grief over the death of loved ones regardless of their age. However, our attitude toward family members and close friends may not be the same as our attitude toward death in general, or the death of people we do not know well (Tomer, 2000). Is there any difference in the responses people have to the death of a child or young adult compared to the death of an older adult?

According to Jecker and Schneiderman (1996), people tend to view the death of a child or young person as a catastrophic event, but they are more likely to think the death of an older adult is sad but acceptable. For example, there may be feelings of sorrow, anger, despair, and even a sense of injustice when a child dies because the family could not obtain a bone marrow transplant. In contrast, there may be a sense of loss over an older adult age 70 or 80 who dies because of age-based rationing of kidney dialysis, but people are less likely to consider this a tragic event. Even when medical intervention has little chance of success, medical teams may treat young persons more aggressively than they do older persons. Why is this so, and is this way of thinking typical in all societies?

Jecker and Schneiderman (1996) contend that one justification for the attitude that death is unfair when people are young is that young people have not yet had a chance to experience events such as falling in love, becoming a parent, or fulfilling life ambitions. Also, a common view in contemporary American society is that the younger generation represents society's future and young people have more potential contributions to make. In contrast, older adults have already had opportunities to experience meaningful events. Furthermore, they have made whatever contributions to society that they are going to make. In some sense, older adults symbolize the past, and upcoming younger generations are expected to improve upon the contributions that older generations have made.

Jecker and Schneiderman (1996) emphasize that not all societies hold this view. For example, in ancient Greek society and among some groups living in Africa today, the death of a small child is considered less tragic than the death of a mature adult who has built a network of meaningful relationships and earned respect and honor in the community.

Even so, if all human beings are considered equally worthy, shouldn't medical technology that could prolong life be available regardless of age? There is little doubt that ethical questions about who has access to both basic and more specialized health care will become increasingly important in modern societies with aging populations but only a limited supply of sophisticated and expensive medical technology. Under such conditions, a society's attitude can influence the way health resources and life-prolonging techniques are allocated among different age groups. Nonetheless, we do not usually think in terms of age when it comes to losing family members or close friends.

Loss of a Spouse

The marital relationship is often longstanding, so death of a spouse has a clear impact on the one left behind. More research has been conducted on the effects of losing a spouse than on losing others who hold meaningful places in our lives. However, much of what is known about loss of a spouse can be applied to the loss of any close relationship. Losing a spouse, partner, significant other, sibling, or close friend becomes more and more probable as people progress through the adult years.

The term **widowhood** refers to the status of a person who has lost a spouse through death and has not remarried. Becoming a widow or widower, the respective terms for a woman or a man who loses a spouse, involves the event of a spouse's death, followed by a funeral and then a period of bereavement. However, when a spouse suffers from a long-term illness and has a lengthy dying trajectory, the process of becoming a widow or widower may start before the actual event of the spouse's death (Lopata, 1995).

The Bereavement Process   How do people deal with the loss of a spouse or any close relationship? Early in the bereavement process, feelings of grief include disbelief, confusion, numbness, sadness, and in some cases anger and guilt. The widowed individual, or for that matter any person who loses a close companion, may feel abandoned, lonely, depressed, and preoccupied with thoughts of the events surrounding the loved one's death (Lund, 1996). However, there are no set rules about the exact nature or intensity of people's reactions to losing a spouse. Some feel anger or guilt, while others feel a sense of relief, especially if the spouse had a long and painful dying trajectory. Some suffer from overwhelming sadness and depression while others view their situation as an opportunity for growth (Lund, 1996).

There is considerable variation not only in the nature but also in the time course of the reactions people have to the loss of a loved one (Wortman & Silver, 1990). For some individuals, feelings of grief are intense but subside quickly. For others, feelings of grief are less intense but they resurface months or years later

(Lund, 1996). A common view is that people who do not show signs of distress within the first weeks or months following the loss of a loved one will not be successful in "working through" to a resolution of the bereavement process because feelings of distress will "leak out" at some later time, possibly causing physical and mental health problems. Contrary to this view, however, Wortman and Silver (1990) point out that a minority of individuals do not express intense distress either shortly after a loss or later on, but their long-term adjustment does not differ much from that of individuals who do express intense distress.

Some studies indicate that feelings of psychological and physical distress taper off after 12 months, but never to a level as low as that of individuals who are not bereaved (Gallagher-Thompson, 1995). Most bereaved individuals manage to get through one day at a time but for many, the bereavement process can take up to 2 years (Martin-Matthews, 1996). Eventually, life may become enjoyable once again. Even so, widowed individuals often report, "You never get over it—you learn to live with it" (Lund, 1996).

Successful mastery of the bereavement process is thought to involve three tasks: (a) accepting the loss intellectually (being able to make sense of why the loss occurred), (b) accepting the loss emotionally (no longer feeling the need to avoid reminders of the loss), and (c) recovering to a normal level of functioning (see Wortman & Silver, 1990).

For the most part, the nature and length of the bereavement process is related to the bereaved individual's previous experiences and personality traits, the social support available from close friends and family members after the loss, the circumstances surrounding a spouse or loved one's death, and the bereaved individual's competence in handling the tasks of daily living on his or her own (Lund, 1996). For example, the sudden death of a spouse who seemed to be perfectly healthy would be particularly difficult for the widow or widower who was highly dependent on the deceased spouse or did everything in the company of the deceased spouse and had no close social relationships outside the marriage. Also, it is important to recognize that loss of a spouse or significant other can occur in the context of other stressors (Wortman & Silver, 1990). For example, a spouse's long illness may result in financial hardship for the surviving spouse, or the surviving spouse may suffer physically or psychologically from a long stretch of unrelieved intensive care for the deceased spouse. Furthermore, losing a spouse can be more stressful if the surviving spouse is also responsible for the care of dependent children or older parents (Martin-Matthews, 1996).

We still have much to learn about the similarities and differences in the bereavement processes of young and older individuals who lose spouses (Gallagher-Thompson, 1995). Comparisons of widowed younger and older adults are complicated by many factors. Younger widowed adults have probably been married for fewer years than older widowed adults, and they are more likely to have responsibilities for dependent children and jobs. These responsibilities can be stressful, but on the positive side, children and co-workers may provide comfort and emotional support. In contrast, widowed older adults may have fewer responsibilities, but at the same time they may not have as many opportunities for social and emotional support. The loneliness that bereaved older adults feel may be especially intense because many are left to live on their own for the first time in decades.

The experience of widowhood can vary for different ethnic groups. In some groups, it is assumed that if a spouse dies, the widowed older adult will move into the same house with adult children and be taken care of by them. A widowed older adult, especially a woman, may be expected to devote all of her attention to her grandchildren. In other groups, widowed older adults are expected to carry on alone, developing new interests and new social networks. Also, in some ethnic groups, family members tend to live close by and may be available to offer emotional support. In other groups, adult children and other family members are scattered across the country and remain in the vicinity for only a short time following the funeral.

Comparing Widows and Widowers   Is loss of a spouse experienced any differently by women and men? Sheer numbers could play a role in this regard. Older widows (women) in the United States greatly outnumber older widowers (men). As of 2001, almost half (46 percent) of women age 65 and older were widows, whereas only 14 percent of men age 65 and over were widowers, and there were over four times as many older widows (8.49 million) as there were older widowers (2.0 million) (A Profile of Older Americans, 2002). Reasons for this gender imbalance are that women tend to marry men older than they are, women have a longer life expectancy than men, and women are less likely than men to remarry once they are widowed.

Not only are older widowers more likely to remarry, but many pick women younger than they are. This is one reason older men are more likely than older women to live in the community with a spouse until the end of their days and wives will probably care for older husbands at some point (Moen, 1996). In contrast, older women are more likely than older men to live alone once they become widowed.

Davidson (2001) interviewed 25 widows and 26 widowers over the age of 65 who lived in the United Kingdom and had been alone for at least two years. Asked what they thought about remarriage, more women than men stated they were hesitant to consider remarriage because they were reluctant to give up their new-found freedom to do whatever they want even though they felt guilty that this was probably selfish. Unfortunately, when widowed women begin to suffer from health problems, many find it difficult to continue living on their own. The fact that more nursing home residents are women than men is undoubtedly related to the longer life expectancy of women and the lower likelihood that older women have a living spouse to serve in a caregiving role if necessary.

Widowed older adults must assume responsibility for tasks that spouses performed for years or decades. Many in the present generation of widowed older women depended on their husbands to take care of taxes, insurance, and other financial arrangements. When they lose their spouses, they are faced with the daunting task of handling these things by themselves. This gender

Often, widowed older men must assume responsibility for household tasks that their spouses were in charge of throughout the years they were married.

division may be less marked in the future now that more women are participating in the paid labor force and presumably have greater financial independence and know-how.

Many in today's generation of older widowers depended on their wives to cook and take charge of other household tasks. For the first time, they are faced with learning how to prepare nutritious meals and perform household duties that they took for granted. To the extent there is less gender-based division of labor among young and middle-aged couples, future generations of older widows are likely to have greater skills in financial management and future generations of older widowers may have more expertise in the kitchen.

Although widows and widowers both go through a period of bereavement, the process has a more negative emotional impact on men than it does on women. Men derive more of their social and emotional support exclusively from a spouse than women do (Moen, 1996), and men who lose a spouse are more likely than women are to suffer from depression (Umberson, Wortman, & Kessler, 1992). In addition, the overall rate of mortality increases in the first six months after the death of a spouse, but the risk is much greater for men who lose their wives than it is for women who lose their husbands (Wortman & Silver, 1990).

Women often find that as time goes by, their social interactions with married couples become less and less frequent (Norris & Tindale, 1994). This can be especially difficult for a woman who is the first in her circle of married friends to lose a spouse. Eventually, however, many widowed women form a network with other widows with whom they can socialize and from whom they can derive emotional support. Widows who keep active and see friends seem to adjust best (Quadagno, 2002). Fewer men have informal support groups consisting of widowers.

Widowed men often find social connections through remarriage. Even so, remarriage for a widower or a widow can meet with resistance from adult children, who are unable to conceive of an older parent being in love with someone else or who fear that the older parent's remarriage will jeopardize a possible inheritance. In addition to objections from children or other family members, another barrier to remarriage is a common reaction of a grieving spouse to idealize the deceased mate to the point of sanctification (Lopata, 1995). For example, a widower may remember his late wife as being perfect and having no irritating habits. It would be difficult for a living woman to meet these unrealistically high standards.

Typically, older widows are at a greater economic disadvantage compared to older widowers. In some instances, widowed women face financial difficulties immediately, especially if a spouse suffered from a lingering illness and incurred many medical expenses (Quadagno, 2002). For women more than for men, losing a spouse is associated with a significant drop in income (Moen, 1996). As described in Chapter 10, Social Security payments from the federal government are reduced when either member of an older couple dies. In addition, payments from a husband's private pension may cease upon his death. Although the majority of women age 65 and over may not be poor, many are "within poverty's reach" (Moen, 1996). Reduced economic resources can limit a widow's social life if she does not have sufficient funds for travel, eating in restaurants, or even entertaining friends at home. Advance financial planning is the key to minimizing the negative economic impact of widowhood. Future generations of women who are financially savvy may not suffer negative economic consequences with widowhood to the same extent the present generation does.

Loss of Other Meaningful Relationships

The losses experienced in older adulthood are not limited to widowhood. With regard to the marital relationship, loss can occur not only through death but also through divorce. As of 2001, 10 percent of older women and 9 percent of older men were divorced or separated (A Profile of Older Americans, 2002). These percentages are higher than they were in 1994, when only 6 percent of older women and 5 percent of older men were divorced or separated (A Profile of Older Americans, 1996). The increase can be attributed partly to a higher rate of divorce occurring in young and middle-adulthood, which is then reflected in a larger percent of older adults who are divorced (Hooyman & Kiyak, 2002). However, a small but growing number of people are divorcing in older adulthood after long-term marriages (Cooney, 1995), and such individuals probably go through bereavement as they adjust to the single life after decades of couplehood. After a divorce, older adults, and especially older women, experience a drop in financial status that can severely limit their daily activities and living situation (Kausler & Kausler, 1996).

In addition to losing marital or other partners, older adults with brothers and sisters experience loss of their siblings. Sibling relationships, which Chapter 9 discussed in detail, are based on a common family history, and many siblings find renewed closeness in later life. Relationships between older adult sisters are especially close and involve social and emotional support associated with feelings of well-being (Cicirelli, 1995). With the death of a sibling, the surviving brother or sister may feel intense grief and a sense of incompleteness, especially if the relationship was close. Because a deceased sibling's spouse and children are usually considered to be the primary mourners, the surviving bereaved sibling may not be given as much emotional support from family members as might be needed (Cicirelli, 1995).

Some older adults experience the loss of adult children. This is especially devastating because it goes against the natural order whereby members of the oldest generation are expected to predecease their children. We know less about older parents' bereavement following the death of an adult child than we do about their reactions to the death of a spouse. Also, some people reach their older adult years before they experience the loss of their parents. In the future, it may become more common for adults in their 60s and 70s to experience the loss of parents in their 80s, 90s, or older.

Finally, older adults lose friends. Long-standing friendships are based on a common history over an extended time, and rarely can they be replaced with newer friendships. Depending on how long the friendship has endured, it may be just as close or closer than a sibling relationship. The loss of close friends will most certainly be followed by bereavement not unlike that found with the loss of close siblings.

In sum, nobody is immune to the experience of bereavement. Over the course of a lifetime, one can suffer the loss of family members and close friends. With the loss of loved ones, especially spouses and companions, older adults must restructure their lives. The surviving member of a couple may be forced to learn new skills. After a period of bereavement, older adults must build or strengthen new social ties and perhaps substitute new activities and goals. New relationships may not substitute for those lost, but being able to form them can be important in determining an older adult's success in adapting to a changed environment.

AGING IN THE FUTURE

It may seem contradictory to speculate about the future after discussing death, dying, and loss. However, this seems less so if we stop to consider that death and bereavement are not separate from living but rather they are critical episodes within the experience of living (Kastenbaum, 1999). Given the premise that the life of every individual will end and that every living person will experience loss, let's look at some views on what the later stages of life may be like in the future.

We will center our discussion on two phases that have been described with regard to older adulthood: the **third age** and the **fourth age** There are no strict chronological boundaries, but the third age usually coincides with the young-old (65–74) years. (See Chapter 1 for further description of the young-old age category.) It can last for several years or extend as long as two decades (Baltes, 1997; Weiss & Bass, 2002). The fourth age coincides with advanced old age (Baltes, 1997). After contemplating what the future may hold for people in the third age and fourth age, we will make a final visit to the Selective Optimization with Compensation and Ecological Models.

The Third Age

According to Weiss and Bass (2002), the first age, youth, is a phase of life during which individuals prepare for the activities of maturity, namely employment and childrearing. In the second age, maturity, individuals give their time almost exclusively to those activities. The third age represents a phase in life before morbidity (illness) limits activity and mortality (death) brings everything to a close. In the third age, individuals are able to live life as they please before they enter the fourth age, which usually brings decline.

In some sense, the third age is an extension of middle age but without the work or childrearing responsibilities. Ideally, third agers have adequate pensions and accumulated savings that enable them to maintain the same standard of living they had prior to retirement. Furthermore, their health and vitality are sufficiently high so that there are no major limitations in their activities. In short, the third age is the time between retirement from the paid workforce and the start of age-imposed limitations.

What kind of lives do third agers lead? Their choices appear to be unlimited and include traveling, playing golf, visiting children and grandchildren, or just staying home and occasionally getting together with family and friends. Many third agers pay strict attention to physical fitness by walking, swimming, or participating in other sports and to cognitive fitness by exercising their memory and attending lectures, movies, or plays that stimulate their thinking. Occasionally, there may be crises such as family illness or the divorce of an adult child that requires their help. In general, however, third agers drift along, leading pleasant lives with some degree of routine (Weiss & Bass, 2002). Some do volunteer work or pursue interests they put off earlier in life. Others launch new careers for the love of it, and this may or may not be associated with income. In short, older adults in the third age enjoy great freedom.

Weiss and Bass (2002) contend that the third age as just described has become available to larger numbers of Americans for two main reasons. First, a large portion of middle-class retired older adults enjoy a high standard of living thanks to generous company pensions, carefully accumulated savings and investments, and substantial financial gains from homes bought years earlier for low prices and sold years later for extremely high ones. Second, increases in life expectancy due to medical advances in treating and preventing diseases that used to afflict individuals in their older adult years have made it possible for more people to maintain their health in this phase of life (see Chapter 3 for more description). For example, a man who may have had a debilitating or fatal heart attack at age 65 in years past may now enjoy an active lifestyle thanks to new medications and advances in coronary bypass surgery. The vitality of many people during this phase illustrates a phenomenon referred to in Chapter 3 as compression of morbidity, which means that illness and physical limitations are pushed to a later point in the life course. Clearly, the third age as just described does not include older adults whose work careers were less steady, those who held low-paying jobs throughout their lives and now have difficulty making ends meet, or those who suffer from poor health.

What is the future outlook for the third age? Clearly this is speculative, but there are indications that fewer people will fit Weiss and Bass's (2002) characterization of the carefree third ager who enjoys a leisurely lifestyle. To be sure, advances in medical care will make it possible for more individuals to remain in good health in their young-old years, but retirement in the early or mid-60s may be a thing of the past (see Chapter 10 for further discussion). The chronological age needed to qualify for full Social Security pension benefits from the federal government is increasing from 65 to 66 and then 67. Furthermore, fewer companies will offer the generous private pension plans that so many of today's third agers enjoy (see Chapter 10 for discussion of pensions). Middle-class wage earners in today's young adult and middle-aged cohorts are less accustomed to saving money and more comfortable with incurring debt. In addition, the cost of health care is soaring at the very time cutbacks are being made in the health insurance benefits companies pay both workers and retirees. In sum, it is becoming more and more difficult for families to stay ahead financially let alone save enough money to live for two or three decades in retirement.

In the future, Riley's (1994) model for an age-integrated social structure with a balance among work, education, and leisure throughout life (described in Chapter 10) may apply to more members of the young-old age group. Young-old adults will probably continue to work for a longer time. They may cut back on their working hours, but there will be less demarcation between the working years and retirement years. Furthermore, fewer individuals will work for years at one job for a company that will eventually reward them with a guaranteed lifetime pension. People are likely to remain in the labor force to later ages, and they will probably change not only jobs but also careers during the course of their working lives. Consequently, people of all ages will have to update their skills through education to keep current with technical and other advances in the workplace. Recent legislation makes it possible for adults in their late 60s to continue working without being penalized by losing Social Security benefits.

Although Social Security benefits will be paid when workers reach their late 60s, fewer private companies will offer generous lifetime pension benefits. This means that in the future, people will need to shoulder the financial responsibility for their own retirement. To accomplish this, they will have to develop a plan early in their work careers that will enable them to phase out their working hours or retire altogether from the paid labor force later. It is likely that more women will have work careers from an earlier age, which should result in a better financial situation in their later years. With regard to couples, women's increased participation in the labor force may make it possible for men to decrease their working hours. Thus, there may be greater similarity between the working lives of women and men throughout the adult years (O'Rand, 1996).

In addition to being in charge of their own financial well-being, third agers may also have an increased level of responsibility for others. With the high divorce rate among adult children, third agers may be called upon to help financially, especially when there are grandchildren. Also, third agers themselves are more likely to be divorced. Many will have been married more than once so they are likely to have stepchildren and step grandchildren. There may be urgent calls for help from adult children and stepchildren with full-time careers when grandchildren and step grandchildren have school vacations or cannot attend day care due to illness.

Another responsibility likely to fall more heavily on the shoulders of third agers in the future is care of the older generation. The term sandwich generation (described in Chapter 9) generally refers to the middle-aged generation, most often women who care for both children and older parents. At present, however, more middle-aged women work full time. With the increase in life expectancy, more people in their 60s will be in good health and many will have parents in their 80s and 90s. If these older parents live in the community, they may need help with transportation and household duties. In the future, there may be more gender crossover, with caregiving for the oldest generation more evenly distributed across young-old men and women (Moen, 1996).

The beanpole family structure (described in Chapter 9) means that each family will have more living generations but there will be fewer members in each one. Because families will have fewer children, fewer third agers will be available to share in caregiving responsibilities for elderly parents. Furthermore, third agers themselves may still be working part time or possibly full time. Perhaps grandchildren and great-grandchildren will take on a greater share of the caregiving responsibilities for the oldest generation. Working conditions may be sufficiently flexible so that individuals of all ages will be able to help the oldest family members on a regular basis and not just when there is a health crisis.

In sum, the days of a footloose and fancy-free third age may be numbered. In the future, third agers may have less time for the pursuit of carefree leisure. This might sound negative, but there could be a silver lining. Weiss and Bass (2002) claim that many third agers find life enjoyable but do not feel as though they are fully engaged or contributing to society. In the coming years, they may not have to worry about remaining engaged and there will be less fear of boredom because many of them will be working at least part time, and they will be called upon to help both the younger and older generations. In short, they will have more responsibilities, but their lives may also have more purpose.

The Fourth Age

The fourth age is the phase of advanced old age often marked by the 80th birthday onward (Baltes, 1997). It overlaps with the late old-old age category and the oldest-old age category, which is the fastest-growing segment of the population in the United States and other technologically advanced countries. (See Chapter 1 for further description of these age categories.) Those who reach the age of 80 have an excellent chance of living an additional seven years or longer.

The fourth age often brings declining independence for all but the most fortunate and the need to face issues related to deteriorating health. Thus, there is good reason for concern about the quality of life in this phase of older adulthood (Baltes, 1997; Lawton, 2001). In studies conducted both in the United States and Germany, a sizeable proportion of fourth agers were found to suffer from some degree of dysfunction that forced them to limit their level of activity (Baltes, 1997). The risk of dysfunction and inactivity was greater for women, who are more likely than men are to be living alone.

In the fourth age, dysfunction may be not only physical but also cognitive. For example, the risk of dementia such as Alzheimer's disease (see Chapter 11 for more discussion) increases dramatically from the decade of the 60s to that of the 90s. Although the majority of fourth agers will be spared, more people will be reaching the phase of life when the risk of dementia is very real. It is crucial that researchers be given sufficient resources to continue their investigation into ways to prevent or treat the symptoms of dementia. With regard to mental health issues such as depression (see Chapter 11), future fourth agers will probably be more willing to seek help when necessary, and hopefully they will have access to mental health services that enable them to experience pleasure and satisfaction in this final phase of life.

In addition to the availability of such services, what other factors play a role in determining the quality of life in the fourth age? The secret to success may lie at least partly in living environments that enable individuals with some physical or sensory limitations to remain as independent as possible. For example, improved visual cues may make it safer for those individuals in their 80s and older who continue driving. Large signs that clearly mark danger zones should be posted far in advance of any hazard. Perhaps devices could be installed in cars to assist older drivers who have hearing difficulties. For example, a sound sensor that responds to sirens could be programmed to trigger a flashing light on the dashboard to ensure that older drivers pull over in time.

For older adults who choose not to drive or who should not drive, other forms of transportation must be available. In this regard, older adults who live in urban areas with efficient public transportation systems are likely to fare better than those in suburbs, small cities, or rural areas. There will be a greater need for reasonably priced door-to-door car or van service. For older pedestrians, "walk" signs must be set to allow sufficient time for crossing the street, and benches should be strategically placed in shopping districts and malls.

Fourth agers who live in the community in their own houses or apartments are likely to need in-home services, especially if family members do not live nearby or cannot assist them on a regular basis. They may need to have groceries and other items delivered to their homes, especially when the weather limits their mobility. A number of grocery chains have implemented online grocery shopping and home-delivery service for a set charge and minimum order. Unfortunately, some have discontinued such service because the demand has not been sufficient to make such a venture cost-effective. It remains to be seen whether an increasing number of fourth agers who need this type of service will make it a worthwhile business in the future. If not, fourth agers might need to employ personal shoppers who can deliver groceries, clothing, or other items to their homes or perhaps accompany them on shopping trips or to medical appointments or other activities. In addition, there may be increased demand for day care or daytime activities and programs in community centers that provide both social and cognitive stimulation. As well, there will be a greater need for door-to-door transportation to these centers so that older adults who no longer drive do not become housebound.

Although the majority of fourth agers will probably live in the community, this is a phase of life in which a substantial number will live in institutional settings such as nursing homes or assisted living facilities, or in independent adult congregate living facilities. (See Chapter 10 for a description of these living environments.) For these individuals, there will be some services on the premises, and transportation by van may be scheduled at intervals or by reservation. The challenge for older adults who reside in these facilities is remaining integrated into the community and not becoming isolated from the outside world.

In the future, there could well be a greater demand for living environments that are not institutional but at the same time offer some level of support. For example, apartment buildings might have the facilities to offer at least one meal a day on the premises and van transportation to stores or medical appointments. Ideally, such buildings would be located within safe walking distance of grocery stores, enclosed bus stops, schools where residents could play a volunteer role if they so choose, and shaded parks with adequate benches.

The growth of technology should be a boon to individuals in the fourth age, and the personal computer will most likely be an essential part of daily life. At present, approximately 70 percent of Americans in their 30s and 40s live in a home where a computer is available, and level of education is an important predictor of computer use (Cutler, Hendricks, & Guyer, 2003). Future cohorts of older adults will have a higher level of education compared to the present cohort. Accordingly, older adults should not be any different from middle-aged adults in their use of computers and related technology. E-mail keeps family members in touch even if they live at a distance, and it enables older adults to keep up with friends when they cannot visit in person. In addition to e-mail, telephones with visual capabilities will allow older adults to feel in touch with the outside world even if they cannot leave the house as often as they would like. Some forms of health care may even be delivered via such technology. For example, there have already been efforts by medical personnel to use computer technology to keep in touch with isolated older adults who live in rural areas. With further advances in technology, computers could be an efficient means of reaching older adults in urban areas as well. In addition, computers make it possible for pharmacists to keep track of patients' medications, thereby minimizing the chances of unwanted or dangerous drug interactions. In short, technology is set to play an ever-more important role in keeping fourth agers safe and in touch with family, friends, and health-care providers.

With regard to health care, a concern of increasing significance in the fourth age is cost. Although the federal health insurance program, Medicare (see Chapter 3), is available to older Americans once they reach the age of 65, there are costly deductibles and co-payments. In the future, affordable health care, including access to reasonably priced prescription medications, should contribute to a higher quality of life for more older adults.

In the future, advance planning will become increasingly important not only for finances but also for living environments. Many middle-aged adults are beginning to think in terms of their future housing needs. Some are modifying their present residences or designing new homes that can be configured to accommodate the changing physical needs that they anticipate in the later years. Less attention has been paid to the delivery of in-home services that may be necessary for fourth agers who plan to continue living in these carefully designed homes.

With gradual increases in life expectancy have come improvements in health and vitality for individuals in the third age and a chance for more of them to spend time in the fourth age. Despite the many theories about biological aging, scientists have yet to discover a way to halt the process or extend the human life span beyond 120 years. What has transpired, however, are discoveries that make it possible for more people to live closer to the maximum human longevity. Hopefully, the additional years will be ones of quality.

REVISITING THE SELECTIVE OPTIMIZATION WITH COMPENSATION AND ECOLOGICAL MODELS

Throughout this book, we have used two theoretical models to examine what it means to age successfully. The Selective Optimization with Compensation (SOC) and Ecological Models are by no means the only ones that could have been employed for this purpose, but together they provide a framework for conceptualizing aging as a process of adaptation.

Perhaps in no other aspect of the aging process is such a framework more valuable than when considering situations of loss. The SOC Model would emphasize the strategies aging individuals use to compensate for loss. For example, the older adult who is approaching the end of life may selectively concentrate on aspects of life and relationships that are most meaningful. After a period of bereavement, the older adult who suffers the loss of a spouse or other loved one must recreate an optimal life by selecting goals that will help compensate for those that are no longer possible. The Ecological Model would focus somewhat more heavily on environmental characteristics. For example, the older adult who experiences a decline in health is likely to achieve the best level of adaptation in an environment that continues to offer some degree of challenge but provides greater physical support than was needed previously.

The older adult who suffers the loss of a loved one may find it easier to adapt in an environment that offers an increased level of social support.

As people travel through life, they will experience loss. This may be loss of physical or cognitive capabilities, particularly in the fourth age, or loss of close relationships. It is remarkable that most older adults are able to adjust and derive a sense of life satisfaction in the face of loss.

KEY POINTS

- In the United States and other developed countries, death occurs most frequently in older adulthood. However, an individual's dying trajectory can be sudden or gradual.
- In the United States, people can make plans about their property by drawing wills and plans about their health care by signing living wills and designating a durable power of attorney for health-care matters.
- Older adults are closest to death, but as a group, they tend to express less anxiety about, or fear of, death compared to middle-aged adults. However, within the older group, those with strong religious beliefs (not necessarily frequent church or synagogue attendance) have less death anxiety than those with weak religious beliefs.
- Kübler-Ross noted five stages that can occur in the dying process: denial, anger, bargaining, depression, and acceptance. These stages can be experienced by the dying individual and by family members and close friends. However, not all people progress through these stages in a set order and not everyone goes through every stage.
- Hospice is a recent humane approach that provides palliative (pain-reducing) care for dying patients and addresses the needs of those who are terminally ill and the needs of their families.
- Euthanasia (both active and passive) and assisted suicide are ways of ending life that continue to be hotly debated from both a legal and ethical standpoint.
- Bereavement is the situation and long-term process of adjusting to the death of someone to whom a person feels close. Grief is the affective, or emotional, response to bereavement. Mourning refers to culturally patterned ways of behaving and the rituals followed when there is a loss.
- Comparisons between men and women who lose a spouse indicate that men (widowers) are less likely than women (widows) to suffer economically, more likely than women to remarry, and less likely than women to have a social network outside a marital relationship. Widowed men are more likely than widowed women to suffer from depression and are more at risk for mortality.
- The third age usually coincides with the young-old years and is the span of time between retirement and the start of age-imposed limitations. Many of today's third agers are in good health, are free from work and childrearing responsibilities, and have great freedom to do what they please.

- The fourth age is the phase of advanced old age marked by the 80th birthday onward, so it overlaps with the late old-old and oldest-old age categories. This rapidly growing segment of the U.S. population usually experiences some degree of decline in health and some loss of independence.

KEY TERMS

active euthanasia   459

assisted suicide   459

bereavement   460

durable power of attorney
in health-care matters   454

dying trajectory   451

fourth age   467

grief   460

hospice care   458

Kübler-Ross's five stages of death
and dying   456

living will   453

mourning   460

passive euthanasia   459

Patient Self-Determination Act
(PSDA)   453

third age   467

widowhood   461

will   451

To learn more about the issues discussed in this chapter, point your browser to http://www.infotrac-college.com and use the passcode from the InfoTrac College Edition card that came with your book. InfoTrac College Edition gives you access to complete articles from many different journals.

References

A Profile of Older Americans (1996). Document PF3049 (1296). Washington, DC: American Association of Retired Persons.

A Profile of Older Americans: 2000. Administration on Aging (AoA), U.S. Department of Health and Human Services (http://www.aoa.gov/aoa/stats/profile/html).

A Profile of Older Americans: 2002. Administration on Aging (AoA), U.S. Department of Health and Human Services (http://www.aoa.gov/aoa/stats/profile/html).

Abeles, N. (1997). *What practioners should know about working with older adults.* Washington, DC: American Psychological Association.

Abraham, J. D., & Hansson, R. O. (1995). Successful aging at work: An applied study of selection, optimization, and compensation through impression management. *Journal of Gerontology: Psychological Sciences, 50B,* P94–P103.

Adam, J. (1978). Sequential strategies and the separation of age, cohort, and time-of-measurement contributions to developmental data. *Psychological Bulletin, 85,* 1309–1316.

Albert, M. (1995). Alzheimer's disease. In G. L. Maddox et al. (Eds.), *The encyclopedia of aging* (2nd ed., pp. 56–57). New York: Springer.

Allaire, J. C., & Marsiske, M. (1999). Everyday cognition: Age and intellectual ability correlates. *Psychology and Aging, 14,* 627–644.

Allen-Burge, R., Storandt, M., Kincherf, D. A., & Rubin, E. H. (1994). Sex differences in the sensitivity of two self-report depression scales in older depressed inpatients. *Psychology and Aging, 9,* 443–445.

American Psychiatric Association (1994). *Diagnostic and statistical manual of mental disorders* (4th ed.). Washington, DC: American Psychiatric Association.

Anderson, S. A., Russell, C. S., & Schumm, W. R. (1983). Perceived marital quality and family life-cycle categories: A further analysis. *Journal of Marriage and the Family, 45,* 127–139.

Anstey, K. J., Luszcz, M. A., & Sanchez, L. (2001). A reevaluation of the common factor theory of shared variance among age, sensory function, and cognitive function in older adults. *Journal of Gerontology: Psychological Sciences, 56B,* P3–P11.

Antonucci, T. C. (1986). Hierarchical mapping technique. *Generations, 10(4),* 10–12.

Antonucci, T. C., & Akiyama, H. (1987). Social networks in adult life and a preliminary examination of the convoy model. *Journal of Gerontology, 42,* 519–527.

Antonucci, T. C., Sherman, A. M., & Akiyama, H. (1996). Social networks, support, and integration. In J. E. Birren (Ed.), *Encyclopedia of gerontology: Age, aging, and the aged* (Vol. 2, pp. 505–515). San Diego: Academic Press.

Aranda, M. P., & Knight, B. G. (1997). The influence of ethnicity and culture on the caregiver stress and coping process: A sociocultural review and analysis. *The Gerontologist, 37,* 342–354.

Arbuckle, T. Y., & Gold, D. P. (1993). Aging, inhibition, and verbosity. *Journal of Gerontology: Psychological Sciences, 48,* P225–P232.

Ardelt, M. (2000). Antecedents and effects of wisdom in old age. *Research on Aging, 22,* 360–394.

Arlin, P. K. (1990). Wisdom: The art of problem finding. In R. J. Sternberg (Ed.), *Wisdom: Its nature, origins, and development* (pp. 230–243). New York: Cambridge University Press.

Atchley, R. C. (1971). Retirement and leisure participation: Continuity or crisis? *The Gerontologist, 11,* 13–17.

Atchley, R. C. (1994). *Social forces and aging* (7th ed.). Belmont, CA: Wadsworth.

Atchley, R. C. (1996). Retirement. In J. E. Birren (Ed.), *Encyclopedia of gerontology: Age, aging, and the aged* (Vol. 2, pp. 437–449). San Diego: Academic Press.

Atkinson, R. C., & Shiffrin, R. M. (1968). Human memory: A proposed system and its control processes. In K. W. Spence & J. T. Spence (Eds.), *The psychology of learning and motivation: Vol. 2* (pp. 89–105). New York: Academic Press.

Avolio, B. J., & Waldman, D. A. (1990). An examination of age and cognitive test performance across job complexity and occupational types. *Journal of Applied Psychology, 75,* 43–50.

Bäckman, L., Small, B. J., & Wahlin, A. (2001). Aging and memory: Cognitive and biological perspectives. In J. E. Birren & K. W. Schaie (Eds.), *Handbook of the psychology of aging* (5th ed., pp. 349–377). San Diego: Academic Press.

Bäckman, L., Small, B. J., Wahlin, A., & Larsson, M. (2000). Cognitive functioning in very old age. In F. I. M. Craik & T. A. Salthouse (Eds.), *The handbook of aging and cognition* (2nd ed., pp. 499–558). Mahwah, NJ: Erlbaum.

Baddeley, A. D. (1986). *Working memory.* Oxford: Oxford University Press.

Baddeley, A. D. (1990). *Human memory: Theory and practice.* Boston: Allyn & Bacon.

Badley, E. M., & Rothman, L. M. (1996). Arthritis. In J. E. Birren (Ed.), *Encyclopedia of gerontology: Age, aging, and the aged* (Vol. 1, pp. 111–121). San Diego: Academic Press.

Bahrick, H. P. (1979). Maintenance of knowledge: Questions about memory we forgot to ask. *Journal of Experimental Psychology: General, 108,* 296–308.

Bahrick, H. P., Bahrick, P. O., & Wittlinger, R. P. (1975). Fifty years of memory for names and faces: A cross-sectional approach. *Journal of Experimental Psychology: General, 104,* 54–75.

Baines, S., Saxby, P., & Ehlert, K. (1987). Reality orientation and reminiscence therapy: A controlled crossover study of elderly confused people. *British Journal of Psychiatry, 151,* 222–231.

Ball, K., Beard, B., Roenker, D., Miller, R., & Griggs, D. (1988). Age and visual search: Expanding the useful field of view. *Journal of the Optical Society of America, 5,* 2210–2219.

Ball, K., & Owsley, C. (1991). Identifying correlates of accident involvement for the older driver. *Human Factors, 33,* 583–595.

Ball, K., Owsley, C. Stalvey, B., Roenker, D. L., Sloane, M. E., & Graves, M. (1998). Driving avoidance and functional impairment in older drivers. *Accident Analysis and Prevention, 30,* 313–322.

Ball, K., & Rebok, G. W. (1994). Evaluating the driving ability of older adults. *Journal of Applied Gerontology, 13,* 20–38.

Baltes, M. M., & Carstensen, L. L. (1996). The process of successful ageing. *Aging and Society, 16,* 397–422.

Baltes, M. M., & Lang, F. R. (1997). Everyday functioning and successful aging: The impact of resources. *Psychology and Aging, 12,* 433–443.

Baltes, M. M., & Zerbe, M. B. (1976). Independence training in nursing home residents. *The Gerontologist, 16,* 428–432.

Baltes, P. B. (1987). Theoretical propositions of life-span developmental psychology: On the dynamics between growth and decline. *Developmental Psychology, 23,* 611–626.

Baltes, P. B. (1993). The aging mind: Potential and limits. *The Gerontologist, 33,* 580–594.

Baltes, P. B. (1997). On the incomplete architecture of human ontogeny. *American Psychologist, 52,* 366–380.

Baltes, P. B., & Baltes, M. M. (1990). Psychological perspectives on successful aging: The model of selective optimization with compensation. In P. B. Baltes & M. M. Baltes (Eds.), *Successful aging: Perspectives from the behavioral sciences* (pp. 1–34). Cambridge, England: Cambridge University Press.

Baltes, P. B., Dittmann-Kohli, F., & Dixon, R. A. (1984). New perspectives on the development of intelligence in adulthood: Toward a dual process conception and a model of selective optimization with compensation. In P. B. Baltes & O. G. Brim, Jr. (Eds.), *Life-span development and behavior: Vol. 6* (pp. 33–76). New York: Academic Press.

Baltes, P. B., & Lindenberger, U. (1997). Emergence of a powerful connection between sensory and cognitive functions across the adult life span: A new window to the study of cognitive aging? *Psychology and Aging, 12,* 12–21.

Baltes, P. B., & Schaie, K. W. (1974). Aging and IQ: The myth of the twilight years. *Psychology Today, 7,* 35–40.

Baltes, P. B., & Schaie, K. W. (1976). On the plasticity of intelligence in adulthood and old age: Where Horn and Donaldson fail. *American Psychologist, 31,* 720–725.

Baltes, P. B., & Smith, J. (1990). Toward a psychology of wisdom and its ontogenesis. In R. J. Sternberg (Ed.), *Wisdom: Its nature, origins, and development* (pp. 87–120). New York: Cambridge University Press.

Baltes, P. B., & Smith, J. (1995). Developmental psychology. In G. L. Maddox et al. (Eds.), *The encyclopedia of aging* (2nd ed., pp. 267–270). New York: Springer.

Baltes, P. B., & Staudinger, U. M. (1995). Wisdom. In G. L. Maddox et al. (Eds.), *The encyclopedia of aging* (2nd ed., pp. 971–974). New York: Springer.

Baltes, P. B., Staudinger, U. M., & Lindenberger, U. (1999). Lifespan psychology: Theory and application to intellectual functioning. *Annual Review of Psychology, 50,* 471–507.

Baltes, P. B., Staudinger, U. M., Maercker, A., & Smith, J. (1995). People nominated as wise: A comparative study of wisdom-related knowledge. *Psychology and Aging, 10,* 155–166.

Baltes, P. B., & Willis, S. L. (1982). Enhancement (plasticity) of intellectual functioning in old age: Penn State's Adult Development and Enrichment Project (ADEPT). In F. I. M. Craik & S. Trehub (Eds.), *Aging and cognitive processes* (pp. 353–389). New York: Plenum Press.

Bandura, A. (1977). Self-efficacy: Toward a unifying theory of behavioral change. *Psychological Review, 84,* 191–215.

Barer, B. M. (1994). Men and women aging differently. *International Journal of Aging and Human Development, 38,* 29–40.

Bargh, J. A., Chen, M., & Burrows, L. (1996). Automaticity of social behavior: Direct effects of trait construct and stereotype activation on action. *Journal of Personality and Social Psychology, 71,* 230–244.

Baron, R. A., & Byrne, D. (2000). *Social psychology* (9th ed.). Boston: Allyn & Bacon.

Barzel, U. S. (1995). Osteoporosis. In G. L. Maddox et al. (Eds.), *The encyclopedia of aging* (2nd ed., pp. 722–723). New York: Springer.

Bedford, V. H. (1989). Understanding the value of siblings in old age. *American Behavioral Scientist, 33,* 33–44.

Beller, S., & Palmore, E. (1974). Longevity in Turkey. *The Gerontologist, 14, Pt. 1,* 373–376.

Bengston, V. L., & Kuypers, J. A. (1971). Generational differences and the developmental stake. *Aging and Human Development, 2,* 249–260.

Bengston, V., Rosenthal, C., & Burton, L. (1996). Paradoxes of families and aging. In R. H. Binstock & L. K. George (Eds.), *Handbook of aging and the social sciences* (4th ed., pp. 253–282). San Diego: Academic Press.

Berardo, D., Shehan, C., & Leslie, G. (1987). A residue of tradition: Jobs, careers, and spouses' time in housework. *Journal of Marriage and the Family, 49,* 381–390.

Berg, C. A., & Klaczynski, P. A. (1996). Practical intelligence and problem-solving: Searching for perspectives. In F. Blanchard-Fields & T. M. Hess (Eds.), *Perspectives on cognitive change in adulthood and aging* (pp. 323–357). New York: McGraw-Hill.

Berg, C. A., & Sternberg, R. J. (1992). Adults' conceptions of intelligence across the adult life span. *Psychology and Aging. 7,* 221–231.

Bergman, C. S., & Plomin, R. (1996). Behavioral genetics. In J. E. Birren (Ed.), *Encyclopedia of gerontology: Age, aging, and the aged* (Vol. 1, pp. 163–172). San Diego: Academic Press.

Berry, J. M. (1999). Memory self-efficacy in its social cognitive context. In T. M. Hess & F. Blanchard-Fields (Eds.), *Social cognition and aging* (pp. 69–96). San Diego: Academic Press.

Berry, J. M., & Jobe, J. B. (2002). At the intersection of personality and adult development. *Journal of Research in Personality, 36,* 283–286.

Berry, J. M., West, R. L., & Dennehy, D. (1989). Reliability and validity of the Memory Self-Efficacy Questionnaire (MSEQ). *Developmental Psychology, 25,* 701–713.

Bieman-Copland, S., & Ryan, E. B. (1998). Age-biased interpretation of memory successes and failures in adulthood. *Journal of Gerontology: Psychological Sciences, 53B,* P105–P111.

Binstock, R. H. (2002). In memoriam: Bernice L. Neugarten. *The Gerontologist, 42,* 149–151.

Birren, B. A., & Stine-Morrow, E. A. L. The development of the division on adult development and aging (Division 20): History and reminiscences. Unpublished manuscript.

Birren, J. E. (1974). Translations in gerontology—from lab to life: Psychophysiology and speed of response. *American Psychologist, 29,* 808–815.

Birren, J. E. (1996). History of gerontology. In J. E. Birren (Ed.), *Encyclopedia of gerontology: Age, aging, and the aged* (Vol. 1, pp. 655–665). San Diego: Academic Press.

Birren, J. E., & Fisher, L. M. (1990). The elements of wisdom: Overview and integration. In R. J. Sternberg (Ed.), *Wisdom: Its nature, origins, and development* (pp. 317–332). New York: Cambridge University Press.

Birren, J. E., & Schroots, J. J. F. (1996). History, concepts, and theory in the psychology of aging. In J. E. Birren & K. W. Schaie (Eds.), *Handbook of the psychology of aging* (4th ed., pp. 3–23). San Diego: Academic Press.

Birren, J. E., & Schroots, J. J. F. (2001). The history of geropsychology. In J. E. Birren & K. W. Schaie (Eds.), *Handbook of the psychology of aging* (5th ed., pp. 3–28). San Diego: Academic Press.

Black, J. E., Greenough, W. T., Anderson, B. J., & Isaacs, K. R. (1987). Environment and the aging brain. *Canadian Journal of Psychology, 41,* 111–130.

Blanchard-Fields, F. (1994). Age differences in causal attributions from an adult developmental perspective. *Journal of Gerontology: Psychological Sciences, 49,* P43–P51.

Blanchard-Fields, F. (1996). Causal attributions across the adult life span: The influence of social schemas, life context, and domain specificity. *Applied Cognitive Psychology, 10,* S137–S146.

Blanchard-Fields, F. (1997). The role of emotion in social cognition across the adult life span. In K. W. Schaie & M. P. Lawton (Eds.), *Annual review of gerontology and geriatrics* (Vol. 17, pp. 238–265). New York: Springer.

Blanchard-Fields, F. (1999). Social schematicity and causal attribution. In T. M. Hess & F. Blanchard-Fields (Eds.), *Social cognition and aging* (pp. 219–236). San Diego: Academic Press.

Blanchard-Fields, F., & Abeles, R. P. (1996). Social cognition and aging. In J. E. Birren & K. W. Schaie (Eds.), *Handbook of the psychology of aging* (4th ed., pp. 150–161). San Diego: Academic Press.

Blanchard-Fields, F., Baldi, R., & Stein, R. (1999). Age relevance and context effects on attributions across the adult lifespan. *International Journal of Behavioral Development, 23,* 665–683.

Blanchard-Fields, F., Jahnke, H., & Camp, C. J. (1995). Age differences in problem solving style: The role of emotional salience. *Psychology and Aging, 10,* 173–180.

Blanchard-Fields, F., & Norris, L. (1994). Causal attributions from adolescence through adulthood: Age differences, ego level, and generalized response style. *Aging and Cognition, 1,* 67–86.

Blazer, D., Burchett, B., Service, C., & George, L. K. (1991). The association of age and depression among the elderly: An epidemiological exploration. *Journal of Gerontology: Medical Sciences, 46,* M210–M215.

Blazer, D. G., & Koenig, H. G. (1996). Suicide. In J. E. Birren (Eds.), *Encyclopedia of gerontology: Age, aging, and the aged* (Vol. 2, pp. 529–538). San Diego: Academic Press.

Blumenthal, J. A., & Madden, D. J. (1988). Effects of aerobic exercise training, age, and physical fitness on memory-search performance. *Psychology and Aging, 3,* 280–285.

Botwinick, J. (1971). Sensory-set factors in age difference in reaction time. *Journal of Genetic Psychology, 119,* 241–249.

Botwinick, J. (1984). *Aging and behavior* (3rd ed.). New York: Springer.

Brandtstädter, J. (1999). Sources of resilience in the aging self: Toward integrating perspectives. In T. M. Hess & F. Blanchard-Fields (Eds.), *Social cognition and aging* (pp. 123–141). San Diego: Academic Press.

Brandtstädter, J., & Greve, W. (1994). The aging self: Stabilizing and protective processes. *Developmental Review, 14,* 52–80.

Brandtstädter, J., & Renner, G. (1990). Tenacious goal pursuit and flexible goal adjustment: Explication and age-related anaysis of assimilative and accommodative strategies and coping. *Psychology and Aging, 5,* 58–67.

Brandtstädter, J., Wentura, D., & Greve, W. (1993). Adaptive resources of the aging self: Outlines of an emergent perspective. *International Journal of Behavioral Development, 16,* 323–349.

Bransford, J. D., & Johnson, M. K. (1972). Contextual prerequisites for understanding: Some investigations of comprehension and recall. *Journal of Verbal Learning and Verbal Behavior, 11,* 717–726.

Brody, E. M., Litvin, S. J., Albert, S. M., & Hoffman, C. J. (1994). Marital status of daughters and patterns of parent care. *Journal of Gerontology: Social Sciences, 49,* S95–S103.

Burgio, K. L., & Burgio, L. D. (1991). The problem of urinary incontinence. In P. A. Wisocki (Ed.), *Handbook of clinical behavior therapy with the eldery client* (pp. 317–336). New York: Plenum Press.

Burgio, L. D., & Engel, B. T. (1990). Biofeedback-assisted training for elderly men and women. *Journal of the American Geriatrics Society, 38,* 338–340.

Burke, D. M., MacKay, D. G., Worthley, J. S., & Wade, E. (1991). On the tip of the tongue: What causes word finding failures in young and older adults? *Journal of Memory and Language, 30,* 542–579.

Busse, E. W. (1995). Primary and secondary aging. In G. L. Maddox et al. (Eds.), *The encyclopedia of aging* (2nd ed., p. 754). New York: Springer.

Butler, R. N. (1963). The life review: An interpretation of reminiscence in the aged. *Psychiatry, 26,* 65–76.

Butler, R. N., Lewis, M. I., & Sunderland, T. (1998). *Aging and mental health: Positive psychosocial and biomedical approaches* (5th ed.). Boston: Allyn & Bacon.

Camp, C. J., Foss, J. W., Stevens, A. B., Reichard, C. C., McKitrick, L.A., & O'Hanlon, A. M. (1993). Memory training in normal and demented populations: The E-I-E-I-O model. *Experimental Aging Research, 19,* 277–290.

Campbell, L. D., Connidis, I. A., & Davies, L. (1999). Sibling ties in later life: A social network analysis. *Journal of Family Issues, 20,* 114–118.

Cantor, M. (1979). Neighbors and friends: An overlooked resource in the informal support system. *Research on Aging, 1,* 434–463.

Carr, C., Jackson, T. W., Madden, D. J., & Cohen, H. J. (1992). The effect of age on driving skills. *Journal of the American Geriatrics Society, 40,* 567–573.

Carstensen, L. L. (1991). Socioemotional selectivity theory: Social activity in life-span context. In K. W. Schaie & M. P. Lawton (Eds.), *Annual review of gerontology and geriatrics* (Vol. 11, pp. 195–217). New York: Springer.

Carstensen, L. L. (1992). Social and emotional patterns in adulthood: Support for socioemotional selectivity theory. *Psychology and Aging, 7,* 331–338.

Carstensen, L. L. (1995). Evidence for a life-span theory of socioemotional selectivity. *Current Directions in Psychological Science, 4,* 151–156.

Carstensen, L. L., & Fredrickson, B. L. (1998). Influence of HIV status and age on cognitive representations of others. *Health Psychology, 17,* 494–503.

Carstensen, L. L., Gottman, J. M., & Levenson, R. W. (1995). Emotional behavior in long-term marriage. *Psychology and Aging, 10,* 140–149.

Carstensen, L. L., Gross, J. J., & Fung, H. H. (1997). The social context of emotional experience. In K. W. Schaie & M. P. Lawton (Eds.), *Annual review of gerontology and geriatrics* (Vol. 17, pp. 325–352). New York: Springer.

Carstensen, L. L., Isaacowitz, D. M., & Charles, S. T. (1999). Taking time seriously: A theory of socioemotional selectivity. *American Psychologist, 54,* 165–181.

Cattell, R. B. (1963). Theory of fluid and crystallized intelligence: A critical experiment. *Journal of Educational Psychology, 54,* 1–22.

Cavanaugh, J. C., Grady, J. G., & Perlmutter, M. (1983). Forgetting and use of memory aids in 20- to 70-years olds' everyday life. *International Journal of Aging and Human Development, 17,* 113–122.

Cerella, J. (1994). Generalized slowing and Brinley plots. *Journal of Gerontology: Psychological Sciences, 49,* P65–P71.

Cerella, J. (1995). Reaction time. In G. L. Maddox et al. (Eds.), *The encyclopedia of aging* (2nd ed., pp. 792–795). New York: Springer.

Chap, J. B. (1986). Moral judgment in middle and late adulthood: The effects of age-appropriate moral dilemmas and spontaneous role taking. *International Journal of Aging and Human Development, 22,* 161–172.

Chen, Y. P. (1996). Economics: Society. In J. E. Birren (Ed.), *Encyclopedia of gerontology: Age, aging, and the aged* (Vol. 1, pp. 469–476). San Diego: Academic Press.

Cherniack, N. S., & Altose, M. D. (1996). Respiratory system. In J. E. Birren (Ed.), *Encyclopedia of gerontology: Age, aging, and the aged* (Vol. 2, pp. 431–436). San Diego: Academic Press.

Cherry, K. E., & Jones, M. W. (1999). Age-related differences in spatial memory: Effects of structural and organizational context. *Journal of General Psychology, 126,* 53–73.

Cherry, K. E., & LeCompte, D. C. (1999). Age and individual differences influence prospective memory. *Psychology and Aging, 14,* 60–76.

Cherry, K. E., & Smith, A. D. (1998). Normal memory aging. In M. Hersen & V. B. VanHasselt (Eds.), *Handbook of clinical geropsychology* (pp. 87–110). New York: Plenum Press.

Choi, I., Nisbett, R. E., & Norenzayan, A. (1999). Causal attributions across cultures: Variation and universality. *Psychological Bulletin, 125,* 47–63.

Chui, H. (1995). Vascular dementia. In G. L. Maddox et al. (Eds.), *The encyclopedia of aging* (2nd ed., pp. 951–954). New York: Springer.

Cicirelli, V. G. (1993). Attachment and obligation as daughters' motives for caregiving behavior and subsequent effect on subjective burden. *Psychology and Aging, 8,* 144–155.

Cicirelli, V. G. (1995). Siblings. In G. L. Maddox et al. (Eds.), *The encyclopedia of aging* (2nd ed., pp. 857–859). New York: Springer.

Cicirelli, V. G. (1997). Relationship of psychosocial and background variables to older adults' end-of-life decisions. *Psychology and Aging, 12,* 72–83.

Cicirelli, V. G. (2002). Fear of death in older adults: Predictions from terror management theory. *Journal of Gerontology: Psychological Sciences, 57B,* P358–P366.

Cicirelli, V. G., Coward, R. G., & Dwyer, J. W. (1992). Siblings as caregivers for impaired elders. *Research on Aging, 14,* 331–350.

Clarke, E. J., Preston, M., Raksin, J., & Bengston, V. L. (1999). Types of conflicts and tensions between older parents and adult children. *The Gerontologist, 39,* 261–270.

Cleveland, J. N., & Shore, L. M. (1992). Self- and supervisory perspectives on age and work attitudes and performance. *Journal of Applied Psychology, 77,* 469–484.

Cohen, G. D. (1990). Psychopathology and mental health in the mature and elderly adult. In J. E. Birren & K. W. Schaie (Eds.), *Handbook of the psychology of aging* (3rd ed., pp. 359–371). San Diego: Academic Press.

Cohen, G., & Taylor, S. (1998). Reminiscence and ageing. *Ageing and Society, 18,* 601–610.

Collins, K., Luszcz, M., Lawson, M., & Keeves, J. (1997). Everyday problem solving in elderly women: Contributions of residence, perceived control, and age. *The Gerontologist, 37,* 293–302.

Collins, L. M. (1996). Research design and methods. In J. E. Birren (Ed.), *Encyclopedia of gerontology: Age, aging, and the aged* (Vol. 2, pp. 419–429). San Diego: Academic Press.

Comjis, H. C., Penninx, B. W. J. H., Knipscheer, K. P. M., & van Tilburg, W. (1999). Psychological distress in victims of elderly mistreatment: The effects of social support and coping. *Journal of Gerontology: Psychological Sciences, 54B,* P240–P245.

Connidis, I. A. (1989). *Family ties and aging.* Toronto: Butterworths.

Connidis, I. A. (1994). Sibling support in older age. *Journal of Gerontology: Social Sciences, 49,* S309–S317.

Conwell, Y. (1994). Suicide in elderly patients. In L. S. Schneider, C. F. Reynolds, III, B. D. Lebowitz, & A. J. Friedhoff (Eds.), *Diagnosis and treatment of depression in late life* (pp. 397–418). Washington, DC: American Psychiatric Press.

Cooney, T. M. (1995). Divorce. In G. L. Maddox et al. (Eds.), *The encyclopedia of aging* (2nd ed., pp. 286–287). New York: Springer.

Cordoni, C. N. (1981). Subjective perceptions of everyday memory failure. (Doctoral dissertation, Duke University.) *Dissertation Abstracts International, 42,* 2047B.

Corey-Bloom, J. (2000). Dementia. In S. K. Whitbourne (Ed.), *Psychopathology in later adulthood* (pp. 217–243). New York: John Wiley.

Corr, C. A., Nabe, C. M., & Corr, D. M. (2003). *Death and dying: Life and living* (4th ed.). Belmont, CA: Wadsworth.

Corso, J. F. (1995). Hearing. In G. L. Maddox et al. (Eds.), *The encyclopedia of aging* (2nd ed., pp. 449–452). New York: Springer.

Costa, P. T., Jr., & McCrae, R. R. (1985). Hypochondriasis, neuroticism, and aging. *American Psychologist, 40,* 19–28.

Costa, P. T., Jr., & McCrae, R. R. (1991). *NEO Five-Factor Inventory.* Odessa, FL: Psychological Assessment Resources.

Costa, P. T., Jr., & McCrae, R. R. (1992). *Revised NEO Personality Inventory (NEO-PI-R) and NEO Five-Factor Inventory (NEO-FFI) professional manual.* Odessa, FL: Psychological Assessment Resources.

Cousins, S. O. (2000). "My heart couldn't take it": Older women's beliefs about exercise benefits and risks. *Journal of Gerontology: Psychological Sciences, 55B,* P283–P294.

Cowgill, D. O. (1986). *Aging around the world.* Belmont, CA: Wadsworth.

Cox, H. G. (1990). Roles for aged individuals in post-industrial societies. *International Journal of Aging and Human Development, 30,* 55–62.

Craik, F. I. M. (1994). Memory changes in normal aging. *Current Directions in Psychological Science, 3,* 155–158.

Craik, F. I. M., & Byrd, M. (1982). Aging and cognitive deficits: The role of attentional resources. In F. I. M.

Craik & S. Trehub (Eds.), *Aging and cognitive processes* (pp. 191–211). New York: Plenum Press.

Craik, F. I. M., Byrd, M., & Swanson, J. M. (1987). Patterns of memory loss in three elderly samples. *Psychology and Aging, 2,* 79–86.

Crimmins, E. M., Reynolds, S. L., & Saito, Y. (1999). Trends in health and ability to work among the older working-age population. *Journal of Gerontology: Social Sciences, 54B,* S31–S40.

Crispell, D., & Frey, W. H. (1993, March). American maturity. *American Demographics,* 31–42.

Cristofalo, V. J., Tresini, M., Francis, M. K., & Volker, C. (1999). Biological theories of senescence. In V. L. Bengston & K. W. Schaie (Eds.), *Handbook of theories of aging* (pp. 98–112). New York: Springer.

Cross, S., & Markus, H. (1991). Possible selves across the life span. *Human Development, 32,* 230–255.

Cuddy, A., & Fiske, S. T. (2002). Doddering but dear: Process, content, and function of stereotyping older persons. In T. D. Nelson (Ed.), *Ageism: Stereotyping and prejudice against older persons* (pp. 3–26). Cambridge, MA: MIT Press.

Cumming, E. M., & Henry, W. (1961). *Growing old: The process of disengagement.* New York: Basic Books.

Cutler, N. E. (1996). Pensions. In J. E. Birren (Ed.), *Encyclopedia of gerontology: Age, aging, and the aged* (Vol. 2, pp. 261–269). San Diego: Academic Press.

Cutler, S. J., Hendricks, J., & Guyer, A. (2003). Age differences in home computer availability and use. *Journal of Gerontology: Social Sciences, 58B,* S271–S280.

Czaja, S. J. (2001). Technological change and the older worker. In J. E. Birren and K. W. Schaie (Eds.), *Handbook of the psychology of aging* (5th ed., pp. 547–568). San Diego: Academic Press.

Czaja, S. J., & Sharit, J. (1993). Age differences in the performance of computer based work as a function of pacing and task complexity. *Psychology and Aging, 8,* 59–67.

Czaja, S. J., & Sharit, J. (1998). Ability-performance relationships as a function of age and task experience for a data entry task. *Journal of Experimental Psychology: Applied, 4,* 332–351.

Danner, D. D., Snowdon, D. A., & Friesen, W. V. (2001). Positive emotions in early life and longevity: Findings from the Nun Study. *Journal of Personality and Social Psychology, 80,* 804–813.

Davidson, K. (2001). Late life widowhood, selfishness, and new partnership choices: A gendered perspective. *Aging and Society, 21,* 297–317.

Davison, B. J., Kirk, P., Degner, L. F., & Hassard, T. H. (1999). Information and patient participation in screening for prostate cancer. *Patient Education and Counseling, 37,* 255–263.

Denney, N. W. (1982). Aging and cognitive changes. In B. B. Wolman (Ed.), *Handbook of developmental psychology* (pp. 807–827). Englewood Cliffs, NJ: Prentice Hall.

Denney, N. W., & Palmer, A. N. (1981). Adult age differences on traditional and practical problem-solving. *Journal of Gerontology, 36,* 323–328.

Dennis, W. (1966). Creative productivity between the ages of 20 and 80 years. *Journal of Gerontology, 21,* 1–8.

Dick, L. P., Gallagher-Thompson, D., & Thompson, L. W. (1999). Cognitive-behavioral therapy. In R. T. Woods (Ed.), *Psychological problems of ageing: Assessment, treatment, and care* (pp. 253–291). Chichester, England: John Wiley.

Diehl, M., Coyle, N., & Labouvie-Vief, G. (1996). Age and sex differences in strategies of coping and defense across the life span. *Psychology and Aging, 11,* 127–139.

Diehl, M., Willis, S. L., & Schaie, K. W. (1995). Everyday problem solving in older adults: Observational assessment and cognitive correlates. *Psychology and Aging, 10,* 478–491.

Diener, E., & Suh, M. E. (1997). Subjective well-being and age: An international analysis. In K. W. Schaie & M. P. Lawton (Eds.), *Annual review of gerontology and geriatrics* (Vol. 17, pp. 304–324). New York: Springer.

Dilworth-Anderson, P., Williams, S. W., & Cooper, T. (1999). Family caregiving to elderly African Americans: Caregiver types and structures. *Journal of Gerontology: Social Sciences, 54B,* S237–S241.

Dixon, R. A. (1999). Exploring cognition in interactive situations: The aging of N + 1 minds. In T. M. Hess & F. Blanchard-Fields (Eds.), *Social cognition and aging* (pp. 267–290). San Diego: Academic Press.

Dixon, R. A., & Gould, O. N. (1996). Adults telling and retelling stories collaboratively. In P. B. Baltes & U. M. Staudinger (Eds.), *Interactive minds: Life-span perspectives on the social foundation of cognition* (pp. 221–241). New York: Cambridge University Press.

Dixon, R. A., & Gould, O. N. (1998). Younger and older adults collaborating on retelling everyday stories. *Applied Developmental Science, 2,* 160–171.

Dixon, R. A., Hultsch, D. F., & Hertzog, C. (1988). The Metamemory in Adulthood (MIA) Questionnaire. *Psychopharmacology Bulletin, 24,* 671–688.

Dorfman, R., Walters, K., Burke, P., Harden, L., Karanik, T., Raphael, J., & Silverstein, E. (1995). Old, sad, and alone: The myth of the aging homosexual. *Journal of Gerontological Social Work, 24,* 29–44.

Dowd, J. J. (1975). Aging as exchange: A preface to theory. *Journal of Gerontology, 30,* 584–594.

Drevenstedt, J., & Russell, D. (1986). Disorders of the later years. In R. H. Price & S. J. Lynn (Eds.), *Abnormal psychology* (2nd ed., pp. 296–335). Chicago: Dorsey Press.

Duberstein, P. R., & Conwell, Y. (2000). Suicide. In S. K. Whitbourne (Ed.), *Psychopathology in later adulthood* (pp. 245–275). New York: John Wiley.

Duberstein, P. R., Evinger, J. S., & Conwell, Y. (2002). Religion and completed suicide. Presented at the American Psychological Association Convention, Chicago.

Dupree, L. W., & Schonfeld, L. (1999). Management of alcohol abuse in older adults. In M. Duffy (Ed.), *Handbook of counseling and psychotherapy with older adults* (pp. 632–649). New York: John Wiley.

Dye, C. J. (1978, February). Psychologists' role in the provision of mental health care for the elderly. *Professional Psychology*, 38–49.

Earles, J. L., & Kersten, A. W. (1998). Influences of age and perceived activity difficulty on activity recall. *Journal of Gerontology: Psychological Sciences, 53B*, P324–P328

Ebersole, P., & Hess, P. (1998). *Toward healthy aging: Human needs and nursing response* (5th ed.). St. Louis, MO: Mosby.

Einstein, G. O., & McDaniel, M. A. (1990). Normal aging and prospective memory. *Journal of Experimental Psychology: Learning, Memory, and Cognition, 16*, 717–726.

Einstein, G. O., McDaniel, M. A., Manzi, J., Cochran, B., & Baker, M. (2000). Prospective memory and aging: Forgetting intentions over short delays. *Psychology and Aging, 15*, 671–683.

Ekerdt, D. J. (1986). The busy ethic: Moral continuity between work and retirement. *The Gerontologist, 26*, 239–244.

Ekerdt, D. J. (1995). Retirement. In G. L. Maddox et al. (Eds.), *The encyclopedia of aging* (2nd ed., pp. 819–823). New York: Springer.

Ekerdt, D. J., & DeViney, S. (1993). Evidence for a preretirement process among older male workers. *Journal of Gerontology: Social Sciences, 48*, S35–S43.

Ekerdt, D. J., DeViney, S., & Kosloski, K. (1996). Profiling plans for retirement. *Journal of Gerontology: Social Sciences, 51B*, S140–S149.

Elias, M. G., Elias, P. K., & Elias, J. W. (1977). *Basic processes in adult developmental psychology*. St. Louis, MO: Mosby.

Ellis, H. C., & Hunt, R. R. (1993). *Fundamentals of cognitive psychology* (5th ed.). Madison, WI: WCB Brown & Benchmark.

Engel, B. T. (1995). Incontinence. In G. L. Maddox et al. (Eds.), *The encyclopedia of aging* (2nd ed., pp. 501–502). New York: Springer.

Erber, J. T. (1974). Age differences in recognition memory. *Journal of Gerontology, 29*, 177–181.

Erber, J. T. (1976). Age differences in learning and memory on a digit symbol substitution task. *Experimental Aging Research, 2*, 45–53.

Erber, J. T. (1979). The institutionalized geriatric patient considered in a framework of developmental deprivation. *Human Development, 22*, 165–179.

Erber, J. T. (1989). Young and older adults' appraisal of memory failures in young and older adult target persons. *Journal of Gerontology: Psychological Sciences, 44*, P170–P175.

Erber, J. T. (1995). Remote memory. In G. L. Maddox et al. (Eds.), *The encyclopedia of aging* (2nd ed., pp. 806–808). New York: Springer.

Erber, J. T. (2001). Remote memory. In G. L. Maddox et al. (Eds.), *The encyclopedia of aging: A comprehensive resource in gerontology and geriatrics* (3rd ed., pp. 873–875). New York: Springer.

Erber, J. T., & Danker, D. C. (1995). Forgetting in the workplace: Attributions and recommendations for young and older employees. *Psychology and Aging, 10*, 565–569.

Erber, J. T., & Rothberg, S. T. (1991). Here's looking at you: The relative effect of age and attractiveness on judgments about memory failure. *Journal of Gerontology: Psychological Sciences, 46*, P116–P123.

Erber, J. T., & Szuchman, L. T. (2002). Age and capability: The role of forgetting and personal traits. *International Journal of Aging and Human Development, 54*, 173–189.

Erber, J. T., Szuchman, L. T., & Prager, I. G. (1997). Forgetful but forgiven: How age and life style affect perceptions of memory failure. *Journal of Gerontology: Psychological Sciences, 52B*, P303–P307.

Erber, J. T., Szuchman, L. T., & Prager, I. G. (2001). Ain't misbehavin': The effects of aging and intentionality on judgments about misconduct. *Psychology and Aging, 16*, 85–95.

Erber, J. T., Szuchman, L. T., & Rothberg, S. T. (1990a). Everyday memory failure: Age differences in appraisal and attribution. *Psychology and Aging, 5*, 236–241.

Erber, J. T., Szuchman, L. T., & Rothberg, S. T. (1990b). Age, gender, and individual differences in memory failure appraisal. *Psychology and Aging, 5*, 600–603.

Erber, J. T., Szuchman, L. T., & Rothberg, S. T. (1992). Dimensions of self-report about everyday memory in young and older adults. *International Journal of Aging and Human Development, 34*, 311–323.

Erikson, E. H. (1950). *Childhood and society*. New York: Norton.

Erikson, E. H. (1963). *Childhood and society* (2nd ed.). New York: Norton.

Fees, B. S., Martin, P., & Poon, L. W. (1999). A model of loneliness in older adults. *Journals of Gerontology: Psychological Sciences, 54B*, P231–P239.

Field, D., & Minkler, M. (1988). Continuity and change in social support between young-old and old-old or very-old age. *Journal of Gerontology: Psychological Sciences, 43*, P100–P106.

Fillenbaum, G. G. (1995). Activities of daily living. In G. L. Maddox et al. (Eds.), *The encyclopedia of aging* (2nd ed., pp. 7–9). New York: Springer.

Finch, C. E., & Seeman, T. E. (1999). Stress theories of aging. In V. L. Bengston & K. W. Schaie (Eds.), *Handbook of theories of aging* (pp. 81–97). New York: Springer.

Fingerman, K. L. (1996). Sources of tension in the aging mother and adult daughter relationship. *Psychology and Aging, 11*, 591–606.

Fingerman, K. L. (1998). The good, the bad, and the worrisome: Emotional complexities in grandparents' experiences with individual grandchildren. *Family Relations, 47,* 403–414.

Fingerman, K. L., & Griffiths, P. C. (1999). Season's greetings: Adults' social contacts at the holiday season. *Psychology and Aging, 14,* 192–205.

Finkelstein, L. M., Burke, M. J., & Raju, N. S. (1995). Age discrimination in simulated employment contexts. *Journal of Applied Psychology, 80,* 652–663.

Fisk, A. D., & Fisher, D. L. (1994). Brinley plots and theories of aging: The explicit, muddled, and implicit debates. *Journal of Gerontology: Psychological Sciences, 49,* P81–P89.

Fitzgerald, J. M. (2000). Younger and older jurors: The influence of environmental supports on memory performance and decision-making in complex trials. *Journal of Gerontology: Psychological Sciences, 55B,* P323–P331.

Fleeson, W., & Heckhausen, J. (1997). More or less "me" in past, present, and future: Perceived lifetime personality during adulthood. *Psychology and Aging, 12,* 125–136.

Fletcher, W. L., & Hansson, R. O. (1991). Assessing the social components of retirement anxiety. *Psychology and Aging, 6,* 76–85.

Flippen, C., & Tienda, M. (2000). Pathways to retirement: Patterns of labor force participation and labor market exit among pre-retirement population by race, Hispanic origin, and sex. *Journal of Gerontology: Social Sciences, 55B,* S14–S27.

Flynn, J. R. (1999). Searching for justice: The discovery of IQ gains over time. *American Psychologist, 54,* 5–20.

Folstein, M. F., Folstein, S. E., & McHugh, P. R. (1975). Mini-Mental State: A practical method for grading the cognitive state of paients for the clinician. *Journal of Psychiatric Research, 12,* 189–198.

Fortner, B. V., Neimeyer, R. A., & Rybarczyk, B. (2000). Correlates of death anxiety in older adults: A comprehensive review. In A. Tomer (Ed.), *Death attitudes and the older adult: Theories, concepts, and applications* (pp. 95–108). Philadelphia: Brunner-Routledge.

Franks, M. M., & Stephens, M. A. P. (1996). Social support in the context of caregiving: Husbands' provision of support to wives involved in parent care. *Journal of Gerontology: Psychological Sciences, 51B,* P43–P52.

Fredrickson, B. L., & Carstensen, L. L. (1990). Choosing social partners: How old age and anticipated endings make us more selective. *Psychology and Aging, 5,* 335–357.

Friedhoff, A. J. (1994). Consensus panel report. In L. S. Schneider, C. F. Reynolds, B. D. Lebowitz, & A. J. Friedhoff (Eds.), *Diagnosis and treatment of depression in late life: Results of the NIH consensus development conference.* Washington, D.C.: American Psychiatric Press.

Fries, J. F. (1995). Compression of morbidity/disease postponement. In G. L. Maddox et al. (Eds.), *The encyclopedia of aging* (2nd ed., pp. 213–216). New York: Springer.

Fries, J. F. (1997). Will future elderly persons experience more years of disability? Yes. In A. E. Scharlach & L. W. Kaye (Eds.), *Controversial issues in aging* (pp. 214–218). Boston: Allyn & Bacon.

Fritz, C. L., Farver, T. B., Hart, L. A., & Kass, P. H. (1996). Companion animals and the psychological health of Alzheimer patients' caregivers. *Psychological Reports, 78,* 467–481.

Fronstin, P. (1999). Retirement patterns and employee benefits: Do benefits matter? *The Gerontologist, 39,* 37–47.

Fung, H. H., Carstensen, L. L., & Lutz, A. (1999). The influence of time on social preferences: Implications for lifespan development. *Psychology and Aging, 14,* 595–604.

Gallagher, D. E., & Thompson, L. W. (1983). Treatment of major depressive disorder in older adult outpatients with brief psychotherapies. *Psychotherapy: Theory, research, and practice, 19,* 482–490.

Gallagher-Thompson, D. (1995). Bereavement. In G. L. Maddox et al. (Eds.), *The encyclopedia of aging* (2nd ed., pp. 105–108). New York: Springer.

Gardner, H. (1983). *Frames of mind: The theory of multiple intelligences.* New York: Basic Books.

Gardner, H. (1999). Are there additional intelligences? The case for naturalistic, spiritual, and existential intelligences. In J. Kane (Ed.), *Education, information, and transformation* (pp. 111–131). Upper Saddle River, NJ: Prentice Hall.

Gatz, M. (Ed.). (1995). *Emerging issues in mental health and aging.* Washington, DC: American Psychological Association.

Gatz, M., & Finkel, S. I. (1995). Education and training of mental health service providers. In M. Gatz (Ed.), *Emerging issues in mental health and aging* (pp. 282–302). Washington, DC: American Psychological Association.

Gatz, M., & Hurwicz, M. L. (1990). Are old people more depressed?: Cross-sectional data on center for epidemiological studies depression scale factors. *Psychology and Aging, 5,* 284–290.

Gatz, M., & Karel, M. J. (1993). Individual change in perceived control over 20 years. *International Journal of Behavioral Development, 16,* 305–322.

Gatz, M., Kasl-Godley, J. E., & Karel, J. J. (1996). Aging and mental disorders. In J. E. Birren & K. W. Schaie (Eds.), *Handbook of the psychology of aging* (4th ed., pp. 365–382). San Diego: Academic Press.

Gatz, M., & Pearson, C. G. (1988). Ageism revised and the provision of psychological services. *American Psychologist, 43,* 184–188.

Gatz, M., & Smyer, M. A. (1992). The mental health system and older adults in the 1990s. *American Psychologist, 47,* 741–751.

Gatz, M., & Smyer, M. A. (2001). Mental health and aging at the outset of the twenty-first century. In J. E. Birren & K. W. Schaie (Eds.), *Handbook of the psychology of aging* (5th ed., pp. 523–544). San Diego: Academic Press.

Gendell, M., & Siegel, J. S. (1996). Trends in retirement age in the United States, 1955–1993, by sex and race. *Journal of Gerontology: Social Sciences, 51B,* S132–S139.

Giambra, L. M. (1989). Task-unrelated thought frequency as a function of age: A laboratory study. *Psychology and Aging, 4,* 136–143.

Giarrusso, R., & Bengston, V. L. (1996). Self-esteem. In J. E. Birren (Ed.), *Encyclopedia of gerontology: Age, aging, and the aged* (Vol. 2, pp. 459–466). San Diego: Academic Press.

Giarrusso, R., & Silverstein, M. (1995). Grandparent-grandchild relationships. In G. L. Maddox et al. (Eds.), *The encyclopedia of aging* (2nd ed., pp. 421–422). New York: Springer.

Gilbert, D. T., & Malone, P. S. (1995). The correspondence bias. *Psychological Bulletin, 117,* 21–38.

Gilligan, C. (1982). *In a different voice: Psychological theory and women's development.* Cambridge, MA: Harvard University Press.

Gilmore, G. C. (1996). Perception. In J. E. Birren (Ed.), *Encyclopedia of gerontology: Age, aging, and the aged* (Vol. 2, pp. 271–279). San Diego: Academic Press.

Gladwell, M. (1997, October 20 & 27). The Alzheimer's strain. *The New Yorker,* 122–139.

Gold, D. T. (1989). Sibling relationships in old age: A typology. *International Journal of Aging and Human Development, 28,* 37–51.

Gold, D. T. (1990). Late-life sibling relationships: Does race affect typological distribution? *The Gerontologist, 30,* 741–748.

Goldmeier, J. (1986). Pets or people: Another research note. *The Gerontologist, 26,* 203–206.

Goldsmith, R. E., & Heiens, R. A. (1992). Subjective age: A test of five hypotheses. *The Gerontologist, 32,* 312–317.

Gomberg, E. S. L. (1996). Alcohol and drugs. In J. E. Birren (Ed.), *Encyclopedia of gerontology: Age, aging, and the aged* (Vol. 1, pp. 93–101). San Diego: Academic Press.

Gordon-Salant, S. (1996). Hearing. In J. E. Birren (Ed.), *Encyclopedia of gerontology: Age, aging, and the aged* (Vol. 1, pp. 643–653). San Diego: Academic Press.

Green, D. M., & Swets, J. A. (1966). *A signal detection theory and psychophysics.* New York: John Wiley.

Greenberg, B. (1998, March 11). 93-year-old Macy's worker charms customers, rings up sale. *The Miami Herald,* p. 14A.

Grisso, T. (1986). *Evaluating competencies: Forensic assessments and instruments.* New York: Plenum Press.

Gross, J. J., Carstensen, L. L., Pasupathi, M., Tsai, J., Skorpen, C. G., & Hsu, A. Y. (1997). Emotion and aging: Experience, expression, and control. *Psychology and Aging, 12,* 590–599.

Guo, X., Erber, J. T., & Szuchman, L. T. (1999). Age and forgetfulness: Can stereotypes be modified? *Educational Gerontology, 25,* 457–466.

Gutmann, D. (1977). The cross-cultural perspective: Notes toward a comparative psychology of aging. In J. E. Birren & K. W. Schaie (Eds.), *The handbook of the psychology of aging* (pp. 302–326). New York: Van Nostrand.

Haight, B. K., Michel, Y., & Hendrix, S. (1998). Life review: Preventing despair in newly relocated nursing home residents short- and long-term effects. *International Journal of Aging and Human Development, 47,* 119–142.

Hakamies-Blomqvist, L., Mynttinen, S., Backman, M., & Mikkonen, V. (1999). Age-related differences in driving: Are older drivers more serial? *International Journal of Behavioral Development, 23,* 575–589.

Haley, W. E., Robb-Belcher, C., Becker, M. A., & Polivka, L. A. (1999, August). Attitudes about mental health services among older adults. Poster presented at the annual meeting of the American Psychological Association, Boston.

Hall, C. S., Lindzey, G., & Campbell, J. B. (1998). *Theories of personality* (4th ed.). New York: John Wiley.

Hannah, M. T., Domino, G., Figueredo, A. J., & Hendrickson, R. (1996). The prediction of ego integrity in older persons. *Educational and Psychological Measurement, 56,* 930–950.

Harkins, S. W., & Scott, R. B. (1996). Pain and presbyalgos. In J. E. Birren (Ed.), *Encyclopedia of gerontology: Age, aging, and the aged* (Vol. 2, pp. 247–260). San Diego: Academic Press.

Harootyan, R. A. (1996). Volunteer activity by older adults. In J. E. Birren (Ed.), *Encyclopedia of gerontology: Age, aging, and the aged* (Vol. 2, pp. 613–620). San Diego: Academic Press.

Harris, M. B. (1994). Growing old gracefully: Age concealment and gender. *Journal of Gerontology: Psychological Sciences, 49,* P149–P158.

Hartley, A. A. (1993). Evidence for the selective preservation of spatial selective attention in old age. *Psychology and Aging, 8,* 371–379.

Hartley, A. A. (1995). Attention. In G. L. Maddox et al. (Eds.), *The encyclopedia of aging* (2nd ed., pp. 91–93). New York: Springer.

Hasher, L., & Zacks, R. T. (1979). Automatic and effortful processes in memory. *Journal of Experimental Psychology: General, 108,* 356–388.

Hasher, L., & Zacks, R. T. (1988). Working memory, comprehension, and aging: A review and a new view. In G. H. Bower (Ed.), *The psychology of learning and motivation: Vol. 22* (pp. 193–225). New York: Academic Press.

Hawkins, H., Kramer, A., & Capaldi, D. (1992). Aging, exercise, and attention. *Psychology and Aging, 7,* 643–663.

Hayflick, L. (1994). *How and why we age*. New York: Ballantine Books.

Hayflick, L. (1995). Biological aging theories. In G. L. Maddox et al. (Eds.), *The encyclopedia of aging* (2nd ed., pp. 113–118). New York: Springer.

Hayflick, L., & Moorhead, P. S. (1961). The limited in vitro lifetime of human diploid cell strains. *Experimental Cell Research, 25,* 585–621.

Hayslip, B., Jr. (1996). Hospice. In J. E. Birren (Ed.), *Encyclopedia of gerontology: Age, aging, and the aged* (Vol. 1, pp. 687–702). San Diego: Academic Press.

Heckhausen, J. (1997). Developmental regulation across adulthood: Primary and secondary control of age-related changes. *Developmental Psychology, 33,* 176–187.

Heckhausen, J., & Baltes, P. B. (1991). Perceived controllability of expected psychological change across adulthood and old age. *Journal of Gerontology, 46,* P165–P173.

Heckhausen, J., Dixon, R. A., & Baltes, P. B. (1989). Gains and losses in development throughout adulthood as perceived by different adult age groups. *Developmental Psychology, 25,* 109–121.

Heckhausen, J., & Krueger, J. (1993). Developmental expectations for the self and most other people: Age grading in three functions of social comparison. *Developmental Psychology, 29,* 539–548.

Heckhausen, J., & Schulz, R. (1993). Optimisation by selection and compensation: Balancing primary and secondary control in life span development. *International Journal of Behavioral Development, 16,* 287–303.

Heckhausen, J., & Schulz, R. (1995). A life-span theory of control. *Psychological Review, 102,* 284–304.

Helson, R., Kwan, V. S. Y., John, O. P., & Jones, C. (2002). The growing evidence for personality change in adulthood: Findings from research with personality inventories. *Journal of Research in Personality, 36,* 287–306.

Herr, J. J., & Weakland, J. H. (1979). *Counseling elders and their families*. New York: Springer.

Hertzog, C. (1990, April). Methodological issues in cognitive aging research. Invited address to the 3rd Cognitive Aging Conference, Atlanta, GA.

Hertzog, C., Hultsch, D. F., & Dixon, R. A. (1999). On the problem of detecting effects of lifestyle on cognitive change in adulthood: Reply to Pushkar et al. (1999). *Psychology and Aging, 14,* 528–534.

Herzog, A. R., House, J. S., & Morgan, J. N. (1991). Relation of work and retirement to health and well-being in older age. *Psychology and Aging, 6,* 202–211.

Hess, B. B., & Markson, E. W. (1995). Poverty. In G. L. Maddox et al. (Eds.), *The encyclopedia of aging* (2nd ed., pp. 748–751). New York: Springer.

Hess, T. M. (1999). Cognitive and knowledge-based influences on social representations. In T. M. Hess & F. Blanchard-Fields (Eds.), *Social cognition and aging* (pp. 239–263). San Diego: Academic Press.

Hess, T. M., & Auman, C. (2001). Aging and social expertise: The impact of trait-diagnostic information on impressions of others. *Psychology and Aging, 16,* 497–510.

Hess, T. M., & Blanchard-Fields, F. (1996). Introduction to the study of cognitive change in adulthood. In F. Blanchard-Fields & T. M. Hess (Eds.), *Perspectives on cognitive change in adulthood and aging* (pp. 3–24). New York: McGraw-Hill.

Hess, T. M., Bolstad, C. A., Woodburn, S. M., & Auman, C. (1999). Trait-diagnosticity versus behavioral consistency as determinants of impression change in adulthood. *Psychology and Aging, 14,* 77–89.

Hinrichsen, G. A., & Dick-Siskin, L. P. (2000). General principles of therapy. In S. K. Whitbourne (Ed.), *Psychopathology in later adulthood* (pp. 323–350). New York: John Wiley.

Hooker, K. (1992). Possible selves and perceived health in older adults and college students. *Journal of Gerontology: Psychological Sciences, 47,* P85–P95.

Hooker, K. (1999). Possible selves in adulthood: Incorporating teleonomic relevance into studies of the self. In T. M. Hess & F. Blanchard-Fields (Eds.), *Social cognition and aging* (pp. 97–122). San Diego: Academic Press.

Hooker, K., & Kaus, C. R. (1994). Health-related possible selves in young and middle adulthood. *Psychology and Aging, 9,* 126–133.

Hooyman, N., & Kiyak, H. A. (2002). *Social gerontology: A multidisciplinary perspective* (6th ed.). Boston: Allyn & Bacon.

Horn, J. L., & Cattell, R. B. (1967). Age difference in fluid and crystallized intelligence. *Acta Psycholologica, 26,* 107–129.

Horn, J. L., & Donaldson, G. (1976). On the myth of intellectual decline in adulthood. *American Psychologist, 31,* 701–719.

Howard, D. V. (1996). The aging of implicit and explicit memory. In F. Blanchard-Fields and T. M. Hess (Eds.), *Perspective on cognitive change in adulthood and aging* (pp. 221–254). New York: McGraw-Hill.

Hoyer, W. J., & Rybash, J. M. (1996). Life span theory. In J. E. Birren (Ed.), *Encyclopedia of Gerontology: Age, aging, and the aged* (Vol. 2, pp. 65–71). San Diego: Academic Press.

Hoyert, D. L., Arias, E., Smith, B. L., Murphy, S. L., & Kochanek, K. D. (2001). Deaths: Final data for 1999. *National Vital Statistics Reports, 49(8)*. Hyattsville, MD: NationalCenter for Health Statistics.

Hultsch, D. F., Hertzog, C., Small, B. J., & Dixon, R. A. (1999). Use it or lose it: Engaged lifestyle as a buffer of cognitive decline in aging? *Psychology and Aging, 14,* 245–263.

Hummert, M. L. (1990). Multiple stereotypes of elderly and young adults: A comparison of structure and evaluations. *Psychology and Aging, 5,* 182–193.

Hummert, M. L. (1999). A social cognitive perspective on age stereotypes. In T. M. Hess & F. Blanchard-Fields (Eds.), *Social cognition and aging* (pp. 175–196). San Diego: Academic Press.

Hummert, M. L., Garstka, T. A., Shaner, J. L., & Strahm, S. (1994). Stereotypes of the elderly held by young, middle-aged, and elderly adults. *Journal of Gerontology: Psychological Sciences, 49,* P240–P249.

Ingersoll-Dayton, B., Morgan, D., & Antonucci, T. (1997). The effects of positive and negative social exchanges on aging adults. *Journal of Gerontology: Social Sciences, 52B,* S190–S199.

Ingram, R. E., & Price, J. M. (2001). The role of vulnerability in understanding psychopathology. In R. E. Ingram & J. M. Price (Eds.), *Vulnerability to psychopathology: Risk across the lifespan.* New York: Guilford.

James, J. W., & Haley, W. E. (1995). Age and health bias in practicing clinical psychologists. *Psychology and Aging, 10,* 610–616.

James, L. E., Burke, D. M., Austin, A., & Hulme, E. (1998). Production and perception of "verbosity" in younger and older adults. *Psychology and Aging, 13,* 355–367.

Jansari, A., & Parkin, A. J. (1996). Things that go bump in your life: Explaining the reminiscence bump in autobiographical memory. *Psychology and Aging, 11,* 85–91.

Jecker, N. S. (1996). Ethics and euthanasia. In J. E. Birren (Ed.), *Encyclopedia of gerontology: Age, aging, and the aged* (Vol. 1, pp. 505–508). San Diego: Academic Press.

Jecker, N. S., & Schneiderman, L. J. (1996). Is dying young worse than dying old? In J. Guadagno & D. Street (Eds.), *Aging in the twenty-first century: Readings in social gerontology* (pp. 514–524). New York: St. Martin's Press.

Johnson, M. M. S. (1990). Age differences in decision making: A process methodology for examining strategic information processing. *Journal of Gerontology: Psychological Sciences, 45,* P75–P78.

Johnson, R. W., Sambamoorthi, U., & Crystal, S. (1999). Gender differences in pension wealth: Estimates using provider data. *The Gerontologist, 39,* 320–333.

Jones, E. E. (1979). The rocky road from acts to dispositions. *American Psychologist, 34,* 107–117.

Jones, H. E., & Conrad, H. (1933). The growth and decline of intelligence: A study of a homogeneous group between the ages of ten and sixty. *Genetic Psychological Monographs, 13,* 223–298.

Jones, J. H. (1993). *Bad blood: The Tuskegee syphilis experiment.* New York: Free Press.

Kahana, E. (1982). A congruence model of person-environment interaction. In M. P. Lawton, P. G. Windley, & T. O. Byerts (Eds.), *Aging and the environment: Theoretical approaches* (pp. 97–121). New York: Springer.

Kahn, R. L., Goldfarb, A. I., & Pollack, M. (1964). The evaluation of geriatric patients following treatment. In P. H. Hoch & J. Zubin (Eds.), *Evaluation of geriatric treatment.* New York: Grune & Stratton.

Kane, R. L., & Friedman, B. (1996). Health care services. In J. E. Birren (Ed.), *Encyclopedia of gerontology: Age, aging, and the aged* (Vol. 1, pp. 635–641). San Diego: Academic Press.

Kastenbaum, R. (1996). Death and dying. In J. E. Birren (Ed.), *Encyclopedia of gerontology: Age, aging, and the aged* (Vol. 1, pp. 361–372). San Diego: Academic Press.

Kastenbaum, R. (1999). Dying and bereavement. In J. C. Cavanaugh & S. K. Whitbourne (Eds.), *Gerontology: An interdisciplinary perspective* (pp. 155–186). New York: Oxford University Press.

Kastenbaum, R., & Candy, S. E. (1973). The 4% fallacy: A methodological and empirical critique of extended care facility population statistics. *Aging and Human Development, 4,* 15–22.

Kaszniak, A. W. (1995). Parkinson's disease. In G. L. Maddox et al. (Eds.), *The encyclopedia of aging* (2nd ed., pp. 727–729). New York: Springer.

Kausler, D. H. (1982). *Experimental psychology and human aging.* New York: John Wiley.

Kausler, D. H. (1991). *Experimental psychology, cognition, and human aging* (2nd ed.). New York: Springer-Verlag.

Kausler, D. H. (1994). *Learning and memory in normal aging.* San Diego: Academic Press.

Kausler, D. H., & Kausler, B. C. (1996). *The graying of America: An encyclopedia of aging, health, mind, and behavior.* Urbana, IL: University of Illinois Press.

Kemper, S. (1994). Elderspeak: Speech accommodations to older adults. *Aging and Cognition, 1,* 17–28.

Kemper, S. (1995). Language production. In G. L. Maddox et al. (Eds.) *The encyclopedia of aging: A comprehensive resource in gerontology and geriatrics* (2nd ed., pp. 538–540). New York: Springer.

Kemper, S., & Harden, T. (1999). Experimentally disentangling what's beneficial about elderspeak from what's not. *Psychology and Aging, 14,* 656–670.

Kemper, S., & Mitzner, T. L. (2001). Language production and comprehension. In J. E. Birren & K. W. Schaie (Eds.), *Handbook of the psychology of aging* (5th ed., pp. 378–398). San Diego: Academic Press.

Kendig, H., & Pynoos, J. (1996). Housing. In J. E. Birren (Ed.), *Encyclopedia of gerontology: Age, aging, and the aged* (Vol. 1, pp. 703–713). San Diego: Academic Press.

Kimmel, D. (1992). The families of older gay men and lesbians. *Generations, 16,* 37–38.

King, D. A., & Markus, H. E. (2000). Mood disorders in older adults. In S. K. Whitbourne (Ed.), *Psychopathology in later adulthood* (pp. 141–172). New York: John Wiley.

Kinsella, K., & Gist, Y. J. (1998, October). Gender and aging: Mortality and health. *International Brief, IB/98–2*. Washington, DC: U.S. Census Bureau.

Kite, M. E., & Johnson, B. T. (1988). Attitudes toward older and younger adults: A meta-analysis. *Psychology and Aging, 3*, 233–244.

Kite, M. E., & Wagner, L. S. (2002). Attitudes toward older adults. In T. D. Nelson (Ed.), *Ageism: Stereotyping and prejudice against older persons* (pp. 129–161). Cambridge, MA: MIT Press.

Kivnick, H. Q., & Sinclair, H. M. (1996). Grandparenthood. In J. E. Birren (Ed.), *Encyclopedia of gerontology: Age, aging, and the aged* (Vol. 1, pp. 611–623). San Diego: Academic Press.

Kleemeier, R. W. (1962). Intellectual change in the senium. *Proceedings of the Social Statistics Section of the American Statistical Association, 1*, 290.

Kliegl, R., Smith, J., & Baltes, P. B. (1989). Testing-the-limits and the study of adult age differences in cognitive plasticity of a mnemonic skill. *Developmental Psychology, 25*, 247–256.

Kline, C. (1975). The socialization process of women: Implications for a theory of successful aging. *The Gerontologist, 15*, 486–492.

Kline, D. W., & Scialfa, C. T. (1996). Visual and auditory aging. In J. E. Birren & K. W. Schaie (Eds.), *Handbook of the psychology of aging* (4th ed., pp. 181–203). San Diego: Academic Press.

Kline, D. W., & Scialfa, C. T. (1997). Sensory and perceptual functioning: Basic research and human factors implications. In A. D. Fisk & W. A. Rogers (Eds.), *Handbook of human factors and the older adult* (pp. 27–54). San Diego: Academic Press.

Knight, B. G. (1996). *Psychotherapy with older adults* (2nd ed.). Thousand Oaks, CA: Sage.

Koenig, H. G., & Blazer, D. G., II (1996). Depression. In J. E. Birren (Ed.), *Encyclopedia of gerontology: Age, aging, and the aged* (Vol 1, pp. 415–428). San Diego: Academic Press.

Kogan, N. (1990). Personality and aging. In J. E. Birren and K. W. Schaie (Eds.), *Handbook of the psychology of aging* (3rd ed., pp. 330–346). San Diego: Academic Press.

Kogan, N., & Mills, M. (1992). Gender influences on age cognitions and preferences: Sociocultural or sociobiological? *Psychology and Aging, 7*, 98–106.

Kohlberg, L. (1969). Stage and sequence: The cognitive-developmental approach to socialization. In D. A. Goslin (Ed.), *Handbook of socialization theory and research* (pp. 347–480). Chicago: Rand McNally.

Kral, V. A. (1962). Senescent forgetfulness: Benign and malignant. *Canadian Medical Association Journal, 86*, 257–260.

Kramer, A. F., Humphrey, D. G., Larish, J. F., Logan, G. D., & Strayer, D. L. (1994). Aging and inhibition: Beyond a unitary view of inhibitory processing in attention. *Psychology and Aging, 9*, 491–512.

Krause, N., & Borawski-Clark, E. (1994). Clarifying the functions of social support in later life. *Research on Aging, 16(3)*, 251–279.

Krause, N., & Rook, K. S. (2003). Negative interaction in late life: Issues in the stability and generalizability of conflict across relationships. *Journal of Gerontology: Psychological Sciences, 58B*, P88–P99.

Krueger, J., Heckhausen, J., & Hundertmark, J. (1995). Perceiving middle-aged adults: Effects of stereotype-congruent and incongruent information. *Journal of Gerontology: Psychological Sciences, 50B*, P82–P93.

Kübler-Ross, E. (1969). *On death and dying*. New York: Macmillan.

Kübler-Ross, E. (1974). *Questions and answers on death and dying*. New York: Macmillan.

Kwong See, S. T., Hoffman, H. G., & Wood, T. L. (2001). Perceptions of an old female eyewitness: Is the older eyewitness believable? *Psychology and Aging, 16*, 346–350.

Kyucharyants, V. (1974). Will the human life-span reach 100? *The Gerontologist, 14, Pt. 1*, 377–380.

Labouvie-Vief, G. (1997). Cognitive-emotional integration in adulthood. In K. W. Schaie & M. P. Lawton (Eds.), *Annual review of gerontology and geriatrics* (Vol. 17, pp. 206–237). New York: Springer.

Labouvie-Vief, G. (1999). Emotions in adulthood. In V. L. Bengston & K. W. Schaie (Eds.), *Handbook of theories of aging* (pp. 253–267). New York: Springer.

Labouvie-Vief, G., & Diehl, M. (2000). Cognitive complexity and cognitve-affective integration: Related or separate domains of adult development? *Psychology and Aging, 15*, 490–504.

Lachman, M. E. (2003). Negative interactions in close relationships: Introduction to a special section. *Journal of Gerontology: Psychological Sciences, 58B*, P69.

Landsfield, P. W. (1995). Stress theories of aging. In G. L. Maddox et al. (Eds.), *The encyclopedia of aging* (2nd ed., pp. 903–905). New York: Springer.

Lang, F. R., & Baltes, M. M. (1997). Being with people and being alone in late life: Costs and benefits for everyday functioning. *International Journal of Behavioral Development, 21*, 729–746.

Lang, F. R., & Carstensen, L. L. (1994). Close emotional relationships in late life: Further support for proactive aging in the social domain. *Psychology and Aging, 9*, 315–324.

Lang, F. R., Staudinger, U. M., & Carstensen, L. L. (1998). Perspectives on socioemotional selectivity in late life: How personality and social context do (and do not) make a difference. *Journal of Gerontology: Psychological Sciences, 53B*, P21–P30.

Langer, E. J., & Rodin, J. (1976). The effects of choice and enhanced personal responsibility for the aged: A field experiment in an institutional setting. *Journal of Personality and Social Psychology, 34*, 191–198.

LaRue, A., Dessonville, C., & Jarvik, L. F. (1985). Aging and mental disorders. In J. E. Birren and K. W. Schaie

(Eds.), *Handbook of the psychology of aging* (2nd ed., pp. 664–702). New York: Van Nostrand Reinhold.

Lavelle, M. (1997, March 9) On the edge of age discrimination. *New York Times Magazine*, pp. 66–69.

Lawton, M. P. (1989). Environmental proactivity in older people. In V. L. Bengston & K. W. Schaie (Eds.), *The course of later life: Research and reflections* (pp. 15–23). New York: Springer.

Lawton, M. P. (1999). Environmental design features and the well-being of older persons. In M. Duffy (Ed.), *Handbook of counseling and psychotherapy with older adults* (pp. 350–363). New York: John Wiley.

Lawton, M. P. (2001). Quality of life and the end of life. In J. E. Birren & K. W. Schaie (Eds.), *Handbook of the psychology of aging* (5th ed., pp. 592–616). San Diego: Academic Press.

Lawton, M. P., & Brody, E. M. (1969). Assessment of older people: Self-maintaining and instrumental activities of daily living. *The Gerontologist, 9*, 179–186.

Lawton, M. P., Greenbaum, M., & Liebowitz, B. (1980). The lifespan of housing environments for the aging. *The Gerontologist, 20*, 56–64.

Lawton, M. P., Kleban, M. H., Rajagopal, D., & Dean, J. (1992). Dimensions of affective experience in three age groups. *Psychology and Aging, 7*, 171–184.

Lawton, M. P., & Nahemow, L. (1973). Ecology and the aging process. In C. Eisdorfer and M. P. Lawton (Eds.), *The psychology of adult development and aging* (pp. 619–674). Washington, DC: American Psychological Association.

Layton, B. (1975). Perceptual noise and aging. *Psychological Bulletin, 82*, 875–883.

Lee, J. A., & Clemons, T. (1985). Factors affecting employment decisions about older workers. *Journal of Applied Psychology, 70*, 785–788.

Lehman, H. C. (1953). *Age and achievement*. Princeton, NJ: Princeton University Press.

Levenson, R. W., Carstensen, L. L., & Gottman, J. M. (1993). Long-term marriage: Age, gender, and satisfaction. *Psychology and Aging, 8*, 301–313.

Levinson, D. (1978). *The seasons of a man's life*. New York: Knopf.

Levitt, M. J., Weber, R. A., & Guacci, N. (1993). Convoys of social support: An intergenerational analysis. *Psychology and Aging, 8*, 323–326.

Levy, B. (1996). Improving memory in old age through implicit self-stereotyping. *Journal of Personality and Social Psychology, 71*, 1092–1107.

Levy, G., & Langer, E. (1994). Aging free from negative stereotypes: Successful memory in China and among the American deaf. *Journal of Personality and Social Psychology, 66*, 989–997.

Light, L. L. (1991). Memory and aging: Four hypotheses in search of data. *Annual Review of Psychology, 42*, 333–376.

Lindenberger, U., & Baltes, P. B. (1994). Sensory functioning and intelligence in old age: A strong connection. *Psychology and Aging, 9*, 339–355.

Lisansky-Gomberg, E. S. (2000). Substance abuse disorders. In S. K. Whitbourne (Ed.), *Psychopathology in later adulthood* (pp. 277–298). New York: John Wiley.

Litwak, E., & Longino, C. F., Jr. (1987). Migration patterns among the elderly: A developmental perspective. *The Gerontologist, 27*, 266–272.

Longino, C. F., Jr. (1995). Geographic mobility. In G. L. Maddox et al. (Eds.), *The encyclopedia of aging* (2nd ed., pp. 402–403). New York: Springer.

Longman, P. (1997). Should there be an affirmative action policy for hiring older persons? No. In A. E. Scharlach & L. W. Kaye (Eds.), *Controversial issues in aging* (pp. 40–43). Boston: Allyn & Bacon.

Lopata, H. Z. (1995). Widowhood. In G. L. Maddox et al. (Eds.), *The encyclopedia of aging* (2nd ed., pp. 969–971). New York: Springer.

Lovelace, E. A., & Twohig, P. T. (1990). Healthy older adults' perceptions of their memory functioning and use of mnemonics. *Bulletin of the Psychonomic Society, 28*, 115–118.

Lowenthal, M. F., & Haven, C. (1968). Interaction and adaptation: Intimacy as a critical variable. *American Sociological Review, 33*, 20–30.

Lubart, T. I., & Sternberg, R. J. (1998). Life span creativity: An investment theory approach. In C. E. Adams-Price (Ed.), *Creativity and successful aging: Theoretical and empirical approaches* (pp. 21–41). New York: Springer.

Lund, D. A. (1996). Bereavement and loss. In J. E. Birren (Ed.), *Encyclopedia of gerontology: Age, aging, and the aged* (Vol. 1, pp. 173–183). San Diego: Academic Press.

Madden, D. J., & Allen, P. A. (1996). Attention. In J. E. Birren (Ed.), *Encyclopedia of gerontology: Age, aging, and the aged* (Vol. 1, pp. 131–140). San Diego: Academic Press.

Madden, D. J., Blumenthal, J. A., Allen, P. A., & Emery, C. F. (1989). Improving aerobic capacity in healthy older adults does not necessarily lead to improved cognitive performane. *Psychology and Aging, 4*, 307–320.

Magai, C., & Passman, V. (1997). The interpersonal basis of emotional behavior and emotion regulation in adulthood. In K. W. Schaie & M. P. Lawton (Eds.), *Annual review of gerontology and geriatrics* (Vol. 17, pp. 104–137). New York: Springer.

Maier, H., & Smith, J. (1999). Psychological predictors of mortality in old age. *Journal of Gerontology: Psychological Sciences, 54B*, P44–P54.

Mancini, J. A., & Bleiszner, R. (1989). Aging parents and adult children: Research themes in intergenerational relations. *Journal of Marriage and the Family, 51*, 275–290.

Markus, H. R., & Herzog, A. R. (1991). The role of the self-concept in aging. In K. W. Schaie & M. P. Lawton

(Eds.), *Annual review of gerontology and geriatrics* (Vol. 11, pp. 110–143). New York: Springer.

Markus, H. R., & Nurius, P. (1986). Possible selves. *American Psychologist, 41,* 954–969.

Marsiske, M., Klumb, P., & Baltes, M. M. (1997). Everyday activity patterns and sensory functioning in old age. *Psychology and Aging, 12,* 444–457.

Marsiske, M., & Willis, S. L. (1995). Dimensionality of everyday problem solving in older adults. *Psychology and Aging, 10,* 269–283.

Martin-Matthews, A. (1996). Widowhood and widower-hood. In J. E. Birren (Ed.), *Encyclopedia of gerontology: Age, aging, and the aged* (Vol. 2, pp. 621–625). San Diego: Academic Press.

Masoro, E. J. (1995). Body composition. In G. L. Maddox et al. (Eds.), *The encyclopedia of aging* (2nd ed., pp. 124–125). New York: Springer.

May, C. P., & Hasher, L. (1998). Synchrony effects in inhibitory control over thought and action. *Journal of Experimental Psychology: Human Perception and Performance, 24,* 363–379.

Mazur, D. J., & Merz, J. F. (1995). Older patients' willingness to trade off urologic adverse outcomes for a better chance at five-year survival in the clinical setting of prostate cancer. *Journal of the American Geriatrics Society, 43,* 979–984.

McAdams, D. P. (1996). Narrating the self in adulthood. In J. E. Birren, G. M. Kenyon, J. E. Ruth, J. J. F. Schroots, & T. Svensson (Eds.), *Aging and biography: Explorations in adult development* (pp. 131–148). New York: Springer.

McAdams, D. P., de St. Aubin, E., & Logan, R. L. (1993). Generativity among young, midlife, and older adults. *Psychology and Aging, 8,* 221–230.

McCann, R., & Giles, H. (2002). Ageism in the work-place: A communication perspective. In T. D. Nelson (Ed.), *Ageism: Stereotyping and prejudice against older persons* (pp. 163–199). Cambridge, MA: MIT Press.

McCay, C. M., Crowell, M. F., & Maynard, L. A. (1935). The effect of retarded growth upon the length of life span and upon the ultimate body size. *Journal of Nutrition, 10,* 63–79.

McCrae, R. R. (2002). The maturation of personality psychology: Adult personality development and psychological well-being. *Journal of Research in Personality, 36,* 307–317.

McCrae, R. R., & Costa, P. T., Jr. (1982). Aging, the life course, and models of personality. In T. M. Field, A. Huston, H. C. Quay, L. Troll, & G. E. Finley (Eds.), *Review of human development* (pp. 602–613). New York: John Wiley.

McCrae, R. R., & Costa, P. T., Jr. (1991). Adding liebe and arbeit: The full five-factor model and well-being. *Personality and Social Psychology Bulletin, 17,* 227–232.

McCrae, R. R., & Costa, P. T., Jr. (1997). Personality trait structure as a human universal. *American Psychologist, 52,* 509–516.

McCrae, R. R., Costa, P. T., Jr., Lima, M. P., et al. (1999). Age differences in personality across the adult life span: Parallels in five cultures. *Developmental Psychology, 35,* 466–477.

McDonald, L. (1996). Abuse and neglect of elders. In J. E. Birren (Ed.), *Encyclopedia of gerontology: Age, aging, and the aged* (Vol. 1, pp. 1–10). San Diego: Academic Press.

McDowd, J. M. (1997). Inhibition in attention and aging. *Journal of Gerontology: Psychological Sciences, 52B,* P265–P273.

McDowd, J. M., & Shaw, R. J. (2000). Attention and aging: A functional perspective. In F. I. M. Craik & T. A. Salthouse (Eds.), *The handbook of aging and cognition* (2nd ed., pp. 221–292). Mahwah, NJ: Erlbaum.

McEvoy, G. M., & Cascio, W. F. (1989). Cumulative evidence of the relationship between employee age and job performance. *Journal of Applied Psychology, 74,* 11–17.

McKnight, A. J., & McKnight, A. S. (1993). The effect of cellular phone use upon driver attention. *Accident Analysis & Prevention, 25,* 259–265.

Meacham, J. A. (1990). The loss of wisdom. In R. J. Sternberg (Ed.), *Wisdom: Its nature, origins, and development* (pp. 181–211). New York: Cambridge University Press.

Medvedev, Z. A. (1974). Caucasus and Altay longevity: A biological or social problem? *The Gerontologist, 14, Pt. 1,* 381–387.

Meeks, S. (2000). Schizophrenia and related disorders. In S. K. Whitbourne (Ed.), *Psychopathology in later adulthood* (pp. 189–215). New York: John Wiley.

Menec, V. H., Chipperfield, J. G., & Perry, R. P. (1999). Self-perceptions of health: A prospective analysis of mortality, control, and health. *Journal of Gerontology: Psychological Sciences, 54B,* P85–P93.

Mergenhagen, P. (1994, June). Rethinking retirement. *American Demographics,* 28–34.

Meyer, B. J. F., Russo, C., & Talbot, A. (1995). Discourse comprehension and problem solving: Decisions about the treatment of breast cancer by women across the life-span. *Psychology and Aging, 10,* 84–103.

Miller, G. A. (1956). The magic number seven plus or minus two. Some limits on our capacity for processing information. *Psychological Review, 63,* 81–97.

Mishkin, B., Mezey, M., & Ramsey, G. (1995). Advance directives in health care: Living wills and durable power of attorney. In G. L. Maddox et al. (Eds.), *The encyclopedia of aging* (2nd ed., pp. 26–28). New York: Springer.

Mitty, E. L. (1995). Nursing homes. In G. L. Maddox et al. (Eds.), *The encyclopedia of aging* (2nd ed., pp. 693–699). New York: Springer.

Moen, P. (1996). Gender, age, and the life course. In R. H. Binstock & L. K. George (Eds.), *Handbook of aging and the social sciences* (4th ed., pp. 171–187). San Diego: Academic Press.

Monroe, S. M., & Simons, A. D. (1991). Diathesis-stress theories in the context of life stress research: Implications for depressive disorders. *Psychological Bulletin, 110,* 406–425.

Montepare, J. M., & Lachman, M. E. (1989). "You're only as old as you feel": Self-perceptions of age, fears of aging, and life satisfaction from adolescence to old age. *Psychology and Aging, 4,* 73–78.

Morrell, R. W., Park, D. C., Kidder, D. P., & Martin, M. (1997). Adherence to antihypertensive medications across the life span. *The Gerontologist, 37,* 609–619.

Mroczek, D. K., Hurt, S. W., & Berman, W. H. (1999). Conceptual and methodological issues in the assessment of personality disorders in older adults. In E. Rosowsky, R. C. Abrams, & R. A. Zweig (Eds.), *Personality disorders in older adults: Emerging issues in diagnosis and treatment* (pp. 135–150). Mahwah, NJ: Erlbaum.

Mroczek, D. K., & Kolarz, C. M. (1998). The effect of age on positive and negative affect: A developmental perspective on happiness. *Journal of Personality and Social Psychology, 75,* 1333–1349.

Murphy, M. D., Sanders, R. E., Gabrieskeski, A. A., & Schmitt, F. A. (1981). Metamemory in the aged. *Journal of Gerontology, 25,* 268–274.

Myers, G. C. (1990). Demography of aging. In R. H. Binstock & L. K. George (Eds.), *Handbook of aging and the social sciences* (3rd ed., pp. 19–44). San Diego: Academic Press.

Myers, G. C. (1995). Demography. In G. L. Maddox et al. (Eds.), *The encyclopedia of aging* (2nd ed., pp. 260–264). New York: Springer.

Myers, G. C., & Eggers, M. L. (1996). Demography. In J. E. Birren (Ed.), *Encyclopedia of gerontology: Age, aging, and the aged* (Vol. 1, pp. 405–413). San Diego: Academic Press.

National Academy on an Aging Society (1999, December). *Hearing Loss,* Number 2.

National Academy on an Aging Society (2000, April). *Diabetes: A Drain on U.S. Resources,* Number 6.

National Institute on Aging (1998). *Progress Report on Alzheimer's Disease* (http://www.alzheimers.org/pubs/pr98.html).

National Vital Statistics Report (2002, September 16), Vol. 50, No. 15 (http://www.cdc.gov/nchs/fastats/lifeexpec.htm).

Neimeyer, R. A., & Fortner, B. (1995). Death anxiety in the elderly. In G. L. Maddox et al. (Eds.), *The encyclope dia of aging* (2nd ed., pp. 252–253). New York: Springer.

Neugarten, B. L. (1977). Personality and aging. In J. E. Birren & K. W. Schaie (Eds.), *Handbook of the psychology of aging* (pp. 626–649). New York: Van Nostrand Reinhold.

Neugarten, B. L., Havinghurst, R. J., & Tobin, S. S. (1968). Personality and patterns of aging. In B. L. Neugarten (Ed.), *Middle age and aging* (pp. 173–177). Chicago: University of Chicago Press.

Neugarten, B. L., & Weinstein, K. K. (1964). The changing American grandparent. *Journal of Marriage and the Family, 26,* 199–204.

Newton, N. A., & Lazarus, L. W. (1992). Behavioral and psychotherapeutic interventions. In J. E. Birren, R. B. Sloane, & G. D. Cohen (Eds.), *Handbook of mental health and aging* (2nd ed., pp. 699–719). San Diego: Academic Press.

Norris, J. E., & Tindale, J. A. (1994). *Among generations: The cycle of adult relationships.* New York: W. H. Freeman.

O'Connor, B. P., & Rigby, H. (1996). Perceptions of baby talk, frequency of receiving baby talk, and self-esteem among community and nursing home residents. *Psychology and Aging, 11,* 147–154.

Okun, M. A., & Keith, V. M. (1998). Effects of positive and negative social exchanges with various sources on depressive symptoms in younger and older adults. *Journal of Gerontology: Psychological Sciences, 53B,* P4–P20.

Olshansky, S. J., Carnes, B. A., & Grahn, D. (1998). Confronting the boundaries of human longevity. *American Scientist, 86,* 52–61.

Olshansky, S. J., Hayflick, L., & Carnes, B. A. (2002, June). No truth to the fountain of youth. *Scientific American,* 92–95.

O'Rand, A. (1996). The cumulative stratification of the life course. In R. H. Binstock & L. K. George (Eds.), *Handbook of aging and the social sciences* (4th ed., pp. 188–207). San Diego: Academic Press.

Owens, W. R., Jr. (1953). Age and mental abilities: A longitudinal study. *Genetic Psychology Monographs, 48,* 3–54.

Palmore, E. (1975). *The honorable elders: A cross-cultural analysis of aging in Japan.* Durham, NC: Duke University Press.

Palmore, E. (2001). The ageism survey: First findings. *The Gerontologist, 41,* 572–575.

Panek, P. E. (1997). The older worker. In A. D. Fisk & W. A. Rogers (Eds.), *The handbook of human factors and the older adult* (pp. 363–394). San Diego: Academic Press.

Park, D. C., Morrell, R. W., Frieske, D., & Kincaid, D. (1992). Medication adherence behaviors in older adults: Effects of external cognitive supports. *Psychology and Aging, 7,* 252–256.

Pashler, H. (1994). Dual-task interference in simple tasks: Data and theory. *Psychological Bulletin, 116,* 220–244.

Passuth, P. M., & Bengston, V. L. (1988). Sociological theories of aging: Current perspectives and future directions. In J. E. Birren & V. L. Bengston (Eds.), *Emergent theories of aging* (pp. 333–355). New York: Springer.

Peck, R. C. (1968). Psychological developments in the second half of life. In B. L. Neugarten (Ed.), *Middle age and aging* (pp. 88–92). Chicago: University of Chicago Press.

Peng, K., & Nisbett, R. E. (1999). Culture, dialectics, and reasoning about contradiction. *The American Psychologist, 54,* 741–755.

Perdue, C. W., & Gurtman, M. B. (1990). Evidence for the automaticity of ageism. *Journal of Experimental Social Psychology, 11,* 177–186.

Perls, T., & Silver, M. H. (1999, November/December). Will you live to be 100? *Modern Maturity.*

Perry, E. L., Kulik, C. T., & Bourhis, A. C. (1996). Moderating effects of personal and contextual factors in age discrimination. *Journal of Applied Psychology, 81,* 628–647.

Piaget, J. (1952). *The origins of intelligence in children.* New York: International Universities Press.

Pillemer, K., & Bachman-Prehn, R. (1991). Helping and hurting: Predictors of maltreatment of patients in nursing homes. *Research on Aging, 13,* 74–95.

Pillemer, K., & Hudson, B. (1993). A model abuse prevention program for nursing home assistants. *The Gerontologist, 33,* 128–131.

Pillemer, K., & Moore, D. (1989). Abuse of patients in nursing homes: Findings from a survey of the staff. *The Gerontologist, 29,* 314–320.

Pillemer, K., & Suitor, J. J. (1992). Violence and violent feelings: What causes them among family caregivers? *Journal of Gerontology: Social Sciences, 47,* S165–S172.

Poon, L. W., Sweaney, A. L., Clayton, G. M., & Merriam, S. B. (1992). The Georgia Centenarian Study. *International Journal of Aging and Human Development, 34,* 1–17.

Pratt, M. W., Diessner, R., Pratt, A., Hunsberger, B., & Pancer, S. M. (1996). Moral and social reasoning and perspective taking in later life: A longitudinal study. *Psychology and Aging, 11,* 66–73.

Pratt, M. W., & Norris, J. E. (1994). *The social psychology of aging: A cognitive perspective.* Cambridge, MA: Blackwell.

Pratt, M. W., & Norris, J. E. (1999). Moral development in maturity: Life-span perspectives on the processes of successful aging. In T. M. Hess & F. Blanchard-Fields (Eds.), *Social cognition and aging* (pp. 291–317). San Diego: Academic Press.

Pruchno, R. A., & Rose, M. S. (2000). The effect of long-term care environments on health outcomes. *The Gerontologist, 40,* 422–428.

Puder, R., Lacks, P., Bertelson, A. D., & Storandt, M. (1983). Short-term stimulus control treatment of insomnia in older adults. *Behavior Therapy, 14,* 424–429.

Pushkar, D. Etezadi, J., Andres, D., Arbuckle, T., Schwartzman, A. E., & Chaikelson, J. (1999). Models of intelligence in late life: Comment on Hultsch et al. (1999). *Psychology and Aging, 14,* 520–527.

Pynoos, J., & Golant, S. (1996). Housing and living arrangements for the elderly. In R. H. Binstock & L. K. George (Eds.), *Handbook of aging and the social sciences* (4th ed., pp. 303–324). San Diego: Academic Press.

Quadagno, J. (2002). *Aging and the life course: An introduction to social gerontology* (2nd ed.). Boston: McGraw-Hill.

Quadagno, J., & Hardy, J. (1996). Work and retirement. In R. H. Binstock & L. K. George (Eds.). *Handbook of aging and the social sciences* (4th ed., pp. 325–345). San Diego: Academic Press.

Quinn, M. J. (1995). Elder abuse and neglect. In G. L. Maddox et al. (Eds.), *The encyclopedia of aging* (2nd ed., pp. 304–306). New York: Springer.

Reedy, M. N., Birren, J. E., & Schaie, K. W. (1981). Satisfying love relationships across the life span. *Human Development, 24,* 52–66.

Reese, S. M. (2003, January/February). You can't say no to blood. *AARP Modern Maturity,* 56–62.

Reitzes, D. C., Mutran, E. J., & Fernandez, M. E. (1996). Does retirement hurt well-being?: Factors influencing self-esteem and depression among retirees and workers. *The Gerontologist, 36,* 649–656.

Reitzes, D. C., Mutran, E. J., & Fernandez, M. E. (1998). The decision to retire: A career perspective. *Social Science Quarterly, 79,* 607–619.

Rendell, P. G., & Thomson, D. M. (1999). Aging and prospective memory: Differences between naturalistic and laboratory tasks. *Journal of Gerontology: Psychological Sciences, 54B,* P256–P269.

Revenson, T. A. (1989). Compassionate stereotyping of elderly patients by physicians: Revisiting the social contact hypothesis. *Psychology and Aging, 4,* 230–234.

Rhee, C., & Gatz, M. (1993). Cross-generational attributions concerning locus of control beliefs. *International Journal of Aging and Human Development, 37,* 153–161.

Rhodes, S. R. (1983). Age-related differences in work attitudes and behavior: A review and conceptual analysis. *Psychological Bulletin, 93,* 328–367.

Ribot, T. (1882). *Diseases of memory.* New York: Appleton.

Richman, L. (1969). Sensory training for geriatric patients. *The American Journal of Occupational Therapy, 23,* 254–257.

Riegel, K. F., Riegel, R. M., & Meyer, G. (1967). A study of the dropout rates in longitudinal research on aging and the prediction of death. *Journal of Personality and Social Psychology, 4,* 342–348.

Riggle, E. D. B., & Johnson, M. M. S. (1996). Age difference in political decision making: Strategies of evaluating political candidates. *Political Behavior, 18,* 99–118.

Riggs, K. M., Lachman, M. E., & Wingfield, A. (1997). Taking charge of remembering: Locus of control and older adults' memory for speech. *Experimental Aging Research, 23,* 237–256.

Riley, M. W. (1994). Aging and society: Past, present, and future. *The Gerontologist, 34,* 436–446.

Roberts, B. W., & DelVecchio, W. F. (2000). The rank-order consistency of personality traits from childhood to old age: A quantitative review of longitudinal studies. *Psychological Bulletin, 126,* 3–25.

Roberts, J. C. (1995). Eye: Structure and function. In G. L. Maddox et al. (Eds.), *The encyclopedia of aging* (2nd ed., pp. 354–359). New York: Springer.

Rodin, J., & Langer, E. (1980). Aging labels: The decline of control and the fall of self-esteem. *Journal of Social Issues, 36,* 12–29.

Rogers, W. A. (1997). Individual differences, aging, and human factors: An overview. In F. D. Fisk & W. A. Rogers (Eds.), *Handbook of human factors and the older adult* (pp. 151–170). San Diego: Academic Press.

Rogers, W. A., & Fisk, A. D. (2001). Understanding the role of attention in cognitive aging research. In J. E. Birren & K. W. Schaie (Eds.), *Handbook of the social psychology of aging* (5th ed., pp. 267–287). San Diego: Academic Press.

Rollins, B., & Feldman, H. (1970). Marital satisfaction over the family life cycle. *Journal of Marriage and the Family, 32,* 20–28.

Rook, K. S. (1984). The negative side of social interaction: Impact on psychological well-being. *Journal of Personality and Social Psychology, 46,* 1097–1108.

Rook, K. S. (1987). Reciprocity of social exchange and social satisfaction among older women. *Journal of Personality and Social Psychology, 52,* 145–154.

Rook, K. S. (1997). Positive and negative social exchanges: Weighing their effects in later life. *Journal of Gerontology: Social Sciences, 52B,* S167–S169.

Ross, L. (1977). The intuitive psychologist and his shortcomings: Distortions in the attribution process. In L. Berkowitz (Ed.), *Advances in experimental social psychology: Vol. 10* (pp. 173–220). New York: Academic Press.

Roth, D. L., Haley, W. E., Owen, J. E., Clay, O. J., & Goode, K. T. (2001). Latent growth models of the longitudinal effects of dementia caregiving: A comparison of African American and White family caregivers. *Psychology and Aging, 16,* 427–436.

Rotter, J. B. (1966). Generalized expectancies for internal versus external control of reinforcement. *Psychological Monographs, 80* (Whole No. 609).

Rowe, J. W., & Kahn, R. L. (1998). *Successful aging.* New York: Pantheon Books.

Rowles, G. D., & Ravdal, H. (2002). Aging, place, and meaning in the face of changing circumstances. In R. S. Weiss & S. A. Bass (Eds.), *Challenges of the third age: Meaning and purpose in later life* (pp. 81–114). New York: Oxford University Press.

Rubin, D. C., Rahhal, T. A., & Poon, L. W. (1998). Things learned in early adulthood are remembered best. *Memory & Cognition, 26,* 3–19.

Rubin, E. H., Storandt, M. Miller, P., Kincherf, D. A., Grant, E. A., Morris, J. C., & Berg, L. (1998). A prospective study of cognitive function and onset of dementia in cognitively healthy elders. *Archives of Neurology, 55,* 395–401.

Rubin, K. H., & Brown, I. D. R. (1975). A life-span look at person perception and its relationship to communicative interaction. *Journal of Gerontology, 30,* 461–468.

Ruthruff, E., Pashler, H. E., & Klaassen, A. (2001). Processing bottlenecks in dual-task performance: Structural limitation or strategic postponement? *Psychonomic Bulletin & Review, 8,* 73–80.

Ryan, E. B. (1992). Beliefs about memory changes across the adult life span. *Journal of Gerontology: Psychological Sciences, 47,* P41–P46.

Ryan, E. B., Bourhis, R. Y., & Knops, U. (1991). Evaluative perceptions of patronizing speech addressed to elders. *Psychology and Aging, 6,* 442–450.

Ryan, E. B., Hamilton, J. M., & Kwong See, S. (1994). Patronizing the old: How do younger and older adults respond to baby talk in the nursing home? *International Journal of Aging and Human Development, 39,* 21–32.

Ryan, E. B., Hummert, M. L., & Anas, A. P. (1997, November). The impact of old age and hearing impairment on first impressions. Paper presented at the Gerontological Society of America Convention, Cincinnati, OH.

Ryan, E. B., Hummert, M. L., & Boich, L. H. (1995). Communication predicaments of aging: Patronizing behavior toward older adults. *Journal of Language and Social Psychology, 14,* 144–166.

Ryan, E. B., & Kwong See, S. (1993). Age-based beliefs about memory changes for self and others across adulthood. *Journal of Gerontology: Psychological Sciences, 48,* P199–P201.

Rybash, J. M., Hoyer, W. J., & Roodin, P.A. (1986). *Adult cognition and aging: Developmental changes in processing, knowing, and thinking.* New York: Pergamon Press.

Ryff, C. D. (1989). Happiness is everything, or is it? Explorations on the meaning of psychological well-being. *Journal of Personality and Social Psychology, 57,* 1069–1081.

Ryff, C. D., Kwan, D. M. L., & Singer, B. H. (2001). Personality and aging: Flourishing agendas and future challenges. In J. E. Birren & K. W. Schaie (Eds.), *Handbook of the psychology of aging* (5th ed., pp. 477–499). San Diego: Academic Press.

Salthouse, T. A. (1982). *Adult cognition: An experimental psychology of human aging.* New York: Springer-Verlag.

Salthouse, T. A. (1984). Effects of age and skill in typing. *Journal of Experimental Psychology: General, 113,* 345–371.

Salthouse, T. A. (1990). Cognitive competence and expertise in aging. In J. E. Birren & K. W. Schaie (Eds.),

Handbook of the psychology of aging (3rd ed., pp. 310–319). San Diego: Academic Press.

Salthouse, T. A. (1991). *Theoretical perspectives on cognitive aging.* Hillsdale, NJ: Erlbaum.

Salthouse, T. A. (1996a). Reaction time. In J. E. Birren (Ed.), *Encyclopedia of gerontology: Age, aging, and the aged* (Vol. 2, pp. 377–380). San Diego: Academic Press.

Salthouse, T. A. (1996b). The processing-speed theory of adult age differences in cognition. *Psychological Review, 103,* 403–428.

Salthouse, T. A., & Maurer, T. J. (1996). Aging, job performance, and career development. In J. E. Birren & K. W. Schaie (Eds.), *Handbook of the psychology of aging* (4th ed., pp. 353–364). San Diego: Academic Press.

Schacter, D. L. (1987). Memory, amnesia, and frontal lobe dysfunction. *Psychobiology, 15,* 21–36.

Schaie, K. W. (1965). A general model for the study of developmental problems. *Psychological Bulletin, 64,* 92–107.

Schaie, K. W. (1977–1978). Toward a stage theory of adult cognitive development. *Aging and Human Development, 8,* 129–138.

Schaie, K. W. (1989). The hazards of cognitive aging. *The Gerontologist, 29,* 484–493.

Schaie, K. W. (1990). Intellectual development in adulthood. In J. E. Birren & K. W. Schaie (Eds.), *Handbook of the psychology of aging* (3rd ed., pp. 291–309). New York: Academic Press.

Schaie, K. W. (1994). The course of adult intellectual development. *American Psychologist, 49,* 304–313.

Schaie, K. W. (1995). Research methods in gerontology. In G. L. Maddox et al. (Eds.), *The encyclopedia of aging* (2nd ed., pp. 812–815). New York: Springer.

Schaie, K. W. (1996). Intellectual development in adulthood. In J. E. Birren & K. W. Schaie (Eds.), *Handbook of the psychology of aging* (4th ed., pp. 266–286). San Diego: Academic Press.

Schaie, K. W., & Willis, S. L. (1986). Can decline in adult intellectual functioning be reversed? *Developmental Psychology, 22,* 223–232.

Schaie, K. W., & Willis, S. L. (1996). Psychometric intelligence. In F. Blanchard-Fields & T. M. Hess (Eds.), *Perspectives on cognitive change in adulthood and aging* (pp. 293–322). New York: McGraw-Hill.

Schaie, K. W., & Willis, S. L. (1999). Theories of everyday competence and aging. In V. L. Bengston & K. W. Schaie (Eds.), *Handbook of theories of aging* (pp. 174–195). New York: Springer.

Schaie, K. W., & Willis, S. L. (2000). A stage theory model of adult cognitive development revisited. In R. L. Rubinstein, M. Moss, & M. H. Kleban (Eds.), *The many dimensions of aging* (pp. 175–193). New York: Springer.

Schiffman, S. (1996). Smell and taste. In J. E. Birren (Ed.), *Encyclopedia of gerontology: Age, aging, and the aged* (Vol. 2, pp. 497–504). San Diego: Academic Press.

Schneck, M. K., Reisberg, B., & Ferris, S. H. (1982). An overview of current concepts of Alzheimer's disease. *American Journal of Psychiatry, 139,* 165–173.

Schneider, B. A., & Pichora-Fuller, M. K. (2000). Implications of perceptual deterioration for cognitive aging research. In F. I. M. Craik & T. A. Salthouse (Eds.), *The handbook of aging and cognition* (2nd ed., pp. 155–219). Mahwah, NJ: Erlbaum.

Schneider, E. L. (1997). Will future elderly persons experience more years of disability? Yes. In A. E. Scharlach, & L. W. Kaye (Eds.), *Controversial issues in aging* (pp. 210–212). Boston: Allyn & Bacon.

Schneider, L. S. (1995). Efficacy of clinical treatment for mental disorders among older persons. In M. Gatz (Ed.), *Emerging issues in mental health and aging* (pp. 19–71). Washington, DC: American Psychological Association.

Schone, B. S., & Weinick, R. M. (1998). Health-related behaviors and the benefits of marriage for elderly persons. *The Gerontologist, 38,* 618–627.

Schooler, C., & Mulatu, M. S. (2001). The reciprocal effects of leisure time activities and intellectual functioning in older people: A longitudinal analysis. *Psychology and Aging, 16,* 466–482.

Schroots, J. J. F. (1996). Theories of aging: Psychological. In J. E. Birren (Ed.), *Encyclopedia of gerontology: Age, aging, and the aged* (Vol. 2, pp. 557-567). San Diego: Academic Press.

Schulz, R. (1976). The effects of control and predictability on trhe psychological and physical well-being of the institutionalized aged. *Journal of Personality and Social Psychology, 33,* 563–573.

Schulz, R. (1994). Introduction: Debate on generalized theories of slowing. *Journal of Gerontology: Psychological Sciences, 49,* P59.

Schulz, R., & Hanusa, B. H. (1980). Experimental social gerontology: A social psychological perspective. *Journal of Social Issues, 36,* 30–46.

Schulz, R., & Heckhausen, J. (1996). A life span model of successful aging. *American Psychologist, 51,* 702–714.

Schulz, R., & Salthouse, T. (1999). *Adult development and aging: Myths and emerging realities* (3rd ed.). Upper Saddle River, NJ: Prentice Hall.

Schwenk, M. A. (1979). Reality orientation for institutionalized aged: Does it help? *The Gerontologist, 19,* 373–377.

Segall, M. H., Dasen, P. R., Berry, J. W., & Poortinga, Y. H. (1999). *Human behavior in global perspective: An introduction to cross-cultural psychology* (2nd ed.). Boston: Allyn & Bacon.

Shanas, E. (1979). Social myth as hypothesis: The case of the family relations of old people. *The Gerontologist, 19,* 3–9.

Sharps, M. J., Price-Sharps, J. L., & Hanson, J. (1998). Attitudes of young adults toward older adults: Evidence from the United States and Thailand. *Educational Gerontology, 24,* 655–660.

Siegler, I. C. (1995). Functional age. In G. L. Maddox et al. (Eds.), *The encyclopedia of aging* (2nd ed., p. 385). New York: Springer.

Siegel, J. M. (1993). Companion animals: In sickness and in health. *Journal of Social Issues, 49,* 157–167.

Siegler, I. C., & Botwinick, J. (1979). A long-term longitudinal study of intellectual ability of older adults: The matter of selective subject attrition. *Journal of Gerontology, 34,* 242–245.

Sigelman, C. K., & Rider, E. A. (2003). *Life-span human development* (4th ed.). Belmont, CA: Wadsworth/ Thomson Learning.

Silver, J. H., Bubrick, E., Jilinskaia, E., & Perls, T. T. (1998, August). Is there a centenarian personality? Presented at the 106th Annual Convention of the American Psychological Association, San Francisco, CA.

Silverstein, M., & Zablotsky, D. L. (1996). Health and social precursors of later life retirement-community migration. *Journal of Gerontology: Social Sciences, 51B,* S150–S156.

Simons, R. L. (1983–1984). Specificity and substitution in the social networks of the elderly. *International Journal of Aging and Human Development, 18,* 121–139.

Simonton, D. K. (1990). Creativity in the later years: Optimistic prospects for achievement. *The Gerontologist, 30,* 626–631.

Simonton, D. K. (1997). Creative productivity: A predictive and explanatory model of career trajectories and landmarks. *Psychological Review, 104,* 66–89.

Simonton, D. K. (1998). Career paths and creative lives: A theoretical perspective on late life potential. In C. E. Adams-Price (Ed.), *Creativity and successful aging: Theoretical and empirical approaches* (pp. 3–18). New York: Springer.

Sinclair, A. J. (1995). Diabetes mellitus. In G. L. Maddox et al. (Eds.), *The encyclopedia of aging* (2nd ed., pp. 274–276). New York: Springer.

Sinnott, J. D. (1989). A model for solution of ill-structured problems: Implications for everyday and abstract problem-solving. In J. D. Sinnott (Ed.), *Everyday problem solving: Theory and applications* (pp. 72–99). New York: Praeger.

Sinnott, J. (1996). The developmental approach: Postformal thought as adaptive intelligence. In F. Blanchard-Fields & T. M. Hess (Eds.), *Perspectives on cognitive change in adulthood and aging* (pp. 358–383). New York: McGraw-Hill.

Skoog, I., Blennow, K., & Marcusson, J. (1996). Dementia. In J. E. Birren (Ed.), *Encyclopedia of gerontology: Age, aging, and the aged* (Vol. 1, pp. 383–403). San Diego: Academic Press.

Slawinski, E. B., Hartel, D. M., & Kline, D. W. (1993). Self-reported hearing problems in daily life throughout adulthood. *Psychology and Aging, 8,* 552–561.

Slotterback, C. S. (1996). Projections of aging: Impact of generational differences and the aging process on perceptions of adults. *Psychology and Aging, 11,* 552–559.

Smeedling, T. M., Estes, C. L., & Glasse, L. (1999, August). Social Security in the 21st century. More than deficits: Strengthening security for women. *Gerontology News.*

Smith, A. D. (1996). Memory. In J. E. Birren (Ed.). *Encyclopedia of gerontology: Age, aging, and the aged* (Vol. 2, pp. 107–117). San Diego: Academic Press.

Smith, J., & Baltes, P. B. (1990). Wisdom-related knowledge: Age/cohort differences in response to life-planning problems. *Developmental Psychology, 26,* 494–505.

Smith, J., & Freund, A. M. (2002). The dynamics of possible selves in old age. *Journal of Gerontology: Psychological Sciences, 57B,* P492–P500.

Smith, J., Staudinger, U. M., & Baltes, P. B. (1994). Occupational settings facilitating wisdom-related knowledge: The sample case of clinical psychologists. *Journal of Consulting and Clinical Psychology, 62,* 989–999.

Smyer, M. A. (1993, August). Mental health services in nursing homes: Still crazy after all these years. Presidential Address for Division 20 of the American Psychological Association, Toronto, Canada.

Smyer, M. A., & Allen-Burge, R. (1999). Older adults' decision-making capacity: Institutional settings and individual choices. In J. C. Cavanaugh & S. K. Whitbourne (Eds.), *Gerontology: An interdisciplinary perspective* (pp. 391–413). New York: Oxford University Press.

Smyer, M. A., Brannon, D., & Cohn, M. D. (1992). Improving nursing home care through training and job redesign. *The Gerontologist, 32,* 327–333.

Smyer, M. A., & Qualls, S. H. (1999). *Aging and mental health.* Malden, MA: Blackwell.

Snowdon, D. A. (1997). Aging and Alzheimer's disease: Lessons from the Nun Study. *The Gerontologist, 37,* 150–156.

Solomon, D. H. (1999). The role of aging processes in aging-dependent diseases. In V. L. Bengston & K. W. Schaie (Eds.), *Handbook of theories of aging* (pp. 133–150). New York: Springer.

Somberg, B. L., & Salthouse, T. A. (1982). Divided attention abilities in young and old adults. *Journal of Experimental Psychology: Human Perception and Performance, 8,* 651–663.

Sontag, S. (1972, September 23). The double standard of aging. *Saturday Review,* 29–38.

Spearman, C. E. (1927). *The abilities of man.* New York: Macmillan.

Spitze, G., & Logan, J. (1992). Helping as a component of parent-adult child relations. *Research on Aging, 14,* 291–312.

Spitze, G., & Miner, S. (1992). Gender differences in adult child contact among Black elderly parents. *The Gerontologist, 32,* 213–218.

Stains, L. R. (2002, March-April). Look who's back! *AARP Magazine,* 36–38.

Sternberg, R. J. (1985). *Beyond IQ: A triarchic theory of human intelligence.* New York: Cambridge University Press.

Sternberg, R. J. (1996). *Successful intelligence: How practical and creative intelligence determine success in life.* New York: Simon & Schuster.

Sternberg, R. J. (2004). *Psychology* (4th ed.). Belmont, CA: Wadsworth/Thomson Learning.

Sternberg, R. J., & Lubart, T. I. (2001). Wisdom and creativity. In J. E. Birren, & K. W. Schaie (Eds.), *Handbook of the psychology of aging* (5th ed., pp. 500–522). San Diego: Academic Press.

Sternberg, R. J., Wagner, R. K., & Okagaki, L. (1993). Practical intelligence: The nature and role of tacit knowledge in work and at school. In J. M. Puckett & H. W. Reese (Eds.), *Mechanisms of everyday cognition* (pp. 205–227). Hillsdale, NJ: Erlbaum.

Sternberg, R. J., Wagner, R. K., Williams, W. M., & Horvath, J. A. (1995). Testing common sense. *American Psychologist, 50,* 912–927.

Sterns, A. A., & Sterns, H. L. (1997). Should there be an affirmative action policy for hiring older persons? Yes. In A. E. Scharlach & L. W. Kaye (Eds.), *Controversial issues in aging* (pp. 35–39). Boston: Allyn & Bacon.

Stevens, A. (1994). *Jung.* New York: Oxford University Press.

Stine, E. A. L., Soederberg, L. M., & Morrow, D. G. (1996). Language and discourse processing through adulthood. In F. Blanchard-Fields & T. M. Hess (Eds.), *Perspectives on cognitive change in adulthood and aging* (pp. 255–290). New York: McGraw-Hill.

Stine-Morrow, E. A. L., Loveless, M. K., & Soederberg, L. M. (1996). Resource allocation in on-line reading by younger and older adults. *Psychology and Aging, 11,* 475–486.

Stoller, E. P., & Longino, C. F., Jr. (2001). "Going home" or "leaving home"? The impact of person and place ties on anticipated counterstream migration. *The Gerontologist, 41,* 96–102.

Strawbridge, W. J., Wallhagen, M. I., Shema, S. J., & Kaplan, G. A. (2000). Negative consequences of hearing impairment in old age: A longitudinal analysis. *The Gerontologist, 40,* 320–326.

Stroop, J. R. (1935). Studies of interference in serial verbal reactions. *Journal of Experimental Psychology, 18,* 643–662.

Sullivan, R. J. (1995). Cardiovascular system. In G. L. Maddox et al. (Eds.), *The encyclopedia of aging* (2nd ed., pp. 133–138). New York: Springer.

Sullivan-Marx, E. M. (1995). Delirium. In G. L. Maddox et al. (Eds.), *The encyclopedia of aging* (2nd ed., pp. 256–259). New York: Springer.

Sunderland, A., Watts, K., Baddeley, A. D., & Harris, J. E. (1986). Subjective memory assessment and test performance in elderly adults. *Journal of Gerontology, 41,* 376–384.

Svanborg, A. (1996). Postponement of aging. In J. E. Birren (Ed.), *Encyclopedia of gerontology: Age, aging, and the aged* (Vol. 2, pp. 333–340). San Diego: Academic Press.

Szinovacz, M. E., & DeViney, S. (1999). The retiree identity: Gender and race differences. *Journal of Gerontology: Social Sciences, 54B,* S207–S218.

Taranto, M. A. (1989). Facets of wisdom: A theoretical synthesis. *International Journal of Aging and Human Development, 29,* 1–21.

Tasker, G. (2003, October 14). My grandfather (or grandmother) the alcoholic. *The Miami Herald,* pp. 10E–12E.

Thomas, J. L. (1990). The grandparent role: A double bind. *International Journal of Aging and Human Development, 31,* 169–177.

Thompson, E. E., & Krause, N. (1998). Living alone and neighborhood characteristics as predictors of social support in late life. *Journal of Gerontology: Social Sciences, 53B,* S354–S364.

Thorson, J. A., & Powell, F. C. (2000). Death anxiety in young and older adults. In A. Tomer (Ed.), *Death attitudes and the older adult: Theories, concepts, and applications* (pp. 123–136). Philadelphia: Brunner-Routledge.

Thurstone, L. L. (1938). *Primary mental abilities* (Psychometric Monographs, Whole No. 1). Chicago: University of Chicago Press.

Thurstone, L. L., & Thurstone, T. G. (1947). *Primary Mental Abilities Test.* Chicago: Science Research Associates.

Tomer, A. (2000). Death-related attitudes: Conceptual distinctions. In A. Tomer (Ed.), *Death attitudes and the older adult: Theories, concepts, and applications* (pp. 87–94). Philadelphia: Brunner-Routledge.

Tonna, E. A. (1995a). Arthritis. In G. L. Maddox et al. (Eds.), *The encyclopedia of aging* (2nd ed., pp. 79–80). New York: Springer.

Tonna, E. A. (1995b). Musculoskeletal system. In G. L. Maddox et al. (Eds.), *The encyclopedia of aging* (2nd ed., pp. 656–658). New York: Springer.

Tower, R. B., & Kasl, S. V. (1996). Gender, marital closeness, and depressive symptoms in elderly couples. *Journal of Gerontology: Psychological Sciences, 51B,* P115–P129.

Troll, L. E., & Skaff, M. M. (1997). Perceived continuity of self in very old age. *Psychology and Aging, 12,* 162–169.

Tucker, J. S., Friedman, H. S., Tsai, C. M., & Martin, L. R. (1995). Playing with pets and longevity among older people. *Psychology and Aging, 10,* 3–7.

Tucker, J. S., Wingard, D. L., Friedman, H. S., & Schwartz, J. W. (1996). Marital history at midlife as a predictor of longevity: Alternative explanations to the protective effect of marriage. *Health Psychology, 15,* 94–101.

Tuckman, J., & Lorge, I. (1953). Attitudes toward old people. *Journal of Social Psychology, 37,* 249–260.

Tulving, E., & Thomson, D. M. (1973). Encoding specificity and retrieval processes in episodic memory. *Psychological Review, 80,* 352–373.

Tun, P. A. (1998). Fast noisy speech: Age differences in processing rapid speech with background noise. *Psychology and Aging, 13,* 424–434.

Tun, P. A., & Wingfield, A. (1997). Language and communication: Fundamentals of speech communication and language processing in old age. In A. D. Fisk & W. A. Rogers (Eds.), *Handbook of human factors and the older adult* (pp. 125–149). San Diego: Academic Press.

Tun, P. A., & Wingfield, A. (1999). One voice too many: Adult age differences in language processing with different types of distracting sounds. *Journal of Gerontology: Psychological Sciences, 54B,* P317–P327.

Tun, P. A., Wingfield, A., Rosen, M. J., & Blanchard, L. (1998). Response latencies for false memories: Gist-based processes in normal aging. *Psychology and Aging, 13,* 230–241.

Tuokko, H., Frerichs, R., Graham, J., Rockwood, K., Kristjansson, B., Fisk, J., Bergman, H., Kozma, A., & McDowell, I. (2003). Five-year follow-up of cognitive impairment with no dementia. *Archives of Neurology, 60,* 577–582.

Turk-Charles, S., Meyerowitz, B. E., & Gatz, M. (1997). Age differences in information-seeking among cancer patients. *International Journal of Aging and Human Development, 45,* 85–98.

Turker, J. (1996). Premature aging. In J. E. Birren (Ed.), *Encyclopedia of gerontology: Age, aging, and the aged* (Vol. 2, pp. 341–354). San Diego: Academic Press.

Umberson, D., Wortman, C. B., & Kessler, R. C. (1992). Widowhood and depression: Explaining long-term gender differences in vulnerability. *Journal of Health and Social Behavior, 33,* 10–24.

United Nations Population Division, Department of Economic and Social Affairs (2002). Population ageing, 2002. United Nations Publication (ST/ESA/SER.A/208).

Van Dras, D. D., & Blumenthal, H. T. (2000). Biological, social-environmental, and psychological dialecticism: An integrated model of aging. *Basic and Applied Social Psychology, 22,* 199–212.

Vaupel, J. (1995). Life expectancy. In G. L. Maddox et al. (Eds.), *The encyclopedia of aging* (2nd ed., pp. 559–560). New York: Springer.

Vercruyssen, M. (1997). Movement control and speed of behavior. In A. D. Fisk & W. A. Rogers (Eds.), *Handbook of human factors and the older adult* (pp. 55–86). San Diego: Academic Press.

Verhaeghen, P., Geraerts, N., & Marcoen, A. (2000). Memory complaints, coping, and well-being in old age: A systemic approach. *The Gerontologist, 40,* 540–548.

Vinick, B. H., & Ekerdt, D. J. (1991). Retirement: What happens to husband-wife relationships? *Journal of Geriatric Psychiatry, 24,* 23–40.

Waldman, D. A., & Avolio, B. J. (1986). A meta-analysis of age differences in job performance. *Journal of Applied Psychology, 71,* 33–38.

Walker, A. J., Acock, A. C., Bowman, S. R., & Li, F. (1996). Amount of care given and caregiving satisfaction: A latent growth curve analysis. *Journal of Gerontology: Psychological Sciences, 51B,* P130–P142.

Walker, A. J., Martin, S. S., & Jones, L. L. (1992). The benefits and costs of caregiving and care receiving for daughters and mothers. *Journal of Gerontology: Social Sciences, 47,* S130–S139.

Wechsler, D. L. (1997). *Wechsler Adult Intelligence Scale-Third Edition.* San Antonio, TX: Psychological Corporation.

Weg, R. B. (1996). Sexuality, sensuality, and intimacy. In J. E. Birren (Ed.), *Encyclopedia of gerontology: Age, aging, and the aged* (Vol. 2, pp. 479–488). San Diego: Academic Press.

Weindruch, R. (1996, January). Caloric restriction and aging. *Scientific American,* 46–52.

Weiner, B. (1993). On sin versus sickness: A theory of perceived responsibility and social motivation. *American Psychologist, 48,* 957–965.

Weisenberger, J. M. (1996). Touch and proprioception. In J. E. Birren (Ed.), *Encyclopedia of gerontology: Age, aging, and the aged* (Vol. 2, pp. 591–603). San Diego: Academic Press.

Weiss, R. (1997, November). Aging: New answers to old questions. *National Geographic, 192,* 10–31.

Weiss, R. S., & Bass, S. A. (2002). Introduction. In R. S. Weiss & S. A. Bass (Eds.), *Challenges of the third age: Meaning and purpose in later life* (pp. 3–12). New York: Oxford University Press.

West, R. L. (1996). An application of prefrontal cortex function theory to cognitive aging. *Psychological Bulletin, 120,* 272–292.

West, R. L., Welch, D. C., & Thorn, R. M. (2001). Effects of goal-setting and feedback on memory performance and beliefs among older and younger adults. *Psychology and Aging, 16,* 240–250.

Whitbourne, S. K. (1999). Physical changes. In J. C. Cavanaugh & S. K. Whitbourne (Eds.), *Gerontology: An interdisciplinary perspective* (pp. 91–122). New York: Oxford University Press.

Whitbourne, S. K., & Hulicka, I. M. (1990). Ageism in undergraduate psychology texts. *American Psychologist, 45,* 1127–1136.

Williams, S. A., Denney, N. W., & Schadler, M. (1983). Elderly adults' perception of their own cognitive development during the adult years. *International Journal of Aging and Human Development, 16,* 147–158.

Willis, S. L. (1996). Everyday cognitive competence in elderly persons: Conceptual issues and empirical findings. *The Gerontologist, 36,* 595–601.

Wilmoth, J., Skytthe, A., Friou, D., & Jeune, B. (1996). The oldest man ever? A case study of exceptional longevity. *The Gerontologist, 36,* 783–788.

Wingfield, A. (1995). Language comprehension. In G. L. Maddox et al. (Eds.), *The encyclopedia of aging* (2nd ed., p. 538). New York: Springer.

Wingfield, A. (1996). Cognitive factors in auditory performance: Context, speed of processing, and constraints of memory. *Journal of the American Academy of Audiology, 7,* 175–182.

Wingfield, A., Prentice, K., Koh, C. K., & Little, D. (2000). Neural change, cognitive reserve, and behavioral compensation in rapid encoding and memory for spoken language in adult aging. In L. T. Connor & L. K. Obler (Eds.), *Neurobehavior of language and cognition: Studies of normal aging and brain damage* (pp. 3–21). Boston: Kluwer Academic Publishers.

Wingfield, A., & Stine-Morrow, E. A. L. (2000). Language and speech. In F. I. M. Craik & T. A. Salthouse (Eds.), *Handbook of aging and cognition* (2nd ed., pp. 359–416). Mahwah, NJ: Erlbaum.

Wingfield, A., Tun, P. A., & Rosen, M. J. (1995). Age differences in veridical and reconstructive recall of syntactically and randomly segmented speech. *Journal of Gerontology: Psychological Sciences, 50B,* P257–P266.

Wolf, R. L. (1996). Understanding elder abuse and neglect. *Aging,* No. 367, 4–13. Administration on Aging, U.S. Department of Health and Human Services.

Wong, P. T., & Watt, L. M. (1991). What types of reminiscence are associated with successful aging? *Psychology and Aging, 6,* 272–279.

Woodruff, D. S., & Birren, J. E. (1972). Age changes and cohort differences in personality. *Developmental Psychology, 6,* 252–259.

Woodruff-Pak, D. (1988). *Psychology and aging.* Englewood Cliffs, NJ: Prentice Hall.

Woodruff-Pak, D. S. (1989). Aging and intelligence: Changing perspectives in the twentieth century. *Journal of Aging Studies, 3,* 91–118.

Woodruff-Pak, D. S., & Papka, M. (1999). Theories of neuropsychology and aging. In V. L. Bengston & K. W. Schaie (Eds.), *Handbook of theories of aging* (pp. 113–132). New York: Springer.

Woods, R. T. (1999). Mental health problems in late life. In R. T. Woods (Ed.), *Psychological problems of ageing* (pp. 73–110). Chichester, England: John Wiley.

Wortman, C. B., & Silver, R. C. (1990). Successful mastery of bereavement and widowhood: A life-course perspective. In P. B. Baltes & M. M. Baltes (Eds.), *Successful aging: Perspectives from the behavioral sciences* (pp. 225–264). Cambridge, England: Cambridge University Press.

Wykle, M. H., Segall, M. E., & Nagley, S. (1992). Mental health and aging: Hospital care—a nursing perspective. In J. E. Birren, R. B. Sloane, & G. D. Cohen (Eds.), *Handbook of mental health and aging* (2nd ed., pp. 815–831). San Diego: Academic Press.

Yesavage, J. A. (1982–1983). Development and validation of a Geriatric Depression Screening Scale: A preliminary report. *Journal of Psychiatric Research, 17,* 37–49.

Yoon, C., Hasher, L., Feinberg, F., Rahhal, T. A., & Winocur, G. (2000). Cross-cultural differences in memory: The role of culture-based stereotypes about aging. *Psychology and Aging, 15,* 694–704.

Zacks, R. T., Hasher, L., & Li, K. Z. H. (2000). Human memory. In F. I. M. Craik & T. A. Salthouse (Eds.), *The handbook of aging and cognition* (2nd ed., pp. 293–357). Mahwah, NJ: Erlbaum.

Zarit, S. J., & Haynie, D. A. (2000). Introduction to clinical issues. In S. K. Whitbourne (Ed.), *Psychopathology in later adulthood* (pp. 1–26). New York: John Wiley.

Zarit, S. H., Johansson, L., & Jarrott, S. E. (1998). Family caregiving: Stresses, social programs, and clinical interventions. In I. H. Nordus, G. R. VandenBos et al. (Eds.), *Clinical geropsychology* (pp. 345–360). Washington, DC: American Psychological Association.

Zarit, S. H., Stephens, M. A. P., Townsend, A., & Greene, R. (1998). Stress reduction for family caregivers: Effects of adult day care use. *Journal of Gerontology: Social Sciences, 53B,* S267–S277.

Zwahr, M. D., Park, D. C., & Shifren, K. (1999). Judgments about estrogen replacement therapy: The role of age, cognitive abilities, and beliefs. *Psychology and Aging, 14,* 179–191.

Name Index

Subject Index

Note: page numbers in *italics* refer to illustrations

Integrated Coverage of Applications to Everyday Life